Problems and Perspectives
of Fundamental Theology

edited by
René Latourelle and *Gerald O'Collins*

translated by
Matthew J. O'Connell

PAULIST PRESS • *New York/Ramsey*

Originally published as *Problemi E Prospettive Di Teologia Fondamentale,* copyright 1980 by Editrice Queriniana, Italia. English translation © 1982 by The Missionary Society of St. Paul the Apostle in the State of New York

Library of Congress
Catalog Card Number: 82-81192

ISBN: 0-8091-2466-1

Published by Paulist Press
545 Island Road, Ramsey, N.J. 07446

Printed and bound in the
United States of America

Contents

Part 4
ECCLESIOLOGICAL PERSPECTIVES

Introduction

The theological disciplines, like the other sciences, feel periodically the need of a breather, of pausing at some vantage point, in order to get a better view of the road already traveled, to decide on direction, and to study the difficulties that are becoming visible on the horizon. This need is felt with special intensity in fundamental theology, since it stands at a point where a number of other disciplines, themselves constantly changing, intersect. The present book represents a kind of "state of the question," an effort on the part of fundamental theology to locate and define itself at the beginning of a new decade. What precisely is fundamental theology at the present time? What direction is it likely to take in the eighties?

What we have in mind here is not an absolute beginning but a joint reflection by colleagues (most of the contributors are men who have long been engaged in teaching). It is intended as a continuation of similar work done elsewhere: bulletins on fundamental theology in, for example, the *Revue thomiste* or the *Recherches de science religieuse*[1]; the symposia held at Gazzada in 1964 and at Rome in 1969[2]; surveys published by *Concilium* in 1965 or in collective works such as *Bilan de la théologie au XXe siècle* and *Correnti teologiche postconciliari*[3]; books and articles giving a historical synthesis,[4] to say nothing of the many articles in dictionaries and encyclopedias. In our judgment, the number and seriousness of the problems that fundamental theology faces justify a new effort at a collective restatement of the question and a collective reflection on answers.

In this volume a number of voices are heard (nineteen, to be exact); the book is the result of collaboration on an international scale. The chapters, therefore, are not like sections of a musical composition from the pen of a single composer. The aim is rather to let various voices be heard, to let various witnesses speak from their personal experience; in this way we shall learn the perspectives, tendencies, and problems characteristic of each cultural and theological horizon. In this context, to force guidance on the contributors would doubtless have produced a more unified book, but it would also have undermined our plan from the outset. Our primary purpose in this volume has been to serve the Church.

The freedom left the contributors does not mean anarchy, and the book follows an overall plan. We have focused on four series of problems, all of them of a general kind. Any study of the detailed problems of fundamental theology would have required an encyclopedia, not a single volume. Here is

1

the framework that has been adopted: (a) problems of identity and method, as seen first in a historical and then in a systematic perspective; (b) questions of hermeneutics; (c) christological approaches; (d) problems of ecclesiology, but only those closely connected with revelation (credibility, tradition, magisterium, theology) or with other religions and other Churches. It may surprise the reader that the theme of revelation and faith has not been treated as such. But studies of this subject, before and after Vatican II, are legion; moreover, the essays in the first part of this book call attention not only to the agreement reached on matters of substance but to most of the new aspects highlighted in recent studies. Within each section of the book, we proceed from the more general to the more specific.

A project of this kind entails and imposes limitations of which we are quite aware: the number of pages, the number of contributors, the number of themes discussed. We would like to have been able to include many other well-deserving names. One thing is sure: the omissions in this book never represent negative judgments.

Here, now, is a brief description of each essay; the summaries will help guide the reader through the book.

The *first part* studies the problems of identity and method which fundamental theology faces.

Jean-Pierre Torrell studies current trends in the fundamental theology of the postconciliar period and distinguishes four aspects that are of greater importance: the persisting uncertainty about the nature of fundamental theology; the entrance of Protestant theologians into a discipline that seemed hitherto to be a Catholic preserve; the revival of interest, among both Catholics and Protestants, in apologetics conceived as the work of justifying faith; finally, after the Modernist interim, reflection on the difficult problems relating to "experience." This essay by the man who has written the bulletins on fundamental theology for the *Revue thomiste* since 1964 serves as a real introduction to the book as a whole.

David Tracy emphasizes the public nature of fundamental theology as a theological discipline that studies and systematizes the questions and answers emerging from the contemporary situation as well as from the religious tradition. By reason of its public (the "academic" world), its mode of reasoning, its ethical and religious perspectives, and its attitude toward the truth it pursues, it is distinct both from systematic theology and from practical theology. It cannot, however, be autonomous. Fidelity to its internal dynamics requires a link with systematic theology, just as systematic theology must acknowledge that many of the problems it encounters or raises belong to fundamental theology.

René Latourelle endeavors to define the characteristics of present-day fundamental theology as this has gradually been elaborated after a development that extends through almost three decades and corresponds to a threefold movement of theological discourse: a period of reaction against classical apologetics; a period of expansion that affects the concept of fundamental theology, its privileged themes, its addressees, a period in which the tasks of fundamental theology are related to a center and put in a hierarchic order. After having been a country without borders, it seems now to be concentrating on the essential questions that identify it and give it its specificity. Finally, the author turns to the pedagogical problems raised by the new Apostolic Constitution *Sapientia Christiana*.

Carlo M. Martini shows how the Church, from her beginnings, was conscious that Christian life matured according as, and to the extent that, reflection on the faith developed and deepened. This last is a discourse of a "fundamental" kind, in which experience and thought support each other and are never separated. From this point of the view, our four gospels, regarded as handbooks for initiation, represent stages or plateaus on the Christian journey. Mark represents the catechumenal stage; he highlights the wonderworking power of Jesus and the revelation of the mystery of God in the life and death of Christ. Matthew represents the catechetical initiation to life in the Church and emphasizes the continuity of the divine plan in the history of Israel. Luke focuses on witness and shows how the gospel fits into the plan of universal salvation; this is the level of a thinking that is more directly along the lines of contemporary fundamental theology, the latter being understood as a process of becoming aware of the "solidity" of the Christian faith. Finally, John, who is more contemplative, shows the unity of the divine plan and the manner in which revealed truth makes itself known in the realities of our world. All this adds up to an essentially concrete type of initiation in which progress toward the gospel goes hand in hand with the manifestation of the gospel's credibility, following the rhythm of experience; it is an experiential showing rather than an abstract proving.

The *second part* of the book tackles questions of hermeneutics: at the levels of *scripture*, of *history*, and of the *themes* proper to fundamental theology.

René Marlé studies the heremeneutical problem by taking as his starting point the phenomenon of scripture, the latter being regarded as a producer of *texts* or as the unique *text*, namely the Bible, which faith takes as its point of reference (the two ways of looking at scripture are interconnected). After showing how the hermeneutical problem arises out of a certain number of distances that must be traversed or differences that must be confronted, the author explains how the problem is connected with the complex functioning of the "rule of faith." He then considers hermeneutics as rendering a service to the word and to the confession of faith, as the roots of hermeneutics in personal and social life become increasingly clear.

Ignace de la Potterie takes up a problem that is central in all of modern thought: the problem of the relationship of absolute truth and historical contingency. The question was raised in the time of modernism but it is emerging again today with heightened intensity. The author studies the principal models of this history-truth relation: truth separated from history (Platonic tradition, rationalism, extrinsicism), truth embodied in history (historical positivism, the Hegelian current or other currents of thought inspired by Hegel), truth immanent in the human being (atheistic existentialism of Max Stirner, Christian existentialism of Sören Kierkegaard). Finally, the author calls attention to the way in which Christianity has made its own original and organic synthesis of the various aspects of truth which are present in the preceding models: transcendence, historicity, interiority. This synthesis has taken concrete form in Jesus Christ, who in his person is both mystery and truth-revelation.

In the last essay of this part, Prosper Grech asks to what extent and under what conditions modern fundamental theology can still make use of the themes of the traditional treatise *De Christo legato* (Christ the Legate of God): the historical value of the gospels, the messianic consciousness of Jesus, his christological titles, miracles and resurrection. After examining the difficulties which recent critical thought has raised against the old treatment of these themes and after judging the weight of the difficulties, the author shows how each of the classical themes can be reintroduced provided it is given an entirely new basis and is rethought and re-elaborated in the light of the findings of history, exegesis, hermeneutics, and the sciences of language.

The *third part* of the book is devoted to problems of christology, but always in the perspectives and with the concerns of fundamental theology: christology and philosophy, christology and anthropology, christocentrism as a methodological principle, relationship of Christ to the Old and New Testaments, access to the person of Jesus through the gospels, the resurrection and the textual documentation of it.

Xavier Tilliette examines the question of whether a philosophical christology is possible. The assertion of such a possibility is only an apparent paradox, since not only Christian philosophy but modern philosophy as well give Christ a place of considerable importance that is not always measurable by the number of explicit statements made about him. The author thinks he can find implicit in "the Christ of the philosophers" a discipline that moves along two lines: a philosophy that leads to Christ, a Christ who enlightens philosophy. Out of the interaction of these two movements is born a philosophical christology that is of value both to christology and to philosophy.

Gustave Martelet takes two facts as his starting point: the first is of the cultural order, the second of the christological order. The first is the drift of modernity away from the faith; the second is the difficulty contemporary christology finds in really coming to grips with the historical development of the race. It is this difficulty that the author attempts to explain and overcome in his essay: "Christology and Anthropology: Toward a Christian Genealogy of the Human."

Tullio Citrini studies the presence of christology in fundamental theology, not as a simple fact but as a principle of the critical elaboration and structuring of theological discourse. The author shows how only by winding paths and after transcending false dilemmas (christocentrism or theocentrism, christocentrism or ecclesiocentrism) has there developed an effective use of christocentrism) as a methodological and operational principle for tackling and treating the problems of fundamental theology.

Pierre Grelot takes up the problem of the Old Testament—New Testament relationship in Jesus Christ. After describing two approaches that have each led to an impass, he explains how history, Law and promises find their fulfillment in Jesus Christ. He then shows how in the person of Jesus the Old Testament reaches the ultimate limits of its internal dynamism: that is, in the way Jesus lived, preached and died "as a Jew" and in accordance with the scriptures; and how, on the other hand, by living personally in God's presence as his Son, Jesus establishes the type of existence which is characteristic of the new covenant. The Old Testament—New Testament relationship also entails consideration of other themes: the divine pedagogy, and the three possible types of figurative interpretation of the Old Testament, along with the doctrine of the four senses of scripture which is based on these possibilities.

Jacques Guillet's essay, "Access to the Person of Jesus," identifies this theme in a concrete manner and develops various aspects of it. The issue is not simply access to Jesus via history (Guillet here compares the respective approaches of Rudolf Bultmann and Heinz Schürmann) but also access to the risen Lord and, above all, access to the person of Jesus and to his consciousness (both impenetrable and transparent) of himself as Son which caries him at one and the same time toward his Father and toward "others," i.e., the whole human race, for the purpose of making forgiveness available to them. Access to the person of Jesus requires both the revelation of the risen Lord and contemplation of the prophet of Nazareth.

It is impossible to pass over in silence the subject of the resurrection. In dealing with the tremendous number of contemporary books and articles on the resurrection it is possible to classify the questions raised and to distinguish those relating to the texts, those relating to the event itself, and those relating to the theological meaning of the affirmation made by faith. Giuseppe Ghiberti devotes his attention primarily to the written documentation, that is, the texts which bear witness to the event: formation and development of traditions, description of the original nucleus of primitive faith and of its essential characteristic, which is the indissoluble union of faith and event. Finally, the author points out some of the problems most widely discussed today: language and interpretation of the texts, reconstruction of textual sequences from the beginnings to the final text, relation to history, relation of the earthly body to the glorified body, nature of the appearances.

The *fourth* and last *part* of the book is devoted to problems of ecclesiology. We must insist once again that the intention here is not to produce a treatise on ecclesiology but to deal with those aspects of ecclesiology that are inseparable from reflection on the fundamental problems of religion, revelation, and the mediation of faith.

In a comprehensive vision Avery Dulles presents the Church as sacrament and foundation of faith. The old apologetics of the Church, he says, proved ineffective. Newman's intuitions with respect to the way in which human beings come to faith, and, more recently, the heuristic theory of Polanyi can help understand better the dynamics of conversion and the ways by which God invites us to accept the testimony of the Church. Contemporary fundamental theology sees the Church as a sacrament and a community that make the presence of salvation known to us and invite us to be converted. This vision of the Church, which has important consequences for ecumenism, urges theologians to make their own this sacramental understanding of faith, which entails participation in the life of the ecclesial community.

Karl Rahner calls attention to the difficulty, even the practical impossibility, of uniting in a single awareness both the Christian faith and the data of modern science with its spectacular range and expansion. In a climate of opinion that is marked by skepticism and relativism the magisterium of the Church, viewed as a formal principle of authority, has lost a great deal of its credibility. It is becoming increasingly necessary that preachers bring out the *internal* credibility of the Church's dogmas and of the official texts in which her teaching is conveyed. In the light of what Vatican II has to say about nonchristians and nonbelievers, Rahner analyzes the situation of those Catholics who in good faith do not unreservedly accept one or other dogma, without at the same time denying it completely. He insists that in such cases a basic, unqualified acceptance of the option of faith can coexist, at the explicit and conscious level, with a less complete sense of certainty regarding these dogmas which belong to the content of faith.

With the Declaration *Nostra aetate* of Vatican II as his point of reference, Pietro Rossano examines the theological problem created by the existence of other religions. He takes up the following aspects of the problem: the "religious"dimension of the human person as evaluated in theological perspective; the various religions seen as the fruit of the human being's religious quest; the problems which the religions create for the theologian (unity and plurality, elements of "revelation," ways of salvation, and so on); the specific problems posed by each religion; the rereading of the Bible and Christian sources in the light of our present experience of the interfaith movement. Finally, he makes some points and suggestions regarding the mode of the Church's presence in the world.

The old apologetics, says Heinrich Fries, maintained that only the Roman Catholic Church possessed fully the four marks of the true Church; the other Christian confessions, therefore, could not claim the title "Church." Down to Vatican II the problem of the distinction between "the Church and the Churches" was generally solved by insisting that we could not speak of "Church" in the plural. By emphasizing the many factors in common rather than the differences that separate, *Lumen gentium* makes it possible for the Decree on Ecumenism to speak of various "Churches and Communities," even though they be separated from Rome. Since Vatican II the term and concept "Church" can be used analogously and in the plural. Plurality in unity shows that all these Churches have their place in the one Church of Christ. In this connection Cardinal Joseph Ratzinger recently made the point that "the Churches must remain Churches in order to become the one Church."

Gerald O'Collins takes as his starting point the large number of traditions in the areas of teaching, life and worship that each generation experiences and passes on in the Church, and he asks that principles be applied in order to discern and preserve "the purity of the Gospel" (Trent), "the Catholic faith that comes to us from the apostles" (Roman Canon) or *the* Tradition within the traditions. He goes on to examine seven criteria (the Magisterium, the canon of St. Vincent of Lerins, the "sense of the faith," continuity, the symbols of the faith, apostolicity, the scriptures), and shows how they all converge on a single criterion, which is the presence and power of the risen Lord.

Juan Alfaro studies the problem of the mediatorial role of the Church in regard to the Christian faith, with the inevitable repercussions which the exercise of this function has on theological discourse. This problem is in turn situated with the larger problem of the faith-reason relationship. After specifying the nature of theological work (fides quaerens intellectum) the author studies the functions proper to theology in relation to the Magisterium: understanding the very existence of a Magisterium within a revelation that is constituted by the unique event of Christ; interpreting the content of the Magisterium's definitions along three lines: retrospective, introspective, prospective.

The voices heard in this volume are different but not discordant. In fact we think the book as a whole is marked by a surprising harmony. Amid the diversity of the presentations substantial points of agreement emerge. Here are some of them: (a) an awareness on the part of all that mental attitudes have changed and that those currently addressed by fundamental theology, be they believers or nonbelievers, are people "marked" by the immense range of contemporary knowledge and the uncontrollable acceleration of progress; (b) fundamental theology, with its greater awareness of the complexity of the problems it studies, is generally also more modest and more concerned to find meaning and intelligibility than arguments that will overwhelm; (c) fundamental theology recognizes that it has a dogmatic function, just as dogmatic theology cannot help having an apologetic or fundamental dimension; (d) on various sides, scholars are moving away from the idea of fundamental theology as a land without borders and seeking to get back to a discipline that is more clearly identified and more focused on essential questions; (e) for this reason, christocentrism seems indispensable as a principle of analysis and structuration; (f) emphasis is everywhere put on the need of attention to the human person as the subject to whom revelation, signs, and faith are addressed; (g) all the problems of fundamental theology are affected by questions of history, philosophy, language, and hermeneutics; (h) more than in the past, fundamental theology is aware of the relation faith has to practice or active participation in ecclesial life; (i) by that very fact, it is also more attentive to all forms of dialogue (with the other religions that proclaim salvation, with the other Churches, with the other disciplines). In our opinion, these points of agreement represent substantial progress and a valuable promise for the future.

René Latourelle and Gerald O'Collins
Gregorian University, Rome

Part 1

Problems of Identity and Method

1
New Trends in Fundamental Theology in the Postconciliar Period

Jean-Pierre Torrell

The apparently unchallenging title given me by the editors of this volume conceals, in fact, a rather difficult task. For this reason I must begin by carefully defining the limits of my essay so that readers will know what they may and may not expect.

First of all, it will be helpful to point out that the expression "new trends" is more applicable to this entire collection of studies than it is to my contribution in particular. Only a reading of the whole book will show what fundamental theology has been doing in the postconciliar period and in what direction it is moving. This opening essay can do no more than highlight certain characteristics, generally regarded as more important, of the work done in this area during the time under consideration. In addition, readers will see that the novelty of the trends indicated is at times a quite relative matter, since it is a fact that in fundamental theology as in other areas of theology there are certain unchanging constants. The only thing that has really changed is the way in which we rediscover them and approach them, for this is indeed conditioned by a new context. It would perhaps be more accurate, therefore, to speak of "present" trend rather than properly "new" trends.

On the other hand, given the diversity of subject matter covered by the label "fundamental theology" (I shall return to this point, but the table of contents of this volume is enough to show what I mean), it is clear that the selection of themes judged important by one author will not be identical with the selection made by another. From the very beginning, then, I am quite ready to admit that my selection is determined by my own view of fundamental theology. While seeking, therefore, to omit nothing of importance (I am not sure, of course, that I have succeeded, apart from taking into account what I have already said in essays similar to this one), I have not hesitated to offer a critical evaluation, in the light of my conception of fundamental theology, of the positions I am reviewing here. I ask the reader's indulgence if I refer rather frequently to those other reports of mine.[1]

In order to mitigate the one-sidedness (and perhaps partisan character) of this report, I have thought it useful to begin by calling attention to some other surveys similar to mine. These too are stamped with the individuality of their authors, but at times they touch on points which complement those treated here, and can therefore help offset the fragmentary character of my selection of themes.

In addition to the special issue of *Concilium* which is already somewhat dated and to which I shall be returning,[2] I may call particular attention to the state of the question as defined by Heinrich Fries in 1975.[3] He describes there the considerable demands being made of fundamental theology nowadays, while at the same time he bemoans the fact that no one seems capable of giving a convincing response. He also refers to the difficulty of speaking today about certain subjects, such as miracles or the absolute character of Christianity, whereas other themes, such as the anthropological approach, have become congenial to us. He also regards it as important that the range of collaborators with fundamental theology has been extended or restored, for this discipline must now be concerned not solely with philosophy but also with the science of religions, modern ideologies, Marxism, psychoanalysis, hermeneutics, linguistics, theories of science, and so on.

This last point is also made, along with many others, in the more recent and much more extensive essay of Heinrich Stirnimann.[4] Reviewing new trends in fundamental theology, Stirnimann sketches a historical conspectus in which he distinguishes five successive but somewhat overlapping stages. (1) To begin with, there was a revitalization of the traditional approach; this was begun by A. Gardeil and R. Garrigou-Lagrange, and a good example of it can be seen in the manuals of Adolf Kolping. (2) Next came the anthropological trend, whose initiator and most notable representative is Karl Rahner. (3) This was followed by a period in which primacy was given to the history of salvation (Oscar Cullmann was the prime mover here); this period saw biblical categories taking control of fundamental theology. (4) A period of hermeneutical restructuring came next and brought a complete reversal. (5) This hermeneutics seems to have yielded place in turn to a new trend which is difficult to describe in precise terms but which is recognizable by the use made of such key words as "analysis," "linguistics," "logic," and "history of science."[5]

Fries and Stirnimann both provide their readers with valuable aid in getting their bearings in the recent history of fundamental theology. If I now offer another view, it is not so much that I want to challenge theirs (which I regard as shedding a good deal of light) but that I wish rather to avoid repeating it and perhaps to complete it by drawing attention to other aspects. There are many points which I ought to raise in this survey, but I shall limit myself to only four which seem to be the most important:

I. A persisting uncertainty about the nature of fundamental theology.
II. The presence on the scene of Protestant theology.
III. The revival of apologetics.
IV. Theology and experience.

I. Uncertainty Regarding Fundamental Theology

Anyone who casts an eye over recent work in fundamental theology must be struck by the persistent recurrence of questions about its identity, object and method. Without going back beyond the Council, we find Johann Baptist Metz saying in 1965, in an editorial launching the section on fundamental theology in *Concilium,* that this discipline, more perhaps than any other, is in need today of "a new understanding of itself."[6] At almost the same time, Karl Rahner was throwing out his idea of a basic course of theology which would have for its purpose to survey everything which "at the existential and prescientific level can *justify* the faith of an educated modern person." This indication of purpose was accompanied by a statement of the subjects to be treated or omitted; his procedure entailed a major reversal of received ideas, the chief of which, perhpas, had to do with the method to be followed.[7]

Three years after the appearance of Rahner's essay, and almost simultaneously, two periodicals, *Concilium* and *Gregorianum,* published contributions which gave insight into the prevailing state of mind. *Concilium* devoted an entire issue to fundamental theology, its recent history, its problems, and the way in which it was being taught throughout the Christian world. The editors of the issue justified the undertaking by pointing out that "its [fundamental theology's] specific tasks make this branch of theology more deeply involved in constant change than others."[8] *Gregorianum,* for its part, published the papers of a meeting of several professors at the Gregorian University who were in search of this discipline's lost identity.[9] The relative agreement among the participants in the meeting meant that some points of agreement emerged, but in the papers of this meeting as in those published by *Concilium,* we can discern a real uncertainty with regard to the concept behind the term "fundamental theology."

This indecision is explained to some extent by the historical background as detailed in certain essays, such as that of Claude Geffré, who recalls the recent history of fundamental theology,[10] and especially that of Henri Bouillard, which sheds more light because it goes further back and reminds us of the anti-deistic context which conditioned the appearance on the scene of the rationalist apologetics that was the not-too-distant ancestor of our present-day fundamental theology.[11]

At the beginning of the seventies Father Bouillard is able to distinguish three trends among the practicioners of fundamental theology. 1. First of all, there were those whose outlook in fundamental theology was primarily dogmatic and who made divine revelation the central point in their thinking. "They show how [revelation] took place in the history of salvation which reaches its climax in Jesus Christ, then how this revelation has been transmitted by means of ecclesial tradition, scripture and the Magisterium, and finally how it is accepted by faith and rendered explicit by theology." Among the representatives of this position the author singles out René Latourelle in his *Theology of Revelation* and, with the nuances proper to each,

Karl Rahner in the work mentioned above, Hans Urs von Balthasar in his *Herrlichkeit* [Glory], and Henri de Lubac in parts of his many writings. This is the position toward which I myself incline.[12]

2. Next come those who preach a fundamental theology "which is apologetic in purpose," that is, "which endeavors to explain, in terms intelligible to nonbelievers, what believers consider to be the rational foundations of their faith." Bouillard locates himself among the representatives of this second position, which "does not rely on the authority of scripture and the Church but advances by way of philosophical reflection and an examination of historical facts."

3. Thirdly, there are the theologians in whose view fundamental theology should be conceived "as an investigation of the foundations of theological science, analogous to that which is carried on by the exact sciences and yielding an axiomatic, formal theory of the fundamental categories of theology; such a study would be based on modern logic, semantics and linguistic analysis."[13] This is the kind of project G. Söhngen presents in his article "Fundamentaltheologie" in the *Lexikon für Theologie und Kirche*. It is also the kind of project which H. Stirnimann's essay (later than Bouillard's) makes the reader think of at more than one point.[14]

This picture resembles a French garden in that it points out avenues through a reality which would otherwise be pretty much an expanse of matted underbrush. As a matter of fact, the picture only partially represents the reality which, taken in its full dimensions, is much less orderly. The reader need only page through the issues of *Concilium* on fundamental theology to verify this for himself.

If we place ourselves at the vantage point of strictly external criticism, it is already possible to distinguish two periods within the position taken by *Concilium* itself. The two are clearly indicated by the general title given to the issues dealing with fundamental theology: "Borderline Questions" was the general heading for the issues from 1965 to 1972, while "Fundamental Theology" was the general rubric adopted beginning with issue no. 85 in 1973.

The aim of the first series had been explained by J. B. Metz in the editorial with which he launched it.[15] As he describes them there, borderline questions include but go beyond the questions proper to fundamental theology. By and large, they correspond to the subject matter of the conciliar Constitution *Gaudium et Spes* on the Church in the Modern World (the Constitution was at that very time being composed under the working title *Schema XIII*). Given this perspective, we are not surprised to find a wide variety of themes being selected for subsequent issues. One or other article (sometimes even a whole issue, such as no. 46) may treat subjects belonging by full right to fundamental theology, but we also come upon others that belong purely and simply to dogmatic theology or moral theology.

From the beginning, therefore, we can see, on the one hand, a certain practical confusion about the precise boundaries of the area covered by fundamental theology, and, on the other hand, some theoretical difficulty in defining the proper object of this discipline.[16] These initial fluctuations did not disappear when the title of the second series of issues was changed. Although the series now bears the overall title of "Fundamental Theology" and does include from time to time articles on problems specific to this discipline, it continues nonetheless to deal with borderline questions (Church-world). It can be said without being paradoxical that this second series, which in theory should have been devoted to problems characteristic of fundamental theology, is the series that has least to say about these problems.

In the preceding remarks I am certainly not questioning the interest of the subjects treated in these issues of *Concilium* nor denying the need of treating them. I am simply calling attention to the fact that fundamental theology cannot deal with anything and everything without losing its identity. We need to look elsewhere to find the reason for the uncertainty and indecision which I mentioned at the beginning of this section. Lacking a sufficiently clear and exclusive choice at the very outset, the theologian will be constantly tempted to include in fundamental theology a number of subjects which seem to have in common only the fact that they have no specific place elsewhere in theology. Such an approach cannot ensure the unity of a discipline, but rather destroys it. We are faced once again with the defect which Ambroise Gardeil criticized long ago when he spoke of a "sacred pantology."[17] Henri Bouillard has more recently reminded us, and with good reason, of the dangers of such a procedure.[18] We must be forthright and say that from the viewpoint of methodology such an approach is a step backwards.[19]

Among more recent studies in this area we find the name of J. B. Metz occurring once again, with his book *Faith in History and Society.* The book's subtitle: "Toward a Practical Fundamental Theology," shows clearly that it comes within our purview here.[20] Metz here tries to refine his conception of political theology in the light of the criticisms it has met; he also proposes to consider this political theology as being a practical fundamental theology that is conceived as an invitation to Christianity. Despite the inherent interest of its contents, however, this book (which includes, among other things, some articles that have already appeared in *Concilium*) does not advance the definition of our discipline. The author is still persuaded that the subject matter of fundamental theology is provided by questions raised by the encounter of Church and world; the main preoccupation is still with borderline questions.[21]

Much more interesting, in my opinion, is H. Stirnimann's essay, which, like the German original of Metz's book, was published in 1977.[22] It is by far the most important study that has appeared in the postconciliar period, not only by reason of its bulk but even more because of its considerable historical information, its rigorous thinking, and the significant proposals the author makes with regard both to scholarly research and practical teaching. Very briefly, the study is intended as a solidly grounded proposal in the service of an ecumenical fundamental theology; in fact, in his essay the author carries on a dialogue with non-Catholic theologians. More specifically, the author defines fundamental theology as the reflective, critical study of the foundation of theology. This involves him immediately with three major groups of problems: those of revelation, those of tradition, and those of theological method (and connected questions).

These have always been the themes of fundamental theology, but Stirnimann approaches them in the light of four main concerns which reflect the whole new climate of contemporary theology: 1. Faith and reason; 2. Faith and understanding; 3. Faith and praxis; 4. Faith and experience. The fourfold repetition of the word "faith" in this listing is a way of calling attention to a basic point Stirnimann makes: the impossibility of a neutral, purely academic approach to theology (and therefore to fundamental theology). Theology can be done only on the basis of a lived faith and must lead to practice and commitment in accord with this faith.[23] Located as it is between a general dogmatics and a metatheology which represent two extremes to be avoided, this ecumenical fundamental theology is likely to prove a difficult balancing act.

Nonetheless, even though we must ask a few critical questions of the author, it must be acknowledged that his essay treats the various aspects of the subject in a masterful way.[24]

II. Presence of Protestant Theology

The most important event in the recent history of fundamental theology is undoubtedly the entry of Protestant theologians into an area that used to be regarded as the private preserve of Catholic theologians.[25] The first of our contemporaries to travel this new path is Gerhard Ebeling who in 1970 published his "Reflections on an Evangelical Fundamental Theology"[26] and shortly afterward in 1975, various essays on fundamental theology in the third volume of his *Wort und Glaube* [Word and Faith].[27] The 1970 article was very influential and is readily acknowledged as a point of departure both by Catholic theologians (such as Stirnimann and Metz) and by Protestant theologians. In fact, Wilfrid Joest refers explicitly to Ebeling in his own *Fundamentaltheologie* of 1974.[28] Max Seckler seems quite justified, therefore, in hailing Ebeling as "the first Protestant fundamental theologian" while describing Joest's word as "the first Protestant fundamental theology."[29]

Flattering though these evaluations are (and even justified, as far as recent theology is concerned), they are not completely accurate. According to Ebeling himself, the terms "foundations," "fundamental doctrine" and even "fundamental theology," as well as the realities corresponding to such terms can be found in the works of Protestant authors from as early as the second half of the eighteenth century. More than that, Ebeling claims that the introduction of the very name "fundamental theology" for a special discipline within Catholic theology was effected under the influence of a usage already widespread in the Protestant world.[30] This point, which Ebeling says is in need of further verification, receives broad confirmation from the extensively documented historical sketch which Stirnimann gives of the beginnings of fundamental theology. At the decisive point in this history, when the theologians of Tübingen were constructing their great works, they found not only suggestions but in many cases a model in parallel Protestant writing. Similarly, the prehistory of fundamental theology, in the form of an apologetics meant as a weapon against a spreading rationalism, was not begun (contrary to a widespread view) by Catholic authors but by Anglican and Protestant authors.[31]

Consequently, when nowadays such authors as Ferdinand Hahn,[32] Johannes Flury,[33] Horst Beintker,[34] or in French, the theologians writing in *Etudes théologiques et religieuses*[35] turn to fundamental theology and apologetics, their action represents less a novelty than a spectacular return to a venerable heritage of the Reformed tradition. In this renewed sharing of interests by Protestant and Catholic theologians Stirnimann sees a sign of promise for the future of the ecumenical fundamental theology for which he himself is calling.

If we turn now to the themes and tasks which the authors just mentioned see as proper to fundamental theology we find them listing a whole series of questions which is identical at a number of points with the questions put forward by Catholic authors. Hahn, for example, whose article is entitled "Exegesis and Fundamental Theology," speaks of the indissoluble bond linking these two disciplines and takes the question of the historical Jesus as a concrete example.[36] Flury, who cannot help feeling a certain admiration for the compact structure of Catholic fundamental theology (as expressed, for example, in the documents of Vatican II), gives preference to the themes characteristic of dialogue with unbelievers and with philosophy. Beintker mentions chiefly questions having to do with relations between faith and reason. Joest, for his part, uses the name "fundamental theology" to refer to a doctrine about the foundation and methods of theology. By this he means a foundation, a critical reflection on theology's understanding of itself, on the methods used in theology as a whole, on its object and function, on the foundations and norms of its statements, and on its relation to science generally.

Ebeling too is much concerned about the epistemological and methodological task of fundamental theology. In regard to what he calls the main business (*Hauptgeschäft*) of fundamental theology, namely "as radical as possible a statement of the problem of truth," he formulates three requirements that must be met: a methodical determination of the conditions for a historical and systematic verification of theological statements; a determination of what is specific to Christianity; and a working out of the major guiding distinctions, such as God-world, nature-grace, sin-forgiveness, law-gospel.[37]

We may be allowed to doubt the necessity of including all the last-named themes in fundamental theology, but on the other hand we can only applaud the increasingly pronounced tendency to give serious thought to the problems of theological criteriology. Protestant writers will render an important service to their Catholic colleagues by reminding them of this area which they have too often neglected.

III. Revival of Apologetics

The reader may be surprised to see apologetics put down as a *new* trend. Is this not in fact a very old trend, but definitively discredited now by reason both of its weaknesses and of its excesses? This is indeed a rumor that has been abroad among Catholic theologians for some thirty years now. But it is not a very well-founded rumor, and serious theologians have never questioned the need for the apologetic task. In fact, some of them—Henri Bouillard, for example—have gone on successfully defending the view that fundamental theology is apologetic in nature, its ambition being to discourse in ways acceptable even to unbelievers.[38] And yet it must be admitted that this type of thing has been in disfavor among Catholic theologians for some time now; if it should manage to win favor again, we would indeed have to speak of a revival or return.

Here again, Protestant theologians have played an important role. In addition to the Protestant theologians, chiefly German-speaking, whom I mentioned in the previous section, we may name here a whole series of English-speaking authors, Protestant and Anglican, for whom this type of undertaking has continued to be, or has become once again, a living reality.[39] Paul Tillich, whose *Systematic Theology* is presented unambiguously as an apologetic theology, is doubtless the best known of these writers. But there are others, such as Schubert Ogden,[40] Gustaf Aulén,[41] and John Macquarrie,[42] who with more or less direct reference to Tillich pursue a similar course: to show that there is a correspondence (Tillich speaks of a "correlation") between human existence and the gospel message.[43] Each author's work is marked by emphases peculiar to him, but none of them doubts the importance of the task.[44]

On the Catholic side, apologetics is once again being looked upon with greater favor, at least when it comes to declarations of principle. In the article of which I spoke earlier, Henrich Stirnimann vigorously defends the cause of this discipline. Far from referring to something negative (as current usage of the term would suggest), apologetics is on the contrary an eminently positive procedure based on faith. It is in no sense a dishonest technique using any and every argument in order to prevail at any price. As an undertaking that has for its purpose to defend the faith and show its reasonableness, apologetics is an integral and indispensable part of the discourse of faith. The manner in which the great apologetes of the past carried out this task is enough to show its beauty and fruitfulness. We need think only of Pascal or Kierkegaard, both of whom did more for the Christian faith than armies of professors of theology.[45] Stirnimann indeed, does not think that apologetics should be confused with fundamental theology or that it is even a part of it, but his concern in maintaining this position is to distinguish the specific task proper to each, and not to deny the specific task of apologetics.[46]

Johann Baptist Metz is no less clear. He too recalls the bad press which apologetes have had until recently as professional defenders of the Church who are inspired by a shortsighted ideology and a real mania for always having the last word, and always suspected of insincerity and of looking solely for tactical advantage. Yet Metz does not hesitate to make this uncompromising assertion: "The apologetical approach forms the basis of all genuine Christian theology. As an attempt to justify or defend Christian hope, it is as old as Christianity itself and the controversies in which the Christian religion has always been engaged."[47] The example of St. Justin, apologete and martyr, is enough to confer a patent of nobility on this task. At the same time, it shows that the duty of giving an account of the faith is not a purely intellectual or theoretical matter, but extends to the testimony of one's life and even to dying for the cause. "Apology" or defense is here very close to "following of Christ" and therefore includes a praxis.

On the basis of New Testament language, which emphasizes the public and quasi-juridical character of such a defense,[48] as well as of the example of Justin as he followed in the footsteps of Christ and his apostles, Metz stresses the point that this praxis implies taking a position with regard to political power and its embodiments. He even thinks he can see here something like a scriptural basis for his own practical fundamental theology. One may feel free not to follow him as far as this, and yet continue to regard his rehabilitation of apologetics as a very positive contribution.

Other examples of this new interest in apologetics might be cited.[49] Neither may we overlook the undeniable apologetic dimension in the work of certain great contemporaries of ours: Teilhard de Chardin and Karl Rahner, for example. Far from lessening the excellence of their work, the presence of the apologetic aspect shows clearly the extent to which every original reflection on the faith inevitably leads to the question of faith's justification, not only in the eyes of unbelievers or non-Christians but even in the eyes of the faithful themselves. Well before Justin and the Apologists appeared on the scene St. Paul had expended greater energy than anyone in defending what is specifically Christian.[50]

"Always be prepared to make a defense to any one who calls you to account for the hope that is in you" (1 Pet 3:15). These attractive words of scripture have always been regarded as the very charter of all theological work,[51] but they apply in a special way to the task of showing the legitimacy of faith. It is not surprising, then, that this verse from Peter should be a privileged point of reference for apologetes[52] and that we should find it being quoted on every side in our time. It states a task that came into existence with the Christian faith itself and is destined to last as long as that faith does.

IV. Theology and Experience

This is a trend that affects theology generally and not just fundamental theology. But since one function of fundamental theology is reflection on problems of epistemology and criteriology, it is clear that the renewed place given to experience in theology must be of concern first and foremost to fundamental theology.

The attention given to experience in theology is not as recent a phenomenon as we might be tempted to think. Without stopping to speak of the books of Ambrose Gardeil on mystical experience, which were addressed to a problem quite different from our present one,[53] we must at least mention the magisterial book of Jean Mouroux, in which experience was expressly presented as an introduction to a theology.[54] Shortly thereafter, in 1965, Henri Bouillard gave expression to an idea that has always been dear to him, when he described human experience as the starting point of fundamental theology.[55]

However, it is chiefly since 1970 that the appeal to experience has become a real commonplace. Beginning in 1970 we find a number of titles by English-speaking authors from North America and elsewhere; for example, Gregory Baum, Gabriel Moran, and Avery Dulles.[56] In Europe the same interest began to show itself at about the same time; I may mention especially an essay of Piet Schoonenberg[57] and an important conference which Gerhard Ebeling gave at Göttingen in 1974 and published a year later in the third volume of his *Wort und Glaube,* along with several other studies in fundamental theology.[58]

At this point I must allot a special place to a little book that appeared in France in 1972 and that by its brilliant writing contrasted favorably with the usual literary mediocrity of contemporary theological publications. But *Une foi exposée,* by Patrick Jacquemont, Jean-Pierre Jossua and Bernard Quelquejeu, was distinguished by more than its style. Its originality was also, and more profoundly, in its method: reflection by the authors on their experience as Christians, and its purpose: to render an account of a lived faith.[59] Jean-Pierre Jossua became the theoretician of this undertaking and isolated its characteristics in a study that appeared a little later on.[60]

Along the same lines I may mention J. B. Metz's defense of this type of essay in an article in which he put forward the thesis that a theologian's own life can be regarded as a kind of theological locus.[61] Finally, the term and the theme have also found their way into the work of specialists, for example, in that of Heinrich Stirnimann (who has written a number of things not mentioned here[62]) or in the "Chronicles" in which I have drawn attention to this phenomenon and suggested some criteria for discernment.[63] Then too there is the special issue of *Concilium* on "Revelation and Experience" (no. 133; New York, 1979).

To speak of a revival of interest in experience or a new attention being given to it is clearly to suggest the reappearance of a theme already known to theology. And in fact G. Ebeling reminds us in a timely way that *exper-*

ientia was one of Martin Luther's key words: *experientia sola facit theolgum* (experience alone makes a theologian).[64] But neither does Ebeling forget to point out that neither the word nor the reality was unknown to the medieval theologians. He mentions Bonaventure and Gerson;[65] he could also have cited Thomas Aquinas, some of whose themes closely resemble those of Luther[66] and who also uses the expression *cognitio experimentalis* (experiential knowledge or knowledge springing from experience).[67] Schleiermacher, closer to us in time, is evidently still the important name in Protestant theology; he repeats Luther's formula almost verbatim.[68] Georg Hermes (first half of the nineteenth century) may be rather forgotten now,[69] but the Modernist appeal to experience is still present in the minds of all.

As a cause of this new interest in experience Ebeling mentions the pressure of an environment that for three centuries now has been heavily influenced at every point by the methods of the experimental sciences. This factor doubtless played a decisive role in changing mentalities, but, nearer to us in time, and at least in French-speaking countries, we cannot underestimate the role played during the past fifty years by Catholic Action movements. Their well-known method with its three points: see, judge, act, has influenced not only the members of the movements but also their chaplains and, indirectly, even the theologians. The latter, often called upon to provide a theological "reading" of the "facts" put forward by the members, were surprised to discover not only a Christian and even a mystical life of unsuspected richness, but an implicit theology which when explicitated could be a source of great enthusiasm.[70]

The call for "a theology based on life," which was first formulated in these circles, preceded and surely influenced the desire of many contemporary theologians to practice their discipline in close connection with a vital environment. The essays I mentioned above (those of Jossua and his colleagues, as well as that of Metz) seem to me to be an echo—distant indeed and indirect, as well as highly filtered and controlled—of those initial, more informal essays. Nowadays the theology of liberation can be considered to be in part an extension, on a large scale, of the method that seeks to ground theology in life. Now it is a matter no longer of a few individuals or even of a much larger group, but of the life of the Church throughout an entire continent; the goal, however, is the systematic elaboration of the faith that is implied in the Church's life and practice.

The concept of experience, however, is one of the most "problematic" ones we have,[71] and it is here that fundamental theology has something special to contribute, both in clarifying the meaning assigned to the term and in formulating criteria for judging the possible normative value of experience in theology. Among the theologians who have addressed themselves to this task I must mention Ebeling who sees experience in general as structured by a fourfold relationship: (1) to life; (2) to history; (3) to reality; and (4) to perception. All this, which holds for secular experience, applies also to religious experience at its own proper level, which is that of the ultimate, the decisive, the unconditional, and of supreme interiority. In fact, it is in the concrete unity of Christian experience that experience of God, experience of the world and experience of the self are brought together. The first of these three experiences is evidently the decisive one, and faith, says Ebeling, is the lived experience, in harmony with God, of total human experience.[72] Normative values in this area are given us through the experience that is received by the handing on of the word of God in its original source, but this transmitted experience itself becomes perceptible only in Christian experience that is lived in union with Christ.[73]

Stirnimann in turn, but more briefly, raises three main questions: 1. Must theology be related to experience? The answer is evidently Yes. 2. Of what kind of experience are we speaking? The answer is quite similar to Ebeling's: an experience of the world and of life, with experience in, with, and through faith being at the center. 3. What normative value do various possible experiences have? Here again the answer is clear: Individual experience cannot serve as the ultimate norm; the only possible norm is that which is the foundation of faith itself, namely, the event of God's Word becoming a reality in Jesus Christ.[74]

At a time when I was as yet unacquainted with Ebeling's thinking or Stirnimann's suggestions, I had myself, in a first approach to the subject, proposed that particular Christian experience (the experience of an individual, a group or even a local Church) be tested in the light of the total Christian experience. The experience of the Church (which in turn has for its norm the foundational experience that is transmitted through scripture) is thus the vital environment for, and the framework within which to judge, the concrete experience of believers. Within this ecclesial experience, however, a place must be provided for two internally coordinated sources of critical evaluation: on the one hand, the service rendered by theology and, on the other, the hierarchical ministry in the exercise of its prophetic function. The second of these two has the final word, but neither one can carry out its work of discernment except in continual dependence on the foundational experience.[75]

In all likelihood, this appeal to experience as "locus of theology" and "theological locus"[76] marks only the beginning of a movement that will spread in the coming years. It is a promise of hope for theology which may find renewed vitality in it, but it is also a task laid on fundamental theology which must further define the norms for the utilization of experience.

2
The Necessity and Insufficiency of Fundamental Theology

David Tracy

Each theologian often seems dominated by a single concern. For some that concern takes the form of a particular thematic focus (salvation—reconciliation—liberation) around which cohere all uses of the broad range of the Christian symbol-system and the broad range of experience disclosed by those symbols. For others the wide-ranging character of the symbol-system and the equally wide-ranging and more elusive nature of the forms of experience and language involved in theological discourse occasion the need to reflect first on the character of theological discourse itself before proceeding to more thematic interests. Moreover, the distinct but related crises of meaning of both Judaism and Christianity in the modern period and more recently the crisis of the Enlightenment model of modernity itself intensify the need for clarification of the character of any claims to public truth. The related phenomena of historical and hermeneutical consciousness are the chief but not sole forces to occasion the question of the character of theological language moving to the center of reflective attention for many theologians in our period.

This general and familiar set of questions may take the more specific form of seeking ways to express anew the authentically *public* character of *all* good theology, whether fundamental theology, systematic theology or practical theology; whether "traditional" or "contemporary." In initially general terms, a public discourse discloses meanings and truths which in principle can transform all human beings in some recognizable personal, social, political, ethical, cultural, or religious manner. The key marks of "publicness," therefore, will prove to be disclosure and transformation.[1] For example, Christian theological discourse—here understood as a second-order, reflective discourse upon the originating Christian religious discourse—serves an authentically public function, precisely when it renders explicit the public character of the meaning and truth for our actual existence embedded in the Christian classical texts, events, images, symbols, doctrines, and persons.

When one focuses on the character of theology as an academic discipline and as a social reality one cannot but note certain complexities in the character of the discipline itself.[2] For distinct theologies and distinct disciplines in theology are related to distinct social realities as their primary reference group. It is true, of course, that the university setting of much contemporary theology forces to the center of theological attention the public character of any theological statement. The same setting, in its reflection upon theology as an academic discipline, impels the contemporary academic theologian to reflect upon the social realities involved. Since the very choice of the word "public" as a focus for theology logically involves a relationship to *social* realities ("publics") it may prove helpful to reflect first from the viewpoint of sociology of knowledge on what difference an emphasis upon one or the other of the three publics of theology (society, academy, church) actually makes for a particular theology.[3] My hypothesis is that the most helpful way to clarify this complexity is to propose the existence of three distinct but related disciplines in theology: fundamental, systematic, and practical theologies. There is first a need to state the basic meaning of each discipline and the fundamental differences of emphasis that occur in each. The major differences may be grouped under the rubrics of (1) different primary reference groups; (2) distinct modes of arguments; (3) distinct emphases in ethical stance; (4) distinct self-understandings of the theologian's personal faith or beliefs; (5) distinct formulations of what counts as meaning and truth in theology. As will become apparent in further analysis, these differences of types of theology reformulated as distinct disciplines within theology need not lead to the radical conflict or sheer chaos of entirely different understandings of theology itself. Yet a shift of emphasis on any one of the five questions listed above does in fact affect the very notion of what constitutes an authentically theological statement. Whether those same shifts of emphasis lead to real or apparent conflicts in each issue only further analysis of each type and its relationships to the other two can determine. My wager here is that to change the more global analysis of conflicting "types" or "models" for theology to a proposal for distinct disciplines within theology itself may lead to a clarification of both the real and the merely apparent differences within each type in theology on those five issues which affect any theology.

I. Fundamental, Systematic, and Practical Theologies: Five Problems

A. *In terms of primary reference groups, fundamental theologies* are related primarily to the public expressed but not exhausted in the "academy."

Systematic theologies are related primarily to the public expressed but not exhausted in the "church," here understood as a community of moral and religious discourse and action.[4]

Practical theologies are related *primarily* to the public of society, more exactly to the concerns of some particular social, political, cultural, or pastoral movement or problematic which is argued or assumed to possess major religious import (e.g., some particular movement of liberation or some major pastoral or cultural concern).

B. *In terms of modes of argument, fundamental theologies* will be concerned principally to provide arguments that all reasonable persons—whether "religiously involved" or not—can recognize as reasonable. It assumes, therefore, the most usual meaning of public discourse—i.e., that discourse available to all persons *in principle* and explicated by appeals to one's experience, intelligence, rationality, and responsibility and formulated in explicit arguments where claims are explicitly stated with warrants, backings, and rebuttal procedures.[5]

Systematic theologies will ordinarily show less concern with such obviously public modes of argument. They will have as their major concern the representation, the reinterpretation of what is assumed to be the ever-present disclosive and transformative power of the particular religious tradition to which the theologian belongs.

Practical theologies will ordinarily show less explicit concern with all theory and theoretical argument. They will assume in some manner *praxis* as the proper criterion for the meaning and truth of theology—praxis here understood as *practice* informed by and informing (often transforming) all prior theory in relationship to the legitimate and self-involving concerns of a particular cultural, political, social or pastoral need which bears genuine import.

C. In terms of *ethical* stances, other real differences emerge.

Fundamental theologies will be concerned *principally* with the ethical stance of honest critical inquiry proper to its academic setting.

Systematic theologies will be concerned *principally* with the ethical stance of loyalty to or *creative fidelity to some classical religious tradition* proper to its church relationship.

Practical theologies will be concerned *principally* with the ethical stance of responsible *commitment* to and usually involvement in a particular *praxis* situation; indeed, often to the goals of a particular movement and/or group addressing a practical problem.

D. In terms of religious stances, certain differences also emerge.

Both *systematic* and *practical* theologians will ordinarily assume personal involvement in and commitment to either a particular religious tradition or a particular *praxis*-movement bearing religious significance (often—as in Johann Baptist Metz, Jürgen Moltmann, James Cone, Rosemary Ruether, and Juan Luis Segundo—to both).

Fundamental theologians in fact ordinarily share that commitment but *in principle* will abstract themselves from all religious "faith commitments" for the legitimate purposes of critical reason. They will insist upon the need to articulate the arguments for theological discourse as public arguments in the obvious sense of argued, reasonable positions open to all intelligent, reasonable, and responsible persons.

E. Perhaps most importantly, in terms of *expressing claims* to *meaning* and *truth,* claims to a genuinely public character, the following differences also seem present and will receive the major attention of the present analysis:

(a) *Fundamental theologies* will ordinarily be principally concerned to show the adequacy (or inadequacy) of the truth-claims, usually the cognitive claims, of a particular religious tradition to some articulated paradigm of what constitutes "objective argumentation" in some acknowledged discipline in the wider academic community. Usually that other discipline will be philosophy or the philosophical dimension of one of the social sciences; hence the frequent use of the phrase "philosophical theology" to describe the same kind of task here labeled "fundamental theology."

(b) *Systematic theologies* will ordinarily assume (or assume earlier arguments for) the truth-bearing nature of a particular religious tradition. They will thereby focus upon reinterpretations and new applications of that tradition for the present (in that sense, systematic theologies are principally hermeneutical in character).

(c) *Practical-theologies* will ordinarily analyze some radical situation of ethical-religious import (sexism, racism, classism, anti-Semitism, economic exploitation, environmental crisis, etc.) in some social, scientific, cultural analysis, or even prophetic manner. They will either assume or argue that this situation is *the* (or at least *a* major) situation demanding theological involvement, commitment and transformation. In terms of truth-claims, therefore, involvement in transformative *praxis* and theological articulation of that involvement will be assumed or argued to bear predominance over all theoretical claims to truth.

If the situation described above is at all accurate, then it becomes clear that a radical if not chaotic pluralism of paradigms on what constitutes theology as a discipline and the public character of theology is likely to occur. It thereby becomes necessary to study more closely what kinds of arguments cross the more radical lines of difference and then what kinds of public discussion of the remaining major differences might profitably occur.

II. Some Constants and Differences in Theological Discussion

A. *Constants:* The route from a chaotic pluralism to a responsible one within any discipline demands that all conversation-partners agree to certain basic rules for the discussion. In fact, for theologians such agreement does occur in spite of their otherwise vital differences. Central among those already existing rules would seem to be the following:

All theologians agree to the appropriateness (usually the necessity) of appeals to a defended interpretation of a particular religious tradition and a defended interpretation of the contemporary "situation" from which and to which the theologian speaks. Moreover, even within the very general confines of this fundamental agreement, two further constants occur before the major differences surface.

1A. *First Constant: Interpretation of a Religious Tradition*

In keeping with the demand that a theological position warrant its position with appeals to a religious tradition all theologians are inevitably involved in interpretation. This in turn implies that some method of interpretation of religious texts and history will be implicitly or explicitly employed and defended. Since the general issues of hermeneutical and historical interpretation can be argued on extra-theological grounds it seems imperative for each theologian to explicate her/his general method of interpretation.[6] Included in that explication should be explicit argument defending any claim that the general rules of interpretation must be changed to interpret religious texts or events.

In sum, each theologian should feel obliged to develop explicit "criteria of appropriateness" whereby her/his specific interpretations of the tradition may be critically judged by the wider theological community. For example, consider the present theological discussion in Christian theology between some major forms of "existentialist" interpretations of the New Testament and some major forms of "liberation" or "political" interpretations of the same document. The latter insist upon the need to employ such Old Testament categories as the Exodus symbol in order properly to interpret the New Testament envisionment of human salvation as communal, political, and social liberation. The former insist that a distinctive characteristic of the New Testament basic vision of salvation is precisely its radicalization of interest in the individual, now become an authentic self. All or most of the prevailing differences outlined earlier are in fact usually involved in those conflicting interpretations of the basic understanding of salvation in the same document. Still it remains legitimate, even imperative, if a public discussion of these differences is to occur, that all interpreters agree to bracket all other differences for the moment so that a purely hermeneutical argument on which interpretations the texts in fact support without further extra-hermeneutical backings or warrants. Once that specific argument is clarified, the conversation-partners may *then* move on to the equally relevant issue of the present truth-status of the interpreted meanings. If that conversation does not occur, however, then it is all too likely that not merely hermeneutical differences but all the issues at once—and all the differences obscuring this crucial constant—will emerge to obscure the adjudicable conflict of interpretations and assure a talking-past one another's theological position.[7]

2A. *Second Constant: Interpretation of the Religious Dimension of the Contemporary Situation*

In keeping with the demand that a theological position appeal to some analysis of the contemporary situation,[8] all theologians are also involved in another constant of theological discussion.

This second "constant" is more elusive than the first since some theologians argue for the admissibility of appeals to contemporary "experience" as warrants for a theological statement while others deny this. On theological grounds, some theologians, for example, share the more affirmative and universal understanding of the Johannine understanding of world—or, alternatively, of the Jewish and Christian affirmation of the essential goodness of creation and thereby consider the "world" a fully appropriate locus for theological reflection.[9] Other theologians are far more impressed with the negative understanding of "world" in the more sectarian and exclusivist aspects of the Johannine tradition—or, alternatively, more convinced of the centrality of the sense of radical fallenness than of essential created goodness. The latter will ordinarily reject to various degrees of radicality any appeal to the "world" (e.g., to "common human experience") as warrants for a theological statement. Even in the latter case, however, some understanding of the contemporary "situation" and some (here usually negative) appraisal of that situation will be employed explicitly or implicitly to influence the reinterpretation of the tradition. The influence of the cultural shock of the post World War I crisis of European civilization was obviously influential upon (not, of course, determinative of) Karl Barth's rigorous stance against appeals to common human experience or religious experience in his crisis—theology of *Romans*. The shock of an encompassing technology is obviously influential upon the anti-world stances of such distinct prophetic voices in contemporary theology as Daniel Berrigan, Jacques Ellul, John Howard Yoder and William Stringfellow. Whether positive or negative in the appraisal of the contemporary situation, every theologian in fact is involved in some implicit or explicit assumptions about that situation and thereby—even when the present culture is judged demonic (which, let us recall, is an explicitly religious category)—in some analysis of a religious dimension of the present culture. Yet even before the arguments for and against that position are advanced, an agreement can be reached, I believe, on the following propositions:

Whatever *specific* interpretation of the phenomenon "religion" a theologian follows, she/he assumes or argues for an understanding of "religion" as, in some manner, involving particular "answers" from particular religious traditions to certain fundamental questions of the meaning of human existence. This implies, negatively, a reasoned refusal to consider adequate strictly reductionist interpretations of "religion"—i.e., religion is really "art" or "ethnic" or "bad science" etc., without remainder. This position implies that although the theologian will often share specific methodological commitments with her/his colleagues in "religious studies," the scholar in religious studies may, but the theologian must, bear the obligation to raise to explicit consciousness the question of the "truth" of, first, any interpretation of the most pressing, fundamental "questions" in our contemporary situation and, second, the "answers" provided by a particular religious tradition.

If this is accurate, then even before the difficult question of what constitutes a genuinely public claim to "truth" in theology is addressed, there is a common assumption among all theolgians on the need to provide some analysis of the contemporary situation insofar as that situation expresses a genuinely "religious" question, i.e., a fundamental question of the meaning of human existence. A public discussion within the wider theological community is entirely appropriate, therefore, on (a) whether the "situation" is accurately analyzed (usually an extra-theological discussion) and (b) why this situation is said to bear a "religious" dimension and/or import and thereby merits or demands a properly theological response.

If, to cite a "liberal" example, social scientific evidence refutes a particular model of the "secularization of Western society" employed in such earlier "secular theologies" as those of Harvey Cox or John Robinson, then this obviously affects one's appraisal of the further arguments on the religious dimension of that secularization. If, to cite a radically conservative example, the complexity of present technological society is not adequately analyzed by either Jacques Ellul or by some theologians employing distinct interpretations of Heidegger's understanding of technology, then this obviously affects one's appraisal of the adequacy of the theological analysis of the religious (here often as "demonic") character of present technology.

Although the presence of these two sets of demands and criteria by no means resolve all the important differences among models for "theology" as a discipline, they do clarify certain crucial constants which cut across theological boundaries. The second set of questions, moreover, may serve to indicate when a position in "religious studies"—whether sociology of religion, psychology of religion, or philosophy of religion is *also* on this account an implicitly or explicitly theological position.[10]

B. *The Major Differences: What Constitutes*
   a Public Claim to Truth in Theology

Every theologian does provide both (a) interpretations of a religious tradition and (b) interpretations of the religious dimension of the contemporary situation and thereby provides some interpretation of the meaning and meaningfulness of the religious tradition for the present situation. It is also clear that the logic of those interpretations forces the question of the *truth* of the questions *and* answers of the tradition and the questions *and* answers in the situation to the forefront of any genuinely theological discussion. This is especially the case when one also recognizes that the central subject-matter of all theology—the reality of God—demands by the very universality of its claims to meaning and truth a public explication of truth claims. Precisely here radical pluralism in theology erupts with a vengeance. Yet to pose this question to all three models for theology outlined earlier seems entirely appropriate if one grants the fact that each theology in fact asserts in some manner the "truth" of its position. The *constant* in this second and more complex discussion, therefore, is the articulation of some truth-status to any particular theological position. My wager is what if that articulation can be clarified further, then the significant differences among theological models might surface. Minimally, this clarification would allow for a clearer discussion of all claims to truth in the inevitable clashes which ensue. Maximally it may serve to warrant my proposal that there are three distinct but related disciplines constituting theology.

III. The Necessity of Fundamental Theology

Fundamental theologies share the two "constants" articulated above. Yet their defining characteristic is a reasoned insistence on employing the approach and methods of some established academic discipline to explicate and adjudicate the truth-claims of the interpreted religious tradition and the truth-claims of the contemporary situation. With historical origins in the *Logos* theologies of Philo and Justin Martyr, these theologies ordinarily possess a strongly "apologetic" cast, sometimes reformulated as "fundamental" theologies.

The major discipline usually employed is, of course, philosophy or the "philosophical" dimension of some other discipline. Philosophy as itself a self-constituting discipline continues to be the discipline especially well-suited for the task of explication and adjudication of such truth-claims as those involved in "religious answers" to "fundamental questions." Granted the pluralism of method and approaches within "philosophy" itself, still any genuinely philosophical discussion will inevitably raise and explicate the issue of truth. For example, in recent theologies there exist various implicit or explicit criteria for the truth of the theological claims; some employ a correspondence model—whether verification, falsification, or neo-Scholastic; others employ a coherence model—whether the strict coherence model of Thomas Torrance of the rough coherence model of Reinbold Niebuhr; others employ an experiential model for truth—whether in "softer" ontic claims to existential meaningfulness or harder ontological claims to adequacy to human experience; others employ a disclosure model—whether the modest Anglo-American linguistic model of either Ian Ramsey or several theologies of story or the strong claims for truth as disclosure-concealment of Heideggerian theologies; others employ a *praxis* or transformation model—whether the implied transformation of radical alienation through personal involvement of many liberation theologians or the explicitly transformation model for religious meaning and truth present in Bernard Lonergan's notion of "conversion"; others employ in effect a consensus model of varying degrees of sophistication. In any case, an explicitly philosophical analysis of the model implicity or explicitly employed and its success or failure in application cannot but advance the analysis. Systematic and practical theologies may be more implicit than explicit on the criteria for truth in theology. Fundamental theologies must prove explicit—and help to explicate the criteria implicitly present in all theological proposals.

In fundamental theologies, therefore, arguments will be formulated in harmony with the rules of argument articulated by a particular philosophical approach. The theologian will employ those arguments first to explicate the truth-claims and then to adjudicate them. The most obvious strength of this position is its ablity (indeed its insistence) that all theological statements be explicated and defended in a fully public way. More exactly, the word "public" here refers to the articulation of fundamental questions and answers which any attentive, intelligent, reasonable, and responsible person can understand and judge in keeping with fully public criteria for argument. The argument for this approach to theology takes various forms. Ordinarily, however, the following positions will be held:

(a) There are inner-theological reasons for this task. More exactly there exist warrants in the Christian tradition for a task like that of fundamental theology. Above all, the Christian doctrine of God renders explicit a particular interpretation of the whole of reality. That interpretation logically demands public, philosophical analysis of that universalist interpretation by all reasonable persons. Hence the tradition—within theology itself—for arguments on the existence and nature of God. The doctrines of creation and the universal salvific will of God provide further warrants for this exercise. The universalism of the basic Johannine and Lucan traditions, the clear implications of Paul's charge in Romans I that all are "without excuse" and the Lucan Areopagus speech in *Acts* provide scriptural warrants for this understanding of theology's task. The emergence of Logos theologies in Justin, Clement and Origen, the philosophical theologies of Augustine, Aquinas, et al, the traditions of different "apologetic" theologies, "natural" theologies, "philosophical" theologies and "fundamental" theologies throughout the history of Christian theology provide warrants from the tradition for this task.

In sum, either the public character of the fundamental questions which religion addresses (from the side of the "situation") or the fully public character of the answers which any major religious tradition articulates (from the side of the tradition) demands a theological discipline which will investigate and correlate both questions and answers in both situation and tradition. That discipline is here called fundamental theology.

(b) From the "existential" viewpoint of the fundamental theologian, moreover, even if *in fact* the theologian is a believer in her/his tradition, *in principle* as theologian (i.e., as one bound by the discipline itself to interpret and reflect critically upon the claims of both tradition and the situation), the theologian should argue the case (*pro* or *con*) on strictly public grounds that are open in principle to all rational persons. In all such arguments in fundamental theology personal "faith" or "beliefs" may not, therefore, serve as warrants or backings for publicly defended claims to truth. Instead, some form of philosophical argument (usually either implicitly or explicitly metaphysical) will serve as the major warrant and backing for all such claims.[11]

These last two factors (understood in the context of the larger, inner-theological argument) clearly distinguish this model of theology from the two remaining models and clearly relate it primarily to the public of the academy where disciplined and critical reflection is demanded.

IV. The Necessity for Fundamental Theology of Systematic Theology

The defining existential characteristic of this model for theology is its insistence that the theologian as theologian is a faithful member of the religious tradition. Her/his major task is the reinterpretation of that tradition for the present situation. All serious reinterpretation of the tradition for the situation is called systematic theology.[12] Since there are no reasons why anyone holding this position need reject the two "constants" outlined in section A, disagreements between this position and the first must take a different form. One form of the argument for systematic theologies which are ordinarily church theologies can, in fact, be articulated on public, philosophical grounds. For the moment its skeletal character and its intuitive appeal need initial and summary form.

(a) There are inner-theological reasons for doing systematic church theology. Indeed, the doctrine of God which so informs the fundamental theologian's insistence that public discussion of the reality of God as the referent of both our fundamental trust in the worthwhileness of existence and the reality of the whole articulated in various metaphysical systems also informs the systematic theologian's more "confessional" perspective. Here, however, the understanding of the Christian doctrine of God will yield a different emphasis. Like the fundamental theologian who relates the reality of God to our fundamental trust in existence (our common faith), the confessional systematic theologian will relate that reality to the Christian understanding of a fully authentic faith. Indeed what Christian theologian will not agree that Luther speaks for the entire Christian tradition when he states: "Faith and God—these two belong together"?

Like Luther, the confessional systematic theologian will insist that the "faith" in question must be authentic Christian faith with its trust in and loyalty to the God of Abraham, Isaac, Jacob, and Jesus Christ or one will not (or, more cautiously, will not theologically know that) the doctrine of God articulated in a particular theology is real or an idol. The inner-Christian drive to universality, the common faith disclosed by Christianity and the sense of a whole still present in our broken world drives the fundamental theologian to critical philosophical reflection. In an analogous manner the biblical fear of idolatry, the biblical sense of a fallenness that affects even reason, the biblical insistence that philosophical wisdom cannot judge the gift of faith drives the systematic theologian to a confessional position.[13] The confessionalist may appeal for warrants to aspects of John and especially to the main themes of Paul which the more universalist fundamental theologian will account for otherwise. It would be too strong to say that sin more than grace, radical redemption rather than the good of creation, the cross more than resurrection or incarnation will determine the confessionalist systematic position. Yet usually the sense of sin will be strong and the symbol of cross will play a central illuminative role for major neo-orthodox Protestant confessionalist positions just as a strong sense of the "supernatural" and a "high" incarnational christology will play equally central roles in confessional Anglican and Roman Catholic theologies.

(b) Nor is the confessionalist position likely to lack intellectual resources from the contemporary intellectual situation to warrant its claims to publicness. Indeed, as the most sophisticated model for a confessional theology in contemporary theology, H. Richard Niebuhr's subtle and careful position,[14] demonstrates a confessional position in theology can unite with a profoundly modern sense of historical relativity without collapsing into the privateness of either Christian sectarianism or secularist relativism. The perspectivism which informs all claims to universality (including those, as the confessional theologian is sure to observe, of all metaphysical systems) plays as the basic *leitmotif* from the viewpoint of the present situation. When joined to a strong biblical sense of idolatry grounded in a profoundly Christian theological sense of the sovereignty of God, the public plausibility of the confessionalist position seems secure. Christian theology, therefore, should not hesitate to begin with its own "inner history" and reflect upon its own "special occasion" or "illuminating event" as the properly "self-evidencing" reality of its foundation.

Nor will this confessional position be merely private or untested: not only will it allow for a "rational image" which permits abstraction of "general ideas" which are illustrated on other occasions; not only will it allow the views of others (histories external to the community) inform but not determine its own self-understanding, but it will also demand a constant dialectic between formulations of the revelatory tradition and the contemporary experience of the theologian. Christian systematic theology, therefore, is as fully aware of its perspectival character as any other historically conscious position on modern culture. Christian theology therefore consists in explicating in fully public terms and in accordance with the demands of its own primary confessions, the full meaning and truth of the original "illuminating event" which occasioned and continues to inform its understanding of all reality. Claims that a discipline, any discipline, can achieve more publicness than this for its truths are misguided: for all metaphysical or generally philosophical claims to universality are suspect to an historically conscious mind and all theological claims to the formulation of universal truth must be put under the strictly theological hermeneutics of suspicion of idolatry.[15] Whatever publicness is humanly achievable to disciplined reflection, so the argument runs, is accomplished by all good Christian confessional systematic theology related principally to the "public" of the church and articulated in the academy.

The systematic theologian might also argue that it is a mistaken judgment to assume that only the model for objective, public argument employed in fundamental theologies can serve as exhaustive of what functions as genuinely public discourse even for the "academy." Indeed, as Hans-Georg Gadamer, for example, has argued on strictly philosophical grounds, "belonging to" a tradition (presuming it is a major tradition which has produced classics) is unavoidable when one considers the intrinsic, indeed ontic and ontological historicity of our constitution as human selves.[16] Moreover, "tradition" is in fact an enriching, not impoverishing reality. Any serious recognition of the radical finitude of any single thinker's reflection and the wealth of experience, insight, judgment, taste, and common sense which enculturation into a major tradition provides enriches participants willing to be "formed" by that tradition. Any major Church tradition meets these general qualifications for an authentic tradition: the reinterpretation of that tradition by committed and informed thinkers of the tradition is the goal and drive of all good systematic church theology. In that wider cultural sense, such reflection is private, not public.

(b) Finally, the Enlightenment "prejudice against prejudices" (as prejudgments) which is said to inform the earlier model for public truth disallows crucial human possibilities for meaning and truth. In art, this prejudice against prejudice disallows an experience of the disclosure of the truth by the authentic work of art. In effect, Enlightenment prejudices can destroy the truth-disclosure of the work of art by removing the event-character of the work of art as a disclosure of truth. The work of art then becomes merely another object-over-against-an autonomous subject. Since the subject already possesses exhaustive criteria for "truth" he/she may feel free to judge all artistic truth on "unprejudiced" grounds: eventually as a matter of taste for "*de gustibus non disputandum.*" On this reading, the "enlightened" bourgeois critic with an all-embracing subjective taste is the one guilty of privateness, not the critic who recognizes the essentially public character of any genuine work of art or any authentic religion. Indeed it is all too easy in the modern technological situation where appeals to "reason" can become defined ever more narrowly even purely instrumentally for the interpreter of both art and religion to become a philistine. There is a long and slippery slope from Schleiermacher's "cultured despisers" to contemporary understandings of the entire realm of culture as both private and marginal to the wider public of society. Every society's self-understanding in the academy can be affected when the "humanities" become marginal to the "harder" pursuit of reason and truth in the scientific community. The presence of the philistine in art is well recorded since Matthew Arnold's time. The presence of the modern philistine in religion is a story yet to be told. For the philistine by definition must disallow a disclosure of any further meaning and truth than that already articulated in ever more "objective" criteria. The rest is a matter of private taste, personal preference, and consumer needs. In an analogous fashion, religion like art is argued to disclose new resources of meaning and truths to anyone willing to risk allowing that disclosure to "happen" by faithful attendance to (and thereby involvement in an interpretation of) that truth-disclosure of genuinely *new* possibilities for human life in a classical religious tradition of taste, tact, and genuinely common (as communal) sense.

(c) On this understanding, the theologian's task must be primarily hermeneutical. Yet this is not equivalent to being unconcerned with truth, unless "truth" is exhaustively defined on strictly Enlightenment and increasingly instrumental terms. Rather the theologian by risking faith in a particular religious tradition, has the right and responsibility to be "formed" by that tradition and community. Then a *communal* taste, a faith-ful tact, a reverential and public judgment may be expressed through the reinterpretations of the tradition in new systematic theologies.

(d) Moreover, since every interpretation involves *application* to the present situation, every theological interpretation will be a new interpretation. The "criteria" for judging its appropriateness *and* its truth, therefore, will be the general criteria for good interpretation. These criteria include the "disclosure" possibilities of new meaning and truth for the situation to which the interpretation is applied.

(e) This argument is dependent upon the assumption that "classics," defined as those texts and events and persons which formed communities of interpretation and are assumed to disclose permanent possibilities of meaning and truth, actually exist. If classics do not exist we may have *tradita* but no authentic tradition as *traditio*. Since even their most skeptical critics grant that the Hebrew and Christian traditions include classical texts, the hermeneutical theologians can argue that they perform an analogous public function for both society and academy to the philosophical interpreter of the classics of philosophy or the literary critic of cultural classics.

Any text, event, or person that reaches the level of *classic* expression of a *particular* person, community, or tradition serves an authentically *public* character.[17] One need not accept the Romantic notions of classic and genius justly criticized by Hans-Georg Gadamer to accept this argument on the ontological truth-status of the classic. Indeed all that need be accepted is the following thesis: A systematic theologian's commitment and fidelity to the *particular* classical religious tradition should be trusted on two conditions: first, *once* it reaches a proper depth of personal experience in and understanding of (*fides quaerens intellectum*) that very tradition which "carries one along"; second, *once* appropriate forms of expression (genre, codification, systematic exigency) have been developed to represent that tradition's basic experience and self-understanding of an appropriately public manner.

This application of the notion of a classic to systematic theology does involve public criteria of a depth-dimension of personal experience in and understanding of a particular classical religious tradition; criteria of proper forms of expression to assure that the first factor does not become merely private or idiosyncratic. Each of these factors demands, of course, further technical analysis on experience and its intensification on genres, and on the fully positive character of tradition as *traditio* before they can be accepted as other than a statement of a thesis on the public character of systematic theologies.

All first-rate systematic theology, on this reading, will serve exactly the same public function as any other classical expression. For when studying Karl Barth, Karl Rahner, Rudolf Bultmann, Hans Urs von Balthasar, Bernard Lonergan, Paul Tillich, Franz Rosenzweig, one notes in their best systematic works the same reality at work: precisely an experience and understanding of a classic religious tradition, once united with an intense, intellectual struggle to find proper, second-order genres and modes of reflection to *apply* that tradition anew, free their work to perform its authentically public character as the faith of a particular tradition finding public, not particularist expression.

In sum, if this brief analysis is accurate, then a case can be made for the public character of the systematic theologian's work as a hermeneutical theologian. "Truth" in systematics will ordinarily function as some form of a "disclosure" model implied in all good interpretation. With that working-model for the universality of the hermeneutical task as the "true" task of disciplined reflection, precisely a fidelity to and involvement in a classical religious tradition ("faith" or "belief-in") will function as a correct theological stance.

It follows that the primary referent group of the systematic theologian will be the church.[18] It does not follow that this will render systematic work private for society and academy—provided the case for the authentic publicness of the real disclosure of truth always already present in every classical text is recognized. For the present, the analysis may simply serve as a statement of a thesis they may prove intuitively correct or intuitively dubious to the reader. If the thesis is wrong, then systematic theology should be eliminated and only fundamental and/or practical theologies really function as theological disciplines.

And yet, as even this brief analysis should show, that counter-thesis is erroneous. Fundamental theology cannot live on its own. It finds that its own inner drive to truth and concreteness necessitates its move to systematics. Correlatively systematic theology cannot live on its own terms alone either. Systematics finds that its very commitment to true interpretation (not mere repetition) of the tradition drive it to interpret not only the tradition but the present situation. Thereby systematics reopens within its own horizons to the legitimate questions and concerns of fundamental theology. The same drive to the truth of concreteness impel both systematic and fundamental theology to recognize the grounding of their own theories and methods in a *praxis* deeper than all theory, and their own drive to concreteness imply their sublation by practical theology.[19] We are left with a paradox which the classical theological tradation recognized on its own terms: fundamental theology is necessary but not sufficient for theology; systematic and practical theologies are sufficient but must recognize as a necessary aspect of their own sufficiency the questions and concerns of fundamental theology.

3

A New Image of
Fundamental Theology

René Latourelle

Fundamental theology, to a greater extent than other disciplines, is condemned by its very nature to insecurity. It must be constantly creating its own tomorrow. As a boundary discipline that keeps an eye on the human sciences (history, philosophy, linguistics, psychology, sociology, ethnology), it shares the eventful life of these sciences. If it is to give an account of Christianity in response to the demands of the human spirit it must respond to the sciences which that spirit is constantly developing or renewing. As a "theological" science, it is affected by all the renewals in theology, especially in the area of exegesis. In consequence, fundamental theology must periodically reexamine itself, face new hazards and change course abruptly, lest it simply disappear.

The postwar period has seen one of these striking changes of course, as classical apologetics has been transformed into fundamental theology. The change of name is only the surface sign of a much deeper mutation that affects the very constitution of this science. To tell the truth, we must say that fundamental theology now carries a new passport, since the changes that have occurred affect its name, its content, its method, or, in short, its very identity. On the other hand, since the problems it faces remain substantially the same (revelation and credibility), it would be unjust to turn our back on the past and to act as if the present represented a totally new beginning. Since the fundamental theology of today, like the apologetics of yesterday, is formed in the image of its age and the age's requirements, it would be more accurate to speak of a "new image" of fundamental theology. Once again, the important thing is to understand and explain rather than to condemn.

The formation of this new image of fundamental theology has taken place during the postwar years. It occupies a period of three decades that correspond to a threefold movement of theological reflection: a phase of reaction against classical apologetics; a phase of expansion that coincides with the definitive victory of the name "fundamental theology" over the name "apologetics"; and, finally, a phase of focusing and of hierarchical organization of the tasks of fundamental theology. If we schematize this development and make Vatican II our reference point, we may speak of a preconciliar, a conciliar and a postconciliar phase. I prefer to speak of three phases or periods rather than of three chronologically distinct stages, since what we are dealing with is three waves that overlap as they succeed one another. When the second wave forms, the movement of the first may still be felt, and while the second is still unfolding, the third has already begun to form.

I. Phase of Reaction Against Classical Apologetics

"Traditional" or "classical" apologetics with its three steps: religious proof, Christian proof, and Catholic proof, was not the outcome of critical reflection on the object, finality and method of apologetics. It came into being rather as the result of a historical *need*, that is, of the struggle against the Protestants of the 16th century, the libertines and practical atheists of the 17th century, and the deists and Encyclopedists of the 18th century. The libertines and atheists had to be met with a rigorous theodicy and shown the necessity of religion. Against the deists, who were satisfied with a natural religion and who rejected every notion of a historical revelation, the need was to show that Christianity is the true religion, on the ground of cogent proofs that Jesus Christ speaks in the name of God. Against the Protestants, finally, it was necessary to show that of the various Christian confessions the Catholic Church is the sole true Church. In the realm of faith Protestants emphasized subjective elements, and in particular the action of the Spirit that makes us cleave to the word of God and gives us certainty regarding its origin. Catholic apologetics, on the other hand, stressed objective criteria. As seen by Vatican I, these criteria are chiefly miracles and prophecies.

Behind this three-stage process lies the conviction that faith is the necessary outcome of the proof of Christianity, while entrance into the Church follows from the proof of Catholicism.[1] This tripartite procedure, which was already in existence in the 16th century, became sacrosanct as a result of the publication, in 1754, of Luke Joseph Hooke's *Religionis naturalis et revelatae principia* [Principles of Natural and Revealed Religion]. The term "apologetics" became current around 1830, but it was only at the beginning of the present century that books appeared which not only undertook a rational, systematic justification of the decision to believe, but also endeavored, at the same time, to define the epistemological status of apologetics as a science distinct from both philosophy and theology. I mention, as landmarks, the classical works of A. Gardeil and R. Garrigou-Lagrange.[2]

The postwar context has been quite different from the one that saw the birth of classical apologetics. A vast renewal has taken place in theology, and in those areas, in particular, which are most closely connected with apologetics. I am thinking, specifically, of the renewal in biblical and patristic studies which have shown revelation and faith to be much richer, more concrete, more personal, and more flexible realities; of the renewal in the methods and techniques of exegesis; of the many-sided progress made in the linguistic sciences; of the contribution made by the philosophies of the human person as the subject who accepts revelation and faith; and, finally, of the ecumenical renewal, which has turned an aggressive and polemical attitude toward Protestants into an attitude of openness and dialogue. Beyond a doubt, there has been a change of mentality. This quite new cultural and religious context soon caused the weaknesses and limitations of the old apologetics to become visible. Here are some of the criticisms raised against it.

1. Classical apologetics aims to show the *credibility* of revelation, but it makes the attempt before undertaking a serious study of the reality toward which it intends to take a critical stance. And yet it is certainly not irrelevant to point out that the revelation in question here is not revelation of a philosophical kind, one whose "pattern" may be anticipated; it is rather something of a quite determinate kind that comes to us via history and the Incarnation. Only revelation can tell us what revelation is. For this reason, an apologetics that is built on the narrow foundation of a quasi-nominal definition is an undertaking in which the real problems may simply be bypassed.

In any event, it is surprising to see the structure of treatises that were being used as late as 1950–1955. These treatises spoke first of "revelation in general" and "signs in general"; then they undertook to study the revelation of Jesus Christ and the signs that accompanied this revelation. But, in point of fact, the only revelation we know, and indeed the only revelation that exists, is the manifestation of God in Jesus Christ. This is the primordial mystery, and provides the matrix for all others; it is the decisive event in the history of salvation. The first need of apologetics, therefore, is to study this intervention of God in the person of Jesus Christ, in all its richness and all its dimensions. Similarly, the only valid treatment of the signs of revelation is one that shows them as unified in the person of Christ. This revelation, then, is the *basic datum* on which the believer must reflect with a view to grasping its historical actuality and its meaning.

2. The question of *meaning* is the focus of the second criticism leveled against classical apologetics. After establishing by external arguments that Jesus is the messenger of God and that he founded a Church, classical apologetics concluded that we must receive from this Church everything that we are to believe. In drawing this conclusion, classical apologetics overlooked the fact (at least in practice) that the Christian message is supremely intelligible and that its very fullness of meaning is already a motive for accepting it in faith. Revelation is "believable" not only because of eternal signs but also because it reveals human beings to themselves; it is even the only key to an understanding of the mystery of the human person. We may not, therefore, isolate the historical factness of revelation from the meaning of the revelation. Apologetics did not dare tackle this question, probably in order that it might not seem to infringe on a domain reserved to dogmatic theology.

3. Many practicioners of traditional apologetics dealt only with the

messiahship of Jesus. They thought it sufficient to show that Jesus presented himself as a divine legate who had come to speak in God's name. The other testimonies of Jesus regarding his person were the preserve of dogmatic theology. But, once again, such a position is unacceptable. First of all, it forces us into repeated and unjustifiable reductions of the picture of Jesus that is given to us in the gospels, which confess him to be the Christ, the Son of man, and the Son of God. Secondly, this approach makes a simple legate responsible for the radical demands proper to one who claims to be supreme judge of all human beings. Finally, it makes unintelligible the miracle of a glorious resurrection, a miracle without parallel in the history of salvation. The dichotomy between divine legate and Son of God is artificial; it is contrary to the testimony of Jesus regarding himself and even more to the way the kerygma presents him.

4. A fourth criticism has to do with the minimal attention, or, better, the complete lack of attention, in classical apologetics to the conditions required for the acceptance of revelation and the signs of it on the part of the person to whom these are addressed. With scientific objectivity as its excuse, apologetics neglected one whole side of credibility. If, however, the object of apologetics is not an abstract credibility but the human credibility of revelation, then it cannot be content to study revelation and its signs in the abstract: "Apologetics must pay equal attention to the conditions which determine the subject's effective reception" of revelation and its signs.[3] In other words, there is such a thing as an objective study of the believer's subjectivity. If apologetics were to neglect the subject, "it would soon fall into a barren extrinsicism." On the other hand, if it were to ignore the *facta divina* and "seek to restrict itself to the subject," it would degenerate into meaningless language.[4]

Objective apologetics and subjective apologetics are not two strategies for conversion, nor two methods applied successively, but two aspects of a single, integral apologetics. In this perspective, the consideration of subjective attitudes and conditions is not simply an introduction to the proof (an apologetics of the threshold), but is rather coextensive with the entire demonstration and plays a part in the structure of each argument. At the beginning, it takes the form of a reflection on the human person as possessed of a mysterious openness to a possible word of God in history. Then, in the treatment of each and every sign, it intervenes to show that the decipherment of the signs requires a number of dispositions; otherwise the signs will remain phenomena that are not only anomalous but exasperating as well. Finally, the consideration of subjectivity comes into play in the acceptance of the word, for this acceptance is an option, a decision, a gift of the whole person to the God who likewise gives himself wholly. The need of taking human subjectivity into consideration was brought out by Blondel and is now taken for granted.

5. Until well into the twentieth century apologetics continued to lash out at its adversaries: Protestants, deists, rationalists. In the present ecumenical atmosphere this attitude is no longer defensible. The primary con-

cern is not to refute, but rather to create conditions in which access and listening are possible. In seeking to defend itself the old apologetics turned in on itself and blocked others out. Happily, it has now laid aside the cutting, polemical tones that discredited it in the past. Instead of formulating its statements in terms of oppositions, it does so now as positions and propositions. It has shifted from pleading a case to offering a dispassionate yet critical explanation. Besides, the enemy today dwells as much in the heart of the believer as in the heart of the unbeliever. The men and women of the twentieth century are interested less in refutations than in having their problems faced and in receiving a responsible explanation of the credentials of Christianity. This is a task apologetics would have to accept, even if there were no adversary.

The difficulties I have been listing are less an indictment brought against apologetics from outside than a self-criticism on the part of those whose mission it was to teach apologetics in the postwar years. As these teachers sought to determine the status of their discipline in a new and quite different context of life and thought, they were obliged to engage in a number of adjustments which amounted to many liberating choices. This much is certain: on the eve of the Council there was agreement among these teachers on a number of points.

Negatively, first of all, they recognized: (*a*) that apologetics is not an art nor a pastoral method for obtaining conversion, but a science that has its object, finality and method; (*b*) that it is not a system of defense against adversaries; (*c*) that it is not simply a philosophico-historical treatise; (*d*) that it is not reducible to a study of the fact of revelation, while prescinding from the mystery this revelation implies and from the means it contains; (*e*) that it cannot abstract from the conditions required in the human subject and limit itself solely to historical proofs; (*f*) that it cannot be satisfied with the same "apologetics," which has now been discredited by centuries of polemics.[5]

Positively, they recognized: (*a*) that apologetics is a real theology, elaborated in the light of faith, or, in other words, that it is a search for the intelligibility proper to faith as found through a study of the most basic Christian reality: revelation and its acceptance by faith; (*b*) that the privileged object with which this discipline deals, namely revelation, ought to be seen in its *totality,* that is, in its dimension of mystery, in its historical manifestation, in the signs of this manifestation, in the objective forms in which it finds expression and perdures through the centuries (tradition, scripture, magisterium); consequently, the apologetic and dogmatic treatments of revelation are seen not as opposed but as complementary and necessary; (*c*) that while the study of the credibility of revelation is indispensable, the theme is one that must include the study of Christianity as a historical phenomenon and as an interpretation of human existence; (*d*) that a reflection on the nature and method of theology is indispensable; in other words, that an epistemology and a methodology are necessary; and (*e*) finally, that the apologetic task is essentially an ecclesial one:[6] it is a service to the Church.

II. Phase of Expansion

The second phase in the postwar history of fundamental theology began around the sixties and culminated in the promulgation of the conciliar Constitution on Divine Revelation (*Dei Verbum*). After it had exorcised the ghost of the old apologetics and had dissociated itself from the very name with which it had been linked, the "new style" apologetics experienced the joy of a second spring. Books and articles on revelation proliferated; commentaries on *Dei Verbum* were legion. This period was marked by an *expansion* of the discipline, and this expansion could be seen at every level: broadening of its role, additions to its privileged themes, dialogue with new interlocutors. All this found concrete expression in the definitive adoption of the name "fundamental theology" as indicative of its new image and new identity.

1. To begin with, the very *concept* of fundamental theology was broadened. Significant in this regard is the vision manifested by the definitions or, more often, the descriptions that follow upon one another from 1960 to 1970.

In this exposition I am interested less in being complete that in pointing out significant milestones in a development.

As early as 1969 *N. Dunas* was insisting that the term "fundamental theology" is not a label stuck on to basically heterogenous disciplines that are brought together for the sake of convenience. The first year of theological study is "fundamental," he said, because it studies the dogma which is first in the order of knowledge. Fundamental theology "is concerned with the theological criticism of the dogma which for us is the foundation of all the others: the dogma of revelation . . . it is a critical theology of God's word in its being and manifestations, its sources and means of expression." "This critical reflection which proceeds from faith and is carried on for the benefit of faith can develop only if it remains within the light of faith. It is therefore integrally theological."[7]

In 1962 *Y. Congar* distinguished two conceptions of fundamental theology. We may understand it, first of all, he said,

> as an integral part of theology, that is, as one of the special treatises, or a set of special treatises, that are part of the complete theological program: fundamental theology would include not only an apologetics, that is, a study of the reception of God's word by the human person, but also a *treatise* on this word of God both in its original state as revelation and in its state as tradition and dogma.[8]

As thus understood, fundamental theology studies the word of God under both the dogmatic and the apologetic aspect.

But fundamental theology can also be conceived as the defensive and justificative aspect of theology. In this view, says Congar, theology does not exercise its full powers, but only one of its functions, as the theologian endeavors to mediate between the world of faith and the world of critical reason. "He takes the signs God gives of his approach to human beings, and the call God addresses to them, and tries to make these valid to the human consciousness."[9]

> He works on behalf of faith and under the direction of faith, but he brings into play only such data as are acceptable to human reason. Working as it were under the judgment of critical reason and in dialogue with the unbelievers of his day, the theologian must undertake a critique of the foundations of faith and theology, which is to say: a critique of the word of God.[10]

This second conception is a fairly good description of our apologetics in its defensive phase.

In 1964 *J.-P. Torrell* expressed the view that there is no place for distinguishing, as Congar does, two conceptions of fundamental theology. There is actually only a single fundamental theology that "without any break in continuity, undertakes to defend on the plane of reason, but under the direction of faith, the ideas it has first had to establish critically by using all the resources of the fully supernaturalized rational mind."[11] Fundamental theology, says Torrell, carries out its work in two stages: the first is dogmatic and consists in "receiving from the Church the notions to be studied (revelation, tradition, dogma, faith, credibility) and then developing them critically so as to gain as exact a knowledge of them as possible." This stage is already "a first intellectual grasp of the datum, a grasp that, given the primordial character of these notions, becomes extremely important for its own sake."[12]

It is not enough, however, to show the internal intelligibility of these mysteries as seen by faith; the latter must also be established before the bar of reason, and this brings us to the second stage of fundamental theology (the one Congar describes as: fundamental theology as a potential part of theology), that is, to "the specifically defensive phase of fundamental theology in which the theologian must justify his faith, both philosophically and historically, to one who does not share it."[13] This is the place for speaking about the mission of Christ and the Church and about the Church as a motive for believing. It is also the function of fundamental theology. Torrell observes, to construct an *epistemology* (determination of the status of theology as a science; its relation to faith, philosophy, the sciences, etc.) and a *methodology* or study of the concrete procedure followed by theology.[14]

In that same year, at the international symposium held at Gazzada (September 6–11, 1974), I myself expressed similar views. The first year of theological studies (I said) "deserves the name 'fundamental' because it studies the first and most basic reality of Christianity,

> namely revelation or God's word to the human race. . . . Now this reality, like others in Christianity (for example, the Church) has

two sides to it: it is simultaneously a *historical event* that can be located in time, and a *mystery of faith.* This particular reality is the primordial mystery, the matrix for all the others. . . . On the other hand, revelation is also the first decisive Christian event, the one that is the condition and justification of faith. . . . Revelation even owes its richness, to some extent, to the fact that it is both mystery and event.[15]

Consequently, fundamental theology, like every authentic theology, will endeavor to understand this basic Christian reality, but in its totality, as both mystery and event. Its method will be at once dogmatic and apologetic, because the very nature of revelation requires this joint treatment.[16]

The first volume of *Mysterium salutis* [The Mystery of Salvation], which appeared in 1965, is entitled: "The Foundations of the Dogmatic Theology of the History of Salvation." The Introduction tells us that the volume is in fact a fundamental theology. However, the topics studied in this collaborative venture (revelation, the permanent presence of revelation in scripture and tradition, the actuation of this revelation by the Church, faith) show clearly that "fundamental theology" is understood here as a set of prolegomena to dogmatic theology, in the spirit of the first two chapters of *Dei Verbum.* The important problem of credibility is passed over. The point to which I must call attention here, however, is the extensive development of the subject of revelation.

In 1968 *V. Boublik* divided fundamental theology into two parts. The first is dogmatic and aims at an understanding of revelation; the second is apologetic and takes up the problem of credibility, but on an expanded scale, that is, as including historical, philosophical, and semeiological approaches.[17]

H. Bouillard has returned several times to the subject of fundamental theology. Each time, the discipline becomes wider in scope; this change in Bouillard's conception of it corresponds pretty much to the development of contemporary theological thinking on the meaning and status of fundamental theology. In 1964, in his *The Logic of Faith,* he ends a chapter on the nature of apologetics by saying: "It would be better if the manual of apologetics we have been planning here were to be described as a manual of fundamental theology. The reason should now be clear. It would supply the fundamentals to which dogmatic and moral theology must always return. For it would enshrine the true sense of dogma and the logical basis, the rationale, of Christian life."[18]

In 1965 Bouillard proposed the title "Prolegomena to Dogma" as a description of the study of those basic Christian realities that are the foundations of theology: revelation, tradition, scripture, magisterium. He reserved the named "Fundamental Theology" for *apologetics* or the study of the "rational foundations of the decision to believe."[19] In 1969, during a seminar at the Gregorian on fundamental theology, he expressed the view that fundamental theology deals with three essential factors: revelation, the faith that accepts revelation, and credibility or the relationship between faith and revelation.[20]

Finally, in 1972, in an article entitled "La tâche actuelle de la théologie fondamentale" [The present task of fundamental theology], Bouillard extended the scope of fundamental theology. Here he understands it to be the locus of a "dialogue between the Christian faith and the secular culture which believers and unbelievers alike share."[21] "If it is to set such a dialogue in motion," he says, "fundamental theology cannot any longer limit itself to the classical treatise on revelation; it must rather become coextensive with theology in its entirety"[22]; "it must become a function of all theology[23]; for it must show "how the Christian message with its various component parts gives an answer to the radical questions implicit in human existence."[24] This vast project can be carried out, provided we are able to synthesize in a single work "a summary of the content of the Christian faith and a summary of its justification."[25] This is also the idea behind Rahner's "foundational course in theology."[26]

In *Sacramentum mundi* (1968),[27] and then in *Concilium* (1969),[28] *H. Fries* assigns to fundamental theology (which has replaced apologetics, but without denying the latter's purpose) a twofold task. The first is to reflect on revelation itself, which is the basic reality of Christianity, the object of the believer's faith, and the principle and foundation of all the theological disciplines. In this part of its work, fundamental theology seeks to understand revelation in itself, in its essential content, in its communication to human beings, and in its transmission. It also studies the conditions required in human beings if they are to accept a possible revelation of God within history; it is not possible to separate a discussion of God as revealer from a discussion of the human person. The second task of fundamental theology is to study the signs or testimonies that bear witness to the fact of revelation and, consequently, to its credibility. Fundamental theology is thus to be seen as an indispensable reflection on the conditions for the possibility of faith. In the *Concilium* article Fries emphasizes the necessity of showing that the Christian message deciphers the meaning of the human condition at the latter's most mysterious level. All that God has revealed is meant to help us to "know who he [man] is and to turn the world into a human reality. The content of the Christian faith is meant to tell us who man is and what his existence means."[29]

According to *C. Geffré* fundamental theology may be defined as the discipline in which theology exercises its critical and hermeneutical function. In its *critical* function fundamental theology analyzes the historical conditions for the possibility of faith and the conditions for the reception of revelation through faith. By doing this, it shows that Christian faith is reasonable and therefore worthy of belief. In its *hermeneutical* function fundamental theology endeavors to bring out the meaning of revelation in terms of the understanding human beings have of themselves and their relation to the world. Geffré thinks that while these critical and hermeneutical functions are coextensive with theology in its entirety, they find "a particularly explicit expression in the two major sections of any fundamental theology: revelation and faith."[30] More recently, in 1977, Geffré has defined fundamental theology as "the critical study of the foundations of Christian existence, that is, on the one hand, revelation as the basis of faith and, on the other, faith as receptive of revelation."[31]

At this point I must say something about the important article of *H. Stirnimann,* the scheme of which shows analogies to that of G. Söhngen.[32] After a substantial and stimulating sketch of the history of fundamental theology,[33] Stirnimann explains what he means by fundamental theology. First of all, fundamental theology is not to be confused with apologetics, which is a defense of the faith, or with dogmatic theology. Fundamental theology must provide an introduction to the entire universe of theology (dogma, moral, exegesis, liturgy, history of the Church, missiology, pastoral theology). Starting from the principles of theology, fundamental theology justifies the diversity of theological disciplines and methods; it introduces the student to theological work and ensures the unity of the latter. But the task of fundamental theology is not exhausted by questions of method; it must also reflect critically on the foundations of faith and find expression in appropriate language.[34]

Concretely, fundamental theology tackles three series of problems: (*a*) revelation; (*b*) the Church; it does not provide a complete ecclesiology but deals with the Church as a community of believers and as the place where the revelation is transmitted; (*c*) questions of method (epistemology, theological sources, methodology, encyclopedics). These foundational problems, which may not be evaded, are seen in the light of four concerns that may be expressed in four pairs of terms: faith and reason, faith and understanding, faith and practice, faith and experience.[35] As thus understood, fundamental theology is distinct both from a general dogmatics and an abstract meta-theology.[36] In the final section of his article, Stirnimann sketches a six-chapter program for the teaching of fundamental theology.

Stirnimann's plan represents, in my judgment, both a broadening and a reduction of fundamental theology. There is an evident broadening of scope to be seen in his resolutely ecumenical outlook; in his sensitivity to modern problems of language, philosophy, hermeneutics, history of religions, praxis and experience; and, above all, in his concern for method. I would even say that fundamental theology, as Stirnimann conceives of it, is more like a discourse on theological method than a critical reflection on the foundations of faith.

On the other hand, by separating apologetics from fundamental theology Stirnimann deprives the latter of some of its traditionally most important themes: the deeper study and development of the basic concepts of Christianity on the basis of scripture, tradition and the magisterium; reflection on God's decisive intervention in history in the person of Jesus, who is the fullest form of this intervention; the relation between the gospel and Jesus, between text and event; a study of the signs which enable us to identify Jesus as God among us (works and miracles, loving self-donation in the passion; the resurrection; etc.). In short, a fundamental theology thus conceived is in danger of losing its specific character and becoming a reflection on a theological activity that has become more conscious of itself.

For *J.-B. Metz* the mission of fundamental theology is "to stimulate faith to a greater awareness of its responsibilities in the modern world."[37] This statement, which sets forth a program for the volumes on fundamental theology in the *Concilium* series, can be summed up in the term "borderline questions." These volumes, Metz goes on to say, "aim at tackling all the problems raised today as we endeavor to acquire a deeper understanding of the foundations for our faith and our proclamation of the message."[38] But as we read these volumes of *Concilium* we may well ask ourselves whether we are still in the area of fundamental theology and not rather in a domain *without borders.*

2. It is not only the concept of fundamental theology that has been expanded to such an extent that the nature of fundamental theology as a special discipline is threatened. There has also been an expansion in regard to the *two privileged themes* of classical fundamental theology: revelation and its credibility.

Since 1940 there has been a ceaseless proliferation of studies on the subject of revelation. This outpouring has been stimulated by Protestant scholarship which has been especially productive in this area; it has also been favored, in Catholic circles, by the biblical and patristic renewals and by the development of the theologies of faith, preaching and mission, which have all acted as catalysts.[39] It can be said that this renewal of the theology of revelation, which began with the work of H. Niebecker (1940), R. Guardini (1940), K. Rahner (1941), and L.-M. Dewailly (1945), and was patiently carried forward for two decades in increasingly numerous monographs, reached its culmination and was in a sense canonized in the conciliar Constitution *Dei Verbum* of November 18, 1965.

In the Constitution revelation is presented not only under its objective aspect as doctrine or message, but also as an act of God, namely, the self-manifestation and self-giving of God himself in Jesus Christ. Christ is God's epiphanic word; that is, he does not simply bring revelation, he *is* the revelation. Revelation as described by *Dei Verbum* is truly the Christian revelation, and not just any revelation of a philosophical or gnostic kind. This is a revelation of which Christ is both subject and object, that is, both revealer and revealed; he is its mediator, summit, fullness and sign. One of the merits of the Constitution is that it also presents Christian revelation not as an isolated phenomenon, unconnected with anything else, but as an "economy," that is, as a vast, mysterious plan which God carries out through the centuries in ways he alone knows. This economy is initiated by the Father; it enters history and then reaches its culmination in Jesus Christ, who is the fullness of revelation. It continues, under the action of the Holy Spirit, in the ecclesial community, by means of tradition and scripture and moves toward an eschatological completion. All the components of this economy are articulated each with the others; they support and shed light on one another; they are organized into a synthesis in which Christ and the Spirit are the source of unity and development. The Constitution also stresses the historical, interpersonal, dialogical, christological and ecclesial dimensions of revelation.[40]

By thus expanding the idea of revelation, and by doing so in fidelity to the data of revelation itself, the Constitution has effected a liberation. It has also rendered a valuable service to fundamental theology by bringing together in a single vision various themes that in the past were either scattered or artificially combined: for example, a treatise on inspiration that belonged to the treatise on scripture; a treatise on tradition that was put sometimes with ecclesiology, sometimes with the treatise on the sources of theology.

The theme of credibility has been expanded in no less spectacular a manner. While not denying what legitimacy there was in the traditional treatment of credibility in terms of the historical proofs or signs of revelation (miracles, prophecies, message, resurrection), fundamental theology in the conciliar age cannot fail to see the limitations of that treatment. There was an inadequate knowledge of the methods and techniques of modern exegesis; a simplistic use of certain arguments (for example, the argument based on the fulfillment of the messianic promises); a unilaterally apologetic vision of the signs of revelation; an overemphasis on a few signs (miracles, prophecies) to the detriment of the really important signs: Christ and his Church; an isolation of the signs from the person who gives them, and of the signs from the message that gives them their full meaning; an insufficient consideration of the sign of holiness or of the harmony between the message and the life; little or no attention paid to the conditions required in human beings for the reception of the signs and, correlatively, a tendency to overvalue their power to convince the subject; and so on.

These complaints are the negative side. Much more importantly, the fundamental theology of the conciliar age has become aware that if the theme of credibility is to be properly handled, it must embrace far broader horizons. In this expansion of perspective, three main areas of attention may be distinguished.

A first has to do with the problems of history and hermeneutics. Theologians have been quick to realize that the knowledge of Jesus by means of the gospels (in which revelation finds its maximal concentration) is not an enterprise that may be taken for granted. If it be the fact that God has "revealed" himself in Jesus: in this man's words and works and entire presence in the world, then it is of supreme importance to know whether, how, and to what extent we can make real contact with this epiphany of God, at least in its historical reality. It follows that the problem of access to Jesus via the gospels is absolutely fundamental to any reflection on the credibility of Christianity. For, if we are unable to determine the relationship between history and kerygma, event and text, it is useless to proceed any further in our study of Jesus, since the original event, which is the source of Christianity, is inaccessible.

In the case of Jesus this historical problem is accompanied by a hermeneutical problem. We know that the rereading, in the light of the resurrection, of the event which was Jesus and his earthly life set in motion a whole process of interpretation that is now woven into the very texture of the gospels. How, then, can we get back to the Jesus who lies beneath the superimposed layers of apostolic preaching, ecclesial interpretation and actualization, and the editorial activity of the evangelists? The real relation between the text and the event that is Jesus is being determined only gradually by the joint efforts of historical and hermeneutical scholarship. This first problem connected with credibility has already given rise to an immense literature.[41]

The second area of attention is *anthropology,* in response to the objection raised against the old apologetics, that it had separated the fact and the content of revelation and had studied the event without any concern for the meaning it has for human beings. A hermeneutics focused solely on the origin of Christianity in Jesus would be sterile, because Jesus is not simply a breakthrough of God into human history; he is rather a breakthrough that reveals human beings to themselves, decoding them, as it were, and transfiguring them. It is therefore not enough simply to show that the gospels give us access to Jesus of Nazareth. It must also be shown that the Christian message concerns human beings and the basic questions they ask themselves. This demand on the part of the contemporary human person finds expression in varying ways, but it is clear and insistent. People today expect to be shown that Christ alone supplies the key to the human cryptogram. This anthropological aspect of credibility had already been emphasized by Blondel in his *L'Action* and has been extensively developed by R. Guardini, K. Rahner, H. Bouillard, H. U. von Balthasar, M. Zundel, G. Marcel, J. Mouroux, M. Légaut, and J. Ladrière, even if within quite divergent philosophical horizons.

The third area of attention is the *signs* of revelation. The problem here is the *identification of Jesus as God-among-us.* Since Jesus is the human, bodily form in which God encounters human beings and manifests himself to them, the salvific presence of God in the world is, strictly speaking, to be authenticated only through the mediation of the man Jesus. He is the mystery, the riddle to be solved. Fundamental theology is therefore returning to a study of the signs, but now it does so with a more watchful critical eye; it is better equipped in the exegetical and historical domains; it is more conscious of the complexity of the problems it tackles and, consequently, less categorical in its claims.

This study of signs, too, is influenced by the hermeneutical problem in the interpretation of the texts that relate the signs. But the thing most characteristic of this study as conducted nowadays is a concern to connect the signs with the person who gives them. The signs which make it possible to identify Jesus are not extrinsic to him: they are the living Jesus himself in his totality, in the many aspects of his epiphany to the world. Such a theology of the signs takes into account the resistances offered by human beings in our day, and especially their antipathy to miracles. This is why it endeavors to bring out the internal *coherence* of the signs among themselves, or, in other terms, the fact that there is an "economy" or plan to them. It is also why this study of the signs lays great emphasis on the testimony given by a holy life. For, once the gospel was promulgated and the Spirit had been given, the great sign of salvation is a life lived according to the gospel, that is, the transformation of the human person into a new creature that lives by the Spirit, and the transformation of a human race that is gathered in unity and love. All this is done without therefore downplaying the other signs, such as miracles.[42]

3. Finally, the range of *those whom fundamental theology addresses* has also been broadened. Fundamental theology intends to be a theology *in dialogue:* not only with believers but with all forms of religion and unbelief. Who, concretely, are these new partners in dialogue?[43] They are the great religions of salvation: Hinduism, Buddhism, Islam, Judaism. They are the various forms of contemporary unbelief that draw their inspiration from Marx, Freud and Nietzsche. They are the vast areas of indifference that have been created by the secularized world of technicity and progress. They are also the cultures, civilizations and human types which all these represent, together with the problems they offer.

Finally, the partner in dialogue is believers themselves, not only because believers experience within themselves the same doubts as unbelievers, but also because present-day believers live amid a world of unbelief and indifference and inevitably are influenced by these. "That which feeds the thinking and the attitudes of unbelievers also keeps uncertainty and doubt alive in many Christians."[44] When we dialogue with unbelievers, we are dialoguing with ourselves. But this means that reflection on the rational bases of the decision to believe is not a game for intellectuals but a necessity of life.

If we now list together the points which make the fundamental theology of the conciliar age appear to be passing through a phase of immense expansion, we will understand the reason why the term "fundamental" has been adopted to describe it. Here, in concise form, are the points to which I am referring: (*a*) fundamental theology studies revelation in its totality as both event and mystery and, consequently, regards the compenetration of the dogmatic and apologetic viewpoints as necessary; (*b*) it exercises a critical function (analysis of the conditions for the possibility of the act of faith) but also a hermeneutic function (quest of the meaning of the Christian message for the human beings of our time); (*c*) it is coextensive with the whole of theology, insofar as it is a dialogue between faith and the secular culture of the age; (*d*) it must construct an epistemology and methodology of theology as a science; (*e*) its privileged themes are revelation and credibility; (*f*) it looks upon revelation as being simultaneously an act of God, history and mystery, and an economy; (*g*) fundamental theology sees the necessity of a threefold approach to the problem of credibility: historical and hermeneutical, anthropological, and semeiological; (*h*) in the study of the signs of revelation (which it links with Christ and the Church) it pays equal attention to the objective and subjective poles; (*i*) being ecumenical in its concerns it desires to carry on a dialogue with the other religions of salvation, with all forms of unbelief and indifference, with all cultures and civilizations, with the believer and also the unbeliever who dwells within the believer; (*j*) working as it does within faith, it must lead to a praxis, which itself in turn is a condition for understanding; (*k*) it is located at the point where the question of God and the question of man in Jesus Christ meet; (*l*) it fully merits the name "fundamental," which is now officially recognized and used in documents emanating from the Sacred Congregation for Catholic Education.[45] With certain exceptions, contemporary practitioners maintain that fundamental theology represents the integration, expansion and deepening of apologetics, rather than a break with it.

III. Phase of "Focusing"

In the years after the Council, that is, at the time when the reform of ecclesiastical studies was being carried out, fundamental theology was threatened by two equally deadly perils. It was threatened, on the one hand, by a dismemberment, a scattering of its traditional themes; and, on the other, by an excessive expansion which was turning it into a kind of "sacred pantology" and threatening to strip it of its specific character.

Paradoxically *Dei Verbum* fostered, to a degree, the dismemberment of fundamental theology. Since Christ is the "fullness of revelation," there was a strong temptation to shift the theme of revelation over to christology. On the other hand, it seemed natural to let the exegetes handle the technical questions that fell within their competence: historical value of the gospels, the themes of miracle and resurrection. Then the course entitled "Introduction to the Christian Mystery" absorbed everything else! As a result, in many places fundamental theology was either dismembered or else simply disappeared as an autonomous discipline, thus depriving theology of one of its essential tasks.[46] The process of disintegration was speeded up by paucity of qualified teachers.

On the other hand, the post-conciliar years also saw an ever-increasing *expansion* of the field claimed by fundamental theology. This expansion was made necessary by the renewal of biblical and historical studies, by the new ecumenical openness, and by the development of the human sciences, but it nonetheless had a deadly effect. Fundamental theology developed an annexationist attitude and was in danger of turning into an encyclopedic study of all the sciences: philosophy of religion, psychology of religion, sociology of religion, history of religions, confrontation with the various forms of atheism and with politico-social reality, critique of history, critique of language, problem of acculturation. Because it wanted to include and embrace everything, fundamental theology was at the point of losing its unifying center and specific character. Because it was so concerned with borderline questions it was forgetting that which should be its central concern, namely, revelation.[47]

In the face of these two dangers the need was felt almost everywhere of *finding a center or focus* and of *introducing a hierarchic order* into the subjects to be handled. In any case, it is typical that in recent articles on the problems of fundamental theology we hear more and more of a "search for identity," of a "unifying center" or "focal point," of a "structure" or "basic structure." Typical also of this felt need of unity and structure is the fact that the articles mentioned sometimes offer outlines of a revised treatise on revelation or even of an entire fundamental theology.[48]

At this moment of indecisiveness it will not be unhelpful to recall the urgency and necessity of a fundamental theology. In a recent article H. Fries states that fundamental theology is the theological discipline the need of which is felt most keenly today,[49] because the most pressing problems of the present time regarding God, Christ and the Church are problems belonging to fundamental theology. H. Bouillard, H. Stirnimann, J.-B. Metz, J.-P. Torrell, A. Manaranche and G. O'Collins use language that is no less categorical and emphatic.

If we are tempted to forget this urgent need of fundamental theology, various Protestants are there to keep reminding us of it. Thus Schubert Ogden, an American, writes: "The safest generalization about Protestant theology since World War II is that it has evidenced a growing concern with its inescapable apologetic task. . . .No theology today can be adequate which restricts itself to this dogmatic task alone."[50] Similar statements may be found in the writings of G. Aulén, J. Macquarrie, and L. Gilkey. P. Tillich explicitly offers his *Systematic Theology* as an apologetic theology. The term "fundamental theology," which until recently was missing from the Protestant vocabulary, has now made its appearance in G. Ebeling[51] to describe the hermeneutic function of theology, that is, theological reflection on the language of faith and human language and on the reconciliation of these two universes that are seemingly without any points of contact. Such a reflection is a precondition for the work of dogmatic theology, because it performs a task that must be done before any theology can begin. The term "fundamental theology" which Ebeling used became popular, for we find W. Joest using it in 1974, F. Hahn in 1975, J. Flury in 1975, and H. Beintker in 1976. This revival of Protestant interest in the problems of apologetics and fundamental theology is less a real novelty than a return to a traditional concern of the Reformers.[52]

In order to bring out the urgent need of the essential work proper to fundamental theology, we may look at the matter from the viewpoints of revelation and of faith. We can say that, as seen from the standpoint of revelation, fundamental theology is a discourse in which theology reflects on God's free intervention in Jesus Christ, or, in other words, on the self-manifestation and self-giving of God that are the utterly unique and original core of Christianity. But this free and staggering initiative which God takes in the flesh and language of Jesus Christ must carry in and with it the signs of its own authenticity. If Jesus is truly among us as the Son of the Father, as the Wholly Other, there must be some way of discovering and identifying him as such; he must allow something of his glory as Messiah and Lord to be seen. Otherwise the epiphany of God in Jesus Christ is, in the strict sense of the word, "unbelievable," and if the Church is unable to say on what evidence it relies when it asserts that "Jesus *is* Lord," its basic claim collapses.

In parallel fashion, we may say that *the decision to believe* must be shown to be a truly human option, that is, as something reasonable and meaningful. For, on the one hand, faith as the act of adhering to Christ is not an inescapable conclusion but a human person's surrender to God, a gift of the entire person to the God who gives himself entirely to us in Jesus Christ. On the other hand, while faith is an unreserved surrender of the human person to God, it is not an unthinking abdication of the self or a declaration of bankruptcy on the part of reason which is incapable of establishing the human rightness of its choice but falls back on fideism. The person must have knowledge *before* believing and *in order to* believe. Faith, in its root, is an act of understanding. It is indeed an option for Christ, but an option made in a clearsighted manner. Human beings who commit themselves to Christ must have valid reasons for doing so: reasons which can be spelled out in a coherent manner. The believer can "test" the soundness of his reasons for committing himself. The ordinary believer cannot usually give a detailed explanation of these reasons. It is for the theologian, as a servant of the believing community, to show that the option of faith has *meaning,* that it is *meaningful.*

When fundamental theology is thus seen in the light of its essential task, which is to explain revelation as "credible" and faith as "reasonable," or, if you prefer, to show that revelation and its acceptance by faith are *meaningful* for human beings, it is evidently not an optional undertaking that may be left to the good will of the theologians. On the contrary, it is a necessary task of which the Church cannot deprive itself without betraying its mission both to the faithful and to unbelievers who approach it with questions. If the Church were to cease reflecting on the reality of revelation as God's intervention in Jesus Christ and on the decision to believe as a meaningful decision, it would be signing its own death warrant.

In my view, this task cannot be taken over by dogmatic theology or by exegesis in the form of "occasional thoughts." The questions fundamental theology faces are too important by reason of their number and seriousness to be dealt which "in passing." I am thinking, for example, of the relationship of Christianity to history, along with the whole spate of questions this relationship raises; the relationship of Christianity to other religions; the relations between revelation, tradition, and scripture; the problem, which is such a complex one today, of the signs of revelation (for example, miracles and the resurrection of Jesus); and so on. These questions must be treated from a specific standpoint and in light of the concerns of one who, by profession, stands at the boundary where history, philosophy, exegesis and theology meet. If these questions are not faced in all their breadth and depth and

if they are not given satisfactory answers, then they cause doubts and un-
easiness to fester in the depths of hearts, and these doubts will then lead to
crises and cause shipwrecks.

It is a fact, of course, that a certain type of apologetics which was
marked by aggressiveness and ill-temper and which was ironclad in spiky
armor, has now been discredited. But this rejection must not be allowed to
include in a single sweeping judgment, along with the attitude it denounces,
the "authentic" problems that belong to apologetics. The "problems," after
all, remain with us; they are always "at the door." We may refuse to see
them, but we cannot get rid of them. The tone of apologetics must certainly
change, especially in the contemporary ecumenical climate, but the function
that fundamental theology must henceforth make its own, is a permanent
thing. In addition, the questions it deals with form a *totality* that has its own
proper unity and makes fundamental theology a distinct province of theology.

This leads us to ask: What is *specific* to fundamental theology? That is:
What is the problem that fundamental theology alone is to handle: a problem that dogmatic theology does not face as such and without which there
would be no reason for the existence of a fundamental theology? This problem is a single complex one: the *credibility-of-the-revelation-of-God-in-Jesus-
Christ*. The problem is not simply that of revelation as a mystery of faith,
because the reality here is not only a mystery in the strict sense but also a
breakthrough of God into the history, flesh and language of the human person. On the other hand, the problem is not simply that of the credibility of a
message or doctrine, because the revelation in question is not the revelation
of an ideology but of a historical and personal reality which changes the
meaning of history and the human person: I mean the epiphany of God in
Jesus.

The specific object of fundamental theology, therefore, is revelation as
"believable"; the "believable," in this case is also the "believed," namely Jesus Christ who is both the fullness of revelation (revealer and revealed) and
the sign of this revelation which he is in his own person (bearer of his own
identity). Consequently, the unifying center of fundamental theology as well
as the specifying component of this theology is this central assertion which
Christianity makes: "God is among us in Jesus Christ," and which it regards as an assertion that is "provable" and "believable." It is true that it is
for dogmatic theology, as a hermeneutic of the human person and his problems,[53] to show the meaning of each of the Christian mysteries. But this
function represents only one aspect of the total problem of credibility. Just
as fundamental theology has a dogmatic concern (which does not specify it)
when it studies the notion of revelation, so dogmatic theology has an apologetic perspective which is coextensive with it but does not specify it. For
fundamental theology the problem of the *credibility of Christian revelation
as a whole* (with its particular mysteries) is the essential task and specifying
element.[54] The questions asked in fundamental theology have to do not only

with "what we believe," but also and above all with "why we believe."

I must now add that the two terms which make up the unified pair: *revelation-credibility* have to be understood in a broader sense that goes far beyond the meaning the words had in the old apologetics.

The starting point of fundamental theology is not revelation "in general," but the particular revelation which Christianity pointed to as the condition for its existence and the content of its faith. On this point, fundamental theology can rely on the vision and procedure of *Dei Verbum.* The Constitution first sets forth the mystery of revelation (its nature, object, finality, economy, mediators). It then considers this revelation in its historical development: promise and preparation in the Old Testament; epiphany of God in Jesus Christ, together with the signs of this epiphany; and, finally, the acceptance of this revelation by human beings through faith. The Constitution goes on to deal with the transmission of the revelation by means of tradition and the inspired scripture: both of these give life to God's people and in turn draw life from it; both are interpreted by the Church in the exercise of its teaching authority, a Church which is both hearer and servant of the word.

Recent theology emphasizes other aspects of revelation that are omitted or receive but little attention in *Dei Verbum.* I may mention, by way of example, the social dimension of revelation.[55] Even more important is its "experiential" character. Under this heading, there are a number of aspects to be considered: the primordial and normative experience of Jesus, the prophets, and the apostles; the religious language of scripture, which is the language closest to the original experience; the various religious experiences that are fed and transformed by the original experience (the experiences of the mystics, of charismatic groups, and so on).[56] The more theology is able to develop the multiform riches of this primordial mystery, the better it will be able to deal correctly with the problem of its credibility and the better it will be able to situate other religious experiences without downgrading these but also without downgrading itself and losing sight of its own uniqueness.

A dogmatic theology of revelation does not exclude an apologetics of revelation. In developing a theology of revelation the new fundamental theology has no intention of becoming a substitute for apologetics, but aims only at supplying something that was lacking in traditional apologetics.[57] The problem of credibility remains intact and must be treated in the most rigorous way possible. More than this, it must be undertaken on a broader basis and with the aid of renewed techniques.

The problem is this: Does the central assertion of Christianity about God present and manifested in Jesus Christ have a *meaning*? That is, is it an acceptable, intelligible assertion? In answering this question the theologian must be able to show not only that Jesus belongs to human history as does any historical person, but also that he is "accessible" via the only witnesses, we have, namely, the gospels. It must be shown not only that he is accessible in his message and actions, but also that he "deciphers" the human condition in all its dimensions and brings it to completion in a way utterly unforeseeable. It must be shown not only that Jesus was a great prophet among his fellow human beings, but also that his life, death, and resurrection contain signs of his "identity" as God among us.

In short, an answer must be given to three questions: Is Jesus accessible in his historical reality? Do Jesus and his message give the answer to the radical question of the meaning of human existence? And: Is Jesus identifiable as God among us? Classical apologetics was interested in the third question, that of the signs, but paid little or no attention to the first two questions. Yet, if we are to do justice to all aspects of the problem of credibility, we must assign equal importance to the historical, anthropological and semeiological approaches. In addition, contemporary alertness to problems of history and problems of the human person shows the urgent need of the historical and philosophical approaches.[58]

These, then, are the questions which, in my view, belong to the very substance of fundamental theology, give it its reason for existence and its special character, and establish it as a special province of theology. In a word, these are the questions that *identify* and *specify* fundamental theology. They represent as it were the look which fundamental theology directs toward its own very *core*. Other questions represent fundamental theology as a discipline concerned with borderline questions, a discipline that engages in dialogue with other religions, other philosophies, other cultures, other sciences. This look toward the *outside* is necessary, to be sure, but it must not distract fundamental theology from its basic task, which is to study the revelation of God in Jesus Christ insofar as it is something accessible, meaningful, identifiable, and therefore "credible."

The problem of the "centering" or "focusing" of fundamental theology thus raises at the same time the problem of a "hierarchic ordering" of the questions to be treated. It also brings up the problem of their pedagogical organization in a theological curriculum.

IV. Pedagogical Organization

If we judge by what I have been saying about a renewed and expanded fundamental theology, then it follows that each theological institution must have a body of teachers who are quite familiar with the most recent findings of exegesis and history and who are fully acquainted with modern philosophies, the religions of salvation, the problems of linguistics, and so on and so on. These professorial prodigies, each a Pico della Mirandola, should then be confronted with students who are no less exceptional.

Evidently, we must immediately make a distinction between fundamental theology as an ecclesial function and a province of theological science, and, on the other hand, the more limited problem of pedagogical organization at a specific theological institution (a seminary or university faculty). Just as no single physician can possess medical science in its totality, neither can any theologian or even any theological institution claim to handle all the themes of fundamental theology in their full scope. Such a possession of knowledge can only be collegial, that is, a possession of the Church as a social body.

Within these limitations there are questions which are best treated at the beginning of the theological curriculum; I am referring to the questions that constitute the core of fundamental theology, namely, the problem of revelation and its credibility. Even the treatment of this problem is a vast undertaking that calls for close collaboration between exegetes and theologians, especially as regards the historical and hermeneutical approach to the gospels. The anthropological approach, which consists in showing that the Christian message provides the key to the mystery of the human person and gives an answer to the person's basic problems, may seem to be a gigantic and even utopian enterprise, since it amounts to teaching the whole of dogmatic theology. But I think there is a middle ground between an exhaustive treatment of this theme, such as only dogmatic theology in its entirety can offer, and the complete omission of it.

Fundamental theology can supply *in summary form* what dogmatic theology will then develop fully, just as (looking in the opposite direction) dogmatic theology leaves the subject of revelation to fundamental theology. It is possible to show, in a succinct manner, how the Christian message clarifies the essential problems of the human condition: relations with the world (work and human advancement), with other human beings (love, justice, solidarity), with the person himself or herself (identity, solitude, suffering, death), with God (the authentic image of God and of the relationship he wishes to have with us). If these questions are not treated at the beginning of theological studies or (and this is a much more serious matter) if they are watered down or evaded, fundamental theology will, in my judgment, fail in its task, and the theologian will fail to give the Church the service he owes it.

The same questions can be taken up again and gone into more fully in the second and third cycles where they can be given monographic treatment. There is also another series of problems, no less essential, which are best presented at the end of the theological course (second and third cycles), whether because of their intrinsic difficulty or because their proper treatment presupposes an overall grasp of theology or simply because there is no time to treat them at an earlier stage. Such are, for example, the problem faced by fundamental theology when it engages in "dialogue" with other religions and other theologies; the problems of language and the special problems of anthropology and christology; and, finally, the problems of epistemology and methodology that have become so wide-ranging and complex nowadays that we wonder whether they should not constitute a special sector of theology as a "science" within the concert of sciences, rather than *one* of the problems of fundamental theology.

The old curriculum that was regulated by *Deus scientiarum* and put all theological studies into a single four-year cycle, made it difficult to handle such a vast range of material; it also made it simply impossible to put the various questions in a proper sequence and hierarchical order. But what was impossible in other years has now become feasible, ever since the publication of the Apostolic Constitution *Sapientia Christiana.*

These few remarks are not meant to complicate further the already burdensome task of professors of fundamental theology, but only to show how the new looser and more flexible program of studies can give free rein to a discipline which, more than others, needs space to breathe freely and exercise a creative liberty.

V. Conclusion

After a period of reaction against classical apologetics, and after a change of name that points to a deeper change in status, due to an expansion of its task, its privileged themes, and its addressees, contemporary fundamental theology is better structured and has a better grasp of its specific mission; in consequence, it is experiencing a new spring.[59] Treatises reflecting its new image are less ambiguous and more sharply defined. Fundamental theology is now a specialized field of theology. Its purpose, like that of the other specialized disciplines, is to understand better the mystery of God. Dogmatic theology breaks this mystery down into more particular mysteries, but fundamental theology contemplates it in its totality; it does so in an introductory treatise that proposes the mystery of faith as "credible" and the object of a "meaningful" decision. If this kind of study did not exist, it would have to be invented.

4

Christian Initiation and Fundamental Theology: Reflections on the Stages of Christian Maturation in the Primitive Church

Carlo M. Martini

Was the primitive Church familiar with the idea that there are stages in the process of Christian maturation? In other words, did it maintain that the initiation to knowledge of the gospel and the integration of it into Christian life did not take place in a short space of time, for example, during the preparation for baptism, but required a long period of time and successive stages of development? And is it possible to specify these stages with some exactness, so as to determine whether, and in which of them, it can be said that there is a stage of reflection on the experience of faith which is analogous to certain typical phases of "fundamental theology"?

I. Awareness of a Process of Christian Maturation

It is not difficult to find in the New Testament an awareness that the experience of faith has its stages. We hear of those who are being "taught the word" (Gal 6:6; Greek *catēchoumenos,* one who is being instructed, a catechumen), of the "enlightened" (Heb 6:4; 10:32), of the "perfect" or "mature" (1 Cor 2:6; 14:20). In Ephesians 4:13–14 there is a contrast between "children, tossed to and fro and carried about with every wind of doctrine" (the description presupposes that they are baptized Christians, who therefore have passed through their catechumenal initiation) and "mature manhood . . . the measure of the stature of the fullness of Christ." In Hebrews 5:12–14 the situation of those who need someone to teach them again "the first principles of God's word" is contrasted with that of persons who "ought to be teachers"; the condition of those who "need milk" is contrasted with that of those who, on the contrary, can digest "solid food" and

"have their faculties trained by practice to distinguish good from evil."
Paul's prayers for the communities give us a glimpse of a journey toward
"the knowledge of his [God's] will in all spiritual wisdom and understanding" (Col 1:19), "increasing in the knowledge of God" (Col 1:10).

In addition to these lexical references to the progressive maturation of
the baptized person, there are passages in the New Testament which describe in quite explicit terms some successive phases of initiation to the
Christian mystery. In the second chapter of Acts, for example, the first sermon of Peter (Acts 2:14–36) is followed by a statement of the good dispositions of those who have heard the word (2:37) and a call for repentance and
the baptism that will bring the gift of the Spirit (2:38). After then saying
that baptism has in fact been administered (2:41), the text notes that those
who had been baptized continued to listen to the teaching of the apostles
(2:42) and "devoted themselves to . . . fellowship, to the breaking of bread
and the prayers" (ibid.).

This means that even after the catechumenate there was a period of instruction, joined to a more intense participation in community life. The Letter to the Hebrews expressly distinguishes (6:1–6) between an initial
teaching about Christ, in which basic information about Christian life is giv-
en, and a more complete and thoroughgoing instruction.

Since, then, the primitive Church did have an awareness that there is a
Christian journey with its successive stages, we may ask a further question:
Did there exist, in the New Testament period, something like a "handbook"
(one or several of them) that could suitably introduce Christians to these
various stages? One response to this question is the working hypothesis that
the "four gospels" (in the order: Mark, Matthew, Luke, John) may be regarded as showing the spirit proper to successive stages in this journey.
There are, of course, many reasons for the diversity of the gospels, and these
have been amply documented by critical study, for example, the multiplicity
of sources and underlying traditions, the various audiences for whom the
gospels were composed, the theological outlooks of the authors, and so on.
But, in explaining the diversity, it seems that there is also a place for the
specific intention of each gospel to be of service at a particular stage in
Christian development.

Mark is the earliest of the gospels, and it is easy to see how well suited
it is for an initial catechumenal instruction in preparation for baptism. It develops an outline of the life of Jesus which it shares with the kerygmatic discourses in the *Acts of the Apostles*, and by so doing it provides the basic
material for an introductory instruction on Christianity as summed up in
the person and work of Jesus. *Matthew* emphasizes the theme of community
and has an extensive collection of the parenetic sayings of Jesus; as such, it
is rather well adapted for the formation of those who have received baptism
and must be initiated to the duties of a life lived in common. The Lukan
corpus (*Luke* and *Acts*) not only gives an account of evangelization as carried on by Jesus himself but also adds a narration of the testimony given by
the envoys of Jesus, it is thus especially helpful in preparing the baptized to

proclaim the word of God to others. Finally, *John*, the gospel of the "elder," represents the mature reflection of a Christian consciousness on the mystery of revelation; it is suitable especially for the instruction of those who have passed through the successive stages of Christian experience and wish now to contemplate this experience as a single whole in the light of faith.

The gospels thus provide us with the hypothesis of four successive stages in Christian growth: catechumenal initiation, introduction to community life, preparation for evangelization, and contemplative maturity. We are already in a position to give a first answer to the question of how these various stages can be taken as typical phases of fundamental theology and its reflections on the various requirements for the act and exercise of faith.

In the catechumenal stage the gospel of Mark focuses attention on the power of Jesus as wonder-worker and on the new revelation of God that takes place in the life and death of Jesus. In the second stage, which is that of catechetical initiation to ecclesial life (and corresponds to the gospel according to Matthew), the emphasis is on the continuity between the Christian community and the saving plan of God as this was worked out in the history of Israel. In the stage of witnessing (Luke) evangelization is shown as playing a role in God's providential plan of salvation for all human beings. Finally, in the contemplative stages the unity of the plan of salvation emerges, as does the transparent presence of the revealed God in the life of the redeemed.

Each of these aspects of Christian life helps clarify the foundations of faith. The latter are perceived gradually as Christian experience fills out and becomes mature. There is no question, then, of an abstract presentation of these foundations, but only of a concrete initiation that leads at one and the same time to the reality in which Christians believe (the "gospel," the revelation of God's mercy in the person of his Son) and the motives for belief, which are clarified in the course of the experience. But, in addition to this first and rather generic series of steps in reflection on the foundations of belief, I think it possible to go further and locate in more precise terms the specific phases of fundamental theology.

II. The Gospels and the Stages of Christian Maturity

We can turn again to the New Testament and ask how a good deal of the information it gives about the various aspects of Christian experience can be better understood by locating it within the dynamics of progressive growth that I explained earlier. In my opinion, the main questions to be asked of the texts are these: What type of prayer corresponds more closely to each stage? What sacramental experience is characteristic of each? What "gifts" and "services" are to be best associated with one or other stage? What type of cultural reflection on the concrete religious experience of individual and community is characteristic of these stages and constitutes the object of an appropriate instruction (*didaskalia*)?

I cannot give here an answer to each of these questions, even though they are interconnected. I shall concentrate on the final question.

(a) *The catechumenal experience (Mark).* This is the period or stage of conversion. The catechumen must experience an upheaval of his or her mental world, a change of horizon, a "conversion." There must be a real transformation of subjects and their world. Those whose focus had previously been on themselves or on a set of false values, even if of a religious kind, must now opt clearly for the God who has revealed himself in Jesus Christ. The kind of reflection typical of this stage seems to me to be the one described in Mark 7:21–23: "For from within, out of the heart of man, come evil thoughts, fornication, theft . . . pride, foolishness. All these evil things come from within, and they defile a man." What we have here is a psychological and moral meditation on the pagan sympathies and schemings of the heart. It is based on the principle of interiority: "Out of the heart of man come evil thoughts." The focus of attention is thus no longer on external behavior, as it was in pagan religious thinking, but on interior dispositions. Mark 7:22 gives a list of the wicked complicities which human beings can recognize within themselves and from which they can hope to be liberated solely through baptism. The result is a recognition of the necessity of salvation and, once the catechumen has been educated in the school of the Master's public life, the baptismal prayer: "Jesus, Son of David, have mercy on me!" (Mk 10:47). This in turn prepares the way for recognition of the mystery of God as at work in the death of Jesus: "Truly this man was the Son of God!" (Mk 15:39).

(b) The second stage consists in an introduction to the various *ecclesial experiences (Matthew).* The intellectual reflection proper to this stage seems to be that found in a formative catechesis that includes an initiation to the realities of community life. Those who have been baptized must learn what it means to live as children of God in the visible Church. They must be given a fuller explanation of God's kingdom, how human beings enter it, how it spreads, what difficulties it must overcome, and so on. These are the very subjects treated in the five great discourses of Matthew's gospel (chapters 5–7; 10; 13; 18; 25). Matthew, the *catechist's gospel,* gives in thematic order all the sayings and deeds of the Lord that help complete the instruction of the baptized. In keeping with the final words of Jesus: "Lo, I am with you always, to the close of the age" (Mt 28:20), newly baptized Christians must learn to realize that the Lord is not only the One whom God has sent but also the One whom they encounter in their communities. The experience of community is an authentic experience of God; Christians must therefore learn how to deal with others in the community through forgiveness, the law of the value of the lowliest, and mutual acceptance. In this context chapter 18 of the first gospel may be regarded as typical.

(c) The third stage (*Luke*) introduces us to an understanding of the mystery of the kingdom in its *relationship with history.* The need here is to give an answer to the following question especially: What is the significance and task of the Christian community in the world? The community that has made its members integral parts of itself feels ready to bring the gospel "to all that are far off" (Acts 2:39): "You shall be my witnesses . . . to the end of the earth" (Acts 1:8). But how can such a commission be carried out unless Christians first define themselves clearly in relation to the world and to history? There is need, consequently, of a systematic reflection on the phenomenon of Christianity as considered not only in its sources but also in its internal coherence, its continuity with the past, and its significance for the present and future stages of history, and this in relation not only to the Jewish world but also to all the cultures and religious traditions "under heaven" (cf. Acts 2:5). This is precisely the kind of meditation Luke intends to give to Theophilus, as he proposes to show the latter the "truth" (RSV) of received teachings or how "well founded" (JB) they are (Lk 1:4).

Let us go into this last point a little more fully. The Greek word *asphaleia* in Luke 1:4, which might also be translated as "the solidity" (of the teachings received), suggests the "security" of those who feel safe and at ease (cf., e.g., 1 Thess 5:3). It is, in other words, the "solidity" proper to things that gives a sense of security. As used in a material sense, it can mean, for example, the solidity of the locked doors of a prison (Acts 5:23). In the moral sphere, it is, for example, the irrefutable certainty with which Peter can proclaim, in his sermon on Pentecost, that "God has made him both Lord and Christ, this Jesus whom you crucified" (Acts 2:36).

The context in which Peter makes this statement is significant. The entire sermon (Acts 2:14–36) shows that such "security" does not depend solely on an accurate grasp of the paschal happenings. It flows rather from the insertion of these into the larger context of the history of salvation, both as immediately experienced (the Pentecostal event: Acts 2:1–21) and as embracing the past (David: Acts 2:25–31, 34–35; Jesus: Acts 2:22–24, 32–33, 36). And in fact it is only after having placed the Jesus event in this kind of framework (Acts 2:14–35) that Peter proclaims a truth which all should assert with absolute assurance: namely, that God has made Jesus both Lord and Messiah (2:36).

Luke's intention, therefore, is to bring his readers to acknowledge the solidity of the facts of salvation. He does this not by providing them with a simple chronicle, however accurate, but by helping them grasp the overall framework of the history of salvation as this moves from Adam to Jesus and then on to Paul and the communities he founded, without neglecting in the process the providential action of God in the world of the pagan religions (Acts 17:22–31). And indeed it is not only the actions of Jesus that are part of the divine plan and show that God was with him. The experiences of the primitive community and their evangelizing activity also reveal the plan of God in Jesus for the salvation of all human beings (cf. Acts 4:12). From the account of these events the reader is able to see how all that has been "accomplished among us" (Lk 1:1) is part of a single divine plan that embraces even the pagans.

Luke's intention, then, is not to give the initial instruction that is provided to catechumens (he supposes that this has already been received, cf.

Lk 1:4). His purpose is rather to make his readers reflect on the meaning of events "from the beginning" (Lk 1:2) down to the foundation of flourishing Christian communities throughout the Mediterranean basin. He wants to show that here at the heart of Greek and Roman culture the ecclesial fulfillment of the evangelical ideal—especially its fulfillment by the Gentile Christian communities that owe their origin to Paul and have their own preaching and manner of life—is authentic: it is conformed to God's plan and is a legitimate development of principles laid down by Jesus and the Twelve. This Christian experience is "solid" and withstands a dispassionate and penetrating examination of the facts.

I think we can see in this outlook and in the instruction that is characteristic for this stage, the beginnings of the kind of reflection on Christian experience in its totality that is the prelude to contemporary ways of structuring a "fundamental theology." As far as Matthew's gospel was concerned it was necessary to ask only in what relation the Jewish Christian community stood to the promises God has made to Israel. In Luke the perspective widens to include the communities that are being formed within the bosom of paganism and that look to embrace the entire world. These latter communities desire to reflect seriously on the solidity of the foundations of their hope.

(d) The final stage, which is that of the gospel according to John, is an experience of *contemplative simplification,* in which the emphasis is on the basic values of faith and love. Strictly speaking, what we have here is not a real religious reflection in the narrow sense, but rather a contemplation of the mystery of the historical Christ in his relations with the Father and with the Church that has the Spirit as its life-giving principle. I cannot go into this point here and shall therefore pass on to some conclusions regarding the theme with which we are concerned.

III. Some Conclusions

If it is thus possible to determine to some extent the successive stages of formation in a personally experienced Christianity, as well as the type of cultural reflection more especially appropriate to each stage, especially the third, then we can now draw two conclusions.

The first is that fundamental theology is not born of a felt need of abstract speculation, but rather springs directly from a progressive awareness of Christian experience. For this awareness leads Christians to inquire into their relationship to the world that is as yet unbelieving and is to be evangelized, and to give this world an "account for the hope that is in you" (1 Pet 3:15). We should note that this last text, so typical of the attitude proper to fundamental theology, is written in the context of persecution. But Luke's work too, that is so much concerned with evangelization and witness, highlights the theme of persecution. Thus fundamental theology comes to birth not among a fearful minority that must justify itself to itself, but in a com munity that is open and bent on evangelizing, and therefore subjected to trials and testings.

If fundamental theology owes its origin to this type of Christian experience, then a second, obvious conclusion follows that has a bearing on the renewal of fundamental theology. This theology will be linked to a clear consciousness of the Church's evangelizing mission and not simply to a posture of "defense," as happened at times in the apologetics of the past. Such an attitude of defensiveness may well be justified in certain situations, but fundamental theology will acquire renewed vitality rather in situations of open and courageous confrontation with various cultures and mentalities. In this confrontation Christians will have to explain in depth, to themselves and to others, their attitude as evangelizers and will thus be forced into an enlightening and profitable reflection on the "solidity" of their own experience.

Part 2

Hermeneutical Questions

5
Hermeneutics and Scripture

René Marlé

I. Introduction

The hermeneutical problem is one of those central problems that can be discussed without end. It stands at the meeting point of several disciplines and concerns the philosopher as well as the theologian, the linguist as well as the sociologist or psychoanalyst.

Linking it, as in the title of this essay, with the phenomenon of writing (Scripture/scripture) makes it possible to state immediately the approach to hermeneutics that is intended here. This is certainly not the only possible approach, but it has the advantage of taking as the point of departure a datum that conditions the very rise of the problem and brings out its urgency quite clearly, and this by reason of the two meanings which the term "writing/scripture" can have. "Writing" can refer to the production of *texts,* but it can also refer to the special text with which the faith of believers is correlated, namely, the *Bible.*

In both of its meanings, writing, in different but connected ways, calls for and directly involves hermeneutics. In relation to the first meaning of the term writing, hermeneutics develops as a response to a cultural need. In relation to the second (*the* Writing which is the Bible), hermeneutics is part of fundamental theology and of the structures fundamental theology calls for nowadays. We shall see, moreover, that the singular problem raised for theology by the existence of writings which faith regards as sacred has been and continues to be a powerful stimulus to a deeper study of the general problem raised by all writing (textual production), just as, conversely, reflection on this general problem, as well as current practices and the theories accompanying them, all help the theologian to approach the problem of reading and interpreting the sacred writings with new perspectives or a new methodological stringency.

For this reason the two points of view I have mentioned will be constantly intersecting or calling for each other in the course of this essay.

I. The Hermeneutical Problem as a Problem of Distances and Breaks

(1) *Writing and the Breach Caused by Time*

Why do we write, except to capture facts or thoughts so as to keep them from being carried away by time, to save them from forgetfulness and death? At the same time, however, when we put them in writing, we place them outside of current reality. They evade death only "potentially." Of itself, writing rather entombs them until a new intervention, which we call reading or interpretation, comes along and restores them to life.

How does the act of reading or interpretation accomplish this? Hermeneutics is meant to supply an answer to this question. The concern that gives rise to hermeneutics seems to be as old as writing itself or at least as old as the various literatures. Hermes, under whose patronage this activity is usually put, was regarded by the Greeks as the inventor of writing and, at the same time, of language and trade. His function was to make the thinking of the gods known and understood; consequently, he presided as it were over all kinds of exchanges, that is, over everything that establishes communication despite distances and differences. In any case, it was a time when myths had become unreal, with a consequent loss of ability to shape the life of the people, and when these myths were beginning to turn into literature, that Plato undertook to restore their meaning with the help of a whole system of interpretation. Aristotle was to formalize this system and thus bring it to completion. He authored a treatise *On Interpretation* (*Peri Hermēneias*).

The healing power of hermeneutics becomes necessary, then, as soon as the breaks in continuity which are caused by time and to which writing as such bears witness, have made their appearance. Hermeneutics becomes especially needed whenever a more radical break in continuity takes place in the course of history.

(2) *The End of an "Economy."*

The manifestation, death and resurrection of Jesus Christ certainly represent such a break. Our very calendar is based on it. These events are also connected with what may be called a crisis in writing and with the most decisive of all developments of the hermeneutical question.

This is so because, as everyone knows, the "New Testament" was not originally a book or part of a book, but rather a norm for reading; it provided a new way of relating oneself to the ancient Writings and even to "the letter" wherever found, a new way of understanding and interpreting these. St. Paul speaks eloquently of this new factor, which is revolutionary in the full sense of the word: it represents a change of epoch or "eon," which also means a change of regime or "economy" and can be described as the transition from the "letter" to the "spirit." But this latter transition is identically a transition from death to life.

Even after his death, on his return to new life, Jesus discloses the lost meaning of the ancient writings by "interpreting" them to his disciples on the road to Emmaus (cf. Lk 24:27). This meaning proves to be wholly contained in his Pasch or Passover, that is, in his own "passage," which in a sense puts death to death.

From that time forward, the act of interpretation and the theory developed for its grounding and proper execution (in other words, hermeneutical reflection) will be the most important work of the Christian mind and one of the fundamental ways in which faith finds its expression. H. de Lubac has made us sensitive to the theological significance of the interpretation of scripture to which the Fathers and theologians devoted themselves so unwearyingly, at least until the appearance of the Summas during the central Middle Ages.[1]

(3) *The Breakup of the Ecclesial Body*

At the end of the Middle Ages, the greatest of all ecclesial crises, and one that would lead to a rupture from which the Church has still not recovered, was due in the last analysis to differences in the manner of understanding the Church's relation to scripture. At bottom, the opposition between the Reformers and the Roman Church is an opposition between two theories of the interpretation of scripture or, in other words, between two hermeneutical doctrines. To the Reformer's "scriptural" principle of "scripture alone" (*Sola Scriptura*) the Council of Trent opposed the principle of "scripture and tradition." In the view of the Reformers the scriptures, when accompanied by "the interior witness of the Holy Spirit," would make their own meaning known to the mind of the believer. Scripture is not only an object of faith; it is also the sole rule of faith and for this reason must be "interpreter of itself" (*sui ipsius interpres*). For the Council of Trent, on the other hand, it is not possible to find the authentic meaning of scripture except within the Church and under the influence of the Church's tradition as authenticated by the magisterium. The opposition has been reinforced, at a surface level, in the doctrine of verbal inspiration maintained in certain forms of Protestant fundamentalism, and in the "two source" doctrine of one kind of Catholic theology (Vatican Council II reacted against this doctrine). But in any case the opposition continues to be a radical one, as we shall see again later on, for it concerns, as the hermeneutical question always does, the very thrust and meaning of faith.

(4) *The Cultural Breach of Modern Times*

Another break in continuity, this time one that was exclusively cultural, at least in the beginning, served as a springboard for a renewal of the hermeneutical problem. For those who experienced this cultural break it was in its own right a privileged theme of their speculations as well as a goal which they sought to promote in all their undertakings. The science of history, for which the way had been paved by the growth of objective knowledge and the development of the natural sciences, then came along to increase our sense of distance from objects which this science was learning to define ever more fully. This historical approach has tended to spread throughout the whole field of culture and to present itself as almost the very shaping form of this culture.

It was not long before others began to point out the one-sidedness and limitations of the kind of relationship which the positive science of history establishes with its objects. One philosopher reminded his contemporaries that another type of relationship is possible, one that enables us to overcome distances which science is constantly extending. "Explanation," which leaves the knowing subject still external to the object, is not yet "understanding," which implies a certain involvement of this subject in the act and object of its knowledge. Dilthey (1833–1911) develops these ideas in his work as a philosopher of history and is one of the pioneers in modern hermeneutics.

These philosophical notions should have been of the greatest interest to theologians. For in fact faith was directly affected by the breaches in continuity that were now taking place. A new kind of relationship was being introduced into the data of tradition in general and into the object of scripture in particular. This relationship is no longer solely, and in any event no longer directly, one of sympathy and connaturality. The way travelled in setting up the relationship generally passes by way of criticism which establishes the object's autonomy and measures its distance from us. The basic harmony that had long existed between the teaching of faith (as gotten from the Bible) and the culture as a whole existed no longer. The reader no longer starts out as one who is located in the universe proper to what he is reading; he exists elsewhere, in a world outside what he is reading, a world constituted by the new culture that has been brought into being precisely by this emancipation. No one spoke as yet of an "epistemological break," but that was in fact what had occurred in the entire thinking of the age. In the world of theology hermeneutical thinking would take the form of an attempt to respond to a challenge of the day, an attempt to recover once again a meaning lost in the archives of history—unless it be taken as a manifestation of the power of discovery and creation that is present in a community whose writing/scripture exists simply to attest that this community represents the end of the "letter" and is, in short, a resurrectional community.

(5) *Epistemological Break in the Modernist Period*

Even if (let me repeat) the term itself was not used, it was in fact an "epistemological break" that led to the Modernist crisis in the Catholic Church at the beginning of this century and inaugurated a new kind of hermeneutical thinking, the depth of which would be difficult to exceed.

Alfred Loisy had clearly realized the shifts that would be caused in every area by his approach to scripture and especially the gospels along the lines of modern historical science. In reply to a letter from Maurice Blondel in which the latter spoke of how disturbed he was by his reading of *L'Evangile et l'Eglise* [The Gospel and the Church], Loisy wrote: "I do not think my book implies a denial of any dogma; it implies only the need of revising the entire teaching of theology from the standpoint of history so as to render it truer in positive terms, and from the standpoint of philosophy so as to render it more intelligible at the level of theory."[2] Dogma has not been touched, but one may ask whether it has any longer a place and a meaning, inasmuch as a question of truth and intelligibility has been raised from which dogma is absent.

The question is in fact identical with the hermeneutical question since it is a question of the relationship to be developed to the documents of history and specifically to the scriptural documents, in order to grasp, even in our day, their true meaning. Maurice Blondel clearly grasped this point; he wrote his *History and Dogma: The Philosophical Deficiencies of Modern Exegesis*[3] precisely in order to place Loisy's problem in a new context, for he did not find the terms in which Loisy put it to be satisfactory from the viewpoint either of philosophy or of faith. His aim was to provide a kind of "prolegomena to all future exegesis," that is, "a critical reflection on the very conditions of a science of revelation and of any sacred literature." The solution was found by bringing to light a complex operation which involves not only ideas but in the last analysis images as well; this operation is a living tradition, which is the deeper life of a social body and continuer of the original life of the society, while also being a power that produces ever new fruits.

(6) *Two Irreconcilable "World Pictures"*

Blondel's solution could not be offered in Protestantism. And yet the problem created by the modern breach of cultural continuity was no less real there, and indeed all the more so since there had been much more receptivity to the critical approach. More than one exegete and theologian had become convinced that this criticism, along with the positivist historical viewpoint to which it gave rise, was the only acceptable way of dealing with past realities and that a contemporary mind should find it fully satisfying. This was tantamount to admitting that there is no longer any object for faith, but only for science; in other words, that what had inspired the life of all generations of believers was now completely dead. The hermeneutical problem was solved, or rather eliminated, before it was even raised.

But not everyone accepted this verdict. By the end of the last century Martin Kähler was already maintaining that "the historical Jesus of modern authors conceals from us the living Christ" to whom scripture bears witness.[4] Then, right after the first World War and without spending much time justifying his attitude, Karl Barth performed a kind of act of violence as he offered an interpretation of scripture that broke radically with the purely positive approach of the historians and, even in its novelty, marked a return to the basic exegetical procedures of the Fathers and especially of the Reformers.[5]

However, Rudolf Bultmann is the first who believed that the hermeneutical problem and the theoretical reflection that it calls for must be central to his work as an exegete and theologian. He too has formulated this problem in terms of a break or breach of continuity: a break between the mythical "world picture"within which the New Testament message was formulated, and the contemporary "world picture" that derives its structure from science and technical methods. This is the initial observation that commands the thesis of a necessary "demythologization."[6]

In explaining his position to those (especially Karl Jaspers) who had not grasped the real issue, Bultmann emphasized the point that the problem of demythologization is in his eyes only a particular formulation of the hermeneutical problem and is intended to put us on the road to a solution of it: "The real problem is the hermeneutical problem, that is, the problem of how the Bible is to be understood and how the Church is to preach, so that both Bible and preaching can be understood as a message addressed to the people of today."[7]

Bultmann thus clearly makes the hermeneutical problem a problem of getting across distances, or, if you prefer, a problem of restoring relevance and life to something that by itself would remain alien and dead. Bultmann also regards it as one of his fundamental duties as an exegete to work out a theory that will enable him to give a satisfactory solution to the problem. As we all know, the idea of demythologization brings out only one aspect of this theory. It must not be separated from the aspect represented by the goal of "existential interpretation," which brings into play a whole set of concepts and systems of analysis that Bultmann has taken over from Heidegger. Bultmann believes that the latter supplies him with the needed means of bridging the gulf between our universe and the New Testament universe and of bringing out the meaning which the New Testament "message" still has for the lives of people today.

Bultmann has remained almost obsessed by the hermeneutical problem and has constantly gone into it from ever new angles. Yet he has always done so in the light of the realization afforded him by his exegetical practice of the distance that separates us from these ancient writings which it is his task (he believes) not only to reconstruct in their literal meaning but also to "translate," in the deepest sense of this word.

II. The Hermeneutical Problem as a Problem of Differences within the Scriptural Object

(1) *The Call for a "Canon within the Canon"*

It is not only the cultural differences caused by the movement of history that raise the hermeneutical problem for exegetes and theologians. The problem is also raised in another way: by the differences within the corpus of scripture, differences made ever clearer by advances in critical exegesis. Can reason, first of all, and then faith be satisfied with the chaotic landscape with which certain scholarly works seem to leave us? Must they not also take account of the fact that this heap of materials left by analysis has, after all, been passed down to us as forming a book which is made up of a structured set of documents? And could faith possibly respond to a message that turns out to be a pile of fragments and even full of contradictions? Can faith be a response to anything but a message that has a *unified* meaning which it declares itself ready to accept and profess?

Where and how, then, is this unified, living, meaningful message to be found? Where and how is an organizing principle, the real organizing principle, of this multiplicity to be found? Where and how is the unity of witness, to which the unity of faith corresponds, to be grasped?

By raising these questions we are forced to confront a problem of method or, if the reader prefers, of procedure or movement, that will make it possible once again to effect a *passage*, namely, the passage from a mute multiplicity that is of interest only to a collector of old stones, to a living unity that is capable of challenging us. We might also call it a problem in reading: How are we to read an assemblage of seemingly disparate texts, in such a way that they will really be saying something to us and sketch out for us a *single* course of thought and action? What viewpoint must we adopt or rather what viewpoint does this collection of texts (which comes to us as a collection) require us to adopt, and what stance must we take, if we are to be in a position to receive a possible message and really hear what the texts intend to say?

These questions are sometimes summed up in the phrase "Canon within the Canon." The formulation is one that has inevitably elicited reservations or indignation. Are the exegetes arrogating to themselves (some people ask) the authority to make a selection from the heritage which has been passed on to Christians through the centuries and which Christians have always regarded in its totality as an expression of God's very own word? But such a reaction only shows that the speaker has not properly understood the question. There is in fact no thought of making a selection. The point of view is not the external one of quantity, but the internal one of organization and importance. Given the divergent data of scripture, the strata which analysis uncovers in it, and, at a certain level, the contradictions it manifests, there seems to be need of a *canon for reading* or, to use other terms, a hermeneutical rule that will enable us to penetrate beneath the surface to the hidden principle of a possible structure for the text.

(2) *Recourse to an "Elsewhere" That Is Not Scripture?*

Once the need has been recognized of looking for a criterion to be used in reading that will enable us to grasp the unity of a meaningful message, there remains the question of how to go about this search and how to determine the new viewpoint without which scripture remains a collection of irreducibly disparate testimonies.

The response that may immediately come to a Catholic mind is the need of recurring to the tradition of the Church as authenticated by the magisterium. If need be, the Catholic can point out that tradition thus understood is not necessarily a reality external to scripture, and that the magisterium which makes it possible to recognize in an "authentic" way the meaning of scripture and tradition is not on that account superior to these.

No, tradition is primarily, if not exclusively, a faithful reading of scripture, and the magisterium is the servant of both tradition and scripture.

Clearly, however, there would still be the need of determining how the reading of tradition itself is concretely to be performed, since the documents of tradition reflect no fewer differences than does scripture itself. In addition, how are the documents of the magisterium itself to be interpreted, since these too are varied, complex, and located in particular contexts? It is not so easy, therefore, to avoid the necessity and even the duty of interpreting. Even literalism is a form of interpretation; it is even one of those that does the greatest violence, since it arbitrarily dismisses the context in which propositions, texts, and documents are always located.

In any case, recourse to an "elsewhere" that is not scripture means introducing a hermeneutical principle which no rational motive alone can rebut. And in fact it is for quite different reasons that Protestant theologians reject this principle: they reject it for explicitly confessional reasons, which is to say reasons directly connected with a conception of faith itself. For that matter, it can be said that the adoption of a certain position on this point was constitutive for the Reformation and the Churches to which it gave rise.

(3) Scripture as Its Own Interpreter

As Gerhard Ebeling has explained on a number of occasions, the *Scripture Alone (Sola Scriptura)* principle of the Reformation is identical with the explicitly hermeneutical principle *Scripture the interpreter of itself (Scriptura sui ipsius interpres)*. As such, *Sola Scriptura* "is a credal utterance."[8] It expresses a decision to acknowledge scripture, and it alone, as the supreme and decisive norm of faith. The decision implies that scripture may not be judged by any other tribunal and that it itself is judge of everything, including the way in which we approach it in order to understand it and translate its meaning.

Given this viewpoint, it follows that if a canon of interpretation is to be found in scripture, only scripture itself can tell us what it is. Consequently, in the formula "Canon within the Canon" the word "within" must be given its full force. What is being sought is really a canon that is *inside* the canon of scripture: not in the sense of an area with narrower boundaries within the larger area, but in the sense of a principle for reading and interpretation that is supplied by the *content* of the canon of scripture. As Ebeling again says: "Instead of reasoning from two separate principles ['formal' and 'material']," scope should have been left for "the movement of thought which would have enabled the canonical writings to establish their own canonicity and to make its meaning clear."[9] The *Sola Scriptura* of the Reformation implies the conviction that the content of scripture has no need of being established on any other basis than itself:

The central issue in this debate about the subject of Scripture is whether, to put it briefly, the very *object* of Scripture is to establish the authority of the content of Scripture. This means, to define whether, and in what way, Scripture itself is the determining factor of its own content, and what Scripture as Scripture can do to establish its own validity.[10]

In Ebeling's view, the decision to look in the canon itself, and only there, for the principle of its interpretation is not simply the expression of an option based on faith. As he sees it, this decision alone does full justice to the hermeneutical enterprise. For he regards the two as intrinsically connected. The "essential function" of the *Sola Scriptura* principle, he explains, is to help "to preserve intact the distinction between text and interpretation," or, in other words, to respect fully the authority of the text itself. For Ebeling "the Catholic conception is in danger of ascribing to an interpretation the value of an authoritative text."[11] In his view, once the Church is no longer seen as wholly the creation of the word of God that is attested in scripture, the logic of the Catholic system leads almost inevitably to making the Church first a partner of the word and then finally its judge or its object.

> If "Scripture and Tradition" thus understood are regarded as an expression of the conflict about the subject of Scripture, then the Church must be regarded as the subject of Scripture, which, in respect of its basis and origin, is contained in Scripture itself, although, in respect of its continuing sacramental activity as the effective operation of divine grace, it has an independent position alongside Scripture as that to which Scripture in its teaching and ministry refers, and in which the vast variety of its utterances (*credenda* and *agenda*) has a common point of reference.[11a]

The already established presence of the Church (it might be said) hinders the movement of interpretation that should proceed from the signifying power of the text taken in itself.

(4) *The Gospel of Justification as Principle of Discernment*

Ernst Käsemann presents similar considerations when he formulates the necessity of a "Canon within the Canon" to which, in his view, the practice of critical exegesis inevitably leads.

> The problem of the Canon cannot be dealt with solely as a historical problem, but involves a discussion of the value of Scripture for the Church and its preaching and teaching. It is, therefore, in the last analysis identical with the problem of the correct interpretation of Scripture. No decision by the Church, no ecclesial tradition, no antecedent judgment can relieve us of the duty of learning this correct interpretation from Scripture itself, although these other authorities can be of some help. Exegetically, and historically as well,

it can be maintained that Scripture refers us clearly enough to its own center, which is given in the gospel and on the basis of which it is to be interpreted.[12]

This obligation of finding within the canon itself the canon or norm of its reading was linked by Ebeling with the principle of *Sola Scriptura,* which he showed to imply the principle of *Scriptura sui ipsius interpres.* Käsemann believes he can specify this "Canon within the Canon," which he has established as necessary and which he finds justified in scripture itself. This "Canon within the Canon" is the doctrine of justification by faith as Paul especially formulates it with perfect clarity. This doctrine not only provided him with a "hermeneutical approach" but also "consistently determined his interpretation of scripture and from the perspective of the antithesis of law and gospel, gave it a critical determination." This doctrine, which in fact supplies him with a principle of discernment, makes it possible, for example, to come to a "varying evaluation of Abraham and Moses, and finally permits him to play off scripture against scripture." Therefore the conclusion: "It would hardly be going too far to talk in epigrammatic terms about a canon within the canon."[13] Käsemann also shows that the doctrine of justification is only a restatement of the first commandment or, in other words, of the assertion that God alone is God. The "Canon within the Canon" is a principle that must lead us to encounter this God in his unshared authority and all-powerful grace.

(5) *A Complex Hermeneutical Principle*

What I have been saying should be enough to show that the hermeneutical problem takes us to the very heart of confessional differences. This is further evidence of the importance of the problem. Not the least of the services it can render is to help us at the ecumenical level to get beyond superficial differences (often factitious to some extent) and reach the point where the fundamental choices are made; I am referring to choices with regard to the understanding of faith *as such* and not simply of its different "objects."

Moreover, since the question of the "Canon within the Canon" has provided a number of contemporary Protestant theologians with an occasion for formulating in a clear manner what they regard as an exigency (even a constitutive one) of their faith, it is appropriate that we ask ourselves to what extent the idea of a "Canon within the Canon" can be accepted as a problem by a Catholic theologian (this, before any judgment is offered on the solution given by Käsemann and others).

Speaking very generally, I think it difficult to deny the need of determining a canon or norm for reading the complex and to some extent composite document which the Bible, or even the New Testament alone, is. Those who stubbornly refuse to admit such a need would find themselves quickly contradicted by their own practice. Is it not true, for example, that the Church in its liturgy accords an honor to the gospels which it does not accord to the other canonical writings in the same degree? In its preaching, too, and its catechesis the Church does not refer to all scriptural texts without distinction. In other words, texts are assigned a certain hierarchic order of importance; this supposes that the texts are not looked at in a one-dimensional way, so to speak, but that some stand out more than others. The Church's reading of the scriptures is thus guided by a vision of at least a rudimentary internal structure.

On the other hand, a Catholic theologian cannot accept the rigid restriction of the hermeneutical principle to within the canon, the jealous guard mounted over the exclusive authority of the canon. The hermeneutical principle to which he appeals and which he would perhaps prefer to call his "rule of faith," and which is in fact at the same time a rule of interpretation, functions in a manner too complex to admit of that kind of rigid limitation. In this functioning a number of authorities play a role, although they refuse to admit that there is in any sense a rivalry among them. The problem of the interrelationship of the various authorities to which faith gives answer might possibly be regarded as equivalent to the problem of the "Canon within the Canon," as this is raised by some Protestant theologians.

It is important, moreover, to note, right from the beginning, that the treatment of the hermeneutical problem as a problem of the functioning of the authority of the Bible in its relation to other authorities equally acknowledged by faith, is not a problem peculiar to Catholic (or Orthodox) theologians. The Faith and Order Commission of the World Council of Churches dealt with it in an important document at the time of its triennial conference at Louvain in 1971.[14] But the Catholic theologian does, it seems, have special reasons for facing up to this problem, not only because it takes him to the very heart of his tradition, but also because it makes him bring out the exigencies of this tradition in a relatively new situation that is characterized, here again, by the ever clearer emergence of differences and pluralism. In such circumstances he is less than ever able, or allowed, to think of the rule of faith as functioning automatically.

(6) *The Interplay of the Various Authorities*

It can be said with regard to all of the confessions, that from a properly theological point of view the hermeneutical problem is the problem of how we can and ought to encounter, discover and recognize the *auctoritas Dei revelantis* [the authority of God revealing] which gives rise to and is the ground of faith. In the last analysis the only reason men believe is *propter auctoritatem Dei revelantis,* as the most classical of doctrines expressed it. But where and how are we to perceive this authority?

As a matter of fact, this authority reaches us through various channels, various kinds of testimony, which are not unrelated each to the others, but at the same time are not purely and simply coextensive. For the believer there is, of course, only one absolute authority, that of God. We may even say that faith is an assertion of this oneness, in keeping with the first commandment. But this unparalleled authority reaches us only as refracted through a number of "authorities," which are consequently relative, even if indispensable. For the Catholic there are, in addition to the scriptures which are God's word, the Church and its tradition and magisterium, which do not find expression in words alone, any more than Christ, the Word of God, expressed himself only in his preaching. From another standpoint we may add to the list of authorities: reason and science, which define the truth, at least from one viewpoint. Whatever be the form it takes truth is also "authoritative," and we must also recognize and take account of this authority on our journey of faith.

What position are we to take in regard to these various authorities? How are we to bring them into play simultaneously, in order to see refracted through them the indisputable authority of God, which alone is of concern to faith (and perhaps to the human person, whose freedom it guarantees)? This is one of the most meaningful ways, it seems to me, of raising the hermeneutical problem within the perspectives proper to the Catholic faith.

Vatican Council II was the first to turn us in this direction. After emphasizing the need to "carefully investigate what meaning the sacred writers really intended, and what God wanted to manifest by means of their words," the Council adds this complex and especially concise statement:

> But, since holy Scripture must be read and interpreted according to the same Spirit by whom it was written, no less serious attention must be given to the content and unity of the whole of Scripture, if the meaning of the sacred texts is to be correctly brought to light. The living tradition of the whole Church must be taken into account along with the harmony which exists between elements of the faith.[15]

Clearly enough, the necessary task is defined here rather than done for us. Since the Council a number of theologians have studied the demands which the task lays on us and the possibilities it opens up for us. Thus, in his book *Dogma unter dem Wort Gottes* [Dogma under the Word of God], Walter Kasper points out how scripture and dogma are referred each to the other:

> The principle of the analogy of faith means, in broad terms, that each witness to the faith is true only in the context of all the other witnesses to the faith. This means not only that scripture must be interpreted in the light of dogma, but also that dogma must be interpreted in the light of scripture. . . .Every advance in exegetical knowledge is at the same time an advance in the interpretation of dogma. It is this dynamic and historical organization of the relations between dogma and exegesis that gives concrete form to the unity-in-tension which exists between gospel and dogma.[16]

Michel de Certeau adopts a broader perspective in his consideration of the several authorities which faith respects, and show how this very plurali ty enables us to do greater justice to the indispensable authority of God: "The only sign proportionate to the authority of God is a *pluriform sign* that comprises various types of authority in the Church and finds expression in a variety of languages and is distributed among distinct functions."[17] The reason for this is that, far from reducing others to a subservient position, authority "authorizes," that is, "*renders possible* what was not possible before."[18] Authority is therefore not to be identified with anything verifiable in positivist terms. Even Jesus constantly relates his authority to the mysterious authority of the Father. A "flattening out of christology" that would forget this aspect would make "Christian fidelity nothing more than conformity to a place and a circling about in this one narrow spot."[19] De Certeau goes on to say that the latter temptation

> is sometimes met with today in individuals who adopt narrowly historicist or sociological points of view and locate authority solely in past events (the life of Jesus) or in primitive writings (the gospels) or in magisterial formulas (dogmatic definitions) or in a particular function in the Church (the pope).

And he adds: "This is to misunderstand the 'rule of faith' which refers each authority *to other authorities,* by reason of their relation *to the Father.*"[20]

Hermeneutical reflection thus leads to the threshold of the mystery of the Trinity. But this should not surprise us, if it be true that in theology this reflection aims at discovering as clearly as possible the source of the functioning of the "rule of faith".

(7) *The Unity in Difference of the Two Testaments*

I have been making the point that the complex interplay of authorities in the functioning of the rule of faith amounts to a Catholic statement of the hermeneutical problem. The unity in difference of the two Testaments is another formulation of the problem, but a formulaton connected with the Christian faith as such. Consequently, the specific way in which this problem is resolved will depend on how this faith itself is understood. In the stimulating conclusion of his book *Histoire et Esprit* [History and Spirit], which is subtitled "Origen's Understanding of Scripture,"[21] Henri de Lubac brings out brilliantly the important consequences for all of theology and spirituality that are entailed in the way the relationship between the two Testaments is understood. This importance is evident within Catholicism, but it is also to be seen in the divergent views (divergent in relation to the Catholic tradition but also to one another) adopted by the major Churches of the Reformation. Following Origen and the Fathers of the Church generally de Lubac himself gives a fine example (which I would like to call "Catholic") of the complex articulation of the two Testaments. It is an articulation that provides the basis for a complete theology that is resolutely "spiritual" while being at the same time rooted in the soil of history, developed under the dynamic power of the Pasch or Passover of Christ, and deriving from this Pasch the rule for its own functioning.

In other perspectives and in connection with a theory of reading and of the writing we call a book, Paul Beauchamp analyzes the makeup of the Old Testament and sees in it a book that has already found its closure and that communes with itself as it were in the sapiential "writings," but still is able to produce, at its limiting boundary, the apocalypses. The latter sum it up, in a sense, while at the same time turning it toward a *telos* that is both present and future and that supplies the real key to the book. But is not the New Testament embedded as it were within the Old Testament apocalypse? The reading Beauchamp offers of the Old Testament is, in the final analysis, a Christian reading. He does not attempt to hide this fact but rather justifies it. In a sense he has taken sides, he had made a "choice" which "consists in applying and risking the hypothesis of our faith."[22] But this hypothesis proves to be faithful to the picture the Old Testament gives of itself. The content of the New Testament is not projected into the Old, so that when all is said and done the Christian finds there only what he himself had put there. On the contrary, his faith bids him respect the intention and terms of the older book. It is precisely this respect that proves advantageous to Christian faith. This faith is now seen to be based on something outside of itself, while at the same time it alone is seen to be able to give an understanding of its own foundation. "It is an essential attribute of faith that it calls for, brings to light, and projects outside and apart from itself whatever is necessary for its existence but from which it is also distinct, since nothing can keep it in bonds."[23]

Influenced as they are by an interpretation of the Pauline dialectic of law and gospel that runs the risk "of confusing the Jewish generation of gospel times with the Old Testament and of reading into the content of the Book the conflict going on between two groups of Jews who were transmitters of the Book,"[24] Lutheran exegetes and theologians are often inclined to lay more stress on the opposition of the two Testaments than on the "marvelous exchange" that goes on between them. A Dietrich Bonhoeffer, however, discovered in his prison cell the important fact that the "ultimate things" of the gospel are rooted in the "penultimate things" to which the Old Testament bears witness: "In my opinion it is not Christian to want to take our thoughts and feelings too quickly and too directly from the New Testament. . . .We still read the New Testament far too little in the light of the Old."[25] This conviction sprang from a life according to the gospel and deeply involved in human history, while at the same time it provided the foundation for that life. It is indeed very true that the understanding of the unity amid difference of the two Testaments is the expression not only of a basic option in regard to the hermeneutical problem but also, as in all these cases, of an option with regard to human existence and the nature of faith.

Looking beyond the divergences or variations of accent that can be observed within the Christian world, we may ask whether it is not the difference which is displayed within the Book that radically distinguishes Christianity (and Judaism, in its own way) from Islam, that other "religion of the Book."

It is this same internal difference that makes possible the emergence of a living, creative word, which it is the mission of hermeneutics to serve and of which I must now speak in a third section of this essay.

III. Hermeneutics in the Service of the Word and of the Confession of Faith

(1) *Hermeneutics as a Theory of the Speech Act*

When we consider hermeneutics as a service of the word and of the confession of faith, we continue to dwell under the sign of difference. The difference that comes into play here and must be evaluated is that of the word and of language: the word that is a utilization of language but at the same time embodies a movement of transcendence in relation to language. In such a perspective hermeneutics might be defined as the theory of a particular practice, namely the speech act, which is always also the taking up of a position with regard to truth. Hermeneutics is a service to the word to the extent that it establishes an accurate theory of it, cooperating, should occasion arise, in its emergence, and supporting it in its functioning.

For some years now this service has been especially necessary, because the original function of the word is being stifled, devalued, and even rejected outright, either by a civilization in which method or information play the dominant role, or by an exclusive emphasis on praxis, or by a cultural trend that, outside of closed functional systems, acknowledges only a limitless dispersion of meanings in a kind of shattering of all things human. Hermeneutics is then easily judged to be simply the residue of a humanist, and therefore more or less idealist, culture that is now to a great extent outdated. Hermeneutics would be one of the last forms taken by theology, that holdover from another age.[26]

It may be, then, that hermeneutics really reflects a choice: a choice in behalf of the human person (even before being a choice in favor of the God question) that represents a definitive openness to a confession of faith.

(2) *Contrasting Aspects of the Word*

In order to bring out the singular character of the biblical word, Bultmann contrasts the biblical conception of the word to that which was current in Hellenism. Hellenism was interested primarily in the word's more or less static content of meaning. The Bible on the other hand focuses its attention essentially on the speech event. In the Bible the word takes the form basically of assertion, call, and commandment. Even in the preaching of Jesus the important thing is not *what* he says but the fact *that* he says it *at this moment.* The word always functions in the instant, at one particular point.

By its very nature it bears witness to a creative freedom and power.[27]

As seen in these perspectives, the word does not dwell in the body of a human being. It does not come forth out of the darknesses of history. It does not even dwell, properly speaking, in the body of Jesus, nor come forth from the silence of his death. Evidently, in such an analysis, it is not an entire hermeneutic alone but an entire theology that is implied.

In the course of his ceaseless reflection on language and the word, G. Ebeling has complemented or corrected Bultmann's analyses in important ways. He shows how the word is connected with the emergence of the individual, but also how this emergence always occurs in a situation, within a history, a community, a tradition. In this way, he makes it clear that the speech act opens upon an entire universe and makes possible the promotion of an entire set of values: truth, human understanding, peace, and so on. But then hermeneutics turns out to be not at all a purely intellectual undertaking. It endeavors to have the word function in a manner ever more faithful to its basic purpose; as such, hermeneutics is a work of, and a way to, harmony and peace, as well as being a service to truth. For, in Ebeling's view, the truth as conveyed by the biblical word (which is the archetype of all words) is the contrary less of error than of falsehood, the falsehood that is so closely associated with death-bringing folly (Rom 1:22–25), and even with criminality (Jn 8:44). Hermeneutics deals with the truth of the concrete human person as well as with the truth of God.

(3) Toward a Correct God-talk

If all this be the case, then it is easy to see that hermeneutics is of great concern to the enterprise which aims to speak of God: I mean theology. To the extent that hermeneutics keeps watch over the speech act, in order that the latter may properly carry out its role of speaking the truth and making it truly "heard," hermeneutics evidently has a part to play in the search for ways that will enable this speech, possibly in a roundabout fashion, to express God ever more perfectly by bringing into play, as faithfully as it can, the creative but always in some degree baffling power of his own Word.

G. Ebeling, who is the theologian par excellence of hermeneutics, observes that it is typical of the contemporary approach to link the question of God to the question of the word and language. That is how Bultmann approached it in one of his first major articles, as the title of that article clearly shows: "What Does It Mean to Speak of God?"[28] Bultmann here shows the involvement of the human person in this speaking, which confronts the person as an objective that is at once impossible and necessary, and which can be attained only with the help of a power that the person can neither program nor authenticate.

Ebeling appreciates but also criticizes the way in which Bultmann thus cuts off talk about God from all its human supports, especially by setting up a radical opposition between "speaking of" and "speaking about." Ebeling stresses the point that there is always a speaking of God, not in a pure *act* of grace and freedom, but in the acceptance of a tradition of *meaning,* which alone can give content to the word. As thus viewed, the hermeneutical problem doubtless becomes a less simple one, since hermeneutics exists not only to make possible an opening and, if conditions allow, an emergence, but also to accompany a work.

(4) *The Opening to the Confession of Faith*

As a theory of the word, hermeneutics brings out the transcendence of the word, which is simply the transcendence of speaking human subjects in relation to their conditionings, especially their linguistic conditioning. As I pointed out, in this area hermeneutics has to carry on a persevering struggle against certain trends in contemporary culture that would prefer to ignore or downplay any creative meaning, or to conceive of the emergence of speaking subjects in so discontinuous, fragmentary, and in the last analysis anarchic a way that the existence of a tradition and community of faith becomes unthinkable. By opening up the field of truth in which speaking subjects can involve themselves and within which they can make decisions, hermeneutics does more than simply provide the vigilance required for speaking properly of God. It can also open the way to the Catholic confession of faith. This is because faith and word are so closely connected: *Credidi, propter quod locutus sum* ("I believed, and therefore I spoke") (Ps 116:10, cited in 2 Cor 4:13).

Few authors have expressed as eloquently as Paul Ricoeur this bond of mutual interest that exists between faith, or more accurately the community of faith, and the human word, which hermeneutics should be regarded as serving. For Ricoeur, who in this context sets himself against the "abstraction" of which some structuralist ideologies approve, "the basic postulate" of a fruitful interpretation "is that we readers should belong to the same tradition as the text itself." In the case of at least some texts "our relationship . . . is not one of subject to object, but of historical being to historical being." In such cases, "the text was written and is now being read within one and the same tradition."

> Antecedent to any distance that intervenes there is a mutual belonging of text and interpreter, thanks to which the interpretation remains the act of a community that interprets itself when it interprets the texts on which its existence is based. . . .There is always an interpreting community that is itself interpreted in the text which it reads; the real hermeneutical circle operates at the level of the community, which is at one and the same time interpreter and interpreted.

The truth that is confessed by faith is also "a road to follow—a road of love—and thus makes possible a *common journey.*"[29] It is this journey that hermeneutical work helps to map out.

IV. Conclusion

With the phenomenon of writing/scripture/scripture as our starting point we saw the hermeneutical problem taking shape via a certain number of distances to be bridged or differences to be faced. We saw next that this problem is connected with the complex functioning of the "rule of faith." Then we saw it to be involved in the coming into existence of the word, in the work of speaking about God, and in the commitment of believers to a confession. As we advanced, we saw its profound roots in personal and social existence becoming increasingly clear. It became ever more obvious that hermeneutics is a demanding task in which the individual can aspire only to some small share, at a certain point, according to one or other approach. The task will never be completed, any more than will the building up of the Church, to which hermeneutical work is one way of contributing.

Bibliography

1. *General works*
    R. Marlé, *Introduction to Hermeneutics,* tr. by E. Froment and R. Albrecht (New York, 1967). Idem, *Herméneutique et Catéchèse* (Paris, 1970). G. Ebeling, "Hermeneutik," in K. Galling (ed.), RGG, 3 (Tübingen, 1969), 242–62.

2. *For a study of the historical development of the problem*
    H. de Lubac, *Histoire et Esprit. L'intelligence de L'Ecriture d'après Origène* (Paris, 1950). Idem, *Exégèse médiévale. Les quatre sense de l'Ecriture* (4 vols.; Paris, 1959–64). Idem, *The Sources of Tradition,* tr. by L. O'Neill, (New York, 1968). M. Blondel, *History and Dogma* in *The Letter on Apologetics & History and Dogma,* tr. by A. Dru and I. Trethowan (New York, 1964).

3. *Philosophical Studies*
    H.-G. Gadamer, *Truth and Method,* tr. by G. Barden and J. Cumming (New York, 1975). P. Ricoeur, *Freud and Philosophy. An Essay on Interpretation,* tr. by D. Savage (New Haven, 1970). Idem, *The Conflict of Interpretations. Essays in Hermeneutics,* tr. by D. Ihde (Evanston, 1974).

⑥
History and Truth

Ignace de la Potterie

The problem of the relationship between history and truth is a vast one. It may seem at first sight to be of concern only to the historian and the philosopher.[1] But it has arisen in no less urgent a way for the theologian and the exegete. We may therefore say with P. Gisel that it dominates all modern thinking in our Western world.[2] The cardinal question that the theologian must face is that of the connection between absolute truth and historical contingency in the economy of revelation and the history of salvation. This was one of the central issues in the controversy among Catholic theologians in the Modernist period.[3] The same question is at the bottom of a problem which has been a critical one in exegesis since the time of D. F. Strauss: the relationship between the Jesus of history and the Christ of faith. Thus we find it often said: Doesn't the mind find it scandalous to speak of revelation and *truth* having a *historical* origin? "How can the salvation of all human beings be made to depend on the particular, contingent event that is Jesus Christ?"[4]

The question can be asked in still other terms: Is it legitimate to speak of truth as having a "place" and therefore as being historically localized? P. Gisel recently asked this question once again and resolutely chose a negative response: "In theology truth is not a question of *place* (of localization whether metaphysical or historical: *There* is the truth). . . .In radical terms, the question is never: Where is the truth? (*where* is God? which is, significantly, the question asked by the secretly skeptical and even dolefully orphaned modern mind)."[5] But we should note that it is not a good idea to identify the two questions: "Where is truth?" and "Where is God?"

This way of putting the question situates us directly in a particular philosophical tradition that goes back to Plato and Parmenides. But from the standpoint of the theologian and the exegete the problem of the relation between history and truth no longer arises within the framework of Platonic metaphysics (where the truth is *in God*), but rather in direct relation to the gospel, according to which "the truth is *in Jesus* (Eph 4:21). Here we have the fundamental novelty of Christianity. Christians can no longer ignore "the place . . . (of) history as the *primordial theophanic locus* of biblical revelation,"[6] and therefore as also the privileged place for encountering the truth.

We can already see how important it is, in the dealing with the problem that concerns us here, to make very clear the *kind* of truth of which we are speaking. Are we thinking of metaphysical truth? Historical truth? Scientific truth? The truth of conscience? The truth of action? The truth of faith? In each of these instances the relation of truth to history will be different. This explains why some modern thinkers emphasize the historicity of truth, while others no less vigorously maintain the radical non-historicity of truth.[7]

In the following pages my aim is to clarify the issues by making a detailed analysis of the principal models of the relationship between history and truth. In the final stage of my argument (section IV) I hope to show that the Christian conception of truth is the only one to satisfy all the requirements, legitimate but partial, laid down by the other points of view, since it alone brings into unity the contingency of history and the transcendental dimension of truth.

I. Truth Separated from History

1. *The Platonic Tradition*

(*a*) According to Greek philosophy truth is the innermost reality of things, their nature, their ultimate essence; in the last analysis it is identical with the idea of the thing. In Platonic dualism truth is intelligible realities that are distinct from phenomenon; it is being as opposed to becoming; it is the world of the Ideas, which is also the world of the divine.[8] In the well-known myth in the *Phaedrus* (248b) Plato speaks of "the Plain of Truth." According to the mythic tradition on which Plato is here dependent and which goes back to archaic Greece, the Plain of Truth exists outside the flow of time, at the level of eternity.[9] The road leading to it is therefore an ascending road; in the hermetic writings it is called "the road *toward* the truth."[10]

In this dualistic and idealistic metaphysical conception truth evidently no longer has any contact with history, since the latter is produced by human beings and belongs to our earthly world which is subject to the law of change and becoming. Truth, on the other hand, being found above, in the "place beyond the heavens" where "the gods dwell,"[11] is outside of history; it is changeless and immortal.

(*b*) Among the Fathers of the Church who were more directly influenced by this Platonic tradition truth is directly identified with God or with the Word of God. "God is truth," say Gregory of Nyssa and Maximus the Confessor.[12] In Origen, as in his teacher, Clement of Alexandria, truth is identified rather with the heavenly Christ, the eternal Logos, who is the mind or thought of God.[13] According to Origen's commentary on John, Christ in God, or the Word, is "Truth in itself and substantial (*hē auiouleih-*

eia he ousiōdēs), and he is so to speak the prototype of the truth that is found in spiritual souls."[14]

In his conception of truth, then, Origen remains in the tradition of Platonism, which identified truth with being and with the divine world. At the Catechetical School of Alexandria, just as at the School of Athens, men were convinced that Truth eludes the grasp of history. This emerges very clearly in Origen's commentary on Jn 1:17. The fact that the evangelist here speaks of a "becoming" with reference to truth caused a problem for the Alexandrian thinker. He answered by saying that John is not speaking here of the truth of Christ (the Logos) but of the truth of human beings who participate in the truth of Christ.[15] This type of thinking certainly had advantages: it reminded Christians that the events of salvation do not have their ultimate meaning within history, or, to put it differently, that the meaning of history lies outside of history. It also highlighted the transcendence of Christ. But it also brought a danger with it, inasmuch as it was an invitation to see in Jesus only a divine being. Origen could therefore be reproached with "undermining the historical Christ."[16] When the ultimate conclusions of such a view were drawn, they could easily lead to monophysism.

2. *Rationalism*

Platonic idealism, with its strong metaphysical structure and its keen sense of the transcendence of God, could not survive as such in the modern age that is so profoundly rationalistic and positivistic. The remark was made quite recently that "philosophers shifted from the problem of the *locus of truth* (Plato) to that of the *criterion of truth* (Descartes and Kant)."[17] Modern thought has in fact been essentially critical. Nonetheless, the rationalism of the last few centuries does have something in common with the philosophy of the Parmenides and Plato, since it too identifies being and thought (the men of the Enlightenment would have said being and reason) and since it too isolates truth from history. In this view, *purely rational* truth alone can dominate the confused and uncertain material of sense experience.[18]

Descartes may be regarded as the father of rationalism. For him, mathematical truth is the model of all truth: "Those who seek the straight path of truth must not spend time on any object regarding which they cannot have a certitude equal to that of the proofs in arithmetic and geometry."[19] For practical purposes, then, Descartes limits the object of metaphysics to clear and distinct ideas. A similar point of view is to be seen in Leibniz, according to whom the knowledge of truth has nothing in common with experience: "Reason pure and simple, as distinct from experience, only deals with truths independent of the senses."[20] Philosophical presuppositions of this kind directly paved the way for Lessing's well-known axiom at the time of the Enlightenment: "Accidental truths of history can never become the proof of necessary truths of reason."[21]

All this had inevitable corollaries for the problem of the historical Jesus and his relation to truth. No longer would thinkers speak, as in the Platonic tradition of the Fathers, of the truth of the Logos in an ontological and transcendent sense, but only of the much more abstract *rational and universal truths* which we know thanks to Jesus. The result is that here again, but in a quite different sense than in Platonism, Christ, whose divinity is now denied, "is radically cut off from history with its contingency and servitudes. He comes on the scene as a superman who brings a truth that is valid at all times and outside of time. . . .Time and history are in principle completely neutral and irrelevant and set no conditions; truth is universal."[22]

3. *Extrinsicism*

The philosophical rationalism which dominated the entire thinking of the last century had almost inevitable repercussions on the theology of the age. We see a progressive conceptualization of truth and a propositional approach to revelation and faith. This is especially noticeable in the way in which theologians spoke of truth. Whereas Scripture and the older tradition always used *alētheia* or *veritas* in the singular and meant by the term the definitive revelation Jesus had made, nineteenth-century theology became increasingly accustomed to using the word in the plural and speaking of *the truths* of faith[23]; such a practice meant a risk of absolutizing in formulas the revelation of God in Jesus Christ.[24] The language used becomes abstract: "Ineffable truths proposed *by . . . divine revelation.*"[25] The connection of Christian truth with Jesus Christ and the history of salvation is hardly perceived any longer; reference is made rather to the "divine," in a quite vague sense: "truth *divinely* revealed."[26] The name "extrinsicism" aptly describes this tendency, since both the relation of history to truth and the relation of the saving events to the Christian faith are extrinsic ones.

This is one of the two types of thinking which M. Blondel criticized so severely back in the time of Modernism.[27] He spoke of "ideologists claiming to impose their systems upon the concrete truth of history."[28] Such people regarded biblical criticism as a waste of time:

> From the point of view of the proof the important thing is to establish *that* God has acted and spoken, not to examine *what* he said and did through human agencies. . . .The Bible is guaranteed *en bloc,* not by its content, but by the external seal of the divine: why bother to verify the details? It is full of absolute knowledge, ensconced in its eternal truth: why search for its human conditions or its relative meaning?[29]

At this point, I shall bring the first part of my essay to a close. We have thus far met, in their historical order, three successive types of thinking in which truth and history remain extrinsic to one another: Platonism among the ancients, rationalism and extrinsicism in modern times. The models to which I now turn move in a direction diametrically opposed to the preceding.

II. Truth Immersed in History

A number of writers have pointed out that the beginning of the contemporary age was marked by the advent of the historical sense and the scientific spirit. This same advent can be seen in the way the word "truth" is
used: for the modern mind the "true" is what has passed the test of *scientific
verification* or is guaranteed by solid *historical documentation*. Since I am
studying the relation between truth and history, I shall dwell only on the
second of these two criteria.

G. B. Vico († 1744) was certainly one of the precursors of the tendency to identify the true with historical truth. He proposed to replace the classical metaphysical principle: "Being and the true are convertible (*ens et
verum convertuntur*)," with this other formula which perfectly expresses the
modern mind's felt need of concreteness and historicity: "What is *true* is
convertible with what is *made (verum et factum convertuntur)*"[30]; you really
know a thing only when you yourself have produced it.[31] Since human beings have brought history and civilization into existence, these are the things
they can know best. "Truth" in Vico's eyes, then, is human truth, the truth
that human beings gradually bring into being by their activity in the course
of history. There is already visible here the operational conception of truth
that is so widespread today. For this reason scholars have thought to see in
Vico's theory an anticipation of the historicist positivism of the last century
as well as of the secularized idealism of the Hegelian type (Croce) or of
Marxism. This judgment is surely mistaken, since Vico, a Christian, had a
firm belief in the action of Providence within history.

But for us here this point of interpretation is of little importance. The
chief thing we must note is that the modern view of truth as immanent in
history was to develop in two opposite directions: for some, the truth of history consists in the "truth" of *past* facts ("what really happened"); this current of thought was to lead to the historicist positivism that dominated
historical study in the nineteenth century and still exercises an influence today. For others, on the contrary, truth is always the object of study, action,
or the carrying out of a plan, and will be attained only in the *future*, when
the unfolding of history reaches its end; this is the idealist current, which
has been influenced chiefly by Hegel.

In each of these two currents of thought—the retrospective and the
prospective—truth is deeply marked by a coefficient of historicity, to such
an extent that the two notions of truth and historicity end by being for practical purposes coextensive. This is a point I shall now show briefly, while
also showing what happens in each current of thought when it comes to
conceiving the truth of Jesus Christ.

1. *Historicism*

(*a*) There is almost universal agreement today that the historiography
of the second half of the nineteenth century should be labeled "positivist."

As early as M. Blondel, and then in many writers of the last fifty years, this tendency is called "historicism."[32] The word refers to the "retrospective" type of thinking I spoke of a moment ago. Here is B. Croce's definition of it: historicism "is the position that *reality* is *history* and nothing but history."[33] Taking his lead from the works of E. Troeltsch, P. Gisel has quite recently described historicism in comparable terms: it is the tendency to make *fact* and *truth* completely identical.[34] Of course, the question would have to be asked: What "facts" are we talking about?

As for "truth": what does this word signify? In his book *The Meaning of History* H. I. Marrou brings out very clearly the "theory of truth" that was implied in positivist historiography: it endeavored "to model history [and, therefore, 'the facts'] on the sciences of nature" and "to make objectivity the supreme and, in a sense, the sole criterion of truth."[35] According to historicism the only truth is historical truth, the latter being understood in the technical sense; there is no history but critical history.[36] Critical history is concerned solely with phenomena; that is, it takes into consideration only facts that are documented and can be controlled by all, thus guaranteeing in the highest degree the "scientific" objectivity of history. This conception of history is positivist in its tendency, since it assimilates historical facts to physical objects. It completely neglects the human factor in history. But this factor plays an essential role in history, first of all, in the unfolding of the "facts" themselves (since these form, concretely, the web and texture of human life[37]), but also in those who observe the facts and in the historian who studies and interprets them.

(*b*) In the last century this historicist approach predominated in the many studies of the life of Jesus (cf. the Liberal school): the aim was "to recover, with the help of the then widely used critical historical methods, the 'real' picture of the man in whom Christianity originated."[38] Such was also the goal of A. Loisy whose intention was to apply the historical method in a strict and exclusive way to exegesis: "Historical phenomena with their relativity and limitations are the *complete object* of scientific and historical study. An analysis that would look only for the truth behind the phenomena, that is, a sort of other world to which the phenomenal representation is related, is definitively excluded and outdated."[39]

When applied to the Jesus of the gospels such a method can discover only the external aspect of his person; it is unaware of the mystery, the inner life of Jesus, and therefore of his "truth" as well. In other words, the critical historical method is necessarily limited and reductive. It plays a legitimate and even necessary role, provided it recognizes its limitations, but it becomes unacceptable when it claims to be the sole method and seeks to be applied in every possible area, or when it condemns every other approach, for example, that of faith.[40]

Despite the many critiques of which it has been the object, historicism is not dead. Is it not present to some extent in recent christologies that are interested almost solely in the earthly Jesus as recoverable solely by use of the historical method, and even more in books that offer us a "materialist reading" of the gospel? It is not surprising that people should now be finding in Jesus only a human figure (a prophet, the friend of the poor, etc.) and should be doubting the incarnation and divine sonship of Jesus.

The unadmitted presupposition of this approach is that truth is to be found solely by scientific history and cannot be attained by faith. In consequence, Jesus is seen, and cannot but be seen, solely as a man of the *past*. In a sense, therefore, we must "forget him."[41] Given this perspective, it is clear that the hermeneutical problem of the *present meaning* of Jesus is insoluble: he is looked upon only as an eminent man of another age, an astonishing model of moral life or social action (in this respect, the historicist view of Jesus today is oddly like that of the last century's liberal theology). But in regard to all forms of historicism Hegel's very relevant critique will always be valid: "If you adopt solely the historical viewpoint in dealing with religious truth, you simply destroy the religious truth."[42]

Does this mean that in order to discover the precise relation between truth and history (as seen from the religious standpoint), we must now turn to Hegel and those who derive from him?

2. *The Hegelian Heritage*

This second current of modern thought moves in a direction contrary to the first and can therefore help to counterbalance the excesses of the first. It too considers human beings in their historicity but draws conclusions opposite to those of historicism. The perspective here is either idealist or pragmatist. According to the idealist, truth takes the form of hope, of openness to the future, of an ever new possibility offered to the human person. Truth is identified with the movement into the future, with the development of the Idea, and will be fully itself only at the end of history. For pragmatists, on the other hand, the true is identified with the useful, with praxis, with what the human person accomplishes for the transformation of society.

(a) Hegel is the starting point for this entire current of thought. In the *Phenomenology of Mind* he gives this well known definition of truth: "The truth is the whole. The whole, however, is merely the essential nature reaching its completeness through the process of its own development"[43]; or again: true reality is "the process of its own becoming, the circle which presupposes its end as its purpose, and has its end as its beginning; it becomes concrete and actual only by being carried out, and by the end it involves."[44] The idea of the *becoming* of being is evidently very fundamental here; Hegel conceives truth as the becoming, the gradual realization, and the growing awareness of the Idea, the Absolute. At first sight he seems to be placing himself at the other end of the spectrum from Platonism, since in the Platonic tradition Truth is transcendent and changeless. And yet it was in Plato that the master and teacher of German idealism found an outline of his own system, except that he then introduced into it the logic of historical development. Consequently, in Hegel the world of the Ideas (which for Plato was "the Plain of Truth") is no longer separated from our earthly world. Instead, the Idea is located at the end of history, where it becomes the pole that draws all of history to itself; this pole becomes the object of the striving of the Spirit which is always seeking itself and gradually finding itself.[45] The Hegelian conception of truth is thus a form of idealism, but one into which historical development has been boldly integrated: truth is the movement of the Idea by which the latter strives for its own fulfillment and "by which the consciousness freely attains to its truth."[46]

What judgment may be passed on such a bold synthesis? Here is a recent appreciation from P. Gisel: "With Hegel we must maintain the reconciliation of history and truth. This reconciliation is the starting point for the Christian affirmation."[47] Is this indeed the case? One of Hegel's merits was, admittedly, that he so strongly emphasized the dynamic nature of truth and its eschatological tension. But he made truth so immanent to the unfolding of history that he undermined both the divine transcendence and the absolutely unique character of the incarnation as the center of history.[48]

(b) I need say only a few words about posthegelian currents of thought, and especially the one that derives from Karl Marx. There is now agreement that Marx should be regarded as a representative of the Hegelian Left. He criticizes Hegel's idealism, denying the importance of the idea, rejecting all metaphysics, and paying no heed to transcendence. As he sees it, truth is not an ideal which we must try to translate into reality. It is rather, "in the strictest sense, political, that is, mediated by history."[49] Truth is reducible to *praxis,* to social or political effectiveness; it is "produced" by history. This is the point of Marx' aphorism in his second thesis on Feuerbach: "Men must prove the truth, i.e., the reality and power, the this-sidedness of their thinking in practice."[50] J. Lacroix rightly comments: "This form of political atheism implies a real transformation of the meaning of truth."[51]

(c) Here, then, as in the preceding current of thought, there is a kind of identification pure and simple between truth and the positive side of history. Historicism saw truth solely in the verifiable events of the past; Hegelian and posthegelian thought sees truth in the historical process. When radicalized, these two forms of thought lead to a completely secularized concept of truth, in which there is no longer any room for any kind of openness to God on the part of truth.

III. Truth Immanent in the Human Person

The final modern philosophical system which I must discuss briefly is existentialism. It might be thought that this type of thinking, which is so preoccupied with the human person, is of no concern in discussing the relation between history and truth, but this is not entirely the case. Existentialism is completely aware of the historicity of the human person, but it focuses its entire attention on the concrete existence of the individual. As a result, truth is separated as it were from the flow of history and located in the person; the person is the *place* of truth. Existentialism became possible only because of the anthropocentric climate of modern thought. Its chief danger is evidently philosophical or religious subjectivism[52] and immanentism.

It is essential, however, to make a distinction here between agnostic or atheistic existentialism and Christian existentialism. In the view of the former there is no objective truth that exists outside of consciousness: "Thought and truth are identified; there is an absolute immanence of truth in thought and of thought in truth."[53] Christian existentialists, on the contrary, while emphasizing consciousness of self, always locate themselves as beings related to God, and they admit the existence of an objective foundation of truth. Let us look at a representative of each of these two forms of existentialism.

(a) *An Atheistic Existentialist: Max Stirner (1806–1856)*

This Berlin philosopher, who is much less well known than Nietzsche, his heir, belonged to the extreme Hegelian Left. His philosophy is a form of atheistic materialism and is built around an absolute solipsism: it is a philosophy of self-centeredness.[54] He has been regarded as a forerunner both of existentialism[55] and of anarchism.[56] He certainly represents an extreme form of philosophical immanentism.It is worth our while to spend a few moments discussing him, especially because of his surprising thoughts on truth,[57] in which we see an anticipation of Nietzsche's view of truth as power.

We may start with a kind of description that Stirner himself gives of truth: "All truths that are *below* me are dear to me; any truth that is *above* me, any truth I would be *obliged to follow,* I do not acknowledge. For me there is no truth, because nothing is beyond my grasp. Neither my own essence nor the essence of man is beyond my grasp."[58] Each individual is thus his own law, his own absolute norm. Truth for the individual consists in the consciousness of being master, the consciousness of ownership. This explains the title of Stirner's book: *The Ego and His Own.* The idea of truth is thus closely connected with that of *power:* "The true is what is mine; the false is anything that owns me."[59] We can now perceive the full significance of the decisive statement: "I am the criterion of truth."[60]

Such statements may seem to us to be inspired by a monstrous pride; in any event, they show clearly the logical outcome of an existentialist philosophy that rejects all transcendence and is determined to be radically immanentist. It is not part of my brief here to offer a philosophical critique of the system; for this I refer to the first-rate book of G. Penzo.[61] But I must show how the problem of the relation between history and truth is seen in such a context as this.

Existentialism has at least one important point in its favor: it has shown, against Platonism, rationalism and historicism, that truth is not a purely objective datum, entirely independent of the human person.[62] In other words, it is accurate to say that (in a sense that must be further specified) the human person is the "place" of truth, but not in the exclusive and radical way proposed by a man like Stirner, in whose view truth is not only cut off from any and all transcendence (since transcendence does not even exist) but is just as much isolated from human history. For the relationship of individuals to society around them is dictated solely by self-centeredness or the will to power. Since the self is the sole criterion of truth, human beings lock themselves up within themselves as in a fortress; they make absolutes of themselves and attribute to themselves prerogatives that are properly divine.[63] Since history exists only in function of the self, it cannot be a place of truth, but is as it were absorbed into the truth of the self. We can see why Stirner's egoism might be regarded as a new form of idealism;[64] here again there is an almost complete break between history and truth.

(b) *A Christian Existentialist: Sören Kierkegaard (1813–1855)*

Stirner was a forerunner of existentialism, but its real founder was Kierkegaard. The Berlin philosopher was an atheist, the Danish thinker a real believer. While in Stirner's view existence and subjectivity meant in the last analysis an egoistic turning in on the self ("the individual"), the latter is always, for Kierkegaard the Christian, an "individual before God."[65] Unlike Stirner, who carries certain principles of Hegel to their logical extreme, Kierkegaard is in reaction against the Hegelian system. He criticizes the classical definition of truth (*adaequatio rei ad mentem*) as understood in idealism, which reduces reality to thought: "Truth in its very being is not the duplication of *being* in terms of *thought,* which yields only the *thought of being.*"[66] Kierkegaard looks for another kind of truth, one that is directly related to the *concrete existent* being and its human subjectivity.

According to Kierkegaard there are several ways of getting at truth: the objective way of thought and the exact sciences; and the subjective way which alone is of concern to us in the moral and religious sphere. In the latter sphere, we attain to truth only if we appropriate it to ourselves and live it out. This, it seems, is the meaning that must be ascribed to two famous aphorisms of Kierkegaard: "Truth is subjectivity," and "Subjectivity is truth."[67] The important thing is not so much the *object* of belief, but the way in which a person believes, the *how* of belief: "Subjectivity and the subjective 'how' constitute the truth."[68] Everyone knows the example which Kierkegaard himself gives: if a man says he is a Christian but in fact simply has a mental idea of the true God, he does not really pray; if the man is a pagan but addresses his idol with a passion of the infinite, this man prays to God in truth.[69]

It was almost inevitable that such statements should be frequently misunderstood; the author was thought to be saying that the object of faith was a matter of indifference and that truth consisted solely in the authenticity and depth of religious feeling.[70] And we must admit that a number of formulas seem to justify this interpretation. But we must keep in mind that Kierkegaard's purpose was not to work out a complete theory of truth[71]; he was simply bringing home forcefully to his readers the importance of the existential dimension in our journey toward religious truth. A number of more recent critics have shown convincingly that Kierkegaard's conception of truth is not the radically subjectivist one attributed to him.[72] According to H. Bouillard, this is what Kierkegaard is really saying:

> He has constantly before his eyes both Christ and the authority of the Bible. . . . Christ is the sole object of an authentic faith. But we do not attain to truth in the religious order except in the degree that we commit ourselves to this truth and bear witness to it by transforming our own lives to accord with it. In the realm of belief objectivity is attained at the term of interiority. There is a *how,* Kierkegaard writes, and when it is given, the *what* is also given; this how is the how of belief. When interiority reaches its acme, it is once again objectivity.[73]

But we must now ask the question which is the direct object of this study: What is the relation between history and truth as Kierkegaard sees it? We must begin by removing a possible ambiguity: when Kierkegaard identifies truth and subjectivity, his intention is not to enclose human beings within themselves; on the contrary, he thereby situates them before God and emphasizes God's transcendence to the point of paradox. He also professes the existence of the incarnate Word and even makes this existence the content of faith. It is true, however, that he does not give sufficient place to the economy of revelation and the place of Jesus in the history of salvation: "Christ, as Kierkegaard conceives of him, is hardly involved in history; he remains tangential to our world. Thus his doctrine of the incarnation is seriously deficient and has trouble defending itself against the charge of docetism."[74]

And yet we must not underestimate Kierkegaard's contribution to the study of religious truth. In opposition to Hegelian immanentism he maintains an authentic transcendence; above all, he emphasizes the importance for faith in interiorizing the truth, thus showing himself the heir of a long tradition that goes back to Saint Augustine.[75] On the debit side, we must regret that he has not adequately shown Christian truth to be based on an objective datum and to be intrinsically connected with the events that are the foundation of the history of salvation.

IV. The Christian Synthesis: The Historicity, Transcendence, and Interiority of Truth

1. *Christian Truth*

We begin with an important premise: that Christianity, or, better, the Christian faith, uses the word "truth" in a sense that is proper to itself. Contemporary theology does not seem to be very aware of this fact. This Christian use of the word differs from the use made of it in classical metaphysics, on the one hand, and in the sciences or history, on the other. The specifically Christian conception of truth comes from scripture, but it has remained alive and operative throughout the tradition.[76] I shall describe here only its major characteristics.

The word "truth" in its specifically Christian use, does not refer to God in himself, in his transcendence, but to the revelation of God. This revelation of God's saving plan reached its highest point of intensity and completeness in Jesus Christ, but it has continued to be ever more fully grasped due to the Holy Spirit who acts in the hearts of believers to make them share ever more fully in the very life of the Son of God. In the course of tradition, this truth-as-revelation has been given a whole series of other names which brings out different aspects of it: the mystery of truth, revealed truth, the word of truth, the truth of the gospel, the light of truth, Christian truth, the rule of truth, the doctrine of truth, the way of truth, and others.

Let us now compare this Christian idea of truth with the idea of it in the systems we have been reviewing, and ask ourselves what relation it sees as existing between history and truth. It is notable, to begin with, that the Christian viewpoint differs essentially from the preceding inasmuch as it avoids the various partial approaches characteristic of them. The Christian approach is synthetic. With the idea of revelation as its starting point, it gathers into an organic unity the different aspects of truth we have been seeing in the preceding models: the transcendence of truth that was characteristic of Platonism; the historicity of truth, emphasized by the moderns; finally, the dimension of interiority, highlighted by existentialism. But the factor that unifies all these into a synthesis is the idea of revelation: only revealed truth, the truth that comes from God, represents an integration of all the points of view. This is what I must now show.

2. *The Four Dimensions of Christian Truth*

The image of four dimensions is suggested by Ephesians 3:18 ("to comprehend . . . what is the breadth and length and height and depth"), where Paul is trying to bring home to Christians the dimensions of the saving mystery and of Christ's love. Since the notions of *mystery* and *truth* belong to the same semantic field in the biblical and Jewish tradition,[77] it is legitimate to use the Pauline image as a way of describing the different dimensions of Christian truth.

(a) *Historicity of Truth: (1) The Economy of Revelation*

I said at the beginning that philosophers and theologians alike are debating the historicity or non-historicity of truth; and I made the point that everything depends on what kind of truth is under discussion.[78] From the Christian viewpoint there can be no doubt: since the word "truth" means "revelation" to a believer, it is obvious that this revelation takes place in *history.* As Vatican Council II reminded us: "This plan of revelation is realized by *deeds* and *words* having an inner unity. . . . But this *revelation,* then, the deepest *truth* about God and the salvation of man is made clear to us in Christ, who is the mediator and at the same time *the fullness of all revelation.*"[79]

But it is necessary at this point to forestall a misunderstanding: when, in a Christian context, we speak of the historicity of truth, it should be clear that we are not using the word "truth" as equivalent, purely and simply, to "historical truth" as historians do; in other words, we are not speaking solely of "the truth (reality) of facts."[79] If we were, then Christian "truth" would be nothing more than a series of past events that are studied under their phenomenal aspect and in their succession. Christian truth would be the prisoner of the horizontal world of history; truth-as-revelation would cease to exist, and we would be in danger of slipping into historicism. Christian truth, of course, is located *also* on the level of history, since divine revelation is realized in deeds and words that are the very stuff of human life. But to the horizontal dimension of historical truth Christian truth adds a new, vertical dimension that is essential to it. This dimension does not fall within the realm of scientific history. Truth can be described as the presence and self-manifestation of mystery at the very heart of historical events.[80]

The New Testament supposes at every point that revelation has this temporal structure. For Paul, preaching Jesus Christ means making known "the *mystery* which was kept secret for long ages but is *now (nun) disclosed* and through the prophetic writings is made known to all nations" (Rom 16:25–26). This coming of Jesus Christ, at the end of the Old Testament, marks "the fullness of *time*" (Eph 1:10; cf. Gal 4:4). The same idea is repeated in the Prologue of St. John: "For the law was given through Moses; grace and *truth came* through Jesus Christ" (Jn 1:17).[81] John is here distinguishing the two major stages of revelation: that of the Law, which was represented by Moses, and that of "the fullness of *truth*" (cf. Jn 1:14, 17), which is realized in Jesus Christ. The Greek verb *egeneto* in v. 17, which is here used absolutely, as it is also in vv. 3, 6, and 10, describes a historical *happening*, an *event* of the past, namely, the supreme moment of the entire economy of revelation: the *coming* of the Word, "full of grace and truth" (Jn 1:14). What precisely is meant by speaking of the "truth" of Jesus, the incarnate Word? The use of parallelism shows that "truth" here is equivalent to the "glory" of the Word made flesh, the glory that he has "as . . . the only Son from the Father" (v. 14): it is the revelation and manifestation, in the man Jesus, of his divine sonship.

In later tradition the word "truth" will not often have the same fullness of meaning that it has in St. John. On the other hand, the identification of Christ and truth will be repeated in every age. It will be enough here to cite the recent Council once again: "Christ Himself is the Truth and the Way. The preaching of the gospel opens them up to all."[81a] The text also uses the word "truth" in a very traditional way, whereas usually it designates "the preaching of the gospel"or "the true faith."[82]

(b) *Openness to Transcendence*

After what I have said thus far, it should be clear that Christian truth is more than the simple historical truth of the Christian *facts.* Precisely because these facts manifest a mystery, they are open to transcendence. This connection between history and transcendence even works in two directions as it were: from above down and from below up, or from God to the human race and from the human race to God.

(1) In the official texts of the Church we almost never find a pure and simple identification of the truth and God, as we do in the Platonic tradition. The relation between God and truth is to be seen rather in a descending movement: the movement of revelation toward the human race, the entrance of the truth into history. At the point of departure, in God himself, there is "mystery of truth,"[83] the saving plan of God; this plan is written in a heavenly book, "the book of truth."[84] But the plan must be revealed, and it is in this context that God is called "God of (the) truth,"[85] or even, but more rarely, "the Father of truth."[86] The meaning of these two expressions emerges clearly in the *Second Letter of St. Clement:* "In like manner, brothers and sisters, after (the word of) *the God of truth* I read you this exhortation . . ."(19,1); "To the only and invisible God, to *the Father of truth* . . . who made the truth and eternal life known to us through him" (20,5). The "God of truth" is God and he has revealed himself to us in his Son, and whose word of truth (the scriptures) continues to be heard in the Christian assembly.

The inverse formula is even more frequent: "the truth of God" (or, in prayers, "your truth," *veritas tua* or *tua veritas).* We find it especially in the Psalms.[87] This fact explains why it occurs frequently in the liturgy, as in this prayer from the Gregorian Sacramentary: "Lord, let your truth shine in our hearts" (*Veritas tua, quaesumus, Domine, luceat in cordibus nostris).*[88] Christian truth is truth as revelation that comes to us from God.

(2) To the descending movement of truth as revelation from God there corresponds a complementary ascending movement: Christian truth always directs the believer on earth to God, since it is in our midst as the manifestation of his plan of salvation. Even for the wise man of the Old Testament "to understand the truth" meant "to understand what the Lord purposed for him."[89] According to St. John, Jesus is "the truth," and as such becomes for us "the way" *to the Father* (14:6). In like manner, the Prologue says that for his disciples and witnesses Jesus was the one who is (literally) "turned toward (*eis*) the bosom of the Father" (1:18). By this very fact, he was "full of grace and truth," for this life "turned toward the bosom of the Father" was, at the level of the earthly existence of Jesus, the image and revelation of the life of the Word. "The Word was turned toward (*pros*) the Father" (Jn 1:1–2, literal); he is "eternal life turned toward (*pros*) the Father" (1 Jn 1:2, literal).

Descending christology and ascending christology go together, therefore, and must always retain their dialectical relationship to each other. If the circularity of the two approaches is not respected, there is danger of losing sight of one of the two essential components of Christian truth: either its element of historicity or its constant reference to the very life of the Word in God.

(3) We can also see how that the dualism of antiquity (whether platon-

ic or gnostic) and Christianity have very different ideas of the transcendence proper to truth. In the dualist syntheses, truth belonged solely to the world of ideas, to the "Plain of Truth," to the Pleroma. The way of salvation was therefore a "journey *toward* the truth."[90] For the Christiañ faith, on the contrary, "the truth is in Jesus" (Eph 4:21); the term refers not to the eternal Logos but to the incarnate Word. Truth is no longer a metaphysical entity cut off from history and banished to the world above; the Christian truth is in history but at the same time it leads beyond history, for it is an opening to transcendence:[91] in the light of Christ it opens up for us a *way to achieve* communion with the Father.

(c) *Historicity of Truth: (2) Its Eschatological Ambition*

Throughout their earthly journey Christians have their eyes fixed on both a before and an after. The historicity of truth thus involves a tension in two opposing directions, for the Christian condition is marked in its entirety by both an "already" and a "not yet." As I pointed out earlier, truth directs us on the one hand to the origins, to the foundational event of Christianity, to the historical revelation given in Jesus; at the same time, however, it has an eschatological direction, a constant polarization toward the future and "the glorious manifestation of our Lord Jesus Christ."[92]

(1) According to Wisdom 3:9 it is only at the final judgment that the just will be able to "understand truth."[93] In the New Testament, too, full knowledge of the truth is reserved for the end time. The author of the Second Letter of Peter recognizes that even now Christians "are established in the truth that you have" (1:12), but that at the same time this "truth that you have" is incomplete: it is like "a lamp shining in a dark place, until the day dawns and the morning star rises in your hearts (1:19) on the great day of the parousia. John too, despite his tendency to anticipate eschatological realities, accepts the same notion, which he develops especially in the last and most solemn promise of the Paraclete: "When the Spirit of truth comes, he will guide you into all the truth" (16:13).

This important text has not always had the influence that it deserves. We should note, however, that it played a decisive role in the theology of Tertullian. He translated the verb *hodēgein* in Jn 16:13 by *deducere* (lead, guide)[94] and from it derived a new title for the Paraclete: *deductor omnis veritatis* (leader to all truth).[95] At the Second Vatican Council this same verse of John inspired one of the finest formulations in the *Constitution on Divine Revelation:* "As the centuries succeed one another, the Church constantly *moves forward toward the fullness of divine truth* until the words of God reach their complete fulfillment in her."[95a] I must stress once again the fact that this constantly deeper grasp of the truth is the work of the Holy Spirit; this is the very reason why St. John calls him "the Spirit of truth."

(2) Among the types of thought examined earlier the Hegelian system is the one that shows the closest analogy to biblical teaching on the eschatological dimension of truth. As a matter of fact, it is quite probable that the Hegelian identification of truth and becoming is Christian in origin. It is to

Hegel's credit that in contrast to certain positivist or excessively notional conceptions of truth he saw truth as always subject to the action of the Spirit and as open to the end state. At the same time, however, his idealist approach differs considerably from the Christian. His concept disregards excessively the historical objectivity and uniqueness of the Christ event and therefore the value of the facts of Jesus' life as *sign* and *revelation*. Nor does Hegel respect adequately the mystery and transcendence of Jesus who calls himself *the* Truth. Ever since this self-manifestation of Jesus' truth is already present in the world, and we need not wait for history's end before attaining it.[96] On the other hand, "the absolute Spirit" of Hegel is too immersed in history for us to be able to see in it the Spirit of truth who comes from God, that is, the Paraclete whom Christ sends from the Father (Jn 15:26).

(d) *Interiority of Truth*

The Christian synthesis would be incomplete if it laid stress only on the historicity of truth, its openness to transcendence, and its eschatological orientation. The dimension of the interiority of truth is also essential to this synthesis, as Kierkegaard has opportunely reminded us.

(1) In the New Testament it is above all St. John who emphasizes this aspect: truth is not simply the revelation which Christ brought by manifesting himself; under the action of the Spirit human beings must also appropriate this truth for themselves. In the Johannine writings "to do the truth" (*poiein tēn alētheian*) (Jn 3:21; 1 Jn 1:6) means precisely to make the truth of Jesus *one's own,* so as thereby to reach the light. According as they accept or reject the truth, human beings form two groups in relation to the light that has come into the world (Jn 3:19–21). As the evangelist sees it, the devil's most tragic trait is that "there is no truth *in him*" (Jn 8:44). In a similar fashion, John states that if anyone claims to know God but does not keep God's commandments, "the truth is not *in him*" (1 Jn 2:4). Genuine believers are those who love their brothers and sisters in the light of truth, "because of the truth which abides *in us*" (2 Jn 1–2); their love is exercised simultaneously "in deed and *in truth*" (1 Jn 3:18): The authentic Christian "is of the truth" (Jn 18:37; 1 Jn 3:19): in their entire behavior such Christians make evident the influence of the truth that is in them.

The same theme is repeated in the later tradition. According to Clement of Alexandria, "our title of 'children' translates into a word the springtime that extends throughout our lives; the truth that is *in us* does not grow old; and our entire manner of life is watered as it were by this truth."[97] In the Latin West the two great teachers of Christian interiority are St. Augustine and St. Gregory. Let us recall a principle that is very characteristic of the metaphysics and theology of the Doctor from Hippo: "Go not abroad, enter into yourself: truth dwells in the interior man; and if you find your nature to be changeable, then rise above even yourself."[98] Gregory the Great, for his part, speaks of "the inward truth" (*intima veritas*),[99] and sees fervent Christians as "souls utterly resplendent with the light of truth."[100] This idea of the interiority of truth was especially dear to Pascal and Port-

Royal circles, as may be seen from the striking formulation: "The heart is the natural place of truth."[101]

(2) After citing these few texts, I can now compare the Christian theme of the *interiority* of truth with the Kierkegaardian theme of truth as *subjectivity*. The difference between the two is undeniable. Even if we agree with many modern scholars that Kierkegaard was not indifferent to the object of belief, it remains true, as far as I can see, that he gives the name "truth" only to subjectivity as such. Here is a text that is especially enlightening on this point: "There is no objective truth, but the truth consists in personal appropriation."[102] The name of truth is given only to experience, to the inner "life" of the subject, to the subject's "passion of the infinite."[103]

The situation is quite different in the early Christian tradition (cf. St. John and St. Gregory), which speaks not of *interiority* (which would already be truth) but of the *interiorization* of *truth,* that is, of a movement *ab extra ad intra* (from without to within) and also (in virtue of this assimilation) of the active presence of Christ's truth within us, but this truth remains something distinct from us. The believer must indeed make the truth his own, but the truth has an objective existence antecedent to and independent of this appropriation.[104] Faith consists precisely in accepting this truth within us. And if the truth has power to transform us gradually into *children of God,* this is because it is a truth that comes from elsewhere: from Christ and the Father, or, in other words, because it is the revelation of Jesus Christ, *the Son of the Father.*

V. Conclusion

An overall impression emerges from these analyses. When the Christian conception of the relation between truth and history is compared with that of the systems examined earlier, it resembles a synthesis set alongside the elements that go into such a synthesis. As compared with the Christian model, the other models make us think of an organic whole that has been reduced to fragments, of a shattered unity. On the other hand, it can hardly be denied that in modern theology the notion of truth has not preserved the synthetic character it has in scripture and early tradition. It has become overly conceptual and thus has cut itself off from the history of salvation and from the lived faith of Christians. The Platonism of the ancient Fathers and the major currents of modern thought have been important in helping bring to light all the dimensions of Christian truth. The philosophy of history of a Hegel or a Marx and the philosophy of existence of a Kierkegaard have emphasized aspects of truth that belong to the authentic Christian heritage. But they have done so in ways that are incomplete or else wholly secularized. G. Fessard is one of the contemporary thinkers who have been endeavoring to restore the synthesis.[105]

I hope to have shown that the genuine Christian conception of truth is an inclusive one, being at one and the same time recollection of the past, openness to the mystery of God, eschatological tension, and existential appropriation. Only in faith, hope and charity can these four dimensions of Christian truth be organized into a synthesis. In this sense I may conclude with J. Ladrière that "only a theological hermeneutics is an adequate hermeneutics; its starting point is an existential presupposition, namely, the acceptance of Christian revelation."[106]

7
The Christological Problem and Hermeneutics

Prosper Grech

The revision of the treatise traditionally known as *De Christo Legato Divino* [Christ the Legate of God] is one of the more important problems facing contemporary fundamental theology. The endless discussions of the historicity of the gospels and the person and teaching of Jesus that went on from Reimarus to Wrede are well known from Albert Schweitzer's masterly presentation of them in his standard work of 1906.[1] Now Rudolf Bultmann in his many publications has again called into question not only the historicity of the gospels but also the legitimacy of basing our faith on the results of historical research. Moreover, in his existential hermeneutics he has proposed a radical reinterpretation of the Christian message itself.

The writings of this outstanding theologian have given rise to so much controversy among theologians and philosophers and historians, both Protestant and Catholic, that we may well ask whether the treatise I just mentioned can still have any place in our fundamental theology, or at least how the argument of it must be reformulated in the light of the results that have thus far emerged from the controversy. In this article I shall examine: (I) the traditional argument; (II) the criticisms leveled against it; (III) the validity of these criticisms; and (IV) the possibility of reformulating the argument in light of the present state of theology.

I hardly need say that the limited space at my disposal allows only a schematic presentation. However, in the footnotes I shall mention the more important publications so that those who wish may pursue the matter further.

I. The Traditional Argument

I shall summarize the argument as given by P. Parente in his *Theologia Fundamentalis* (Turin, 1955), pp. 44–62 and 82–89, since this is the best brief presentation of the way in which preconciliar Catholic theologians dealt with the knowableness, testimony, and trustworthiness of the historical Jesus and with his place in the argument for the credibility of the Christian faith.

(1) The source for our knowledge of the beginnings of Christianity is the New Testament and in particular, for our knowledge of its founder, the four gospels of Matthew, Mark, Luke, and John.

(2) These gospels are authentic, that is, they were written by those to whom they have traditionally been attributed. They are textually intact. They are historical (a point proved by various arguments), so that with the aid of all four of them we can form a material and psychological picture of Jesus and his life, and can reconstruct, in particular, his teaching and activities during the final three years of his earthly existence. The same degree of historicity is assigned to the fourth gospel as to the other three.

(3) From these sources we know that Jesus claimed openly to be the Messiah, the Son of God, and an envoy from God. Since Jesus was a holy man and psychologically normal, these claims of his are objectively true.

(4) The miracles and prophecies of Jesus, and especially his resurrection from the dead, are to be regarded as the divine seal of approval on the objective truth of his claims and as therefore the basis for the *credentitas* of his words [i.e., his words are not only credible but must be believed].

(5) The apologetic argument concludes to the credibility of the Christian faith and also to the fact that this doctrine not only may but must be accepted. The judgment of credibility and credentity is to be distinguished from the act of faith proper, which is elicited "under the command of the will that is moved by God through grace" (St. Thomas Aquinas) and consists essentially in the assent of the intellect to the divine truth. The *fides quae creditur* calls for the submission of the intellect; the *fides qua creditur*, or the act of faith, is made reasonable by means of the apologetic argument.

II. Criticisms of the Traditional Argument

Parente's book was written at a time when Catholic theologians were still doing battle with a rationalist, liberal and modernist theology. The studies which Bultmann, Dibelius, and Schmidt had undertaken a few decades earlier[2] received hardly any attention.

(1) *Criticisms of the Historicity of the Gospels*

At the end of the second decade of this century, four positions were current among Protestant critics.[3] There were the old-school rationalists, heirs of H. E. B. Paulus, who gave a rationalistic explanation of the supernatural element in the stories about Jesus or else regarded such stories as fiction. The liberals, for their part, while retaining a boundless confidence in the historicity of the gospels, likewise eliminated the supernatural element and reinterpreted Jesus as a moralist who preached the fatherhood of God and the brotherhood of all human beings. Renan's life of Jesus was typical of this school.[4] Against this trend Johannes Weiss[5] and, later, Albert Schweitzer, emphasized the eschatological aspect of the preaching of Jesus;

for them, Jesus is not primarily a moralist but a prophet of the last things. The fourth current of thought was that of Strauss who, instead of rationalizing the supernatural, interpreted it as a religious myth.[6] In addition, scholars like Martin Kähler[7] tended to separate the Jesus of history from the Christ of faith and to minimize the importance of historical research for faith. They emphasized the creative role of the first Christian community. The history-of-religions school, for its part, assigned a large role to the influence of the Hellenistic religions and gnosticism in the development of Christianity,[8] while the philosophical theories of the time, especially idealism, were used in interpreting the Christian message.

Such was the state of scholarship when Bultmann came on the scene. The positions adopted by the *Formgeschichte* school are so well known that no lengthy exposition of them is required in this article.[9] Basically, this approach maintains that after the death of Jesus his sayings and deeds were passed on orally in a manner that accorded with the literary genres, or forms, to which they belonged. Each "form" had its own life setting or life situation in the first community; the latter, however, did not function as an agent of transmission, but also exercised a creative power. It put into the mouth of Jesus sayings that were composed in the service of some vital interest. In like manner, the deeds attributed to Jesus were not all historical; the accounts had a theological purpose.

The authors of the Synoptic gospels, like the author(s) of the Q source, collected all these elements of the tradition (in the last analysis, these writers were editors rather than authors in the strict sense) and wrote their gospels. These last are not to be considered biographies of Jesus but simply testimonies of the primitive Church. It is impossible, therefore, to reconstruct the life of Jesus, nor can we ever be certain that a saying or action attributed to Jesus is or is not authentic. The more Palestinian the tone or atmosphere of a logion or story, the more likely it is to be truly historical.

In the years after the Second World War, form history came to be almost universally accepted as a method of studying the literary units in the Synoptic gospels. Insofar as form criticism contained a judgment on the historicity of the gospels, the exegetes fell into two classes: those who were unwilling to deny the historicity until they had good reason for doing so,[10] and others who gradually became universal skeptics. Many Catholic exegetes belonged to the first category, although sympathizers with the second group were not lacking among them.

Meanwhile, the form critical method became so widespread that even the Second Vatican Council had to take it into account in its *Constitution on Divine Revelation:*

> Holy Mother Church has firmly and with absolute constancy held, and continues to hold, that the four Gospels just named, whose historical character the Church unhesitatingly asserts, faithfully hand on what Jesus Christ, while living among men, really did and taught for their eternal salvation until the day He was taken up

into heaven (see Acts 1:1–2). Indeed, after the ascension of the
Lord the apostles handed on to their hearers what He had said and
done. This they did with that clearer understanding which they
enjoyed after they had been instructed by the events of Christ's ris-
en life and taught by the light of the Spirit of truth. The sacred
authors wrote the four Gospels, selecting some things from the
many which had been handed on by word of mouth or in writing,
reducing some of them to a synthesis, explicating some things in
view of the situation of their churches, and preserving the form of
proclamation but always in such fashion that they told us the honest truth about Jesus. For their intention in writing was that either
from their own memory and recollections, or from the witness of
those who themselves "from the beginning were eyewitnesses and
ministers of the word" we might know "the truth" concerning
those matters about which we have been instructed.[10a]

The citation shows that while the Council stresses the essential truth-
fulness of the gospel narrative, it also makes certain concessions to form
criticism, especially with regard to the *Sitz im Lebem* or life situation, the
reinterpretation of the sayings and actions of Jesus in the light of the resurrection, and the kerygmatic form of the gospels.

But Bultmann's radical skepticism had created such confusion among
the critics that criteria were needed for distinguishing the authentic from the
nonauthentic sayings of Jesus. These criteria, which were set forth clearly
for the first time by Norman Perrin,[11] are four in number. The first criterion
is *antiquity*: a saying is more likely to be authentic, the older it is, that is, the
more Semitic its character. The second is multiple *attestation*: the more
sources a saying is found in, the more likely it is to be authentic, in comparison with a saying that is found in only a single source. The third criterion is
dissimilarity: an authentic saying should be unlike either contemporary rabbinical sayings or the teaching of the post-resurrection Church. The final
criterion is *consistency*: sayings that have been shown to be authentic by the
first three criteria attest to the authenticity of other sayings that are consistent with them.

Minimalist critics begin with a universal doubt and admit the authenticity only of those sayings that pass the test of the criteria. The maximalists
begin by supposing the authenticity of all and then excepting such sayings
or parts of sayings as have a redactional or excessively ecclesiastical tone. As
far as the miracles of Jesus are concerned, even Bultmann admits that some
cures or exorcisms took place, but few Protestants admit truly supernatural
events that can be proven.[12]

(2) *The Messianic Consciousness of Jesus*
    The discussion of the question of Jesus' awareness of himself as Messi-
ah, and of the value of his declarations on this point, is nothing new. The

writings of the eighteenth century are full of it. After the advent of form criticism, however, the controversy came to be focused on certain points. The criterion of dissimilarity, explained above, led the critics to regard as creations of the post-Easter Church those more or less explicit statements of Jesus that show him as Messiah, Son of God, and Son of man in a messianic sense. Here is how Bultmann sums up the results of his own studies:

> We can say nothing with certainty about the origin and development of his messianic consciousness. It is really a question whether Jesus ever considered himself to be the Messiah or whether, on the contrary, he became Messiah only in the faith of the community. Most scholars are increasingly choosing the first of these alternatives. To my mind, however, the second seems to be the necessary conclusion to be drawn from an analysis of his own words. In any case, it is clear that Jesus did not manifest the traits which, for the Jewish mind, were connected with the title of Messiah, and that his activity is accurately described by saying: "He was a prophet."[13]

Exegetes who adopt the strict Bultmannian position write off the confession before the Sanhedrin as being a confession of the Church rather than of Jesus himself. They apply the words "Get behind me, Satan!" (Mk 8:33) to the confession made by Peter in Mark 8:29 and thus make them a thoroughgoing denial of this title by Jesus.[14] The sayings about the Son of God (e.g., Mt 11:27) are either insertions by the Church or generic proverbs.[15] The title "Son of Man," moreover, was either never used by Jesus,[16] or, if it was, it referred to a third person who was still to come.[17]

Exegetes of this same school but who adopt a more moderate position, such as E. Käsemann,[18] maintain that Jesus' preaching of the kingdom is inseparable from his person and that, although his words do not contain an explicit christology, he did act and speak with such authority that his hearers easily took him to be the Christ. These critics thus admit an implicit christology in the sayings of the historical Jesus.

(3) *Relevance of Knowledge of the Historical Jesus for Faith in Christ*

Bultmann is not worried that by undermining trust in the historicity of the gospel narrative he may also have undermined the believer's faith in Christ. He can adopt this position, not by making a virtue of necessity, but because he is convinced that history and faith are separable and that, except for the fact of the existence of Jesus and of his crucifixion, no other historical facts are of any value when it comes to accepting the kerygma regarding the Christ of faith.[19] It is true, of course, that the primitive community presupposed the identity of the risen Christ with the Jesus of history; Jesus is the messianic Son of man and the risen Lord. But, according to Bultmann, Jesus was not a Christian (a Christian being one who believes in the risen

Christ), but still belonged to Judaism. The question arises, therefore, whether the relationship between the two is simply a matter of the existence of Jesus or whether it extends also to the content of his message. Paul and John (I am still giving Bultmann's views) are quite unconcerned about the "how" and the "what" of his activity; they are interested only in the fact of his existence or, at most, in the fact of his crucifixion as well.

Those, therefore, who go beyond the simple fact that Jesus lived and are concerned about his manner of life, do so for either of two reasons: they suppose that the message of the historical Jesus founds and legitimates the kerygma, or they maintain that the kerygma is already implicit in the teaching of Jesus. Bultmann does not accept the first of these two reasons, because (as he sees it) it is the kerygma that has been projected back into the life of Jesus, and not vice versa (the doctrine of Jesus elevated to the rank of kerygma). Bultmann accepts the second alternative (that the teaching of Jesus is implicitly the kerygma of the risen Christ) only insofar as this position is an assertion of historical continuity; if, however, this second alternative goes further and maintains that the teaching of Jesus is complete in itself and already confronts the hearer or reader with a decision and a choice, then this position cannot be accepted because it really renders superfluous the kerygma regarding the risen Christ.

The exact position of Bultmann is that the kerygma cannot proclaim a figure of the past. It must present Christ as a present reality, and he is this (in Bultmann's understanding of the resurrection) in the preaching of the Church. If we look back to historical events, and especially if these are of a supernatural character, in order to ground our own faith, we destroy the essence of this faith, since faith is a leap in the dark and not a vision based on provable miracles.

This is the best place to explain that when Bultmann speaks of faith he is not talking about *fides quae,* that is, an assent to a truth which the intellect cannot comprehend. Such faith would require an irrational "sacrifice of the intellect." He is talking rather of *fides qua,* the act of believing in the saving event, the experience that transforms me existentially in an encounter with the kerygma of Christ. This act cannot have any foundation, even in history; otherwise the "scandal of the cross" would be eliminated. The content of the *fides quae,* on the other hand, must be demythologized if it is to be accepted.[20]

In order that we may better understand Bultmann's concept of faith we must go back to its sources. Bultmann was a disciple of Wilhelm Herrmann, and the latter, after examining the Thomist concept of faith, writes as follows:

> We must break away altogether from this idea. . . . Christian faith looks, in the first instance, not to any doctrine, but to a fact which stands firm and sure in the life of the man who is summoned to believe. . . . All Christian faith is thus a confidence in an event

which has taken place in the Christian's own life. No discussion concerning the credibility of a report or inquiries into the truth of a doctrine can supply faith with its real object, at least not that faith which regards itself as an experience of divine help, and not simply the work of men.[21]

M. Kähler had already written:

Do I really need to know more of him [Jesus] than what Paul "delivered to [the Corinthians] as of first importance, what [he] also believed, that Christ died for our sins in accordance with the Scriptures, that he was buried, that he was raised on the third day in accordance with the Scriptures, and that he appeared" (1 Cor 15:3ff.)? This is the witness and confession of faith which has overcome the world (1 John 5:4). If I have all this I do not need additional information on the precise details of Jesus' life and death.[22]

(4) *The Miracles: Historicity and Apologetic Value*
Among the eighteenth-century exegetes two tendencies emerged in explaining the miracles reported in the gospels. The classical rationalists of Paulus' type maintained that the miraculous occupied only a secondary place in the story. A change in the course of nature can neither explain nor deny a spiritual truth and therefore is of no value from the religious point of view. Moreover, when uneducated onlookers saw something extraordinary happening they immediately assigned it to divine intervention. Jesus effects his healings with special medicines or by a power we today would call "parapsychological."[23]

The rational explanations offered by these exegetes were often puerile. The explanation given by Strauss and his school was less superficial. According to them any story of a miracle was mythical in character: By "myth" in the New Testament they meant that the religious ideas of the primitive community were given the garb of history; such myth was shaped by the unconsciously inventive power of legend and then embodied in a historical person.[24] The primitive community was trying to express the theological idea that Jesus was greater than Moses or Elijah; they did so by narrating deeds that surpassed the wonders worked by those earlier figures. The New Testament account represents in many instances what we today would call midrash.

With the advent of form criticism Strauss' notion of myth was retained. On the other hand, we now also find statements such as this one of Dibelius: "The extraordinary acts that are told of Jesus are accordingly not something that was imposed on his portrait later on; from the beginning they formed an essential part of the tradition about him" and it would be a mistake "to reject the whole report as unhistorical," simply because the report of them is in the service of the proclamation of the kingdom of God.[25] For all that, the similarity of these stories to parallels in Hellenistic or Rabbinical literature not only casts serious doubt on the historicity of the former but also means there is nothing supernatural about the events narrated:

> The miracle stories of the gospels are especially close to Hellenistic tales of the marvelous. . . . The narratives have three parts: 1. a description explaining the situation of the sick person. . . . 2. The marvelous cure . . . generally quite succinct . . . with the elements of magic, so typical of the Hellenistic wonderworker, being eliminated from the picture of Jesus. 3. The presence of witnesses. . .; and finally the sick man himself attests to the efficacy of the cure by performing some action or other.[26]

But even if these miracles really took place, says Bultmann, their probative value for faith is null:

> The conception of miracles as ascertainable processes is incompatible with the hidden character of God's activity. It surrenders the acts of God to objective observation, and thus makes belief in miracles (or rather superstition) susceptible to the justifiable criticisms of science.[27]

Moreover,

> the man who wishes to believe in God as his God must realize that he has nothing in his hand on which to demand a proof of the Word which addresses him. For the ground and object of faith are identical. Security can be found only by abandoning all security, by being ready, as Luther put it, to plunge into the inner darkness.[28]

(5) The Resurrection

This subject will be treated at length elsewhere in this volume. Here I shall limit myself to brief remarks on the hermeneutical aspect. Bultmann does not repeat the explanations of the rationalists who claimed that the body of Jesus had been stolen and who gave other rationalistic interpretations. In Bultmann's view no dead human being has ever risen, and the people of our day will never be able to believe in a physical resurrection of the Lord. Christ lives, but in the kerygma, in the preaching of the Church which begets life by means of faith in the personal, existential salvific event. Here is Willi Marxsen's now classical interpretation of what Bultmann is saying:

> In this connection I think we must simply agree with the proposition: "Jesus arose into the *kerygma*," even though its terminology is incorrect. But Bultmann himself says that this proposition must

be understood rightly; so he interprets it at once, and in so doing he modifies it by not repeating the concept of "rising again." According to Bultmann the proposition must be understood to mean "that Jesus is really present in the kerygma, and that it is *his* word which involves the hearer in the kerygma"; and in fact there is meaning in this proposition only in this sense: for if "resurrection" is mentioned in the *kerygma,* then a theme of the other interpretative derivation is taken up, that theme which (at least in the beginning) did not occur at all in what had been our interpretation. For this very reason we shall not speak of "resurrection into the kerygma"... but ... of the *living* presence of Jesus who was crucified.

Thus we can, in the first instance and provisionally, declare the content of the function brought into being by the vision to be that the purpose of Jesus is continued [*die Sache Jesu geht weiter*]. What is at stake is that Jesus' *kerygma* continues to be preached. However, a new element appears, namely, that the continuation of the preaching occurs without the earthly Jesus being visible or present. And this takes place in such a manner that the old "purpose" brought by Jesus is also not considered apart from him.[29]

(6) *Genesis and Interpretation of the Christological Titles*
In the view of those who, like Bultmann, do not allow that Jesus bestowed messianic titles on himself, these titles were given to him by the primitive community. The Palestinian Church took these titles either from the Bible or from contemporary apocryphal literature: such titles as Son of Man, Messiah (which in the Hellenistic world became "Christ" and a quasi proper name), Servant of God, Lord (without any cultic connotation), and Son of God (without ontological connotations). When these titles passed over to the Hellenistic world (Bultmann still does not distinguish between Judaic Hellenism and pagan Hellenism), they underwent the influence of the popular religions, the mystery religions, and gnosticsm, and as a result acquired fully mythological connotations. "Lord," for example, became a cultic title; "Son of God" was made equivalent to *theios anēr* [divine man] in an ontological sense; preexistence and the notion of an incarnate God were derived from the gnostic myth of the redeemer.[30]

Even if Jesus had presented himself as Son of man, he would have done so under the influence of "mythological" ideas:

At any rate, the early Christian community thus regarded him as a mythological figure. It expected him to return as the Son of Man on the clouds of heaven to bring salvation and damnation as judge of the world. His person is viewed in the light of mythology when he is said to have been begotten of the Holy Spirit and born of a virgin, and this becomes clearer still in Hellenistic Christian communities where he is understood to be the Son of God in a metaphysical sense, a great, pre-existent heavenly being who became man for the sake of our redemption and took on himself suffering, even the suffering of the cross. It is evident that such conceptions are mythological, for they were widespread in the mythologies of Jews and Gentiles and then were transferred to the historical person of Jesus. Particularly the conception of the pre-existent Son of God who descended in human guise into the world to redeem mankind is part of the Gnostic doctrine of redemption, and nobody hesitates to call this doctrine mythological.[31]

The fact that a doctrine is "mythological" does not mean to Bultmann that it should be rejected. But in the approach taken by existential hermeneutics every concept must be translated into terms that are intelligible to our contemporaries, along the lines of the early Heidegger. The demythologizing interpretation of the christological titles and the cross of Jesus subjectivizes these so that they provide terms which can give objective expression to the salvific event or, better, to the experience of salvation which takes place in each believer at the moment of encounter with the kerygma. As Luther had already said: "Christ is not called Christ because he has two natures; what difference would that make to me? He bears this glorious and consoling name because of the function and work that he took upon himself. It is from this that his name is derived."[32]

Bultmann goes even further. In order to believe, it is not necessary to know that Jesus is the Christ and that his cross is the cross of Christ, and *then* to let oneself be saved by him. The process is in fact diametrically opposite: "You cannot first believe in Christ and then in the strength of that faith believe in the cross. To believe in Christ means to believe in the cross as the cross of Christ. The saving efficacy of the cross is not derived from the fact that it is the cross of Christ: it is the cross of Christ because it has this saving efficacy. Without that efficacy it is the tragic end of a great man."[33]

The act of affirming that God acts in Christ, and the surrender of my self-understanding so as to accept the grace of God, are not two acts in a sequence, the one objective and the other subjective; they are one and the same act. To assert further that Christ is God means that I encounter God in my surrender to the kerygma about Jesus. "All these assertions are an offense (*skandalon*), which will not be removed by philosophical discussion, but only by faith and obedience. . . . It is precisely its immunity from proof which secures the Christian proclamation against the charge of being mythological."[34]

(7) *Other Hermeneutical Approaches to the Life of Jesus*

As we shall see below, Bultmann was almost alone in saying that the particulars of the life of Jesus were without relevance to faith in Christ. Not even his own disciples followed him on this point. On the other hand, his existential hermeneutics opened the door to other interpretations that were dependent on the various contemporary schools of philosophy. The first such interpretation comes from the same existential circles, but it is based on the later Heidegger's philosophy of language rather than on *Sein und Zeit* [Being and Time], as Bultmann's own interpretation had been. Ernst Fuchs and Gerhard Ebeling speak of a linguistic event rather than a salvific event, and of the faith *of* Jesus rather than faith *in* Jesus. The words spoken by Jesus are an interpretation of his own experience of God, and his intention in speaking them is to reproduce the same experience in his hearers. Only then can one call oneself a Christian, when, *by means of* the words of Jesus, one reproduces in oneself the attitude of faith proper to Jesus himself.[35]

From British neopositivism comes the christology of Van Buren, for whom Jesus is the essentially free man, the man free for others to the point of dying for them.[36] Marxism is the source of the social interpretation of a Fernando Belo who portrays Jesus as the first Marxist of history.[37] A kind of neo-Hegelianism has given rise to the more serious christologies of Pannenberg and Moltmann with their emphasis on the eschatological dimension.[38] The process theology of Whitehead has yielded an evolutionary christology which some Catholics interpret in the light of Teilhard de Chardin.[39] Three programmatic articles of Hulsbosch, Schoonenberg, and Schillebeeckx in the *Tijdschrift voor Teologie*[40] gave rise to an interpretation of descending christology that had implications for the doctrine of the Trinity as well, thus leading to the reprimand from the Sacred Congregation for the Doctrine of the Faith in 1973.[41]

(8) *Conclusion*

In presenting the confrontation between Catholic theology and the radical theology of the postwar period I have concentrated on Bultmann because his is the extreme position, denying, as it does, point by point what is stated in Parente's apologetic argument. He challenges the historical value of the gospels and especially of the sayings of Jesus. He denies the messianic consciousness of Jesus. He separates the Jesus of history from the Christ of faith and makes knowledge of the former irrelevant to faith in Christ. He reduces the miracles to a minimum not only as far as their historicity is concerned but also and especially as far as their probative value is concerned. He does the same to the resurrection, giving an interpretation of it that strips it of all theological value. He explains the historical beginnings of christology in such a way as to make it the accidental product of religious eclecticism at a particular historical moment and to deprive it of any objective ontological status. Finally, he opens the door to all sorts of explanations of Jesus that often fail to shed light on the traditional Christian faith by integrating new intuitions into it, but seem instead to be mere palliatives which attempt to replace a lost faith in Christ.

Although these two positions at opposite ends of the spectrum (Parente and Bultmann) continue to be maintained, recent years have seen second thoughts on both sides. The result has been a dialogue which is constructive for fundamental theology as well.

III. The Critics Reconsider

It was inevitable that Bultmann's clear position should elicit reactions in the various areas affected by his theories: historical criticism, theology and philosophy. I shall review the more important results of post-Bultmannian criticism, with a view to determining the limits within which it is possible to reformulate the arguments traditionally used in our fundamental theology.

(1) *The Historicity of the Gospels*
The doubt cast by form criticism on the historicity of the gospels is due to the assertion that the post-Easter Church invented stories about Jesus and sayings of Jesus—even putting the sayings of some "prophets" in the mouth of Jesus—in order to authorize its own behavior in a specific life situations. Every "form" is connected with a specific life situation: liturgical, controversial, communal, and so on. This is an a prioristic presupposition on Bultmann's part that is far from being historically documented. In fact, post-Bultmannian studies show a strong tendency to deny this presupposition. Let us look at some prominent examples.

(a) The first step was the rediscovery of *Jesus' own life situation* as distinct from that of the Church. Joachim Jeremias in his now classical book on the parables of Jesus[42] had already gone back beyond the editorial interpretation of the parables to that of the community during the oral stage of transmission, and beyond this again to the original meaning the parables had in the concrete life situation of Jesus himself. We may not agree with Jeremias on the application of individual parables, but the critics have accepted his overall method. He has shown that when the redactional and traditional interpretations (each representing a different life situation) have been set aside, it is possible to get back to the parable in its original form and vital context.

This method was then carried further by Heinz Schürmann in an essay entitled "The Pre-Easter Origins of the Sayings Tradition."[43] Here he asks what the vital context of the sayings was in the life of Jesus himself. He emphasizes the point that Jesus requires faith in his words or in his person, and that this faith is developed both by a life in common and by the various evangelizing missions launched by the Master himself during his life. Consequently, various sayings of Jesus may be reported in the gospel as referring to the life of the post-Easter Church, but this simply represents an application to the community and its apostolic mission of sayings uttered in a comparable situation prior to the resurrection. The sayings are therefore not invented but rather applied by the Church in the light of the paschal event.

(b) In a recent book that applies the latest linguistic studies of the Güttgemans school to New Testament research,[44] Klaus Berger likewise criticizes Bultmann on two basic points. The first is the claim that the distinction of forms derives less from their content than from their function and effect in the structure of discourse. The second is the (erroneous) assertion that a form is inseparably connected with a specific life situation. For, in fact, one form can be used in various situations, and a single situation can call for various forms. The forms were therefore not invented to meet a particular, limited need.

(c) Everyone knows by now of the work done by Riesenfeld and Gerhardsson[45] on the methods of oral transmission used by the rabbinic scholars. In 1961 Gerhardsson published a book entitled *Memory and Manuscript* in which he applies to the transmission of the sayings of Jesus the technique used in rabbinic teaching, namely, the learning of a teacher's doctrine by heart with the help of mnemonic and rhythmic formulas. Jesus would have dealt in a similar way with his disciples who, in a sense, formed a school. This does not mean that Jesus was a halakic teacher; he would, however, have resembled a haggadic who taught in parables. His sayings would have been transmitted in a similar manner after the resurrection; this would assure the substantial fidelity of the transmission, even though account must also be taken of the adaptation of the sayings to the situation of the Church.

Despite two weighty objections, Gerhardsson's theory has met with growing agreement. The difficulties comes, first, from the fact that the rabbinical documentation which the author uses to prove his thesis comes from the years after 70 A.D. To this the author answers that we find the method used in the school of Jamnia, and that it does not appear on the scene as a totally new method; this becomes especially clear when we find sayings being reported of rabbis who were contemporaries of Jesus, such as Hillel and Shammai. In addition, there are many indications in Josephus and in the New Testament itself that the method was also in use before 70. But (and this is the second objection) was Jesus a rabbi? Was his style not rather that of an eschatological prophet? To this Gerhardsson answers that the point is not to define the class to which Jesus belonged, but rather the teaching method used in his day by any teacher who had something to communicate to his disciples, especially if he was sending them out to preach in his name to the neighboring countryside.

(d) Bultmann's argument that the primitive Church was not interested in the biography of Jesus has been countered recently by G. N. Stanton in his *Jesus of Nazareth in New Testament Preaching.*[46] Stanton studies the discourses in Acts: these are kerygmatic but they always contain a reference to the earthly life of Jesus. The author shows that this reference is only a hint of a longer discourse; it is also pre-Lukan, having as its vital context the missionary preaching carried on in circles that had not known Jesus in person. The reference also counters Bultmann's hypothesis that Paul in his letters could do without the historical Jesus.

(e) We may pass on now to the criteriology of the sayings of Jesus. A great deal has been written on this subject. F. Lambiasi has reviewed all recent studies in his book *L'autenticità storica dei Vangeli* (Bologna, 1976), along with sensible comments of his own. In addition to the studies reviewed in Lambiasi's book, the most serious work done thus far is to be found in the published results of a seminar conducted by F. Mussner: *Rückfrage nach Jesus* (edited by K. Kertelge [Freiburg, 1974]).

In general terms, we can say of the validity of the criteria that they are useful in confirming the authenticity of a saying, but incapable of excluding any saying as unauthentic. The following are the reasons for this assertion. The criterion of antiquity is based on the Semitic flavor of a saying. But, in addition to the fact that the "Semitic flavor" might point to a Palestinian community and not necessarily to Jesus himself, we know from Hengel's studies that a good deal of Greek was spoken even in the Palestine of Jesus' time. The Acts of the Apostles mention the presence of Greek-speaking Christians in Jerusalem itself in the very earliest days of the Church. A saying with a "Greek" flavor is therefore not necessarily later in time than one with a Semitic flavor.

With regard to the criterion of multiple attestation, the greater the number of sources, the better, of course. But let us not forget that some of the finest parables, which no one has ever thought of denying, are to be found in Luke alone!

The criterion most hotly debated is that of dissimilarity. If a saying is unlike those of the contemporary rabbis, the only thing proved is originality. But similarity need not prove a lack of authenticity, since there was nothing to prevent the sayings of Jesus from sometimes echoing rabbinical teaching. Dissimilarity to the teaching of the primitive Church is a begging of the question, for only if one begins with the assumption that Jesus did not have a christology or ecclesiology is it possible to deny the authenticity of sayings on these two subjects; but that is the point to be demonstrated! The question of authenticity depends a great deal, therefore, on the a priori from which one starts. The two contrasting classical positions are those of N. Perrin who assumes that a saying is doubtful until the contrary is proved, and of J. Jeremias who puts the burden of proof on those who deny authenticity. In view of the recent studies reviewed above and of the a prioristic positions of the strict Bultmannian school, I cannot but think that Jeremias is correct.

(f) But, even granting the validity of this last statement, the fact remains that form criticism and the principle of an interpretative tradition have been accepted by all, even, as we saw, by the Second Vatican Council. What method is there, then, for distinguishing interpretation from transmission and getting back to the original nucleus of a saying? We have seen that the famous four criteria are of quite limited value. Perhaps we will be on a somewhat more solid ground if we say that first of all elements which are redactional (recognizable by style, vocabulary, or thought) must be eliminated from a saying. If we think of John or of the extracts from Q in Matthew, or if we compare the three Synoptics with one another, we can see that such an operation is feasible.

In studying the degree of interpretation involved in the transmission of the sayings and actions of Jesus, not enough attention has as yet been paid to the analogy between the targumization of the Torah and the "targumization" of the sayings of Christ in the Church's tradition. After all, Christ was understood to be a new Moses. We may therefore expect that in transmission his words were treated in the way that the *meturgeman* (translator) treated the words of Moses when re-expressing the lawgiver's thought in Aramaic. At times, the translation (transmission) was very literal; at other times, interpretive glosses were added or the words were paraphrased in order to adapt them to contemporary problems; at still other times, an explanatory midrash drawn from scripture itself or from the community's tradition was added, but there was always a substantial fidelity to the original words or events. In applying this analogy, account must be taken, of course, of the situation of the post-Easter Christian community.

(g) Recent scholarly study of the miracles of Jesus was focused chiefly on their nature as *signs* and on the theological interpretation of them in the process of transmission and at the redactional level.[47] The starting point is the realization that the message of the kingdom of God, on the one hand, and the miracles of Jesus, on the other, are so interrelated that the former does not make sense without the latter. Even if the number of the authentic sayings of Jesus be reduced to the minumum which Perrin's criteria calls for, these sayings continue to presuppose that Jesus has worked wonders; both Bultmann and Dibelius admit as much.[48] Christ transmits his revelation by means of both words and actions that explain each other; we may think in this context of certain sayings such as the message to John the Baptist (Lk 7:22), the saying about Capernaum and Chorazin (where we do not read of any miracle having been done: Luke 10:13-15), and the sign of exorcisms (Lk 11:15).

On the other hand, the gospels do not present us with a simple chronicle of miracles but rather with accounts that are primarily theological in purpose. We may say that the gospel account has the same relation to the interpretation of Christ in the apostolic kerygma that the deeds accomplished by Christ had to his preaching of the kingdom. When we say that in the context of Jesus' life a miracle is a "sign," we mean that it is an extraordinary action which immediately catches the attention of the bystanders and shows Jesus to be personally endowed with special powers. The attribution of these powers to Beelzebul or to God depends on the crowd's faith. A sign has to be "read," and the key to the reading is almost always to be found in associations with the action of Yahweh in the Old Testament or with eschatological prophecies. Anyone who "reads" the sign properly cannot but conclude that the saving power of God that operated throughout the history of Israel has now reached its soteriological culminating point in the person and work of this man who proclaims the coming of the kingdom so long desired.

The gospel *story,* however, unlike a narrative chronicle, chooses its vocabulary, phrases, structure, and Old Testament citations in order to elaborate an interpretation of the fact and enable the reader to grasp the meaning of the fact in relation to the risen Christ. The narrators are convinced that the event actually took place and are interested less in *how* than in *why* it occurred. A gospel miracle, therefore, has a theological aspect that presupposes faith, but it also has an "apologetic" aspect that precedes faith. Both aspects are clearly in John in the episode of the man born blind (ch. 9) and the resurrection of Lazarus (ch. 11).

There is still the difficulty of determining "what really happened" in the miracle stories. But as long as a careful study has not been made of the extent of Christian "midrashic targumization," it is very difficult to determine in particular cases just how a miracle occurred. This difficulty does not, however, weaken the conviction that Christ did in fact perform extraordinary works. Whether or not such works are to be called "miracles" in the modern sense of the term depends on the a priori mindset of the person who reads the stories. An agnostic or someone who, like Bultmann, rejects the miraculous as such because it demands a *sacrificium intellectus* could at most admit that something happened, while denying that God was its cause, and could therefore admit its mythical or theological value but certainly not its apologetic value. For someone, on the other hand, who sees God as "all in all," miracles present no difficulty. But at this point the problem ceases to be one of historical criteriology and becomes a philosophical problem, and this is not the best way to look at reality.

Since recent literature on miracles is so very extensive, I refer the reader to L. Sabourin's recent book, *The Divine Miracles Discussed and Defended* (Rome, 1977). Sabourin provides a very full bibliography as well as documentation on some contemporary cases of miracles. He also discusses in detail the similarity with Hellenistic miracles and concludes, with various recent studies, that it is not impossible that in writing on Apollonius Philostratus for polemical reasons deliberately imitated the gospel stories.

For recent studies on the resurrection the reader should consult G. Ghiberti's essay in this volume.

(2) *The Jesus of History and the Christ of Faith: Reconsiderations*

Bultmann's claim that the Jesus of history has no relevance for the Christ of faith has not found acceptance even among his own disciples. The first to respond negatively was Ernst Käsemann who in a programmatic address of 1954 sought a fourth way in addition to those of Bultmann, rationalism, and the supernaturalism that calls for a *sacrificium intellectus*.[49]

As Käsemann sees it, the Jesus of history was important to the early Church because it did not want mythology to supplant history or a gnostic heavenly being to take the place of the man from Nazareth. Most importantly, however, it is the cross and resurrection of Christ that are the center of our faith. History is therefore taken over into the kerygma. The firm grounding in history that we find in the Synoptic gospels amounts to a clear assertion that salvation is *extra nos*. The life of Jesus is constitutive for our faith because the Christ of faith and the Jesus of history are one and the same person. It is true that the Easter faith is the foundation of the kerygma, but that faith is not first nor the sole source of the content of the kerygma. On the contrary: the Easter faith represented an awareness of the fact that God acted before we became believers, and it bore witness to this priority by incorporating the life of Jesus into its proclamation. Study of the life of Jesus is therefore theologically legitimate; it is also possible, within the limits of a radical criticism, because many historical details have been preserved in the gospels.

Käsemann holds that even if the historical Jesus never explicitly claimed to be the Messiah, he nonetheless spoke and acted with such authority that all could catch a glimpse of the superior being that he was. Only in the proclamation of the post-Easter Church did the implicit become explicit, and the *semel* of Jesus become the *ephapax* of Christ. This explicitation does not represent a faith cut out of whole cloth but has its basis in the authority of the historical Jesus.

Eleven years later, when the debate was well under way, Käsemann wrote a second article in which he asks why the Church could not carry on its proclamation in the form of letters alone.[50] Even John felt the need of expressing his ideas in a gospel. In the first days, the kerygma could be broadcast through the work of charismatic preachers, but the rise of "enthusiasm" in the Church and the multiplication of kerygmas caused the need to be felt of anchoring the kerygma in history and thus providing a criterion for the discernment of spirits. The work of the charismatics alone would have reduced the kerygma to a docetism; gospels alone would have turned it into an ebionitism. But the evangelists succeeded in locating history within the kerygma. Bultmann accuses Fuchs and Ebeling of making the kerygma superfluous; he himself, however, makes the gospels superfluous.

Joachim Jeremias responded even more strongly to the Bultmannian challenge.[51] He agrees with Bultmann in emphasizing the *sola gratia* and in downgrading human efforts in relation to it, but he says that Bultmann is in danger of emptying the gospel message of its central content, namely, the incarnation ("And the Word was made flesh"), of substituting Paul for Jesus, and of returning to docetism. Our faith has its origin not in the kerygma but in the historical fact of the life of Jesus. It is difficult to understand why the Bultmannians lay so much emphasis on the presence of the kerygma in the gospels when the influence of Paul on the gospels is so slight. The gospels give us a fairly faithful description of the pre-Easter situation. But the return to the historical Jesus is not required solely by a greater fidelity to the sources. The kerygma itself tells us that God reconciled the world to himself by means of a historical event. Without Jesus, Paul is incomprehensible. There is need, therefore, of continuing to study the life of Jesus with all the means at our disposal: this is our way of saying "Yes" to the incarnation at a particular moment of history. If we separate the kerygma from history we fall into the excesses either of docetism or of ebionitism. The historical Jesus is related to the Christ of faith as summons to response.

So far did the reaction against Bultmann go that the three principal representatives of the so-called "New Hermeneutics"—James Robinson, Ernst Fuchs, and Gerhard Ebeling—even call themselves "neo-liberals." Robinson writes:

> The purpose of a new quest must derive from the factors which have made such a quest possible and necessary, a generation after the original purposes had lost their driving force and the original quest had consequently come to an end. A new quest must be undertaken because the *kerygma* claims to mediate an existential encounter with a historical person, Jesus, who can also be encountered through the mediation of modern historiography. A new quest cannot verify the truth of the *kerygma,* that this person actually lived out of transcendence and actually makes transcendence available to me in my historical existence. But it can test whether this kerygmatic understanding of Jesus' existence corresponds to the understanding of existence implicit in Jesus' history, as encountered through modern historiography. If the *kerygma's* identification of *its* understanding of existence with *Jesus'* existence is valid, then this kerygmatic understanding of existence should become apparent as the result of modern historical research upon Jesus. For such research has as a legitimate goal the clarification of an understanding of existence occurring in history, as a possible understanding of my existence. Hence the purpose of a new quest of the historical Jesus would be to test the validity of the *kerygma's* identification of *its* understanding of existence with *Jesus'* existence.[52]

In other words, an encounter with the kerygma is not enough, since there was a variety of kerygmas even in the early Church: the gnostic, the Jewish-Christian, the Pauline, the Johannine, and so on. Comparison with the Jesus of history is the criterion that helps me decide the validity of the direction of the existential self-understanding in which I am engaged. "As a matter of fact, history is not the objective happening of the past, but an act of commitment that I make in a dialogue with the past which is meant to bear fruit and in which the self is actualized and existentially revealed to itself."[52a]

Fuchs and Ebeling take as their starting point the concept of language that is found in the later Heidegger; according to this the linguistic event of encounter with being finds expression in words which are an interpretation of language itself and therefore of being. In Jesus "faith becomes word," faith here being understood as the global attitude of Jesus toward the future of God. "Even if our knowledge of Jesus is defective in many respects, we are able to identify clearly the main purpose of his life." To believe *in* Christ means simply that through the words and general attitude of Jesus we reproduce in ourselves the same attitude of faith that we find in him. Our encounter with God thus takes place in the historical Jesus.[53]

(3) *The Messianic Consciousness of Jesus*

The problem of the self-consciousness of Jesus, or, in theological terms, what Jesus claimed to be or whether he required faith in his person, is perhaps the most difficult of the problems facing historical criticism and fundamental theology. The main cause of the difficulty is twofold. There is the difficulty of applying the criterion of dissimilarity to the "christological" sayings of the Synoptic gospels: are they completely authentic, or are they put into the mouth of Jesus by the faith of the early Church, or are they authentic sayings that have been reinterpreted in the light of the resurrection? The difficulty is also due to an incorrect statement of the problem, on the part both of those who want to find the whole dogma of Chalcedon contained in the words of Jesus, and on the part of those whose rationalist approach makes them treat the gospels like an onion to be peeled: they remove layer after layer until there is nothing left.

There are few, even among the most committed Catholics, who claim to find in the sayings of Jesus an explicit christology of a post-paschal type. It is only the most diehard disciples of Bultmann who deny all messianic consciousness to Jesus. The vast majority today accepts the formula of Käsemann: by his manner of speaking and acting Jesus made it easy for people to infer that he was the Messiah; it is therefore possible to speak of a christology that is implicit by comparison with the explicit christology of the Church after Easter. In this middle group we find concessions being made that are more or less generous depending on the tendency of the author. In this essay I can only sketch briefly the positions held today regarding the christological titles found in the gospels: Son of man, Christ, and Son of God.[54]

(a) The title *Son of man* is found almost exclusively in the four gospels, and there always on the lips of Jesus himself, sometimes as a parallel to "I." The questions debated today are these: What does the title mean? Did Jesus really use it, or did the Palestinian Church put it in his mouth? If he did use it, was he referring to himself or to a third person?

In response to the first question: there are some today who say that in Aramaic "Son of man," in addition to its general meaning of "human being," can also be simply the equivalent of "I"; however, the instances used to prove this thesis are rather late and uncertain.[55] The title is more commonly understood by reference to the figure in Daniel 7 and in the Ethiopic Book of Enoch. That Jesus himself spoke of the Son of man few would deny today, in view of the indisputable fact that the title is found only in the mouth of Jesus; some scholars, however, would limit this authenticity to sayings that refer to the future, and would exclude those that refer to the present or to the "suffering Son of Man" (Mk 10:45). Bultmann, however, and others with him, are of the opinion that Jesus was speaking not of himself but of a third person who was to come.[56] Even Jeremias is hardly able to convince his colleagues that Jesus was referring to himself in a different way.[57]

(b) No less discussed is the title *mashiach*. Jesus never says that he is the Messiah. Wrede explains this by the famous "messianic secret," which would therefore be an editorial contribution of Mark.[58] The two passages in which Jesus accepts the title when given him by others (Mk 8:29–30; 14:62), namely, the confession of Peter and the admission by Jesus to the Sanhedrin, are sharply challenged by the more radical critics. By a bit of sleight-of-hand in their literary criticism, these critics see Peter's confession as answered by Jesus in v. 33 with the words, "Get behind me, Satan!"; in their view, the intermediate verses, speaking as they do of a suffering Son of man, cannot be authentic. The confession before the Sanhedrin cannot be historical because it is composed of texts from the Old Testament (Ps 110; Dan 7:12) after the model of the Church's confessions of faith, and not based on direct testimonies. There is an abundant literature on these two texts,[59] but the arguments of the radicals are too contrived to win wide acceptance. The majority of critics maintain that Jesus does not refuse the title of Christ, but also that he does not accept it in the sense given it by the Jews.[60]

(c) The title *Son of God,* which forms part of the confession to the Sanhedrin in Mark 14:62, is rejected for the same reasons as the title of Messiah, while the saying in Matthew 11:27 is regarded as being too Johannine in tone. But, after the studies of de Kruijff and Jeremias,[61] and especially after the discovery of the Qumran Florilegium (4QFlor) which cites 2 Samuel 7:14 and Psalm 2 as referring to the Messiah, the critics are beginning to see the admissibility of the hypothesis that Jesus spoke of himself as Son (though, of course, not in an ontological sense).

But the limitation of the study of Jesus' self-consciousness to an analysis solely of the titles represents too restrictive an approach. In his book on Jesus, Bornkamm (who does not admit the authenticity of the three titles I have discussed) ends his chapter on the messianic consciousness of Jesus by saying:

> The result of these deliberations is in no way merely negative, but is pre-eminently positive as well. They recall us to the recognition which has governed our whole treatment of the message and history of Jesus, namely, that the Messianic character of his being is contained *in* his words and deeds and *in* the unmediatedness of his historic appearance. No customary or current conception, no title of office which Jewish tradition and expectation held in readiness, serves to authenticate his mission, or exhausts the secret of his being.... We thus learn to understand that the secret of his being could only reveal itself to his disciples in his resurrection.[62]

This judgment represents the consensus of the vast majority of more moderate post-Bultmannian critics. I too could subscribe to it if I were not convinced that the criticism of the three messianic titles is too radical and cannot provide a plausible historical explanation of the condemnation of Jesus for being "King of the Jews."

(4) *The Demythologizing Approach*

The programmatic writings in which Bultmann explained his theory of existential demythologization[63] unleashed a real storm of controversy. In addition to the volumes published under the title of *Kerygma und Mythos,* hundreds of books and articles have appeared on the subject.[64] Bultmann is attacked by philosophers of the Left, for example, Jaspers, Buri, and Ogden, who think the theory of demythologization does not go far enough, and by theologians like Karl Barth, Schniewind, and the Catholics, who see in Bultmann a return to rationalism and the destruction of the Christian faith that this entails. If truth be told, many a page written in this controversy is full of rhetoric, misunderstanding, and unjustified accusations, or at least of accusations that are justified only because Bultmann joins in paradoxical coexistence a kerygma of a saving act of God and a demythologization that calls for no *sacrificium intellectus.* I shall give here the arguments which, in my view, are on target in this controversy.

Nowadays, all admit the necessity of a hermeneutic that explains the New Testament message to our contemporaries in a language that is intelligible to them. That is precisely what Karl Barth was trying to do in his commentary on the Letter to the Romans. But an interpretation must be a translation, not a betrayal, of the message. Moreover, when we have brought New Testament teaching as much "up-to-date" as we can, there always remains the *scandalum crucis,* which is not reducible to any wisdom of this world (1 Cor 1:20). Bultmann is very conscious of this problem, but he goes astray in dealing with it. When, for example, he speaks as an apologist to nonbelievers, he seeks to strip faith of any objectivization and verification. To do this he must emphasize the immanence of faith; that is, it is impossible to speak *of* God, *of* revelation, except within an experiential relationship. And yet Bultmann himself speaks of kerygma, that is, of a proclamation, and a proclamation that is impossible without conceptualizations and objectivizations, as is customary when human beings talk to each other.[65]

The same holds for Bultmann's distinction between the value of Christ's death *in itself* and its value *for me.* According to Bultmann, the death of Jesus becomes the death of Christ only if I make it my own; it does not redeem me because it was objectively the death of Christ, which precedes the saving event. But then what difference would there be between the death of Jesus and the death of Socrates, in the assumption that I found my authentic existence through the death of the latter? Why could I not say that for me Socrates was Christ?

Furthermore, by reducing the life of Jesus to an existence at a given moment, Bultmann creates a nullity that leads to gnosticism,[66] another myth lacking in the *extra nos* of a history that precedes our faith, that is, lacking an act of God outside of me to which I can respond in a reasonable manner. The irrationality of the act of faith is in fact the weakest point in Bultmann's teaching. He for his part sees in this irrationality the *scandalum crucis,* that is, the scandal of the lack of historical and rational basis for the *fides qua.*

To this we must say: an act without a rational basis is not a human act. Paul locates the *scandalum crucis* rather in the *fides quae:* the revealed folly that confounds the wise.

Despite his emphasis on *sola fides* and *sola gratia* Bultmann really falls into Pelagianism, because, if every intervention of the supernatural in the world is a myth, then the saving act in me cannot be traced back to the real intervention of God within me. But if, in response, one real intervention is admitted that is not mythical, what is the problem with admitting other such interventions? Doesn't it take a *sacrificium intellectus* to believe even in my own act of faith?

In addition, Bultmann's entire theory of demythologization is based on the philosophical premise of the separation of subject and object in knowledge. But is this not to make theology too dependent on philosophical theories that are not admitted by all? In fact, when it comes to philosophies, is not the definition of "modern" man in terms of Heideggerian existentialism too restrictive an approach?[67] This is why since Bultmann we have seen other hermeneutics offered: Marxist, logico-positivist, Gadamerian, and so on, all of them making theology a "handmaid of philosophy."

Finally the individualist, here-and-now type of "saving event" that Bultmann envisages is difficult to reconcile with the idea of a Church, a group that preaches to the nonbeliever. All these criticisms show that Bultmann's paradox lacks internal consistency.

IV. The Reformulation of the Argument in Fundamental Theology

After all that I have been saying, I must ask whether the argument adopted at the beginning of this essay is still valid. In my opinion, the reasoning as such is not incorrect, but it does suffer from a kind of "short circuit" and needs to be completely reformulated. When we read Bultmann's harsh attack on the traditional viewpoint, we might think that not a stone would be left upon a stone of an argument so essential to fundamental theology. However, the second thoughts of the critics during the last twenty-five years have not only salvaged many valuable stones, but have also shown how Catholic theology can reconstruct the argument.

In regard to the historicity of the gospels, we have learned that we cannot do without form criticism and redactional criticism; at the same time, however, we have seen that within due limits the Jesus of history is not utterly beyond our ken. The difficulty is to relate the results to the Church's act of faith in Jesus as the Christ and the Son of God. The weakness of the traditional argument was that it sought to prove too much, as though one could pass directly from a knowledge of the historical Jesus to the full Chalcedonian confession without passing through the post-Easter confession and the testimony of the Spirit. As a result, it was unclear how the act of faith elicited under the influence of grace was reconcilable with the excessive clarity of the historical argument.

The ordinary believer attains to faith in Christ by way of the Church's testimony, the latter usually being imparted in the parish catechism class, even if this believer, as is often enough the case, has never read the gospels and knows very little of the life of Jesus. The act of faith made by such individuals is the work of grace and is no less complete despite the deficiencies in their knowledge of history. But in our present context we are not speaking of the individual believer's act of faith, but of the faith of the Church: of the learning Church in its entirety and of the teaching Church which must justify its testimony by reference to the scriptures and to tradition. It must give the reasons for saying that the salvation in which it believes has come to it in definitive form not through Isaiah or Muhammad or Buddha but through Jesus of Nazareth. The subjective experience of a saving event even by many individuals, without reference to the *extra nos* of God's self-revelation in history, cannot constitute an objectively valid testimony at the level of human communication.

Before tackling the argument in greater detail I would like to examine two New Testament texts that show how this problem was felt in the apostolic Church. The first text is well known: Luke 1:1–4. Here the evangelist gives Theophilus the reasons why he is undertaking to write his gospel. Theophilus had learned from "those who from the beginning were eyewitnesses" about the saving events that had recently occurred. Luke's intention now is to make a careful study of the facts "so that your Excellency may learn how well founded the teaching is that you have received" (Lk 1:4 JB). Theophilus had believed the testimony of the apostles. His faith was already full even though his knowledge of the historical events was not complete. The reading of this new document will give him a basis for seeing that his act of faith was a reasonable one. Here we have two elements in the problem: the testimony of the apostles and the historical narrative.

The second text is less well known but more important: Heb 2:3–4. "How shall we escape if we neglect so great a salvation? It was declared at first by the Lord, and it was attested to us by those who heard him, while God also bore witness by signs and wonders and various miracles and by gifts of the Holy Spirit distributed according to his will." The direct object of our faith is the salvation wrought by God. This salvation was first declared by Jesus. The apostles transmitted it, while the spirit of God bore witness to it externally and internally. To the two elements given in Luke we can now add the object of faith (we may call it the "saving event," *Heilsgeschehen,* in an objective sense) and the testimony of the Spirit. The threefold basis on which our faith in the saving event rests is thus constituted by the word of Jesus, the testimony of the Church, and the co-testimony (*synepimartyrountos,* Heb 2:4) of the Spirit. How are these three elements interrelated?

The mention of "salvation" as the main object of our faith is not something accidental. In my opinion, the problem is improperly stated when it is made one of continuity between pre-Easter and post-Easter *christology,* since, if Peter can say in his sermon in Acts 2:36 that in the resurrection God made Jesus both Christ and Lord (cf. Rom 1:4), then there must be a sense in which the post-Easter christology differs from the pre-Easter christology. Perhaps it would be better to speak of continuity of *eschatology,* that is, of the continuation of God's final and definitive action of salvation, which was preached and promulgated in the person of Jesus on earth and then actuated in his person and work when he had been made Christ and Lord.

As a matter of fact, the main focus, the primary object, of Jesus' preaching was the reign of God, that is, God's decision to reconcile the world to himself. There was a "christology," yes, but only in the framework of the promulgation of the kingdom. Christology became central only after the resurrection. The question asked of Jesus by his listeners when they had heard and seen what he preached and did was the question of his *exousia,* his authority, which was greater than any human authority, even that of the prophets. But the most profound inference that "flesh and blood" (Mt 16:16) could make after observation of the earthly Jesus was that he was the eschatological prophet. The confession of Jesus as Christ and Son of God required a qualitative leap that took place only through a revelation of God mediated by the Holy Spirit (Mt 16:16; 1 Cor 12:2).

As I pointed out a moment ago, the central message of Jesus was the coming of the kingdom, of God's salvific act. He does not define the reign of God but simply exemplifies it by means of his parables, tells us how we must prepare ourselves to receive it, and sheds further light on it by means of his miracles. But then he leaves it up to the action of God. The same thing holds for his own person. He manifests a supernatural power that lends authority to his words, an authority distinct from that of the prophets, who do not speak in their own name, as Jesus does, but proclaim the oracles of the Lord. I do not agree with the more radical critics that Jesus never accepted any messianic title. Apart even from his messianic actions, such as the entry into Jerusalem (which is difficult to demythologize), his discourses were woven through and through with citations and references to the Old Testament, texts—especially those of Zechariah—which were to be little used by the early Church. Moreover, although he was not enthusiastic about the title of Messiah in the sense in which his contemporaries predicated it of him, he did not deny that it was properly his in the sense of Son of man and Servant of Yahweh. But even this "christology" remained open, awaiting a clarifying action on the part of God.

This clarifying action was the resurrection of Jesus. This may be designated as the interpretation both of the kingdom and of the person of Jesus. But we believe even in the resurrection not because of the empty tomb and the testimony of the apostles but because the Spirit bears witness to it. The resurrection, moreover, must not be thought of as something isolated. From the theological viewpoint, the resurrection and the parousia form a single event *ex parte Dei,* even though the parousia is separated from the resurrection in time. The authors of the gospels, and especially Luke, consider the resurrection as marking the beginning of the "reign of God," with the result that in the letters the expression "reign of God" or "kingdom of God" acquires a different meaning than it had on the lips of Christ, and all attention is now focused on the role played by Christ in the saving activity of God. The resurrection begins the "last days" foretold by the prophet Joel and other prophets (Acts 2:17, 24).

Christology in the strict sense, that is, the full knowledge of the person and work of Jesus, begins with the resurrection. This does not mean, however, that during his mortal life Jesus was not already what the Church, enlightened by the resurrection, proclaims him to be. When the Church reflects on the divine powers bestowed on the risen Christ, it concludes that these powers cannot have been bestowed on a purely human individual, and therefore begins to give a fuller meaning to the title "Son of God"; it sees the title as having an ontological meaning that supposes Christ's preexistence with God before the incarnation. Consequently, the question of the continuity between the historical Jesus and the Easter Christ must take the form not of what Jesus *was* before Easter and what he *became* afterwards, but of what his contemporaries knew of him during his earthly life (and therefore what we know of him from a purely historical reading of the gospels) and what they believed about him after the resurrection. A confusion of the ontological and epistemological orders has been the cause of many misunderstandings in this controversy.

The post-Easter Church, then, as the place where God unfolds his definitive act of salvation in time through the agency of the risen Christ (from the apostolic age to our own day) is the further interpretation of the kingdom of God which Jesus had proclaimed. History thus serves us as the place for verifying the beginning of God's salvation in the time of Jesus and as the interpreter of the actuation of this salvation.

These are the facts in their sequence, historical and logical. But let me go back now to the gnoseological order with a view to understanding better the value of knowledge of the Jesus of history for our faith in Christ. At this point we must distinguish the believer and the nonbeliever. The faith of believers is based on the testimony of the Church and the power of the Spirit (1 Cor 2:5). They read the gospels not simply as a document concerning Jesus but as the "life" of Christ that furnishes a paradigm for the life of the Christian. By means of the gospels they can determine whether the Church in its preaching respects the priority of God's saving act, but the gospels also enable them to be sure that the risen Christ preached by the Church is not a myth; that he does not exist solely in the kerygma but is a historically verifiable reality which is the sign *extra nos* of salvation; that he precedes my faith and is not created by my faith.

Nonbelievers read the gospels as historical documents, bearing in mind the while the observations of form criticism and redactional criticism. It is possible in this way for unbelievers to encounter Jesus as he preached in the Palestine of his day; his "life" is a parable that challenges them. But the message and work of Jesus issue a call to the *interior veritas* even of the people of our time, only when these people set aside their spirit of self-sufficiency and recognize their own need of salvation. The rule of God which

Jesus preached and made a reality becomes a promise that will later be fulfilled in the form of a gift, but people receive this gift through the Spirit of Christ, even if they be not conscious of this fact.

As far as the hermeneutical aspect of the Church's statements about Christ is concerned, no one denies that the kerygma must be adapted to the language of our contemporaries. I have already noted the limitations of the existential hermeneutic of Bultmann and Ebeling, but this is not to say that every hermeneutic is to be rejected. I have written elsewhere of the relation between scripture and the interpretation of language.[68] Here I shall simply end this essay by pointing out the limits any hermeneutic must respect if it is to be acceptable to the Church.

Christian faith is based on a public revelation. A revelation is by its nature an action of God in human history. The public nature of revelation entails the objectivizing of the revelation, for only such an objectivization will permit communication among human beings; and if this communication were lacking, the revelation would be purely private and would lose its kerygmatic character.

A hermeneutic that is charged with expressing the essence of this revelation to the contemporary world must do so with fidelity; otherwise it will be a betrayal rather than a translation. There are two pitfalls to be avoided in interpretation: one is to subordinate every event to a philosophical scheme that reduces theology to theodicy, and the other is to express everything in terms of an immanentist religious experience, as Feuerbach does. Each of these approaches necessarily excludes any real intervention of God and, by implicitly claiming that salvation originates within a closed human circle, eliminates any vestige of a genuine revelation. As I indicated earlier, moreover, to reduce hermeneutic to a matter of explaining a purely individual saving event that occurs in the life of each separate person, as Bultmann does, is to destroy the public nature of revelation and exclude the very idea of a Church.

On the other hand, revelation is not a purely intellectual communication of dogmas, even if dogmas constitute a part of revelation. The latter is rather an action of God in human history and in the soul of each individual. The response to this revelation must be not only a submission of the mind but a commitment of the entire person. The subject of the faith experience is the total self. Historically, as I indicated earlier, the faith that Jesus is the Christ and the Son of God arose, first, out of the experience of an *authority* that was more than human; then out of the experience of the transforming power contained in the belief that Jesus is the Christ. The conclusion from the *exousia* of Christ to his *ousia* was a *logical,* not a mythological necessity. Mythology appeals to superstition, not to logic, and the process of rethinking that led to Chalcedon was a logical, not a superstitious process.

The objectivization of an experience and a process of reflection necessarily takes place in the language of the day.[69] The subsequent transferral of the whole business into a different language means a change of expression but not a denial of what has been believed nor a transformation of substance. We must keep in mind, moreover, that no linguistic change and adaptation can ever completely capture in human schemata the transcendence of God's saving act and of the person of Christ; on the other hand, to transcend reason is not to contradict it. Our dogmatic conceptualizations are by their nature partial and analogical; neither are they ends in themselves, but instead tend spontaneously to be transformed back again into an experience of salvation. This cycle of experience—language—conceptualization—experience is characteristic of the Christian's life. It also indicates the limits within which any hermeneutic must operate that is not to be lacking in sincerity.

The life of Jesus is our guarantee that our faith is not unreasonable. Faith in Christ, the Son of God, carries us to heights which our minds can only glimpse, and then only if they bow in humble respect for the mystery.

Bibliography

In addition to the books and articles mentioned in the text and notes of this essay the following are quite important: P. J. Achtemeier, *An Introduction to the New Hermeneutic* (Philadelphia, 1969); G. Aulén, *Jesus in Contemporary Research* (London, 1976); C. E. Braaten (ed.), *The Historical Jesus and the Kerygmatic Christ: Essays on the New Quest of the Historical Jesus* (New York, 1964); H. Braun, *Jesus* (Berlin, 1979); E. Castelli (ed.), *Il problema della demitizzazione* (Rome, 1961); idem (ed.), *Ermeneutica e tradizione* (Rome, 1963); H. Conzelmann, "Jesus Christus," RGG 3:619–53; E. Dhanis (ed.), *Resurrexit: Actes du Symposium international sur la résurrection de Jésus, Rome 1970* (Vatican City, 1974); J. Dupont (ed.), *Jesus aux origines de la christologie* (Gembloux, 1975); G. Ebeling, "Hermeneutik," RGG 3:242–62; idem, *Introduction to a Theological Theory of Language,* tr. by R. A. Wilson (Philadelphia, 1972); E. Fuchs, *Hermeneutik* (Bad Cannstatt, 1958²); idem, *Jesus: Wort und Tat* (Tübingen, 1971); R. W. Funk, *Language, Hermeneutic, Word of God* (New York, 1966); H.-G. Gadamer, *Truth and Method,* tr. by G. Barden and J. Cumming (New York, 1975); P. Grech, "Jesus Christ in History and Kerygma," NCCHS, pp. 822–37; idem, "From Bultmann to the New Hermeneutic," *Biblical Theology Bulletin* 1 (1971), 190–213; E. Güttgemans, *Offene Fragen zur Formgeschichte des Evangeliums* (Munich, 1970); M. Heidegger, *Being and Time,* tr. by J. Macquarrie and E. Robinson (New York, 1962); idem, *Unterwegs zur Sprache* (Pfüllingen, 1959); F. Hahn et al., ed. by K. Kertelge *Rückfrage nach Jesus* (Freiburg, 1974); M. Hengel, *The Son of God: The Origin of Christology and the History of Jewish-Hellenistic Religion,* tr. by J. Bowden (Philadelphia, 1976); W. Kasper, *Jesus the Christ,* tr. by V. Green (New York, 1976); R. Latourelle, *Finding Jesus through the Gospels: History and Hermeneutics,* tr. by A. Owen (Staten Island, N.Y., 1979); X. Léon-Dufour, *The Gospels and the Jesus of History,* tr. by J. McHugh (New York, 1967); L. Malevez, *The Christian Message and Myth: The Theology of Rudolf Bultmann,* tr. by O. Wyon (London, 1958); R. Marlé, *Le problème théologique de l'herméneuti-*

que (Paris, 1963); idem, *Bultmann et l'intérpretation de Nouveau Testament* (Paris, 1966²); I. H. Marshall, *I Believe in the Historical Jesus* (Grand Rapids, 1977); I. de la. Potterie et al., *Da Gesù ai Vangeli* (Assisi, 1971); H. *considered* (Oxford, 1960); J. M. Robinson et al., *The Later Heidegger and Theology* (New York, 1963); idem (ed.), *The New Hermeneutic* (New York, 1964); idem, *Theology as History* (New York, 1966); W. Schmithals, *Introduction to the Theology of Rudolf Bultmann,* tr. by J. Bowden (Minneapolis, 1968); H. Schürmann, *Jesu ureigener Tod* (Freiburg, 1975); E. Schweitzer, *Jesus* (London, 1971); G. Strecker, *Jesus Christus in Historie und Theologie* (Tübingen, 1975); E. Trocmé, *Jesus as Seen by His Contemporaries,* tr. by R. A. Wilson (Philadelphia, 1973); G. Vermés, *Jesus the Jew: A Historian's Reading of the Gospels* (London, 1973).

Part 3

Christological Approaches

⑧
Is a Philosophical
Christology Possible?

Xavier Tilliette

It is perfectly clear that the problem of a *philosophical* christology is part of a wider question: that of the relations between philosophy and theology. It is subject to the breaks, imbalances, challenges, reconciliations and interactions that have marked the relationship between these two more inclusive entities, especially ever since the coming of modern thought, which Schelling described as "free thought,"[1] liberated philosophy from its allegiance to theology. But it is also a fact that a negative attitude holds sway in both camps, and that distance has been transformed into a dilemma which Dostoievsky, for example, sees as a moving choice between Christ and truth.[2]

This incompatibility of Christ and philosophy has led, on the part of theologians, to a reserve and even a distrust toward the "Christ of the philosophers," behind whom they glimpse the God of the philosophers: they suspect this Christ of being a fraudulent imitation that is tacitly opposed to the Christ of John, Paul, and Augustine. So instinctive is this reaction today that it even determined the tone of the Gallarate Colloquium of 1975 on *The Christ of the Philosophers*.[3] It became clear on that occasion that historiography has not yet grasped the very important role Christ has played in the philosophies of the secularist era. This extraordinary eclipse of the real facts shows that the philosophy of the philosophers themselves is not always identical with the impression others gain of it, with "philosophy" as a frame of mind. In any case, the recent divorce of philosophy and christology is in keeping with the now long past anathemas of St. Paul.

But the long tradition of Christian thought, of Christian philosophy, speaks a different language. Upon the clean break made by St. Paul it grafted a new wisdom, a new philosophy. "Our philosophy" soon became a synonym for Christianity. The terms "Christ" and "philosophy" were brought together and harmonized; each drew the other to itself. The *Philosophia Christi,* so dear to Erasmus,[4] means both the wisdom and the knowledge of Christ: that is, at one and the same time, the knowledge and wisdom that has Christ for its object (an object whose riches it will never exhaust), and the knowledge and wisdom that Christ himself offers, namely, the message of the gospel and the beatitudes, the revelation of all these things to the lowly and the little (thus leading to the paradox of a wisdom that is folly).

The philosophy of Christ is thus a splendid name for a theology that is at once speculative and spiritual. It sums up all the sublime truth that christology offers, without losing sight of the historical revelation of Jesus Christ. It emphasizes, more than any other theological approach, the analogy of faith. As a result, the patristic and great Scholastic theologians developed a philosophical christology that is based on the speculative and existential aspects of Christ and that flows from the practice of an understanding of faith. This inspiration of philosophy by Christ and this aspiration to Christ culminate in the genial work of Cardinal Nicholas of Cusa at the time when christendom was approaching its end.[5] Cusa's work joins in an exemplary way the "sober intoxication" of the mind with the "learned ignorance" of devotion; it is also much more christological than the work of Master Eckhart and the Rhenish mystics. For Cusa Christ is truly the key to knowledge, the key of the door, the key of the arch. But by reason of his speculative daring and virtuosity Cusa, at the threshold of the modern age, makes clear as no one else has the enigmatic situation of a philosophical christology.

This situation is not intrinsically different from the situation of a christology that is theological in its terms and aim. The proclamation of faith that Jesus is the Christ underlies, and considers as resolved, the problem that came to light in the famous and destructive dichotomy (made explicit in the last century but latent in early biblical criticism) between the Jesus of history and the Christ of faith.[6] This duality does not in fact exist for faith. Faith, on which theology feeds, bridges the gulf between the one-time-only, historical, dated appearance of Jesus of Nazareth and the imposing christologies that were immediately developed by the post-Easter community and are to be found in the letters of Paul and the gospel of John. It is precisely this marvelous truth—that Jesus is the Christ—that the first community of witnesses unceasingly voices and proclaims. But this "cry" or proclamation of faith is accompanied by a conceptual elaboration that is extremely early since it is contemporary with St. Paul and St. John and opens the way to later erudite christologies.

This first christology is not speculation (in fact it already rejects the temptation to engage in speculation), but is rather a decisive, because foundational, effort to enunciate the mystery in the full light of understanding. Thus the Logos of Philo, for example, is completely subordinated by St. John to the expression of the revelation: the Word in John is a trinitarian Person who has made his appearance in this world as Jesus of Nazareth. In his Captivity Letters and especially in the hymn in Philippians, St. Paul finds the religious categories that are determinative for christology. He says in so many words that "we . . . take every thought captive to obey Christ" (2 Cor 10:5), and he protests against a "philosophy" that is "according to human tradition, according to the elemental spirits of the universe, and not according to Christ" (Col 2:8).

It seems, then, that there is a break, a separation, and even a confrontation, and this at the very point of origin for New Testament revelation: the incarnation and the scandal of the cross. The wisdom of the wise, the wisdom of the world, is abandoned for the foolishness of the cross, which crowns and symbolizes the human existence of the Son of God. Under these conditions the very idea of a philosophical christology seems inevitably absurd. And yet, as I have just said, such a christology was born out of the very radicalness of the faith. The great texts of St. Paul and St. John have become preferred sources for a philosophy that is obsessed with Christ.

Can philosophy, which is in principle unconnected with theology, that is, with revealed faith, say anything about Christ, independently of the personal beliefs of the philosophers? It seems in fact that philosophy must stop short at the threshold of what is beyond its competence, and that agnosticism should be the rule for it. Philosophy has adopted this reserve in the case, for example, of Descartes, of Husserl, of Heidegger. But we may observe that an inclusion of Christ in philosophy is possible without abrogating this proviso of reserve. Jaspers, who enunciates this reserve in the form of a strict philosophical theorem—no man is God[7]—nonetheless give Jesus a place of honor among the "paradigmatic individuals"[8] of philosophy. Bergson exalts him as a sublime hero, the incomparable exemplar of an open morality,[9] while taking no position on the theological context of the person of Christ. In point of fact, philosophy cannot leave Christ and christology completely outside its purview. To do so, it would have to cancel out its history and even its very origins, to the extent that Christianity has meant a radical reprise of all human thought. But anything that occurs in philosophy is henceforth irrevocable. I am not saying that there are no neutral or indifferent areas, those proper to logic or science. The point is rather that in its general articulation of problems and in the living connection of its parts philosophy sooner or later touches on the ultimate problems and thus comes in contact with religion and especially with the revelation offered by Jesus Christ.

The stupendous initial effort of theology to understand Christ and to make intelligible the appearance on the human scene of a concrete existing Man-God became a definitive acquisition of human thought. It continues in existence, therefore, though latent at times, even after the emancipation and subsequent secession of philosophy. Historical change has led thinkers from a *philosophia Christi* to a *philosophia de Christo,* but, paradoxical as this may seem, the shift has not eliminated the christological element in philosophy. Christ continues to be a preoccupying presence in the construction of philosophy and especially in the vast secularized cathedrals which are the idealist systems.

It is true enough that modern philosophy, having eliminated faith as a premise, has trouble preserving the unity of christology, which is expressed in the combination of the two names Jesus and Christ. In Malebranche,[10] the last representative of Christian philosophy, the Logos, Christ, in his glory and his humiliation, still holds the place of honor, but he is here and there subordinated to the demands of the system. This is so, for example in the theorem on intercession, which states that Christ, by reason of the limitations he accepted in the incarnation, cannot apply himself to all his functions at the same time; thus when he carries out his function as adorer, he does not work at the building of the kingdom, and during this time the damned weep. The Christ of Leibniz,[11] who is a perfect monad, is primarily a revealer, namely Jesus the preacher, but he does not fulfill the role of a hinge or point of articulation between the worlds that the idea of the *Vinculum* would suggest; Blondel took Leibniz severely to task on this point.[12]

In general, then, emancipated philosophies have trouble retaining and integrating all aspects of christology. We may also see a dividing line, but not one that is knife-sharp, between the philosophies whose explicit christology is focused on Jesus or the Master (Teacher, *Lehrer*), and those that focus rather on Christ, the God made man, and his importance for speculative thought. As a matter of fact, in each case we have a point of reference and a touchstone for these various philosophies rather than for christology. The interest in a given picture of Christ did not predetermine the tendency of the particular philosophy; on the contrary, the philosophical tendency predetermined the type of philosophical christology. The well-known and deadly dichotomy already mentioned between the Jesus of history and the Christ of faith is present in the philosophical christologies no less than in the theological christologies; it is even more clearly present in the former because it has been more completely assimilated by reason. But I must add that to the extent that the philosophers take dogma seriously—and the greatest ones do—they do not simply accept the dichotomy, but either endeavor with difficulty to reconstruct a christology on the basis of the existential portrait and words of the Master, or else locate the phenomenal appearance of the Principle within a general process of manifestation.

It is understandable then that in contrast to an (intended) theological unanimity there are also as many philosophical christologies as there are philosophies, each with its own identifying mark and signature. Christ does not enter into philosophy in order to dismantle or shatter it; rather he filters his light into it and subjects it to the law of growth. This is very clear in the great idealist systems. The philosophical approach to Jesus Christ can only be difficult and indirect when the specific illumination given by faith is lacking. This is why Henri Gouhier, the first to use the term "Christian philosophy" and to give some worthwhile specimens of such a philosophy, conceived it as a plurality and allowed it only a relative unity.[13] I think, however, that we can be more daring and that the necessarily inductive procedure of determining the major traits of a philosophical christology should lead to the question in *de jure* terms of the very possibility of such a christology.

The simplest philosophical approach to Jesus Christ, and the one least strewn with pitfalls, seems to be the acceptance of his historical existence, his words, and his teaching. These are an obvious subject for comparison with their philosophical counterparts. Moreover, an appreciation of Jesus' sublime teaching leads the mind quite naturally to the personality of the founder; the same relationship exists between the two as between the philosopher and his philosophy, except that the philosopher whose attention is caught by Christ objectivises a relationship which in his own case more often remains implicit. Thus Spinoza, an outstanding proponent of the Christ of the philosophers, is not interested in "what certain Churches think of Christ"[14]; he wants to listen only to "the mouth of God" and what it has to say.[15] The degree of externality that initially marks Christianity is overcome by claiming Christ for philosophy as a forerunner of perhaps unsurpassable genius. He is therefore given the title of *summus philosophus*[16]: Christ is the supreme philosopher. The formula recaptures, but in a new context, the ancient idea of *philosophia Christi,* with "of Christ" here being a subjective genitive: Wisdom has spoken through the mouth of this man. As a result the chief relationship to be clarified is that of the teaching of Jesus to the *philosophia vera.* The Christian or post-Christian attitude of Spinoza, remarkable indeed for a Jew, led to the development of comparable positions by philosophers such as Kant and Fichte, who are especially open to the teaching of the gospel and the extrinsic revelation it offers. For these men, too, "supreme philosopher" will provide a key for understanding the "mystery" of Christ.

I have elsewhere spelled out Spinoza's conception of Christ and pointed out the problems it raises for the interpreter of Spinoza.[17] Christ is the supreme philosopher; which means that in some sense he is more than simply a philosopher; he is the super-philosopher just as for Bergson he is the super-mystic. He is not a prophet, because God speaks to a prophet through the mediation of visions and dreams; he is greater than the prophets, even so great a prophet as Moses, because God directly revealed his plans to him and spoke through his mouth: to listen to Jesus is to hear the voice of God. What are these hidden plans which Christ unveiled as one who had full knowledge of them, and the motivation of which eluded everyone but him? They have to do with the salvation of the non-philosophers, the "ignorant," by means of charity and submission.

Christ was therefore a sage and a philosopher, since he truly grasped and intellectually understood the doctrine he revealed. He was also more than a philosopher because his third type of knowledge, which includes the two ways of salvation and the connection between them, surpasses that of Spinoza and any other philosopher (implied is: for all time to come). It is inevitable, then, that there be the intriguing discontinuity or shift of levels that we find between the *Tractatus* and the *Ethics,* because if Spinoza could have rationally shown their accord or noncontradiction, he would have reached the same level as the Spirit of Christ. Christ may have given esoteric teaching to a few initiates (Paul, John), but he did not think he had to show the rational appropriateness of salvation through obedience. He was satisfied to use parables and images; he adapted his teaching to the limited understanding and imagination of the people. On the other hand, he did not jealously keep for himself the hidden truth that he possessed. Through his preaching and example he is the pledge and way of salvation for all who believe in his teaching. An imitation of Christ is therefore perfectly legitimate.

Can the philosopher himself bypass the mediation of Christ? Yes, undoubtedly, because "under the guidance of reason" (*ex ductu rationis*) he attains beatitude by his own efforts. No, however, if we take into account that the sage receives the Spirit of Christ and that there is an analogy and conformity between the philosopher and Christ; for, as a matter of fact, Spinoza's philosopher is not cut off, even during his hidden life, from teaching and communication.

Christ would thus be a kind of *primus inter pares* and, by any accounting, an exceptional phenomenon: "Never did anyone speak as this man speaks." But Spinoza stubbornly refuses to investigate the nature of Christ. He does, of course, reject the divine incarnation as he understands it, but the fact remains that the Wisdom of God, the Eternal Son, manifested himself supremely (*maxime*) in Jesus.[18] This manifestation is of a wholly intellectual kind, reducible to a profound, clear, and direct knowledge of God. But the manifestation does point to an embryonic christology; it raises a corner of the veil that covers the mystery.

If we join this idea of the supreme manifestation of God in Jesus with Spinoza's unconditional praise of the Christ of the gospel, we will find ourselves ready to believe that Spinoza came close to repeating the confession of Caesarea and was prevented only by his ancestral idea of an inaccessible and imageless God. But then, we must read him in the most favorable light and perhaps even overdo it a bit. We shall find Fichte adopting an analogous attitude.

But first the dissociation, which is not accentuated in Spinoza because he is engaged in speculation on eternal Wisdom, becomes much greater in the very interesting religious philosophy of Kant.[19] As everyone knows, Kant intended that this philosophy should remain "within the limits of reason alone." His rational religion is a moral religion, that is, morality is the ground and essence of religion, a circle inscribed within ecclesiastical and legal religion. This does not prevent revealed religion from bordering on moral faith and perhaps acting as a protective casing around it. Nevertheless Christianity or any religion whatsoever is judged by its moral content. Now the founder of Christianity was so extraordinary a person precisely because he was an incomparable teacher of morality. Jesus originated the religion that contains moral teaching in its pure state; he was the model of morality. Does this mean that he was God made man, the Son of God? Philosophy cannot take a stand either on the person of the Teacher or on the representations attaching to his person. In this matter prudence must be the rule, and we can do without many superfluous things such as miracles or biblical inspiration; the only decisive proof is written in the soul. It is necessary and enough, therefore, that Jesus in one way or another manifested the moral

Idea. On the other hand, since the moral intention which is the heart of all religion is in conflict with the evil principle, that is, radical evil, the representations associated with Jesus can be a powerful help to the victory of the good principle or the coming of the kingdom of God. These representations are, however, accompanied by restrictions and reservations insofar as they are applied to the person of Jesus. In short, in regard to the domain of history the philosopher abstains from judgment, he beats a retreat; when all is said and done, he has no need of dogmas, once Jesus presents himself as the herald and perfect model of the moral life.

The distinction thus made between the historical Christ and his transcendent image is even more evident in the a priori, nonhistorical part of Kant's work. The terms of the problem reversed here; there is no longer a passage from fact to idea. Transcendental christology is based on "the personified idea of the Good Principle," the idea of a human being who is perfectly pleasing to God.[20] This man is the Word, the Archetype. It can be said that he came down or abased himself to become a man and that by his suffering he demonstrated the unconditional importance of God. This description is evidently based on Jesus Christ, although we may also recall here the persecuted just man of Plato; but the deduction itself is a transcendental one. For it is in our own reason that the idea of the human being morally pleasing to God resides; it is there that it has its objective reality and necessity. The empirical embodiment of the idea is left undecided; it is hypothetical.

But let us suppose a second phase, that is, that at a given moment such an ideal divine man were to come on the scene. We will apply to him the criteria supplied by the ideal, and only these. There is no need, therefore, of bringing in the supernatural (concretely: the incarnation and virgin birth), which would risk introducing a discouraging gap between the Model and its imitators. Of course (Kant adds), the voluntary self-humbling of the Son of God and the spectacle of his self-renunciation can be a powerful stimulus, an incentive by way of moral analogy, to conversion and thereby justification; for the latter is the result of conversion, whether it takes place directly or via the Savior.[21]

If we turn now from transcendental history to positive historical reality, we are confronted with a third appearance of Jesus Christ, an empirical one this time. Kant brings it before us by creating a picture out of the dogmatic aspects of the life of Jesus. But christological dogma is not essential; the essential thing is the preaching of Jesus, his pure moral religion joined to exemplary conduct. The "Teacher of the Gospel" and herald of the moral law preached primarily by his example. He is the supreme Model. Does this mean that he is to be identified with "the Archetype of humanity, begotten by the Father and loved by him"? Kant has no doubt that the Son of God did become incarnate as a human being and that there is a passage from transcendent christology to transcendental christology. But he hesitates to say openly that the Idea and its representation are concentrated wholly in the incomparable individuality of Jesus Christ and that transcendental christology finds its adequate projection in a christology involving a single historical being. This is the step which his philosophy, or any other philosophy perhaps, does not dare to take. Given this position, it is possible either to inflect Kantian christology in the direction of Spinoza (Jesus as supreme but not exclusive manifestation of him who is Son from all eternity) or on the contrary to leave open for revealed faith the possibility of a full affirmation of Christ.

But, better than Spinoza, whose *summus philosophus,* though a unique and incomparable personality, remains nonetheless a historical figure, Kant highlights that which must give the backbone and dynamic vitality to any christology that seeks to be philosophical, namely, the *Idea Christi.* For Kant, in keeping with the fundamental option which his philosophy represents, the Idea of Christ is the Idea of a human being fully pleasing to God, perfectly moral, the *personified* ideal of the Good Principle, onto which is grafted a christology of a transcendental type. Has this human being ever existed? Has he become a reality? The relation of the personified Ideal to the founder of Christianity, the Teacher of the Gospel, is in many respects a relation of coincidence, but there is a gap between model and archetype, and Kant leaves it to statutory religion to bridge this gap. Within the limits of reason alone Christ is God only by default.[22]

The privileged place of a transcendental christology that is conformed to the Idea, and the secondary character of experimental historical verification are displayed almost naively in the writing of the young Schelling, but they are not found as such in Fichte, who is heir rather to the outlook of Spinoza. He is probably such an heir as a result of his instincts. There is no evidence that he was particularly struck by the praise of Christ in the *Tractatus Theologico-politicus.* In any case, he began his own philosophical career with a knowledge of Christ that had been tempered by theological studies and preaching. So great is the impact of his "true" philosophy (the "true" is a point of similarity with Spinoza), namely, the Science of Knowledge (*Wissenschaftslehrer*), that the relation of the philosopher to his philosophy points the way to understanding the founder of the Christian religion. Science of knowledge and christology are presented in analogous terms, and the "problem of the Christ" is not different from the problem of the Teacher of knowledge (*Wissenschaftslehrer*). The unconcealed gap between the historical and the metaphysical[23] and between life and speculation controls the interpretation; and this rule continues unbroken throughout the developing Science of Knowledge. Despite the insights of the *Critique of All Revelation,* therefore, Fichte did not follow the transcendental procedure of Kant. The *Idea Christi* is played down as a late product. The problem that intrigues and stimulates Fichte is the "problem of Jesus"; more precisely, since he spends little time on the person of Jesus as teacher and model of morality, he asks how Jesus, a single individual, poor and helpless, could have anticipated later centuries and promulgated the purest Science of Knowledge. Fichte therefore sees Jesus as the supreme philosopher whose doctrine parallels that of the Teacher of Knowledge.

This is the perspective adopted in the famous commentary on the Prologue of John in the *Anweisung zum seligen Leben* (Initiation to the Blessed Life),[24] although it might seem that the evocation of the Logos should have led directly to the Idea of Christ. In fact, the solemn prologue of John's gospel is here completely subjectivized. The separation between the opening verses (down to "There was a man sent from God") and the subsequent ones corresponds to the separation between the speculative and the historical. The historical is a means: Jesus was indeed by nature the perfect human representation of the eternal Word, but he was this in order to teach us that from the viewpoint of eternity the Word becomes flesh in every human being. Historically speaking, the interior knowledge of union with God (which *is* Christianity) is due solely to Jesus, and this is what makes of him the only and firstborn Son. The philosopher, of course, can independently recover and develop this truth, but even then it presupposes the cultural context of Christianity.

Up to this point we have hardly departed from Spinoza's thinking. Rational beatitude comes from the "spirit of Christ," but in itself it is independent of the existence of Jesus. But it is the historical aspect (especially the latter part of Jesus' life) that intrigues Fichte, as does the significant passage of the Prologue from "he came to his own" down to "the Word was made flesh," which presents a structure suggesting a coalescence of the historical and the metaphysical. It is, then, this prior and basic distinction that needs to be studied more fully, and since for the philosopher the speculative cannot be grasped, the historical calls for further explanation.

It is to this task that the *appendix* of the *Anweisung* is devoted, and, above all, the lectures of the summer semester of 1813.[25] If Jesus is the concrete historical means to knowledge of the truth and, for Christians at least, to beatitude, he is such by reason of his very historicity, which must be elevated to the metaphysical order by making Jesus act as a philosopher, much less by turning him into an object of speculation. No, Christ Jesus is thoroughly historical; he does not derive his knowledge from concepts but simply from his self-consciousness. God is with him; his consciousness is on the same level as God; he is an extraordinary individuality, an ethical genius.

The lengthy and labyrinthine disquisitions of 1813 only supply further evidence of this uniqueness of Jesus. That which to us is metaphysical was for Jesus simply historical; that is, he was immediately conscious of what *we* know by learning; his self-consciousness was the consciousness of union with God. This is what makes him forever superior to the Teacher of Knowledge, who is obliged to demonstrate and reconstruct. His concept was one with himself. How make this compatible with the theory of the Self (*Moi*)? The task would be difficult indeed if Fichte had stayed with the self-posited I, but in fact he had long since shifted the center of gravity. There is nonetheless an analogy with the free act that initiates the discovery of Knowledge (a contingent, non-necessary act, but one which is connected with the thesis of absolute freedom); for the "divine" consciousness of Jesus came into existence at a point in time, after a period of latency and dissatisfaction, just as the Teacher of Knowledge may have groped his way through "obscure feelings." But it presupposes a prior "image" which intuition immediately concretizes. Jesus, whose individuality seemed to set him apart, thereby comes back into the orbit of philosophy, just as the Fichtean philosopher is included in the Science of Knowledge.

The pragmatic history of the self-consciousness of Jesus thus falls quite naturally within the purview of the philosophy of history (provided, of course, that we do not leave the plane of history). Just as the act of reflection transcends the arbitrariness of its appearance in existence and bears witness to the action of an originating freedom which is identical with necessity, so the contingent appearance of Jesus of Nazareth depends on an a priori and points to a necessary person. There is no question of *deducing* Jesus in any proper sense of the term (from this point of view a certain facticity is unavoidable), but only of relating the historical traits of Jesus to a necessary person.[26] In short, Fichte takes hold of the transcendental guiding thread. Human freedom cannot do without an *image* (Fichte's pregnant image) of its destination, and this image presupposes a prior freedom. How is it possible to break out of this circle? By means of an image which is freedom, a freedom that is an image: a true reality, a person. This is why Jesus—and Christianity—began a "new world" that is discontinuous with the old.[27]

This very cursory sketch of transcendental christology only seems to abandon historical determination. For the image is not located outside of Jesus as it were, as an icon of divinity. It is rather the image that sets his goal and coincides with his free being. It is the image we must freely appropriate for ourselves. Nonetheless, the supereminent historical rank of Jesus is confirmed by his transcendental dignity: he is, by divine calling, the herald of the kingdom, since "kingdom" designates the destiny of the human person; he is the first and incomparable citizen of the kingdom; he is the only Son by right of birth, the Son of God and, as such, the means and instrument of beatitude. This is a matter of fact, but there are Christians who do not realize it, and the "image" has not only been broadcasted and popularized, but brought out with superior clarity by philosophy. The historical as such, therefore, cannot be sacralized, transmuted into metaphysics. And the intellectual proof of the reality of the kingdom of heaven has since been established, thus rendering the person of Jesus superfluous for the beatitude of individuals.

As this last phrase suggests, we hardly seem to have broken loose from Spinoza. And yet there is more here than Spinoza. Fichte takes into account the refocusing of doctrine or Christianity on the person of Jesus; in other words, he takes christology into account. He works out a philosophical (non-transcendental) christology that is interesting from two points of view: first, it remains attached to an existent, speaking Jesus; second, it coincides at least in part with dogmatic christology. But this second aspect is ambiguous, since it is not easy to distinguish between that which is simply an interpretation of Christianity, and that which is an integral part of Christianity. Concretely, what can a philosophical christology retain for itself of Christ and his work of redemption? Given its subjective premise, it tries to make faith in Christ and the faith of Christ coextensive. Since this entire doctrine is a genetic explanation of Christianity, it presupposes a dogmatic "argument." For Christians such an argument is indispensable. But it is taken for granted that for the philosopher the Science of Knowledge has replaced religion and therefore, as I said, can do without the person of Jesus, that is, without belief in him.[28] The faith of Jesus himself, that is, his decisive intuition, has been recovered and integrated. But for the disciples of Jesus, too, the proof "of spirit and power" took priority and mediatised faith in Jesus. It was from the latter that dogmas came, for it produced a relationship that rises vertically above time. Jesus, the Christ, is the "Son from all eternity," who is connected with the manifestation and its law. From this, in turn, flows the Trinity, which Fichte presents in an extremely schematic fashion.

The rather reductive philosophical reading of the truths that give rise to christology is surely less important than the project of which it supplies the armature. The reader will have noted the absence of the idea and dogma of the incarnation. Fichte's philosophical christology rests on the true idea of Christ as presented by Jesus; it proceeds from the realized intuition of the kingdom. In short, faith in Christ and the "objective" christology to which it gives rise are makeshifts that serve while waiting for something better. The essential point is that by the divine will Jesus was bearer of the idea, and that is all he was. This idea is a historical idea; it emerged straight from history and is valid for history. But it stands apart from metaphysics: "That Spirit likewise provides the third proof which bears witness to Jesus in cases where Jesus is known historically, and which transfigures him, but which no longer needs him as a link in the chain of insight (*Einsicht*), because this chain proceeds in a purely a priori manner on the basis of the law."[29]

The originality of Fichte's philosophical christology consists in the close connection established between the supreme philosopher or, more accurately, "artistic or practical genius,"[30] and the Idea of Christ, that is, the Son of God who is founder of the kingdom of heaven. This "eternally valid theoretical truth"[31] is identically the evidence which Jesus provides. It is present, indisputable and inescapable, in the consciousness and being of Jesus; and the philosopher, who investigates the law of the phenomenon, necessarily discovers it in the genetic sequence. But as soon as the idea develops into a christology, it loses its intensity; the relation to the person of Jesus weakens, and even the bond between Jesus and the Christ is strained. Admittedly, Fichte uses these two names almost indifferently in his sketch of a christology, but Jesus, who is immersed in his intuition, is less the Christ to himself than he is to his disciples and the community. Nonetheless, of the three major idealist philosophers, Fichte is the one who most closely links the historical Jesus and the Christ of belief. Unfortunately, his christology is atrophied, and guided from a distance by the theorems of the Science of Knowledge.

In Schelling and Hegel the juxtaposition of Jesus and the Christ is obvious, and it is the Jesus of history who suffers in the process. I alluded earlier to the almost candid statements in the *Lectures on the Method of University Studies* which amount to saying that the empirical person is unimportant. Oddly enough, Kierkegaard or rather Johannes Climacus says almost the same thing in the *Philosophical Fragments* where the concrete historicity of the Master is literally volatilized in absolute paradox. It is true that Kierkegaard downplays history in order to strengthen faith, while Schelling, less well intentioned, does it in order to disparage critical work and exalt speculation and the Idea. Christian symbolism comes along at the same time to support the tragedy of the finite, the suffering of nature, which is set in parallel to the Son, who is "God suffering and subject to the conditions of time."[32] The symbolic use of christology can only be an extrapolation, but the context in which this is done is close to being gnostic, and in fact gnosticism is the permanent temptation of theological speculation.

The long journey of Schelling, which is many respects a kind of journey to Canossa, does not concern us here. He endeavors, successfully, to repulse the gnostic invasion; he increasingly proclaims the priority of revealed positivity, and here the positive is to be understood in the strict sense as the historically objective, the attested, the documented, the textually authentic. His intention is not suspect, and his devotion even finds somewhat touching expression (in a subordinationist atmosphere that we can leave aside here). But when the piety of the elderly Schelling forsakes the gospel and the Sermon on the Mount and gives preference to the doctrinal passages of St. Paul and St. John, the motivating impulse is always a secret distrust of the empirical. His enlightened faith passes through and beyond Jesus to the Christ of dogma; the episodes in the life of Jesus that hold his attention are those to which a dogmatic truth is attached. In short, he is drawn by the *being* of Jesus, the very object and content of Christianity, a christological ontology. He looks at the *person,* but only insofar as it is a transcendent personality and moves in a metahistorical realm. Moreover, the earthly appearance of Jesus is only an episode and an avatar, although of fundamental importance in the process of fall and restoration. The second principle emerges by the light of the human figure and human consciousness, at the end of a long subterranean, ecstatic life which is marked by suffering, in the womb of a mythology through the successive phases of which it has passed. But the very remarkable thing is that the entrance into individuality and particularity (these notions sum up the incarnation) took place at the cost of a new interment, a kenosis. The incarnation is necessarily kenotic, in the original sense which Schelling gives to the term: the "Light of the Gentiles" renounces the pagan glory to which his victorious journey had led him, and goes into exile from this splendid divine world which after him will fade away. The death on the cross completes the extinction of paganism and of the many-faceted splendor of the gods.

It would be unjust to condemn Schelling's speculative christology because of the elements of fantasy that appear in it from time to time. These come from the backdrop of the system and do not weaken the realistic intention of the latter. Schelling constantly endeavors to maintain a reference to the Bible and to the letter of the text. This, in fact, is what makes his christology, and indeed the whole of his theology, both attractive and ambiguous. He undoubtedly believes in the divinity of Jesus and therefore in the incarnation, but what he understands by preexistence is not the eternal generation of the Son. It is not fully clear that he finally eliminated "the incarnation from all eternity"[33] of the *Lectures on the Method of University Studies*; in any case, this can be understood as referring to the great plan of the incarnation, to the mystery made manifest of which Ephesians speaks. But everything indicates that Schelling did water down the factual, existential aspect of the incarnation, perhaps in order to ward off the demythologizing criticism of which he had been a precursor. The incarnation is the ceaseless neutralization of the *morphē Theou*. It is kenotic through and through, but Schelling hardly, if at all, faces the difficult problems of the being and consciousness of Christ. His distrust of demythologizing criticism grows keener, as does his very lively fear of being taken for a practicioner of this barren trade.

Seemingly, Hegel too has no interest in the critical approach. He does not call into doubt the existence of Jesus or the sublimity of his manifestation, but neither does he bridge the gap between Jesus and the representation of the Christ. Now, the entire system that is developed is built on a christological schema: from the Calvary of the absolute Spirit to the voluntary descent of the Idea into altereity, into Nature. All of this is so well known that I need not emphasize it here. If we look only at the *Phenomenology* and the *Encyclopedia,* the Christian representations function as symbols which dissolve and are absorbed into absolute Knowledge. But the *Philosophy of Religion* sounds a different note; no longer is a speculative Good Friday distinguished from a historical Good Friday. Here Hegel reflects on Jesus and the message of the Sermon on the Mount; then, with an emphasis which Strauss was to point out,[34] he calls attention to the fact that what is specific about Christianity's belief in the incarnation is that its object is a God-man here and now, a Jesus of Nazareth who has a historical context and date; in other words, the haecceity of the Logos is characteristic of the Christian faith. But—as Strauss again notes[35]—this fundamental aspect of Christianity is always connected with the belief of Christians and with its object and purpose, but not with the consciousness and nature of Christ. There is no explicit joining of Jesus and the christological archetype. But it may be that we must allow here for the irreparable lacunae of a text which, we must remember, is posthumous, largely compiled from the notebooks of students, and, above all, published by Bruno Bauer, a licentiate. The fact remains that in the Christian community belief in the God-man and in his indispensable existential support (the element of particularity and singularity), the crucified Jesus, came into being ineluctably. On the other hand, the appearance of (belief in) the God-man was favored by the course of history, by slow inculcation through the centuries, and by the dissolution of the Roman empire. However, the "superior" reflection which leads to the abolition of the representation of the moral and religious genius does not outweigh the postulate of the unhappy consciousness and the belief in the determinate objective existence of the God-man. It is difficult to get rid of the impression that speculation asserts possession of a higher truth and that it claims to understand faith better than faith understands itself.

I wish to touch only lightly on an endless debate that in the final analysis runs up against the indecipherable personal faith of Hegel—surely a very unhegelian conclusion. But precisely when Hegel's imposing philosophical christology, which provides the main schema for the entire system, is measured against the philosophy of absolute religion, it shows and admits the extreme difficulty it has in harmonizing the *Idea Christi* with the haecceity of Jesus. I do not mean that philosophy must bridge the gap separating it from the confession of faith; I do mean that we expect a christology to dispose us for this considerable step and not to paralyze us. Otherwise it is only a "christology of the philosophers," a substitute for the eternal gnosis.

Despite the diversity among them, the christologies of the three great German idealists points to the philosophical christology whose concept I am establishing. They risk being philosophical by excess and incurring, justifiably, the reproach of presenting an idolatrous "Christ of the philosophers" in contrast to the Christ of Christians. But even a Christ of the philosophers is not an *ens rationis*; he cannot be constructed out of nothing but rather presupposes, at least tacitly, the faith which is contrasted with him. Nor does he necessarily represent a secularization of this faith. There is much that is valid in the effort thus made by reason when stretched to its utmost. The shaky balance of the philosophical christologies is due to the absence of the supernatural dimension, of the sense of mystery which would fill in the gaps reason is forced to leave. But it is not responsible—at least not any more than the limitations of theology are—for the subsequent decline that came precisely with the collapse of the great systems. Christ is only a man, Christ is only an idea: these propositions, which the post-idealist-nineteenth century salvages from the systems, amount in practice to the same thing and are combined at the human level: the socialist Christ, the populist Christ, or the revolutionary Christ is paralleled with the new Prometheus, generic man, or the new man.

Now the thing that is characteristic of philosophical christology as it is reflected in the idealist systems is that, like doctrinal christology, it links the *Idea Christi* with the Christ of the gospels. This is true of highest, christophanic form of speculative christology, namely Hegelianism. This makes its own, at least in the belief of the community, the irreducible particularity of *the* human being who is the vehicle of the Idea. The same holds for Fichte who has no desire to go beyond a consideration of history, but accepts the eternally begotten Son as being coextensive with the phenomenon. Schelling, for his part, attributes the properties of the theogonic principle to the empirical person of the Savior. The trinitarian, cosmic, transhistorical, and eschatological aspects of the Word made flesh are not always brought out better in theological writing than they are here. The theandric idea, so magnificently orchestrated in Russian sophiology, can be regarded as a talisman and a value of philosophical christology, without our therefore having to blind ourselves to the danger of gnosticism that accompanies it.

Anyone who so desires is free to reject out of hand any and every attempt to reach a fuller understanding of the mystery of God incarnate by following the unblazed paths of reason. Such an attitude of protest, so forcefully enunciated by a Kierkegaard, a Dostoievsky or a Chestov, has a certain grandeur. But while philosophical christology runs serious risks when it tries to appropriate Christ for itself, it can also benefit by accepting the light "that enlightens every human being." If Christ is the Alpha and the Omega, if he is the crown upon all that is, then philosophy too must accept this ascendancy. The unfortunate Jules Lequier—philosopher of freedom, geometer and man of enthusiasm—accepted as valid for philosophical thought the motto *Instaurare omnia in Christo* [To unite all things in Christ], "a far-reaching motto, since it excludes nothing."[36]

In a period of triumphal secularization it was the ambition of Maurice Blondel to restore philosophy to Christ by restoring Christ to philosophy. From a formal point of view, his attempt is no different than the enthusiasm of a Fichte or a Schelling as they found in the Prologue of St. John the inspiration for their philosophy and indeed for philosophy as such. And indeed the legitimacy of any christology that aims to be philosophical is based on the universality of the *Idea Christi* with its plurality of aspects (personified ideal, theandrism, mediation, Calvary of the concept). The proof of this is that modern humanisms, the new Prometheanisms, are only christologies turned upside down. But Blondel's intention was different. Later on he developed a philosophy of Christianity that draws a parallel between the enigmas of philosophy and the mysteries of Christianity, the latter providing the solutions of the former.[37] In so doing, he does not surrender the underlying idea of *L'Action*. But the problematic of *L'Action* does not aim to match enigmas and responses. The *Carnets Intimes* show clearly the christological purport of many statements; the rigorous text of the first version of *L'Action* only gives glimpses of it. But the intention is indeed to integrate christology—or, better, some main headings of christology—into an anthropological and metaphysical enterprise by bringing out certain questions if need be, but without forcing them. Very different is the aim of a philosophy of religion, which takes up religious themes for the sake of a better understanding of religion. Here it is for philosophical purposes that a conformity and even an osmosis is established between the working of reason and the truths of faith. It is a fact, of course, that in the mind of a philosopher who is looking for Christ christology is secretly exerting its influence. But the problem is not how christology should be presented in order to meet the needs of philosophy, but rather how philosophy should be presented in order to meet the demands of christology. In fact, the conviction that Christ is either everything or nothing leaves no choice. And even when philosophy tries to maintain its own autonomy, as soon as it admits the *Idea Christi* it changes its identity and moves beyond the singular universal which is the idea.

There is no doubt that under the name of panchristism Blondel has given us only confused rough notions, marked though these are by genius, and that the latent presence of Christ at the end of *L'Action* is not unambiguously clear.[38] It is also certain that many passages of the correspondence, especially on the consciousness of Christ, belong rather to mysticism and theology. But Blondel is the only one—along with Teilhard de Chardin, though the latter is a philosopher only in a qualified sense—to give us a glimpse of what a real philosophical christology would be, like a temple set over against the elaborate tombs of Christ that are the great systems I have discussed. Blondel thus joins an admirable Christian tradition, even while taking account of the patent change in philosophy.

The notion of panchristism, enriched by mystical inspiration and eucharistic contemplation, helps understand the existence of the world and its objective coherence. If the matter of the eye were not solar, how could it perceive the light? If God did not somehow belong to the world, how could he create and know it? But God, without ceasing to be God, has made himself "patient" of the universe, seeing it with our eyes and receiving it through our senses, and this divine passivity is the ultimate basis of sense knowledge.[39] Dostoievsky writes a heartrending lament over the dead Christ and the crime of nature,[40] although nature doubtless exists solely in order to produce this great being. The total Christ of Blondel is not only the fruit and flower of nature; he is also, in the fullest sense, nature's origin and reason for existence. Admittedly, the "firstborn of every creature" is not named, but he is an implicit obsession. One or other phrase might lead us to think that Blondel is speaking of Adam, that is, the first Adam, but he is in fact speaking of the heavenly Adam who became one of us.

The cosmic patience of Christ, the passivity of his kenosis, lead to the passion and the suffering of agony and abandonment. Gethsemani and Golgotha are the places par excellence where the consciousness of Christ gathers up consciousnesses and their lack of consciousness, while at the same time submitting to them and suffering them. The basis of intersubjective consciousness is compassion and charity, because the intersubjective bond is the consciousness of the dying Jesus. This is a mystical, Pascalian perspective which become an element in the highest morality. "Fellow feeling that inflicts the stigmata" (*sympathie stigmatisante*) is the formula for this astonishing insight.

Many other suggestions are to be found in the last part of *L'Action*. Kenosis and passivity are not the only themes of christology; the latter is also present via the method and criterion of a truth that is a way of life. The light shed can also touch all aspects of anthropology: temporality, corporeity, individuality, death, and so on. The subjectivity of Christ is impenetrable and mysterious but it is not completely off limits to us. It yields to the effort of the *idea* that unfolds in a *scientia Christi* and then returns to philosophy in order to give new life to the latter's abiding concern with "God, self, and things."

⑨
Christology and Anthropology: Toward a Christian Genealogy of the Human

Gustave Martelet

I shall begin in a rather unacademic fashion with some brief autobiographical notes on my career as a teacher. As for the subtitle of my essay, its justification, if there is any given, will appear only at the end of this very short study. The essay will have three sections: the first describes the genesis of a point of view; the second is a presentation of content; and the third offers a synthesis.

I. Genesis of a Point of View

1. *Culture and Anthropology*

When I was appointed in 1952 to teach fundamental theology at the scholasticate of Lyon-Fourvière, a position I held for ten years, I was very much struck by a question which had indeed come to mind previously but which I never had time to evaluate in its full depth and extent. How is it that the West and especially Europe, which owes so much of itself to Christianity, could have rejected Christianity or have decided to do so? When I speak of the influence of Christianity on the genesis of Europe I am not, of course, trying to deny the influence of pagan Rome and Greece, or of the Celts, the Germans, and the Goths. I do, however, see Christianity, which for a long time was the cultural mortar holding Europe together, as having played the predominant role. And yet, beginning in the eighteenth century (a point of reference that is beyond challenge), this mortar seems to have cracked, and the cultural edifice it served to hold together has been disintegrating or is even collapsing completely.

Ever since the century of the Enlightenment Europe has been undergoing an extraordinary change. In the Roman Empire of the East and West there had come into existence what could henceforth be called a "patristic culture," that is, a type of culture that was based on a consecration of the human genius to the mystery of Christ. But beginning in the eighteenth century the cultural genius of Europe seems to have devoted itself rather to tearing down Christianity and thereby undermining its own foundations and meaning. This, then, is the paradox: modern Europe is barring Christianity from the cultural plane it has reached and is even developing, in opposition to Christianity, an *antipatristic* culture that says "No" wherever patristic culture had in countless ways said "Yes."

I said to myself: Rather than indulge in sterile lamentation at this situation, why not try to understand it and, if possible, remedy it? In particular, is there not room to judge that a certain silence of Christians on the new values which seem to have intoxicated Europe, is one of the hidden reasons for the very paradox itself? Yes, it undoubtedly is! But, in my opinion, this silence seems in turn to have been the result of an obscuring of the mystery of Christ in Western Christian thought, and this is surely a far more serious matter than the mere silence as such. When Western theology was confronted with the cultural newness that defined the Europe of the Enlightenment, it did not, in my view give the mystery of Christ the place that rightfully belonged to it and that would have enabled Christians to accept the cultural changes going on and then to illuminate them spiritually from within with the help of the transforming integrator. The impoverishment of christology which Rahner has shown so well was harmful not only to theology as such[1] but also to human beings in their vital relations with the faith. There had come to be a divorce between the changing and developing content of cultures and the inadequately grasped and therefore statically conceived meaning of the mystery of Christ. Speculatively daring essays like those of Malebranche were expressed in terms of an excessively abstract metaphsics,[2] while further studies undertaken in Germany,[3] and elsewhere as well,[4] remained unknown, or practically so, to Catholic theology. In any case, the gulf displayed in this theology between culture and faith continued to deepen and has still not been overcome in christology.

Great though it is, the harm done is not irreparable since it is something historical. It came into existence gradually, and a cultural analysis can be made of its causes and phases[5]; it can therefore be "cured"—but only on condition that those attempting the cure open themselves to the depths of him whom historical changes can only reveal more fully to the eyes of faith. This does not mean that christology is henceforth to be absorbed in the recovery of lost values. The point is rather that the unsearchable riches of Christ should be made evident within a world from which christological reflection has too long been absent.

After all, is Christ not the plenitude of what is human, its completion, its "recapitulation," to use Paul's term? Faith in Christ, therefore, far from possibly inducing us to exclude or scorn the human, is on the contrary the most fervent and salvific justification of our humanity. More than this, every *systematic* abandonment of the mystery of Christ in our thinking and acting is paid for sooner or later by a corresponding destructuring of the human. It follows that adherence to Christ by faith and the discovery of the full reality of the human person should be one and the same process, since Christ, the historical Messiah, is also the Truth, Foundation, Reason for being, and supreme Crown of the human person and all that is human. We therefore take Christ seriously as Alpha and Omega of the world and history only when we antecedently reject any idea that he might be a principle of decomposition or progressive disintegration of the person and the human.

Such a vision of Christ evidently presupposes a christology which from the outset rises above the excessively narrow viewpoint of an incarnation that is *exclusively* redemptive. Since I have dealt with this point on a number of previous occasions,[6] I shall not dwell on it here. On the other hand, there is need of explicitating the anthropology implied in such a christology. In my judgment, the lack of such an anthropology is largely responsible for the quarrelsome relationship between culture and faith. This situation can therefore be changed only if we as Christians renew our vision of the human person and modify the traditional anthropology by introducing the genetic dimension that is, for practical purposes, lacking to it.

2. How Speak Genetically of the Human Person?

Since human beings are not amorphous entities we can obviously speak of them in terms of "nature" and, specifically, of "human nature." We can also say of them that they have an "essence" that is unique in kind. On the other hand, to be a human being does not mean answering to a concept or being faithful to a definition, even if the definition be "rational animal" or even "political animal." Human beings exist only insofar as they develop and take shape. We may say that it is of the essence of the human person to *have* or *be* a "becoming" (or to be processual). The reality of the person is neither inert nor fixed; it is dynamic, something that evolves; the reality gradually reveals its virtualities in individuals and through them in the race as a whole. This constant becoming is, of course, not something arbitrary. Human existence has its properties and can be described; it has structures and follows norms. We may say that it has its "lines of life," its low points and high points. It is therefore necessary to call attention expressly to this constitutive fact: that human beings have a continuity amid their becoming, a watershed line, an axis of growth, a "nature," if you want to use the term, provided it be taken in a very general sense that does not exclude becoming and genesis, discovery and invention, development and the future, or, in short, history and a horizon within which the history takes place. From this it follows that we may speak of the generically human and may begin by suggesting what it is with the help of an image that manifests its development.

In full awareness that I am treating a magnetic phenomenon of the upper atmosphere as though it depended directly on the sun, I shall give the term "aurora borealis" the poetic meaning it acquired in the sixteenth century. I use the term to describe the often stormy development of individual human beings and the race as a whole within the pregiven horizon created for them by the existence of the *world,* that is, of *nature*. "Nature" here is not primarily something metaphysical; it is the sensible universe from which the human being is constantly emerging and of which it is an integral *part.* Within this horizon supplied by nature the human entity is one that is rising and, like the aurora borealis of the poets, never ends its morning. We may think it has reached its full noon but we deceive ourselves: it is still just dawning. It is like a sun that is constantly just rising, always incomplete as yet, or, in symbolic shorthand, it is *boreal.* The human being is always at its beginning: it is constantly beginning and then beginning again. Whatever its age it is still as young as an infant, or, more precisely, via any human being the race is always in its first infancy, and when this being dies, it always has the feeling that it has done nothing *as yet.*

The human being represents the appearance in nature of an entity that is closely related morphologically to the primates, while at the same time being irreducible to these. It is physically conditioned and has biological roots, while its psychism is unquestionably similar to that of the animals; yet there is nothing in this being upon which it does not in the last analysis set an indelible mark for which it alone is responsible. However closely it may feel linked to all other living things, it discovers that it has the power, however limited this may be initially, to assert itself as different from the rest of the world. The human being stands amid nature as the living entity that knows and declares itself to be someone and not just something. It says "I" and refuses, no matter what the price, to let itself be absorbed by that which is other than itself. The more mediocre it seems and the more threatened it is (Ivan Denisovich is not a wholly unreal character), the more it has the "Pascalian" power to assert a personhood that is undeniable however much it be flouted. It knows that while the universe of the stars and of other human beings may crush it, the universe of the stars knows nothing of it and the universe of men may be unwilling to know of it, but this being itself at least knows it is being crushed and will emerge from the crushing, even the crushing of its own death.

The indispensable part played by speech in this human emergence has become increasingly clear in our time. Being distinct from every form of signal, however subtle the latter may be, speech presupposes self-awareness.[7] To speak is to learn to make the things and beings one discovers and sees the subject of an expression of which one is oneself the focus. Being the instrument of self-consciousness, speech is thus the great sign of human emergence. Even when far removed as yet from having developed in the form of languages as we know it now, even when as yet almost indiscernible from the paleontological viewpoint,[8] speech is doubtless potentially present as early as the ability to use tools is. It shares the same intentionality as tools. The human individual asserts his threatened uniqueness in the midst of nature either by arming his hands with tools or by turning his mouth into a tool through the signs, very modest ones admittedly for a long time, in which he expresses his subjective superiority. This is why the behavioral similarities being increasingly discovered between the higher animals and human beings remain just that: similarities or analogies. Between the two there is always the gap of the human to which speech points and which itself comes from the *spirit.*

As a quasi-solar entity emerging from the bosom of nature, the human being is a dawn that is never done with asserting its dawnness; this incompleteness is due to the modest and struggling subjectivity that characterizes it over against the often triumphant vastness of the cosmos and of life. And yet the human person is there, at the heart of the world, in an auroral state; now that he has appeared on the scene, the light he brings and sheds can never be eliminated.

But the human being is never excused from an active effort needed if he is to impose his presence on the world; his state of emergence therefore requires a constant act of emergence. The traditional anthropology dating from antiquity has doubtless emphasized the human *state* of emergence in too onesided a manner. Modern man for his part tends to reduce his being to the isolated *act* of emergence. The two must be combined: what one receives and what one accomplishes. Man is an existent that wins its own reality, but it does so on the basis of an irreplaceable gift. Teilhard used to say that "man makes his soul." The formula is perhaps extreme, but it contains a truth: the human person as a subject is never created in advance. He must take responsibility for himself in order to become what he is; he must reach, through a process of becoming, the full dimensions of what he ought to be and of his *generic* reality.

3. *Operational Definition of the Human "Generic"*

"Generic" (adjective and noun) is chiefly a term current in the language of film and has new overtones which, in my judgment, are of some importance. The "generic" (*le générique*) of a film is the collection of human and technical conditions which explain the film's existence. Without the men and women of varied but complementary and integrated abilities whose names and functions the *generic* makes known to us, the film would not have come into existence. Is there not a comparable generic of the human? True enough, the human in its full extent and depth cannot be known in advance. But are there not a certain number of components without which the individual or the race could not exist and whose proper dynamics must be respected if we wish to understand the specific manifestation of the human and contribute to its authentic development? We may not, on the one hand, enclose this manifestation and development in the straitjacket of an arbitrary essence that would allow us to be contemptuous toward existence and history. On the other hand, we may not dissolve the human in an indeterminacy and, eventually, a chaos to which the names "reality" and "life" are erroneously given. We should, however, be able to understand the becoming of the person and the race as showing normative traces of its own meaning. The human person does not manifest this meaning as if the meaning were something determined in advance or were being constructed behind the person's back and independently of the choices he makes. In the case of the human person this mean is rather an axis of development, an inner self-regulation that enables him to become himself by reclaiming as it were the existential fields within which his freedom discovers its own powers and expands them.

The human generic is thus a certain number of components or, if you prefer, *spheres,*[9] the development of which conditions and commands the individual and collective identity of the human being and the human race. The historical manifestation of man in the bosom of nature where his unique powers enable him to win dominance is thus not something chaotic; it is, in the strict sense, *generic,* that is, it enables us to discern the truth of the person and the human, not as a fact that owes its existence to the give-and-take of contingencies, but as an ought-to-be that imposes and reveals its beneficent light to human consciences.

As thus sparingly defined at the beginning of our discussion, the notion of the human generic is still a heuristic notion; its purpose is operational: to help in the analysis, discernment and judgment of the data (presumed to be convergent) of experience and history. It enables us to move away from a petrified concept of "nature" without falling into an existentialism that broadcasts the arbitrary in order to regain contact with life! It should be possible to understand the identity of the human being without ever immobilizing it; to accept that it can change without its falling apart; to discover a norm for its life without shackling its freedom; to discern a law of growth that does not hinder its becoming; to decode its existence without impeding its free movement. Consequently, we should be able to educate ourselves in what is human without paralyzing ourselves as human beings, and to be reconciled to a Christianity that manifests itself in Jesus Christ as the fullness of humanness without therefore suppressing any human responsibilities but, on the contrary, meeting them in a way that saves them.

In the following discussion, which is intended only as a brief sketch, I shall not set myself a goal that in itself is desirable, namely, to show how Christ is related to each of the presumed stages of the human generic. I shall indicate this relation only at the end and in a summary fashion. The development, never complete in itself, of the human generic implies throughout a continuous influence, hidden or explicit, of the Christian mystery; this influence is too complex and too bitterly challenged for me to justify here except by way of a reference at the end.

II. The Existential Components of the Human Generic

We may take as our starting point an area recognized by all as essential for all: the economic. This is not an absolute starting point, as we shall see; it is, however, a starting point too often forgotten by the "classical" thinkers. By bringing it in right at the beginning we shall prevent ourselves from yielding to abstractionism, since we shall be introducing nature itself—I mean here: physical nature—at the basis of human becoming.

1. *The Economic*

When seen from the viewpoint of the human generic, the economic is *the never finished act by which the human being develops nature in order to supply the necessities of life.* *Primum vivere* [the first thing is to maintain life] is a principle already to be found in ancient philosophy. The emergence of the human being is directly dependent on having life. Man has the primordial responsibility of sustaining his existence by turning the elements of the world into food for himself. Instinct alone provides nothing; the instinct of self-preservation dictates certain needs but does not supply the means of meeting them. Man's response in this area is entirely one of discovery, work, and creation: from the elementary forms of food gathering down to the most modern types of industry. This is why the economic sphere is vital and by its nature *generic,* since without the activity man exercises there he would not be able to subsist in the midst of a nature into which he is born defenseless.

Although plants and animals possess after their fashion an organic economy based on carbon, limestone, pollens, or wood, neither plant nor ammonite nor bee nor beaver transforms nature by applying *tools* distinct from themselves. Their tool, if we may so use the word, is their own body. As the only animal that does not identify itself bodily with any of the means it uses in order to extract service from the world, man projects outside of himself each of the instruments he uses in gaining mastery. The presence of tools in nature is his work and his mark; these tools evolve in structure and purposes, and human paleontology, then archeology, have made inventories of them that fill us with astonishment. While, therefore, the need to which man responds in the economic order is *natural* and common to all living things we know of in nature, the way in which he responds is not natural but *human.* It thus *humanizes* nature too, in an emergence which, though conditioned, asserts itself as irreducible to animality, increasingly so as history moves on but also from the very beginning of this history.

Important though it is, and while being *always* present in the human generic, as Marx has shown, the economic sphere does not constitute the whole of the human generic. There are two reasons for this assertion.

If man is so unequipped at the beginning, and if he is the most completely unarmed of all the animals (the rest of them being "adapted" by their nature), this is because of the very greatness that is his. From the beginning he has, in a state of potency, both intelligence and hand, and with these has the instruments for making instruments. For this reason he can be thrown on his own, left to his own resources and his skills. Even after being born, man remains a being that must always be *made* through invention, education, and freedom; he is never constructed in advance by mechanisms and instincts, nor do any of his genes carry the "code" for even the most rudimentary tools. The existence of an economic sphere that is truly his work and becomes inseparable from a multitude of industries, is thus truly a sign of the spirit in man. His subsistence in the midst of nature implies culture. His natural conditioning is constantly transcended without ever being abolished. Spirit in him is fidelity to reality and not primarily abstraction, much less bondage.

Furthermore—and this is the second reason—despite appearances the economic sphere is not the most primordial in man. It itself exists only on condition that man *be*. Consequently, there is a *generic* necessity for an existential component that is even more fundamental than the economic; this component is the sexual.

2. *The Sexual*

Sexuality is to be seen first of all in its elementary relationship to necessities immanent in the law of *primum vivere*. However, this *primum vivere* is a matter less of man's economic *subsistence* than of his *existence* within the order of living things. The sexual thus designates first of all *the fact that man appears and exists in nature—where work brings him subsistence—only if he begets himself as a human being*. From the standpoint of the generic, then, work does not come first or at least does not hold first place alone. The economic is less radical than the sexual, when the latter is understood as the "generative." The economic supposes that man exists, but generation is the human and biological "work" reserved to woman who must perform it if man is to be born and exist. Now, just as the classical thinkers often overlooked the economic when they dealt with the historical genesis of man, in a similar way many modern thinkers—Hegel first among them—seem to forget the irreplaceable role of generation in the real appearance of man on the scene. Prior to economic production, even in a very rudimentary form, and prior to the struggle of master and slave, the very existence of man depends on the recognition, in however elementary a form, of male and female, as well as the acceptance by the female of the fruit of her relationship with the male.[10]

Preoccupied as he was with eliminating the idea of creation from human consciousness, Marx also failed to attend to the phase of generation in the human generic. He probably thought of this *natural* phase as self-evident. While he acknowledged the symbolic value of the natural relationship of man and woman for gauging the quality of any human relationship, he did not make generation his starting point in thinking about the genesis of the human. And yet, however deeply rooted the sphere of the sexual is in the biological order, it is also a specifically human sphere on three accounts. It is human by reason of the love of man and woman; it is human by reason of the prohibition of incest; it is also human by reason of the presence of the child.

The love of man and woman is so much a part of the human generic, as the account in Genesis makes perfectly clear, that we may feel an almost limitless surprise at having inherited an anthropology that seems to have forgotten this fact. As for the prohibition of incest, which ethnology has clarified for us while leaving behind Freud's fantasies about the primitive horde,[11] it removes human genitality from subjection to immediate attractions and compels it to direct itself toward another that is truly other, thus leading to a community which is constantly enlarged.[12] It is the child, however, that represents the most incontestably human element at the very center of the human sexual, in the form of the social in its nascent state.

3. *The Social*

Contrary to the sociological presupposition of modern thought, the social is not primarily a matter of large numbers. The social makes its appearance as soon as a being is born of man and woman and asserts itself over against them as something possessing absolute value. The social thus surfaces, from the generic viewpoint, at the very heart of the familial but without being compelled to remain imprisoned by the familial; it is there that it first asserts itself. If the social means the love of the other for its own sake, insofar as this other has no deeper claim to love than the fact of its being human, then the child is indeed the germinal revelation of the social in man. Clearly, then, generation, while biological in its conditions, is fully human in its effects, since it should lead human beings to treat as a supreme value the being that makes its appearance as one lacking any power over the world but invested nonetheless with the privilege of having emerged from the combined entrails of man and woman. This elementary acknowledgment of the other in the form of the child may undergo the worst kinds of transformation and even be utterly denied; it represents, nonetheless, the basic gesture of the human social body. The latter can exist in the midst of nature only if it imposes its own originality on nature, not simply by reason of *numbers* but in a more hidden manner by reason of the *value* it claims for itself by attributing this value unconditionally to its members.

Such, then, at the generic level, is the social that defines the human: *the unconditional love of the other simply because he is human.* The quantitative extension of the social is the result of history, but its appearance is generic for the human being. The social therefore is not primarily this or that particular form whose existence in the past, present, and perhaps future is made known to us by ethnology and sociology. In this context the social is the foundational condition of society in man, under the form of love for the other who has made his appearance in the world with his own individual face.

The struggle for survival, which in Hegel's view gives rise to the human, is therefore not primary in the generic order of human societies. It is rather the other's radical right to life by reason of his humanness that makes him a fellow human being of mine and, sooner or later, a companion and a brother. This elementary acknowledgment which is constitutive of mankind is rooted much less in the conflict of adults than in the acknowledgment and acceptance of the child. Here the woman plays a primordial role which the warrior and his violent world may forget but of which the woman constantly reminds him. By the fact that they are co-sharers in the generic origin that is my own, all the individuals born of man and woman, whatever be their number, race, culture or sex, have the inherent right to be treated as absolutes. In this light it becomes possible to measure the human value of the societies and empires which man has created for himself in the course of his history.

The social, thus understood, cannot be radically denied by any system, whatever its character. It provides in its turn the generic form and primordial content of the ethical as such.[13]

4. The Ethical

The ethical in man is his passionate concern for man and, as it were, his unconditional and limitless cultivation of what is human. I use the word "limitless" deliberately. For it is probable, that given the greatness of the human when viewed in its total truth, this love of the human will manifest dimensions which will lead consciousness well *beyond* the human but never in a direction *contrary* to it. Man will always be for man the royal way to his fullest truth, as Pope John Paul II has just said of the Church. Even in the transcendings that might be required when the human tends to close in on itself, man will always be the decisive criterion of authentic humanness. Ethical conscience in the full sense of the term exists only to the extent that *this norm—the human as lovable beyond any measure*—is effectively accepted and human beings are faithful to its implications. We shall find here what I spoke of earlier as an axis of growth, a *self-regulation* of the human. This should not be confused, and in fact cannot truthfully be confused, with a *self-sufficiency.* In fact, the self-regulation in question is even opposed to self-sufficiency, as we shall see.

It is clear that the animal world, no matter how high a degree of development its psychism may attain in terms of collective integrations or even a preference for this or that individual, knows nothing of the ethical sphere which marks the crown of the social as I have analyzed it. It is sometimes said of certain animals that "they can all but talk!" True enough, but the important thing is precisely that they cannot speak. They lack in addition that to which speech points, namely, the spirit which is ultimately in charge of the human generic that manifests its originality in the form of culture.

5. The Cultural

As a generic component of man, the cultural emerges directly from the combined spheres of the social and the ethical. As spheres in which man acknowledges man and *each* man shows an unconditioned respect for *every* man because of his inalienable humanness, the social and the ethical command the cultural, which is *the sphere in which human excellence is fostered for its own sake.* If respect for man is not merely verbal, it will inevitably lead to the promotion of man and the human for each and all. I am speaking of what the Germans call *Bildung,* a word that is almost untranslatable into French. It has two overtones: of "construction," inasmuch as man must *make himself* as man in the midst of nature, but also of "figuration" and "image," inasmuch as man must discover his true face in and through culture. *Culture then, is an unending development of man in accordance with the inexhaustible requirements of his own identity.* Human identity, though real, is in fact never finished, and its aspirations, as these have come to light in the course of history, are never completely satisfied. For this reason, as the German Romantics, Herder first among them, saw clearly, culture is always historical in form and understands itself to be a necessary but never satisfactory progress. In this sense, culture, and indeed culture above all, is always "boreal."

Clearly, I cannot analyze here in detail all the main elements of culture as everywhere found (what the French usually call "civilization"). The conquest of fire for the hearth, the shaping of stone, communication by signs (which culminates in spoken language), weapons, tools, adornments, art in the proper sense, the burial of the dead, the domestication of animals, the cultivation of the major grains, villages and cities, writing, the metal trades—little by little all these made their appearance due to the cumulative effort on the part of human beings who, unwearingly and in ways that show an astonishing convergence across space and time, developed themselves as they developed for their own use the most varied elements supplied by the world.[14] Nor is it possible for me here to discuss the generic role in human culture of the major scientific, technical, artistic, literary, juridicial, historical, philosophical and religious disciplines taken in the aggregate. By means of these man provides himself with descriptions of things, of living beings, and of himself: he offers himself an explanation of them and investigates their meaning.

* * *

The cultural thus understood, which has to do with the personal fulfillment of the individual and the collective fulfillment of the race, does not develop in the abstract, but in the midst of nature and in a society that has nothing idyllic about it. The cultural advances or regresses and turns in on itself in a society which is always marked by conflict and in which man is constantly the stake in an interplay of rivalries, powers, and services, but also of servitudes. There is required, therefore, a regulation tailored to this society in which man should always be finding his cultural advancement.

6. *The Political*

In the generic sense of the term, that is, in its constitutive relation to the genesis of the human, the political is *the sphere of the deliberate establishment of the public conditions required for the human.* The political thus implies and supposes the content of all the "prior" spheres of the human generic, as it does that of all the spheres the generic necessity of which will appear later. Within a society in which human beings are born, work for their livelihood, encounter other human beings, and endeavor to promote what they think is the good of man as such, the political sphere is torn apart by the inhuman and even murderous rivalry of forces which claim to be *serving* but in fact often only *dominate* those whom they should be *governing* in a human manner. In this domain, differently than in the realm of the technical, progress is not inherent in history. When the political sphere attains to its own real truth in the service of man, it is the place in which all the rights and duties and all the freedoms and constraints of each and all can and should be harmonized, a way that can be constantly bettered, with a view to shaping a social body. The political sphere therefore supposes that a legitimate and real authority *exists* and *is exercised* for the purpose of justice. The reason for the existence of the political is that the social body, in whose service the state is, may achieve the success, unity, balance, and well-being of which it feels itself capable and to which it thinks it has a right.

I cannot go further into the nature of the political sphere, which is complex in its concrete origins, structures, and historical development, and is so important for individuals, groups, nations, and, in the future, for the very planet itself. However, though I cannot say everything that needs to be said about its significance, development, ambiguities, and greatness, I must point out the limitation inherent in the political sphere when looked at *from the generic point of view* which I am adopting here and *which is concerned with the total genesis of man.*

The political sphere does not play an absolute or unconditioned role in man. I am not denying that man has the right and even the duty of giving to the political the forms and shapes which he regards as best able to ensure the betterment of man and the most authentic kind of justice. But, indispensable though this political service is, it is not coextensive with the service rendered to man at the generic level. This can be shown by analyzing the many ways in which this service has made its appearance in history. I shall show it here, however, by pointing out a limitation which the political is in danger of forgetting nowadays and which it may wrongly think to be extrinsic to its definition.

Now, as a matter of fact, there is a desire and a purpose that constitute the greatness of the political: to establish the public conditions of a human development at the individual and collective levels, a development that will be as full as possible for the community for which the political bears responsibility.[15] It is within the competence of the political to use every kind of means to attain this goal, while maintaining a genuine respect for all. Generically speaking, then, the political is coextensive with man himself. And yet it also has its limitations.

Great though this particular service to man is or ought to be, it exists completely within an englobing reality which it can neither transcend nor destroy and which marks the boundary of its proper powers. This englobing reality is *nature* itself, which provided our starting point when we spoke of the economic and which is always there as the horizon for the cultural dawn of man. Its role is generic; that is, not merely contingent but structural at every point. In relation to man who, as we have seen, is himself the *norm* of becoming and who also rules the political, nature truly represents the *limit* of man whose very *emergence* it conditions. Nature is the parenthesis within which everything is enclosed, a parenthesis that takes the form of the birth and death which no individual and no society can escape. No political power, in particular, can liberate itself from nature, except in myths of "thou sand-year empires," or liberate others from their relation to nature which marks the horizon within which their powers are restricted. Just as man sees the light in conditions determined by nature and then falls under nature's blows, so too do man's works, political or other. This limit applies to all the spheres of human becoming, since all reflect man's mortality. The reason why I recall under the rubric of the political the limitations that are generic and not limited to the political alone, is that the political is par excellence the sphere in which human *power,* thinking itself to be absolute, can become totalitarian and believe that it represents the fullness of man and the human.[16] But the same remark applies to any similar claim that might be made in any sphere whatsoever of the human generic.

In thus speaking of an essential limitation of the power exercised on man's behalf in the political sphere, I have already implied the generic legitimacy of the religious sphere in the service of man.

7. *The Religious*

Often corrupted in the course of history and now regarded by the modern world as a superstructure and a form of alienation, the religious sphere is in fact connected with the *infrastructure* par excellence that nature is for man and history. No human genesis is possible, none even thinkable, apart from nature which conditions and encompasses all of our becoming. I made this point just a moment ago. This sovereignly encompassing reality that conditions man's biological genesis and cultural development is a Given for man. Every man is nature's beneficiary without either belonging to nature or ever being able to become nature's author. It follows immediately that only a recent cultural contingency has managed to hide the fact from us that we depend entirely on what is not of us and what, in the last analysis, is independent of us, as death proves.

From this flows the largely ambiguous aspect of nature as supreme encompassing reality. Though nature is beneficent inasmuch as we could not exist without it, it also shows itself to be terrible and destructive in the form of the catastrophes which we rightly call "natural" and of death which strikes every human being sooner or later. We may reject this negative side of nature, regard it as part of the absurd or irrational, and cease to see it as a problem, but the question remains. By reason of the question it raises for man death is also a question about the world, of which no element may be rejected: neither the life which it makes possible nor the death which it contains. This question of nature and death is the *generic* question beyond all others, because it affects the meaning of the human genus as such by affecting the meaning of every individual in his life-giving but at the same time deadly relation to this world.

Religion as thus understood in its origin, that is, *in its relation to the becoming of man in his totality,* is essential for human consciousness. It is *the sphere in which man takes seriously the fact that he is neither the source nor the real master of what conditions him without belonging to him (as is shown by the fact that he is cast forth from it by death).* The fact that the religious man is sometimes too quick with answers and falls into error in the theoretical or practical responses he gives to this situation in no way detracts from the right and duty he has of raising the question and trying to answer it. Beyond the variety of historical forms which religion has taken in the cultural development of man and which can be studied in their birth, decline or perdurance,[17] there is a generic constant, and this is the important thing here. In the religious sphere man finds himself rescued, by the altereity that is constitutive in him of nature or world, from the self-sufficiency that readily tempts him because of his marvelous emergence from nature or world. But, since the emergence is rendered *problematic* by reason of death, nature shows itself as the witness to an enigma that binds man and world together in relation to the hidden foundation of both.

In addition, if nature, from which man knows himself to be inseparable, can come before him as a sign linking him at a deeper level with an Otherness that transcends both of them, then by what right can he, in his religious relation with this Other, impose arbitrary prohibitions on the latter when he is not this Other's master any more than he is master of nature? But this is precisely what Europe has tried ceaselessly to do ever since the time of Spinoza,[18] by declaring it unthinkable that this Other can make his own identity known to man by the way in which he allows us to fulfill ours. "God's right" to make himself accessible to man in connection with man's emergence at the most generic level is in fact fully grounded, although at the present time it is hardly acknowledged.[19] It is for this reason that, in a sense which I shall now define, the revealed is part of the human generic and must be proclaimed.

8. *The Revealed*

Revelation is in fact that which can happen to us in history if the Other-than-ourselves whom nature assigns to us and toward whom we are moving, takes the initiative, within the religious sphere where he is acknowledged as existent, and unites us to himself by uniting himself to us. Then, a new type of relations, always beneficial to us, can come into existence with this Other par excellence. Though these new relations are *contingent* inasmuch as they do not come from us, they are not *arbitrary from the generic viewpoint*, much less de-structuring, if they show themselves essential to the creative plan that is at the root of our existence and if they bring the fulfillment of the need to exist that defines life but is frustrated by death. The fact that this fulfillment proves to be a *grace* does not turn it into an anomaly. As a matter of fact, nature itself is *for* us and *in* us, essentially a Given that does not originate in us. Revelation therefore simply carries further, *by historical paths* that lead from Israel through Jesus to the Church, a situation of acceptance that is generic to us *at the level of nature*. For, despite all the cultures, however brilliant, we do not become self-sufficient entities, since we die, nor can we claim that nature is self-sufficient, since, as subjects living in the midst of nature, we represent something new there. For this reason, the possibility of a revelation that brings an unending noon to complete a hu man dawn which would otherwise remain "boreal," cannot be *rejected at the generic level* from the viewpoint either of God or of ourselves or of nature.

Grounded as it is in the existential openness which the religious sphere represents within the human, *the revelation of the Wholly-Other-than-man belongs to the human generic itself as something possible and even desirable which the apostolic preaching then proclaims as a permanently staggering FACT.* The very thing which, it is claimed, is most heterogeneous to the human and is therefore rejected, can thus find a place in it as a paradoxical yet constitutive factor in an integral fulfillment of man. This presupposes, of course, that the proclamation of such a mystery brings with it an enlightening vision of the human.

III. Toward a Christian Reduction of the Division Regarding Man

The question with which I began was this: How is it possible that Europe, created as it was in large measure by Christianity, should reject Christianity in the name of the humanness which Christianity had enabled it to discover? Perhaps we are now in a better position to answer this question.

The spectacle of his own growth caused European man to fall into a kind of cultural bedazzlement, of which the idea of progress (cf. d'Alembert and the Encyclopedia) is the great sign. Whether in the political order from the fourteenth century on, or in the cultural realm since the Renaissance, or in the area of scientific development beginning in the eighteenth century, or even in the economic order which, at that same period, began to move forward in rather new and deliberately contrived ways, Western European man has discovered resources and aspirations hitherto unknown to him. With the coming of the Enlightenment he began to think and say that he rises above all limitations shown in any model of himself, and must simply tear up all the rough drawings which had previously established his identity.

Meanwhile, the life of the Church was marked by an excessive socialization of *knowledge* (which depended largely on Aristotle and his geocentrism), of *power* (inadequately distinguished from current secular jurisdictions), and even of *possessions* (resulting in an extreme "temporalization" of the Church). As a result, the Church became defensive and suspicious of a new world which was challenging the status quo in all these areas. These reservations on the part of the Church led, in turn, to increased aggressiveness against her and to the notion that an end must be put to this regressive institution which the new culture could only regard as obscurantist. A climax of rejection was reached by Voltaire in the confessional area, by Feuerbach in the matter of atheism, by Marx from the social standpoint, by Nietzsche from the viewpoint of Christian values, and by Freud from the viewpoint of the unconscious—Nietzsche being the one who carried much further than the others the systematic deconditioning of man in relation to revelation. In any case, the increasingly allergic reaction of European man to the faith—a reaction which I suggested earlier might be called *antipatris-*

tic and which is characteristic of a historical age that seeks to be *post-Chris-tian*—is supported by a certain misunderstanding of the Church in relation to the cultural growth of man.

While man was discovering in every area—economic, social, cultural, political, and affective—new dimensions that really do belong (as we now see) to the human generic, the "world" of the Church was showing itself reserved, suspicious, sometimes wretchedly polemical, and in any case little concerned to engage in a thorough rethinking of man and her own message. The real need was to deepen our vision of man by taking as a starting point the new parameters being constantly discovered and rethinking the message in the light of him who, as "the first-born of all creation," grounds the believer's limitless love of man and his world. But, instead of approaching man and his growth in the light of Christ the Integrator who divinizes and in this way redeems a race that closes itself off against what it thinks too great for itself, Christians repeated over and over, in an excessively *unilateral* way, that man is in every way a sinner and that the Christ he needs is a redeemer and nothing but a redeemer. Christ is, of course, a redeemer—happily so for man!—but the ongoing human revolution was concerned with properly generic values which were in no sense sinful and, if they were to be incorporated into the mystery of Christ, required to be accepted in the name of their humanness. But this was not done in a way that might have reversed the trend toward mutual suspicion and led to the necessary conversions on both sides.

What was not thus done at its proper time has had to be accomplished by energetic renewals that began at last in the pontificate of Leo XIII and that have had their scope further determined and clarified by the most recent of the Ecumenical Councils. But if the cultural division that has been intensifying for several centuries is to be overcome theologically, it is also necessary, in my opinion, to complete a truly generic vision of man with a renewed vision of Christ. There is a powerful source of light at our disposal in attempting this task: the Pauline doctrine of the two Adams, as set forth in the First Letter to the Corinthians.

The *second* and *last* Adam, who is the risen Lord, presupposes and claims for his own the *first* Adam, namely man himself in all generic truth as seen through the eyes of his Creator in the Genesis story. It is obvious that this *first Adam,* who is man himself, is truly *first* only insofar as he opens himself to the *second* (who is likewise "second" only in relation to the "first"). But if man in the course of the history we know as our own is to achieve this indispensable opening of himself to his own Lord, the salvation offered to him in Christ must be marked by the recognition of and a respect for the integral development of man and his humanity. But this requirement, far from falsifying the message, is in fact part of it. The existence of Christ does not show us a God who is suspicious and jealous of man's generic authenticity. On the contrary, it provides the divinely inalienable basis for the right and duty man has of himself becoming completely the *first Adam* as seen in the light of the *second.*

As *second* and as *last* Adam, Christ is the absolute vindicator and supreme guarantor of the total truth of the *first* Adam. He will find rest only when this first Adam attains to his complete identity, with the second Adam helping him on his journey, correcting his mistakes, doing away with his radical powerlessness in the face of death, and liberating him from sin. It is therefore the meaning supplied by the *second* Adam that keeps the *first* from wrongly stopping on the way and turning himself into an idol, thus sacrificing his own most important emergence toward the God who liberates by being adored. For man is greater than all the contents with which he can supply himself in each existential sphere, although in all of these he shows forth the immensity of his genius. He cannot therefore identify himself with any of these spheres, any more than he can with one of the tools he uses. He brings fulfillment to the world that is entrusted to him, and he brings fulfillment to himself as the subject responsible for the world, only by surrendering himself in Jesus Christ to the One who looks upon him as the created counterpart of his own Uncreated Greatness. The resurrection is par excellence the sign given to us of the hyperhumanizing power which God reveals in the *second* and *last* Adam to the benefit of the *first*. In the resurrection the humanity of the Son receives, to the benefit of our humanity, the more than human power of *irreversibly* completing the compromised emergence of man by destroying the death that destroys us. He does not suppress the world, which is necessary for our identity, but he promises to transform it into "new heavens" and "a new earth." Nature will thus become the inalienable body of this humanity that remains in a state of genesis as long as history lasts.

In this manner, the veil can be partially lifted that has been cast over the Church's message by the identifications she has allowed to be made of herself with countless historical forms which were not those of her Savior. Other difficulties will undoubtedly arise and indeed have already arisen. But at least the particular obstacle will be removed which Christian thought itself has left in place by remaining silent about the vision of man which it is her vocation to convey.

Moreover, if we recall that Nietzsche is the most radical of all the opponents of Christianity, we must, in Etienne Borne's words, "pick up the javelin in our turn and throw it farther." A "genealogy of morals" and ultimately of Christianity itself, that aims at eliminating the Christian mystery by means of the Overman myth, must be answered, in my view, by a *Christian genealogy of the human* which I spoke of at the beginning of this essay and the implications of which can perhaps now be better understood. At the very least, a vision of man that is renewed in a Christian manner will make us more capable of accepting, hearing, judging, growing, and, finally, bearing witness in a world which doubts that the integrality of the human opens into the integrality of the mystery of Christ and is based upon it.

10
The Principle of "Christocentrism" and Its Role in Fundamental Theology

Tullio Citrini

I. The Terms of the Problem

The principle of christocentrism in theology generally and in fundamental theology in particular might seem at first sight something which should be taken for granted. The principle formulates, does it not, an absolutely fundamental insight of the faith and in fact enunciates the point which may rightly be regarded as uniquely specific to Christianity? By no means as obvious, in any case, are the analytic development and critical elaborations of the christocentric principle; the history of theology, Catholic and non-Catholic, in our century, provides abundant proof of this.

As a matter of fact, for various, equally necessitating reasons the methodological program that is summed up in the rubric "christocentrism" must face up to several questions: first, what precise reality is meant by the term "Christ," and second, what is the meaning of the "centrality" to which reference is made in the term "christo*centrism*"? Is the Christ of whom we speak the Word of God, the man Jesus, the incarnate Word precisely in the mystery of his unity? The incarnate, crucified, and risen Jesus? The Jesus of history, the Christ of the apostolic kerygma (if so, in what form?) and of faith, the Christ of dogmatic formulations and current theological developments? The answer: "All of these" will be satisfactory only on condition that a logic is delineated which makes it possible to interrelate all these aspects precisely from the viewpoint of the question of christocentriam. Otherwise such an answer is retrogressive in relation to the questions asked, or in any case leaves things in the same state of generality with which we begin. Similarly with regard to the second question indicated above: Does "centrality" refer to an epistemological point of departure? Is it a way of synthesizing theological discourse (or, to change the image, a goal for theological discourse)? Is it a "formal object"? A methodological criterion?

When we come to the question of christocentrism in fundamental theology in particular, our task is really not rendered easier by beginning with the assumed identity of this theology. Everyone knows, in fact, without any need of emphasizing it, what a complex set of problems is located under the name "fundamental theology." The contents of the questions asked in classical fundamental theology have been taken over, but fundamental theology as a whole is still in search of a shape that will bring a certain stability. The apologetic of the Christian sign and the apologetic of ecclesial sign (this last being viewed in an ecumenical perspective) tend to form a single whole. The general problems of the theology of revelation and faith, of tradition and scripture intersect in ever new ways (as *nova et vetera* are brought forth) with those of the philosophy of religion and religions. Apologetic method and hermeneutical method prove to be inseparable. The manner in which relations between the theory of faith and the practice of it are unified is always a topical matter.

If then our discussion is to be meaningful, we must evidently not spend our time on an attempt to explain in advance the concepts of "christocentrism" and "fundamental theology." We will do better to move on while keeping before us these two terms on which we are reflecting.

I shall begin by saying that in the present context christocentrism interests me as a methodological principle that is meant to inform the whole procedure and organization of theological discourse. I am dealing therefore with what A. Grillmeier in a phrase that is perhaps not entirely a happy one has called "subjective christocentrism."[1] Such a concentration of attention is necessary since, when all is said and done, my concern is quite specific; in any case, the problems which can most obviously be discussed anew under the heading of "christocentrism" (centrality of Christ in the plan of salvation and in the universe) are too remote from the perspectives of fundamental theology.[2]

Precisely as a methodological principle christocentrism can, from a certain viewpoint, be regarded as falling within the competence of fundamental theology. But perhaps for this very reason (in addition to the one just mentioned: the remoteness from fundamental theology of the Christ-history and Christ-universe themes) fundamental theology itself has remained practically untouched by the question of *its own* (possible) specific restructuring in terms of christocentrism.[3] This is to say that for my purposes here there has been almost no discussion of what it means, or might mean, for this theological discipline, precisely as *fundamental* theology, to be organized in christological terms.[4]

In fact, the history, in a past not always remote, of certain chapters of what now figures (in a more or less clearly demarcated form) as fundamental theology manifests not only a frequent lack of christocentrism (however this phenomenon be evaluated) but often an astonishing lack of any christological perspective at all.[5] A review, even a very quick one, of some phases of this history can be enlightening in the effort to discover temptations and, conversely (and above all), positive perspectives for a correct christocentrism in fundamental theology.

Let me say it right off: it is in this direction that I propose to move, but without making any great claims. Against the background of what I said above about the utter obviousness of the christocentric principle in theology and about the de facto necessity of a critical decision (still not made) on what the principle means, the aim of these pages can be properly grasped if I immediately raise the question of a "correct christocentrism" without first asking "christocentrism: Yes or No?" This latter question may seem more radical but in fact it is meaningless as long as we cannot first (or better: at the same time) say what the christocentrism is that we are approving or rejecting.

II. A Not-Impartial Look at Catholic Fundamental Theology

1. *Catholic Apologetics in Search of Universality and Unity*

The very possibility of a christocentric perspective is connected with an effective commitment to a theological concern that is universal in scope and has unity for its goal. As far as fundamental theology is concerned it must be admitted here that only gradually over the course of recent centuries has apologetic reflection acquired these qualities of unity and universality. Everyone knows that the controversy started by the Reformation and its global reinterpretation of the meaning of Christian faith gave the cue for a general apologetics. But neither the problem of the *demonstratio catholica* nor the problem ("fundamental," if any is) of the theological loci are broad enough to permit (except possibly in a very indirect way) their being evaluated in terms of the presence and action of the christocentric principle.

If we are to discover the roots of christocentrism in the history of fundamental theology we must begin with the rise of the *demonstratio christiana* in a more or less explicit form as a response to the universal and radical claims made by reason during the Enlightenment. At that time Christianity was being asked to defend not simply one or other doctrine or practice, not simply one or other overall interpretation (Catholic, Protestant, etc.) of the faith, but the whole meaning and value of the kerygma, the coherence and ultimate basis of everything that could be called Christian.

I have the impression, however, that this broadening of the question did not lead automatically to an assertion, much less a theoretical statement, of the christocentric principle in fundamental theology. The reason for this is probably to be found in the fact that the question now being asked of Christianity was felt simply to be broader than before and not as addressed to it in its entirety; it was to the question as thus understood that an answer was attempted. It is probably also possible to assemble evidence bearing witness to the presence, in the apologetics of these centuries, of an awareness of the centrality of the problem of Jesus, with specific reference to the question of Christianity's credibility. But I think it would likewise be easy to assemble no less extensive evidence in favor of the thesis that the problem of Jesus, however important, is only *one of the many* problems of modern apologetics.

The treatise *De Christo legato* continues to be a part of Catholic apologetics as found in the manuals of theology. But while playing a decisive part in the argument as a whole, this treatise does not become the keystone and the methodological hinge of fundamental theology in its entirety. And until it does we cannot speak of christocentrism in a proper sense. Even the degree of interest with which the problem of Jesus is tackled is not demonstrably greater than the degree of interest with which the problem of the Church, felt as ultimate and decisive, was faced from the time of the first Counterreform down to Vatican I and later. What we see, then, is an apologetics which in becoming universal might also have become christocentric but has not in fact done so.

2. *Christocentrism and Credibility*

This apologetics, which is universalist but not a unified whole, brings with it an analogous conception of revelation and faith. The excessive separation between proposition and *res,* a heritage from nominalism that passed not only into theology but, under Descartes' leadership, into the whole modern way of thinking, has permitted the development of an intellectualist and atomistic conception of revelation. This could only have the effect of lessening interest in a unified view of Christianity and therefore in finding a possible center for the whole.

It is a known fact that this undervaluation of Christianity as teaching is matched by an extrinsicist statement of the problem of credibility. The intention here was to avoid conceiving faith in naturalist terms and thus prevent its being made unconditionally available to human criteria and thus to subjectivism (rationalistic and irrationalistic). The result however was an equivocal dogmatic authoritarianism that smacked of arbitrariness.

Apologetics was happy, of course, to use the internal coherence of the Christian proposition as a motive of credibility; this in turn might have led to making Christ central in fundamental theology, since he is the focal point of this coherence. But this synthetic vision was admired as a sign of the passage of divine Wisdom rather than being viewed as an invitation to take seriously the assertion of the luminous character of faith.

It is a very curious fact that "kerygmatic theology," whose apologetico-practical concern should not be undervalued,[6] was presented as a theology which is from many points of view inferior in kind. At the same time, this whole episode played an important role in proposing christocentrism as a program for Catholic theology. In the debate concerning kerygmatic theology—as I shall have occasion again to point out—the opposition was rather between christocentrism and theocentrism. In this confrontation attention was focused not on the formalistic authoritarianism with which the message was proclaimed but rather on the internal logic of the content of the message. But while the kerygmatic approach elicited opposition from this point of view, which then became the subject of the debate, the kerygmatic thesis itself contained and expressed, from its point of view, a quite conscious critique of a credibility presented in excessively extrinsicist terms.[7] The point that is of concern to us here is the fact that according to the very people who defended this approach, a christocentric theology was regarded as to some extent a concession to the general public.[8]

3. Ecclesiocentrism?

The dogmatic authoritarianism that has left such a profound mark on Catholic fundamental theology did not focus attention solely on the *auctoritas Dei revelantis*. To some extent, in fact, the real issue was even more the teaching authority of the Church. This is not the place to discuss and evaluate the motives (good and not so good) of the ecclesiastical authoritarianism that marked posttridentine Catholicism. It is certain however that one result of it, at least in fundamental theology, has been an ecclesiocentrism whose ultimate subordination and finalization to Christ has for the most part left no mark on the structure of the discourse.

This ecclesiocentrism has remained largely associated with the approach, authoritatively sanctioned by Vatican I, that sees the Church as a perennial sign of credibility. Paradoxically, the emphasis on the Church as sign could of itself (as I shall point out later on) have led in a quite different direction than ecclesiocentrism. It would in fact have done so if the originality of the "new" way proposed to Catholic apologetics had meant proceeding not from the credibility of Christ to that of the Church but from the credibility of the Church to that of Christ. For then the essentially mediatorial role of the Church would have been clear, and there would have been justification for emphasizing the importance of immediate access to the sign which the Church is. As a matter of fact, however, when the time came for formally stating this mediatorial character of the Church the language of the Council weakened, and no reference was made to the passage from Church to Christ that would have made this "way" the means of a christocentric revitalization of apologetics. The Church was presented as *divinae suae legationis testimonium irrefragabile* (an irrefutable testimony of her own divine mission), and the way proposed by Vatican I took the form of Deschamps' *méthode de la providence* ("method of Providence"), which allows the more simple kind of Christian to bypass the labor of too detailed and complicated an apologetic inquiry. In other words, what was omitted was nothing less than the sign of Christ, on the grounds that this is too difficult for the simple![9] This was the way offered by the Council of avoiding the danger of falling into the snare of Hermesian doubt. Should I say, as a final touch that brings out the full paradoxical character of the picture, that the Council really did not suggest this new way to apologetics but offered it rather as a way of bypassing apologetics?

4. The Mediation of Scripture

Let me continue to look at things from the viewpoint of the mediations of revelation. Another interesting symptom of the lack of christocentrism can be seen in the area of biblical hermeneutics. In late Scholasticism the nominalistic conception of revelation which I mentioned earlier promoted an elimination of the great christocentric exegesis of the Fathers which H. de Lubac made known to us in recent decades with vast learning and profound wisdom.[10] The phenomenon becomes even more accentuated in the second half of our millennium: a period all the more demanding in this respect as it has made great progress in the techniques of historical and literary study.

The problem of the internal logic of the canon of scripture, which Protestantism brought with it by reason of connatural disposition (precisely as a problem of the canon as such), and which the Enlightenment reawakened in Protestantism in a noisy way,[11] has left Catholic theology utterly untouched. The latter, which has so zealously defended in controversy the inspiration and canonicity of the deuterocanonical writings, has maintained an antimarcionist approach in its discussion of the canon of scripture, though there is more than one reason for doubting that such an approach is any longer relevant.

When Vatican II in Chapters 4–6 of its Dogmatic Constitution on Revelation, *Dei Verbum,* maintains that the Old Testament and the New Testament have different degrees of importance for our faith and that the gospels occupy a well-grounded centrality[12] in the body of New Testament writings, it is simply reasserting an utterly traditional awareness within the Catholic faith. And yet I cannot avoid the impression that this consciousness has not been felt, at least in the short run, as particularly binding from the viewpoint of theological epistemology (even if we prescind from certain episodes, connected with contextual reasons that deserve greater attention, which have in recent years led to somewhat inflated readings of Old Testament themes).

On a more specific level, it is worth noting that Catholic research was almost nonexistent during the vital period of *Leben-Jesu-Forschung* (research into the life of Jesus). Evidently there are reasons for this phenomenon that go far beyond the epistemological and methodological presuppositions of Catholic theology and apologetics. These reasons are only too understandable, be they favorable or not to the good name of Catholic scholarship itself. But perhaps it will not be useless to ask also whether the presuppositions just mentioned (in the area of the hermeneutical problem, to which I have hardly referred) have themselves played no negligible part.

As a matter of fact, over and above the historiographical and technical problems raised by the scholarly study of Jesus and of the historical character of his person, we should not underrate the importance of the Jesus question insofar as it reveals the existence of a problem regarding the theological meaning and value of this historicity. Independently of its many idealistic or positivistic presuppositions and even prejudices of content and method, the *Leben-Jesu-Forschung* more or less expressly discussed, in connection with the problem of Jesus, problems also of the meaning of the history of Western culture, the meaning of history in general, and consequently the meaning of history as a history of salvation. A real debate on christocentrism (or, if you prefer, on Jesus-centrism and to a certain extent on the relation between the two) can be read as implicit in this episode. The absence of Catholicism from the debate is part of the wider reason why Catholic theology did not adequately experience the impact of the Enlightenment.

It is not without reason that the christology of the theological manuals was until a few years ago based on the ontology of Chalcedon; that the historical dimension of the mystery of Christ was treated for the most part as an appendix, and a very summary one, of minor relevance from the theological point of view; that the historical uniqueness of Jesus was not an object of any special consideration. Any christology that started from such premises as these was bound, at the very least, to be rather one-sided: the assertion of the ontological and axiological centrality of the Lord Jesus[13] would not be matched by an adequate emphasis on his centrality at the level of the history of salvation.

5. The God-Question. What Kind of Theocentrism?

Once again: the apologetical debate caused by the challenge of the Enlightenment involved both the person of Jesus Christ and the theistic affirmation; the history of the origin of the classical procedure (as seen in the manuals) in fundamental theology reports as for practical purposes simultaneous the rise of the *demonstratio christiana* and the rise of the more radical *demonstratio religiosa*. However it be evaluated, the view that the God-question is more radical reflects quite clearly a theocentric type of thinking which, from a certain point of view, seems odd in its application in fundamental theology.

My point is that the theocentric orientation of "special" theology, inasmuch as the latter aims to structure itself around the *revealed* person of God, is quite understandable. The debate mentioned earlier on the legitimacy and constitution of a "kerygmatic theology" has shown that this theocentrism has been regarded as difficult to harmonize with a christological approach. But, in fact, the scant Christian originality of the contents of the treatise *De Deo uno et creatore* (God as one and as creator) and, on the other hand, the comparative irrelevance of trinitarian themes for the rest of theology bid us not to overvalue even this reference to the revealed person of God.

In any case, fundamental theology and/or the philosophy of religion which served as a preamble to fundamental theology in the traditional structure of ecclesiastical studies (but does not the same apply to the treatise *De revelatione in abstracto* [Revelation in the abstract]?) have taken as their starting point the assertion of God's existence as an assertion of reason. It is a theocentrism of this kind that seems extraordinary.

I neither want nor ought to undervalue the importance for faith of the defense of the human mind's natural ability to gain a sure knowledge of God (along the lines of the dogma defined by Vatican I with its still thought-provoking reference to biblical teaching). On the other hand, after the controversy of recent decades on the supernatural and after the Constitution *Dei*

Verbum we are certainly inclined to rate much more highly the originality of the Christian revelation of God; to read in a new epistemological framework (and with a new esteem for ancient themes in regard to the divine names and their analogous predication) the meaning of Vatican I's phrase *nullo admixto errore* (with no mingling of error)[14]; and thus to see new reasons for harmonizing theocentrism and christocentrism even, and especially, in fundamental theology.

6. *Anthropocentrism*

Finally, fundamental theology has in more recent times adopted the banner of anthropocentrism. Here the human person is taken not as the goal and not as the measure of faith but as the "hearer of the Word" and the necessary point of departure in any study of the general conditions of faith on the part of the believer. The standard reference is to Karl Rahner and is too well known to require any documentation here.

There is to some extent a spontaneous inclination to compare this anthropocentrism with the "anthropocentrism" of the debate on faith and reason (especially as found in the Constitution *Dei Filius* of Vatican I). Are not both dealing in the last analysis with the condition of the human person before God? Apart from the considerable emphasis placed in contemporary anthropocentrism of the Rahnerian type on the unity of the event of encounter between God and man within the unique existential synthesis of nature and grace, we should probably advert to the sharp emphasis on the divine initiative that is found in this approach. In classical anthropocentrism, on the other hand (though it certainly did not fail to do justice to the doctrine on grace), primary attention was on the modalities of human action ("supernatural end"; "supernatural power"; "two orders of knowledge"[15]).

The anthropocentrism of the theology of the hearer of the Word is paradoxical in that it is "centered" on divine grace. The methodological centrality assigned to the human person as starting point is accompanied by an assertion that the human person in turn must take as his focus of attention an initiative which he cannot produce nor deduce and which is not at his disposal.[16] Moreover, the definition Rahner gives of the human person in this context ("the possible other mode of existence for God in his selfemptying and the possible brother of Christ"[17]) is not only theological but—formally at least—christological.

Do we, then, have a christocentrism here? One writer had said: "The anthropocentrism of Karl Rahner can certainly be interpreted as a christological approach."[18] But we may ask: To what extent is this christocentrism more than purely formal? The presence of man to himself, and human consciousness as openness to a history of grace (a concept summed up in the idea of the human person as hearer of the Word)—these certainly existed prototypically in Christ and in his consciousness and self-consciousness (again, the subject of one of Rahner's best known essays[19]). This reminds us of a whole area of contemporary reflection on christology, that dealing precisely with the consciousness of Christ, which has also been presented, with an eye on fundamental theology, as the origin of all theology (now that we have moved beyond the modernist version of this concept).

But the consciousness of Christ cannot be called the starting point of theology in the same sense that the consciousness of the believer is. The latter is immediately given; in other words it takes subjective precedence. The consciousness of Jesus, "the pioneer and perfecter of our faith" (Heb 12:2), enjoys what might be termed an objective precedence as being the first and basic human locus, not of our awareness of the phenomenon of "faith" but of the communication of revelation.

Moreover, what kind of theologizing (fundamental or other) can take the consciousness of Jesus as its starting point? To whom is this consciousness available? Of what value to a theology that takes an anthropological approach is the human preeminence of Jesus' consciousness if the uniqueness of the latter as the consciousness of the man Jesus depends precisely on utterly singular fact that it is *his* consciousness? And if so, and if the demand that we start with man and the demand that we start specifically with the man Jesus belong to two different logics, then how can the anthropological requirement of fundamental theology lead to christocentrism?

III. The Heart of the Question

This very approximative and to some extent (not indeliberately) partisan survey can help us understand why Catholic theology did not allow adequate room for entertaining the hypothesis of a possible christocentrism. In an attempt to sum up what I have been saying in a single global impression, I might say that the lack of a theology of mediation and mediations (the absence of such a theology in Catholicism, of all systems, is especially paradoxical!) is at the origin of this state of affairs. Is not the false dilemma (or, if not false, at least overemphasized and incorrectly stated) of christocentrism or theocentrism, on the one side, and christocentrism or ecclesiocentrism, on the other, due perhaps to having turned mediations and mediated realities into so many "objects" of theological consideration?

This kind of difficulty should not surprise us if we reflect on the general course taken by gnoseology in the West, just as it is not surprising that the kind of problem which concerns us at the moment is "dated" and a specifically modern problem. On the positive side, we are inclined to see in *Dei Verbum*'s statement about Christ as "the Mediator and at the same time the fullness of all revelation" the keystone of a theoretical renewal of the question about the meaning and possibility of a christocentric approach to fundamental theology.[20]

In fact, "revelation" (seen from various viewpoints, of course) is the specific object of fundamental theology. It is therefore understandable how very christocentrically oriented a fundamental theology will be that takes as the basis of its study an identification in principle of revelation with the person of Jesus Christ (the identification would have to be developed and made specific for a better understanding of it).

I shall attempt now to apply this intuition to the most important areas of contemporary fundamental theology.

IV. Approaches to a Renewal of the Question

1. *A Christocentric Analytic of Faith and Revelation*[21]

A first task of fundamental theology is analytic theological reflection on faith and revelation. The necessity of this analysis as the starting point of fundamental theology and as presupposition of every correct and nonaprioristic apologetics can be taken for granted today.[22]

I have mentioned faith and revelation: the two are strictly correlative and are always given together, but in putting the subject of faith first my intention is to adopt the anthropological starting point. We ourselves, and, as far as theology goes, our faith as believers, is what is immediately given; and by our "faith as believers" I mean a faith that is operative and historically specified. The chapters of a fundamental analytic of faith and revelation endeavor to understand this faith in its formal aspects. In particular, what we call "revelation" is a structural condition for the possibility of faith (the other, equally necessary condition is the grace of the Holy Spirit in the believing subject); it supplies that which is to be believed and is actually believed, without which there can be no act of believing; revelation is also the call to which the phenomenon of faith is related insofar as faith is, in its inmost nature, a response.

For this reason an anthropological starting point does not of itself necessarily lead to a fundamental theology that is anthropocentric. If man by his nature is "ec-centric," this intentional eccentricity is activated in faith: faith exists in the believer and is the act of a believing subject, but the object to which faith is directed and its center of gravity is not the believer himself but the God who has revealed himself in Jesus Christ.

Can faith, which is theocentric, also be properly christocentric, so that the same characteristic will also belong, in consequence, to fundamental theology? In Augustinian terms, what is the relation between *credere in Deum* and *credere in Christum*? I believe we must agree with G. Söhngen in rejecting any christocentrism that would set itself up as an alternative to theocentrism in faith and theology (and, consequently, in a fundamental theological analytic).[23] But precisely by this rejection we affirm a christocentric approach properly so called, while at the same time we advert to the existence of a temptation; not all the ways in which christocentrism can be and has been conceived ("have been": after all, the temptation would not be a strong one if it had not in fact already been experienced in the history of theology) are correct or even sufficiently protected against equivocation.

In particular, the ontological approach of Chalcedon does not seem adequately serviceable here. In other words, the assertion that Jesus Christ is true God is not enough to allow us to conclude that a christocentric theology of any kind is automatically theocentric in an adequate way. The emphasis on "God in Jesus Christ" (Söhngen) is not meant simply to call attention to the divine nature of Jesus or to the divine person of the Word; its intention is to highlight specifically the self-gift and self-revelation, the access to the mystery of God ("God" at this point is still a vague term and requires further specification), that are given *through the mediation* of Jesus Christ. The actual development of this Christian understanding of God belongs in special theology, chiefly in its christological and theo-logical sections. It is for fundamental theology to investigate the mediatorial dynamics involved in this mediation.

Now, when theology develops this understanding, on the one hand its concern is to show that it is precisely God with whom faith is dealing when it takes Jesus Christ as its partner in dialogue; on the other hand, this God cannot be suitably "named" except through the mediation of Christ. To the extent that this mediation is effectively operative and that it is indeed the Christian God who is meant (in other words, the revealed God), theocentrism and christocentrism are inseparable. In this regard it cannot be the task of fundamental theology to distinguish the two levels, in order, as it were, to specify a distance between the "economic" mystery and the "immanent" mystery of God.

But to the extent that it is not possible to speak of the divinity of God (including the Christian God) without using analogy and thus a hermeneutical process which necessarily involves the openness of the human person to mystery and, consequently, a preunderstanding of God as ulteriority and transcendence, we must affirm without reservation the dynamic (judging and transforming) priority of Jesus Christ as "the Mediator and at the same time the fullness of all revelation," over any preunderstanding of this kind. If theocentrism, as opposed to christocentrism, were to be understood as a formula that affirms the priority of this preunderstanding in the process of accepting in faith the revelation of God in Jesus Christ,[24] then over against such a "theocentrism" any theology would have to make christocentrism its primary and indispensable methodological principle.

What of fundamental theology as theory of the theory? When fundamental theology studies the process of mediation, it sees this process as having its supreme form in Christ. This supremacy is not simply comparative, in relation, that is, to all other mediations of God, with that of Jesus Christ being the unnormed norm; the supremacy is, so to speak, absolute, to the extent that absoluteness is an attribute which can be predicated of a mediation. Every mediation necessarily mediates something, and even Christ mediates the mystery of God, to whom he relates himself, as for example, when he says that he is God's Son and when he makes this good news a reality in his life. A mediation is "absolute," however, when it is such that its competence is not measured simply by the fact that it presents itself as the measure not only of the medium used in and the mediating activity of every other mediation, but rather by the fact that for this very reason it is the measure of every preunderstanding of the mediated reality that is gotten by any other way, and even of every preunderstanding of what "mediation" itself means in the case of this particular mediated reality and consequently in every mediational process.[25] Such is the mediation of Christ, and therefore fundamental theology cannot restrict itself to thinking of this mediation as active in "special" theology, but must also look to it as the supreme criterion of its own reflection on the theological mediations (faith and revelation) of God. Christocentrism is thus affirmed as a methodological principle in the fundamental theological analytic itself.

The reference to the theme of mediations and to the hermeneutical structure of the dialogue of faith leads me to consider a question which is complementary to the one I have just been examining: I mean the relation between christocentrism and anthropocentrism. Fundamental theology finds itself led to develop along christocentric lines not only the theme of God's self-revelation but also that of man's faith. But when christocentrism takes this form, are we not simply bringing an anthropocentric theology back in again by another door? Here again I think it must be said that a simple reference to the christological ontology of Chalcedon is insufficient to establish an equation between christocentrism and anthropocentrism. Only satisfaction with a very rudimentary approximation can induce contentment with an undemanding dialectic which by affirming the centrality of Christ as "true God and true man" seeks to reconcile the claims of theocentrism and anthropocentrism and thus to satisfy both without really meeting the requirements of either.

In fact, the need at this point is to back and make positive use—within the framework of a (fundamental) theology of mediation—of the theme of Christ's self-consciousness as the original locus of the formulation of revelation. In thus reviving the theme we must go more deeply into at least two points.

First of all, there is the more basic question of how the revelation of God is present in the consciousness of Christ; account must be taken of the fact that here more than anywhere else the law of reception *ad modum recipientis* (according to the capacity of the recipient) combines with the complementary law according to which *habitus determinatur ab actu, actus ab obiecto* (the active potency is determined by its act, the act by the object).[26] Any theology of revelation and faith must therefore face the decisive test of whether it is able to conceive in plausible terms the union of anthropocentrism and theocentrism in the self-consciousness of Christ ("plausible" means at the very least that the two are not simply juxtaposed). The plausibility will be tested in its turn by whether it achieves a unique synthesis of the two requirements that measure the value of any theological reflection: correspondence to revelation and internal coherence. But since in this case the object of theological reflection is the self-consciousness of Christ precisely insofar as it is the original locus of revelation, correspondence to revelation here coincides with the internal coherence of the discourse (this coherence is evidently not to be conceived as something artificial rational, *du naturel plaqué* [natural after the fashion of a veneer]). From the viewpoint of logic there is a kind of "evidence"—a term that is certainly not neutral, since we are dealing with revelation. This brings us to the other point that calls for deeper study: the mediation by which the self-consciousness of Christ becomes the form of our faith and so is able to make itself available, with the same kind of "evidentness," to fundamental theology.

We are aided at this point by consideration of the fact that the point of departure for a fundamental theological analytic is anthropological, not however in any solipsistic sense but in the sense that an appeal is made to the "us" of faith as grasped at the stage of as yet unrefined precritical consensus. The presence of this consensus does not depend on our ability to understand it or to elaborate critically the conditions for its possibility; in other words, the communion of faith exists prior to any theology, even any fundamental theology. This fact does not do away with the obligation of achieving a theological understanding of the datum. Fundamental theology, which is responsible for this effort at understanding, must establish a "center" for synthesis, which will shed light on the phenomenon of the consensus of faith; consequently, the question of christocentrism arises again here, with a view to its possible further development.

2. Christocentrism and Hermeneutic of the Ecclesial and Scriptural Mediations

The problem of a theological understanding of consensus in the faith is identically the problem of tradition.[27] Fundamental theology is therefore led to consider the connection of our faith with the kerygma of the apostles and of Jesus and with the self-consciousness of Jesus which is the primary locus of revelation. Faith as a dialogical and hermeneutical process is never faced with revelation *simpliciter* (in an unmediated form) but always with a revelation that has been transmitted. The hermeneutic of revelation and the hermeneutic of tradition are in reality one and the same process, and the very identification of the self-consciousness of Christ as the primary locus of revelation occurs within and through an analysis of the processes by which the faith is handed on; it is within this handing on and in confrontation with it that the primacy of Christ is asserted.

On this journey back to the source, then, the effort made to understand tradition is itself christocentric. Here in particular, attention to the *history* of salvation is essential if christocentrism in fundamental theology is not to be reduced to an assertion of the headship of Christ within the schemata of an abstract axiology. In this way the unavoidable question of the historical uniqueness of the person of Jesus finds its proper place in fundamental theology (the question includes, but is not simply identical with, the question of the "historical Jesus"). The precise role of Jesus in the handing on of the faith (as absolute origin for which there is, however, a preparation and a pro-phecy or "fore-speaking" which we must take into account) thus acquires meaning and becomes a source of meaning. This role of Christ conditions the development of the tradition in its entirety by determining its structures: fidelity, sacramentality, characteristic mode of "progress," and even prolepsis or anticipation (relative to the identity of the Christ who has come with the Christ who is to come[28]); it also becomes the focus or center of reference for certain theological unique modalities (for example, the apostolic experience of the risen Jesus, and the first and normative apostolic communication of revelation), which cannot be repeated in later tradition and are not reducible simply to the kind of singularity that is inherent in any and every historical fact.

As anyone can see, for this reason the centrality of Christ and the centrality of scripture in relation to tradition are inseparably connected. The recent change in the way Catholic fundamental theology approaches the problem of tradition and scripture has meant a recovery not only of the meaning of the history of salvation but also (and not accidentally) of a christological orientation.

The question of the canon of scripture is now being seen as inevitably a problem of hermeneutics; this view has been encouraged by an analogous approach to the question of the canon on the part of Protestant theology, which likewise tends to acknowledge that it is facing the same kind of problem.[29] It is not a matter of selecting what is genuine in the biblical canon and what is not, or what is more genuine and what less genuine, on the basis of some christological criterion or other.[30] Nevertheless, it is now acknowledged that the radical way in which Catholics rejected Luther's appeal from the scriptures to Christ (as the final step in the appeal from tradition to scripture and thus from the Church to Christ and the gospel) made it especially difficult for Catholic hermeneutics to accept the great heritage left it by the Fathers in the form of a christocentric reading of the Bible.

In fact, a tradition (and more radically, a faith) that has, and knows it has, Christ as its norm, cannot possibly develop a hermeneutics of scripture that is not christocentric. The very reading of scripture "within the tradition" necessarily involves this kind of christocentrism; there is no *sensus ecclesiae* (subjective genitive) that is not a *sensus Christi* (objective genitive)— but it is this also (and specifically) thanks to its reference to the Bible. Acknowledgment of tradition, acknowledgment of scripture, and acknowledgment of Christ take place simultaneously,[31] although fundamental theology then goes on to analyze this triple process. But it is possible in this regard to speak of christocentrism only to the extent that in this triple acknowledgment the focus on Christ becomes dominant from the methodological point of view as well (and not simply as a radical and ultimate concern).

It seems to me that fundamental theology can with assurance assert this precedence since not only is faith's attention to its mediations a function of its attention to the God who reveals himself in Christ, but, in addition, the mediations have no right to claim an independent content of their own (as theological reflection on the so-called *fides ecclesiastica* has repeatedly reminded us[32]). This acknowledgment of Christ's primacy can be safeguarded against the more tempting forms of equivocation if we do not lose sight of certain points. For example: that the denial of an autonomous content to the ecclesiastical and scriptural mediations is not the same as a challenge to the legitimacy and even the necessity of the lengthy and laborious chapters of fundamental theology that discuss these mediations and the conditions for their existence. Or: that the assertion of an immediate relation to Christ as always given with faith does not mean an uncritical reliance on the supposedly "obvious" sense of the scriptures and the formulations of tradition, but is to be interpreted rather within the framework of a constant commitment to a critical study of their authentic meaning. Finally, and above all: that the primacy of the christological principle is seen in the context of and in diachronic relation to the mediations of tradition and scripture and not apart from or in opposition to these.

This is clearly not the place to go into the problems that arise when an attempt is made to develop an effective christocentric hermeneutics. The most serious of these problems is still that of the relation between the christological methodology required by faith, on the one hand, and, on the other, the requirements of critical scholarship and exegetical methods, and, above all, the inalienably inventive responsibility and independence of the interpreter. An acceptance of the non-contradiction between the former and the latter and of the fact that if faith is really to pay man an attention which is inseparable from its attention to Christ, it must call for the development and exercise of critical scholarship, exegetical method, and the interpreter's independence, is not enough of itself to give a christocentric connotation to the entire hermeneutical enterprise. Or, if you prefer: a christocentrism in this area can be accepted by faith in the same way that Christ's presence to every aspect and dimension of the human is accepted by faith; but there is an irreducible (eschatological) distance between the human requirements of hermeneutics and the evidentuality of their Christian meaning.

This irreducibility prevents a unified (and, in particular, a christocentric) formulation of theological hermeneutics as a doctrinal statement of a method. Or perhaps I might better say that this irreducibility shows the unity and christocentrism in question to be the goal of a tension and a hope. The situation is a somewhat paradoxical one, even if the practice of scholarship generally and of theology in particular is not a stranger to the experience of what it means to "hope for" a method. The tension and the hope bring with them an obligation to formulate prophetically the hoped for christocentric unity and even (why not?) to formulate the methods for formulating it correctly. This area of fundamental theology makes clearer than others do the need (present, in some form or other, in all theologizing) of moving from the speculative perspective to practical theology and to pneumatology. In any event, what must be sought is a fundamental theological hermeneutics in the proper sense, and not simply a juxtaposition of a theology and a rational doctrine (philosophical, linguistic, or whatever).

3. Concentration of Apologetics on the Person of Jesus Christ

The classical place of encounter between the message of faith and the critical activity of man is the most traditional area of fundamental theology, namely, apologetics. Christocentrism in apologetics must bear two points of reference in mind: apologetics is connected with hermeneutics, and it is connected with analytical fundamental theology. Insofar as apologetics obliges the believer to give an account of his own faith and therefore to express his understanding of revelation in response to the question of the credibility of this revelation, it is hermeneutical in character. But insofar as it reflects on all the complex phenomena that can show the credibility of Christianity, and reduces them all to an eloquent unity, apologetics comes to grips in an analytical way with the history of salvation. From this point of view christocentrism means that the "motives of credibility" form a unified sign and that Jesus Christ is at the center of this logical development.

On closer examination, the two perspectives prove to be less distant from each other than might be supposed. An apologetics that is christocentric in the first of the two ways indicated is possible only if the believer (actual or potential) finds himself in the presence of a sign that is structured christocentrically in the second of the two senses indicated. For, in fact, only when the person of Christ stands out as playing the central and decisive role in the context of the phenomena which "signify credibility" can he also appear clad with full authority to the person for whom revelation is meant.

At the apologetic level, too, the concentration on Christ is effected through mediations, but through mediations that show their own validity thanks to an immediate presence of Christ which comes about through the mediations but at the same time transcends these and fills them with meaning. I pointed out above the christocentric significance which the affirmation of this mediatorial dynamics possesses when it emerges in the context of a presentation of the Church as a sign of credibility that is permanent (and therefore available; and consequently, too, in keeping with an anthropological starting point). By "Church" I mean here all that is given "today" as fruit of the gospel, including the scriptures when these are understood not as a documentary mark or trace left by the origins but as a document that is of today (and always).

As I see it, the very consideration of the Church as a sign directs us in turn to the sign which is Christ, and this, once again, along two converging lines of meaning. On the one hand, it directs us to him as to a center constituted by a historical figure which never exists in a punctiform "today" that lacks as it were any memory of a past; as a matter of fact, the setting forth of the Christian phenomenon in the living memory of the ecclesial "today" always takes the form of a christocentric story (it is precisely in this sense that the phenomenon is called "Christian" without any further qualification). On the other hand, consideration of the Church as sign directs us to Christ as to the decisive condition for the meaningfulness and apologetic value of this ecclesial sign itself. Not only does the ecclesial sign not claim to be something absolute, but it is not even able to be autonomously probative; an "autonomy" of this kind might seem to be asserted by the "obvious" meaning of the text of Vatican I which presents the Church as sign (*per se ipsa etc.,* "by its nature . . ."), but certainly the formal assertion of such a claim goes beyond the intentions of the Council.

While it is true that the possibility of doubt with regard to any sign is inseparably connected with the hermeneutical nature of the recognition of credibility (a typical task of apologetics is to point out the incorrectness of attitudes that lead to this kind of doubt), it is also true that the sign which is the Church, when considered as distinct from the sign that is Christ, is characterized by a special ambiguity. This last is familiar to the whole apologetic tradition, but it has come to the fore again in connection with the antitriumphalist movement of Vatican II and has been reformulated by R. Latourelle in the most recent attempt to develop an apologetic discourse precisely on the basis of the Church as a sign.[33] The weakness and ambiguity of the sign is due precisely to the fact that we have distinguished it, even if only methodologically, from the sign which is Christ himself. When christologically supported and christologically understood, the Church appears (*per se? per Christum!*) as a sign of the Spirit.[34]

If we take *eximia sanctitas* (outstanding holiness) as an example that can rightly be regarded as paradigmatic (other elements of the total signs, whether those of Vatican I or not, can be given analogous treatment, and the result will be the same), this holiness can be shown by apologetic examination to be in fact truly unique to the Church, but not so *eximia* as to allow a triumphalistic interpretation of the witness afforded by the Church. Despite all its limitations (which are honestly acknowledged in Catholic teaching on sin and justification), the Church, when brought before the tribunal of the human race and history, and even before that of God, emerges not *anapologētos* (indefensible) but *apologētos* (defensible). The important thing, however, is the manner in which this is done. The Church's apologia cannot be formulated by the Church herself in a *Quis arguet me de peccato?* ("Who will convict me of sin?")—only Jesus can say this of himself—but only by Jesus Christ in the form of a *Nec ego te condemnabo* ("Neither will I condemn you") that renews and creates.

There is a final methodological question which an apologetics that claims to be christocentric cannot avoid, since there is a logic internal to the sign that is Christ which will not allow Jesus to be credible unless he has risen, while the message of the resurrection would not be credible if it were not a message about Jesus. Where, then, is the "center" to be located? What kind of "centrism" are we maintaining? The problem has to do not only with apologetics but with the whole of fundamental theology. When, for example, we speak of the self-consciousness of Christ as the primary locus of revelation, at what moment of its existence is this self-consciousness of Christ being considered? When the mystery of Christ is taken as the illumining center that makes possible the interpretation of scripture and of the handing on of the faith, are we speaking of the "Jesus" who is proclaimed Lord in the kerygma, or/and of the Lord whom the kerygma identifies with Jesus? Does the original (not necessarily in a historical sense) form of the kerygma say that Jesus is Lord or that the Lord is Jesus?

I shall not even discuss the merits of this question, which is such a vast one theologically. It will be enough to say that the significance of any christocentrism (especially in fundamental theology) will depend on the answer given to the question. Closely linked with it is the further question of the relation between faith and reason and, correlatively, the relation between pneumatology and christology. The problem of the relation between subject and original theological and kerygmatic predicate—a problem that brings with it (without being identical with) the problem of the relation between preunderstanding and the originality of the message—is reflected in the joining of Old and New Testaments[35] and of "today" and hope (Church and Kingdom). The problem is thus not one that affects only the christological nucleus of fundamental theology and might therefore be faced "after" the question of the centrality of Christ in relation to the entire economy of revelation and its signs had received an adequate systematic answer. Rather, the problem conditions the entire discourse, so that even after the fact of this conditioning has been noted we can see the ultimate radicality of the question of Jesus, thus confirming (if confirmation be needed) the christocentrism to which fundamental theology is called by internal logic.

Bibliography

The theme of christocentrism is rarely discussed for its own sake. Reference must henceforth be made to H. Küng, "Christozentrik," LTK 2 (1958), 1169–74. For a more recent, thoughtful essay on the subject cf. G. Moioli, "Christocentrismo," *Nuovo Dizionario di Teologia* (Alba, 1977), pp. 210–22. Within the broader framework of the modern problematic in christology A. Grillmeier in particular speaks of christocentrism in his "The Figure of Christ in Catholic Theology Today," in *Theology Today* 1. *Renewal in Dogma,* tr. by P. White and R. H. Kelly (Milwaukee, 1965), pp. 66–108. A panoramic view of contemporary Catholic speculative thinking on a theme that is decisive for the present essay is to be found in T. Citrini, *Gesù Cristo rivelazione di Dio. Il tema negli ultimi decenni della teologia cattolica* (Venegono Inferiore, 1969). The following can help the reader situate the christological theme on the basis of reflection on fundamental theology; R. Latourelle, *Theology, Science of Salvation* (Staten Island, N.Y., 1970); V. Boublik, "Orientamenti attuali della teologia fondamentale," in A. Marranzini (ed.), *Correnti teologiche postconciliari* (Rome, 1974), pp. 139–47; various authors, *Révélation de Dieu et langage des hommes* (Paris, 1972). A christocentric development of fundamental theology from the fresh viewpoint of "the beautiful" is given in H. Urs von Balthasar's well-known *Herrlichkeit. Eine theologische Aesthetik* 1. *Schau der Gestalt* (Einsiedeln, 1961). In his *Christ and the Church: Signs of Salvation* (Staten Island, N.Y., 1972), R. Latourelle presents an apologetics of the Church as sign which is geared to Christ as sign; the development is along contemporary lines and is useful for teaching as well. A plan for the development for a fundamental theology along the lines set forth in the present essay is given by T. Citrini, "La singolarità di Cristo chiave di volta della teologia fondamentale," ScCatt 103 (1975), 699–724.

11

Relations between the
Old and New Testaments
in Jesus Christ

Pierre Grelot

I. The Two Testaments

The use of the word "testament" to translate the Greek *diathēkē* (a juridical disposition that can take various forms) and behind it, the Hebrew *berith,* comes to us from the Latin Bible. It is justifiably used in its proper sense only in a passage of the Letter to the Hebrews which sets down the principle that a testament becomes effective only after the death of the testator,[1] and consequently that Christ had to die in order to leave us his testament (Heb 9:16–17). Even in Galatians 3:15 the term is used in a different perspective. Everywhere modern translators and commentators prefer the word "covenant," although this does not capture all the nuances of the "disposition" made by God in defining his relationship with human beings: that which he made historically at Sinai in regard to the people of Israel alone, and that which he made in Jesus Christ with regard to the whole human race that is called to be saved through grace.

A number of apostolic texts ("apostolic" is here taken in the broad sense of the term) contrast "two covenants" (Gal 4:24), but they adopt varying points of view. In Hebrews Christ is described as the "mediator of a new covenant" (9:15; cf. 8:6), on the basis on an important text from Jeremiah (Jer 31:31; cited in Heb 8:3). By that fact the former covenant is rendered "obsolete" and "old" (Heb 8:13), since it is shown to be incapable of assuring human beings the forgiveness of their sins either through the public worship which it regulated or through the gift of a law which remained external to them (9:1–10; 10:1–4). In 2 Corinthians 3:14, after presenting the preachers of the gospel as "ministers of a new covenant," not a covenant in the form of a *letter* that is written on tablets of stone but one in the form of the *Spirit* who is poured into hearts (2 Cor 3:6; cf.3: 3), St. Paul applies the term "old covenant" to the *text* that is read in the framework of Jewish institutions (2 Cor 3:14). St. Paul is here using a metonymy which the course of his argument explains clearly: we read "the old testament" whenever we "read Moses" (cf. 3:15), that is, for practical purposes, the Torah which formed the charter of the Sinai covenant. This is not to say that the legal aspect of the "disposition" God made in view of the future salvation of the human race defined the whole substance of this disposition. On the contrary in the Letter to the Galatians (3:15–18) Paul explains that this duly ratified (cf. 3:15) divine "disposition" had in fact been initiated, historically, with a promise (3:16), while the Law was given to Israel only later on and without abrogating the "economy" of the promise[2]: the citation of Genesis 15:3 in Galatians 3:6 made it possible to locate the Sinai covenant itself within the economy of the promise. The gospel, for its part, is simply the fulfillment of that promise. Thus the new "economy" inaugurated on earth by Jesus Christ is very closely related to the old economy. It is important to be clear on this point lest Christian theology go astray down either of two opposed blind alleys: either by emphasizing the contrast between the two "covenants" at the risk of cutting them off from one another (this was the basic error of Marcion long ago), or by reintroducing into the Christian faith or the structures of the Church a lot of elements taken over from the old covenant without sufficient attention being paid to the manner in which these have been "fulfilled" in Jesus Christ.

II. The Sources of the Doctrine

Those texts of the Jewish Bible that are focused on the past and the Sinai covenant provide theological reflection with an indispensable starting point, but the foundations of the doctrine are evidently to be looked for in the "apostolic" texts of the New Testament, since as St. Irenaeus puts it, "apostolic tradition" supplies the "rule of faith."[3] In regard however to the point that interests us here, apostolic literature gives evidence of varying points of view, depending on the problems the authors are facing and the angles from which they view the mysterious reality of Jesus, who by his resurrection from the dead has been established as "Lord and Christ" (Acts 2:36). We must not reduce this diversity to unity by applying a preconceived theory that is borrowed perhaps from later theological systems. The "theologians" of the New Testament all have something to say about the relationship of the new covenant to the old, but they do not repeat one another, since the way in which each approaches it lays emphasis on a different aspect.

The earliest texts are those of St. Paul. In these we find two different perspectives at work, depending on whether the texts are part of a polemic against a form of Jewish Christian sectarianism (especially Gal, 2 Cor, and Phil 3), or simply reflect Paul's habitual preaching as based on the texts of scripture. In the first case, the texts underscore the *limitations* and deficiencies of the old covenant as compared with the justification and salvation of which Jesus Christ is sole mediator. In the second case the texts take a more *positive* view of the relation of the old covenant to Christ and give several descriptions of it (preparation, pedagogy, prefiguration).

The vehemence of the saint's polemics may give the impression that his reserved or even negative judgments regarding the former "disposition" are a novelty. But elsewhere too we see him hitting upon new ways of expressing what was already the common possession of the churches. His proclamation of Christ on the basis of the scriptures supposes an antecedent preaching, not only by himself but also by the whole of Jewish Christianity that had not yet split off from the Jewish establishment.[4] Admittedly, this preaching is not directly accessible to us, but we have a summation and concrete presentation of it in the discourses of the Acts of the Apostles, where Luke is recalling Christian origins in order to show the continuity in the life of the Church. We may also look to 1 Peter as a witness to the traditional theology in which the texts of scripture are reread so that they may bear witness to the salvation that has come in Christ.

Apart from these sources which are closely concerned with the Christian reading of the scriptures, the relation between the two testaments can also be studied in a number of works that approach it in quite different ways. The Letter to the Hebrews openly urges its Judeo-Christian readers to abandon Jewish worship; the Letter provides us with what is doubtless the fullest development of the principle of biblical prefigurations. The gospel of Matthew, while continuing to be deeply rooted in the Jewish way of expressing the faith, is also fully engaged in an apologetics which is centered on the idea of the scriptures being fulfilled in Jesus Christ. The two volumes of Luke's work show that the good news which had been proclaimed first to Israel had now reached the nations with the purpose of bringing salvation to all of mankind. In the Johannine corpus the Apocalypse is in large measure a rereading and actualization of the ancient prophetic oracles in terms of the difficulties the Church is facing in its historical course, while the fourth gospel is both the most Jewish and the most anti-Jewish of the New Testament books; in it the estrangement of Christians from the Jewish "nation" is seen as now complete. Finally, 2 Peter provides the first indications of an official list of Christian books[5] which are now ranked with "the other scriptures" (2 Pet 3:16). Clearly, the problem of the relation between the two testaments is approached from quite divergent points of view, so that by this time all the basic principles needed for its theological development are already given. It is time now to review these principles.

III. Jesus Christ and the Fulfillment of the Scriptures

To begin with, deference to the indications given in the New Testament itself[6] bids us define its relation to the Old Testament in terms of accomplishment (*telos, tele-ō*), fulfillment (*plēro-ō, plērōma*), and completion (*teleio-ō, teleiōsis, teleiōtēs*). This Greek vocabulary, which is variously distributed according to groups of books but is sometimes associated in neighboring passages (Jn 19:24, 36: *plēro-ō* 19:28, 30; *tele-ō;* 19:28: *teleio-ō*), supposes a movement of the Old Testament toward the New as a result of something defective, inferior or provisional about the former. The general principle reflected in the vocabulary applies to several areas; an examination of the references makes these clear. However, these areas or spheres have something in common and overlap.

On the other hand, the terms referring to these areas are not quite coextensive with those we use today. For example, the aphorism reported in Matthew 5:17 says that Jesus has come not "to abolish (*katalusai*) the law and the prophets . . . but to fulfill (*plērōsai*) them." But the statements that follow show Matthew to be thinking primarily of the law as a practical rule of life; he apparently has nothing to say about the specific problem of the prophets. However, first of all, the Jewish "torah" included more than what we called "law," and in addition, in the rabbinic tradition the prophets were the primary and normative interpreters of the torah. Secondly, "the law and the prophets" meant for practical purposes the whole of scripture and the entire "economy" to which law and prophets gave a framework (cf. Mt 7:12; 11:13; Lk 16:16; 22:40; Jn 1:45. Lk 16:29, 31 and 24:27 speak of "Moses and the prophets"). In itself, Matthew's aphorism envisages this entire reality, which has been brought to its fulfillment by Jesus.

It is possible, nonetheless, to divide the material of the Old Testament into three main sectors, each of which has been "accomplished": *history,* in which the unfolding of God's plan is manifested; the *law,* which regulates the concrete existence of community and individuals and which includes "the law" and "the worship" (Rom 9:4b); "the *promises*" (Rom 9:4c), which announce in advance the grace of salvation that will be given in Christ.[7]

(a) In order to find traces of the *history* that reaches its fulfillment in Christ we must look for it under a different terminology than ours: the terminology of *time,* which calls to mind not simply chronology but also the concrete content of the events that take place in time. The prophets of old had announced what was to come "in the last days." Jesus "was made manifest at the end of the times" (1 Pet 1:20). He himself proclaimed that "the time is fulfilled" (Mk 1:15). St. Paul echoes him: "When the time had fully come, God sent forth his Son, born of woman, born under the law" (Gal 4:4; *plērōma* is used here, *peplērōtai* in Mk 1:15). Here the entire history of Israel is seen as dependent on the person of Jesus who was to spring from and make his own all that was best in it, as though to recapitulate it in himself.

In a sense, the life of Jesus was an integral part of that history, since it was the life of a Jew "born under the law." But his life also began a new era by introducing into the temporal sequence an existence that "had to" end in death in order that the Messiah of Israel might enter into his glory (Lk 24:25). When "all was finished" (*tetelestai;* Jn 19:28) by this death, "the acceptable time," "the day of salvation" began for all human beings (2 Cor 6:2), in a "now" that is coextensive with the entire temporal duration of the Church (ibid.; cf. Heb 3:13), since the Church derives its very name (*ekklē-*

sia) from the fact that it is convoked (verb *kale-ō*) and gathered together around the risen Christ. Such is "the present time" (*ho nūn kairos* in Rom 3:26; *ho kairos ho enestēkōs* in Heb 9:9), a time qualitatively different from the time of the promises, of the first convenant, and of the law, since the Spirit is now given (Jn 7:39). Yet the present time is itself in tension toward the "day of the Lord" (1 Thess 5:2; 1 Cor 1:8; Phil 1:6; etc.), which will also bring "the close (*synteleia*) of the age" (Mt 28:20).

This ultimate completion was already, of course, the goal which from afar governed the historical development of the old covenant too. But the drama that unfolded in the life of Jesus, within the framework created for the purpose by the promises, covenant, and life which had been bestowed on a chosen portion of the sinful race, now introduced into the heart of time the principle of its eschatological transformation: such is the meaning of the resurrection of Jesus. Now that "new heavens and a new earth" (Is 65:17; Rev 21:1) have come by anticipation to Jesus personally, they can be rendered mysteriously present in the sacred signs of the Church. *Preparatory history*, within which several stages can be distinguished ("before the law," then "under the law": cf. Rom 5:12–14), has been succeeded by *sacramental history* in which "the first fruits of the Spirit" (Rom 8:23) are given to human beings.

This, then, is the first application of the principle of fulfillment. It justifies the kind of theological reflection on history that would already emerge from a critical study of the Old Testament texts. But it also brings out the limitations of the latter by highlighting the element of incompleteness in them. As a history of the unfolding of the "economy of salvation,"[8] the Old Testament does, of course, have its internal coherence and contains within itself the principles for understanding it. On the other hand, its unity is of a dynamic kind, since it is in movement toward a goal (*telos*) that will fully reveal its meaning by embodying the latter in events.[9] Christian faith identifies this goal with the person and life of Jesus from his conception and birth to his resurrection and entrance into glory. By his death he establishes the new covenant that makes possible the ongoing time of the Church and provides a principle for the definitive interpretation of the entire history that preceded and prepared for it.

(b) The second area to which the idea of fulfillment applies is at once more easily grasped and more complex: that of the *law*, a term that includes both precepts and institutions, a "law" and a "worship" (Rom 9:4b). In covering all the practical activities of human beings that it has the function of regulating, the law includes both the moral law by way of the "commandments" and positive law by way of the specific precepts that controlled the life of Israel in particular. In order to come to grips with this complexity, medieval theologians distinguished within the laws found in the Old Testament the moral precepts which the gospel reaffirmed, the ceremonial precepts which it abolished, and the juridical and institutional precepts from among which certain guiding principles were taken over while the practical applications were to be evaluated according to their usefulness.[10] This is not precisely the viewpoint adopted in the texts of the New Testament. On the other hand, we must distinguish in the latter the situation of Jesus from that of the apostolic Church, and within the apostolic Church, the situation of Jewish Christians from that of believers who had come from the non-Jewish "nations."

First, as regards Jesus himself, the rule he gives and which Matthew has preserved (Mt 5:18–19) may be taken as a direct reflection of his personal behavior in relation to the commandments (*entolai*) of the law; not a single one of these is to pass away (*parechomai*); not one of them is to be relaxed (*lyein*); much less is anyone to teach others to do so. But what follows in the five antitheses of Matthew 5:20–48 shows how the principle is to be understood: the followers of Jesus must go beyond the letter of the texts and must follow the interior dynamism of these texts to its ultimate goal, since we are to be "perfect" (*teleios*) as the heavenly Father is perfect. This is how the "fulfillment" (*plerōsai;* 5:17) of the law is to be understood. The goal to be reached is in fact inscribed in the very letter of the law; we are told of it in the "first commandment," that of love for God, to which Jesus likens the law of love for neighbor (Mk 12:28–31).

Jesus himself practices to the full the law as thus refocused. This is why the reign of God can become his sole concern, his sole objective, the sole object of his gospel (Mk 1:15). He is, quite literally, the first to "seek first his [God's] kingdom and his righteousness" (Mt 6:33). He thus opens up a way which, from one point of view, is not new. He does, however, establish a new manner of entering upon the way, one that is characterized by *belief* in the good news (Mk 1:15b). For this reason, love, insofar as it has become *his* commandment, can be described as a *new* commandment; the aim henceforth is to love *as* he has loved (Jn 13:34), to the point of giving oneself for those one loves (Jn 15:12–13).

When we turn to the preaching of the apostles, the "economy" of the law can be interpreted from a different point of view. In order that the law may become "the perfect law, the law of liberty" that is actually put into practice (Jas 1:25), or "the royal law" (Jas 2:8a), those who "fulfill" (*teleite:* Jas 2:8a) it must give primacy to the commandment: "You shall love your neighbor as yourself" (ibid.). For "he who loves his neighbor has fulfilled (*peplērōken*) the law" (Rom 13:8), love being the "fulfilling" (*plerōma*) of the law (Rom 13:10). The agreement of James and Paul on this precise point is not accidental. If the entire law can be summed up (*peplērōtai*) in one word (Gal 5:14), it is because this "word" has become "the law of Christ" (Gal 6:2).

This is a principle which, while sticking close to the (selectively read) text of the Torah, introduces into it a critical norm by which the various components of it can be put into a hierarchical order.[11] It thus becomes possible to establish a distinction between the law as a "religious economy" given by God *to Israel* on Mount Sinai, and the law as a set of commandments which define God's will *for all human beings.* As seen from this second point of view, it is "holy," "just and good," and "spiritual" (that is, connected with the demands made by the Spirit of God) (Rom 7:12.14). For this reason, the gift of the Spirit, which is guaranteed by faith in Christ, makes it possible for the justified Christian to "fulfill" the law (Rom 8:4).

But when the law is considered from the first point of view (as a religious economy given to Israel), it is powerless to procure justification (Rom 8:3; cf. Gal 3:11), because it gives the person nothing but "the knowledge of sin" (Rom 3:20). Nor can it annul the principle of justification by faith which, ever since Abraham, has defined the "economy of the promise" (cf. Gal 3:15–18). The law, from this point of view, has to do only with Israel's status among the other nations and within a divine plan that extends beyond Israel in every direction.

In speaking thus of the law, Paul is not overthrowing it (*katargein*) but, on the contrary, upholding it (*histanai*) (Rom 3:31). He is showing its true finality, since Christ is its *telos,* that is, both its fulfillment and its termination. The law is thus assigned its true function, which is not to bring about salvation but to show the way one must enter upon under the guidance of the Spirit in order to receive salvation as a completely free gift. Thus the "fulfillment" of the law is not to be understood simply at the theoretical level of the virtue of charity which is the "summation" of the law, but also at the practical level of action that makes the law be embodied in acts that are the "fruit of the Spirit" (Gal 5:22–25). But when we speak in this fashion, we are making a basic distinction between the moral precepts of the law, which oblige all human beings and which the "Gentiles" obey "by nature" because these precepts are imprinted on their consciences (Rom 2:14–15), and the particular dispositions which defined the national and religious position of Israel as the people of the Sinai covenant. These latter dispositions, which concern both civic life and worship, cannot be imposed on the Gentiles as a condition for entering upon the way of salvation. The fulfillment of the law, which leaves untouched the value for Jews of its every part, involves not only not relying on the law for justification before God, but also transcending its particularisms and becoming part of the human race at the level of what it has universally in common.

Among all the New Testament theologians St. Paul is the one who has best brought out this aspect of the Christian faith and done so on the basis of scripture itself (cf. especially Gal and Rom). But the Letter to the Hebrews tackles the same problem from another point of view, by concentrating on the "purification" of human beings from their sins and by comparing the former cult with the sacrifice of Christ that has taken place at the end of the ages. The vocabulary of the Letter is obviously different from that of St. Paul. It does not use the verbs *plēro-ō* and *tele-ō,* and focuses its attention on the problem of the "perfection" (teleiosis)[12] which the Levitical priesthood had been unable to obtain (Heb 7:11). From this point of view, the law, understood as regulatory of the worship and economy which had been assigned to the Jewish people, "made nothing perfect (eteleiōsen)" (Heb 7:19). This is why it can be said that with the coming of Christ there is a "setting aside" (*athetēsis*) of the former commandment (*entolē*) (7:18) because of its weakness and uselessness (*anōpheles*). The expression is a very strong one, but it refers to only one aspect of the ancient disposition (*diathēkē* = covenant or testament: compare 8:13 etc., with 9:16–18), namely, the sacrificial cultus, which is made up of oblations that "cannot perfect (*teleiōsai*) the conscience of the worshiper" (9:9). This is the sense in which it is said that the law "can never . . . make perfect those who draw near" (10:1). Christ, on the contrary, who has been made "perfect through suffering" (2:10; cf. 5:9), has by his one offering "perfected for all time those who are sanctified" (10:14). This is why the covenant of which he is the mediator (8:6; 9:15) makes the former one obsolete, to the point that the latter has become, after his sacrifice, "ready to vanish away" (*engys aphanismou;* 8:13).

This approach is quite different from St. Paul's. It focuses on the problem of salvation and sanctification, which the ritual of the former covenant could not bring to human beings but which the blood of Christ has accomplished once and for all (cf. 10:10; 14:29). Consequently, we must not interpret the Letter abusively by speaking too quickly of an *abrogation* of the law. What in fact has fallen into disuse is the part of the law that could not achieve its purpose; once the purpose has been achieved by some other means, the ceremonial prescriptions have lost their reason for existence. "Fulfillment" means that from this point of view the law is definitively obsolete.

(c) The concept of fulfillment applies, finally, to the *divine promises* which stand out as landmarks over the course of the old covenant. But in this area it is no longer possible to rely on an association of the vocabulary of fulfillment with that of promise (*epangellia*) in order to identify passages which are clearly to the point. The theme rather finds indirect expression in several ways. First of all, in St. Paul the economy of the law is described as *subordinated* to the economy of the promise which from Abraham's time to our own contains the economy of the law within itself and involves us directly with the promises through the medium of faith (Gal 3:16–22; Rom 4:13–21). In Christ God has effectively proved himself able "to do what he had promised" (Rom 4:21); redemption, the gift of grace, justification, sanctification, and so on are the fulfillment of the promises made to the Israelites (Rom 9:4d). In a similar manner, the Letter to the Hebrews harks back several times to the fact that we are heirs of the promises (Heb 6:12, 17; 9:15; 10:36); the blessings given to us through the mediation of Christ thus fulfill the expectation which the word of God had awakened in the believers of an earlier time.

We can expand the theme of the promises by applying it to *all of scripture when read as a prophetic proclamation of the Christ who was to come.* This is the perspective in which to read the key text of 1 Peter on the searchings and inquiries of the prophets (1 Pet 1:10–12). When the prophets spoke of salvation, they were foretelling the grace that was meant for us. When they tried to search out the times and circumstances intended by the Spirit of Christ who was in them, they were bearing witness in advance to the sufferings of Christ and his subsequent glory (1:11). It follows that the proclamation of the gospel essentially requires that the conformity to the scriptures which marks the actions, behavior, words, final destiny, death and resurrection of Christ be clearly brought out. In the summary of the Christian creed which St. Paul says he himself had received and then passed on (1 Cor 15:3–5), the formula "in accordance with the scriptures" (*kata tas graphas*) occurs twice. The same care in referring to the scriptures is to be seen in many passages of the letters, the forms of the references being adapted to the conventions of Jewish culture. The point of the references is not to *prove* that the event of Jesus Christ had been *foretold* in its least details, but to establish that it is contained in the various schemata of scripture, either as prophetic proclamations already oriented to the Future of God, or even in the form of stories which bear the stamp of God's ways of governing the world.[13]

It is along these lines that we must understand the "fulfillment of the scriptures" of which the evangelists speak on many occasions (Mk 14:59; 15:28; Mt 1:22; 2:15, 17, 23; 4:14; 8:17; 12:17; 13:35; 24:4; 26:54, 56; 27:7; Lk 4:21; 24:44; Acts 1:16; 3:18; 13:27; Jn 12:38; 13:18; 15:25; 19:24, 36—all with the verb *plēro-ō;* John 19:28—with the verb *teleio-ō*). In the Letters this fulfillment is noted quite often by means of simple citations that are introduced by the formula "as it is written" or "as it is said." The point of these references is not only to show that the mystery of Christ took place in history in conformity with the word of God, but also to show that its ongoing fulfillment in the Church follows a pattern determined in advance. The idea of *fulfillment* is thus *a basic principle applied at every point in the reading of the Old Testament.* The texts of the latter are caught up in a hidden movement that from the beginning was directed toward Christ. But of course this presence of Christ in the letter of the Old Testament was not revealed until the latter was reread retrospectively in the light of Christ himself, since it is from him that the ancient texts acquire their full meaning.

IV. Jesus of Nazareth and the Old "Economy"

Before specifying this full meaning we must first locate Jesus in relation to the Old Testament by asking and answering the following question: How has the "fullness" of the Old Testament been manifested in him in the form of a historical *event* within the "economy of salvation" which in its own way is coextensive with all human history but shows its presence in a kind of series of peaks that runs from the call of Abraham down to the apostolic Church? The question is a traditional one, but biblical criticism has compelled us to approach it in a new way. During the patristic period and even more so during the Middle Ages Christian theology focused its attention mainly on a comparison of the two covenants considered in their overall structures; the purpose was to show that the old was completely ordered to the new. But the theologians of those periods were little interested in the fact that Jesus of Nazareth, "born of woman, born under the law" (Gal 4:4), assumed human "nature" with all the particular determinations imprinted on it by Judaism. And yet this is a point that deserves special examination.[14] For, if we take it seriously, we realize that as far as Jesus was concerned, the old covenant was not simply an *antecedent condition* which prepared for his coming and made possible his preaching of the gospel; it was also *a religious and social reality that to some extent fashioned his personality,* so that the Son of God did not become a "man" in some general or abstract sense, but became a Jew. Thus the Old Testament attained the ultimate goal of its interior dynamic movement *in the person of Jesus* and in the way he lived, preached, and died *as a Jew,* "in accordance with the scriptures."

If we put the question this way, we immediately see arising the false problem that has proved a stumbling block to some theologians: How are we to situate Jesus in relation to the Old Testament and to the New? To which of the two does he belong? Are we to connect his preaching, life and death to the old economy, so that they functioned historically as a simple prelude to the Christian kerygma? In this last question we can recognize the position taken by Rudolf Bultmann in his *Theology of the New Testament.*[15] But there is also an opposite way of presenting Jesus as founder of the Church during his public life, that hides the determining role played by his death and resurrection in the establishment of the new covenant. Then the authentic Jewishness of Jesus is left in the shadow and, with it, his profound relationship to the old law and the institutions it governed, to the sacred history within which his genealogy is so emphatically located (Mt 1:1–17; Lk 3:23–38; cf. Acts 13:17–23), and to the prophetic promises which he inherited in order that he might "fulfill" them.

We must therefore approach the question from a different angle, one that is suggested to us by the kerygmatic proclamation of Jesus Christ in the Acts of the Apostles. Here we find two aspects that are inseparable: "[1] God has made him both *Lord and Christ,* [2] *this Jesus* whom you crucified" (Acts 2:36). This is the perspective in which we are immediately located by the proclamation of the resurrection. This proclamation has to do with a *present* reality that has meaning only as a fulfillment of the promises, namely, the condition of Jesus as "Lord and Christ [=Messiah]." But the proclamation includes a *historical* reference to the earthly life of Jesus that ended with the dramatic event of the cross: the Jesus who is now Lord was once crucified. This means that the drama of Jesus *as a Jew* in confrontation with the official rulers of his people must be taken into account if we are to understand how in his total earthly experience the supreme gift of God to Israel and the decisive confrontation of Israel with its God finally coincided. As Son, Jesus was in God's sight *the Jew* par excellence, who lived his Jewish existence to the full "in accordance with the scriptures." He was not content to point out that "the fulfilling of the law" was to be found in the twofold commandment of love (see above); he also made this double commandment the sole rule of his own life, to the point of giving himself for his fellow human beings. In other words, *the fulfillment of the law* took concrete shape in his own behavior as a human being in history.

Similarly, it was not only in words that he proclaimed the worship "in spirit and truth" which God expects of his true worshipers (cf. Jn 4:21–24). On the contrary, his entire life could be summed up in the unconditional obedience to the Father's will which the Letter to the Hebrews unhesitatingly interprets as his *sacrifice* that was completed by his death (Heb 10:5–9). In this way, the worship of the Old Testament was brought to fulfillment. He was able to make the *reign of God*, which was the central object of Jewish hope, the object of his own good news as well and speak of it as not only near but already begun (cf. Lk 17:21), because he already lived this reign of God within himself. He thus lived *the hope of Israel* to the ultimate degree, in the paradoxical form of a life given to God in which he accepted the risks inherent in his personal mission. But in thus accepting the risk of death (cf. Lk 13:33), he brought to fulfillment the prayer of those who are holy yet suffer, a prayer which the prophets (Is 52:12—53:12) and the psalms (22, etc.) had already made part of the scriptures. In addition, Jesus' faith in the resurrection, which was based on the fact that the God of Israel "is not a God of the dead, but of the living" (Mk 12:27 par.), introduced into his practical behavior an unconditional hope in which the hope of Israel reached its highest point, and this at the very moment when the experience of abandonment was bringing him to the nadir of human distress (cf. Mk 14:34–36 par.; 15:34). For all these reasons taken together, *the fullness of time* was reached when God sent him among us as his Son (Gal 4:4; cf. Mk 1:15). He is thus the focal point of all human history, insofar as the latter is the history of the economy of salvation.

By reason of his situation within Judaism, whose structures, culture and language he made his own, as he did the type of spiritual experience conditioned by the law, the prophets and the psalms, *Jesus belongs fully to the Old Testament.* When we look back at the history, institutions, and writings of the Old Testament as a whole, we can say in all truth that they lead to him, because he freely made his own all the values to be found in them. But just as the bud opens into the flower when its time comes, so Jesus opened up the Old Testament to a Future that was already sketched in a suggestive but limited way in the promises of the prophets. Because he personally, from the very moment of his conception and birth (Mt 1:20; Lk 1:35), lived personally in God's presence as Son, in the fullness of the Spirit (Mk 1:10–11 par.; Lk 4:18–21; Acts 10:38), *he introduced the mode of existence proper to the new covenant.* During his lifetime the relationship of his disciples to him showed in a concrete way what this mode of existence would: one that is both interior and lived in community; the group of disciples, with the Twelve as its core, showed in a preliminary form what the characteristics of the future Church would be.

But in his earthly life Jesus accepted the human condition to the full, and this meant failure and death, death on the cross (cf. Phil 2:6–8). It is for this reason that "God has highly exalted him and bestowed on him the name which is above every name" (Phil 2:9). For *"was it not necessary* that the Christ should suffer these things and enter into his glory?" (Lk 24:26). The resurrection of Jesus, which is an anticipation of the goal to which the prophetic promises had been pointing, must not be separated from this fully given life upon which death placed its seal; in this manner the new covenant was established in blood (Lk 22:20 par.; Heb 9:11–12). But the Spirit could now be given to human beings, from the moment when Jesus was glorified after death (Jn 7:39; cf. Jn 20:22; Acts 2:16–21, 23). *The New Testament thus meshes with the Old without any break in continuity.* At the same time, the blood of Jesus removes the barrier which had set the people of Israel apart in the midst of the other nations, so that he might reconcile them both in one body by his cross (Eph 2:14–16); from that point on, the religious economy in which the law was the principal factor yields its place in the order of salvation to an economy of grace into which entry is gained through faith in Christ Jesus. The person of Jesus thus proves to be the link between the two Testaments. Or, better: the mystery of Jesus is the single reality which both contain; but each gives a different expression of it.

V. The Divine Pedagogy

It is to St. Paul that we owe the *image of the "pedagogue"* as a way of describing the function of the law in the historical unfolding of God's plan (Gal 3:24). But when Paul uses it, he is adopting a very negative point of view, in the context of his polemic against those Jewish Christians who wanted to impose the observance of the Jewish Law on Gentiles who came to the faith. In this polemic Paul was led to compare the structures of the two religious dispositions that came on the scene successively in the economy of salvation: that of the Law, which was inaugurated through an intermediary at Sinai, being "added because of transgressions, till the offspring should come to whom the [divine] promise had been made" (Gal 3:19), and that of faith, which in a certain manner existed prior to that of the Law, ever since Abraham had received the promise (Gal 3:6–9) but which acquired its full form once the blessing of Abraham passed, in Christ Jesus, to all the nations and all of us, through faith, received the Spirit of the promise on an equal footing (Gal 3:14, 22). It can be said, in this perspective, that "before faith came, we were *confined* under the law" (Gal 2:23), like a child who is a minor and who is entrusted to the care of guardians and trustees for whatever period his father determines (Gal 4:2). The function in question is entirely a negative one and brings out *the powerlessness of the Law when left to itself*: people need more than the knowledge of sin in order to be able to overcome it. Rudolf Bultmann has forcefully emphasized this aspect of the Old Testament, although he seems in danger of making it the only aspect.[16] But Bultmann has also said that "in the Old Testament existence under the Law is already thought of as existence under grace,"[17] "grace" being understood as a "grace of forgiveness."[18] But is this enough?

At this point a more robust theological tradition, less obsessed with the problem of justification to the exclusion of all else, provides us with a more nuanced answer to the question of *the presence of Christ and his grace in the Old Testament.*[19] The point of departure for this answer is to be found in several series of New Testament texts that intersect at one very important point. In St. Paul, the doctrine of justifying faith has its prototype in the person of Abraham (Rom 4:1–22). Paul does not claim that by reason of this faith Abraham knew in advance the full mystery of Christ; he says rather that the structure of Abraham's faith was identical with the structure of ours: Abraham believed in the God "who gives life to the dead and calls into existence the things that do not exist" (Rom 4:17), just as we believe in the God who raised Jesus from the dead (4:23). By this faith which anticipated the future revelation of Christ Abraham belonged to the new economy that has now been openly manifested. The same can be said of all those who, because they do "by nature" what the Law requires (Rom 2:14), "are righteous before God" (2:13b). These people are able to act in this manner only because, without their realizing it, they are moved by the Spirit; only the Spirit makes such behavior possible (Rom 8:3–4), by way of a hidden activity that links them to the redemption accomplished by Christ.

In the Letter to the Hebrews, the panegyric on the faith of the ancestors (Heb 11:1–40), who surround us like a great cloud of witnesses (12:1), supposes that although they did not yet benefit from the promise (11:39), they were linked in advance to Jesus, the pioneer of our faith, who brings it to its perfection (12:2). Being the Son through whom God has spoken to us in these last days (Heb 1:2), was he not secretly present in every word that God spoke of old to our ancestors through the prophets (1:1)? In the gospel of John a commentary on the vision of Isaiah (Is 6) does not hesitate to assert that the prophet had seen the glory of Jesus (Jn 12:41); the same statement is made about Abraham who, according to Jesus, "rejoiced that he was to see my day; he saw it and was glad" (Jn 8:56).

All of these statements are intelligible only if we assign to the word of God in the Old Testament—and to the relation to God which this word established—a *positive pedagogical* value which gradually prepared men and women for the future revelation of the Word of God. This notion is shared by the Fathers: from St. Justin to St. Irenaeus, from Origen to St. John Chrysostom (who speaks in this context of the *synkatabasis,* or "condescension," of God). For

> God's plan of justice and mercy, though covered in centuries past with a kind of veil, was not so hidden that knowledge of it was withheld from the minds of the saints who, from the beginning down to the coming of the Lord, made themselves worthy of praise. After all, the salvation that was to come in Christ had been promised both by prophetic oracles and by events that served as signs. Nor did only those who preached salvation obtain it; all those who believed in their preaching likewise obtained it. For it is one and the same faith that justifies the saints of every age, and it is to the one hope of all believers that the entire work of the mediator between God and men, Jesus Christ (1 Tim 2:5), is ordered,

whether we now confess this work as already accomplished or whether our fathers adored it as still to come.[20]

This *existential* view of faith avoids reducing its object to a *notional* content that can be explicitly enunciated; it emphasizes, instead, the *dynamic* aspects of faith from the moment when they first appear in imperfect and provisional form. Pushing to its logical conclusion his principle about the Word as Teacher, Clement of Alexandria does not hesitate to write: "There is in fact only one Testament: The one that has brought salvation since the beginning of the world and has now come down to us—but we must clearly understand that its gifts have varied according to ages and generations."[21] If we read the Old Testament *in the light of Jesus Christ* we will discover the universality of the one economy of grace as present in every age. But then the divine "pedagogy" will be seen as not restricted to the negative role assigned it in the Letter to the Galatians; rather it will be seen to include Jewish institutions, the history of Israel, and the prophetic promises as so many veiled signs in which we find positive traces of the mystery of salvation that has now come to pass.

VI. Revelation under the Veil of Symbols

It is not enough to state in a general way the principle just enunciated; it must also be shown what kind of concrete application it found in the experience of believers through the successive stages of God's plan that are represented by the two Testaments. At this point we encounter *the figurative interpretation of scripture,* the theory of which has been sketched for us, in several different perspectives, by several of the New Testament authors. Two of these sketches especially call for our attention: that of St. Paul and that of the Letter to the Hebrews.

(a) That of *St. Paul* is the simpler of the two. It is not to be identified with the use of *allegory,* which is in fact mentioned only once (Gal 4:24). Allegory is a procedure taken over from Greek rhetoric; it allows one to superimpose one or more meanings on the details of a text in order to express what is in one's own mind. Philo made extensive use of it as a way of linking his philosophy to a commentary on the Torah; Paul has recourse to it in conveying his understanding of the connection between the two Testaments. On more than one occasion he sets up very important parallels between the two Testaments, but without explaining the rules of method he is following. He does, however, give such an explanation on one occasion, when outlining a homily on the events of the Exodus (1 Cor 10:1–12). He underscores the action of the Spirit in the experience of the Red Sea crossing and of the time in the desert (10:1–4) and, by the same token, the anticipated presence of Christ (10:4), and explains that all this happened to "our fathers" (10:1) as so many "warnings [lit. 'types,' *typoi*] to us" (10:6); all this happened "as an example" or "figuratively (*typikōs*) and was "written down for our instruction, upon whom the end of the ages has come" (1 Cor 1:11).

This symbolic interpretation of texts is based on a "linear" conception of history in which the great stages of God's plan, embodied in the experiences of his people and recorded as such in the sacred books, show an *analogous structure* which permits us to see in the Old Testament stages a figural forecast of the New Testament stages. The faith of the Old Testament, which is focused on "the end of time" as on its goal, was thus directed to the mystery of Christ without explicitly adverting to this fact. The faith of the New Testament, for which "the end of time" has already begun in Christ, looks expressly to Christ as the one mediator; at the same time, however, this faith gives expression to the content of the mystery of Christ on the base of the "prefigurative" events. This notion of biblical "figures" is also applied to the great human experiences which serve as a background in the time of the former covenant; thus St. Paul applies it in Romans 5:14 to the mystery of the origins of the race, where Adam was "a type of the one who was to come," that is, of Christ.

The same terminology appears again in 1 Peter 3:20–21, where the rescue of Noah in his ark is seen as a prefiguration of baptism, since baptism "corresponds to" the story of Noah or is its "counter-figure" (*antitypos*). This view of symbol, which is the basis for a theological interpretation of history, evidently presupposes that the time of preparation and the time of the Church are alike related to Christ as to the single center from which they derive their meaning: the time of preparation as prophetic history, and the time of the Church as "sacramental" history. On both sides historical experience is inseparable from the experience of faith for which it acts as concrete support.

(b) The idea of prefigurations appears again in the *Letter to the Hebrews,* but here it is structured quite differently.[22] On the one hand, we find again the same symbolic relation between the history of the Old Testament (with the institutions developed during it) and the sacrifice of Christ, who has come "in these last days" (Heb 1:2). He has appeared as high priest of "the blessings which were to come" (9:11, JB) and of which the Law, that is, the old economy as a whole, contained only the shadow (10:1). The imperfect *sketch* or draft preceded in time the *reality* that has been revealed at the end of the preparatory period. On this point, then, the teaching of the Letter is identical with that of St. Paul, although it is applied to the *cultic* experiences of the Old Testament rather than to the latter's *historical* experiences. It should be noted, however, that the prefiguration of Christ's sacrifice by that of Isaac on the pyre is also mentioned and that the author sees in the latter a "symbol" (*parabolē*) (11:19).

On the other hand, the author is heavily influenced by an "exemplarism" that derives from the Platonic tradition but has been transformed under the influence of biblical conceptions. It is in this exemplarist perspective that he uses the key-word *typos,* no longer with the meaning of "prophetic figure" but with the meaning of "model." At Sinai Moses erected the tent of the sanctuary in accordance with the "model" or "pattern" shown to him on the mountain (8:5, citing Ex 25:40). But this model was in fact the *heavenly* sanctuary into which Christ entered at the end of his sacrifice (9:11–12; cf. 9:24). In comparison with this sanctuary and the sacrifice offered in it the worship of the Old Testament was only a copy (*hypodeigma,* 8:5; 9:23), a reproduction (*antitypos,* 9:24), a shadow (8:5; 10:1; cf. Col 2:27). But the substantial image (*eikōn,* 10:1) of this heavenly sanctuary has now been revealed, and Christian experience is a sharing of it: those who have "once been enlightened" (6:4) "have tasted the heavenly gift, and have become partakers of the Holy Spirit, and have tasted the goodness of the word of God and the powers of the age to come" (6:4–5). Thus the "exemplarist" relation between heaven and earth cuts across the "figurative" relation between the history of Israel and the "future" begun by Christ. This Future of God, which is reserved for "the end of time," includes the whole time of the Church: the latter is an abiding "Today" during which believers are called to enter into the "rest of God" (cf. 4:1–11). Such a "typology" is notably more complex than that of St. Paul. It is rather close to the typology which the Johannine Apocalypse utilizes without ever defining its principles.

(c) As a result there are *three lines along which a figurative interpretation can be made* in order to find Jesus Christ and his mystery promised under the veil of symbols in the Old Testament texts.[23] First, the great *historical* experiences of "our fathers" in the time of the patriarchs or throughout the history of Israel, which have already been intrepreted in the sacred books as so many experiences of the "ways of God," can be seen now as marked in advance with the mark of the future Christ and of Christian experience in which the mystery of Christ unfolds in a "sacramental" way. Second, Israel's *institutional* experiences, be they civic (the monarchy) or cultic (for example, the liturgy of the day of atonement: Heb 9), contain veiled prophecies of what Christ has accomplished in full reality as royal Messiah and high priest. Finally, the *prophetic promises,* which focused on eschatological salvation but in the process applied to the end of time an imagery inspired by the history and institutions of Israel, are now understood to have been formulated in prefigurative language. Thus *the theological interpretation of the "prefigurative" realities is essential to the Christian reading of Old Testament texts,* be these narrative texts, or texts dealing with the institutional life, or prophetic texts containing promises of salvation.

These general principles are derived from the New Testament itself. Their application to particular texts is evidently not extended, in the New Testament, to the Old Testament in its entirety. Moreover, it is inevitably marked by the practical procedures used in the culture of the time, whether in rabbinical circles or in Hellenistic circles (allegory, according to Gal 4:24). But the way is thus opened for a Christian "hermeneutic" which is applied at two points: first, to the (historical or institutional) *realities* of which the texts speak, in order to find in these realities a starting point for theological reflection; then to the *texts* themselves as being the normative foundation for such reflection. If it be true that all religious language must inevitably have recourse to symbols in order to speak of God and give expression to his relations with human beings, it is also a fact that in the biblical perspective *the concept of symbol takes on a particular cast* that is due both to the relation between the two Testaments and to the incarnation of the Son of God at the precise point where the two Testaments meet.

VII. The Theory of the Senses of Scripture

On the basis of the foundational reflection that has just been set forth, the Scholastic tradition developed a doctrine of the senses of scripture that served, and still serves, to give Christian hermeneutics its structure.

(a) The texts of the New Testament and especially those of St. Paul and the Letter to the Hebrews were already located at the point where the proclamation of the gospel, which was presented as the "fulfillment" of the entire preparatory economy, came into contact with the methods of reading texts which were current in rabbinical circles (cf. the rules set down by Hillel) or in Hellenistic circles (cf. the allegory practiced by Paul and the exemplarism of the Letter to the Hebrews). These two contacts at the cultural level led to the development of a rather diversified exegetical method which, under the influence of Origen, finally crystalized, in the Latin West, in the doctrine of the "four senses" of scripture.[24]

We should think here not so much of a plurality of "meanings" in the modern sense of this word as of a variety of areas into which the texts of scripture, especially those of the Old Testament, brought the light of revelation. First, there is the area of history as a series of events wherein the unfolding of God's plan has left traces of itself. Then there is the area of the mystery of Christ and the Church (this is the area of *allegory* in Origen's sense of the term). Third, there is the area of Christian experience within the mystery of Christ and the Church (this is the area of *tropology,* sometimes referred to as the "moral" sense). Finally, there is the area of Christian hope (the area of *anagogy,* which henceforth includes invisible realities and leads to the realm of eschatology).

The Old Testament texts and the "realities" to which the texts refer can bring light on all four points, provided we elicit their message by having recourse to the symbolic interpretation whose general rules we saw earlier. Theological reflection which in the patristic period and the high Middle Ages was based on the texts of the Old Testament as the basis for its expression, found in symbolic interpretation a privileged means of expression. This was all the more true of preaching and liturgy.

(b) The problem changed its form once the theology of the schools (Scholasticism) felt the need of sticking closer to the texts in an effort to establish its theses by means of *dicta probantia* or probative statements. The meaning of the *littera* ("letter"), that is, of the text as broken down into propositions, then took priority over any reflections which the reading of the text might awaken in the mind relative to the various objects of which it spoke (history, laws, institutions, promises, etc.). This led to a reclassification of the four senses, the clearest formulation of this being found in the works of St. Thomas Aquinas (especially *Quodlibet* VII, q. 6, aa. 14–16; the commentary on the Letter to the Galatians, chapter 4, lecture 7; the *Summa theologiae* I, q. 1, aa. 9–10).

What St. Thomas calls the "literal sense" is the meaning put into the text by God who is the "principal" author of scripture and inspirer of its human authors, who are the intelligent and free instruments God uses to express his message (they are "prophets" in the very general sense of the term). This "literal" sense is understood as including the whole fullness of meaning which, in the case of the texts of the Old Testament, has been unveiled in Christ.

Once "literal sense" is thus understood, the term "spiritual sense" (or "mystical sense") is reserved for the meaning of the realities (*sensus rerum*) of which the texts speak. These realities are diverse but they are all part of a history (*cursus rerum*) which gives them a context and which God directs toward Christ. As thus understood, the spiritual sense is a matter of theological reflection. It makes it possible, on the basis of the history and institutions of the Old Testament or, more accurately, on the basis of the human experience to which this history and these institutions give a structure, to express in symbolic terms all that has to do with the mystery of Christ and the Church (allegory), with Christian existence and its rules of conduct (tropology), and with the hope toward which Christian life is directed (anagogy).

Admittedly, theology cannot find in this "symbolics" arguments to demonstrate its theses. But the faith does not suffer on that account, since everything essential to it can be found expressed somewhere in the *sensus litteralis* of the texts of scripture. On the other hand, the liturgy, preaching, and the "spiritual" reading of scripture can find in this symbolic approach means of expression that are more diversified than those supplied by the theology of the schools.

This balanced solution was followed, in theory, in posttridentine Scholasticism down to a very recent time. But in fact it suffered gradual attrition as exegetes became increasingly concerned with a *critical reading* that is attentive to the didactic intention of the human authors and not any longer solely to the intention of God who inspired them.

(c) It is in this new perspective that the notion of "literal sense" was reconceptualized in the twentieth century, with the Encyclical *Divino afflante Spiritu* finally setting an explicit seal of approval on it.[25] It is evident that the *intention* of the authors as embodied in the rich and varied human language used by the ancients was the instrument of expression which God used in order to communicate his revelation to the human race.[26] But the interpreter of the texts must also take into account the successive stages and possible degrees of progress of this revelation: the totality of the mystery of Christ cannot be explicitly discovered even in the totality of Old Testament texts, because these are only provisional and more or less deficient expressions. The theology of the Old Testament that is everywhere present in these texts[27] is a "historical" theology, that is, one adapted to the preparatory stages in which Christ was glimpsed only from afar in the faith and hope of the "prophets."

Against the background of such an understanding of the Old Testament, theologians have been led to distinguish in St. Thomas' *littera* (that is, the text of the Old Testament) a "literal" sense, understood in a critical perspective, and a "fuller" sense (*sensus plenior*) which relates to the mystery of Christ and lets its general contours be glimpsed without however conveying as yet the fullness of this mystery.[28] The figurative (or typological) interpretation of Old Testament history and institutions normally falls under this fuller sense, to the extent that such an interpretation is closely based on the *texts*. But, clearly, this interpretation is no more able to ground the theses of theology than it was in the system elaborated by St. Thomas.[29]

We should note that this new recasting of the theory on the senses of scripture, which emerges after 1950, has not been accepted by all exegetes and theologians. Many are satisfied with the very general idea of a *preparation* for Christ in the Old Testament to the extent that the latter represented a *practical pedagogy* which brought human beings to the threshold of the gospel; these exegetes and theologians do not accept the *positive pedagogy of faith and hope* that I presented earlier in this essay.

(d) If I were aiming at completeness, I would also have to take into account the *new methods of reading* that have been proposed rather recently and that go beyond the now "classical" literary and historical criticism: for example, sociological analysis, psychological analysis, and semiotic analysis that is sensitive to the "deep structure" of texts. But the essays made in these various areas are still too recent for me to be able to evaluate them and relate them in an organic way to classical criticism, on the one hand, and on the other, to the theological developments that might profit by them. These "shifts" are not, in themselves, any more alien than the ones whose results we saw emerging in the cultural context of Alexandrian culture (with Origen) or of medieval Scholasticism (with St. Thomas) or of the modern period (when criticism entered the lists).[30] But we must never be too quick to prejudge the results which new methods may make possible, nor the adaptations which these methods themselves may have to undergo in order that they may be properly adapted to the subject matter, which, in this case, is the sacred texts in which faith sees a normative expression of the word of God as it took shape at a given period. If this reservation is called for in exegesis, it is all the more called for in theology, where the translation of the faith into a constructive language must preserve its biblical roots while not losing contact with the language specific to milieus and cultures.

Bibliography

1. The reader may first consult the Theologies of the Old Testament which analyze its particular structures from varying viewpoints; cf. (in order of original appearance): L. Köhler, *Old Testament Theology*, tr by A. S.

Todd (Philadelphia, 1957); O. Procksch, *Theologie des Alten Testaments* (Gütersloh, 1951); P. Heinisch, *Theology of the Old Testament,* tr. by W. Heidt (Collegeville, 1950); P. Van Imschoot, *Theologie de l'Ancien Testament* (2 vols., 1954–56; one volume translated by K. Sullivan and F. Buck, *Theology of the Old Testament* 1. *God* [New York, 1965]); T. C. Vriezen, *An Outline of Old Testament Theology,* tr. by S. Neuijen (Oxford, 1958); W. Eichrodt, *Theology of the Old Testament,* tr. by J. A. Baker (2 vols.; London, 1951 and 1957); E. Jacob, *Theology of the Old Testament,* tr. by A. W. Heathcote and P. J. Allcock (New York, 1958). Cf. also N. W. Porteous, "The Theology of the Old Testament," in *Peake's Commentary on the Bible* (London, 1962), pp. 151–59, and "Old Testament Theology," in H. H. Rowley (ed.), *The Old Testament and Modern Study* (Oxford, 1962), pp. 311–45; and J. L. McKenzie, "Aspects of Old Testament Thought," in R. Brown, J. Fitzmyer, and R. Murphy (eds.), *The Jerome Biblical Commentary* (Englewood Cliffs, N.J., 1968), 2:736–67.

2. Broader studies of the questions raised in this essay: C. Westermann, *Essays in Old Testament Hermeneutics,* tr. by J. L. Mays (Richmond, 1963) (a collection of articles dealing especially with the theme of promise and fulfillment); G. von Rad, *Old Testament Theology,* tr. by D. M. G. Stalker, vol. 2 (New York, 1965), Part 3 (Relations between Old and New Testaments); G. Hasel, *Old Testament Theology. Basic Issues in the Current Debate* (Grand Rapids, 1972) (general presentations of the discussions, with bibliography); G. E. Wright, *God Who Acts* (London, 1952); A. H. J. Gunneweg, *Understanding the Old Testament,* tr. by J. Bowden (London, 1978); G. A. F. Knight, *A Christian Theology of the Old Testament* (London, 1959); W. Harrington, *The Path of Biblical Theology* (Dublin, 1973), pp. 19–113.

3. Studies of a more systematic theological kinds: L. Bouyer, *The Meaning of Sacred Scripture,* tr. by M. P. Ryan (Notre Dame, Ind., 1958); C. Larcher, *L'actualité chrétienne de l'Ancien Testament d'après le Nouveau Testament* (Paris, 1962); P. Grelot, *Sens chrétien de l'Ancien Testament* (2nd ed.; Tournai—Paris, 1962) (with a bibliography of the theological tradition on the subject, pp. 3–88), to which add *La Bible, Parole de Dieu* (Tournai—Paris, 1965). Complete the last-named with the aid of various sections of *Mysterium salutis;* cf., in the French edition, A. Darlapp and H. Fries, *Histoire du salut et Révélation* (= vol. 1); and B. Stöckle and J. Scharbert, "Théologie de l'histoire de l'humanité avant le Christ," which is chapter 12 of vol. 8.

12

Access to the Person of Jesus

Jacques Guillet

What access do we have to the person of Jesus? Who is this person and what is our access to him? Even today these questions are still central in any effort of reflection on the Christian faith. The answer I shall try to formulate here is that of a Christian giving expression to his belief. But it is not entirely cut off from the answers that other people who are not believers may give as they try to locate Jesus, his personality, and his activity within the history of the race and in the human world of our time. When, at Caesarea, Jesus asks his disciples two questions: "Who do men say that I am? . . . But who do you say that I am?" (Mk 8:27–29), he clearly supposes that between the two answers there will be the distance and difference separating error from truth, illusory opinion from authentic knowledge. On the other hand, by the very fact of his juxtaposing the two questions and giving them the same object, Jesus makes it clear that the same question arises both for those who daily share his life and for those who gaze on him from afar, and that the answer given by Peter: "You are the Christ," is valid not only for the Twelve but for all the children of Israel. So too, the way in which Jesus deals with the centurion of Capernaum (Mt 8:10–13) or with the Samaritan woman (Jn 4:29) or with the criminal crucified at his side (Lk 23:39–43) shows that one need not be a disciple or a good Israelite in order to find the way that leads to his person and the manner in which he is to be encountered.

Today less than ever can Christians be unconcerned about those who, without sharing their faith, continue to ask themselves: Who is this man? A Christian may have a further basis for the response, a unique and personal experience to reflect on and propose to others, but for all this the Christian is necessarily in the same position as the outsider who is trying to understand Jesus. Both have the same sources of information: the texts of the gospels and the rest of the New Testament. Both are heirs to the same history: twenty centuries of Christianity. Both often ask identical questions: What does the person of Christ mean to us? What form may his action be taking in our day? When Christians thus become conscious of what they share with non-believers, they are not thereby denying their faith nor trying to minimize its originality. On the contrary, they are trying to live their faith in a better way. Believers know that they can speak of access to the person of Jesus because their faith makes them certain that they can say who this man is. But they are also able to speak of it because there are people capable of understanding what they say and because the road they themselves have traveled, however personal it may be, leads through landscapes which those others are likewise capable of recognizing. The confession of faith finds voice in the languages of human beings; it is understandable by human beings.

Christians can elaborate this argument in an a priori manner by reason of their faith and the data which faith implies; but they can also see the argument justified by the facts. It is a fact that many in our time who are strangers to the faith are profoundly interested in Christ: in what he was, what he sought to do, what the results of his activity were, and what can emerge from the movement he launched.[1]

These preliminary remarks are not meant as an introduction to a comparative study of access to Jesus within the Christian faith and access to him apart from this faith. As a matter of fact, I shall remain situated within the faith and shall be studying, in faith, texts that were born of faith. But just as we who are situated within the faith cannot be indifferent to the route by which unbelievers are seeking access to Christ, so too, in my opinion, when we try to map out our own route in greater detail, we come up with something to say to unbelievers in their quest.

I. Access through History

We do not gain access to Jesus without passing by way of history. However skeptical we may be about the results of historical inquiry, however indifferent we may try to be to secondary contingencies, and however passionate our devotion to what is eternal, the fact remains that the real Jesus, being born into history, left his trail, as it were, in history: a trail we can neither eliminate nor change, a trail that leads, through written documents and a movement originating in him, down to us and our time. We can dream all the dreams we want about Jesus; we can exercise our imagination to the full on him, but the figure with which we emerge will be credible only to the extent that it tallies with the person whom the texts set before us: a real face, a living being. No one denies this truth nor the fact that Jesus was located in history. Yet very different interpretations can be given of the fact. By way of example, I shall present the positions of two thinkers, Rudolf Bultmann and Heinz Schürmann, both of whom have reflected on their principles and methods.

1. *Rudolf Bultmann*

In Bultmann's view, it is impossible to find any certainly authentic saying of Jesus or any indisputable event of his life, concerning which it can be proved that the saying transmitted or the event reported could not have been creations of the Christian community. Where such certitude is lacking, where creation by the community is a plausible hypothesis, the historian has no right to move beyond the saying or the event to Jesus himself, and the believer, far from regretting this gap, should accept the uncertainty.[2] According to this principle, the baptism of Jesus by John is an indisputable fact, because it is improbable that at a time when groups claiming allegiance to the Baptist were still in existence Christian communities would have thought of putting Jesus in a position of inferiority in relation to John, if the fact had not been public and authenticated.[3] On the other hand, we have no way of knowing how Jesus thought and spoke of his death beforehand, because all of his sayings on this event were taken over and revised by the community after their experience of Easter.

This rigorous method does not mean that for Bultmann anything not historically demonstrable is fictitious or that all creations of the community are necessarily falsifications. On the contrary, it was quite natural that after the death of Jesus and the experience of his living presence in the Church the latter should adopt a new language to express a new reality and that his language should be a recasting of the language of Jesus himself, since the point of departure for the new event was the pre-Easter person. In Bultmann's view, the call of Jesus to the radical decision of faith "implies a christology,"[4] a unique relationship between Jesus and God that is of direct concern to all human beings. H. Conzelmann goes along with Bultmann on this point, but speaks of an "indirect christology."[5] It is important to remember these qualifications which Bultmann makes, because otherwise he might appear to be enamored of negation. But it is equally important to understand the principle on which his negations are based.

The principle is of a critical nature: the historian asks for proofs, and the historian of our age needs proofs that are beyond question. But the principle is also, and even more, theological in nature. The starting point of the gospels is the proclamation of the event that has radically changed the destiny of human beings: the Jesus event, the salvation which God has given to us in Jesus. Jesus proclaimed this event as near at hand, radical and definitive; this is the whole burden of his message. The event came with his death and the forgiveness which God has given to us in this death. As long as it was not yet at hand, it had to be prepared for, and this was the point of all the preaching of Jesus that fills the gospels and forms the part of these that is beyond question. But the event, once it occurred, belongs to the sphere of pure faith, and no description of it is possible. It is possible to describe the manner of preparing for it, but it is not possible to describe the actual experience of faith. Faith is more than a secret between God and his creature; it is the very bond uniting creature to God, an abandonment that is complete only if it eludes every representation of it, every justification of it, and even every consciousness of it. Bultmann does not hesitate to say that this rejection of experiential consciousness, of any grasp of faith, is the equivalent in the order of intellection to what faith is for Luther in the order of spiritual experience: a belief that God forgives me at the very time when my heart accuses me, a belief that God saves me in Christ, while I surrender any claim to know the mystery of his person.[6]

And yet we must speak, we must proclaim the event, we must say what happened in and to Jesus and what is repeated daily due to faith in him. The result is a history of Jesus, a narrative of his life, a confession of his work: Jesus enters into history and into the mind and the heart. This process is a necessary one—necessary, but dangerous. It is necessary because through an act of God which we can only acknowledge by faith, salvation has come from Jesus. It is dangerous because to narrate, proclaim and define, while being required by the activity of witnessing, may also be a response to a need of the imagination, a reflection of the will to see, touch, and understand, and a way of avoiding faith. In Bultmann's view, the gospels contain legendary elements that spring from this need to see and narrate: the setting of the baptism of Jesus, the transfiguration, the liturgical narrative of the Supper, the appearances of the risen Jesus. But there are also passages born of authentic faith. The model here is the fourth gospel, in which all the miracle stories lead to Jesus' call for faith.

Bultmann's critique, which is radical at the historical level, thus leads also to a radicalism with regard to faith: a faith that refuses to ask what Jesus was and what he did, so that it may be receptive of the simple fact that in the death of Jesus God forgives us and pronounces that his salvation is ours. There is an access to God through the word and death of Jesus. There is an access to the word of Christ through obedience and faith. There is, however, no access to his person: "person" is a reality of our world, an expression of interhuman relations. To transfer this concept to God is to mythologize: to build another world after the model of our own world as transformed in our dreams. The opposite of myth is faith.

2. *Heinz Schürmann*

Schürmann has never undertaken a systematic study and critique of Bultmann; consequently, the parallel I am setting up here is to some extent artificial. On the other hand, since Schürmann has on more than one occasion tackled problems raised by Bultmann and since he has in particular expressed his views on the principles behind Bultmann's critique, it is worth our while to spend a few moments on Schürmann.

Schürmann challenges Bultmann's basic axiom, viz. the necessity of reaching a *nucleus that is guaranteed* by the "criterion of dissimilarity" against any possibility of later creation by the community. This principle contradicts all the methods of historical research: "What does it mean for a historian to 'prove a fact'? Since when have strict proofs (*Belege*) been required in history? Since when have convergent pointers been insufficient to ground possibilities and lead to probabilities and even to moral certitudes?"[7]

Schürmann is not abandoning the critical approach. Far from it, for he thinks it essential to prove the value of pointers that can be regarded as convergent. "Proofs by convergence may not be based on simple possibilities"[8]; the signs used must be certain, each in its own area, if their convergence is to have probative value.

The principle of classification which Bultmann requires is also open to challenge on the grounds that it establishes a radical break between Jesus, the Jewish milieu in which he comes on the scene, and the Christian milieu that comes after him. To regard as belonging to Jesus only what cannot be the result either of an antecedent Jewish influence or a subsequent Christian development is to deprive him of all human and religious roots; and at the same time to refuse him all influence on his disciples and the community they formed after him.

> As a result of the very method used here, the "guaranteed nucleus" of the Lord's words that has been established by the critical principle used in classification can yield only a very distorted image of Jesus: a "wholly other" Jesus who has absolutely no contact with the Jewish milieu to which he belonged (a conclusion that is disturbing from a psychiatric point of view) and who gives not the slightest impetus to any historical movement (a conclusion that is unthinkable from the historical point of view).[9]

On the basis of these principles Schürmann has for years undertaken a series of studies whose common thrust is to bring out, in addition to the basic continuity between the message of Jesus himself and the preaching of the early Church, the essential links connecting the actions and words of the Christian community with the person of Jesus, his initiatives, behavior and self-consciousness.[10] Behind the consciousness of the post-Easter community that it has been sent to proclaim the message of salvation in Christ lies the original experience of the disciples who were sent forth by Jesus during his lifetime.[11] Behind the celebration of the breaking of bread in the first communities the accounts of eucharistic institution give us a clear glimpse of what happened at the Supper: Jesus' gift to his disciples of his own life and death.[12] When we look for the source of the Christian confession that "Christ died for our sins" (1 Cor 15:3), it is possible to assemble enough sure and convergent indices as to give us the right not only to suppose "that Jesus understood and faced his own death in an attitude of love, intercession, blessing, and confidence regarding salvation," but also to think that the best explanation of all the "for us" elements of the Christian faith is to be found in the final actions of Jesus, and this means, to begin with, his final meal with his disciples.[13]

We must choose between Bultmann and Schürmann. But the choice is not between the naive and the critical approaches, between progressivism and conservatism. Both exegetes are equally trained in the rules of criticism; both theologians are equally aware of the implications of their choices and the presuppositions behind these choices. Both claim the name of Christian, both base their faith on Jesus. For Bultmann, the "authentic" Jesus, the Jesus of God (if we dare so put it), is the Jesus of the word, of the Sermon on the Mount, of the preaching of the kingdom, of the call to conversion and the proclamation of forgiveness. The Jesus of Schürmann does not speak any differently; he does not propose a different gospel. But he is himself involved in his message, he acts, he gives himself in the whole of his life and being. He has a personality, a recognizable image; he calls men and women to himself.

If we choose Schürmann's method rather than Bultmann's, we must nonetheless never lose sight of what Bultmann asks of us: that the Jesus we seek be not a Jesus of our dreams or our logical and historical reconstructions, but the Jesus who is a call to faith, the Jesus who is the expression of God himself.

II. Access to the Risen Christ

Access to Jesus is by way of his resurrection. Such was the experience of the disciples who, in the process, discovered not an unknown personage but the secret of him whom they had already known but whom they had found increasingly difficult to understand, the better they knew him.

The accounts of this experience itself are extremely reserved and afford us almost no information, thus leaving all our curiosity unsatisfied. The only reactions mentioned in the appearance stories are agitation, fear, and joy (Mt 28:8; cf. Mk 16:8): unsophisticated reactions, all of them, and expressed in trite terms, giving only a remote idea of the impression originally made on the disciples. These few details give no basis for comparing these experiences with those made known to us in the writings of mystics and seers. The only certain fact is that certain witnesses saw him and that their names are known to us: "He appeared to Cephas, then to the twelve" (1 Cor 15:5); "The Lord has risen indeed, and has appeared to Simon!" (Lk 24:34); "Have I not seen Jesus our Lord?" (1 Cor 9:1). Even when the Emmaus story describes the depression of the disciples on their journey and the remarks of their unknown companion, it tells us nothing about their experience of Jesus: "Their eyes were kept from recognizing him" (Lk 24:16); "Their eyes were opened and they recognized him; and he vanished out of their sight" (Lk 24:31).

The texts tell us absolutely nothing about the risen Lord himself, or about his new state or about his feelings. His actions are those of the past: breaking bread (Lk 24:30), eating fish (Lk 24:42). The words he speaks are a repetition of those the disciples had heard before (Lk 24:26; cf. 9:22; 17:25). The risen Christ has no special language of his own; at times he speaks like the Jesus of old, at times as the early Christians will speak. The most revealing example is the dialogue on the road to Emmaus, which exactly reproduces the kerygma found in the missionary sermons in Acts, first in the mouth of the travelers (Lk 24:19–20 = Acts 2:22–23), then in the mouth of Jesus (Lk 24:25–27 = Acts 2:25–28).[14] The same is true, however, of all the missionary mandates that end the four gospels; their vocabulary is that of the kerygma: proclaim (*kērussō:* Mk 16:15; Lk 24:47 = Acts 8:5; 9:20; etc.), to all nations (Mt 28:19; Lk 24:47), baptism (Mt 28:19; Mk 16:16; cf. Acts 2:38, 41, etc.), the forgiveness of sins (Lk 4:47; Jn 20:23; cf. Acts 2:28; 5:31; etc.), in the name of Jesus (Mt 28:19; Lk 24:47; cf. Acts 2:38; 3:6; etc.).

The only traits applied exclusively to the risen Christ are that he appears and that he disappears. But there are no special words even for these phenomena: sometimes he "meets" his disciples (Mt 28:9), sometimes he "draws near" (Lk 24:15), sometimes he "comes" (Jn 20:19, 26) and "stands among them" (lk 24:36; Jn 20:14, 19, 26; 21:4). When the encounter is over, he "parts from them" (Lk 24:51) or "vanishes from their sight" (Lk 24:31), "as they look on" (Acts 1:9). Only one aspect of these departures suggests a procedure not of this world: that of "ascent" (Jn 20:17) or "being carried up" (Lk 24:51), but this vocabulary is theological rather than spatial (cf. Lk 9:51; Jn 1:51; 6:62), and even Luke who most emphasizes the visual and sensible side of the occurrence, points out that in his ascent a cloud hides him (Acts 1:9).

In other words, the witnesses can say only one thing about the risen Jesus: it was he, and we saw him. Even the actions most suggestive of bodily presence and closeness—eating, letting himself be touched—really tell us nothing about the new life of the risen Jesus, except that he is still able to enter into contact with human beings living on earth. This silence about the new state of Jesus is not due to a deliberate reserve or intentional caution. It is due rather to the very nature of the event and, indeed, is highly significant in this regard. It is in the literary order what the open tomb is in the order of events. The victory of the risen Jesus cannot be seen by our eyes of flesh nor grasped by our limited minds. At the same time, however, it is capable of touching us in mind and heart and body and of revealing itself in the midst of our earthly existence.

But then the question remains and even becomes more urgent: What access do we have to the risen Christ, since all the witnesses agree that nothing can be said of him?

But all the witnesses are also in agreement on two further points: that the person who rises from the dead is the very one they had known before, and that his action now consists in accompanying to the ends of the earth the witnesses he sends forth to proclaim his resurrection. The resurrection, then, does not introduce a new person to the story; rather, it places the Jesus of old in an entirely new condition. "Jesus of Nazareth, who was crucified ... has risen" (Mk 16:6): this statement does not mean simply that Christ had to suffer in order to enter into his glory (Lk 24:26), but indicates first and foremost the simple, basic fact that the man who has risen is the very one who had been put to death. If he comes back and eats with his disciples, if he allows them to draw near and touch him, he does so primarily to convince them of a fact calculated to surprise them: that the resurrection, which has rescued him from death, liberated him from our earthly limitations, and rendered him secure against any attack, has at the same time not made any change in what he is, in his relations with his disciples, in his manner of dealing with them, in his heart. In another world, the world of God and life, the Jesus of our world—of Nazareth, of Capernaum, of Bethany, of Calvary—lives on.

Strictly speaking, then, the accounts tell us nothing about the resurrection itself and about Jesus' experience of it. The mystery eludes them. It does so, not as in certain mystical experiences because the experience transcends the power of human language to express it, but because it transcends all experience and occurs as a direct act of God in what for us is the world of silence and the invisible. This silence, this invisible, inaccessible world, is the new world of the risen Jesus; it is the world that leaves its mark on all the appearances, the world from which he comes and to which he returns, the world that gives his character its only new trait. From this event that totally eludes us and from the unimaginable encounter between God and himself, Jesus emerges, if we may so put it, both totally new and perfectly identical with himself.

III. From the Risen Jesus to the Prepaschal Jesus

This experience by the disciples of the risen Jesus has an extremely important consequence for the birth of the Church and the formation of the gospels. If the risen Jesus is identical with the crucified prophet and if the resurrection has changed none of his characteristic traits, it follows that before he died he was already the Christ who appeared on Easter. God, who received him as he breathed his last, and led him into his glory, and now shows him as risen, by that very fact tells us who the risen Jesus is and who he was before his death: they are identically one and the same person. In order, then, to know the risen Lord, there is no point in trying to arrest the appearances in their course, to hold on to and contemplate this figure that comes only to disappear (Jn 20:17), or to look up to heaven (Acts 1:11). We should rather turn back to him whom people could indeed embrace and gaze upon, him who talked and explained himself, who had shared the life of other human beings and died the same death as they. In other words, the resurrection is not an invitation to forget the human life of Jesus, but on the contrary bids us recall his words so as better to understand them; it bids us rediscover his very gestures and unique characteristics. The way to gain access to the risen Jesus is to listen to those who had known him and seen him live his life. This is the fundamental law governing the New Testament and all Christian talk of Jesus; it is at work on all the literary levels at which the faith of the first communities has found expression.

If, then, we take seriously the disciples' experience of the risen Jesus with all that is both decisive and inaccessible about it, Bultmann's basic principle of gospel criticism, the principle of selection, is undermined. The principle is indeed utterly logical and legitimate in the perspective Bultmann adopts, for he sees an unbridgeable gulf between the time of Jesus and the time of the Church. Given this hypothesis, it is absolutely correct that if discourse about Jesus is to remain a discourse of faith, it must abstain from attempting any return to Jesus which would represent an effort to satisfy in an external manner, by way of memory, the need to tell stories, to know and understand, to recapture a "knowledge according to the flesh" (cf. 2 Cor 5:16). But, while the experience of the risen Jesus is wholly restricted to the realm of faith, since it is limited to asserting that he is alive, without trying at all to grasp his new existence, and while even for the first witnesses the recognition of the risen Jesus necessarily meant faith in him (Mt 28:17; Mk 16:11, 13, 14, 16, 17; Lk 24:11, 25, 41), it is also the case that to believe in the risen Christ is identically to discover again the Jesus of old. In short, we do not depart from the realm of faith when we go back to memories of the past; on the contrary, we strengthen our faith, because we thus block any attempt to give Jesus a different face than the one he showed to those who encountered him, and we endeavor to discover in this human face with its particular characteristics and its particular historical date the fullness of the divine glory.

Access to Jesus is thus far from requiring that we choose between the movement of faith that adheres to the Lord, the Son radiant with the Father's love, and the requirements of history with its attention to details, concrete circumstances, and inevitable limitations. On the contrary, the very movement of faith in the risen Christ, the Lord, requires believers to focus their attention on the earthly life of Jesus of Nazareth and see the particular face, the personal physiognomy, of the Easter Lord.

For when we call Jesus "Lord," we are not assigning him a new face, as it were, but simply giving him a new name to match the new relation which the resurrection has established between him and his fellow human beings (Rom 1:4; Acts 2:36). "Lord" is a title that is always applied to a person. By this I do not mean simply that it is another way of naming him, as for example, when we call God "Creator" or Jesus "Savior," by reason of a function that belongs essentially to each. "Lord" is normally inseparable from the person to whom the name is given; it establishes a unique relationship between each believer and the very being and person of Jesus, or—I would go so far as to say—between the singularity of each believer and the singularity of Jesus. When we proclaim that Jesus is Messiah, Savior, Prince of life, we are defining him by his mission and his work. This mission is, of course, inseparable from his person, and to say to Jesus "You are the Christ" is really to say who he is, and to give oneself to him in faith. But in these titles, including that of "Christ," there is something that seems to come from outside of Jesus, a content shaped by earlier languages. But the title "Lord Jesus" does not point to a particular activity of Jesus; rather, it establishes the proper relationship between human beings and Jesus. And that relationship always involves his human singularity. The Lord of Christians is always the Lord Jesus, just as the Lord of the prophets was the Lord Yahweh, the one who had revealed himself to their ancestors, the one whose presence and whose hand upon them they felt (Is 8:11; Jer 15:16–17; Amos 3:7–8).

This movement backward from the risen Lord to the Jesus of the past is matched by an opposite movement forward toward the action of Christ in the community and the world. At the origin of this forward movement there is as it were the same absence of specific content as we have seen to be the case with the figure of the risen Jesus. The latter has no personality distinct from his human one. But the absence of any "risen personality," any action or teaching special to this moment, is a sign that from this moment on his action is no longer limited and his message is capable of reaching all hearts. That is what the gospels will point out, as each comes into existence in the Church. All of the gospels, each in its own manner, will be written in order to show the unity of action and identity of person between Jesus the Galilean and the Lord of the Christian community. The viewpoints and procedures of the various gospels differ, but the basic intention is the same.

Mark tells how, amid many misunderstandings and by often disconcerting paths, the disciples finally recognized in Jesus the Son of God whom Christian faith confesses. In the group gathered by Jesus, Matthew sees the Christian community taking shape with its life, its teaching, and its faith. Luke, by means of constant cross-references between the two panels of his diptych, shows the disciples who are following Jesus to be already living by the power of the word and the dynamism of the Spirit; then, in his history of the early communities, he shows the continuing journey of Jesus and his disciples to suffering and glory. John, though apparently the evangelist most remote from the events and the most free in his expression and way of handling history, is undoubtedly the one most careful to show the continuity between the life lived by Jesus and his disciples and that which goes on through the centuries: this last being a spiritual odyssey involving the revelation of God to his children, the struggle between faith and the powers of darkness, the gift of love. None of the gospels fails thus to identify the Jesus of the Twelve and the Lord of the Church. The place where the two meet is the space thrown open by the risen Christ; the appearance of the crucified Lord who gathers all of mankind into unity.

IV. Toward the Consciousness of Jesus

Access to the risen Jesus is had via the prepaschal Jesus. The point is not to isolate the Galilean prophet, by critical means, from the risen Lord who lives now at the heart of the world. The point is rather to encounter this risen Lord in his full reality, in the hidden substance of his existence. The secret that is constitutive of the person of Jesus, the secret revealed on Easter, is present in him from the moment he first becomes present in the world; it is present in his actions and in his heart, in his behavior and in his self-consciousness.

When we speak of the consciousness of Jesus, we immediately stir up a multitude of questions and open ourselves to countless serious difficulties. The requirements of history, the discoveries of psychology, the imperatives of faith, respect for the mystery—everything seems to forbid us to enter upon a fruitless way, a way that is a dead end. And yet it seems that we must do so, even if just to give a meaning to faith in its most elementary statement: Christ died for us. The event from which we draw our life was first an event that he experienced: the death he knew, the way in which he underwent it. This is a fact of consciousness which we cannot deny without contradicting dozens of texts that give expression to an unshakable conviction:

Christ also suffered for you, leaving you an example (1 Pet 2:21).

Christ also died for sins once for all, the righteous for the unrighteous, that he might bring us to God, being put to death in the flesh but made alive in the spirit (1 Pet 3:18).

Christ died for our sins in accordance with the scriptures (1 Cor 15:3).

At the right time Christ died for the ungodly (Rom 5:6).

These are traditional formulas that Paul reformulates for himself, knowing that he will be immediately understood:

Was Paul crucified for you? (1 Cor 1:13).

By your knowledge this weak man is destroyed, the brother for whom Christ died (1 Cor 8:11).

The love of Christ controls us, because we are convinced that one has died for all; therefore all have died. And he died for all, that those who live might live no longer for themselves but for him who for their sake died and was raised (2 Cor 5:14–15).

The life that I now live in the flesh I live by faith in the Son of God, who loved me and gave himself for me (Gal 2:20).

Christ redeemed us . . . having becoming a curse for us (Gal 3:13).

While we were yet helpless, at the right time Christ died. . . . But God shows his love for us in that while we were yet sinners Christ died for us (Rom 5:6–8).

Either these texts are meaningless or they speak, as of a truth that is unquestionable and essential to Christian life, of a fundamental bond uniting, on the one side, the believer who links his life to Christ, and, on the other, Christ who gives his life for believers. There is evidently consciousness on both sides. Can we, with the help of the gospel testimonies, come into contact with this consciousness in Jesus? Can we, with the help of the testimonies that have come to us from the early Church, understand how the first Christians believed themselves to be, from the very beginning, in touch with that consciousness?

When we make the gospels our point of departure, we must admittedly surrender from the outset any pretense that we can follow the birth and development of the consciousness of Jesus, any desire to explain his life in terms of his experiences and reactions, any thought that we might be able to sketch his portrait or analyze his behavior. This impossibility is to some extent quite radical in character. By this I mean that it is not due only to the genre and style of the evangelists and to the nature of their writings, their need of a quasi-utilitarian objectivity, their lack of interest in the very thing we are calling the consciousness of Jesus. No, the impossibility is due, in a way, to the person himself. It is he himself, we might say, who forbids us to enter into his consciousness.

I do not mean by this that he gives the impression of wanting to reserve for himself an area in which he feels at home, a mysterious zone within which, safe from indiscreet prying and from misinterpretation, he can carry on a higher activity devoted to tasks beyond the comprehension of the profane. I mean rather that he has nothing to hide; that he puts his whole self into every gesture and action. Everything he says is unqualifiedly true, and there is a complete coincidence between himself and everything he says. He does not communicate the truth as though it were a discovery he has made and now wishes to pass on, still less as though it were a lesson he had first learned. He presents the truth as a fact, and as a fact of the same order as his own being: he himself is the truth. The Johannine formulas—I have received from my Father; I say what I have seen; I do what he has told me to do . . . — seem to be describing a complex process that has several phases. But this manner of expressing himself, which is calculated to allow each person his own role and to situate the Father, the Son, and human beings—translates a reality that is utterly simple and that flashes out in every line of the Synoptics. We might call it disinterestedness, fidelity to his mission, sincerity in the presence of truth, courage in the face of fear, the certainty of not being mistaken, the knowledge of human beings and of hearts. It is all this, but it is also something more, something infinitely simple: Jesus says what is and, in saying it, gives himself. Things are not true because he says them, and no one is more objective than he, more focused on reality, more conscious of the special value of each thing that makes up our universe. But it is precisely he who makes this value and this truth appear; it is he who says what they are; he is their truth.

This behavior of Jesus is clearly of the order of knowledge, and expresses his personal consciousness. But it is true that this consciousness is not directly accessible to us; rather it is made known to us as a requirement and a call, and we come into real contact with it only if we give it our response and open ourselves to it in faith. It is a consciousness that is undeniable yet beyond our comprehension, impenetrable yet transparent.

V. A Consciousness for Others

Perhaps we can now understand better how this consciousness, though reserved to the point of total self-effacement, could nevertheless leave such a deep impression on the disciples of Jesus and the early communities. The answer is certainly to be found in the words "for us" that keep recurring in the earliest Christian texts.[15] They seem to express something on which everyone was clear. But when we ask what this conviction of "for us" was based on, we find ourselves embarrassed at first. Logically, the conviction should be based on explicit statements in which Jesus expresses the meaning of his death and attests that at the very moment of death he would be giving his life for others. But such declarations are rare; above all, the most explicit among them are also the ones most suspect of being composed after the fact.[16] A number of exegetes regards as authentic the saying of Jesus in Mark 10:45: "The Son of man also came not to be served but to serve, and to give his life as a ransom for many." Others, however, have their doubts, and we may feel some surprise at the idea that the outlook and behavior of the entire Christian community should be based on one or two sayings which are more or less properly interpreted.

But these sayings, even if their authenticity is proof against all criticism, are valid and can sustain the weight placed on them only if they give expression to a reality that is both accessible and undeniable. Even if it were proved against all possible objections that Jesus explicitly said he was going to give his life in sacrifice in order to establish a covenant between God and the human race and in order to forgive all the sins of human beings, his statement would be only an unintelligible riddle if it came at the end of a life in which such concerns had had but little place. On the other hand, while explicit statements to this effect are rare and not always clear, the fact is certain that in all of his activity and throughout the whole of the period in which his life could be seen by others and was lived in the daily presence and fellowship of the Twelve, all of his actions and words are controlled by an abiding movement toward God and toward human beings, by a total, unreserved, and spontaneous gift of his entire being. In all that he is, Jesus is a man "given." The holy men and prophets of Israel, servants of the Lord, likewise felt called to give their lives in the service of their people and to intercede for the guilty (1 Kings 18:42; Is 37:4; Jer 14:7–12; Amos 7:2, 5). But this was part of their vocation, not of their inmost nature, and they were often torn between their mission and their spontaneous instincts that bade them seek vengeance or flee from their responsibilities (cf. Jer 17:12–18). Jesus too utters exclamations of weariness (Mk 9:19) and cries of anguish and distress (Mk 14:33–40). He would not be a human being—would he even be God?—if he were not sensitive to the wickedness of men and women, their cruelty, their capacity for destructiveness and evildoing. But Jesus endures this fear and this weariness within his ongoing activity, within the movement that constantly carries him toward us without ever turning back.

This movement toward us is inseparable from the movement that carries him toward his Father; indeed, he translates into human terms the gaze with which God embraces the world. In his prayer (Mk 1:35–37; 6:46–51; 14:35; Lk 6:12–13; 9:18, 28; 22:32) and in his thanksgiving (Lk 10:21; Jn 11:41) Jesus never comes before the Father without bringing to the encounter the human beings with whom he deals. However extensive the degree of later elaboration and of the stereotypical is in the Johannine "comparisons"[17]: "As the Father and the Son, so I and you (i.e., the Son and other human beings)," the language is not really new in relation to the real experience of the Jesus of the Synoptics. It gives expression to an existence and a being that are completely "de-centered" and perfectly natural and free in this de-centering. Whether or not Jesus, when giving his body and blood at the Supper in the form of bread and wine, actually spoke the "for you" of Paul (1 Cor 11:24) and Luke (22:19), which is missing in Matthew and Mark, is really a secondary question. Even if the disciples did not hear the words that evening, they had only to link the actions at the meal and the subsequent death of Jesus to all that his life had been, in order to be able to say with an absolute certainty communicable to all that "Christ died for us."

VI. Access to Forgiveness

"Christ died for us" can be rephrased as "Christ died for our sins" (cf. 1 Pet 2:21 and 3:18). The two formulas are practically equivalent and can be interchanged. The equivalence is perhaps the thing that best helps us understand how, beginning with the resurrection, the disciples of Jesus could bring out the full meaning of their Master's life and death and could give, to all who joined their ranks (Acts 2:41), access to the inner reality of this death and to this personal gift. The essential thing is doubtless the experience which they had seen others having while they were in the company of Jesus before his death and which they themselves had personally in their dealings with him after his resurrection: the experience of forgiveness.

The manner in which Jesus dealt with sinners is one of the most notable traits of his earthly life and one of the most certain data of his story. Sinners had come to John the Baptist in order to confess their sins (Mk 1:5). Jesus, however, although he too, like John, has begun with a summons to repentance and baptism (cf. Jn 3:22–24), adopts a new manner of life and action once the prophet has been arrested (Mk 1:14): he leaves the Jordan and the area of water-springs, ceases to baptize, and proclaims the Good News, the gospel of the reign of God. He takes to the roads in order to seek out sinners; he welcomes those whom society rejects: the tax collectors and the prostitutes (Mk 2:15; Mt 21:31); he even chooses one of the Twelve from among these outcasts, becomes notorious for keeping company with them, allows a sinful woman to touch him at length (Lk 7:39). He even makes this scandalous conduct the very reason for his mission: "I came not to call the righteous, but sinners" (Mk 2:17).

This typical behavior brings out what is original in his activity and distinguishes it from others. The sinners who sought out John asked him what they should do (Lk 3:10, 12, 14). But Jesus does not come primarily to tell them what they ought to do, or what the role of human beings is in salvation. He comes primarily to forgive; he comes to bring that which human beings need beyond all else and cannot provide for themselves: the forgiveness of God. He comes also to bring the sign and proof of this forgiveness: he eats and drinks with sinners, he takes the place for which he has come.

This behavior of Jesus is unthinkable apart from a two-directional consciousness: of God who forgives and of the human person who receives the forgiveness. For Jesus to be able to say to someone: "Your sins are forgiven" (Mk 2:5; Lk 4:48), he must have, if we may so put it, something even more than certainty: he must have immediate evidence. His words are not an exhortation to confidence; they are an authoritative statement, an event that is of decisive importance for the one receiving the forgiveness, for the one bestowing it, and for those witnessing it. If Jesus is to have this evidence, he must have direct access to God and must know not only that God is determined to pardon (something many prophets understood) but also that this determination has here and now become a reality in our world. Once we have enumerated these conditions, the linkage of which is certain, we have grasped an aspect of the consciousness of Jesus.

Once again, however, we achieve this contact only in an indirect way. Jesus does not tell us what he feels as he forgives, and his words are almost impersonal: "Your sins are forgiven." The *divinum passivum* is a Jewish way of expressing an action reserved to God while avoiding the use of his name out of respect for his greatness and a fear of distorting the reality. Here again we experience this unique characteristic of Jesus: his manner of being himself and doing what no one else can do, but at the same time being completely self-effacing. It is a characteristic which John expresses in a definitive formula: "I am he, and . . . I do nothing on my own authority" (Jn 8:28).

Jesus is himself when he forgives, and he is the one who does the forgiving: the paralytic is forgiven as a result of his words, just as he is healed as a result of his words ("I say to you," Mk 2:10–11). It is on his own initiative that Jesus sets out to find sinners; he is himself, spontaneously so, and being perfectly natural when he welcomes the tearful woman who was a sinner and offers her as an example. But this movement that is so profound a part of him is at the same time a reflection and expression of God's forgiveness. The three parables which Luke places together in Chapter 15 and which, he tells us, were intended as a response to the murmurs of the scribes and Pharisees, are specifically intended to help us imagine God's joy at finding one of his lost children. The response of Jesus is thus the response of God; the spontaneous movement in Jesus mirrors an essential reaction of God: his expectation and his joy. The connection between the behavior of Jesus toward sinners and the three parables on divine joy is one of the most striking testimonies we have to the personal mystery of Jesus, to his relationship with God, and to the experience that is constitutive of his being. As a man wholly himself in all his actions and wholly free in all his decisions, he is, in his spontaneous freedom, the expression and revelation of someone other than he: the Person who stands at the heart of all his life and experience, the Father.

Perhaps these examples, more than others, make it possible for us to approach the consciousness of Jesus. No more here than elsewhere, indeed, does he open his heart to us and confide in us about his feelings. Nonetheless, in these parables he is describing his own life and revealing to us the secret of his mission. No one but he can speak in this way, because the only persons involved are himself and God. On the other hand, he does not say a word about himself; he does not even seem to be unveiling a secret for us but only to be stating a basic truth: Is it not as natural for a father who has seen his son go away to live in expectation of his return, as it is for a woman who has lost a coin to look under all the furniture? And yet! If the consciousness of Jesus is difficult of access for us, it is not because it is closed to us or deliberately evades us, but, on the contrary, because it is utterly simple and devoid of any self-centered reflection on itself, any inquisitiveness with regard to itself. Jesus is a particular individual, a Galilean of the first century, and yet he spontaneously identifies himself with the consciousness of every human being. Without ever forcing the issue, without ever inviting people to have extraordinary experiences, without needing to use any language but that of the simple, he makes the Father known to them (Mt 11:25).

The revelation and bestowal of forgiveness was a striking trait of Jesus before Easter, and it was also one reason for his being put to death. It continues to be a basic trait of the risen Lord. For in the preaching of the gospel, no matter how far back we trace it, the call to conversion has always been based on the forgiveness of sins which the risen Jesus brought to us: "The God of our fathers raised Jesus whom you killed. . . . God exalted him at his right hand as Leader and Savior, to give repentance to Israel and forgiveness of sins" (Acts 5:30–31). The experience of forgiveness is one of the points at which the identity of the pre-paschal and post-paschal Jesus shows up clearly. In fact, Jesus rises in order to forgive: he does not reproach his disciples for their past actions, but only for being so slow to believe in his resurrection (Lk 24:25, 45). He reminds Peter of his denial, his triple denial, but only in order three times to bestow on him his mission as shepherd (Jn 21:15–17) and to assure him that he has now become capable of following the Lord (Jn 21:19; cf. 13:36–38) and of glorifying God (cf. 12:33). The resurrection is not the vengeful return of an offended God in order to show his power and claim his rights; on the contrary, it is the supreme proof of his forgiveness. Human beings have put his only Son to death; now he restores this Son to them forever. God's action is the contrary of what Jesus himself told his adversaries in order to frighten them from proceeding to their fatal action: "What will the owner of the vineyard do? He will come and destroy the tenants" (Mk 12:9).

But while the entire preaching of the post-Easter Church is based on the certainty of forgiveness, a forgiveness received by the discouraged disciples but intended even for all those who had been responsible for the death of Jesus, there is no text that shows Jesus actually bestowing and expressing this forgiveness. Any such experience of forgiveness from him goes back to the days before Easter, to the time when he welcomed the tax collectors and the prostitutes. We need the resurrection in order that we may be sure of God's acceptance of the whole human race, but we also need the story told by witnesses of his life, the account of their experiences with him, in order that this acceptance by the risen Lord may truly be for us a living gesture, an encounter with the God who has become for us a real person with a "face" of his own.

Access to the person of Jesus supposes both the revelation of the risen Lord and the contemplation of Jesus, the man of Nazareth and Galilee, Jerusalem and Calvary.

Contemporary Discussion of the Resurrection of Jesus

Giuseppe Ghiberti

The Problem

Without aiming at a complete presentation of the problems treated and the methodology used in studying the claimed resurrection of Jesus, it is possible to identify at least some of its basic aspects.

Some of the questions that spontaneously come to mind when the resurrection is asserted are these: Did the event take place? How did it take place? What did it mean for its subject, Jesus? What did it mean for early Christianity and what does it still mean today? There is here a set of problems that concerns every area of theological reflection and looks for help to many auxiliary disciplines. The problems are a challenge, first of all, to the exegete, then to the systematic theologian, the fundamental theologian, and the theoretician of theology.

Given the wide range of problems, a study that seeks to be of service to fundamental theology must focus chiefly on the following questions: What conditions must be fulfilled if we are to consider it proved (and in what sense can we talk of "proof") that Jesus of Nazareth did in fact rise from the dead and that this fact is the foundation of the Christian faith (in what sense a "foundation," and what kind of "faith")?

The first party to be heard from in this enterprise is certainly the exegete. Yet it is not necessary for us to review his procedures in their entirety. It will be enough, in the main, to take the conclusions he reaches;[1] for the rest, we must check on certain specific passages. The other partner in the dialogue is the contemporary world with its own intellectual approach to reality.

It is perhaps a sign of our times that the dialogue with the exegetes should clearly be given pride of place. Those for whom the biblical message is intended today are, of course, not the exegetes, but our contemporaries. But it is a fact that many of the objections raised in the past to the resurrection of Jesus resulted from a defective approach to the text in which the resurrection was first reported. In every age, and ours is no exception, a proper approach to the Bible and an accurate analysis of its contents is the best preparation for dialogue with the contemporary mind and its demands.

For this reason I shall at every point be paying close attention to the New Testament data, which have always been the source of the claims made by faith. Once the New Testament data have been carefully defined, it will then be profitable to look at the systematic analyses that have been attempted.

Now that the overall perspective has been clarified, I shall, in the light of the questions asked above, outline the course to be followed in this study and indicate the questions I shall be trying to answer.[2]

Two realities, themselves in dialogue with each other, must be kept before us. The first is the New Testament datum: something of the past that continues to speak to the people of our day in their quest. The second is the faith that has been maintained since the beginning: this is still a reality today and is by its nature problematic for human experience. We must analyze the first and face the problems raised by the second.

I. Analysis of the New Testament evidence. When we examine the writings that make up the New Testament, we find an unfolding history of testimonies to the resurrection of Jesus (testimonies that become increasingly specific), as well as a development in the literary genres that report these testimonies. The basic passages can be catalogued in a series of texts and phases. Once the individual testimonies have been examined, it will be necessary to systematize the data that have emerged, and to see their implications. This, then, is the scheme I shall follow:

1. The first need is to list the texts and present them in a cursory manner. The second is to justify the method used in approaching them. Important problems immediately make their presence known; these will be examined in greater detail in the last part.

2. The individual areas of New Testament testimony to the resurrection will be examined by applying the various methodologies in use nowadays. These areas will be presented to some extent in the light of results now regarded as sure, to some extent in the light of problems that are still open. These areas are: testimonies from the preliterary phase; the testimony of Paul, with reference both to the explicit terms he uses and to the overall background of his thinking; the testimonies of the gospels, insofar as they report (in the accounts of Mark, Matthew, Luke, and John) the various experiences of the empty tomb and the appearances, but also insofar as they report what preceded these experiences (individual teachings; overall context of the gospels); the testimonies in the remaining New Testament literature, namely, the Apocalypse and the Catholic Letters.

3. A systematization of the data that have emerged from the analysis of the texts shows above all, that the reports focus primarily on Jesus himself (I. 4. A). This intention is present in the texts. The focus on Jesus finds expression in terms of: regain of life; victory over death; revivification of the dead body (which is missing from the tomb); a new life with more-than-earthly characteristics (account is here taken of the exceptional traits that

marked the existence of Jesus even before his passion); beginning of new relations with his old interlocutors and, from now on, with every human being, in preparation for his return.

The starting point for the proclamation of Jesus's resurrection is the experiences of the various persons who have become witnesses to it (I. 4. B). The gospels describe these experiences in terms of finding the tomb empty of the corpse that had been laid in it and of meeting ("seeing") him whom they recognize as the man who had been crucified and as the one with whom they had been in fellowship and who, while living an authentically corporeal life, is beginning, in these encounters, a new type of relationship with the human world. The gospels also describe the initial frame of mind of the future witnesses as utterly without any expectation of meeting the crucified Jesus again.

The effect of these experiences is a faith that marks subsequent testimony to the resurrection (I. 4. C). This faith is progressively clarified with the help of categories that are applied to the past and to additional new and enlightening experiences. Faith sees in the risen Jesus a new dimension of existence; it also sees him continuing his active presence in the world, in the form of dialogue with and intimate presence to individuals, of guidance, help, and assurance given to the life of the ecclesial community, and of lordship over the history of the race.

II. The difficulties raised by reflection of the datum of faith are of two kinds: those that emerge directly in the process of examining the biblical text, and those that emerge in the course of reflection on the data of the message.

1. The biblical text conveys its message adequately only when we avoid the pitfalls of a faulty methodology that is not in keeping with the nature of the text. The hermeneutical problem must also receive a thorough response, so that we may adequately grasp the relation between representation and intention, between cultural schema (which acts as channel of transmission) and the nucleus of the message. Involved here, among other things, is the problem of the language used in connection with the resurrection. Especially discussed today are the intentions of the New Testament witness in regard to the empty tomb, as well as their understanding of the encounters with the risen Jesus as expressed in terms of "vision." Finally, when the text has been properly interpreted in the light of its history and prehistory within the development of testimonies to the resurrection, we must inquire of it what was the original content of the Christian faith in the resurrection and what are the factors that must be regarded as also foundational for faith today.

2. Specific problems that emerge in the course of reflection on the data of the message are: those having to do with the anthropological categories used in the message: such categories as body, death, and restoration of life; those referring to participation in the life of Christ and, conversely, to the participation of the risen Lord in the life of human beings, within the ongoing history of the human race and the Church.

III. Final synthesis of the New Testament proclamation of the resurrection of Jesus.

1. The recognition of the fact of the resurrection: how the first witnesses came to it, and then the very first generations of Christians.

2. The terms in which the fact itself is stated: the historiographical intention shown by the documents; distinction between affirmation of the occurrence and attempts to reduce it to the categories of natural experience (the limits of historical discourse); various degrees of discernibility of the occurrence (sure, probable, and improbable elements).

3. The treatment of the fact, with attention to the experiences as such, and especially to the dynamics of the appearances and to the order in which the experiences occurred, with particular reference to Jerusalem and Galilee as contexts.

4. Meaning of the fact of the resurrection as a fulfillment of promises, as foundation of christology, and as beginning of a new economy of relations between God and the human race.

Since I have had the opportunity to deal with this subject in a publication devoted to biblical studies,[3] I shall here simply outline the exegetical treatment, thus providing a basis for some concluding remarks that deal with the problems faced in fundamental theology.

I. Analysis of the New Testament Evidence

1. *The Texts*

The passages most generally acknowledged as testimonies to the resurrection of Jesus are the gospel accounts of the Easter experiences (Mk 16; Mt 28; Lk 24; Jn 20–21). Apart from the gospels the text most familiar to us is certainly 1 Corinthians 15. In this first set of texts there is a significant fact: the story does not make frequent use of the vocabulary most appropriate for the resurrection (*anistēmi* and *egeirō:* rise and raise up), which becomes present only at moments of reflection on the facts that have been narrated. There is a spontaneous passage from the facts to thinking and speaking about the resurrection, but the realities experienced are quite different depending on whether it be the tomb of a dead man who is no longer there or encounters with this same dead man who has now returned to life. "Resurrection" becomes the general title given to these stories because it specifies them by indicating from the outset their subject, which is not described but is already known. A typical example is the dialectical movement of the entire fifteenth chapter of 1 Corinthians: from a dominant emphasis on "visual" experiences the writer moves on to a conclusion which has to do with the transformation that has been produced in Christ and a theory on the destiny of the human person.

Next in order of familiarity comes another series of passages which no longer tell a story but rather express faith in the resurrection, usually in short, stereotyped formulas. There are traces of this in the gospels, especially in the predictions of the resurrection (cf. Mk 8:31; 9:31; 10:33–34 par.). Outside, the gospels we find more of the types of formulation known as acclamations, confessions, and hymns.

The subject matter of these is twofold: an affirmation of the fact of the resurrection, and a proclamation of the glorious state in which Christ exists as a result of the resurrection. In the first case (this is especially true of the confessions), the vocabulary is usually that specific to the resurrection (cf. above); these passages account for most of the use of such vocabulary. In the second case (cf. the acclamations and hymns) the language is more varied, inasmuch as the reference is no longer to the victory over death but to the exaltation that followed upon this victory.

It is doubtful whether we can legitimately speak of a third series of passages that deal with the resurrection. This series would be made up of quite varied statements on the dignity of Christ that are connected not with his preexistence but with his earthly life.[4] For the most part there lies behind them a reference to the resurrection, but the reference is not very proximate. This is the point at which discourse on the resurrection expands into discourse on christology; it is not surprising, therefore, that many critics do not regard these as passages on the resurrection.[5]

I have pointed out a movement from language dealing specifically with resurrection to language based primarily on other categories. Though examination might yield a different result, it seems that reference to the fact of Jesus' passage from a state of death to one of new life is expressed for the most part in the first vocabulary (that of resurrection), while the second type of vocabulary is used for the situation in which Jesus finds himself as a result of the resurrection.

Up to this point, the norm I have used for distinguishing among the testimonies to the resurrection has been an empirical one: their familiarity. Meanwhile, however, a classification based on literary genre has spontaneously made its appearance, as has reflection on the language used in these various testimonies; but every consideration based on the date of their origin has been excluded. As matter of fact, the attempt to determine the historical sequence of the testimonies is significantly more problematical. True enough, by taking as the point of reference the New Testament authors and the date at which their works were composed it is possible to distinguish between prepauline, pauline, and gospel testimonies. But the problem of the redaction of not a few letters in the Pauline corpus and of the "Catholic" letters is still an open one, as is the more radical problem of the origin of the traditions reported in the gospels, which are relatively late.

2. *Method for Dealing with the Texts*

In recent years biblical exegetes have reflected a great deal on the laws and rules governing their discipline. It was necessary for them to take their bearings at the end of a lengthy period of analytical research that had lasted from the last century up to the First World War and had already been given a new shape to some extent by the shattering effect of form criticism. The exegetes also had to give answer to those who were bemoaning what they saw as a climate of lassitude and inability to say anything new. Stimuli and suggestions during the post-Second World War period have come especially from redaction criticism, the "new hermeneutics," and structuralism.

It is fitting that in the service it should render to fundamental theology exegetes should use, above all, the critical historical method. The first key to an understanding of the real intention of a text is the determination of the process by which the text was formed. When this operation has been accomplished, all that the text has to say will certainly not have been discovered, but at least the circumstances in which it originated will have been reconstructed.

As a matter of fact, this method has been used in the studies that have appeared during the last thirty years. On the other hand, studies that follow the method of structural analysis are, for the moment, still very rare. And of those that have appeared none are comprehensive in character.[6]

By and large, however, Yves Congar's words are still completely relevant:

> The time is past when it could be thought that a grasp of the meaning and significance of a biblical text required only a good knowledge of the ancient languages and of the biblical world. This may indeed have been enough at one time. But the problems being raised today call in addition for a full philosophical or philosophico-theological reflection on the nature of witness, on the relationship between fact and meaning. . . .[7]

His observation that "we have hardly begun this work" is perhaps still true fifteen years later and warns us not to accept as sufficient even the most complete technical methods of exegetical study.

3. The Areas of New Testament Testimony

(A) Preliterary Testimony

An analysis of the New Testament enables us to identify with a high degree of probability literary units that originated in a time preceding the formation of the written document. Of special interest for us here are the confessions of faith (cf. Rom 10:9; 1 Thess 4:14; 1 Cor 15:3–5), acclamations (cf. Rom 10:9 again; also 1 Cor 12:3 and 16:22), and hymns (cf. Phil 2:6–11; 1 Tim 3:16b; 1 Pet 3:18–19).

In many instances these venerable remnants of very early Christian thought and life had the liturgical assembly for birthplace and vital environment. Worship dictated the concerns, selected the themes, and conditioned the forms that we see in these units. What these passages show us is that the earliest Christian liturgy concentrated with deep feeling in the mystery of Jesus' victory over death.

Basic elements of these texts are the conviction of the fact of the resurrection, the new description of God (he who raised Jesus from death), and the new description of Christ (the risen Lord who lives now in the glory of the Father).

In these testimonies we see no concern to demonstrate the fact. The one exception is 1 Corinthians 15:3–7, in which the list of eyewitnesses of the appearances is also to be regarded as prepauline. I shall be speaking frequently of this passage later on. But the absence of any mention of concern with proof does not mean that the concern itself was absent (there may be supplementary signs of it), still less that the testimonies of such witnesses were assigned only a secondary value. The first points of reference are memories passed on (it seems) without any need of combating particular doubts (see 1 Cor 15, for example), but conclusions may be drawn about the framework of faith in which the transmitted, believed, and proclaimed fact is located. A picture is given of God as Father of the risen Jesus, and of Jesus himself as in dialogue with the Father who rescues him from death and raises him to glory, thus fulfilling the most profound longing of human beings, who see in this intervention by God the ultimate and truly fundamental substance of salvation.

The set of "missionary sermons" in the Acts of the Apostles (2:14–36; 3:12–26; 4:8–12; 5:29–32; 10:34–43; 13:16–41) calls for a rather different treatment. Their content is not limited to the final events in the life of Jesus but includes, in varying degrees, the chief moments of his public life and brief references to the condition of Jesus after death. As far as their literary genre is concerned, these passages are proclamation or kerygma.

These passages are of interest because on the one hand they repeat the themes (usually with additions) of the lengthier confessions (e.g., 1 Cor 15:3–7) and because on the other the scheme they follow is in basic accord with the structure of the Synoptic gospels. The difficulty with these passages is due to the obvious mingling of traditional and redactional elements in the sermons as they now stand. Since no agreement has been reached on how to determine what belongs to Luke in these texts and what Luke took from older traditions, judgment on the preliterary stage of these witnesses to apostolic preaching is rather uncertain. Yet the essential themes behind the structure and formulation under discussion are certainly older than the written document.[8] The end result is preaching that has as its focus a presentation of the decisive moment of Jesus' earthly life: the resurrection means leaving death behind and entering into eschatological life; it is God's definitive seal upon the legitimacy of Jesus' mission; it explains clearly all of Jesus' behavior during his lifetime; it inaugurates a new condition that is rich in consequences not only for Jesus himself but for other human beings as well; and it is the basis for his role as eschatological judge.

The schemata here are very rich and clearly based on historical experience; there is little concern for the apologetic aspect (it could be said that acceptance of the statements is not too problematic), and there is an extensive openness to theological interpretation. With due allowance being made for Lukan additions, these testimonies to the earliest presentation of the resurrection are also the richest. This fact is explicable in the light of the literary genre: not summary formulas serving as mnemonic devices, but schemata for teaching that can be adequately developed.

(B) Pauline Testimonies

It is widely held that the resurrection of Jesus has a central place in the proclamation and theology of Paul; and this opinion is well founded. Yet we should not be surprised that in its discussion fundamental theology does not turn chiefly to the Pauline literature.

The most important text is in 1 Corinthians 15, a chapter which presents a very wide range of material: there is a statement of the earliest tradition (vv. 3–7), a testimony to Paul's personal experience (vv. 8–11), and a series of reflections, marked by a lively dialectical movement and rhetorical skill, on the reasons for affirming the resurrection of Jesus in connection with the resurrection of the dead (vv. 12–34). The modalities of this connection—which itself is supported by motives drawn from our solidarity with him who is present among us as the second Adam and "a life-giving spirit" (v. 45)—are explained in the second part of this chapter, which is richer in original teaching (vv. 35–58).

Verse 14, the one perhaps most cited in attempts to sum up Paul's thinking, is a trenchant statement: "If Christ has not been raised, then our preaching is in vain and your faith is in vain." And yet undue stress should not be laid on this verse, since, as the entire Pauline corpus shows, the apostle did not feel any need of involving himself in a defense of this fundamental tenet. Only at the beginning of this chapter does he offer facts in support of it, and even here we do not get the impression that he is facing any sharp challenges. We need only compare this passage with the way he handles himself in other circumstances and in dealing with other problems, even in non-polemical writings, for example, in Romans. This lack of challenge is all the more surprising since the difficulties he had to face for a long period of years really turn on the consequences of the fact of the resurrection, for example, its saving efficacy and the demands of a consistent faith. Paul bases the novelty of his preaching on the newness effected in Christ by the resurrection, but the aspect of it that is challenged is Paul's attitude of freedom and independence with regard to the Mosaic Law and its "works." We might expect opposition to be focused more directly on the claim that governs his entire system.

His writings contain other surprises. Unlike any other New Testament writer he appeals to his own personal experience of encounter with the risen Jesus (cf. 1 Cor 9:1; Gal 1:15–17; 1 Cor 15:8). The purpose of these appeals is not to confirm the fact of the resurrection but rather to justify his claim to be a witness of the risen Lord and so to have apostolic authority.

It strikes us as strange that this experience, which plays so decisive a role in Paul's life, is not seen as the beginning of a special relation between Paul and the mystery of the resurrection. The specific vocabulary of resurrection (*egeirō,* almost exclusively) occurs with only average frequency (apart from 1 Cor 15) and then usually in formulas that are either archaic or else based on stereotyped models.[9] Beyond a doubt, Paul's emotional participation in the mystery of the suffering Jesus is far more intense than his participation in the mystery of the resurrection.

Paul certainly makes other references to the resurrection, but these are part of his christological teaching and thus not of primary concern for fundamental theology.

These various observations lead us to conclude that the circles which Paul addressed were not primarily faced with a challenge to the claim of Jesus's resurrection. This does not mean that at this period (50–65 A.D.) so basic an element in the preaching of Christianity went in fact unchallenged; it means only that the circles in which Paul moved paid no special attention to the challenge. In fact, what Paul is faced with in 1 Corinthians 15 is not a denial of the resurrection of Christ but of resurrection generally. It might be said that the pagan world was ready to accept miracles as marvelous and extraordinary happenings, but not resurrection as the common human destiny; in this unwillingness they apparently did not realize the connection between the two aspects (Christ's resurrection and resurrection generally). His Hebrew hearers and readers, on the other hand, seem not to have been disturbed by discourse on the possibility of a human person being restored to life or to have raised any objection to the resurrection of Jesus—perhaps because their roots were not in the sector of Judaism that experienced the struggle to get rid of the preacher from Nazareth.

A panoramic view of the Pauline writings shows no special apologetic preoccupation in the presentation of the resurrection of Jesus. However, on the relatively few occasions when the question came up, Paul did have to come to grips with the problem of the risen body and with the law of conformity to Christ in all aspects of his life and destiny. These are themes to which I shall return later.

(C) *Gospel Testimonies*

a. *The Easter Experiences*

These testimonies are the richest as far as the source of our contact with the resurrection event is concerned. In them a piece of news has been turned into a story.

In the final chapter of each Synoptic gospel and in the last two chapters of John a number of concerns are brought together and given expression in a schema that is henceforth standard; it is not found elsewhere in the New Testament but is a set form in the gospels.

The story of those facts about the earthly life of Jesus that faith regards as important ends with the recollection of the surprise of certain women visitors (and, secondarily, some men visitors) to the tomb of Jesus: they found it empty, but then received indications that this fact was due solely to the resurrection of Jesus. Another series of memories is of meetings with the risen Jesus; among these, the meetings of the privileged group among the disciples were especially important.

Only John 21 departs from this scheme, devoting its attention wholly to the account of a single appearance. Outside of the gospels the schema does not occur, because the experiences at the tomb are not mentioned elsewhere, while the appearances are not narrated but only stated (there is a partial exception in Acts 10:41: ". . . to us who were chosen by God as witnesses, who ate and drank with him after he rose from the dead").

The isolated character of the gospel traditions causes certain difficulties. There seems to be a discrepancy between the detailed recollections in the gospel traditions and the sharply reduced indications found in the other sources. It must be acknowledged that (to judge by the documents) there were initially just statements of the fact of the resurrection and that only later on were traditions collected which reflected the response to the fact. This means that the theology connected with these recollections likewise came later as did the interest in other problems, for example, the theology of the bodily nature of the risen Jesus and various concerns of an apologetic nature and polemical origin.

(A) When we turn to the *empty tomb,* we may sum up the experience of it in a sentence that is Luke's redactional work: "Moreover, some women of our company amazed us. They were at the tomb early in the morning and did not find his body; and they came back saying that they had even seen a vision of angels, who said that he was alive" (Lk 24:22–23). This is the summary which two disciples give to Jesus as he accompanies them in the guise of a stranger on the road to Emmaus (their report continues in v. 24 with a reference to the trip of some disciples to the tomb). It contains the basic elements of the tradition. It represents primarily an experience of some women (Mark and Matthew do not seem to know that some disciples were also involved) on the occasion of a visit they made to the tomb (with the pious intention of paying respect to the corpse which was all that was left of their beloved Rabbi). The surprising and unexpected thing is that the tomb is found open and the body missing. The function of the angels present is to give an authoritative and unequivocal interpretation of the absence of the body. The references to Jesus being alive are exclusive to Luke (24:5, 23), but they translate in an accurate and practical way the statement of the resurrection that is contained in the kerygmatic formulas (Lk 24:6–7, 26, 46; but cf. also Mk 16:6 and Mt 28:6). The episode ends with the women reporting back to the disciples the experience they had had. Mark 16:8 suggests that this message was not in fact delivered by the women, but there are also hints (cf. 16:7) that Mark knows the common tradition.

The tradition is sufficiently well defined in the gospel accounts. There is discussion of the Johannine variants (cf. Jn 20:1–18). Did John rework an older version that came to him in a form similar to that found in Mark? Or did he incorporate into his account varying repetitions of the same fact, with these repetitions reflecting stages in the development of the tradition?[10] If the last-named hypothesis could be defended, it would be very important for fundamental theology because it would show that the only concern of the earliest stage was to show that the tomb was really empty (cf. Jn 20:1–2). It would be easier to understand the shift in the angelic intervention from the field of factuality to that of theological motif. It is in fact possible that the discovery of the empty tomb caused not only joy but also apprehension and then gave rise to a strongly polemical atmosphere.

In discussion of the particulars within this manifold tradition it is not legitimate to place on the same level the appearance of the angels and the absence of the corpse of Jesus, for the latter certainly is originally intended in the account. The hypothesis that the report was unreliable requires that the gospel critic explain this tradition as a dramatization of a theological theme that had no basis in reality. Despite comparable situations in other New Testament books, this explanation must be regarded as unfounded. Silence regarding the fact is not necessarily due to ignorance of it, since in Acts the author certainly knew the fact and yet did not think he had to make explicit mention of it.

(B) The *appearances* of the risen Jesus are less susceptible of reduction to a fixed schema; on the other hand, the event as such of these appearances is attested to a significantly greater degree than the empty tomb. I shall leave aside the appearances to "private" individuals (the women, Mary Magdalene, the disciples at Emmaus) as well as the appearance, attested but not narrated, to Peter, and I shall consider only the appearances to the whole group of disciples. I shall also leave aside the attestation in the late ending of Mark (16:9–20), since the traditions behind it are mixed and difficult to untangle.

For the appearances there is no longer a single time and place. From Resurrection Sunday itself (Lk 24; Jn 20:19–23) we pass to some undefined date (Mt 28 and Jn 21, although the final redaction of Jn 21 seems to suggest that more than a week has passed), to "eight days later" (Jn 20:26–29) and finally to the entire period of "forty days" (Acts 1:3). We move from the Galilee of Matthew (but presupposed also by Mark; cf. 16:7) to the exclusively Jerusalemite setting of the stories of Luke and John 20 (recall also the appearances near the tomb). John 21 tells of a meeting in Galilee, but it is not clear whether he intends to salvage a Galilean tradition as a counterbalance to the preference previously shown to the Jerusalem setting.

The major appearances show a certain similarity due to the repetitions of certain motifs, such as the self-manifestation of Jesus in order to overcome the persistent doubts of those he encounters, or the authoritative commissions which the risen Jesus gives to his disciples and which are foundational for the future, or the promise of an assistance which originates in the divine world but is also explicitly connected with Jesus, who is now active in that world.[11]

These stories are not consistent and uniform from the formal standpoint;[12] this becomes evident especially when they are compared with the appearances to "private" persons, but a great deal of variety can also be seen in the last stories that bring the Easter narratives to an end. The relation between tradition and redaction in the formation of the scenes as we now have them is rather difficult to establish.

At the same time, however, it is not thinkable that the element of tradition should be limited to the simple theme of "appearance" and that everything else should owe its existence to the theological intentions of the various authors. Admittedly, even important details such as the place that provides the scene for the encounter with the risen Jesus are at times a concern of the evangelist. Nonetheless, it seems impossible to remove from the tradition the reference to the appearances having taken place in either Jerusalem or Galilee. Other details, including the times of the appearances, are more difficult to pin down.[13]

It is, however, clear, and important, that apart from circumstantial particulars reports have been transmitted in a free manner which provide us with valuable information. This is true above all of the attitude of the human beings who encounter Jesus.

It is an inescapable conclusion that the insurmountable difficulty of describing the experience of a completely new kind of encounter (I shall be returning to this point) may well have been partially resolved by an interpretation which at an early date focused attention on certain motifs that were destined to become traditional. In such an extraordinary case we cannot be surprised at the variety of depictions; on the other hand, every constant is extremely important.

b. *Before the Easter Experiences*

The final testimonies of which I have been speaking come at the end of the gospels. It may be assumed that what preceded had as one of its functions to prepare the reader to understand these final mysterious pages. But this argument must be balanced by another consideration: that which the gospels tell us of the earthly experience of Jesus has already been interpreted in light of the knowledge that this Jesus was to rise again after dying. Such are the reasons which justify, and at the same time account for the reservations regarding, an appeal to the gospel stories of Jesus' life prior to his suffering and death.

Jesus explicitly predicts the main lines of the way his life would end; he does so on three occasions which the Synoptic gospels report in a threefold tradition, using on each occasion a formulation that is substantially the same. These predictions are missing from John. John does, however, show familiarity with the basic elements of those predictions: Jesus is aware of the murderous intention of his enemies, and he foresees that he will be "lifted up" from the earth. The glorification of which he speaks in these contexts (and in many other circumstances as well) is best explained by accepting his consciousness of his coming resurrection.

The case of John introduces us to a second class of texts that is much less limited. The gospels show us Jesus speaking in a way that betrays so full a grasp of his own mystery that it must include a knowledge of his victory over death and of his divine dignity.

The interest of this behavior is matched by the difficulty of giving a precise interpretation of it in terms of our experience. It must be acknowledged that the evangelists have reformulated many of the remembered words and sayings of Jesus, as they fitted them, for example, into kerygmatic schemata. Therefore a literal interpretation of these items of information can be misleading. It is certain on the other hand that Jesus had an extraordinary kind of knowledge of his future destiny.[14] Therefore an interpretation of these notices as pure inventions of the early community is no less misleading. Both extremes are to be avoided.

It is perhaps not absolutely necessary to define the degree and manner of Jesus' knowledge of his coming resurrection. It is important, however, to determine how much the disciples grasped of what he said. The gospels agree in constantly pointing out how very little the disciples understood of the interior drama of Jesus' life and of the hints he gave of it. Their expectations created a world that was focused on quite different values. Many aspects of the inner life of Jesus remained incomprehensible to them, and many of his cautions were ignored. It seems that the gospels would have us conclude that Jesus was in great measure isolated as he underwent his final experiences and that when the end came the disciples were unprepared and did not understand.

A more radical question has to do with the nature and content of the cultural categories which Jesus and his disciples used in regard to survival generally and to the destiny of the Messiah in particular. Only a thorough discussion of Hebrew anthropology and of Old Testament messianism could lead to answers here. We shall be concerned with these matters to some extent when the problem comes to the fore later on.

(D) *The Remaining New Testament Literature*

The material provided by the Apocalypse and the Catholic Letters is not unimportant, but neither is it sufficiently original, on the points that concern us here, to call for extended attention. It is my opinion that the Catholic Letters were not written at a very early date. There is therefore nothing new to be found in the indications they give which confirm the presence of a fixed and unchallenged faith in the resurrection of Jesus. On the other hand, I must point out the extent to which the specific vocabulary of the resurrection is missing from this literature (cf. 1 Pet 1:3; 3:21). It will therefore be in typically doctrinal contexts (christological and soteriological discourse; parenetic instruction in preparation for the parousia) that the categories of faith in the resurrection come to the fore.

The Apocalypse calls for somewhat more detailed discussion. The terminology of resurrection has given way to a vocabulary dealing with life. The presence of Jesus in history and in the Church is due to the fact that though he certainly died, he also returned to life and now is eternally alive (cf. Rev 1:18–19; 2:8). These expressions convey the fact of the resurrection, faith in it (a completely unchallenged faith), and at the same time an interpretation of the fact: "The resurrection is, as it were, a fruit of the divine eternity. Jesus rose because of the life-giving powers which he possessed and still possesses by reason of his divinity."[15] As lord of life and death, Jesus also has the power to judge, a power he acquired through his resurrection.

Many elements in this thinking are a heritage from very early times; others are formulated in the light of Johannine theology, to which the final amalgam is due. But the discourse moves in the world of New Testament christology rather than that of fundamental theology.

4. Systematization of the Data That Have Merged

(A) The Primary Intention: Proclamation

Like the whole of the New Testament literature of which they are a part, the texts with which I have been thus far concerned are proclamatory. Their primary subject is the newness that has come in Jesus and around him as a result of his resurrection.

We have seen the resurrection asserted in various ways: as center and content of a faith not further determined; as consequence of unanticipated experiences related to the death of Jesus; as revelation that explains other aspects of salvation.

The event, unlike the death on the cross, is not directly described. We can think of it as located in time and space, but the total silence that surrounds the event in itself makes us believe not only that it was not experienced by any witness but that it was beyond the range of possibility for human experience.

Instead, the results of the event are related: some are seen in the Easter experiences, others are understood as the result of reflection on the experiences themselves.

The atmosphere in which the fact is proclaimed is largely one of surprise and a sense of newness. The surprise is certainly due in part to the lack of preparation on the part of the witnesses, but it is due above all to the radically new reality with which they come in contact. The witnesses try to force it into the categories of the extraordinary as allowed by the mind of the time, but these prove inadequate: the risen Jesus is not the ghost of a dead man who thus establishes contact with the living; nor is he a dead man who returns to life and at the same time to the relations he once had with those around him. Read Luke 24:39 and John 20:17, and note, in general, the kind of stupefaction that is the source of an indecisiveness which does not disappear even in moments of great joy (as in Lk 24:41; Jn 21:12; Lk 28:17). The newness is concentrated above all in Jesus himself. A vital process that came to a definitive end in death is seen to be active once again in this man who is recognizable as the one who had been crucified.

But the newness is inherent in the very life that is renewed: he who deliberately submits to a testing (cf. Luke and John) in order to show that the disciples' interlocutor in this unanticipated encounter is the very same person with whom they had lived familiarly of old, has in his victory over death extended the range and dimensions of the life he now lives.

He has not changed the basic modalities of this life: they are still those of human life. This accounts for the insistence that the absence of the corpse from the tomb is to be understood as an effect of the resurrection. There is perhaps an apologetic intention in the stress laid on this part of the gospel message, but even more probably there is a concern to bring out the fact that the bodily life of the risen Lord who will soon be encountered is not alien or less real by comparison with the Jesus whom the disciples had followed as their teacher along the roads of Palestine.

This life, then, which has overcome death and is no longer subject to it, is connected with the pre-Easter life of Jesus by unbroken relationships and a continuous personal identity; on this point there need be no doubts or misunderstandings. In one respect, however, the new life differs from earthly human life: it leads no longer to the abyss of death but to a state of glory in an eternal closeness to the Father. This is brought home by the statements celebrating the triumph of the risen Lord who is now enthroned at the right hand of the Father, where he exercises the powers and prerogatives belonging to him.[16]

The same point is also made by details in the descriptions of the appearances: not only the apocalyptic-style appearances of, e.g., Matthew 28:16–20, but also those in Luke and John which show that Jesus now transcends certain limitations of the bodily condition. In the pre-Easter stage of his life Jesus had already shown himself in possession of a sovereign power over the physical world, a power which at times extended to his own body; thus the evangelists had told of an incident in which Jesus walked on the waters of the sea (Mk 6:45–52; Mt 14:22–23; Jn 6:16–21). But the episode is difficult to interpret and, in any case, the condition it reflects was not habitual, whereas the exceptional state of Jesus after the resurrection is his regular state. The risen Jesus shows that he can enter into contact with the earthly order, but at the same time he shows that he does not belong to that order in the proper sense.

Such is the mystery that emerges from the message. The New Testament does not "solve" it; it simply supplies the evidence showing how the non-earthly character of Jesus' new life does not mean a break in his relations with the earthly world, but only gives those relations a new aspect.

The fact that the appearances of Jesus in the gospel always have a quality of the unexpected has accustomed us to focus our attention on the surprise felt by the disciples. But we should not lose sight of the fact that the appearances also assure them that he is always close at hand—though they may not realize it—in the everyday situations in which there is no sign of this presence. He is certainly present, and in a genuinely human way, as he was to the disciples on the road to Emmaus.

The other New Testament writings use a different language than the gospels, and their treatment is more thematic. The Pauline writings speak of a bond of solidarity between Christ, the new Adam, and the human race. In 1 Corinthians 15 the emphasis is chiefly on solidarity in resurrection, with Christ, the first-born, sharing his resurrection with other human beings at the moment when history reaches its end and goal. The same solidarity in resurrection is applied in Romans 6 to the liberation from sin which the baptismal rite confers on those who become alive in Christ (cf. vv. 3–11).

The efficacious intervention of Christ in behalf of the human race is also called by the more familiar name of "salvation." This can be already seen in the archaic formula in 1 Corinthians 15:3 where the destruction of sin is linked with the death of Christ, but in close connection with the resurrection. Romans 4:25 then provides confirmation of this connection ("who was put to death for our trespasses and raised for our justification"). Just as the condition of resurrection and our need of justification are ongoing, so too is the activity of the risen Lord in bringing the gift of justification to every individual.

This whole teaching is not contradicted by the thinking that lies behind the Lukan account of the ascension (Lk 24:50–51; Acts 1:9–11). This is the only time that the New Testament speaks of a real ascension. Elsewhere we find only the formula of exaltation or glorification, as expression of a cosmic christology; there is no description of a visible event. But even in Luke the "taking" of Jesus to heaven does not mean that the risen Lord no longer comes in contact with those "here below"; it is meant only to bring home the fact that the time of earthly familiarity with him has come to an end (this applies even to the intermediate phase of the Easter appearances) and that the Church now begins the period when it lives in expectation of his return.[17] In Luke's view the sending of the Spirit will be the pledge of the Lord's presence to the Church.

The changed life of Jesus and his liberation from the earthly order do not create a gulf between his present condition and the condition of human beings who are still within history. In addition to the dialogue between the absent-present Jesus and every individual, and in addition to the presence to the Church of him who promised to be "with you" (Mt 29:20), Christ carries on a dialogue with history as he guides it to an expectation of and preparation for his return. The Easter stories and the gospels as a whole end with this perspective of the end of time and the return of Christ. This is also the perspective of the kerygma, insofar as we can reconstruct this on the basis of, for example, Acts 3:19–21; 10:42; 17:30–31 (cf. also 1 Thess 1:10). The emphasis of the return of Christ as judge is also a christological and parenetic theme: it shows the risen Jesus as invested with sovereign power and exercising the most jealously reserved divine prerogative, and it warns believers and the entire world to be subject to his lordship, lest his return bring condemnation.

The set of themes that come together in the message conveyed by the texts on the resurrection may seem inherently heterogeneous. But in fact there is an element common to all of them: the conviction that the Father's intervention in freeing Jesus of Nazareth from death wrought a profound renewing change in him and set a seal on the work he had done by his coming into the world and that this same renewal has touched everything that exists—both man and the rest of creation—establishing a new covenant and inaugurating a new creation.[18]

The primary intention of giving expression to a faith is utterly clear; far less emphatic is the intention of justifying or defending this faith. The starting point for the message is twofold: a matter of fact, namely the authenticated return among the living of the Jesus who had been crucified; and an experiential situation, namely the inability of human beings successfully to escape the power of death and to free themselves from the condemnation laid on sin and from their own radical weakness and isolation. The resurrection of Jesus shows that in him the victory over death has been won; it also offers human beings the gift of liberation from sin, doing away with their isolation by restoring them to communion with the divine world and giving them the pledge of their own victory over death.

But even though the intention of combating tendentious interpretations of the Easter experiences is not primary, it does begin to be present, in varying degrees and on various occasions, in almost all of the gospel accounts. The centuries directly following upon the one that saw the compiling of the New Testament have left us documentation showing that polemics on these points continued, not however within Christianity but rather in dealing with Jewish and pagan adversaries.[19]

(B) *The Experiences of the Witnesses*

The New Testament texts dealing with the human beings who had the Easter experiences are to be found in the gospels, in 1 Corinthians 15:5–8, and in the kerygmatic discourses of Acts (2:32; 3:15; 4:20; 10:41; 13:41). Real accounts are to be found, however, only in the gospels, while 1 Corinthians offers a bare list of names, even if one that is especially detailed and divided. Acts repeats only the Lukan motif of "eating and drinking" with the risen Jesus and for the rest emphasizes the duty the disciples have of telling what they had seen and heard (4:20). But in the dialectical movement of the discourses the service rendered by the witnesses is important in supporting what is said and in moving the hearers to acceptance of the message.

Some women are certainly among those who experience the *tomb*. The memory of a visit paid to the tomb by one or more disciples also rests on a tradition, though one that is less well attested than that concerning the women. If it be maintained that the disciples in John 20:3–10 are the result of a Johannine accommodation to a tradition like the one in Luke 24:12 which names only Peter (but then Lk 24:24 would require explanation), this tradition might be regarded as the equivalent (though differently developed) to that of the appearance to Peter. Many hypotheses, none of them certain!

Less problematic is the tradition regarding the women, who as witnesses are not as important (or as reliable, from the juridical viewpoint) as the chief disciples and who are therefore less likely to have been invented. I have already spoken of the elements in the witnesses' experiences and of the divergent interpretations of them. The point of departure is an observation that becomes the occasion for a kerygmatic intervention in which, it seems, a (weak) apologetic concern is not lacking and which excludes other interpretations of the absence of the corpse.

The commission to bring the news to the disciples is a mixed motif: its purpose is to link the theme of the discovery of the empty tomb to that of the appearances and, at the same time, to introduce the predictions of Jesus into the Easter experiences. The theme is probably parenetic as well. Here for the first time we have the demand that anyone who has come in contact with the risen Jesus should exert himself to share the experience with others (theme of responsibility for the message). But in this instance the "others" are the disciples; that is, those envisaged in the commission to the women are the authorities for whom is reserved the decisive experience that will be foundational for the future existence of believers.

There is thus a mass of theological themes which already betray a good degree of elaboration and are not of very direct interest to fundamental theology.

In the *encounters with the risen Jesus* the points regularly made regarding the earthly participants underscore the inadequacy of their response to the appearance of Jesus: surprise, fear, doubt, and disbelief. It can be debated whether all this represents a single theme, various aspects of which are given concrete expression, or whether there is rather the theme of the sense of human inadequacy (and fear) when faced with the manifestation of the divine, to which theme is then added the theme of the difficulty of giving a faith response to the supreme moment in the revelation of salvation, that is, the moment when Jesus offers himself for acceptance in his presence as the risen Lord.[20]

Common to all the accounts is the theme of the difficulty human beings have in registering or understanding the resurrection, as well as the theme of the difficulty met in coming into contact with the risen Jesus. It also seems to be the common persuasion that the meeting with the risen Jesus can take place only in a climate of faith, as though it were a question of a new type of perception. Thus the problem arises of the relation between this faith and the apprehension of the resurrection.

As described in the gospels, the appearances always have an element of sense experience. However the nature of this be explained, it gives rise to an interpersonal relationship. It is difficult to pin down the precise connection between these two. We may note only that no appearance ends with a refusal of faith, no matter what difficulties may have been encountered initially. This is the first time in the gospels that an initiative which God takes in Christ meets only with success. But we should also note that no appearance is offered to enemies of Jesus or even to nonbelievers and the indifferent.

Each of these points is important, and all of them together combine to show the most important point of all: the necessity of faith. The element of sense experience links the appearances to the order of this world and brings out the genuinely corporeal nature of the risen Jesus. Faith is a condition for grasping the nature and meaning of the resurrection. But faith is also a fruit or result. The Easter stories have as one of their concerns to present future readers with a gallery of models for the ways of reaching faith in the risen Jesus.[21] But those to whom Jesus makes his major appearances are not simply models; they also play a constitutive role in the dynamics leading future believers to the faith.

In the course of the appearances these favored disciples receive a commission to teach (Matthew and the ending of Mark), bear witness (Luke), and continue the mission of Jesus for the same goals, in the same ways, and with the help of the same powers (Matthew and John[21a]), to such an extent that the acceptance of their mission becomes an integral part of the acceptance of Jesus himself. Their testimony thus becomes capable of grounding the faith of those who have not seen the risen Lord, and of making the latter responsible for accepting or refusing this faith.

This very important task is entrusted to the Twelve, and it is under their authority that the task is carried out in the Church. This perhaps explains, at least in part, why the only witnesses of the return of Jesus to life in his resurrection are those who have already lived with him and believe in him and, in particular, why the witness to the final appearance is the specially appointed group of apostles.

Along with this projected vision of the future the gospels show another, rather realistic vision of the present condition of the witnesses to the Easter experiences. Their situation at the beginning is marked by a lack of preparation for the great new event. This can be seen from their inadequate reaction not only to the discovery of the empty tomb but even more to the presence of Jesus. It makes sense, of course, to seek out the conceptions present at the end of the Old Testament period and in the New Testament world that might have promoted the formation of the categories of the Easter faith, but we must not forget that the gospel testimonies show the first people to encounter the risen Jesus as far from envisaging even the possibility of the realities with which they were now coming in contact. They have made their own the most widespread and triumphalistic form of messianic expectation, one that is a self-centered interpretation of royal messianism (cf. also Acts 1:6).[22] This prevents them from understanding the deeper meaning of many of Jesus' actions, and does not dispose them, after his death, to make any effort to sublimate his failure, so far removed are their presuppositions from any possible adjustment to the reality they are now experiencing.

The new order that begins with the resurrection of Jesus is suddenly so radically different from what they had expected and longed for, that we can imagine how forceful and overwhelming the entry of the risen Jesus into their lives must have been.

(C) *Faith as Fruit of the Encounter with the Risen Christ*

The message conveyed by the testimonies to the resurrection of Jesus has experience for its starting point, gives expression to a belief, and is also intended to elicit a commitment of faith. The experience of Jesus as risen is validated at the moment when faith intervenes, but it is communicated when this faith finds expression. But to find expression it must be formulated.

We have already seen the wide range of expressions the New Testament has for the proclamation of the victorious renewal of life in Christ. But these very expressions already represent the end result of a process. What course did this process of formulation take? I shall put off to a later point the elements involved in this problem; for the moment I wish only to identify the initial data that emerge from the text.

It is perhaps not useless here to make the obvious distinction between the coming into existence of faith and the working out of its formulations. I shall not touch on the problem of how necessary it may be for a movement of faith to be formulated somehow from the very beginning, even if only in the most rudimentary interior language of individual consciousness. I regard it as beyond question, however, that there is a distance to be traveled between the intuition at work in faith's initial surrender and its expression in a complete formulation. The entire New Testament discourse on the resurrection corresponds to the phase in which a summary is being made of a more or less extensive process of formulation that has already produced its results. It is understandable that the intermediate steps should be of great interest to anyone who is endeavoring to recapture the pregnant experience of the first hour.

The gospel descriptions do not connect the Easter faith with the experience of the empty tomb. (The only exception to this generalization is the case of the beloved disciple [Jn 20:8] who travels a unique road of his own in his vital relationship with Jesus.) Faith occurs when Jesus puts himself in contact with the witnesses.

As a matter of fact, according to the mind of the gospels a foundation has been laid, well before the experience of the empty tomb, for acceptance of the resurrection: namely, the words of Jesus himself and especially the scriptures (John in particular emphasizes this; cf. 20:9). We do not know the extent to which this recollection may have served in the later process of formulation, which attributes so much importance to scripture. There is an echo of it in the well-known phrase that is repeated in 1 Corinthians 15:3 and 4: "according to the scriptures." But the difficulty immediately arises of determining which scriptures are meant and by what title the scriptures are a basis for faith in the risen Jesus. Our later reflections will be concerned with this problem, in several stages.[23]

Meanwhile, however, it was not the scriptures nor even the experience of the empty tomb that led to faith, but the encounter with Jesus himself. We have already seen some particulars on this point. Let us move on now, realizing that any analysis must be profoundly inadequate.

When Jesus takes the initiative, he is met initially, according to the accounts, by a negative response, chiefly interior, on the part of those to whom he appears. The situation is resolved by the recognition of Jesus. The determining factor here is doubtless the disciples' direct perception of Jesus, but

Luke and especially John point out how Jesus presents himself in a context of special reference to the personal relations linking him with his friends. We receive the impression that acceptance of the risen Lord comes at a moment in which this close communion with this disciples is being renewed. This may be a reason why only the friends of Jesus had the Easter experiences. It is a question whether an equally striking, or even more striking experience would have given rise to faith in someone who was indifferent or hostile. The same question can be asked with regard to our own journey of faith: what effectiveness can even the most forceful and persuasive signs have if there is not a favorable frame of mind (and what must the character of such openness be)?

The experience of recognition is described as a gradual process. Is this due solely to the impossibility of giving a single description of a personal experience which is so new, individual and unrepeatable? Or is it due also to a desire to show that not even encounter with and recognition of the risen Jesus immediately overcomes all resistance or suddenly eliminates every human weakness? In any case, the accounts of the major appearances seem to suppose that at the end submission and openness to the demands of the risen Jesus are complete.

Nonetheless, the faith of the first witnesses needed to grow still more. John felt no difficulty about adding Chapter 21 after the conclusion contained in Chapter 20. The fact that the disciples had been confirmed by an appearance which is narrated twice and that they had already begun to carry out the commission received on the occasion which they report to Thomas, is not considered to be inconsistent with the unenthusiastic attitude of Peter and the other six who go fishing and fail to recognize Jesus when he speaks to them. Then, too, in Luke Pentecost is expressly seen as a completion for the disciples of the fruits produced by the appearance of Jesus. But we cannot go further and describe the increase which Pentecost brought, because we do not have a detailed grasp of what Pentecost was.

I would have liked to follow the development of faith in the first witnesses even after the Easter events. In doing so, the difficulties increase still more, but it seems clear, in the light of the Acts of the Apostles, that the vicissitudes of life in the first community were a stimulus to a deepening of the primitive faith. The tribulations Paul endured in winning acceptance, through his apostolic authority, of a way of life in keeping with faith in the salvation brought by Christ serve as an example, The very process of testifying to and communicating the faith brought an intensification of that faith in the witnesses themselves.

II. Problems Raised by Reflection on the Datum of Faith

The close dependence, even for fundamental theology, of discussion of the resurrection on the biblical text is felt in dealing with the difficulties that arise. A first set of difficulties has to do directly with the interpretation of this text: as a general problem and in application to the quintessential points made in the testimony to the resurrection. A second series of problems has to do rather with anthropological and soteriological aspects of the Easter message. In this second set of difficulties the biblical datum certainly plays a part, but the difficulties arise from the philosophical and theological categories that must come into play in the reading of the text.

1. *The Methodology of Biblical Exegesis*

At the beginning of this essay I spoke of the value, for our study, of the critical historical method. But insofar as this method is a technical one, it is not yet a method that assures trustworthy results. Technique is blind. When it has yielded initial findings, diacritical tools, capable of making distinctions, must be applied in order to turn these findings to account. Finally, in this entire application of methods the attitude of the student plays a determining role.

The critical historical method has ascertained that the testimonies to the resurrection are testimonies springing from faith and that they influence not only confessional formulas and theological assertions but even the stories of the Easter events. At this point, therefore, the question inevitably arises: What reliance can we place on the trustworthiness of the redactions?

In answer it may be said that the separation of theological element from historiographical intention may be difficult but it is not impossible, at least as regards the essential points. Or it may be said that the entire message is focused upon and subordinated to a theological intention and that, in the extreme case, the separating out of the factual datum is not even important. There is a preunderstanding that plays an extraordinarily determinative role in the methodology used. This is true not only of the gospel stories but also of the interpretation of all the statements made about the reality of the risen Christ; there are incalculable consequences for the overall conception of christology and for the very relationship of faith that unites the believer with his Lord.

In the present context I can only refer the reader to the treatises that deal specifically with this problem and with the problem of the "historical Jesus."[24] I intend simply to call attention to the danger of applying indiscriminately the rule which says that a text bearing the marks of a fully developed theological reflection (a text that is *theologisch reflektiert,* as the Germans say) lacks any historical value. The two qualifications—historical and theological—do not belong to the same order and it is therefore impossible to set up a law of reciprocal exclusion. It is legitimate indeed to suggest the hypothesis that a theological purpose may have determined some or many details of the presentation. But the conclusion that this is indeed the case can only be based on proof. Otherwise the Lukan and Johannine narratives should in principle be neglected as part of a first reading of the gospels and relegated to the phase of theological investigation. Theology and history are categories not easily separable; frequently the one finds expression in the other.

For this reason the preceding reflections on methodology do not apply solely to the reading of the biblical text as a historical document. Christological, ecclesiological, and anthropological preunderstandings likewise make their effects felt throughout the entire biblical theology of the resurrection of Christ.

2. *The Problem of Language*

In my first approach to the New Testament data I observed that discourse on the resurrection of Christ finds expression in varying terminologies. I mentioned three especially: the vocabulary of "resurrection," which for us is the more technical and evocative terminology (in the New Testament this means chiefly the verbs *egeirō* and *anistēmi*, with the nouns derived from them); the vocabulary of Jesus' exaltation or glorification after death (a diversified vocabulary, drawn frequently from the psalms and especially from Psalms 110 and 2); the vocabulary of life.

The fact of this diversity is perfectly clear. An explanation may be found in the inadequacy of any language to express an unprecedented reality and in the necessity of varying the linguistic tools depending on the variety of expressions sought for faith in the mystery. Each of these tools is in fact incomplete. The basic meaning of "resurrection" is the return to a standing position of a person who had been sitting or lying down or stretched out; more specifically, it is the return to a state of activity on the part of someone who had been hindered from it, especially by illness (he had therefore been lying down); more specifically still, it is the return to the condition and posture of life on the part of one who had been (lying) immobilized by death. "Exaltation" means the elevation of someone from a condition of lowliness (normal or subnormal) to one of excellence above the normal, with possible overtones of various kinds (especially of glory, authority, sovereignty). "Life" in itself does not call attention to any transition, but in using it of Jesus, early Christianity expressly or by implication contrasts "life" with "death" and thus connotes the third meaning (above) of "resurrection."

The limited denotation of these various terms is clear. Even when the reference is clearly to resurrection from death, it is not clear what the terminus of this resurrection is: a return to the normal conditions of our present life with its temporal limitation, or a return to a higher kind of life that is endless. When Jesus is said to be "exalted," the kind of existence meant is not clear, since one possibility is the glorification of a dead person, even a saint, who is nonetheless not alive. In Easter contexts and in the kerygmatic discourses the vocabulary of "life" suggests a rich content, since it makes us think of the fullness of life enjoyed by one who had been dead. But this full meaning is possible only in contexts in which all the other vocabularies also play their part.

The distribution of this vocabulary in the New Testament is so varied that a preference for the one or the other, depending on the literary genre, cannot compel us to think that conceptions of divergent origin are at work, which modern hermeneutics might legitimately set in opposition.

The discussion that has gone on in scholarly circles in recent years has reflected heterogeneous interests. Some find in it the justification for a christology of exaltation that does not take the event of "the resurrection from the dead" as its point of departure. Others simply investigate the history of linguistic models in an effort to understand better the density of meaning these had when used by the first believers. Still others are interested in these various models because they are seeking helps for contemporary preaching and the service of the faith in our world.[25]

3. *The Empty Tomb*

It is perfectly clear that the tradition about the empty tomb is less well attested than the tradition of the appearance. The question arises whether this restricted attestation is due to a limited knowledge of this tradition (and of the event behind it) or whether there are signs suggesting that knowledge of it may be seen even in passages which do not narrate the discovery.

The value of the traditions telling us what happened at the empty tomb is disputed. The formulation of the traditions is certainly governed by a theology; but is there also present the intention of reporting an incident that really happened as described?

The possibility of giving a negative answer to this last question opens the way for discussion of another possibility: that the tomb was not really without a corpse (assuming that this was even the tomb described by the gospels). More radically still: Is it possible to conceive a proclamation of the resurrection of Jesus that did not involve a return to life of the same body that had been crucified? I shall put this last question aside until later.

In regard to the spread of knowledge of the empty tomb study has moved in three directions: Did Paul have this knowledge? Do the kerygmatic discourses in Acts presuppose it? Within the traditions transmitted by the gospel is the connection between the traditions regarding the appearances and the traditions regarding the women at the tomb a primitive one? Exegetes discuss all these problems today, and no really dominant trends have surfaced.[26] None of these three questions are decisive for us here, but I must emphasize the antiquity of the tradition about the empty tomb and the serious likelihood that 1 Corinthians 15:3–5 bears witness to a knowledge of the empty tomb on the part of Paul.

The theological intention of the stories of the empty tomb is, above all, to assert the identity of the risen Christ with the crucified Jesus and to suggest that his definitive victory over death has ushered in the last times. But this intention makes sense only if it is accompanied by the intention of reporting a real event. The literary hypothesis which interprets these stories as an "etiological legend" to explain the fact that the Jerusalem community worshiped at the tomb, does not deliberately imply a negative attitude to an objective foundation for the "legend."[27]

In view of the rather tenuous links between the empty tomb and the origin of the primitive Easter faith, the discussion of this tradition has been less intense than the discussion of the appearances. The lack of strongly held views (itself a result of the fact that a less important issue is at stake) means that historical study of the point proceeds in an atmosphere of greater calm. This advantage is counterbalanced by the fact that there are greater difficulties connected with the empty tomb than with the appearances. But, in conclusion, the ancient tradition cannot be adequately explained unless we admit that the community in which the traditions arose (Jerusalem) knew the place of Jesus' tomb and the fact that the tomb had been found empty.

4. The Appearances

The abundance of testimony shows how much importance was attributed to the fact. But the abundance does not eliminate difficulties. Once again, we may distinguish some difficulties that are involved in the approach to the text, and others that bring a wider problematic into play. Two problems seem of special concern to fundamental theology.

The first of these questions is this: What was the intention behind the composition of these stories? If we may judge by the themes presented (I have already spoken of these several times), we must conclude that there was more than one concern. It has recently been suggested that the appearances were originally narrated simply as "formulas of legitimation" in order to lend authority to those who would be preaching the gospel. This explanation is applied to the list in 1 Corinthians 15:5–8 and then to the detailed narratives, which naturally involve other intentions as well.[28]

The explanation is not satisfactory. Before any question arises of grounding anyone's authority, the appeal to the appearances is made in order to give support to the kerygma. Important for this purpose is the theme of recognition, and this prior to any apologetic concerns; in other words, before any need of legitimating the authority of the one who speaks and before any need of demonstrating that the appearances were not illusions, it is important to present the experience of recognition of the risen Jesus as this took place in personal encounter with him. The ecclesiological theme of mission and preaching is posterior to this prior theme, as a commitment that springs from the recognition and is posterior to it, just as it is posterior to the faith it presupposes as its foundation.

A more thorny question is the nature of the experience the witnesses had. The question arises even in the reading of the gospel texts, and first of all in the interpretation of *ōphthē* in 1 Corinthians 15:5–8.

The contemporary discussion of this question was launched at the beginning of the Second World War by a contribution from E. Hirsch. In the New Testament (Hirsch says) "the ways of conceiving the 'seeing' of Jesus" followed a downward path: in the gospel stories (which contain "the Church's official Easter legend") "Christ is seen and observed as a bodily being and by the bodily senses," whereas Paul had used the proper description for appearances, speaking of them as "visions (*Gesicht*) that are contemplated by the mind in a state transcending normal consciousness."[29] W. Michaelis tries to follow a middle path: the only thing that is important is that the appearances are revelations.[30]

It was easy to radicalize the problem by introducing the Bultmannian thematic. When the Marburg exegete seemed to suggest that there was nothing but the kerygma, Karl Barth objected that the first thing to be affirmed is the resurrection itself and not faith in it or the preaching of it: the disciples contemplated the glory of the risen Word as something in space and time, something perceived by hearing and touch and experienced in an earthly manner, just as the death of Jesus had been experienced.[31]

Especially influential has been the work of W. Marxsen. According to Marxsen behind the entire passage of 1 Corinthians 15:3–8 can be seen a single vision, the one given to Peter, to whose mission it led. What we have here, then, is a functional formula: *in order to* say that this person has a mission, it is said that he saw Jesus. But all that history tells us is that Peter was the first to believe and that the ground given for this belief was that he had seen Christ. Paul's experience provides confirmation here. His vision, too, is functional in relation to his mission. And in fact the faith-experience of the Corinthians tells them only that Paul is sent as an apostle. The historical facts behind the preaching of the resurrection are not themselves part of the faith. The content of this preaching need not include the *way* in which the crucified Jesus returned to life. This said, Marxsen also offers concessions, but these do not change the substance of his position: "There is no doubt at all that Paul was convinced that the resurrection of Jesus had taken place. But neither in 1 Corinthians 15 nor anywhere else does he offer factual evidence."[32]

Marxsen thus makes his own, in a lively dialectical form, the essence of one of Bultmann's classical positions. But at no small cost: Marxsen does not study the prehistory of the confession of faith (in which history an assertion of Christ's resurrection probably existed without any reference to witnesses and therefore without any functional motivation coming into play), nor does he study the history of the word *ōphthē* (which perhaps suggests points not in agreement with those of Marxsen), nor does he take sufficient account of the *Sitz im Leben* of the formula that is followed in the list of witnesses in 1 Corinthians 15 (perhaps it would emerge that the formula is less one which gives backing to the ecclesial function of all or some of the witnesses, than it is a means of founding a certainty about the resurrection of Christ as an event that really happened).[33]

A great deal of light has been shed on the matter by a short paper of A. Pelletier on the prehistory of the word *ōphthē* in the vocabulary of the Septuagint. The way the word is used in 1 Corinthians 15 with an accompanying divine name ("Christ") recalls the first theophany granted to Abraham in Genesis 12:7. The formulation of the Easter faith is connected with the Greek formulary for the theophanies of the Old Testament. If we take into account that Jesus had a human body, we can understand the new realistic details found in the gospel accounts. The New Testament writers "are thinking of something more than a reanimation of the body of Jesus. . . . They are proclaiming Christ's passage to a glorious life."[34]

This broad participation in the discussion shows how complex its subject matter is. The linguistic tools which the New Testament writers use are much more highly developed than we might think, and they clearly intend to take advantage of all the possibilities offered by these tools. What is expressed is an entering of Jesus into relations with the eyewitnesses through a contact that makes possible both a faith and the preaching of it, and this faith has for its object something that is accepted and attested "as having happened to the historical Jesus."[35]

The wealth of content is well illustrated by a passage from H. Schlier, which will conclude my discussion on a positive note:

> The usual meaning of the concepts of "appearance" and "see" is transcended in still another way. *Ōphthē,* "he appeared," also means, according to its contexts in the gospels, that the risen Lord manifests himself through words and signs. And "see" expresses the corresponding experiences which the witnesses have. It can therefore be said that the resurrection of Jesus Christ takes place at the historical level as an "encounter" (*Begegnis*). Jesus takes the initiative in this meeting that is granted to the witnesses. In its every aspect—word and sign, greeting and blessing, call, address, and instruction, consolation and command and mission—it is a pure gift. It is, we might say, the definitive assurance of his boundless attachment to them and the completion of his total self-giving. But if this is what his "appearance" is, then the "seeing" of the risen Lord is also hearing, acceptance, and personal participation.[36]

5. *The Origin of Faith in the Resurrection*

This question, which is connected with the preceding one, has received its most typical contemporary formulation in a recent paper of R. Pesch, that has given rise to extensive discussion. I shall refer here only to Pesch's initial contribution, since its concerns are those of my own essay.[37]

Pesch's frame of reference is fundamental theology, which even in its most recent spokesmen[38] has been maintaining that the process which gave rise to and provided the basis for the Easter faith began with the appearances of the risen Jesus (therefore there is no appeal to an argument based on the empty tomb, which has its place only in the world of the kerygma). Now, the Easter appearances or christophanies must be carefully analyzed to determine their historical probative value. All of the appearances, as far as the basic experience is concerned, are reducible to the protomanifestation of Christ to Peter as reported in 1 Corinthians 15:5. But this report functions not as a testimony to the resurrection but as a legitimation formula. Pesch here accepts Wilckens' thesis and the documentation applied in K. Berger's book on the resurrection visions.[39] The word *ōphthē* refers only to a revelation, not to a vision of faith. It also specifies and legitimates the authorized witnesses to the kerygma contained in this revelation. On the other hand, nothing is said to tell us how these witnesses came to believe; this is already presupposed.

Whence then did faith in the resurrection take its rise? Its origin (says Pesch) is to be found prior to the Easter experiences, prior even to the experience of the crucifixion. As a matter of fact, Christ's disciples had at their disposal categories for interpreting the fate of Jesus as death and resurrection, martyrdom and justification by God. The proof of this is the existence of Jewish traditions on prophetic individuals such as Enoch and Elijah. In fact, according to traditions behind such passages as Mark 9:11–13; 6:14–16, the fate of the Baptist seems to have been confused with that of Elijah. Jesus himself, who was close to the Baptist, is in possession of these categories and is convinced that he is the eschatological prophet. Thus when his death on the cross occurs, his disciples can proclaim his mission, which fulfills every expectation, and his significance for salvation with the interpretative words: "He is risen!" There may, therefore, have been "visions" after the death of Jesus, but the basis of faith in the resurrection is to be looked for in his disciples' familiarity with him before his death, when all of their experience of his activity found expression in messianic terms.

The hypothesis is an interesting one, but it depends on a series of claims that can hardly be regarded as self-evident. The secondary character of the assertions about the empty tomb is accepted; the intention of describing the appearances as objective experiences is denied; the appearances are reduced to the proto-manifestation to Peter, and the latter in turn to a legitimation formula. No less problematic are these further claims: the category "resurrection of the just man" (immediately after his death) is at hand in the environment of Jesus due to the presence there of typical Jewish traditions; these traditions are applied to the Baptist, but they are much more readily to be applied to Jesus; there is continuity between the earthly experience of Jesus, the faith that came to birth in the apostles at that time, the fate of Jesus after death, and the early Church's faith in the resurrection. Many of these assertions are quite open to criticism; in particular: the skepticism regarding the appearances, and the underlying conception of historical and rational criticism; the presence of an expectation of resurrection; and the continuity with the life of the earthly Jesus.[40] In addition, it is rather strange to see a writer pass so easily from an unsparing critique of the meaning value of the appearances to a ready acceptance of a continuity (even if a differentiated one) of Jewish apocalyptic concepts and Jesus' eschatological claims with the Easter faith. Then there is the basic question: To what is the resurrection being reduced: to a cultural schema which serves to interpret a conviction? or to a real event that takes place in the career of Jesus after his death and in the history of the human race where it has power to change the destiny even of the latter?

The skepticism with which exegetes in particular[41] have reacted to Pesch's hypothesis shows how unsound some parts of it are. Objection is raised especially to his interpretation of the appearances. However worthwhile it may be to pursue the idea of a possible embryonic faith on the part of the disciples even before the crucifixion of Jesus, it seems beyond denial that the New Testimonies intend to show us the Easter faith (which they begin to discuss in an analytic way) as the fruit of encounter with the risen Lord.

6. *Specific Problems*

Many fields are involved, for example, philosophical reflection, biblical theology, the speculative dimension of theological thinking.

(A) I shall not concern myself here with anything that does not directly have to do with fundamental theology. A general observation of the *anthropological categories* involved in the discussion gives reason to bemoan the lack of a philosophy sufficiently developed to serve in reflection on the biblical text. This was a complaint voiced even ten years ago by J. Guitton in an essay which he contributed to the Roman symposium on the resurrection.[42] He offered a pioneering essay on the resurrection that was based on previously developed concepts of "body" and "becoming." Modern philosophy (Marcel, Merleau-Ponty, Bruaire, and others), supported by the experiences of artists (such men as Ingres, Rodin, and Cézanne), bids us think of the body as primarily a language, a means of communication for the soul. Becoming takes the form not only of evolution on the horizontal plane but also of a vertical development (studied by Plotinus, Leibniz and Blondel, among many) by way of a passage from the level of "somatized" life to that of reflective consciousness and then to that of the pneuma; what is meant is the kind of process that might be discovered by a profound, purified study of sex in its metaphysical and mystical meaning (corrupted by sin) that paves the way for anastasis or resurrection. Thanatology, hagiology, and analogy make it possible to start with the world of human experience (ascetical and mystical) and of animal life (for example, the insects) and hypothesize properties of the body that are still hidden but are destined to emerge in the resurrection, when by the power of the pneuma the cosmosphere will be made completely subject to the noosphere.

(B) The problem of the *body of the risen Jesus* is a more specialized one, because its starting point is the data supplied by the New Testament. The problem has two parts: Does the resurrection, as presented by the New Testament, necessarily involve the corpse of Jesus? What is the nature of the risen body of Jesus? The first problem is a more directly biblical one, the response to the second depends more on philosophy.

The exegetical problem must be handled in the light of 1 Corinthians 15. Paul first points out that the state of the risen Christ is identical with that which all human beings will achieve in glory. He then describes the nature of the resurrection; the description holds for Christ and all who are destined for glory. Now, in this presentation of the risen body we are given the impression that the newness of the risen body is so great that there is for practical purposes almost no continuity with the body of our earthly life (cf. vv. 37ff.). Are we to say that the intervention of God in restoring life is creative to the point of not involving at all the body that had fallen prey to death and that he simply creates the new body out of nothing? May we go so far as to say that Jesus existed in a risen life and that at the same time his former body was still in the tomb (a tomb necessarily not empty)?

I just remarked that in 1 Corinthians 15 the resurrection body is described as different from the body of earthly life. The statement is not an isolated one, even if the New Testament shows little interest in the problem. In the Second Letter to the Corinthians there is a contrast between the present body, which will be destroyed, and "our heavenly dwelling," which we would like to "put on" even now (cf. 2 Cor 5:1–10). I may also cite Luke 20:27–40, which, to a greater extent than its parallels (Mt 22:23–33; Mk 12:18–27), emphasizes the differences between the present (bodily) condition and the future condition (they "neither marry nor are given in marriage"), which is consequent upon the resurrection (cf. vv. 34–36). We also saw how, in the accounts of the appearances, the evangelists underscore the newness—and therefore difference—of the body of Jesus.

All these points convey a meaning, but this meaning should not lead us to hasty conclusions. They tell us both that the New Testament never thinks of the risen Jesus except as having a real body and that this real body underwent a transformation when Jesus was glorified. The awareness shown of this transformation assures us that the body was not uncritically affirmed simply because the Hebrew mind could not abstract from the body in its thinking about man. The New Testament shows itself cautious and even to some extent critical in its thinking on the subject.

Those, on the other hand, who would regard the bodily dimension as secondary in the resurrection would be guilty of a docetism that runs directly counter to the intention of the texts. They would be emptying the incarnation of its meaning and would be denying the very basis for the renewed contact with the sensible world which is the point of the experience of the appearance.

The biblical witness goes so far as to show (it seems) a continuity between the crucified body and the risen body. In dealing with any resurrection at all, the reference to "our body" suggests an unbroken relation between the person and his own body both before and after death. But it is not possible to say precisely how the texts think such a continuity is to be maintained despite the fact that time brings corruption. In the case of Jesus, however, the emphasis on his exemption from corruption (in the kerygmatic discourses) and on the reason for the absence of the corpse (in the stories of the empty tomb) show the intention of affirming the glorification of the very body that had been the means of the sacrifice of the cross. This is how Luke and John were thinking when they described the circumstances of the appearances. If it be said that this emphasis is due to an apologetic intention (which is probably the case), then it must also be said that there is a deliberate intention to underscore a factual datum precisely because it is factual.

As for reflection on the nature of the risen body we still have a long way to go. X. Léon-Dufour essayed a response to the problem which immediately became famous by reason of the debate it stimulated.[43] He suggests that we abandon the description of the body bequeathed to us by Greek dualist anthropology and opt rather for a vision of the body that is closer to that of the Semites and to that offered by modern genetics. "*My body* is the universe received and made particular in this instant by myself": it is directly related to the universe and it is subject to duration. My corpse, on the contrary, no longer expresses me in a unique way, and it exists not for me but only for others. By his resurrection Jesus escaped death; "he was glorified in his historical body" which was "taken on by the glorified Christ." This was a mysterious process, the essential element of which was "a change in the relationship between the natural body and the self that is expressed in it" (the body is no longer subject to the conditions of space and time, but has become a pure instrument of—unlimited—action for the person). The presence of the body of Jesus Christ is coextensive with the universe; it should not be limited to his individual body. This essay of Léon-Dufour was inspired by the thinking of Edouard Le Roy. The reservations with which it met do not detract from its value as an effort to solve the problem and as showing the need of continued study.

III. Concluding Synthesis

Among the road we have traveled we have seen so many problems and facets of problems that I have decided by way of conclusion simply to summarize the points made.

We have heard a message which puts us in contact with a pluridimensional event that has manifold consequences. Our aim was to study the origin and intention of the message in order to understand its object and to appraise it in terms of its consequences for faith and life.

1. *Learning of the Event*

The event communicated to us is the fact of the resurrection of Jesus. It has been communicated through the transmission of testimony. The testimony in its turn sprang from and was legitimized by a direct awareness. The awareness was the result of observation, not of the event in itself but in certain consequences which were perceived in contexts that permitted no doubt about the proper interpretation of them.

Before the event the witnesses had a knowledge of Jesus that was already accompanied by a degree of "messianic surmise" but not yet by Easter faith.[44] These witnesses also had an interpretation of the "Jesus event" which made it possible for them to open themselves to hope of the resurrection.

Now there intervened an experiential fact which was made up of various signs. It forced itself upon them and was immediately understood as a challenge to take a position. The result was a variety of reactions: lack of understanding, fear, doubts, reservations—attitudes all of which were expressions of the inadequate reaction that preceded faith, enthusiasm, and the complete acceptance of assignments and commitments which would determine the shape of their lives.

The content of these descriptions cannot be easily or completely reconstructed because the initial responses have been overlaid by the weight of later reflection. One point, however, emerges with clarity: the witnesses experientially recognize their interlocutor as the teacher (*rabbuni*) of yore and, as a result, they accept in a global manner what he was and what he now asks of them.

The awareness gives rise to a movement of reflection and communication. The object of the reflection is the experience itself, the purpose being to find a key that will make the experience communicable in language. A name is given to the experiences and to the event known through the experiences. The encounter as such is expressed in terms, preferably, of "vision" and told of by means of scenes in which appearances occur; a complementary experience, the discovery of the empty tomb, is narrated with the help of details of an apocalyptic kind. The event known through the experiences is the fact that for Jesus the usual sequence of death-burial-corruption has been changed, and death-burial has led instead to a new existence for Jesus in which he possesses eschatological perfection, divine glory, and a lasting ability to communicate as a man with the earthly world and to dispose with sovereign freedom of the future of the world, the Church, and individuals. This reading of the event is worked out with the help of linguistic schemata present in their Hebrew heritage and through exploration of Old Testament precedents that were fulfilled in the destiny of Jesus.

Communcation undoubtedly created problems, because the way of learning about the event had meanwhile changed: no longer would others learn through direct experience, recognition, and acceptance of Jesus, but rather through the lives of the witnesses and acceptance of their testimony. The dialectic of signs has changed. Authority now belongs to those who were in contact with the first witnesses, the latter thus becoming the basic point of reference for the authenticity of the faith of future disciples.[45]

2. *The Event in Itself*

The New Testament presentation of the facts that follow upon and attest the resurrection of Jesus is governed by several intentions. To begin with, it bears witness to a faith which it seeks to arouse in the reader by attestation of the new event that has taken place in Jesus. This new event or fact is an object of faith, but the faith makes sense only if the fact is something real.

The affirmation that the fact is indeed something real is itself an affirmation of faith, since the fact as such lies beyond the boundaries of experiential reality. But the affirmation is supported by observations whose function is to signal the change that has taken place in Jesus. The experiences are thus authenticated (at least partially) in the sphere of experiential reality. Because of the relation that exists between function of these experiences and the assent to the event which the Easter descriptions are meant to attest, it must be admitted that the testimonies to the resurrection include a stand on the historical character of what they assert and, in particular, that the narratives of these experiences have a historiographical purpose among others.

Neither the event nor the experiences that follow on it can be wholly reduced to natural categories. Not the event, because it signals a passage from history to metahistory; not the experiences, because they signal an encounter with an ineffable event. (Clearly, the irreducibility predicated of both event and experiences is not identical but only analogous.) Whence the embarrassment of language that is always conscious of being at best only approximative. But this does not mean that it is inaccurate or incapable of conveying aspects which though partial are true.

For this reason and because of the historico-literary difficulty of finding the interpretive key to so many details of the descriptions, exegetes find the reading of the texts difficult and qualify their interpretations according to various degrees of clarity.

3. *The Course of the Experiences*

I have already summarized the elements in the stories of the tomb and the appearances, and I have pointed out the difficulties in the way of determining, for many of the details, the author's intention in setting them down.

But whereas it is easy to reconstruct, to a limited extent, the experience at the tomb, this is not the case with the appearances. Apart from a certain uniformity of pattern in these, there are no points which are clear. Do the two locales, Jerusalem and Galilee, simply indicate the different places in which the two traditions took shape, or (and this is more probable) are they a reminder of the various places in which encounters took place at different times? In this second hypothesis, where did the first encounters take place? The precedence given to Galilee is not fully satisfactory, even if the choice of Jerusalem is perhaps open to a great number of difficulties.

4. *The Significance of the Event*

I have already attempted at several points to draw up short lists of views, and here again I refer the reader to more appropriate sources. I remind them only that we would be going contrary to the intention of the biblical witness if we were to overaccentuate the *for us* or *for Jesus* aspect of the event which is the object of the Easter faith. Salvation does come *to us* through faith in Jesus, but in the Jesus who really underwent death for our sins and who was really raised from the dead for our justification (cf. Rom 4:25). And the resurrection did take place *in Jesus,* but as an integral part and crown of the mission which he received from the Father and which ended with the attainment, in his glorification, of salvation for the human race.

Part 4

Ecclesiological Perspectives

14
The Church:
Sacrament and Ground of Faith

Avery Dulles

I. Apologetics on the Defensive

In the age of Rationalism, beginning with the seventeenth century, fundamental theology took the form of apologetics, which in turn was understood as an approach to faith by the light of unaided reason. While the Deists emphasized the power of reason to establish by intrinsic arguments the doctrines of the true religion, orthodox theologians, both Protestant and Catholic, used reason rather to establish the divine authority of Christ and the Church. Such authority, they maintained, could be certified only by divine signs, and the divine sign par excellence was the miracle—the deed that transcended the powers and laws of nature.

In the apologetics of the Church, two basic approaches were used. Some apologists, such as Giovanni Perrone (1794–1876), moved by preference from Christ to the Church. They attempted to demonstrate, by a historical approach to the New Testament, that Jesus was divinely attested by prophecies and miracles, especially by his resurrection from the dead. From this point, they went on to argue that he founded the Church and guaranteed its teaching by his promise to assist it until the end of time. All, therefore, should believe what the Church proclaims.

The second major approach, exemplified in the work of Cardinal Victor Dechamps (1810–1883), preferred to begin with the Church as a present and obvious fact. The Church by its marvelous qualities—its unity, durability, expansiveness, and holiness—deserves to be called a "subsistent miracle."

Vatican Council I (1869–1870) accepted both approaches as mutually complementary. It taught that the biblical miracles and prophecies are signs of Christ's divine authority,[1] but it also taught that the Church, by virtue of its extraordinary qualities, is a divine sign. "The Church itself, because of its marvelous propagation, its exalted sanctity, and its inexhaustible fruitfulness in all that is good, because of its catholic unity and its unshaken stabil-

259

ity, is a great and perpetual motive of credibility and an irrefutable proof of its own divine mission."[2]

Dechamps himself, and the Vatican Council to the extent that it endorsed his approach, was moving away from the bookish rationalism of the Enlightenment toward a form of apologetic that was more existential. A similar trend may be noted in John Henry Newman, especially in his *Grammar of Assent,* written almost at the same time as Vatican Council I. Logical proofs, he contended, can demonstrate only what is already implicit in the premises, and hence cannot deliver anything radically new and unexpected. Further, such proofs yield only a conditioned and notional assent, falling far short of the real assent of faith. "Inference," he held, "considered in the sense of verbal argumentation, determines neither our principles, nor our ultimate judgments . . . it is neither the test of truth nor the adequate basis of assent."[3] The Church, in Newman's estimation, must demand conversion on the part of all who come to it. "They who have no religious earnestness are at the mercy, day by day, of some new argument or fact, which may overtake them, in favor of one conclusion or the other."[4] Syllogisms, Newman contended, are powerless to effect conversion. "First shoot round corners," he wrote, "and you may not despair of converting by a syllogism."[5] These criticisms, while they do not necessarily conflict with the positions of Dechamps and Vatican I, run counter to the main stream of Christian apologetics since the seventeenth century and prepared the way for a more realistic analysis of the approach to Christian faith.

Newman's critique gained added force from the inefficacy of the standard apologetics. As Newman himself was well aware, David Hume had objected to all arguments that attempted to establish the fact of revelation of the basis of the biblical miracles. Miracles, according to Hume, are known only through human testimony. Since we have no experience of the violation of natural laws, said Hume, "we may establish it as a maxim that no human testimony can have such force as to prove a miracle, and make it a just foundation for any such system of religion."[6] Experience, in fact, gives some support to Hume's position. Generally speaking, historians approaching the accounts of Jesus with detached objectivity have not been convinced that his mission was divinely attested by supernatural miracles, though some secular historians are prepared to admit that Jesus may have performed faith-healings of some sort. As for the Church, many academic historians profess doubts as to whether Jesus intended to found any continuing organization. They are not persuaded that either the longevity of the Church or any of the other attributes pointed out by Dechamps is such as to defy all natural explanations. Thus both the historical and the empirical routes of apologetics are regarded, by many modern scholars, as dead ends.

Early in the twentieth century, Karl Barth contested the value of apologetics as such.[7] His objection was that in seeking to make Christianity acceptable to unregenerate reason, apologetics tended to water down the substance of the faith. In a famous passage from his essay on Schleiermacher, Barth depicted the apologist as one going out to meet the "despisers of religion" carrying a white flag in hand. Insofar as apologetics approaches the nonbeliever it must refrain from appealing to anything known by faith; it must present its case in categories which are accessible to believers and unbelievers alike, prescinding from what is original and distinctive in Christian faith.[8]

While critics such as Barth dismissed apologetics as too rationalistic, others objected that it was too authoritarian. The two systems summarized above share in common the quality that they conclude to the obligation of submitting to the word of a divine legate—whether the primary legate be seen as the historical Jesus or as the Church itself. In either case, reason in the end is induced to subject itself to the word of another. Toward the end of the nineteenth century Maurice Blondel led the protest against the extrinsicism of this logic. In Blondel's estimation, it made an intolerable separation between the fact and the content of revelation; it depicted faith too much on the analogy of a blank check.[9]

In recent decades the force of this objection has been keenly felt. As the Nuremberg trials dramatically demonstrated, terrible crimes have been perpetrated by functionaries who blindly follow the dictates of supposedly infallible leaders. Under what conditions, therefore, can one responsibly substitute another's judgment for one's own? Christians who implicitly accept whatever the Bible says or whatever the Church teaches on the basis of allegedly miraculous accreditation are frequently uncritical, rigid, defensive, and complacent. They take an attitude of arrogant superiority over members of other religious communities. They close their eyes to evils in the Church and resist the very idea of reform. The orientations of Vatican II, which invited Catholics to take a more positive attitude toward the modern world, and which readily admitted the need for reform and updating in the Catholic Church, dealt a severe blow to the apologetics of the Counter-Reformation. As a result of the dual assault from the Barthian and the Blondelian positions, many Christians are asking themselves whether apologetics itself ought not to be abandoned. Many are calling for a new fundamental theology to take the place of the traditional apologetics.[10]

II. The New Fundamental Theology

The older apologetics rested upon a questionable concept of reason, conceived as a power to arrive at truth by strict deduction from indubitable a priori principles. This concept of reason confronted the believer with a dilemma. If the truth of revelation could be established by reason alone, faith was superfluous. If it could not, faith was an overcommitment; for, as John Locke had contended,[11] it would be irrational to give a firm assent to anything which is neither self-evident nor stringently demonstrable.

Newman broke through this dichotomy with his existential logic of convergence, in which certitude depended not simply on objective evidence but upon the presumptions and concerns of the inquiring subject. The decision of faith, for Newman, was a concrete choice in which the decision was achieved by the "illative sense"—a personal power to discern and assess the force of multiple convergent signs that could not be turned into logical premises. Informal inference in religious matters, as Newman explained it, was not an exercise of pure reason in the sense of the Rationalist philosophers. It was the work of the whole person, and might well rest upon a certain incipient faith. Newman is the spiritual ancestor of all those twentieth-century theologians who interpret conversion not as a movement from reason to faith but as an intellectual movement from faith to faith.

Many subsequent epistemologists, with or without direct dependence on Newman, have developed this line of thinking. Michael Polanyi, for example, situates religious conversion within the framework of a logic of discovery, which operates in many other fields, including mathematics and the natural sciences. The heuristic process, according to Polanyi, begins with a phase in which one is passionately concerned and intensely preoccupied with a problem, convinced that a hidden solution exists, waiting to be found.[12] The inquirer experiences a "heuristic tension" because of the gap between what is already grasped and what is waiting to be found. In this situation, one is admonished to "look at the unknown, look at the conclusion"—that is to say, to focus one's gaze in the direction indicated by hidden clues or hunches, perceived for the most part by what Polanyi calls "tacit knowledge." Aroused by passionate obsession with the problem to be solved, the imagination begins to suggest possible forms for an answer. As these suggestions pop into our mind, we sense that some of them "ring a bell"; they strikingly correspond to our inarticulate anticipations. "The gradient of deepening coherence," as Polanyi calls it, "tells us where to start and which way to turn, and eventually brings us to the point where we may stop and claim a discovery."[13] The discovery, when it comes, is "accredited in advance by the heuristic craving which evoked it."[14] The discovery is further authenticated by the release of heuristic tension, resulting in a movement of profound satisfaction, peace, and joy.

Polanyi's heuristic theory, all too briefly outlined here, is admirably suited to account for discoveries which break out of the framework of what had previously been considered possible. His "logic of discovery" has many points of similarity with what Newman previously described under the rubric of the illative sense.

Fundamental theology is only beginning to take advantage of the enormous possibilities opened out to it by the growing body of literature on creativity in the arts and sciences. The heuristic process, as described by many modern theories, offers striking analogies with the process of religious conversion.[15] Theologians, to be sure, will insist that the logic of faith has its own distinctive features. The process of conversion to a revealed religion, interpreted from the point of view of faith, is one borne by the dynamism of grace, having God as its source and goal. The restlessness of heart (which Augustine in his *Confessions* described as *cor inquietum*[16]) is interpreted by theologians as the effect of God's grace calling us to communion with himself. But it resembles Polanyi's tacit knowledge, insofar as in the hunger of the spirit the good news of the gospel is anticipated by our inarticulate spiritual longing. Aroused by grace, we embark on a passionate search, reaching out in darkness toward the "unknown God." Keeping our attention focused on him alone, we allow our imagination to dwell on the images and symbols proposed by various ideologies and religions, assessing their power to satisfy the heuristic tension of the spirit. When at length the desired answer arrives, it manifests itself as something which had been at hand all the time, waiting only to be found. And thus the convert can exclaim, in the language of St. Augustine, "Late it was that I loved you, beauty so ancient and so new, late I loved you!"[17]

The process of religious discovery, here outlined with the help of Polanyi's epistemology, is verified in a preeminent way in the search and discoveries of the great converts to the faith, such as Paul, Augustine, Pascal, and Newman. But it is replicated on a lesser scale by all who struggle to achieve or appropriate a religious faith offered to them by tradition. Involved in the process of personal assimilation is the activation of the human powers of discovery, under the aegis of the divine attraction. Contemporary fundamental theology utilizing modern heuristic theory, can effectively retrieve the classical themes of conversion and grace, and thus unearth an unexpected wealth of meaning in the biblical precept, "Seek and you shall find" (Lk 11:9).

III. The Church and Conversion

In a certain sense, religious conversion is to God alone. The dynamics of conversion would be thrown into confusion if the inquirer focused on anything other than the divine transcendent as the goal of the search. In the light of this orientation to the "unknown God" Jesus Christ can appear as the form in which God is to be found. The Christian is one who believes that God is to be found preeminently in Jesus Christ. Looking to God, who dwells in unapproachable light (1 Tim 6:16), the Christian beholds "the light of the knowledge of the glory of God in the face of Christ" (2 Cor 4:6).

Up to the time of the Easter events, the disciples could attain a certain inchoatively Christian faith by direct perception of the words and deeds of Jesus, but since Easter there has been no access to Jesus as the Christ except through the believing testimony of the Church. The New Testament itself— as a book written in the Church, collected by it, certified by its authority, and interpreted by its tradition—is an instrument by which the Church addresses those whom it calls to itself. Acceptance of the Bible, therefore, cannot be played off against acceptance of the Church. To accept the one is implicitly to accept the other also.[18]

The Church, for the believer, is not so much an object believed as an extension of the believing subject. The faithful comprise the community of those who view reality, under its religious aspects, through the eyes of the Church, convinced that in that way they will see more and see better than they otherwise could. Many rely on the Church almost unconsciously, in much the same way that in seeing or touching we rely, unreflectingly, on our bodily organs. Through faith and sacramental incorporation, the faithful are taken up into the Church—that community which scripture and theology designate by the term, "body of Christ."

Here again the analogy with science is helpful. To learn science is to affiliate oneself with the scientific community. People believe the theories and findings of scientists, if at all, because they implicitly trust the community, its leaders, and its processes. This act of trust, like trust in our own senses, is not blind and unmotivated. It pays off by giving greater intelligibility to our experience and to the data we can glean from the experience of others. This trust in science, moreover, enables us to live more successfully and productively than we could without it.

So, too, in the religious life. To accept the revelation of God in Jesus Christ, as the Church presents him to us, is critically justified to the extent that it assists one to integrate the data of experience, to interpret the course of history, and to cope with what Vatican II referred to as "the riddles of sorrow and death."[19] Christians are convinced that through a faith-relationship to Christ they are led into a richer, more meaningful existence. By placing themselves under the Lordship of Christ they acquire standards and goals, they can labor with new intensity, find deeper communion with others who share the same faith, and be constantly challenged to become their own best selves. While mysteries do not cease to be mysteries, they become luminous and consoling rather than dark and forbidding.

The confirmations that come from lived experience do not dispense us from dependence on authority. On the contrary, they reinforce our prior conviction that such trust is warranted. Our own partial and limited insights in religious matters call for direction from those who have perceived divine things with special clarity. Just as the scientist, the philosopher, or the artist depends upon geniuses of the past, so the religious person perseveres willingly in discipleship, reverently listening to the word handed down through the community of faith—a word which provides models and precepts for a fruitful relationship to God. We are in need of continual recourse to the great religious leaders in order to purify and revitalize our own religious vision. The great classics of faith, held out to us by the Church, continue to sustain our vision and commitment. Among these classics, of course, the Bible holds a privileged position as the fundamental record of the originating vision.

A religious faith such as Christianity rests more heavily on testimony than does a scientific or philosophical theorem. Science and philosophy refer to what is constantly available—the regular order of nature and the unchanging structure of reality. The beliefs of a scientific community or a philosophical school can be tested, up to a point, for their consistency with the empirical data. Religion, too, seeks to interpret life-experiences that are always repeatable, but a historical faith such as Christianity bases its convictions on unique, unrepeatable, past events. In other words, Christianity articulates a specific historical revelation. It emerges from a particular history in which God is believed to have disclosed more of himself and of his saving plan than could be inferred or verified from daily experience. In biblical religion we have a combination of unique events and an interpretation which claims to be inspired. The apostolic witness was shaped by something more than normal human powers of apprehension: "Flesh and blood has not revealed this to you, but my Father who is in heaven" (Mt 16:17). To gain access to Jesus as the Christ, we must accept both facts and interpretation, and neither of these can be grasped apart from the testimony of the Christian community and its acknowledged leaders. To make an act of Christian faith, therefore, is to submit (not blindly but with open eyes) to the testimony of the Church, and to aggregate oneself, at least in spirit, to that Church. Christian faith is by its very nature ecclesial faith as well.

It would be an exaggeration to maintain that the testimony of the Church could be adequately understood on the analogy of a scientific theory, which presents itself as a mere object of investigation for those who might be interested. The Church claims to be the bearer of a message which is the power of salvation to those who accept it. In proclaiming the gospel, the Church is confident that God is powerfully at work in it, so that its word is capable of becoming, on such an occasion, the very word of God. The testimony of the Church, therefore, has an active dynamism that profoundly alters those whom it encounters. Far from submitting pliantly to the demands and expectations that others place upon it, the Church addresses them with a strange and puzzling message—one that disconcerts its hearers and throws all their previous assumptions and values into question. The dynamism of the Christian proclamation, if it is received in faith, lays bare the deep intention of the inquirer's search for God. The conversion to which the seeker is open does not actually come to completion until it encounters the word of God. God's word is recognized not so much by any explicit criteria as by its capacity to interpret and fulfill the inarticulate aspirations of the sincere inquirer.

IV. The Church as Sacrament

Thus far we have spoken as though the Church were simply the bearer of a verbal message concerning Jesus. Christian witness, however, is never a mere matter of words. It is conveyed "by words and deeds, which are intrinsically bound up with each other."[20] The words, taken in isolation, would be empty, but in their concrete context they are living and effective, powerful to transform those who adhere to them. For this reason the Church is more than a messenger or herald; it bears witness not only by what it says but also by what it does and is. In other words, the Church is an effective sign of the Christ whom it proclaims.

For contemporary ecclesiology the concept of sacrament is fundamental.[21] A sacrament, according to the traditional understanding, is a visible sign of an invisible grace. It contains and transmits the grace that it signifies. All these characteristics of sacrament are preeminently verified in Christ, and, after him, in the Church. Christ is the sacrament of God—the one in whom God's redemptive love becomes present in a historically tangible manner in the world. The Church, in turn, is the sacrament of Christ—the living symbol that he is still actively present in the world through his "alter ego," the Holy Spirit.

For a proper understanding of the dynamics of conversion it is crucial to advert to the role of the Church as sacrament of Christ.[22] It is a symbol, not in the weak sense of merely standing for an absent reality, but in the strong sense of making palpable the divine reality that is present and hidden within itself. Laden with a mystery too great for definition or description, the Church communicates the reality it signifies by means of symbol, and does so, in the first instance, by being itself a sacrament. It is, as Paul VI said in an address at Vatican Council II, "a reality imbued with the hidden presence of God."[23]

In contrast to propositional speech, symbol imparts its meaning not by explicit denotation but by suggestion and evocation. Working on the imagination, emotions, and will, and through them upon the intelligence, the symbol changes the point of view, the perspectives, the outlook of the addressee. They grasp what is meant by sharing in the world indicated by the symbol. Symbolic knowledge is in the first instance participatory and implicit; only through a subsequent process of reflection does it become, in some measure, objective and explicit. The symbol, as Paul Ricoeur has said, "gives rise to thought."[24] To accept a symbol is to take the risk that in following out the line of action and consideration suggested by the symbol one will achieve a richer and more authentic penetration of the real.

If it be conceded that the Church is sacrament or symbol in the sense just described, one can better understand the relationship between the Church and conversion. As symbol, the Church beckons to its prospective members to embark upon the way of life for which it stands, to make a free and loving commitment to its living Lord. All who answer the Church's call become involved in the reality of the Church itself and by that fact they too are taken up into the sacramental sign. They are inwardly changed by participation in the life of faith that corporately animates the Church. The Church does not so much convert them as initiate them into a process of ongoing conversion under the aegis of the Church's Lord.

Although no other community besides the Church is, properly speaking, a sacrament, every genuine community depends for its existence upon the transmission of inarticulate lore through commitment and participation. A family, a nation, or any true community is known only from within, through personal familiarity. Its members know it as no outsider could. In order to impart this participatory knowledge, every community has its symbols, its heroes, its slogans, its rituals, and its traditions. Even a scientific community aims to impart much more than a body of explicit doctrines or explicit rules. The new members of the community are formed in discipleship, in order that they may be able to carry on the tradition by original and self-modifying acts, transforming themselves and contributing to the transformation of the community. Any community not open to such continuing self-modification would be spiritually dead.

The Church, as a religious community, labors to form its own members in the traditions handed down from the past. It passes on with great earnestness its standards of belief and conduct. Formation, however, is only the first stage in the process. As Rosemary Haughton has said: "Formation is for the unconverted. It is designed to create conditions for the converting encounter."[25] Through prayer and the sacraments, as acts of the Church, the Christian is brought into a personal and transforming contact with the God who stands above and beyond all that the Church can clearly say of him. The Eucharist, according to Mrs. Haughton, is a converting event, an encounter with grace, an ecclesial occasion for being caught up into the consuming and transforming love of Christ.

Michael Polanyi speaks in similar terms of the paradox of dwelling in the Church as a community in order to break out of it by direct relationship to God:

> The indwelling of the Christian worshiper is therefore a continued attempt at breaking out, at casting off the condition of man, even while humbly acknowledging its inescapability. Such indwelling is fulfilled most completely when it increases this effort to the utmost. It resembles not the dwelling within a great theory of which we enjoy the complete understanding, nor an immersion in the pattern of a musical masterpiece, but the heuristic upsurge which strives to break through the accepted frameworks of thought, guided by the inanitions of discoveries still beyond our horizon. Christian worship sustains, as it were, an eternal never to be consummated hunch: a heuristic vision which is accepted for the sake of its unresolvable tension. It is like an obsession with a problem known to be insoluble, which yet follows, against reason, unswervingly, the heuristic command: "Look at the unknown." Christianity sedulously fosters, and in a sense permanently satisfies, man's craving for mental dissatisfaction by offering him the comfort of a crucified God.[26]

Fundamental theology, up to the present time, has only begun to ponder the implications of the sacramental vision of the Church. Until very recently the assumption seems to have been that the Church exists simply to hand on a body of explicit teachings and practices. Apologetics, then, was assigned the task of seeking to vindicate the Church's claims to act in the name of an absent God. In the sacramental vision, the Church's task is to bring its members to participate in the life and reality for which it stands— that is to say, in a life of faith in the God who has drawn near to us in love through Jesus Christ. Fundamental theology does not seek to prove by unaided reason that the Christian commitment is a proper one, but rather to make intelligible, with the help of analogies, the process of conversion by which God calls us to himself. The Church, for contemporary fundamental theology, is not understood primarily as a "divine legate" but rather as a symbol or sacrament whereby God intimates his presence and invites us to enter into a transformed life.

V. The True Church

As just suggested, the older apologetics proceeded on the basis of an institutional rather than a sacramental paradigm. It assumed that Jesus, during his lifetime, established a visible society with certain essential structures, and that the Church which preserved these structures without change or diminution must be the true Church in the world today. Relying on the uncontestable biblical and theological datum that the Church must be one, Christian apologists of each denomination labored to prove that theirs was the true Church and that all other denominations were churches falsely so called—mere "synagogues of Satan" (Apoc 2:9).

Many Christians today are ashamed of the rigid dogmatism, the bitter polemics, and the slovenly argumentation characteristic of the apologetics of recent centuries. In trying to correct this, some fall into a kind of relativism or false tolerance which deprives the Christian message of its exigence and authority. Some speak as though churches, like clubs, could be organized at will by any group of like-minded Christians.

The notion of the Church as sacrament preserves the priority of God's action. A sacrament is not an arbitrarily constructed sign, but one that comes into being because of the spiritual reality that is contained in it. The Church, therefore, is present where, and only where, God's irrevocable self-gift in his incarnate Son continues to come to expression in symbolic form. As the work of God, the Church cannot be constructed simply by the free initiative of believers, however pious. The human contribution is necessarily secondary; it is well described as "obedience."

Since human effort is capable of disguising itself as the work of God, it can be important to discern between the true Church and its human counterfeits. In making this discernment, the mind can be assisted by considering those features of the Church which necessarily result from its connection with God's saving work in Christ. The ancient creeds, following certain indications in scripture, described the Church as "one, holy, catholic, and apostolic." These adjectives have been much used—and also misused—in fundamental theology to signalize the true Church. According to the sacramental vision these four attributes are not simply extrinsic criteria based upon positive revelation given in scripture and tradition. They are intrinsically bound up with the very idea of the Church as sacrament.

The Church is and must be *one*. To be an efficacious sign of God's redemptive work in Christ, it must be a fellowship of reconciliation; it must bring its members together into a community of faith, trust, and mutual concern, thus reversing the effects of human sin which have alienated people from God, from one another, and from themselves. The unity of the Christian community is celebrated in many biblical passages such as the high-priestly prayer of Jesus (John 17) and the Pauline Letter to the Ephesians (4:1–16).

The Church is *holy.* That is to say, it does not live, as Church, by merely created principles, but by the power of God's grace. Its life and its unity are from above. Animated by the Holy Spirit, it constantly calls its members out of their sinful, broken existence, so that while remaining in the world, they are no longer of it (cf. Jn 17:14–19).

The Church is *catholic.* Since Christ died not for any particular group or nation, but for the whole human family, the Church as sacrament visibly expresses the universality of his redemptive love. It is not a sect or an elite. It includes men and women, young and old, learned and unlearned, saints and sinners—in short, people of every race, tongue, kind, and condition.

The catholicity of the Church renders its inner unity more resplendent and at the same time more complex. For its unity is a oneness among people who retain their human variety. Catholicity, moreover, stands in some tension with holiness. By virtue of its holiness, the Church must stand against the world as a "sign of contradiction." Without striving for mere bigness, it must retain its own distinctness and integrity. It must fearlessly impose the demands of the gospel, and deliberately marginalize those whose hearts and minds are set not upon God but upon the world of imaginary idols. Yet the Church, as catholic, must reach out even to the unconverted, seeking to form them in ways that will be conducive to conversion. It must be patient toward the weak, as Jesus was.

Finally, the Church is essentially *apostolic*; that is to say, it remains, and must remain, in visible continuity with its own origins. This continuity includes certain institutional elements (apostolicity in doctrine, sacraments, and ministry) but it should not be understood as an unconditional obligation to adhere to its archaic forms. To be an effective sign of sacrament of Christ, the Church subordinates institutional to pastoral concerns as Jesus did in departing from the "traditions of the elders" when the healing of persons so required. Gifted with the power of Christ's Spirit, the Church does not lack the capacity to adapt its institutional forms to the needs of different ages and cultures.

The four "notes" of the Church, viewed in the perspectives of a a sacramental ecclesiology, are not mere indicatives but also imperatives. The sacrament, insofar as it is co-constituted by the human response, is always deficient, always imperfect. Some styles of apologetics have performed a disservice by overemphasizing the oneness between Christ and his Church. They have left unexplained the presence of sin and weakness in the Church, and its capacity to become, in many respects, a countersign. A realistic fundamental theology will reckon with the paradox of an identity in difference, in which the sameness and the contrast mutually condition each other. The Church would not be the sacrament of Christ except for the human response of the faithful who compose it; yet that very response is never what it should be, and to that extent the sacrament itself is tarnished. The identity in difference is simultaneously painful and consoling. Painful, it forbids us to rest in the Church as though it were divinely perfect. Consoling, it enables us to be confident that in spite of the Church's human weakness, Christ remains present with it and in it. His victorious grace is ever greater than the infidelity of his followers.

Thanks to Christ's promise in the gospels, and more fundamentally thanks to the irrevocable character of God's self-gift in his Son, we can be assured that, in spite of all human frailty, the Church itself will not perish. As a sign of God's definitive and victorious love, the Church will endure through the centuries. Though many Christians fall away from the truth of Christ, that truth will remain accessible in history. It will continue to be preached and believed in the Church.

The Catholic Church, while recognizing its own weakness, dares to make the claim that in it the Church of Christ—one, holy, catholic, and apostolic—continues to subsist.[27] It is convinced that its own essential teachings, its hierarchical ministry, and its sacraments are in conformity with Christ's will and institution. Without this confidence, the Church could not properly perform the service of pastoral care and direction committed to it. If the Church could not carry on, through its ministries and sacraments, the sanctifying work of Christ himself, its members would become, in effect, like sheep without a shepherd.

Yet the Catholic Church's claim that in it subsists the Church of Christ provides no ground for smugness or complacency. For effective mission, bare subsistence is not enough. The Church must stir up the charism that is within it (cf. 2 Tim 1:6); it must hear what the Spirit has to say to it (Apoc 2:29, 3:6, 13, 22) in order to become ever more authentically the sign or sacrament of Christ. It must undergo constant conversion to the gospel, purifying itself of its faults, and incessantly pursuing the path of penance and renewal.[28] It must undertake with vigor the task of renewal and reform.[29]

While there is only one Church, in the sense of one bride, one temple, one body of Christ, still there is a multiplicity of ways and degrees in which individuals can be incorporated into it.[30] Some who are incorporated by faith, baptism, and grace may lack the kind of incorporation that is given by Holy Communion and by submission to those pastors who govern by Christ's authority. All must seek to perfect their incorporation, both visible and invisible, both institutional and spiritual.

The diversions among Christians, while they do not destroy the given unity of the Church of Christ, impair the sacramental manifestation of that unity and consequently impede the life of grace. The unity of the "divided" Church must be sought by means that will build up everything that the Holy Spirit has accomplished in the separate communities. Ecumenical activity must seek not to destroy the authentic gifts of any Christian community, but rather to supply what may be lacking and to correct what is amiss, so that the sacrament of unity may be made to shine forth in full radiance. Since Vatican Council II, many members of separated Christian communities have been in dialogue with the Catholic Church. Ecumenists of the vai-ious Churches have engaged in arduous research and discussion, seeking to prepare through convergence and consensus the paths that may one day lead to full visible unity among Christians of different traditions.

Since the present chapter is intended to confine itself to questions of fundamental theology, it would not be appropriate here to pursue the particular dogmatic questions that have come to the fore in the ecumenical conversations of the past two decades. It may suffice to say that ecclesiology has proved central, and that within ecclesiology questions of structure and ministry have commanded the most serious attention. Catholics in dialogue have been pressed by Protestants to defend the necessity of the historic episcopate; they have been pressed by Anglicans and Orthodox, as well as by Protestants, to justify the papal office. Generally speaking, Catholic ecumenists have not been satisfied to respond to these demands by positive arguments drawn from the Bible and early tradition; they have increasingly concentrated on the value of the episcopacy and the papacy as "signs and instruments" of the unity and continuity which belong to the Church of Christ. In other words, they have set forth the importance of these offices within the framework of a sacramental vision of the Church. Without episcopacy and without papacy, as the center of unity of the worldwide episcopacy, the Church would lack something needed for the full and manifest realization of its unity, holiness, apostolicity, and catholicity. Catholic theologians, however, do not deny that the sacraments of the Church may be realized, albeit deficiently, in communities which lack these particular ministries.

VI. The Church and Theological Method

As a reflection on the logic of conversion, fundamental theology should have something to say about the principles of Christian theology. In any system, there is an indissoluble link between the approach to faith and theological method. Deism, for example, insofar as it sought to demonstrate the true religion without reliance on authority, pointed the way to a theology of "pure reason" exemplified by Immanuel Kant and many of the idealist philosophers. The older apologetical theology, maintaining that the process of conversion terminates in an act of submission to authority, led inevitably to a kind of theology that argued from the authoritative statements of the Bible and of the teaching Church. The participatory and symbolic approach for which we have argued in the preceding pages cannot be content with either the rational-deductive or the extrinsic-authoritative styles of theology.

Christian faith, we have contended, is a participatory form of knowledge available within the Church through a lived sharing in the meaning of the Christian symbols. The Christian is one who adheres to Christ and the Church as signs of salvation, or rather, more correctly, to Christ in the Church as a single and all-embracing sign of salvation. Since the sign is a symbol or sacrament, its meaning can never be fully spelled out in explicit language. Yet the symbol does give rise to thought. In moments of reflection, we can to some extent formulate the meaning of the Christian symbols in propositions and formulas, as when we say that "God is love" or that "Christ is Lord." In the course of the centuries, the Church, as a structured community of faith, has enshrined its commitments in credal and dogmatic formulations, as we have already seen in our discussion of the four attributes of the Church listed in the Nicene-Constantinopolitan Creed. Creedal and dogmatic formulas, however, cannot be taken as objective scientific utterances. They do not have a clear conceptual reference, but rather they live off the primary language of revelatory symbolism.

The task of theology is to conduct a methodic or systematic reflection on faith. As an ecclesial discipline, theology is done within the believing community. It endeavors to give a coherent systematization of Christian faith, guided by the symbols and by past formulations, especially those which have normative value in the Church. According to the sacramental understanding, these formulations refer back to the experience of conversion, which continually goes on within the Church. They express certain aspects of a commitment that necessarily remains, in great part, tacit or implicit.

The theologian, according to this view, cannot be content with a merely positive historical method which would argue from authoritative statements as though they could be adequately understood by a mere analysis of their conceptual content. Since the meaning of the formulas is richer than their explicit content, one cannot be satisfied with a deductive method which spells out the logical implications of statements found in the Bible or in past tradition. To be a true theologian one must dwell in spirit within the community of faith; one must participate in the Christian symbols and in their meaning for the community. This kind of participatory knowledge will make it possible to see the formulas in relation to the unexplicit meaning which they carry to those who share in the tradition. Recognizing the Church as the community to which he owes his own faith, the Christian theologian will treat its traditional formulas with great reverence, for only through the expressions of the faith of past believers can anyone today become a Christian. As a participant in the corporate life of the community, the Christian theologian will stand under the guidance of the Spirit who governs the Church at large. Through docility to that Spirit, one may be equipped to perceive the divinely intended meaning of formulas through which the Spirit has spoken in the past. The theologian, then, is not at the mercy of mere words, which are often vague or ambiguous. Through the experience of living in the community, and especially through sharing in its life of worship, the believing theologian has a certain familiarity with the meaning of the symbols not accessible to the outsider.

Theology, then, is an essentially hermeneutical process. It does not begin with a rigid set of premises, whether philosophical or dogmatic, nor with a supposedly immediate experience, untouched by the Christian symbols. The theologian is content to live in the "hermeneutical circle," allowing the experience of faith to illuminate, perfect, and in some cases to rectify, the formulations. The mutual priority of the two poles of Christian experience prevents either from being unilaterally subordinated to the other.

For those committed to the sacramental and participatory understanding of faith, theology has an essentially practical dimension. It cannot be a sterile pursuit of merely theoretical questions unrelated to the actual living out of faith. If faith is a commitment to the meaning of the Christian symbols, and if theology is a reflection on faith, the theologian will always have to ponder how a given doctrine, opinion, or theory will affect the believer's relationship to the community and its sacramental life.

Good theology, since it grows out of the biblical and traditional symbols, illuminates and intensifies the Christian commitment. Rooted in the process of conversion, it interprets and furthers that process. Reflection feeds back into experience, clarifying and heightening it. The best theologian will be one who has personally experienced the transforming power of the Christian symbols, and who knows how to relate those symbols to the God who stands disclosed in them.

Bibliography

Bouillard, Henri, *The Logic of Faith* (New York, 1967). Essays in which the logic of faith is grounded in the logic of human existence, interpreted according to the perspectives of Maurice Blondel.

Congar, Yves, *L'Eglise: une, sainte, catholique et apostolique* (Mysterium salutis 15; Paris, 1970). A dogmatic ecclesiology under the rubrics of the four "notes" of the Church as understood in a contemporary approach.

Dulles, Avery, *A History of Apologetics* (London and Philadelphia, 1970). A one-volume survey which briefly summarizes the trends referred to in this chapter.

———, *Models of the Church* (Garden City, N.Y., 1974). A "sacramental" ecclesiology with a discussion of the problem of the "true" Church.

Latourelle, René, *Christ and the Church: Signs of Salvation* (Staten Island, N.Y., 1972). A study of the signs of revelation in the light of Vatican II.

Newman, John Henry, *Essay in Aid of a Grammar of Assent.* A classic of epistemology, with special attention to the problems of religious conversion.

Polanyi, Michael, *Personal Knowledge* (Harper Torchbooks ed.; New York, 1964). A brilliant and profound study of the logic of discovery, especially as applied to modern science.

Ricoeur, Paul, *The Symbolism of Evil,* tr. by E. Buchanan (Boston, 1967). An inquiry into the symbolic aspects of religious language.

15

Observations on the Situation of Faith Today

Karl Rahner

In the following reflections, which are admittedly somewhat informal and unsystematic, the reference is to faith as understood by the teaching authority of the Catholic Church and by traditional theology. The author is therefore not dismayed by having to reckon with the objection that he is only creating theological problems for himself when he accepts a concept of faith that does not fit in with the meaning given to this term by his contemporaries and many modern theologians.

I. In Search of an Integrated Consciousness

The first point to be considered by a theologian is the now very evident impossibility of achieving a positive integration of faith with the rest of the contents of knowledge (at least among educated persons living in today's world, or in the Western world at any rate). To begin with, then, what is meant by this (reciprocal) impossibility of achieving an integration? Because of the element of chance in the individual's history and the plurality of the sources of his knowledge (beginning with the multiplicity of his senses), the various contents of his consciousness are not integrated among themselves from the outset. Everything does not fit together from the start. A principal function of the knowledge a person has as a subject which despite the multiplicity of realities making it up is *one*, is to synthesize his many and initially very disparate experiences. The person strives for a completely structured vision of the world, a vision in which the object of each single experience has its appointed place; in which all the particulars clarify and explain one another; and in which no contradictions make their appearance. Given the unity of consciousness and the nature of things, it is necessary and intelligible that the realities of the person's secular experience and those of his Christian faith should be integrated to form such a unified vision of the world. The realities of faith do not simply create a world apart, separated from the world of secular experience; this is so if for no other reason than that this faith also presents the believers with claims and demands that must be met in the concrete world of secular experience and action, in the ethical life, and in the ecclesial society, which is a very concrete reality of everyday life. For this reason the striving for a synthesis, an integration of the reality of faith with the reality of secular experience must be accepted as legitimate in principle. The Christian rightly seeks a completely structured and unified "vision of the world," into which his properly Christian faith and the rest of his experience and knowledge (including scientific knowledge) may be integrated.

This "vision of the world" is not simply given in advance, for, if it were, the revelation faith brings would, as such, have to have for its proper content the whole of human knowledge. Not only is this evidently not the case, but in addition revelation and Christian faith show that they actually deny any unified world-vision as created in advance by the unity of the sources of knowledge. Though man does not live by faith alone (this modesty on the part of revelation and faith is not at all to be taken for granted, but the fact is there) and can in fact live this faith only with the help of the rest of his experience, a vision of the world that is completely structured in a clear and intelligible way is nonetheless not given to him in advance but must be sought and constructed as a task rendered obligatory for the Christian by his very faith itself. It is a fact, of course, that in every age this task can be successfully accomplished only to the extent of an asymptomatic approximation to the goal and that, from the viewpoint of the individual and his life work, the goal is one which can be reached only through death. But even at the level of society the goal has never been fully attained. There have always been residues of secular experience (in regard to nature and history) that have not been clearly synthesized with the Christian faith and united with this faith in a single world-vision, although these residues certainly have some relevance to faith. In earlier times, however, these residues of an experience that was a subjective reality but was not positively integrated into a Christian vision of the world were relatively limited, for the reason that people simply did not have knowledge of many secular facts which are relevant to faith but difficult to integrate with it. In the world-picture of a Suárez, for example, while his faith did not from the outset form a unity with his theology and his secular knowledge of faith and history, at least they could without trouble be integrated into a recognizable positive unity. Everything fitted together, and this harmony was not merely postulated in principle by his faith and the radical unity of his consciousness, but was a verifiable fact.

Despite such residues of unresolved problems earlier Christian ages had an unchallenged, unified world picture, a fully structured world view which was not one that an isolated individual had worked out on his own account and at his own risk, but was rather the possession of a whole society. Here, despite individual heretics and dissidents, the world view retained a more or less self-evident and unchallenged dominance, at least in its basic components. And to the extent that people knew and took with existential seriousness (probably only a few did) the fact that there had been and still were other religions and other world views outside the realm of Christian civilization, they were easily able to integrate this fact into their Christian vision of the world. It could be explained in terms intelligible to Christians (original sin, culpable error, and so on), or else the adherents of these other religions and world views could simply be regarded as enemies with whom it was antecedently impossible to hold any dialogue that might prove a threat to the Christian vision of the world. The people of those earlier ages did not look upon those other world views as unintegrated facts which were a threat to their own faith, but rather thought of them in somewhat the way that I know the existence of Tibetan medicine but simply disregard it as irrelevant to my views on medicine, without my having attempted to come to grips with it in a positive way. Of course, even in earlier ages there were short periods when a world picture became unclear or underwent disintegration or there was a struggle between several world pictures, but these critical phases (for example, the transition from the "pagan" world picture of antiquity to that of the Christian West) were relatively brief. In a society that was geographically limited and remained in peaceful possession of its own self-understanding throughout every such process of change, the society's vision of the world was likewise marked by unity and continuity.

Today the situation is quite different, and there is no telling how and when this new situation might yield to another, even if no one is able to say that such a change is simply impossible. The person of today finds it impossible on two accounts to achieve a positive integration between his faith and all the data of his consciousness. The extent of his secular knowledge, and the necessity and real possibility of an existentially authentic dialogue with all the factually given forms of faith and world views, are the two reasons why such an integration is impossible.

II. Can Modern Knowledge and Christian Faith Be Harmonized?

First of all, then, the range of secular knowledge that is possessed or can in principle be easily attained by the individual is so great that a positive synthesis of it with the Christian faith is now a concrete and practical impossibility, at least for the individual.

The amount of knowledge that is supplied by the natural and historical sciences is so immense and is growing so fast that, even if we leave the faith out of consideration, it can no longer be really synthesized in the head of any individual. A system of knowledge into which new information was slowly and carefully integrated has turned for the individual into an exploding chaos in which he can no longer really find his way. Not only does he personally not know an infinity of things which "people" know today, but he is very really and concretely aware *that* he does not know them. (All he has to do is stand in front of a computer!) This is an entirely new and different form of not-knowing, and it is accompanied by a feeling of helplessness and impotence, such as in earlier times a person might possibly have had at the thought of nature in its entirety, but not in the presence of human works.

This present but unmastered mass of knowledge brings with it (I am still prescinding from any confrontation with the faith) a new and specific relationship of the person to knowledge. In earlier times there was an incalculable number of things the individual did not know, but he was not aware that he lacked this knowledge, or, at most, his ignorance, when realized, was extremely unimportant to him in existential terms and was relegated to the periphery of his consciousness. Moreover, what people did know, they knew with certainty and unquestioningly. For this reason the basic form taken by the individual's knowledge was a sure and to some extent unconditional assertion of what he knew.

Today, on the contrary, the individual realizes that he is now surrounded by an immense mass of things "known" but unknown to him personally; he knows how rapidly this mass is constantly growing and how it casts doubt on what he does positively know, reducing it to something provisional and obsolete. In consequence, the normal form taken by contemporary knowledge in any individual is not that of the firm assertion which is proposed as sure, abiding, and more or less unconditional, but rather that of a knowledge felt to be provisional, open to challenge, hypothetical, and valid for the moment. Replacement by knowledge newly gained is looked upon simply as the elimination of a hypothesis hitherto acceptable. The result of this state of affairs is a diffuse, but everywhere operative, skeptical relativism. No longer does man live in firmly built houses made of convictions that are absolutely correct, universally accepted in society, and everywhere taken for granted. He lives rather in tents hastily pitched on a journey into the unforeseeable, precisely because so much is known, new knowledge is so quickly obtained, and each individual is becoming increasingly more ignorant by comparison with the extent of what is in itself immediately knowable and can be "looked up"—this despite the fact that by reason of technological inventions he lives constantly in the presence of what he no longer understands.

Given this situation of the individual in regard to knowledge, it is impossible that his relation to the Christian faith should be simply what it was in an earlier time. A positive, harmonious, and clearly visible synthesis of modern knowledge with the faith so as to form a unified world vision is no longer possible, either subjectively or objectively. The Christian faith can no longer, as it could in earlier times, be experienced in so straightforward and self-evident a way as the ultimate structural principle of all knowledge. Admittedly, one cannot maintain (at least in principle) that there is a clear and certain contradiction of an absolute kind between faith and modern knowledge, although it is not so easy, either psychologically or existentially, to keep one's footing on the rather obscure middle ground between the nonascertainability of an unqualified contradiction and the impossibility of seeing a positive reconciliation and synthesis of the two. But even though such an unqualified contradiction cannot be shown to exist and even though the modern apologia for Christianity is often content with this kind of negative defense, we must at the same time understand and reflect on the fact that a positive synthesis between modern knowledge and the ancient faith is to a large extent no longer possible for the individual.

This statement should be illustrated by concrete cases. Examples should be adduced showing the impossibility of positive reconciliation between contemporary knowledge and Christian faith in the area of the natural sciences as well as in the area of the historical and social sciences. One might ask, for example, whether an individual historian of religions, acting in this capacity, acknowledges as certain the teaching of fundamental theology on the self-understanding of the historical Jesus, a teaching which, in the view of traditional Catholic fundamental theology, must be regarded as historically demonstrable. One might ask whether the modern historian and social scientist can regard as adequately proven (especially given the historical form of the Church) the incomparability of Christianity with the other religions, which the First Vatican Council declared to be a concrete argument of fundamental theology (therefore an empirical historical argument) for the supernatural origin of Christian revelation, an argument that is cogent at all times and within the power of every mind to grasp. One might ask what the modern mind is to make of the claim regarding miracles and prophecies (which people today, unlike Vatican I, pass over in silence). One might ask whether the modern mind unquestioningly regards the spread of the Church as miraculous, her moral condition as one of exceptional holiness, and her activity as limitlessly fruitful in every form of good, so that all this is, for this modern mind, what Vatican I understood it to be: an irrefutable testimony to the Church's divine mission. There are many similar questions that might be asked.

I am not claiming that no meaningful clarifications or responses can be given to these and many, many other questions. The point is simply that even when these answers are correct "in themselves" or at least are assumed to be correct, they do not remove, for the individual, the impossibility of integrating contemporary knowledge and Christian faith into a world vision which can be apprehended as positively unified. There is no means available of changing this situation. It must simply be endured by showing that the real burden it lays on contemporary man would not be removed if he were to surrender the faith and with it the coexistence of Christian faith and modern knowledge, because the coexistence of unconditionally maintained convictions and a limitless range of opinions held only hypothetically and provisionally cannot be eliminated by any means.

We must now look more closely at how the concrete living of the Christian faith is affected when it is forced to exist in such a situation of skeptical relativism and of knowledge that is consciously provisional. The observations I intend to make on this question are very unsystematic; nor do I wish to give the impression that they are exhaustive.

III. The Teaching Authority of the Church

First of all, as a matter of fact the teaching authority of the Church has been given a very secondary existential place in the "system of belief" of a contemporary person. Of course, the acceptance of a teaching office whose occupants teach with binding authority does belong to the Christian faith as understood by Catholics. Where such an office is *denied outright* it is no longer possible to speak of a properly Catholic understanding of the faith. But this authority of the Church and her teaching is certainly not the primary and ultimate foundation of the faith of the contemporary person, but rather a quite derivative element, although from the viewpoint of fundamental theology an element that co-determines the entire faith of the individual Catholic. The teaching authority of the Church is certainly one of the contents of the Catholic faith but, again from the viewpoint of fundamental theology, it is not the beginning of the faith nor its ultimate foundation.

In theory this was always true of Catholic fundamental theology, since the latter justified its teaching on the existence of God and on the possibility and reality of a revelation, as well as its teaching on Jesus Christ as legate of God, *before* presenting an ecclesiology doctrine on the teaching office of the Church and on scripture as inspired source of revelation. But at the practical and kerygmatic level a different mentality was present, at least under the surface. People argued along the lines of St. Augustine's famous statement that he would not believe the gospel if he were not moved to do so by the authority of the Church. They experienced the Church, her authority, and the inflexible absoluteness of her teaching as the sole real bulwark behind which they knew themselves to be protected against their own skepticism and the disintegration of all certitude. They had a direct and unquestioning appreciation of the Church's (rather triumphalistic) emphasis on her being by her nature and history an unassailable motive of faith, and not simply one particular object of this faith, one that in fact holds a relatively secondary place within the total structure and overall justification of the faith.

Even today, of course, there are many people whose psychological bent and social conditioning make them feel the same way. Moreover, there is no way of forecasting whether this experience of the Church may not once again become generally the almost self-evident way of approaching the Christian faith as a whole. This is especially so inasmuch as it is by no means obvious that people should, and in the future will, regard the social conditioning of their convictions as a reason for doubting these and not rather as a reason for accepting them as correct, But, even granting all this and taking it into account, it is a fact that belief in the Church and especially in her authoritative teaching office is today, on the whole, a conviction which plays only a belated and secondary role in the genesis and overall structure of the Catholic faith.

Modern man knows too much about the difficulty of regarding the results of the history of the Church's dogma as derivable, by cogent logic or clear development, from the faith-consciousness of the primitive Church, much less from the teaching of the historical Jesus. Even if such a derivation is objectively possible, he as an individual cannot accomplish it. Nor will recourse to the authority of the Church in her present self-understanding be of help to him in this matter, because he regards this self-understanding as itself the product of a history whose legitimacy he is unable to apprehend with clarity.

Modern man also has a different, more sober, and as it were demythologized attitude to the forms of authority and their representatives, because he has a better grasp than earlier people did of the history of these authorities with its upheavals and blunders; consequently, he is aware of the mistakes and wrong decisions made in the history of the Church's teaching office. The claim that in these undeniable blunders made by the teaching Church there was always question of authentic but nondefinitory doctrinal statements is of course objectively valid, but it is of no ready practical value to an individual today. For even nondefinitory doctrinal statements can in certain circumstances have a very concrete and massive impact on the life of the Church and affect the individual in very real ways (think, for example, of *Humanae vitae* or the declaration that a woman cannot be ordained a priest). In addition, the Roman magisterium in concrete cases obscures rather than explicates the distinction between simply authentic and definitory doctrinal statements, thus giving the impression that in concrete practice it regards all doctrinal statements as irreformable. The result of this practice is to make individuals today suspect that even doctrinal definitions are no better a position than mere authentic declarations issued by the teaching Church.

There is a further reason for this reaction: the simple Christian who is not a professional theologian, though he may be an educated intellectual, often has the impression that in the case of many dogmas modern theology offers interpretations so different from the previous (popular) understanding of these dogmas as to make it difficult to see the identity of new interpretation with old dogma. In principle, such interpretations may be necessary and legitimate and may in fact not be a threat to the continued existence of the old dogma. But the new interpretations certainly do make it difficult for the individual Christian to maintain a straightforward and unembarrassed attitude to the Church's teaching office.

I shall not discuss or attempt to solve here the many problems that all this brings with it. I am interested in only one point: Even existentially, the Church's teaching office is no longer the self-evident reference-point of faith, the self-evident and unproblematic court of appeal to which a preacher can have recourse, but is rather a relatively secondary fact in the constantly renewed genesis of faith and an object of proclamation rather than the foundation of this proclamation.

It follows from all this that anyone proclaiming the faith as taught by the Church must be very cautious about appealing to the authority of the magisterium, especially since in this matter of preaching careful note must be taken of the fact that an appeal to the faith-consciousness of the Church as holding irrevocably to a particular teaching (an appeal that even today still has an apologetic value) is not simply identical with an appeal to the formal authority of the Roman magisterium. Today this authority is factually and in practice a permanent object of proclamation which fundamental theology and apologetics must be constantly making intelligible and credible, but it is not the basis that is always and everywhere presupposed in preaching.

It also follows that the effort to proclaim a particular dogma of the Church in an intelligible and credible way should not be always ending up with an appeal to the formal authority of the Church's teaching office; rather, fundamental theology and apologetics must ground the dogma in question either in itself or in still more general and more basic articles of the Christian faith. This statement is, of course, a truism even for traditional fundamental theology. But until now preachers have usually taken it too much for granted that they are operating within the framework of the Church as something indisputable and self-evident, so that they need only set forth whatever the Church says. But nowadays, even in mystagogical preaching within the bosom of the Church preachers are addressing people whose relation to the teaching office and even to the faith-consciousness of the Church as a whole is not as ingenuous and naive as it used to be. Proclamation "inside" should not differ now from proclamation "to the outside." In principle, dogmatic preaching must have its fundamental-theological aspect; dogmatics and fundamental theology must permeate each other. There can no longer be nowadays, nor may preaching presuppose, a fundamental theology which thinks that it has proved once and for all in a formal way the existence of a binding revelation, so that then it is only necessary and permissible to ask what God is in fact communicating through this revelation. Today the situation is, if anything, reversed: it is the credibility (that is, the meaningfulness, the existential assimilability, and the human indispensableness) of the fundamental dogmas of Christianity that renders credible the existence of (properly understood) supernatural revelation, and not vice versa. The existence of the Church's teaching office and its concrete importance for the faith of the individual, for which it acts as a norm, may not be abandoned even today, but it has a different value and a different place in the structure and "system" of a contemporary person's faith.

To put it bluntly (and a preacher must, if he is to be credible), the Church today is a burden. The burden may not be cast off, since to do so would in the long run deal a deadly blow to the Christian faith (note that a return to the authority of scripture alone involves the same problems and difficulties today, given our contemporary knowledge of the historical conditioning even of the scriptures). Neither may the burden be glossed over; rather we must allow the whole weight of the often very terrible history of the Church to weigh upon us before making an appeal to the authority of the Church. Only when we have honestly and without any triumphalism accepted the scandal of this cross that goes with the faith of the Christian, and only when we make it the starting point of our preaching, can the burden become a blessing and the Church, despite everything, be experienced as the natural place of faith, the place where God's promise of irrevocable power is accepted in Jesus Christ.

IV. The Assent of Faith

There is another and quite different question that calls for consideration when we look at Christian faith as existing in a concrete person within a situation that no longer allows a positive integration of the faith with modern knowledge (in its proper specificity). This situation also threatens the unconditional assent of faith, which is essential to the Christian faith. The assent of faith must be absolute, unconditional, and firm beyond any other assent. To use the formulation of J. Beumer, the act of faith is

> by its nature a complete surrender of man to God. Insofar as this surrender is a free act of the intellect in response to God's revealing word, it possesses the certitude of faith. As regards its object, this certitude implies (beyond the question of the relative certitude of the *Praeambula fidei*) an absoluteness (firmmess) in both the "decision for" (even as norm of knowledge) *(certitudo adhaesionis)* and the (free) apprehension of the formal object of the assent as such (which object gives an absolute, objective guarantee of the truth), namely the true and trustworthy testimony of God *(certitudo infallibilitatis),* so that the believer, even from the cognitive viewpoint, makes that which is attested the absolute point of reference and unnormed norm of his knowledge.[1]

According to traditional teaching, then, faith should be absolutely and unconditionally the first and clearcut fixed point of reference for all human convictions, a point of reference that (because God's very own truth has become the ground and formal object) has no higher human authority over it that could subject it to criticism and cast doubt upon it. I cannot deal here directly with the problems raised by this teaching on the certitude of faith (problems that have always been raised and have long been discussed in traditional theology), or with the answers to these questions as given in various forms in the traditional analysis of faith; I shall simply presuppose that these questions and answers are known.

The basic problem in this area is that the divine truth which is to guarantee the absolute certitude and firmness of faith is always mediated through human knowledge. The question therefore arises: Why does not this human mediation, with its problematic character and its uncertainty, codetermine the concrete faith of the individual, so that it cannot have the certitude the Church claims for it? Even though, as I said a moment ago, I do not intend to deal with this ancient and ever new problem, the mention of it is enough to show that the problem is altered and can become more acute when the concrete situation in which the absolute revelation of God must be communicated in a human way to human beings itself changes and becomes more difficult.

To be more concrete: In an intellectual situation in which in other areas too the firm and unquestioning statement (taking one or other form and possessing, of course, one or other degree of assurance) was the normal form taken by human knowledge, the absolute assent of faith did not stand out as an especially remarkable and unusual phenomenon in the individual's field of consciousness. It presented itself rather as a climactic moment, but not one greatly to be wondered at, in an overall system of statements of a secular kind that were made with calm assurance and presented as unchangeable. But in a consciousness normally marked by a skeptical relativism in secular matters and by knowledge always regarded as provisionally accepted until outdated, such an absolute assent of faith must be felt as an alien body, as a demand which the contemporary person cannot seriously meet, since even in the realm of knowledge he lives in a situation of change, provisionality, and unpredictability. In such a situation the old problems of the analysis of faith take on an entirely new importance and have far different practical consequences than in the past.

In metaphorical terms: in the days when a king was a self-evident and unchallenged figure, the radical necessity of which no critic dared attack (at least not in the world of the individual's real everyday experience), it was also easy to believe in the pope. But now that the kings have all departed, belief in the pope cannot be taken for granted to the extent it was before. Let me drop the metaphor: in the historical and social situation of an earlier time it was easy to regard even the preambles of faith as certain; consequently the preambles posed no threat to faith, although, of course, even the old analysis of faith knew that the certainty and firmness of the assent to the preambles were less than the certainty and firmness claimed by faith itself. Today, however, the concrete individual lives in a cognitive situation in which he is faced with a range of historical and metaphysical problems no single person can master and in which modern knowledge and faith cannot be integrated into a unified world picture. Consequently, not being a professional theologian, he does not have a clear certainty regarding the preambles of faith such as people used to have, and this fact also affects his faith itself. He feels insecure; it is not longer clear to him how he can maintain an absolute and unconditionally firm assent.

At an earlier time, theologians in their analysis of faith could readily say that the knowledge of the preambles of faith was an extrinsic condition for faith and did not, with its merely relative certainty, touch the heart of faith or become part of its very structure; faith was determined only by its own proper internal formal object and was therefore not affected by the relatively lesser certainty of the preambles. (An analogue of this situation would be one in which a person treats a particular couple as his parents with unqualified love and fidelity, although the certitude he has that this couple are in fact his real parents is less than the certitude with which he honors them.) But at that time the certitude of the preambles was felt to be so great and self-evident that people could easily accept the view (which is certainly correct in theory) that the preambles, though certain and experienced as certain, did not form part of the inner essence of faith and could not ground or justify the absoluteness of the assent of faith.

But things are not so simple today, at least once the average person rightly or wrongly regards the certitude he can reach about the preambles as much diminished or even nonexistent. Concretely and in practice this feeling cannot but detract from the certitude of the assent of faith itself, whether or not this further step be logically necessary. For what we are dealing with here is not the abstract nature of faith, but faith as concretely existing in the consciousness of a modern person, and this existence undoubtedly depends on the existence and contemporary form of the preambles in the person's mind. He has the impression that while he may perhaps "in conscience and to the best of his knowledge" (as presently given) provisionally accept the faith after the manner of an "opinion" which can reasonably be maintained for the time being, he must also introduce the same reservation with which he accepts any other human knowledge, namely, that he may acquire a better idea of the matter later on and then have to revise his previous view of the faith. There can be no question, therefore, of an absolute assent that antecedently and in principle forbids such a later revision.

I think that what I have been saying reflects with some exactitude the contemporary state of mind in the Western world, although, of course, there are quite varying degrees of explicit awareness of this epistemological situation in which faith now finds itself.

In the light of faith's own self-understanding what can be said of this threat to faith in our day? Can faith exist even today with the absolute assent and unquestioning certitude it used to claim for itself? Can the spiritual man judge all things and refuse to be judged by any other without making a hopeless attempt to escape from his own historico-cultural situation? What can be said if we do not take as our starting point the presupposition that the traditional distinction between the rational grounds for assent to the preamble of faith, on the one hand, and the inner formal object and motive of faith, on the other, is adequate for answering our problem, which is after all historically conditioned? If I attempt to answer the question thus posed, I am not thereby assuming that my answer is adequate and that quite different considerations might not also be offered in the interests of providing a rounded answer to the question.

V. The Contents of Faith

In this connection it seems worth mentioning at the outset that faith as *fides quae* is a many-sided reality. Although in itself and especially in the contemporary historico-cultural situation it seems necessary and commendable that a credible and effective proclamation should bring out the unity of the faith and the internal cohesion of its individual articles, nonetheless the contents of the faith are in fact varied and complex, especially in the official teaching of the Church. As a result, a particular point may be truly believed with a genuine theological faith, while at the same time another point in this same faith may be dismissed as false. It may perhaps be said that anyone who explicitly and publicly rejects even a single dogma of the Catholic Church is a heretic and no longer belongs to the Catholic Church. But it cannot be asserted that the inculpable dismissal of a particular dogma cannot coexist with a theological faith (infused habit and act). The possibility of a theological faith such as is necessary for salvation is affirmed by the Second Vatican Council even for a "pagan" or an atheist who is true to his own conscience.

If this be so, then it is also thinkable that a Catholic Christian may not be able to give particular dogmas of the Church the unqualified assent which is of the essence of faith, and yet may remain a believer in the theological sense of the word and be a Catholic, provided he does not explicitly and publicly deny a particular dogma and that he is acting in good faith. Many Catholics today are in this situation. Due to their historico-cultural and psychological state in this age of skeptical relativism they are in fact unable, despite their good will, to accept one or other dogma with the absolute assent of faith, and yet no one can therefore automatically say that these people do not possess the faith needed for salvation. It may not be objected that such people are Catholics only if they give an absolute assent of faith to the Church and her teaching office; that if they do so, this absolute assent will implicitly but necessarily extend to everything the Church teaches as irrevocably binding; and that therefore the case I am presenting here simply cannot arise for people who are Catholics and practicing the Christian life in the Church. The objection is invalid because the proposition that the Church is necessary for salvation and has an infallible teaching office is itself a particular article and one that enters the structure of faith at a relatively late point and can therefore be among the articles which a person may inculpably be unable to accept with the absolute assent of faith.

We may therefore say: If there are many people in the Church today who cannot manage a "complete identification with the Church" (to use the current phrase); if they can accept dogmas only with the provisional and conditional assent which they give to statements of purely secular knowledge; and if they live in the Church and "practice" after this fashion, then it cannot be asserted without further ado that they do not possess theological faith or do not belong to the Church. Even a faith that is still developing and is not yet able to give an absolute assent to certain expressions of the one total faith can be a saving and ecclesial faith. The only proviso is that it may not deliberately intend an *unqualified* rejection of a dogma of the Church. But in the majority of cases today there is no such absolute rejection, because even with regard to the teachings which the Church presents as matters of faith, modern man with his generalized skeptical relativism (even toward his own views) is not in a position, or willing, to reject *in an absolute manner* a binding doctrine of the Church just because he is not at the moment positively ready to accept it.

If what I have been saying is correct, then we can have a quite sober estimate of the real faith of very many contemporary Catholics, and yet be optimistic about the salvation of this large number of Catholics and about their membership in the Church. They do not indeed possess fully the faith as (legitimately) described in the theologial manuals. They do not say: I believe firmly, for good, and irrevocably, whatever the Church teaches. Or (if they use such formulas) their declarations are in practice permeated by the skeptical relativism that affects every area of consciousness today. And yet these people are Christians and Catholics.

But the question I asked is still not adequately answered. Can we speak of a theological faith when this "faith" has no contents that are affirmed with an unconditional assent of faith and when absolutely everything that is "believed" is accepted and lived with the attitude of conditionality and tentativeness that is the mark of our age? Or even in such a faith must not at least a few propositions, at some point, somehow, be given the absolute assent without which the traditional teaching on faith has no meaning? Now, one would certainly not do justice to the Church's teaching on faith and would no longer understand the unqualified importance of faith for the salvation of the human person (who determines his eternal destiny only through an unqualified disposition of his own freedom), if one were simply and *completely* to abandon the element of absolute assent in faith. But where and how can a phenomenological description of contemporary faith in the average person and even in the average Catholic still find this type of absolute assent?

It might be said, of course, that given the multiplicity of possible objects of faith, the many-sidedness of the human consciousness, and the impossibility of complete reflection, a Catholic who in principle wishes to be a believer will somewhere, somehow, find an article of faith which he accepts with an absolute assent, even if it is not possible to say exactly *what* this object of faith is. Such a view is certainly not completely mistaken, but, taken by itself, this answer is a little too easy. It is surely possible to say something further on this point and not be satisfied to appeal simply to the idea that in the consciousness of a member of the Christian Church there must inevitably be one or other reality to which he gives an absolute assent.

VI. The Fundamental Option

In order to advance at this point we must reflect on a fact: Human freedom, viewed as not simply a freedom of choice with regard to a particular categorial object present in the unlimited field of consciousness, but also as providing the subject with the possibility of disposing of himself totally in a radical decision, is always unqualifiedly present, in one or other manner, in an adult person. In other words, the human person does not exist as an unchangingly neutral subject who freely posits one act after another in a temporal sequence; the person exists rather as subject who has by a fundamental option made a decision with regard to himself. (This does not mean, of course, that such a basic decision, once made, cannot be changed.) Such an existential-personal decision, despite the fact that it can be revised, is by its nature an absolute decision of freedom; therefore the gnosiological element in it is likewise affirmed absolutely, even though the affirmation is freely made.

Consequently, it is not the case that in a human being who has reached the use of reason and freedom, everything without exception in his consciousness is known and freely accepted in a purely conditional and provisional manner. Even if this were so in the objectivizing and verbalizing concrete consciousness, and even if a particular individual were not able by reflection to discover anything in his concrete consciousness that he affirms as absolutely valid, and were in his reflective consciousness to set the mark of skeptical relativism on every single object, internal or external,—even then there would be no proof that the free fundamental option in which the subject posits and understands himself is not an absolute assent given knowingly and freely. At the very least, the radical protest of the subject against any absolute position, that is, his fundamental choice of universal skeptical relativism, would itself be a position taken absolutely. Freedom cannot escape the necessity of making an absolute decision, because the very effort to refrain completely from such a decision would in concrete reality be itself such a decision.

It must be said, next, that in the concrete real order such a decision is always either faith or unbelief, in the theological sense of these terms. The freedom with which the person disposes of himself in a radical decision is the freedom of a subject with a "supernatural existential," that is, with a permanent real self-offering of God who offers himself to freedom as the innermost subjective principle whereby the person orders himself to the immediacy of God. The radicalization of human transcendence toward the immediacy of God that is given in this constant offer of supernatural grace has the character of revelation in the strict theological sense of the word. Whenever a person in his free and absolute self-understanding does not through culpable fear lock himself up in his own finiteness but trustingly yields to the transcendental movement of his own spirit toward the incomprehensible God, he is accepting himself, even if in an unreflective way, in this transcendentality that is radically oriented by grace to the immediacy of God. In other words, he believes and does so with an absolute assent. Even a person who at the level of his concrete reflective consciousness endeavors to subordinate this consciousness to a universal skeptical relativism is in the primal unreflective exercise of his freedom a believer or an unbeliever by an act of unqualified assent. The inadequate tools of reflection available to him may not enable him to objectivize in a concrete way his absolute option of faith or unbelief, but in fact he either believes or is unbelieving, because a complete existential abstention from decision is impossible for the subject;

the subject in his transcendental openness is necessarily confronted by the gracious self-offering of God and says Yes or No to it.

To this theory, which attempts to show that even amid contemporary skeptical relativism an absolute assent of faith is inevitably possible and is in fact given, it may be objected that it does not render intelligible an absolute assent of faith to a specific (more or less explicit) reality of faith. And yet (the objection says) it is such an assent that is meant in traditional theology when an absolute assent of faith is called for; this or that specific reality is to be believed; "something" must be believed, and Christian faith may not be reduced (as it seems to be in Bultmann, for example) to a formal *fides qua* without any specific *fides quae*. But in the theory just presented (the objection continues) the absolute assent is limited to the acceptance of the subject's own object-less transcendentality, even if this transcendentality is thought of as radically directed to God by means of grace.

What can be said in response to this objection, which raises the suspicion that the theory in question dissolves Christian faith into a sublime existential ontology, since, according to the theory, what is belived is not in fact thought of as presented by a historical revelation?

First of all, the assent of faith of which the theory speaks is clearly based upon the free self-communication of God to the transcendentality of the human person. But wherever there is a free act of God, there is already history in a special but true sense, even if this free act of God does not occur at a particular point in the spatiotemporal world and within the rest of history, but is everywhere and always present as the condition—freely posited and perceived as such—of the possibility of the history of salvation. It is a false dilemma which says that something either belongs to history by having its determinate individual place therein or else belongs to an intrinsically ahistorical "essence."

It must be said, in addition, that the free acceptance of the fact that the person is related by grace to the immediacy of God (an acceptance that is necessarily faith) normally does not take place in an isolated mystical inwardness but, like everything connected with human transcendentality, is mediated to itself by encounter with an aposteriori "object" in the person's ambience and environing world. When the person encounters his historical world in a concrete way, he gains access to himself and thus also to his own transcendentality as radically directed by grace to God in himself. The mediating historical reality need not be of its nature something revealed in the strict theological sense of this term; it may in itself be something profane and secular, provided it be able to mediate an act in which the subject really disposes of himself in freedom and accepts himself as he is and therefore (implicitly) as related by grace to God.

In Scholastic terms: In the present order of salvation, in which by reason of the self-offering of God the human person is always and everywhere ordered to the immediacy of God as his end, every morally good act is in fact a salutary act, even when this morally good act is not expressly related to a revealed reality and a motivation of an objective and verbalized kind (to deny this would be to contradict Vatican II, which asserts that even an atheist or a "pagan" can make a salutary act of faith). Such an object, which has a moral significance and is in any case covered (at least implicitly) by the "authority" of God (this is essential to a morally good act), can be considered as sufficiently a categorical object of revelation, even if it is not as such "revealed" or (better and more accurately) is not reflectively considered to be such. In other words, one can without further ado deny that there is any *moral* object of a morally good act which is not *also* revealed (it makes no difference here just how theology explains the revealed character that already attaches to realities by reason of the natural moral law). But if the object of a morally good act is not simply and wholly outside the dimension of revelation and (this is a point not to be overlooked) is caught up in a global spiritual movement of the subject, a movement radicalized by grace and therefore no longer merely "natural," then it can be safely said that such a mediation of the grace-elevated subject to itself is to a sufficient degree an object of revelation and that not only the *fides qua* but also the *fides quae* lies within the realm of revelation.

This problem calls for a better and clearer treatment and resolution than has been briefly given here. The problem, however, is not simply one which is raised by the thesis that in every person who is not culpably unbelieving an absolute assent of faith is possible and exists, even amid the modern cultural situation of skeptical relativism. Rather, the problem is one that faces every theologian who does not reject Vatican II's optimism with regard to salvation, an optimism which refuses to deny that a real saving faith is possible even where a person inculpably interprets himself in his own mind as a "pagan" or an atheist.

It is possible, therefore, to say the following: There are many Christians and Catholics today who, at least at the level of reflection, do not embrace many individual dogmas of Christianity with an absolute assent of faith and who even reject such dogmas as "opinions," that is, look upon them with a relativistic and skeptical frame of mind, and therefore find themselves frequently confronted with the question of whether they are still Christians and Catholics. According to what has been said in these pages, the answer "Yes, they are" may be given to this question, because even in such individuals there is or can be an absolute assent of faith, inasmuch as the "rejection"of individual dogmas is not accompanied by an absolute assent such as is constitutive of strict unbelief in the theological sense, and inasmuch as the rejection is not in the proper sense a public fact in the Church.

VII. Pastoral Consequences

Given this approach to the problem, there is need in practical theology of giving more careful attention to the question of how such Christians and Catholics are to be dealt with in pastoral practice. They are often called "marginal Catholics," as though they had only a tenuous or even extremely tenuous connection with the Church. What I have been saying should make it clear that such an evaluation of them is itself not as unproblematic as it is often taken to be in pastoral practice.

The real theological difficulty facing practical theology in this matter does not arise when the condition of these Catholics in regard to faith (as I have described) is simply there and is tacitly accepted and tolerated (this is a widespread response to them). The difficulty arises rather when, in order to keep such a Catholic from turning his back completely on the Church, he is explicitly told that he may be and remain in this state, at least for the time being. Is it permissible, for example, to say something like this to an educated modern Catholic: "If you think you do not understand this or that individual dogma, that you cannot develop any inner relation to it, and that you cannot 'believe,' then you should not say that the dogma is false and meaningless and should be rejected out of hand. Abstention from such a judgment is, after all, in keeping with your usual principle of maintaining an attitude of skeptical relativism in intellectual matters generally. In regard to these details of theology you should not jump on your high horse, like a professional theologian who passes final judgment in scientific matters; you do not do that in regard to other metaphysical questions. If you accept the ultimate and basic substance of Christianity: the existence of God, a prayerful attitude to him, a radical trust in Jesus as God's supreme promise of himself to you, and if you unaffectedly cultivate a religious life not only privately but in the Church, to the extent that the Church declares it indispensable (and really, if you look closely, not much is demanded), then you may peacefully regard yourself as a Catholic and unhesitatingly leave to the future that further development of your religious life to which you wish to be open. Intellectual honesty does not require you to turn away from the Church." There can be no doubt that as representatives of the Church today we are often inclined to speak in this way to "the educated people of our time." My reflections in this essay show, I think, that we *may* speak to them in this way (with discretion, of course, and as the individual case requires).

In this context (let me say it explicitly once more), the dogma of the Church's teaching authority is not a special case for which an exception must be made. The absolute teaching authority of the Church is only one of the dogmas to which, despite their truth, a person of our day can only with difficulty give an absolute assent of faith. This particular dogma illustrates what was said earlier of Church dogma generally: Where this dogma has not (yet) been accepted with an absolute assent of faith, there can nonetheless be present (under the conditions named above) an absolute assent of faith in the sense meant by theologians and the Church.

In such a thesis the dividing line between Christians in the Church and Christians outside the Church becomes more blurred than formerly. But in the Church's pastoral practice this dividing line, while usually not consciously adverted to, has always been quite vague and fluid. The thesis I have presented really changes nothing here. It simply makes possible a more peaceful and assured theological conscience (and this is important, after all) when one adopts an attitude of openness and understanding in dealing with very many present-day Christians as they really are. This attitude is certainly adopted very frequently, but we should be able to adopt it in good conscience.

16

Theology and Religions: A Contemporary Problem

Pietro Rossano

A confrontation of theology with the various religions became both inevitable and urgently necessary halfway through the twentieth century. The reasons are well known, and this is not the place to review them. As far as the history of the movement is concerned, it must be recalled that Protestant theologians and Churches began to concern themselves with the subject before the Catholic Church did and that the positions they adopted were of three types. Liberal theology was inclined to regard all religious institutions, doctrines and practices as of equal value. At the other end of the spectrum, dialectical theology passed a negative verdict on all religious manifestations in the name of "faith alone." Running a middle course, "secularization theology" claimed to convey the gospel message independently of any religious expression, while giving pride of place instead to the human and the social in a "Christianity without religion."[1]

This discussion was to be profitable to Catholic theology, which was meanwhile intent on studies in religious anthropology with special attention to the nature of the act of faith, the membership of non-Christians in the Church, and the possibility of salvation for "unbelievers."[2] During this time the main focus of attention in treatises on fundamental theology was still on the section *De vera religione*. The change came at the Second Vatican Council, and the sign and instrument of it was the conciliar Declaration *Nostra aetate* [NA] "on the relationship of the Church to non-Christian religions." The document was published on October 28, 1965, and I think we may say that ever since it has been impressing itself ever more deeply on the consciousness and thinking of the Church. "A fundamental manifesto" is the reaction of Horst Bürkle, Protestant missiologist at Munich; "short but historic" is the judgment of his colleague, Carl Hallencreuz of Uppsala.[3] Thanks to this document—which must be read in the context created by other documents of Vatican II, such as the Dogmatic Constitution *Lumen gentium* on the Church, the Dogmatic Constitution *Dei Verbum* on Revelation, the Decree *Ad gentes* on the Church's Missionary Activity, the Pastoral Constitution *Gaudium et Spes* on the Church in the Modern World, and the Degree *Dignitatis humanae* on Religious Freedom—Catholic theology has taken a decisive step forward, since it now has a solid point of reference which in method and content is in continuity with the patristic and biblical tradition.[4]

This is why I have chosen the Declaration *Nostra aetate* as my own point of reference in outlining this approach to the nature and present-day tasks of the theology of religions. If we look closely at the document and prescind from the lengthy section of the relation of the Church to the Jews (this was the original reason for the existence of the document), we find that it includes the following themes, which are sketched rather than treated fully. After referring to the new situation of the human race on planet earth half-way through the twentieth century and to the Church's consciousness of its duty to mankind, the Declaration goes on to describe the religious sense as an existential component of human nature; the various religions as sociocultural systems (distinct from ideologies) to which human beings turn for answers to the deepest problems of their existence; and the answers given as marked by an "unspent fruitfulness" (no. 2; Abbott, p. 661) and illumined by the light of the Word but also partial and often completely different from the answers given by the Church. Behind all the questions and answers lies the great plan of God for mankind, a plan that extends from creation to the end-time and has for its center Christ "in whom men find the fullness of religious life, and in whom God has reconciled all things to himself" (no. 2; p. 662). The Declaration then describes the nuanced attitude of the Church to each religion according to the differing relation each has to Christ. Finally, Christians are urged to behave without prejudice to the followers of other religions; their concern should rather be to bear witness and proclaim and, at the same time, to engage in dialogue, which requires knowledge, listening, and collaboration.

I. The Religious Dimension of the Human Person in Theological Perspective

One of the first and most striking paragraphs in *Nostra aetate* speaks of the religious quest as a universal psychological constant of the human person:

Men look to the various religions for answers to those profound mysteries of the human condition which, today even as in olden times, deeply stir the human heart: What is a man? What is the meaning and purpose of our life? What is goodness and what is sin? What gives rise to our sorrows and to what intent? Where lies the path to true happiness? What is the truth about death, judgment, and retribution beyond the grave? What, finally, is that ultimate and unutterable mystery which engulfs our being, and whence we take our rise, and whither our journey leads us? (NA, no. 1; p. 661).

Here the religious problem faced by human beings is described in basic terms as an existential quest that in turn implies a number of specific questions. This basic quest or question is specific and proper to the human person and also distinct from other pressing questions raised by human beings.[5]

Psychology speaks of "psychogenic needs" which are distinct from others known as "viscerogenic" (Zunini). Many schools of psychology have applied themselves, with varying methods and ideological presuppositions, to the investigation of this religious dimension of the human person, from its genesis to its symbolic and ritual expressions and its individual and social manifestations, including such as are pathological. It will be enough here for me to refer only to the field of the psychology of religions and to mention the names of W. James, G. W. Allport, S. Freud, C. G. Jung, and E. Fromm. The scholarly explanations given of the human religious phenomenon are quite varied and seem frequently to be determined by ideologies and preconceived visions of the world. This is not the place to list them. It will be enough to observe here that the existence of the religious dynamism inherent in the human person or, in other words, the reality of the religious dimension, does not depend on the interpretations given of it but on the problem it raises. And the problem is the human metaphysical question, the openness to and orientation toward a beyond, toward a something "new" and "different" that brings the human person integrity and contemplation.

Here is where the theological problem arises. The problem is this: What is the significance of the human religious quest for a Christian? What value does it have as seen in the light of biblical revelation? Contemporary theological anthropology shows a unanimity in interpreting the religious quest as an epiphany of human creaturehood and a consequence of the divine image that has been imprinted in the human person.[6] This image and likeness of God in the human being—the point which represents the climax of the biblical story of creation—is the basis for the ontological and dynamic, and therefore interpersonal and dialogical, relation of the human person to God as origin and end. Closely connected with the creation of man in the image of God is the New Testament principle that man is created in Christ, destined for him, and called to put on the image of him who is the perfect icon of God. The result is that there is a christological note in the music of the religious quest. Human beings are directed toward Christ at the very roots of their being and receive his imprint before they even know him. Such a view of the matter eliminates the extrinsicism which has afflicted Catholic thinking on the natural and supernatural and "blinded it for a long time to the full reality of the natural desire [for God]." The expression is Yves Congar's and Henri de Lubac makes it his own.[7] Theological anthropology should therefore no longer be reluctant to interpret the religious quest as a radical openness to and movement toward the mystery of the God who is

One in Three, and toward the ethical good that finds its fundamental expression in the call to love.[8]

This is the context of Karl Rahner's analyses of the human person as endowed with a "supernatural existential" and, as a result of God's self-communication, open to and directed in a transcendental manner toward the Absolute and the Good. Rahner also describes the human person as a "hearer of the word,"[9] that is, of a word that transcends him but has already left its imprint on him, to use an expression inspired by Ferdinand Ebner. Stimulating, too, are the analyses offered by this solitary Austrian Catholic thinker of the "Thou-ness" [*Duhaftigkeit*] of the human person, a term which expresses the idea that the human person carries imprinted within him a call to the Thou: the Thou that is God, from whom the call initially comes, but consequently and necessarily to the Thou that is other human beings.[10]

Religious anthropology and theological anthropology thus find a common interest and a reciprocal stimulus in the area of man's basic religious experience, which proves to be the point of contact for God's self-communication to the human person. The point of contact has countless facets, so to speak, and is reflected in many different ways, depending on the varying spiritual endowments of individuals and peoples.

The inherently supernatural self-communication of God is necessarily individuated in the course of history in the diverse yet similar forms which the religious question takes in various cultures.

II. Necessity and Limits of a "Theology of Religions"

It is a short step from the fundamental religious experience and the theological thinking that accompanies it to the historical religions, that is, the social, cultural and ritual structures that inspire and guide, in varying degrees, the life of the vast majority of the human race. The religions are the fruit produced by the womb which is the fundamental religious experience. Since the human person is by nature a social being who is called and impelled to communion or at least to association with his fellows, it is natural to expect that this social side of his nature will also find religious expressions. As *Nostra aetate* puts it, "men look to the various religions for answers to those profound mysteries of the human conditions which . . . deeply stir the human heart" (NA, no. 1; p. 661). As a matter of fact, religions present themselves, with claims to authority, as "cumulative traditions" in which the religious quest or, in other words, the "personal faith" of individuals, finds satisfaction.[11] The genesis, development, transformation, and dissolution of religions, their historical and social function (the latter may be conservative or progressive), their resistance to modernity and their changing through contact with it: these are phenomena with which the history and sociology of religions deals.[12]

Theology, too, is called on to take a position, from the standpoint of faith, on the religions which the Church finds in the world and which are often opposed to her. Therefore a theologian cannot do without a theology of religions that gives at least a general explanation of the meaning other faiths have for him. But, as Zwi Werblowsky points out, whereas the historian and student of comparative religion stands, by definition and methodological choice, outside and apart from religion,

> theologians operate from *within* a religious system. Trying to give a reasoned account of their faith, theologians have to consider all relevant aspects of reality, and this reality includes the fact of the existence of "other" religions. . . . "Other" religions may be considered as sheer idolatry (possibly wicked and immoral to boot, which is the view the Old Testament takes of ancient Near Eastern religions); as the halting and mostly misguided quest for God by that part of humanity that has not been vouchsafed a direct revelation; as a providential, direct or indirect, *praeparatio evangelica* and as the activity of the *logos spermatikos;* as legitimate, natural and primitive expressions of religion, albeit inferior to the "higher" forms; as manifestations of the mysterious and hidden workings of God in the hearts of "other" men and cultures; as partial and finite ways to the same Infinite One, etc. You can distinguish between "peoples of the book" and the others. What all these have in common is that each view, articulated from within a particular tradition, assumes its own religion to be the summit and apex of the pyramid.[13]

This passage from the present Secretary General of the International Association for the History of Religions contains some inevitable generalizations, but it is also an honest statement of the problem and outlines the wide range of judgments passed by theologians on the religions. The same writer goes on to point out, quite accurately, that even Hinduism, while declaring itself open and tolerant toward every form of religion, nonetheless itself likewise applies an absolute standard, because "it clearly considers itself vastly superior—if only for the simple reason that it proclaims . . . the relativity of all finite ways to the infinite goal, whereas the other (and inferior) religions think of themselves as absolutes. In other words, this type of religion holds its own (relative) relativism to be an absolute yardstick."

As seen by Christian theology the religions are the corporate ways and forms that sum up, as it were, the queries suggested by and the responses given to the basic religious questions which agitate human beings. And because the saving action of God is present to and coextensive with the whole range of the human religious dynamism, it is to be expected that the religions, as socio-cultural structures, will "reflect a ray of that Truth which enlightens all men" (NA, no. 2; p.662). In other words, the religions, as seen from the theological point of view, can be regarded as responses to the interior *instinctus Dei invitantis* through which God calls all human beings to himself To put it in still other terms: from the theological standpoint every religion represents the socially given response of a people to divine enlightenment and the interior self-gift of God and to the call he issues to submit to his reign and share his glory. In all the religions, then, all the components in the fundamental human religious experience find varied expressions. According to a considered statement of Heinrich Fries, the religions "are the result of man's *creatureliness,* his *supernatural elevation* (in Christ), his *fall,* and the desire, consequent upon the fall, for help, salvation, redemption, and grace."[14]

This statement of the Munich theologian calls our attention to the influence exercised on the religions by the fall or sin, a term which in Christian language refers to man's misuse of freedom from the very beginning and his constant temptation to resist the interior action of God who urges him to open himself to God and to other human beings. The religious structures created by the human race illustrate in many ways the misuse of human freedom as well as its lack of docility and obedience to the enlightening and inviting action of the Spirit. The texts of the Council do not gloss over the defects in the religious expressions of the race, but refer expressly to them and see in them a sign of the action of the Evil One (cf. *Lumen gentium,* nos. 16–17; *Ad gentes,* nos. 9 and 11). From a theological standpoint, therefore, "the historical religions and their contents are not a pure expression of the theological truth and reality on which they are based; they also show evidences of religious inadequacy, degeneration, aberration, and excess [*Unwesen*]. This accounts for the ambiguity of the religious mind and the religions."[15]

The religious impact of sin, or of man's rejection of God's interior call, does undoubtedly provide a partial theological answer to the great problem of the plurality of religions and the resultant lack of communication, divergence, and even antagonism among them. But in regard to the plurality of religions, theology can do more than simply remind us of the fact of sin. It also offers considerations based on the variety in creation or, more specifically, on the special genius of each of the peoples who respond in divergent ways to the light flowing from the Word who enlightens every human being, just as the ray of light, touching a surface, "strikes forth various colors wherever it alights," or various musical instruments respond differently even in the hands of one and the same player. The Declaration *Nostra aetate* adverts to the special characteristics of the various religious traditions as they adopt different paths in leading human beings to the Absolute. Islam follows one path, Buddhism and Hinduism another.

Adopting still the theological point of view, we may note that the diversity of human responses to the interior call of the Spirit also depends on the transcendence and incomparable light of the Word, which no human language or culture can express or reflect in an adequate way.

Closely connected with the theme of the plurality of religions is the determining role played by the personalities who are at the origin of a religious tradition or system. The question here is of the founders or reformers of a religion and of their theological status. Martin Buber remarked that the world is still following the path traced by the finger of Moses when he inscribed the laws of the Decalogue. Everyone is aware of the influence exercised by Gautama Buddha in southeastern Asia, to say nothing of such other founders as Confucius, Lao-tzu, Mahavira, Socrates, Zarathustra, Muhammad, Shankara, Nichiren, Guru Nanak, and many others (not to mention Jesus Christ and St. Paul), whose experience became paradigmatic for countless multitudes of followers. A Christian theologian will not be content merely to record the fact that these individuals were extraordinary geniuses, and yet when he tries to go further he finds himself in great difficulty, because the sources at his disposal do not permit solid judgments to be made. In this impasse, which for the moment seems insuperable, it is already a step forward to observe that since Christ is Pantokrator, Lord of the universe and history, we may presuppose that at critical moments of history and society spiritual charisms[16] have been granted to individuals enabling them to bear witness and promote among their fellows values of basic importance for the human person, such as unconditional submission to God, detachment from self and transient things, mastery and ascetical discipline of body and spirit, the law of conscience, social harmony and order, and so on. In the biblical tradition various persons who show the characteristic traits of religious leaders—such men as Melchizedek, Cyrus and Job—are related to Christ as anticipations and prefigurations of him.[17]

The Christian theologian is much better prepared to deal with a problem that is inherent in religious structures and their relation to the individual. I am referring to the relation of the individual, who is endowed with a religious conscience and is the object of God's saving love, to the religious system which receives and conditions him culturally. History affords many examples of divergences between the personal religious conscience and the structures which the cultural context provides for the self-expression and fulfillment of the individual. Cantwell Smith has analyzed this opposition between "personal faith" and "cumulative tradition," which in some cases leads to a historical movement of reform, and in others (which are more frequent) to the abandonment of one religious tradition for the sake of another. There is no doubt that in these cases of opposition Christian theology comes down on the side of conscience, that inner sanctuary where the person stands alone before God (cf. *Gaudium et Spes,* no. 16).

III. Diversified Relation of the Church to the Religions

These few problems connected with the multiplicity of religions are only samples of a whole series of questions that were passionately discussed in the years immediately following the Council. That discussion then seemed to come to a standstill, due perhaps to weariness and a lack of confidence, and the way was left open for a different and more rigorous approach which is the one being followed at the present time. This approach (already present in the conciliar texts) consists of inquiring into the specific attitude of the Church to each of the religions, instead of concentrating on a very general set of themes that do not permit the attainment of any great clarity. It seems more fruitful and certainly more realistic to study the relation of the Church to Judaism, to Buddhism, to Hinduism, and so on, than to linger over such questions as "Are the religions necessary?" "Are they ways to salvation?" Are they vehicles of a revelation and, if so, what is it?" "Can their sacred writings be regarded as inspired?" "What, if anything, can a Christian learn from them?" and so on.

For this reason, before I go on to deal with this broader kind of question, and in order to bring out its scope and importance, it seems opportune to draw at least a sketchy picture of the future development of the theology of religions, that is, the study of the relationship of the Church to each religion. This approach, as I pointed out a moment ago, is suggested by the conciliar texts, especially *Nostra aetate* which begins by referring to the primitive or traditional religions, then moves on to those marked by a greater cultural development: Hinduism, Buddhism, and Islam, and finally speaks of Judaism. The same sequence is followed, but in the opposite direction, in the Constitution *Lumen gentium* (no. 16).

I shall begin with Judaism. It is not without theological reason that within the Roman Curia the Commission for Catholic-Jewish Relations is attached to the Secretariat for Christian Unity. For, according to the Declaration *Nostra aetate* (no. 4), there is a "spiritual bond" and a great "spiritual patrimony common to Judaism and Christianity. "The Jews still remain most dear to God because of their fathers"; like us they take "the revelation of the Old Testament" as their guide and are thus "the root of that good olive tree" onto which the Church has been grafted; their destiny is bound up with the "mystery" of the Church. These were the premises adopted by the Commission for Catholic-Jewish Relations in its document of December 1, 1974, in which it gives practical guidelines for the concrete application of the conciliar Declaration. Meanwhile in various parts of the Christian world, especially in Germany, France and the United States, the first steps are being taken in theological reflection on the "mystery of Israel." The major themes are: the historical and theological connection between the Old and New Testaments, that is, between the two peoples of God and the two covenants; the relationship between Hebrew and Christian messianism; the mission of the Church to Israel and of Israel to the Church and the world; the problem of the interpretation to be given to certain statements of Paul (for example, that the Christian is no longer subject to a law); the theological significance of Chapters 9–11 of the Letter to the Romans; and so on.[18]

Let me turn now to Islam. It is not without significance that the Encyclical Letter *Redemptor hominis* (no. 11) mentions the "esteem" shown by the Council for Islam which shares with the Church the Abrahamic faith in the "one God," living and eternally existent, merciful and omnipotent, who is creator of heaven and earth and has spoken to human beings and to whom these must respond with submission *(islâm)* and faith *(imân)*. Judaism, Christianity, and Islam possess the same salvation-historical structure and face the problem of the Messiah. In the Quran Jesus the Messiah is the virginal son of Mary (which implies an exceptional christology) and is given the title "word of God" and "spirit of God" as well as "judge" of the world. It is beyond doubt that from the historical and theological points of view there were profound links between the three historico-prophetic monotheistic religions, even while each has its own irreducible physiognomy. Christian theological reflection on the phenomenon of Islam and the person of Muhammad began in the first centuries after the Hegira (622 A.D.) but was repressed in the historical clash of the two religions; only in our century has it been possible to engage in this type of reflection once again, thanks to the work of such pioneers as L. Massignon, L. Gardet, C. Journet, Abd-el-Gialil, Moubarac, and others.[19]

Relations between the Church and Judaism or Islam have for a basis the Abrahamic and prophetic monotheism shared by all three religions. Such a basis is completely lacking for a theological approach to Hinduism, Buddhism, the traditional religions of Africa, and such religions as Shintoism, Taoism, Confucianism, and others. Let me take as an example the vast religious amalgam that is Hinduism; in it there has undoubtedly been a slow process of development along the lines of certain schemata that are present in the sources, but no less deniably there has been an influence from both Islam and Christianity, two religions with which India has been in contact for centuries. The Declaration *Nostra aetate* is content to point out with deep appreciation some main aspects of the Hindu religious tradition, such as the "unspent fruitfulness" of its myths, its "loving, trusting flight toward God," and its thirst for liberation and salvation through asceticism and contemplation; but the document refrains from offering a properly theological evaluation. Elements of a theological judgment can however be derived from the theological underpinning of the Declaration; thus the Declaration speaks not only of the history of salvation as this takes shape in Judaism and Christianity (no. 4), but also of the economy of a universal salvation that embraces the whole human race, from creation to the eschatological light of the heavenly Jerusalem (nos. 1, 4); of the universal fatherhood of God (no. 5); and of the enlightenment of every human being by the Word of God (no. 2). These various elements can be integrated with what is said in *Dei Verbum* (no. 3) about the enlightening and saving presence of God to every human person.

All these principles should inspire the theological approaches being taken today to Hinduism and its various spiritual trends. Let me mention by way of example the approach of J. N. Farquhar who sees Christianity as being the crown of Hinduism, and those of H. Le Saux, B. Griffiths and R. Panikkar, who tend to see in the Hindu tradition a particular expression of the transcendent divine mystery.[20] Also worth noting is the position of Richard de Smedt, S.J., who sees in Hinduism a path leading from faith in the omnipresence of God *(Upanishad)* to the recognition of God-who-loves-men *(Bhagavadgita),* to the understanding of love of neighbor through Jesus Christ who is a true incarnation of the divinity (Neo-Hinduism, beginning with Ram Mohan Roy, 1772–1833). "Still to be discovered is God as triper-sonal love, and Christ as this God's theandric witness."[21]

Clearly, if the bases for the theological interpretation of Judaism and Islam are faith in the God of Abraham and this God's intervention in history through the prophets with a view to an eschatological resolution, then the basis for a theology of Hinduism, and analogously of the other religions, must be the trinitarian economy of salvation which has been operative in the human race from the very beginning, together with the fatherhood of God, the light of the Word who enlightens every human being, and the breath of the Spirit "who breathes where he will."

Buddhism, for its part, invites the theologian to meditate on the theme of the apophatic approach to the divine, on the need for salvation in the form of a liberation from suffering, on the eternal repercussions (the "merit"), both positive and negative, of every action, on the truth of what is transient and worldly, and on the need of commitment and contemplation in order to attain to the ultimate truth of being. According to a well-known expression of Romano Guardini, no one has as yet uncovered the religious significance of Buddha; in other words, a thoroughgoing, systematic theological confrontation with Buddhism is still in the future.[22]

The same is to be said of the African religions in which God is seen as the definitive horizon of all existence; here the focus of religious attention is on the life that is shared by cosmos and tribe, with the present time having its archetype and justification in the past.[23] Theological reflection in Asia and Africa is also being devoted to the study of hermeneutical principles and schemata that will make possible a rethinking, re-expression, and new explicitation of the objective elements of the Christian faith in the light of the Afro-Asiatic cultural heritage. To develop a theology of religions does not mean only that the Christian passes judgment on the various religions from the vantagepoint of his own faith; it also means rereading and rethinking his own faith in the light of these religions and of the stimuli and contributions they offer for its growth. This is why there is so much talk today about "theologizing" or "doing theology" in Africa and in Asia as in Latin America.

Need I say that we are moving toward a real catholicity of the Church?

IV. Religions and the Economy of Universal Salvation

The thoughts thus far offered on the theological approach to the religions have highlighted the importance of taking into consideration the economy of universal salvation, at the center of which is the historical event of Jesus Christ, "the son of David, the son of Abraham" (Mt 1:1). The Declaration *Nostra aetate* expressly relates the phenomenon of the religions to this divine plan. But whereas the Jewish and Islamic religions are connected by many threads to the history of the salvation effected in Jesus Christ, the other religious traditions of the human race have their place within the economy or dispensation of universal salvation, according to which God created human beings in order that they might attain to their fulfillment in a relationship with him that is mediated by the Word and the Holy Spirit. This is the *mysterion* hidden in God from before the creation of the world and then manifested or made known to the Church when it was accomplished at a moment in history, "when the time had fully come," by means of Jesus Christ.[24] This plan of salvation has accompanied the human race from the beginning. There is a time before Christ and a time after Christ, but not a time without salvation (*Unheilszeit*) as distinct from a time with salvation (*Heilszeit*). In their thinking the wise men of the Old Testament crossed the threshold of the mystery and gave expression to it with the linguistic tools at their disposal: "God loves the peoples" (Deut 33:3, Heb. text); he "loves the living" (Wis 11:26); "the earth is full of the steadfast love of the Lord" (Ps 33:5), his Wisdom and his Spirit fill the earth (cf. Wis 1:7; Prov 8:31). The first Christian generation and, among the New Testament writers, Paul and John in particular grasped, in their knowledge of Christ, his universal lordship. Thus Peter believed that all salvation in this world comes from Christ (Acts 4:12; 10:34–35). In his Letters to the Ephesians and the Colossians St. Paul proclaims Christ to be the foundation and keystone of all history: everything was created in him, everything has existence in him, everything is moving toward him in whom God wills to reconcile all things with himself (Col 1:15–20; Eph 1:10; 2 Cor 5:18–19, cited in *Nostra aetate* no. 2). St. Paul sees the Spirit as working for the justification of every person who does what is good, that is, who follows the law of love: this is the true circumcision that gives membership in the people of God (Rom 2:25–29). But the apex of contemplation of Christ as universal sovereign (*Pantokrator*) is reached in the New Testament by St. John in the Prologue of his gospel where the action of the Word is described in terms of his "presence" in the world as life and spiritual light of every human being, and of his historical "coming" into the world which is "his home,"[25] and again, and above all, in the Apocalypse where Christ, "the first and the last, and the living one" (1:18), is shown as the Lamb who is slain and is victorious before the foundation of the world (13:8) and who holds in his hand the book containing the secrets of history (5:6–9).

Reflection on this economy of universal salvation that has its center in Christ who died, rose, and is now Pantokrator, has in our day received a strong impulse from theological confrontation with the religions and now calls for a rereading of the entire Bible in the light of universalism. It is usually said that the Bible, especially the Old Testament, is ethnocentric, since its dominant theme is God's action among the Jews. The statement is true as far as it goes, but we must not forget the universalist perspectives to be found in the Bible. The Dogmatic Constitution *Dei Verbum* and the Declaration *Nostra aetate* see clearly present in the sacred books two phases or two aspects of God's action in regard to human beings. There is a universalist side to it and a Jewish-Christian side; there is the covenant granted to Israel and to the Church, and there is what might be called the "sapiential economy" from which all peoples benefit.[26] The term "sapiential economy" refers to God's universal action in the world through his Wisdom and his Spirit, as described in the great collection we speak of as the sapiential books, but also in the first chapters of Genesis, Deuteronomy, the prophets and the New Testament writings. Contemporary exegetes are now in a position to see these two economies as already present in the J, E. P and D documents that are the basis of the Pentateuch.[27] It is a known fact, moreover, that the priestly code knows of a plurality of covenants and that the rabbinical tradition distinguishes between the Mosaic covenant made with the Hebrew people and the Noachic covenant made with all peoples. This is not the place to explain the intricate connection between the economies and the subordinate role of the Hebraic-Christian covenant in the plan of universal salvation, but it will be helpful to note that both economies, the Hebraic and the sapiential, are united, as the New Testament sees it, in the one person of Jesus Christ. He is "the chosen one," "the beloved," "the son" of God who in himself recapitulates Israel, but he is also "the Wisdom" and "the Spirit" of God who are diffused and present throughout the entire world.[28] Justin, Irenaeus, Clement of Alexandria, Origen, St. Augustine, and St. Gregory of Nyssa will find in the christological titles Logos and Wisdom a key for reading and appreciating the entire ethico-religious heritage of antiquity.

V. New Attitude of the Church to the Religions

Closely connected with the new theological understanding of the religions is the broadening and revision of the Church's attitude to them. This way after promulgating the Decree *Ad Gentes* on the Church's Missionary Activity Vatican II then proceeded, in the Declaration *Nostra aetate,* to set down directives for dialogue and to describe its basic spirit. The presence of both documents in the conciliar corpus is enough to show how specious the claim is that mission and dialogue in the Church are mutually exclusive. It should also be noted that whenever *Ad gentes* speaks of mission it always associates with it the word dialogue, while *Nostra aetate,* regarded as the magna carta of dialogue, does not hesitate to speak of the Church's duty to "ever proclaim Christ, 'the way, the truth, and the life' " (no. 2).

The new attitude of dialogue is therefore not asserted to the detriment or restriction of the missionary commitment; it only points to an element and necessary aspect of this commitment. One thing is certain: after Vatican II the "dialogical style" marks the new attitude of the Church to the religions. This attitude owes its existence in our day to a current of thought that is biblico-Christian and existential in origin[29]; it was firmly introduced into the Church by Paul VI in his Encyclical Letter *Ecclesiam suam.* As compared with the past attitude that may be said to have been prevalent, with rare exceptions, from the patristic age to our own time, the concentration on dialogue represents a change in relations between Christians and the followers of the non-Christian religions. By raising the banner of dialogue the

Church declares its intention, in addressing interlocutors of the various religious faiths, of unreservedly respecting not only their physical and human identity but their cultural and religious identity as well.

For the servant of the gospel, therefore, dialogue means the necessity, first of all, of knowing the religious character of his addressee and respecting his spiritual identity. This attitude calls for a high level of spiritual maturity and a "geological patience," to use an effective phrase of Father Monchanin that reflects a lot of personal experience. Dialogue demands a careful hermeneutical effort in order both to enter within the other's horizon of meaning and to bring home to this other the meaning the Christian message has in store for him. Every openness to the objections and values of the other has as a necessary consequence a deeper and wider understanding of the message the Church itself is offering. Many difficult and sensitive problems arise at this point which lie beyond the purview of this essay. It will be enough to recall here the pointed observation of the Protestant missiologist Horst Bürkle with regard to the association of mission and dialogue in the conciliar documents: "Mission and dialogue are thus interrelated in such a way that each protects the other against possible abuses, keeping missionary activity from becoming an export of western ways, and dialogue from degenerating into a barren indulgence in historical comparisons."[30] In other words, in her missionary activity the Church must see to it that the new life she proclaims does not mean a simple transfer of a cultural synthesis but rather a response to the other's question as formulated in the medium of his religion.

VI. Theological Problems Raised by the Religions

After what has been said about the economy of universal salvation as the ultimate foundation for any theological explanation of the religions and for the Church's new and nuanced relation to these, we are in a position to put more accurately and face more realistically the general theological questions usually asked with regard to the religions.

The first of these questions that was very much a focus of attention immediately after Vatican II is whether the religions can be regarded as means and ways of salvation. That is: Can the non-Christians religions be considered ways of salvation which God has established in order to lead human beings to their eternal destiny? Any reply that is to be concrete and at the same time respectful of reality must necessarily distinguish among the religions. Thus there is no doubt that Judaism, containing as it does the Mosaic Decalogue, the Deuteronomic *Shema,* and the message of the prophets, contains more important elements than do other organized religions. Islam, too, thanks to its basic structure, can give expression to a genuine act of faith and explicitly provide the Christian conditions for salvation (cf. Heb 11:6; Rom 2:14, 26; Sura 2:59 and 5:73). Nor can it be denied, for example, that the Bhagavadgita (18:64–65) with its call for a response of affective personal self-surrender to the love of God offers a way that constantly surprises

Christians by its close analogy to the style of the gospel. On the other hand, it is unthinkable that we should not take into account the enormous burden of blindness and darkness that weighs upon certain forms of religion which are swathed in ritualism, alienated by self-centered or earthly perspectives, gone astray in magical practices, and which are asocial if not outright immoral in nature.

All this makes it improbable that an unqualified affirmative or negative answer can be given to the question asked. It may be cautiously asserted that concrete elements of various religions or even, in the better cases, whole religious systems can be providential means and ways of salvation, to the extent that they reflect and give objective form to the light of the Word that enlightens every human being. It is clear, of course, that for a Christian Christ is the only way of salvation. The religions can be such a way to the extent that they receive and express the influence and enlightenment that come from Christ. This is the direction taken by the Council in its statements on the matter (cf. *Ad gentes,* nos. 3, 11; NA, no. 2; *Lumen gentium,* no. 16).

Another question that arises in theological reflection on the religions has to do with their content as possible revelation. The question is whether revelation is present in the religions and, if so, what is this revelation. Anyone who claims, à la Barth, that the human religious phenomenon is by definition darkness par excellence, clearly sets himself outside the framework of Catholic theology. The same is to be said of anyone who joins liberal theology in saying that all religions are parallel or equivalent forms of Christian revelation. The Declaration *Nostra aetate* (no. 2) expresses a general attitude of the Council when it sees in the religions "a ray" of the Word which takes the form of "ways of conduct and life." In fact, the Council itself and later Church documents such as the Apostolic Exhortation *Evangelii nuntiandi* (no. 53) and the Encyclical Letter *Redemptor hominis* (nos. 11–12), while taking no explicit position on the problem, lead the reader to a point from which there seems to be no turning back. A current of theological thought that goes back to John, Irenaeus, Clement of Alexandria, and Origen and that has never run dry at any time in the tradition, leaves no doubt in the matter.

At this point, however, the theologian finds himself looking for a plausible formula that will truthfully reflect the real situation. Here especially it must not be forgotten that all religions are not on an equal footing. As sociocultural structures Judaism and Islam certainly contain elements of biblical revelation; the same can be said of other religions to the extent that in the course of their history they have been influenced by Christianity or by biblical traditions. But what is to be said of all the other cases? It is rather difficult to speak of "fragments" or "particles," because these terms make the Christian spontaneously think of himself as enjoying total possession while others are left with what amounts more or less to crumbs or morsels. Now in fact the Christian knows that he does not represent the fullness and that he does not have the fullness of truth, but rather that Christ is the fullness

(NA, no. 2) and that Christ enlightens equally, even if differently, both Christian and non-Christian.

It may perhaps be legitimate to speak of various aspects or degrees of the divine light which "has shone . . . to give . . . the knowledge of the glory of God in the face of Christ" (2 Cor 4:6). But a rigorous theological discourse would do well to reserve the word "revelation" for the "revelation of Jesus Christ" (Rev 1:1). The word is, after all, one that historically has been specifically connected with the eschatological context provided by the New Testament. When dealing with the other religions it seems more appropriate to speak of "enlightenment" or even of God's "manifestation" of himself through the universe or conscience or other means. This is the terminology of which Paul (Rom 1:19) and John (1:9) make use for the action of God in dispelling the darkness that covers the human race.[31]

Closely connected with the problem of enlightenment and revelation in the religious traditions is that of the theological value of their "sacred books."[32] The point is debated today and has concrete implications for the process of acculturation the gospel message must undergo in the various cultures of the world. Relevant here are the distinctions just made regarding the presence of a revelation in the various religions. Varying judgments must be passed on the Torah, the Quran, the Veda, the Avesta, the Tripitake, the Granth Sahib, and so on. In other words, it is difficult to deny that whatever revelation and enlightenment are present in the religious traditions of a people are also present and even have their privileged form in the sacred books which are the summation of knowledge and the necessary point of reference for the followers of that religion.

A new and unusual question regarding the religions made its appearance recently when the "secularization theologians" began to attack and eliminate the religious fact as something mythical and archaic, a product of emotion and contrary not only to the exigencies of the human person who has come of age and is devoted to scientific method, but also to the Christian faith. In this context they spoke of a "religionless Christianity," as if the Christian had nothing in common with the religions of mankind. But this secularist temptation is losing its attraction for our contemporaries. The reason for this is that more careful studies of human behavior, religious psychology, symbolism, and language itself suggest that the human person whether individually or in society must hold on to some form of symbolico-ritual mediation in order to enter into relations with the invisible and the beyond that is the normal goal of the religious tendency. To those who are urging an areligious reading of the Bible other scholars have pointed out that the entire biblical tradition, from Genesis to the Apocalypse, uses the religious categories of the time in order to express revelation and the relation of God to man and man to God.[33]

The reply to the question of the relation between Christian faith and the religions will inevitably be rather complex and marked by careful distinctions. Even if we leave aside any position that radically denies the religions; even if we exclude the temptation to relativize the religions in order to bring about a "Copernican revolution" in which every religion with its founder is equally concerned with the one Absolute, God;[34] and even if we bear in mind the different relationship the Church has to each of the religions—even then it seems better to approach this large problem from various points of view and to limit myself here to pointing out the different questions to be asked. Contemporary theological thought on the religions is far from being in a position to offer a satisfactory solution to all the questions that arise in connection with this problem.

A first and frankly theological question might take this form: what relation exists between the divine self-communication that takes place in the ecclesial community thanks to faith in Christ and to the sacraments, and the communication that is granted outside this community to all human beings of good will? Another question, more psychological and cultural in character, has to do with the relation between Christian message and religion, between gospel kerygma and human religious experience, whether the latter takes a spontaneous individual or social form, or now bears the imprint of a religious ideology (Buddhism and others). A third question concerns the dynamic and critical role played by the gospel in its contact with the religious syntheses that have arisen in the course of history; the Council sums up this role in general terms: healing, ennobling, and perfecting (cf. *Ad gentes,* nos. 9; 3, 11: *Lumen gentium,* no. 17).

Still other questions have to do with the relation between the contents of the Christian message and the metaphysical, anthropological, and ethical assertions made by the various religions. More specifically, the question here is what the nature is of the contribution which non-Christian religious traditions can make to the Christian message. Do they simply help render explicit or even discover new values present in the message but hitherto unnoticed, or do they rather bring new elements to it, and if so, what is the character of these? Finally, there is always the major question which Paul VI raised at the opening of the 1974 Synod of Bishops: How are the universalist exigences of the mission entrusted by the Christ to the Church to be harmonized with respect for the religious cultures and identities of non-Christians?[35] This problem is an extremely important one, and the Church must think hard about as the year 2000 approaches. Perhaps she may find help to a solution "by linking, without confusing them, a hermeneutic of the biblical message and a hermeneutic of human existence."[36]

Bibliography

Among the introductions to the Declaration *Nostrae aetate* the richest from the biblical and theological viewpoints seems to be T. Federici, *Il Concilio e i non cristiani* (Rome, 1966).

For a general introduction to the theology of religions cf. the entries of P. Rossano in *Nuovo Dizionario di Teologia* (Rome, 1977), and L. Sartori in

Dizionario di Teologia Interdisciplinare (Turin, 1977). Cf. also Carlo Cantone, *Le scienze della religione, oggi* (Rome, 1978); A. Giudici, *Religioni e salvezza* (Turin,1978).
For general treatments of the theology of religions, cf. K. Rahner, "History of the World and Salvation-History" and "Christianity and the Non-Christian Religions," in his *Theological Investigations* 5, tr. by Karl-H. Kruger (Baltimore, 1966), pp. 97–114 and 115–34. P. Damboriena, *La salvación en las religiones no cristianas* (Madrid, 1973). H. R. Schlette, *Towards a Theology of Religions* tr. by W. J. O'Hara (Quaestiones Disputatae 14; New York, 1966); J. Heilsbetz, *Theologische Gründe der* nichtchristlichen Religionen (Freiburg, 1967). M. Maurier, *The Other Covenant: A Theology of Paganism,* tr. by C. McGrath (New York, 1968); G. Evers, *Mission. Nichtchristliche Religion; Weltliche Welt* (Münster, 1974). G. Thils, *Propos et problèmes de la théologie des religions non chrétiennes* (Tournai, 1966). V. Boublik, *Teologia delle religioni* (Rome, 1974). J. Daniélou, "Le problème théologique des religions non chrétiennes," in *Metafisica ed esperienza religiosa* (= Archivio di filosofia; Rome, 1956), pp. 209–33.

The first study to apply a carefully nuanced theological reflection to the different religions is H. Bürkle, *Einführung in die Theologie der Religionen* (Darmstadt, 1977).

17
Church and Churches

Heinrich Fries

In the contemporary fundamental theology the problem of the Church and the Churches occupies a different place than it did in earlier presentations of apologetics.

I. Biblical and Historical Foundations

In the *demonstratio catholica* the starting point for discussion of the theme was the assertion that the Church of Jesus Christ exists only in the singular. In support of this an appeal was made to the numerous passages of scripture which speak of the Church in the singular, especially Matthew 16:17–19, where Jesus expressly speaks of "my Church," that is, of one Church. There was also reference made to the other scriptural images for the Church: flock, plantation, edifice, temple, bride, and body whose head is Christ; all of these point to a Church in the singular, the one Church. This global impression is strengthened by the statements of the Captivity Letters on the Church as body of Christ, as well as by recollection of the various exhortations to unity (especially in Paul), exhortations connected with the struggle against divisions, factions, discord, and disruptions of unity (cf. 1 Cor 1:12–13; Eph 4:1–13).

But alongside these data must be set the historical fact and experience that from a very early time, and precisely in the context of an appeal to the one Church, there arose divisions, separations, mutual recriminations and excommunications. The result was that there were now Churches in the plural. But this plurality was regarded as illegitimate, as a state of affairs that should not be. And this attitude was maintained on both sides. The community from which a group broke off but which was "in possession," as it were, and thought of itself as the old Church, the Church of authentic tradition, also regarded itself as the one true Church of Jesus Christ, from which the "innovators" had separated themselves, losing thereby the right to call themselves the Church of Jesus Christ. But the innovators objected that the old Church had not remained true to its origin, had lost continuity and identity, had ignored the call to conversion and renewal, and had therefore rendered the separation inevitable. For this reason only the new community could be the one true Church of Jesus Christ. In either case, therefore, there could rightfully be only one Church in the singular.

The breakaway from the old Church and the divisions of groups and sectors created no small difficulties in the first period of the Church's history (the ancient Church), as can be seen from the dogmatic controversies on points of Christology and trinitarian doctrine, or the divergences in Church discipline and practice (the disagreement on the date of Easter, the dispute over the baptism of heretics), or the various theologies that came into existence in the Western and Eastern Churches. In the post-Constantinian period and especially in the Middle Ages when the West had become Christian and the Roman Empire had been succeeded by the Christian Empire, the divisions in Christianity also became a political problem which was resolved by the use of power and violence. It was regarded as intolerable that the unity of the now Christian empire—a unity that was based upon and was maintained by the unity of the faith and the Church, despite the tensions that might exist between the *Imperium* and the *Sacerdotium,* the Emperor and the Pope—should be in any way endangered. Both the Church and the state wanted a single Church. Deviations from the faith and divisions into special groups over against the one Church (which had meanwhile become both a universal Church and an inclusive Church) were regarded as not only theologically but even politically suspect and therefore to be ferreted out, condemned, and attacked, and this with no less severity than was used against external enemies. Punishment was inflicted by both Church and state according to a carefully calculated division of powers.

But all these measures were unable to prevent the division of the Church in 1054 into a Church of the West and a Church of the East. After a long period of increasing alienation the two Churches condemned and excommunicated each other, and each maintained that it was the one true "orthodox" Church. Despite the schism neither Church dropped its claim or the predicate "Church." Unity in faith, sacraments, and hierarchic structure (except for recognition of the papacy as jurisdictional court of appeal for the entire Church) remained intact. The differences between East and West did not justify a separation in faith but in fact they led to it. The mutual excommunications and the schism connected with them had for practical purposes the same consequences as a divergence in faith would have: non-recognition, alienation, enmity. The medieval councils aimed at unification changed nothing, since the agreements they reached were not accepted.

In any case, Churches now existed in the plural: the Church of the West, the Church of the East. The plurality was not regarded as in any way a happy one; it was everywhere felt to be a cause of pain; it did, however, seem to be truly possible: the Churches of the East and the West did not deny each other's Church-ness.

This attitude was changed by the separation and division in Western Christendom, that is, by the Reformation and the movement connected with it. Originally the Reformation intended no division of the Church into

Churches; its concern was the renewal of the existing old Church with its pope and bishops, a renewal based on the normative origin, namely, sacred scripture. The failure of these aspirations had many causes and led to the division of Christendom into various confessions: into the ancient Church and the Churches of the Reformation. Unlike the separation into Eastern and Western Churches the separation here affected the faith itself; thus the separation was undoubtedly more thoroughgoing and serious in its effects than the schism between the Eastern and Western Churches.

The ancient Church maintained its claim to be the one Church of Jesus Christ and to have kept her unity unbroken: the unity from which the "innovators" had now departed. The latter, however, claimed that continuity with the original and abiding (*mansura*) Church was to be found in their community, while the Roman Catholic Church had departed from the original norm and had distorted the features of the one true Church or even corrupted them beyond possibility of recognition.

Here, then, is a plurality of Churches that is certainly illegitimate when measured by the will of Jesus and his prayer "that they may all be one" (Jn 17:21) and by the ceaseless exhortations of Paul the Apostle to maintain the unity of the body whose head is Christ. This plurality should not and may not be; it is culpable. This is why each of these Churches, "separated by heresy," claims to be the one Church of Jesus Christ and to possess the singleness which is proper to the Church of Christ and is denied to other Churches. The plurality of Churches became a scandal to the whole of Christendom and the entire world. The confessions, for their part, explained that the separation was necessary for the sake of the truth and "the eternal happiness of souls"; it must be maintained, even if by violence and war.

II. The Marks of the True Church

In this period when the separation caused by the Reformation took place the question arose of the marks of the one true Church of Jesus Christ, the question of the *notae ecclesiae*. It became a basic theme of the theology of that time.

According to the Reformers the true Church of Jesus Christ exists where the gospel is preached in its purity and the holy sacraments are administered in accordance with the gospel (*Confessio Augustana* 7). It must be added that—still in the perspective of the Reformers—the "office of preaching" has been instituted for public service of gospel and sacrament (Article 5) and that the exercise of this office requires a canonical call (*rite vocatus:* Article 14). The other Reformers, including Calvin and the Anglicans, specified the marks of their Churches along similar lines.

The same problem was raised, though in a different way, within the Catholic Church and in the context of a *demonstratio catholica*.

The characteristics or properties (*proprietates*) which the apostolic Creed (the *Apostolicum*) assigns to the Church, namely, unity, holiness, catholicity and apostolicity, were now interpreted as being also notes or marks (*notae*) of the Church. True enough (it was explained), not every characteristic of the Church is also a mark in the sense of *nota,* but every *nota* is certainly a characteristic or property of the Church.

A property of the Church can serve as a note when it is easily recognizable and accessible to all persons, when it belongs exclusively to the true Church, and when it is not temporary but attaches to the Church in a permanent and essential way. Thus in the *demonstratio catholica* a proposition of faith ("I believe in the one, holy, catholic, and apostolic Church") also becomes at the same time the expression of traits which are accessible not solely to faith but to reason and historical investigation. But there are a great many difficulties and problems with this approach, for it is difficult to see how one and the same thing—the properties of the Church—can be believed by the faithful and at the same be recognized as a mark of the Church by anyone and everyone.

The argument of the *demonstratio catholica* runs as follows:

The major premise: From the outset the Church of Jesus Christ has possessed, by institution, four marks which are both permanent characteristics and signs by which it can be recognized. The proof of this statement is given in the witness of the New Testament and the earliest tradition. The marks are the object of both faith and rational knowledge. The thesis is derived from scriptural sources, and this by a process of historical study which is within everyone's power.

The minor premise: These four marks are found, and found exclusively, in the Catholic Church. This proposition can, once again, be ascertained and proved by empirical methods. Admittedly, it is not easy to deliver this proof in an absolutely convincing way and for everyone, so that it will become an argument for credibility. Such a proof supposes many experiences; at bottom, it even supposes faith. Moreover, it is open to the objection supplied by contrary experiences, since it is not a matter of being able to compare a radiantly realized ideal (our side!) with a far from ideal reality (on the other side!).

In order to strengthen both the argumentation and the intention of *demonstratio catholica,* apologetes were not content to show positively that the characteristics in question were to be found in the Catholic Church. They sought to construct a negative argument as well, by showing that the characteristics were either lacking in other Churches or at least not found there in the same pronounced form as in the Catholic Church.

Because of its undeniable difficulties the argument given in the *demonstratio catholica* was simplified, concentrated, and reduced to the so-called *via primatus* [way of the primacy], the *nota romanitatis* [note of Romanness]. The true Church exists where the pope is, so that the Catholic Church is identically the Roman-Catholic Church. A Church that can claim for itself this single, easily recognizable and easily established mark has the other marks as well. For, it was asserted (not argued): The Roman Church and the pope possess the four notes—one, holy, catholic, and apostolic—in a causative way; that is, they produce these in the other Churches, while the other Churches have the marks only by participation. The primacy, or *Romanitas,* thus becomes an easily managed "characteristic and sufficient mark" (*nota characteristica et sufficiens*). But "as the argumentation took refuge in areas less and less open to attack, it became increasingly cogent from the viewpoint of logic but increasingly dubious from the viewpoint of theology."[1]

In summary form, what we have been seeing is this: Only the Catholic Church possesses those marks which are at the same time properties of the Church of Christ: oneness, holiness, catholicity, and apostolicity. This Church is therefore the one and only Church of Jesus Christ.[2] The other confessions have no right to the title "Church," since they lack the marks and properties or have them only partially or in fragmentary form. A plurality of Churches is thus impossible: There is only one Church; there cannot (rightfully) be Churches.

Seen in this perspective, the Catholic Church is

> the broad stream that has carried, and still carries, through the centuries the movement which originated in Christ. The other Churches are streamlets that have branched off from this river; to the extent that they have not silted up and dried out or flowed back again into the great riverbed, they cannot be compared with the river either in external size or in internal power.[3]

This conception of things yields the following consequences:

"Church" exists only in the singular. The plurality of "Churches" is illegitimate, contradicting both the will of Jesus and the very nature of the Church. Christian communities outside the one true Church, which is the Roman Catholic, cannot be given the name of Church, even though they claim it for themselves. With the exception of the Eastern Church they are *sectae acatholicae* (non-Catholic sects), heretical communities, "religious communities" with their ministers of religion.

It cannot therefore be said in a proper sense that the Church is divided and split. The one true Church is not divided but on the contrary is being increasingly strengthened in a unity that, especially since Vatican I, has been turning into uniformity. All that can be said is that the others have separated and dissociated themselves; like the prodigal son in the parable (Lk 15) they have left their father's house.

III. The Church and the Question of Salvation

From the earliest period of the Church's existence the problem of the true Church has been connected with the problem of salvation. The connection found expression in a statement that has never fallen out of use since Cyprian voiced it: *Extra ecclesiam nulla salus*—Outside the Church no sal-

vation. The proposition found its most rigorous formulation and this in relation to individuals, in the *Dictatus papae* of Gregory VII, in the Bull *Unam
sanctam* of Boniface VIII and especially in the Decree for the Jacobites:

> The holy Roman Church, founded by the word of our Lord and
> Savior . . . firmly believes, professes, and preaches that none living
> outside the Catholic Church—not only pagans, but Jews, heretics,
> and schismatics—can have part in eternal life, but will rather go
> into the eternal fire prepared for the devil and his angels, unless
> they become members of the Church before the end of their life.
> So important is the unity of the ecclesiastical body that the sacra-
> ments of the Church profit only those remaining in it, and only on
> them do fasts, almsgiving, and other works of devotion and exer-
> cises of Christian warfare bestow eternal rewards. No one, no mat-
> ter how many alms he may give, and even if he sheds his blood for
> Christ's name, can be saved if he does not remain in the bosom
> and unity of the Catholic Church (DS, no. 1351).

The implications of this axiom for the salvation of those not members
of this Church seemed intolerable, even if they provided an extremely powerful motive for missionary zeal. Anyone not belonging to this Church
must, it seemed, fail to gain salvation. But how can this be reconciled with
the universal salvific will of a God who wills all men to be saved (1 Tim
2:4)? No less open to misunderstanding is the other consequence that seems
to follow from the axiom: that membership in the Roman Catholic Church
assures and even guarantees eternal salvation (although such a proposition
was never formulated).

The difficulty created by this first proposition: "Outside the Church no
salvation," made necessary an explanation which Piux IX formulated as follows: "By faith we must maintain that outside the apostolic Roman Church
no one can be saved, for it is the only ark of salvation, and anyone who does
not enter it must drown in the flood. But we must maintain no less firmly
that no one incurs this guilt in the eyes of the Lord if he lives in invincible
ignorance of the true religion" (DS, no. 2865, introduction).

But in the long view this explanation—that despite lack of membership
in the Catholic Church salvation could be attained if the person was in inculpable invincible error—seemed to supply no satisfactory and adequate
answer. It was very much out of keeping with the nature of salvation as
grace and source of responsibility that its attainment should be based on
something negative and defective, namely, "error."

An attempt was made to overcome this deficiency with the help of an
idea which Pius XII presented in his trailblazing encyclical on the Church,
Mystici corporis (1943), although here again there was an uncompromising
identification of the Mystical Body (understood as the best description of
the Church's nature) with the concrete Roman Catholic Church.

In this encyclical the relation of non-Catholic Christians to the Church is described with the aid of the categories of *desiderium inscium* and *votum* (unconscious desire and wish), and thus in a positive way and not only in terms of error. An explanatory declaration of the Holy Office addressed to Archbishop Cushing then interpreted this *votum* very broadly to include even a *votum implicitum* (DS, nos. 3866–73).

As interpreted by contemporary theology the axiom *Extra ecclesiam nulla salus* is not a personal principle but an instrumental principle. That is, its intention is not to specify who is saved and who is not (no one is competent to make such a judgment), but rather to indicate the means by which salvation comes to human beings. It describes how all the saved are in fact saved: through Jesus Christ and through the Church in which he and his action become concretely present.

According to H. de Lubac, there is therefore no reason why the formula *Extra ecclesiam nulla salus* should not be put "in a positive form and read, appealing to all men of good will, not 'outside the Church you are damned,' but 'it is by the Church and by the Church alone that you will be saved.' For it is through the Church that salvation will come, that it is already coming to mankind."[4] "Only Christ who acts in the Church effects salvation. But his action in effecting salvation is not limited to the Church."[5]

Despite all this, down to Vatican II the problem of the Church and the Churches was decided predominantly along the lines we have just seen in our brief historical survey. In other words: The Church of Jesus Christ is exclusively identical with the Roman Catholic Church. Church exists only in the singular, and a plurality of Churches has no legitimate standing. When the term "the Churches" occurs in nontheological usage, it is inexact; the plurality of "Churches" must be eliminated by reduction to the singular "Church." The other Churches are not "means of salvation" (*instrumenta salutis*); only the Church of Jesus Christ is such a means, and the Church of Christ is identical with the Roman Catholic Church.

IV. The New Situation Created by the Teaching of Vatican II

The Second Vatican Council, though described as "The Council of the Church on the Church," did not by any means make the Church the focal point of Christian faith. Rather, by its comprehensive description of the Church it explained the latter's meaning and function and thus brought out the fact that the Church is not the principal reality but is in the service of this.

Vatican II intended (and proved) to be a council of Church renewal; it intended through this renewal to pave the way for the reunification of divided Christendom. It was therefore decidedly ecumenical and, as such, had to confront the problem of "the Church and the Churches" in a new way. Previous magisterial decisions on the subject had proved unserviceable. They would have conceived of the reunification of divided Christendom as taking only one possible form: a return to the Roman Catholic Church in the form of an unconditional capitulation. For this they were not prepared.

In the question of "the Church and the Churches" Vatican II discovered a principle according to which the Church's identity and continuity were to be preserved not by separating off or denying everything that was not itself but by linking fidelity to itself with openness to others rather than with the denigration of others.

The Constitution *Lumen gentium* does refer to the statements made in the encyclical *Mystici corporis* of Pius XII. But in doing so it also introduces nuances:

> The society (*societas*) furnished with hierarchical agencies and the Mystical Body of Christ are not to be considered as two realities, nor are the visible assembly and the spiritual community, nor the earthly Church and the Church enriched with heavenly things. Rather they form one interlocked reality which is comprised of a human and a divine element (*Lumen gentium,* no. 8; Abbott, p. 22).

The basic idea at work here is the analogy between the mystery of the incarnation and the mystery of the Church, the latter being understood as a community that is both visible and spiritual, as a Church that is earthly but also blessed with heavenly gifts.

Then the text continues:

> This is the unique Church of Christ which in the Creed we avow as one, holy, catholic, and apostolic. After his resurrection our Savior handed her over to Peter to be shepherded (Jn 21:17), commissioning him and the other apostles to propagate and govern her (cf. Mt. 28:18ff.) Her he erected for all ages as "the pillar and mainstay of the truth" (1 Tim 3:15). This Church, constituted and organized in the world as a society, subsists in the Catholic Church, which is governed by the successor of Peter and by the bishops in union with that successor, although many elements of sanctification and of truth can be found outside of her visible structure. These gifts, however, as gifts properly belonging to the Church of Christ, possess an inner dynamism toward Catholic unity (ibid.; Abbott, pp. 22–23).

In both language and intention these sentences reject an extremist type of exclusiveness and identity, and at the same time make room for a positive approach to and recognition of the other Churches. This emerges quite clearly from an important change that had been made in the text. In an earlier version the text read: "Haec igitur Ecclesia . . . *est* Ecclesia Catholica, a Romano Pontifice et Episcopis in eius communione directa" (This Church

... *is* the Catholic Church which is ruled by the Roman Pontiff and the Bishops in communion with him); the later version says: "Haec Ecclesia *subsistit in* Ecclesia catholica, a successore Petri et Episcopis in eius communione gubernata" (This Church ... *subsists in* the Catholic Church, which ... in union with that successor) (No. 7 of the draft). *Est* is exclusive; *subsistit* is positive and open.[6]

In the mind of the Council the *subsistit* has the intention and function of preventing an unqualified identification of the Church of Christ with the Roman Catholic Church and cultivating an openness to the ecclesial reality present in other Christian confessions. According to a Protestant commentary, the statements are so worded "that no trace of arrogance or self-complacency is to be found in them."

There is another point to be noted about this text: it no longer speaks of the Roman Catholic Church. The geographical term "Roman" and the profane designation "Roman Pontiff" are replaced by a reference to the spiritual content of the Petrine office, while express mention is made of the unity between this office and the communion of bishops.

The question of the identification of the Church was taken up again at the Council and set forth in the statements about the Church in the Decree on Ecumenism. Here the reflections on the unity and unicity of the Church reach their climax in the sentence: "The highest exemplar and source of this mystery [of the unity of the Church] is the unity, in the Trinity of Persons, of one God, the Father and the Son in the Holy Spirit" (no. 2; Abbott, p. 344). The agent, on earth and within history, of this living, many-faceted unity of the Church is the Holy Spirit who brings about the communion of believers in Christ and with Christ and is the giver of manifold gifts. This unity finds expression in the confession of the one faith, in the common celebration of the liturgy, and in the fraternal harmony of the family of God (ibid.).

All this makes it clear that the unity of the Church and in the Church cannot be a matter of uniformity but is something vital and free, rich and many-sided. There is, of course, a limit, and it is found at the point when the unity needed in necessary things is threatened, where variety turns into opposition and contradiction and leads to division.

V. The Church and the Churches in the Light of Vatican II

In the light of what has been said about the question of the Church's identity the relation between Church and Churches can also be approached in a new way.

According to the encyclical *Mystici corporis* the relation between the Church of Christ and the Roman Catholic Church is one of outright identity; it follows from this that there is, strictly speaking, no division within the Church. Anyone who does not belong to the Roman Catholic Church simply does not belong to the Church at all. The unity of the Church consists in the unity possessed by the Roman Catholic Church. As long as this latter unity exists, it is not possible, from the theological viewpoint, to speak of a division of the Church.

But the problem remains of how the undeniable Christian-ness of the other Churches is to be evaluated and what is to be thought of the ecclesial dignity of the communions which are formed of Christians outside the Roman Catholic Church and in which these Christians profess the Christian faith and lead a Christian life. An effort was made to solve this problem by asking and answering another question: the question of membership in the Church.

In regard to this second question there were, before the Council, two traditions. The view found chiefly in writing on canon law was based on Canon 87 of the Code of Canon Law. Here it is said that through baptism a human being becomes a "person" in the Church of Christ and acquires all the rights and obligations of a Christian, although the exercise of a right may be hindered either by an impediment (*obex*) which prevents ecclesial communion or by a punishment which is imposed by the Church. "Person"in the sense of juridical personality includes being in the Church and being a member of the Church. Baptism therefore brings membership in the Church of Christ. "The personhood in the Church that is effected by baptism is salutary membership in the Church."[7]

The question then arises of how this general membership of all the baptized is to be distinguished from the specific membership of Catholic Christians. The Code does not go into this question in any detail, but it does suggest that there are degrees of membership: a constitutional membership of all Christians which is based on baptism and distinguishes Christians from non-Christians, and an active membership which can be hindered in one or other way.

In contrast to this first tradition the encyclical *Mystici corporsi* revives an ancient dogmatic and apologetic position and offers the thesis that only they belong to the Church *reapse*, in the proper sense, who have received baptism, profess the true faith, and have not separated themselves, or been separated, from the communion of the Church.

Here, then, we have three criteria of memberships and only when all three are verified is there membership in the Church: baptism; Catholic faith; submission to the ecclesiastical hierarchy with the pope at its head. Excluded from the Church, then, are those who live in schism (the Eastern Church), those who live in heresy (the Christians of the Reformation), and those who live in apostasy (those whom modern secularism has caused to leave the Church). It is said that these three—schism, heresy, and apostasy—by their very nature separate a person from the body which is the Church (the *corpus ecclesiae*). These determinations end with an exceptionally weighty and harsh statement: "Therefore those who are divided from one another in faith or government cannot live in the one same body and by the one same Spirit" (DS, no. 3802). Only indirectly does the encyclical *Mystici corporis* touch on the status of non-Catholic Christians and non-

Catholic communities. It is said that they are in a situation in which they cannot be certain of their eternal salvation; they are therefore urged to get out of this situation.

This negative evaluation is followed by one that reads more positively. This says that non-Catholic Christians are related to the Church by an "unconscious desire and wish" and that when they return they come not as strangers but as people coming back to their paternal home.

J. Ratzinger sums up as follows the criticism leveled at this well-intentioned but unsatisfactory conception:

> Its psychology is based on imagination, inasmuch as it attributes to the separated brethren a desire which in their conscious thinking they expressly deny. In practice it puts non-Catholic Christians and pagans on the same level as far as membership in the Church is concerned, since the pagans too may be said to belong to the Church by desire. The starting point for this entire attempt at a solution is completely of a subjective kind; the salvation of non-Catholics is in practice reduced entirely to a subjective factor: a desire which, in addition, leaves no trace in their consciousness.[8]

Vatican II endeavored to resolve the problems I have outlined, as well as the incongruences created by the old solutions, by approaching them in a different way. This meant chiefly that in describing the relationship between Catholic Church and non-Catholic confessions, communities and Churches the image of membership was no longer used, not even in the form of membership (with whatever distinctions and degrees) and nonmembership. Nor was use made of the "wish and unconscious desire" of Pius XII's encyclical. The Council put the concept of *votum* back where it makes theological sense and can be defended: it was applied to the situation of catechumens. Of the latter it is said that when they have an express intention of being received into the Church they are joined to the Church by this (conscious) *votum* or desire of theirs.

The key concepts that play a determining role in the Council's thinking on the situation of Catholic and non-Catholic Christians are *incorporatio* and *conjunctio*. *Incorporari* (to be incorporated) represents the ecclesial status of Catholic believers, while *conjunctum esse* (to be linked with) expresses, in an open-ended way, the relation of non-Catholics to the Catholic Church.

In what does full affiliation (*plene incorporari*) consist, and to whom is it ascribed? The first factor named (and this priority betokens an exceptionally important ecclesiological principle) is "possession of the Spirit of Christ." Only then are other elements of Church affiliation named:

> They are fully incorporated into the society of the Church who, possessing the Spirit of Christ, accept her entire system and all the means of salvation given to her, and through union with her visi-

ble structure are joined to Christ, who rules her through the Supreme Pontiff and the bishops. This joining is effected by the bonds of professed faith, of the sacraments, of ecclesiastical government, and of communion (*Lumen gentium,* no. 14; Abbott, p. 33).

Aggregation to the Church thus takes place in two ways: at the interior spiritual level and at the visible level.

The mention—and in first place, at that—of the spiritual criterion for belonging to the Church ("possessing the Spirit of Christ") means that we have reached a new stage in understanding of the Church. Previously this understanding was determined solely by what is juridically ascertainable, and the decisive criteria were based on the same. With this new approach, formulated according to the principle of the *hierarchia veritatum* (hierarchy of truths), thinking in this area has acquired a breadth and an openness that are to be regarded not as a denial of Catholic reality but as its fulfillment. The importance of this idea of the Spirit as a criterion can be gauged by looking at it from another viewpoint.

Sin does not eliminate incorporation into the Church (it is an ancient theological principle that sinners continue to belong to the Church), but an incorporation that is hindered by sin not only is not effective but even turns into a judgment on the person: "He is not saved, however, who, though he is part of the body of the Church, does not persevere in charity. He remains indeed in the bosom of the Church, but, as it were, only in a 'bodily' manner and not 'in his heart' " (*Lumen gentium,* no. 14; Abbott, p. 33).

In earlier formulations the distinction between the question of salvation and the question of membership in the Church had not always been made fully clear. Here it emerges unambiguously: "full incorporation" gives no basis for presumption or for false tranquillity and security.

The relationship of the other Christian ecclesial communities to the Catholic Church is described by the words *conjunctum esse* and the *ordinari* which this linkage represents. The links are described in terms not of subjective states of mind but of Christian and ecclesial realities.

The history of the pertinent text (*Lumen gentium,* no. 15) is a very turbulent one. It suggests the intense effort that was made to advance beyond previous positions, as well as the attempt to do justice as far as possible, even in the choice of words and concepts, to the ecumenical and pastoral intentions of the Council. The Christian reality established by baptism and its implications is taken as the basic point of departure. The key text reads as follows:

> The Church recognizes that in many ways she is linked with those who, being baptized, are honored with the name of Christian, though they do not profess the faith in its entirety or do not preserve unity of communion with the successor of Peter. For there are many who honor sacred scripture, taking it as a norm of belief

and action, and who show a true religious zeal. They lovingly believe in God the Father Almighty and in Christ, Son of God and Savior. They are consecrated by baptism, through which they are united with Christ. They also recognize and receive other sacraments within their own churches or ecclesial communities. . . . They also share with us in prayer and other spiritual benefits.

Likewise, we can say that in some real way they are joined with us in the Holy Spirit, for to them also he gives his gifts and graces, and is thereby operative among them with his sanctifying power. Some indeed he has strengthened to the extent of the shedding of their blood. In all of Christ's disciples the Spirit arouses the desire to be peacefully united, in the manner determined by Christ, as one flock under one shepherd, and he prompts them to pursue this goal. Mother Church never ceases to pray, hope, and work that they may gain this blessing. She exhorts her sons to purify and renew themselves so that the sign of Christ may shine more brightly over the face of the Church (*Lumen gentium*, no. 15; Abbott, pp. 33–34).

From this new vision of non-Catholic Christians and their links (despite all the differences and divisions that remain) with the Catholic Church it is only a step to positive evaluation of the communities in which the individual Christian has received his Christian being and in which he now lives it and brings it to fulfillment. If the individual Christian is in possession of all these elements which represent so many links with the Catholic Church, then the same links must be attributed to these communities, and this to the extent of giving them the name "Church."

The step to an express acceptance of this conclusion is taken in the Decree on Ecumenism. Of Christians who live outside the Roman Catholic Church it is said:

All those justified by faith through baptism are incorporated into Christ. They therefore have a right to be honored by the title of Christian, and are properly regarded as brothers in the Lord by the sons of the Catholic Church.

Moreover some, even very many, of the most significant elements or endowments which together go to build up and give life to the Church herself can exist outside the visible boundaries of the Catholic Church: the written word of God; the life of grace; faith, hope, and charity, along with other interior gifts of the Holy Spirit and visible elements. All of these, which come from Christ and lead back to him, belong by right to the one Church of Christ.

The brethren divided from us also carry out many of the sacred actions of the Christian religion. Undoubtedly, in ways that vary according to the condition of each Church or Community, these actions can truly engender a life of grace, and can be rightly described as capable of providing access to the community of salvation.

It follows that these separated Churches and Communities, though we believe they suffer from defects already mentioned, have by no means been deprived of significance and importance in the mystery of salvation. For the Spirit of Christ has not refrained from using them as means of salvation which derive their efficacy from the very fullness of grace and truth entrusted to the Catholic Church (*Unitatis redintegratio,* no. 3: Abbott, pp. 345–46).

This text moves beyond *Lumen gentium* to say that the Church is built up by the gifts of Christ, which are found in their fullness of the Catholic Church but found also, in varying measures, in the other Christian communities, where they exercise their power to form and maintain community. And when it is expressly noted that "all of these, which come from Christ and lead back to him, belong by right to the one Church of Christ," not only is the question of identification once again given an open-ended answer, but the ecclesial character, the Church-ness, of the other communities is highlighted and justified. Explicitly stressed here is also the fact that the existence of Churches thus living by these realities introduces not division but the hope of unity into the Church of Christ. The Decree adds that the divisions among Christians nevertheless prevent the Church from developing her full catholicity; "furthermore, the Church herself finds it more difficult to express in actual life her full catholicity in all its aspects." (no. 4: Abbot, p. 349).

Differences are thus neither denied nor eliminated, but rather located within a shared existence that contains them. In consequence, the word and concept of "Church" is to be used truthfully and by full right, but also in an analogous sense that combines unity with diversity, diversity with unity. In such a perspective as this the Catholic Church is not obliged to renounce its claim to be the Church of Christ, but need neither it challenge the Church-ness of other Churches and communities in order to safeguard its own true ecclesial nature. Rather they too are to be recognized as true Churches, since in them too the gifts are alive and operative by which the Church of Christ lives and is built up and which belong to the one Church.

The passage cited above from the Decree on Ecumenism speaks of "Churches" and "ecclesial Communities," but no differentiation or distribution of the terms is given here, nor should we forcibly introduce one, as is sometimes done. It may be noted, however, that many of these communities of their own accord reject a designation as "Church." This is why the Decree on Ecumenism speaks of the "Eastern Churches" but of the "Churches and separated Communities" of the West.

There is one detail that merits consideration in this context: The statement of Vatican II that the Spirit of Christ uses the separated ecclesial communities as means of salvation is formulated negatively: "The Spirit of Christ has not refrained from using" (*Spiritus Christi uti non renuit*). It is worth noting that the encyclical *Mystici corporis* uses the same verb *renuit* (without the *non*) when it raises the question of the indwelling of the Holy Spirit in those who are completely separated from the Mystical Body and asserts that the Spirit of God refrains from dwelling in them (DS, no. 3808). The encyclical also speaks more generally and says that those who are divided from one another in faith or government "cannot live in the one same body and by the one same Spirit" (DS, no. 3802). The new outlook reached and articulated by the Council represents a great and genuine step forward. It is not a "development" but a clear correction of the earlier view. A new theological principle has been voiced that calls for concrete and many-sided application in the faith and life of the Christian Churches.

VI. The Consequence: Church and Churches in a New Configuration

Taken together, these various statements of Vatican II establish the possibility, and create the conditions, for raising and weighing the question of the Church and the Churches in a different way than in the past: I mean in a positive and affirmative way. The plurality of Churches can no longer be illegitimate, since the Council expressly speaks of the other Christian communities and confessions as Churches and ecclesial Communities.

This action of the Council is an important ecumenical signal. In the past the various confessions were often defined primarily by what distinguished them from others: the non-Catholic or non-Protestant elements. In our time, however, due to many external factors people have been reminded, and the Council explicitly says, that the confessions are linked by common elements which are greater and more important than their differences. In the past these great common bonds were almost lost sight of because of the differences; today the inclination is to look at the differences within the framework of what the confessions have in common. The result is not only a vision more in keeping with reality, but one that has ecumenical significance.

The non-Roman Catholic Churches are now described as Churches and ecclesial Communities, and this very fact is an extremely important basis for ecumenism. It creates the condition needed for heightening the common bonds and achieving a unification in which the very confessions that previously were the typical representatives of separation can increasingly become subjects of a legitimate diversity within unity or, in the words of J. Ratzinger: "The Churches must remain Churches and yet become one Church."

Such statements as these open our eyes for a better understanding of the biblical origins and of history. While the New Testament speaks energetically of the unity of the Church and of Church in the singular, it speaks no less unembarrassedly of Churches in the plural, i.e., local Churches, liturgical assemblies in Corinth, Jerusalem, Rome, and elsewhere. These Churches are not affiliates or mission stations of a principal Church, but Churches in the full sense of the word. They represent the "event" of "Church." In them there occurs and is accomplished that which makes the Church be the Church: the proclamation of the message of Jesus and of the message about Jesus as the Christ, perseverance in the teaching of the apostles, the breaking of bread in the celebration of the Eucharist, and the diaconal ministry (Acts 2:42).

Despite these common elements the communities in question show no uniformity in shape, composition, or even (within limits) organization. There is a difference between the primarily Jewish-Christian and the primarily Gentile-Christian communities.

The form which the Church manifests in the New Testament is that of *the Church in the Churches,* of ecclesial unity in ecclesial multiplicity, and this was seen not as a hindrance but as the expression of a living unity that was based on Christ and his Spirit and that obliged the members to build up the Church.

In other words: the Churches had their place within the one Church; the Church took shape in the Churches.

At the theoretical level, this plurality has never been challenged in the course of history. But we must immediately add, in the words of Joseph Ratzinger:

> This plurality was in fact increasingly eliminated in favor of a centralized system in which the local Church of Rome as it were swallowed up all the other local Churches and thus reduced unity to uniformity. This fact provided important motives for divisions in the Church, but on the other hand it also provides important motives for the Catholic Church of today in relation to the ecumenical movement. The fact that the plurality of "Churches" which should by rights exist in the Church was being increasingly eliminated was one reason why this plurality, for which there was no adequate room in the Church, has now developed outside of it in the form of individual Churches claiming autonomy. By acknowledging this development, the Council shows that unity and uniformity are not the same things and that a primary need is to restore the vital multiplicity of Churches within the unity of the Catholic Church.[9]

This is a task that must be faced and carried out in the Roman Catholic Church. Down to Vatican II and in a context created by the historical effects of Vatican I and its decree regarding the primacy and the infallible teaching office, the various popes named Pius deliberately fostered certain tendencies and translated them into practice in many ways, in accordance with the principle: "The greater the uniformity, the more perfect and convincing the unity." The Catholic Church was thus preoccupied with interpreting the various aspects of unity in the direction of maximal uniformity; this applied even to the language of the liturgy. Catholics still have no real practice in a legitimate multiplicity within the one Church; perhaps they have been struck by the disquieting multiplicity of "denominations" to be found, even today, in the non-Roman Catholic Churches.

Joseph Ratzinger has this to say on the point:

> The Catholic must recognize that his own Church is simply not prepared for the phenomenon of multiplicity in unity and that it is his own task to prepare himself for this possibility and reality. He will thus understand that his own Church has a profound need of renewal and that the renewal will not be accomplished overnight but requires a lengthy process of self-opening, a time of patience during which he has no right simply to "absorb" others because the place in the Church has not yet been created to which they have a right.
>
> The idea of conversion, which is fully meaningful for the individual whose conscience so directs him, must be replaced in principle by the idea of a unity of Churches which remain Churches and yet become one Church.
>
> If the Catholic dares hope for anything, it is that the hour will come when "the Churches" which now exist outside "the Church" will at last enter its unity, in such a way that they will continue to be Churches and will accept such and only such changes in themselves as this unity necessarily requires.[10]

The changes in question may be exemplified by the demand constantly voiced in intraecclesial and ecumenical dialogue: The unification and unity of the Church can come about only on the basis of truth, and not by ignoring the question of truth. On this point too Joseph Ratzinger has something to say that is very much worth noting:

> The claims of truth should not be raised where they are not completely convincing and unrenounceable. It is not legitimate to interpret as the truth something which is in fact a form developed in the course of history and only more or less closely connected with the truth. Precisely when the truth comes into play with its full weight and inexorability there must be a corresponding honesty that shrinks from too ready a claim to possess the truth and is ready to seek with the eyes of love after the full inner breadth of the truth.[11]

We can say therefore that the configuration of Church and Churches which we find in the New Testament is not reflected in the present state of the Church. Consequently, the well-known thesis of Ernst Käsemann—that the New Testament canon provides the basis not for the unity of the Church but for the multiplicity of confessions[12]—is acceptable only if the multiplicity meant is not the present situation of separated confessions which excommunicate one another, but rather the situation which is the object of hope and striving and the goal of ecumenical unity: confessions which are not the mainstays of division but the representatives of legitimate diversity within unity.

The more that people in the Catholic Church recognize the significance of the local Churches "in which and by means of which the Church subsists," and the more they understand and realize that the former mission Churches are becoming independent Churches with their own authentic form and character (the Church in Africa, in Latin America, in the Far East)—the more they will be prepared and ready for the greater ecumenical tasks still ahead: the Churches must remain Churches and yet become one Church.

From all that I have been saying it also follows that ecumenical unity cannot replace the confessions and that the *confessions* must rather, while remaining faithful to what is central in themselves, be the *expression and sign of ecumenical unity.* Then, by an as yet unaccomplished process of properly understood recognition, and in fulfillment of the task and promise of *ecclesia semper reformanda,* "the Church and the Churches" will become a reality.[13]

The General Synod of the Dioceses of the Federal German Republic, in their conclusions regarding pastoral collaboration in the service of Christian unity, expressed as follows the hope of which I have been speaking here: "The Synod hopes for a development in which the oppositions that have hitherto divided the Churches will be dismantled and overcome and the Churches and ecclesial Communities hitherto separated will become representatives of diversity in the one Church of Jesus Christ."[14]

18

Criteria for Interpreting the Traditions

Gerald O'Collins

As John Henry Newman so vividly insisted in *An Essay on the Development of Christian Doctrine,* through the centuries the post-apostolic Church has undergone rich and fruitful changes. He identified this as a necessary thing: "To live is to change."[1] We should expect and actually do find that generation after generation of believers has passed through and expressed for later Christians a huge variety of changing experiences that concern the three levels of the Church's existence: "teaching, life and worship."[2]

But not all the particular traditions handed on from the past are of equal value. Some may turn out to be "the traditions of men" (Mk 7, 8) which distort and misrepresent the Christian message. How then can the present generation of believers go about discerning and interpreting the great mass of traditions it has received from the past? What principles will help us to separate the central from the peripheral traditions, to detect those inherited attitudes and practices in which the Church needs reformation,[3] and to identify and faithfully preserve what the Council of Trent called "the purity of the Gospel,"[4] what the Roman Canon describes as "the Catholic faith that comes to us from the apostles," or what the 1963 meeting of the Faith and Order Commission termed *the* Tradition (with a capital T) within the traditions (with a small t)?

The Commission put the issue this way:

> Do all traditions which claim to be Christian contain the Traditions? How can we distinguish between traditions embodying the true Tradition and merely human traditions? Where do we find the genuine Tradition and where impoverished traditions or even distortion of traditions?[5]

At the third session of the Second Vatican Council Cardinal Meyer of Chicago raised the same issue. He pointed to many limitations and defects which turn up in the traditions of the Catholic Church, a community of pilgrims and sinners: a long neglect of the doctrine of the resurrection, an exaggerated casuistry in moral theology, a non-liturgical piety, the neglect of the Bible and so forth.[6] In the actual traditions of the Church decline and corruption show up, as well as progress.

We can approach the question as follows. When our inherited traditions intersect with our present experiences, two things happen. The various doctrinal, liturgical and moral traditions will help us to discern and interpret what we experience. At the same time our new experiences may call into question and challenge some old traditions concerned with Christian belief, worship and way of life. For instance, a gap may open up between the language of contemporary culture and that of traditional teaching. This kind of tension may be ignored or suppressed, but the price of artificially maintaining old traditions will be a loss of genuine Christian living. Yet sooner or later fresh experiences will always bring home new perspectives on some inherited attitudes and practices. Thus the ecumenical, feminist and charismatic movements, the arms race, widespread injustice and hunger, and other elements in the Church's total environment in their different ways ask the question: Where have Christian traditions preserved "the purity of the Gospel" and where have they obscured it? How can believers discern and interpret their traditions so as to purify and renew them and thus maintain a proper continuity with "the Catholic faith that comes to us from the apostles?"

In this discerning process it would be absurd to expect that the gospel, the tradition, or—to put it in equivalent terms—the truth and saving reality of Jesus Christ could be experienced "neat." The (One) tradition can be found only in and through the (many) traditions. The gospel, transmitted in and by the Church, never exists in some abstract, ideal state, but only as actualized and interpreted through "the preaching of the Word, in the administration of the sacraments and worship, in Christian teaching and theology, and in mission and witness to Christ by the lives of the members of the Church."[7] What criteria are available to recognize and faithfully conform oneself to the tradition within the traditions? *The* Tradition must never be betrayed but the traditions—which run all the way from the preservation of relics, the practice of indulgences and the Latin Mass through methods for appointing bishops to current formulations of doctrine—undergo and should undergo change. We must uphold *tota Traditio* but it would be both a betrayal of Christianity and an impossible task to maintain at all costs *totae traditiones*. But what principles are available to guide our discernment, interpretation and innovations?

1. *The Magisterium*

In the Church's magisterium Catholics enjoy a criterion for maintaining a creative fidelity, as they receive what previous generations have passed on and attempt to discern what the Spirit could be saying to the Churches now. The magisterium will guide the Catholic believer's choices in that permanent dialogue between inherited traditions and new experiences.

Nevertheless, this criterion does not suffice by itself. On given issues the magisterium may never pronounce or only speak after many years have elapsed. In the meantime, however, believers will have to respond and react to the question: Does this or that tradition misrepresent or deviate from the Gospel? Further, the magisterium is a proximate criterion which points beyond itself. The Pope and bishops in their magisterial role do not constitute an ultimate criterion but are bound to adhere and submit to Christ's saving revelation.[8] On this point Vatican II's Constitution on Divine Revelation has been quoted a thousand times but one more time will not hurt: "The task of giving an authentic interpretation of the Word of God, whether in its written form or in the form of tradition, has been entrusted to the living teaching office of the Church alone. . . . Yet this magisterium is not superior to the Word of God, but is its servant."[9]

2. *Universality, Antiquity and Consent*

The Vincentian Canon offers a further criterion for assessing traditions: "What is believed everywhere, always and by everyone—this is truly and properly Catholic."[10] In their own fashion others have articulated part or all of this criterion. Thus St. Augustine wrote: "Securus iudicat orbis terrarum (the whole world judges securely)."[11] But Vincent of Lerins' statement has become the classical one. Let me here indicate rapidly some necessary qualifications and limitations.

There is no escaping the fact that the Vincentian Canon is to a degree a Christianized version of the ancient argument from universality, antiquity and consent: What has been everywhere believed by everyone from time immemorial must be true. Or to put it another way: What was universally believed by everyone at the beginning was the pure, unadulterated truth. Errors come later. Hence we should presume that ancient traditions which were universally and commonly believed carry the truth and that novelties involve falsehood.

To identify the Vincentian Canon as a Christianized version of a classical principle is not *eo ipso* to allege that the Canon is automatically and totally wrong. After all the Greek and Latin thinkers could have some truth on their side. But one should not overlook a very similar appeal to universality, antiquity and consent in writers like Cicero. Precisely on that basis he argued for the existence of the gods and the reality of prescience and foretelling.[12] However, we would get things wrong if we overlooked a point which affects the relationship between philosophy and theology. To a lesser or greater extent, Christian theology will *always* modify ideas which it takes over from philosophy and other sources. Philosophical concepts and principles (such as the criterion of universality, antiquity and consent) cannot be expected to move without change into the theological framework.

What then should be said of the Vincentian Canon? Essentially it appeals to a process of historical verification in support of whatever traditional beliefs and practices are being questioned. To retain some theological validity, however, the Canon requires a number of modifications.

(a) First of all, the Canon needs to be qualified as follows: "What has been believed everywhere, always and by everyone *precisely as part of the saving Gospel of Christ*—this is truly and properly Catholic." Notoriously, Christians have for centuries shared with others false beliefs about the nature of the universe, human procreation and the activities of witches, as well as accepting with their culture slavery and other immoral practices. In the face of such obvious and persistent difficulties from Christian history, we should introduce some such qualification and give the Vincentian Canon a chance.

(b) Further, it is clear that very few traditional beliefs and practices could literally verify the Canon. No one has ever established that some traditional doctrine has been *quite literally and explicitly believed, always, everywhere and by everyone*. It is hard to imagine how this could ever be established. Taking the Vincentian Canon slightly less literally but still pretty rigidly, we could perhaps demonstrate a clear antiquity, universality and general consent for such an utterly basic belief like Christ being Savior of humankind. For other such doctrines and practices as the Real Presence in the Eucharist, Original Sin, the existence of purgatory and the validity of prayers for the dead, we would have very considerable difficulty in showing anything like an explicit acceptance "always, everywhere and by everyone."

We could help matters by adding a qualification: "What has been believed *at least implicitly.* . . ." That addition would give the historian more hope of demonstrating that at least a few traditions were latently and implicitly held "always, everywhere and by everyone."

We could add another qualification: "What has been believed at least implicitly always and everywhere by everyone—*at least that* is truly and properly Catholic." In other words, we could use the Vincentian Canon as an *inclusive,* rather than an exclusive, criterion. It would *not,* therefore, exclude some traditional beliefs which *as a matter of fact* could have been held implicitly "always, everywhere and by everyone," but which we *cannot historically prove* to have been so held.

(c) Even after we have added these different qualifications to the Canon, several questions press themselves on our attention. Who, for instance, is to count as "everyone"? Only those who *on other grounds* we hold to be orthodox believers? Or all practicing Christians? Difficulties over traditions arise precisely when everyone (was and) is not in agreement. If we look back to the christological controversies of the early centuries, we can only wonder what the results would have been had the Vincentian Canon been strictly applied. At their height the Arian party could well have successfully employed such a principle against Athanasius and his followers, who—as John Henry Newman insisted—appeared to be innovating radicals fighting for a strange terminology against the proper traditionalists. In later centuries the prophetic few who campaigned for such reforms as the abolition of slavery would not have helped their cause by appealing to "what has been believed and practiced always, everywhere and by everyone." In short, counting noses might not determine too readily the status of inherited traditions. Even in the milder form of moral unanimity the Vincentian Canon does not fit easily the cases in which prophetic minorities in the Church have challenged certain inherited attitudes and practices and eventually, but only eventually, have been proven right in their discernment of the gospel demands. As Newman remarked, "the number of persons holding an idea is no warrant for its objective character, else, the many never could be wrong."[13] From time to time "the many" have turned out to be wrong in the traditions they have received and handed on—at the level of belief, worship and patterns of behavior.

Frequently "everyone" has been taken in a somewhat restricted way to denote the consent of the Fathers of the Church. Thus some traditional beliefs and practices have been justified by appealing to "the teaching of the holy Fathers," their "ancient tradition," and their "unanimous consent."[14] Whatever the value of such general appeals, Newman and others have pointed out how difficult it is to claim for any specific doctrine whatsoever that *all* the Fathers of the Church *explicitly* and *directly* teach it.

(d) If consent ("everyone") raises problems for the Vincentian Canon, so too do antiquity ("always") and universality ("everywhere"). In assessing inherited traditions what should we accept as counting for "always" and "everywhere"? Will relative antiquity count as "always" or must the tradition in question necessarily go back to the very origins of Christianity? What constitutes the geography of orthodox faith implied by "everywhere"? Newman summed up the problem this way:

> What is meant by being "taught *always*"? Does it mean in every century, or every year, or every month? Does "everywhere" mean in every country, or in every diocese? And does "the *Consent of Fathers*" require us to produce the testimony of everyone of them? How many Fathers, how many places, how many instances constitute a fulfillment of the test proposed?[15]

(e) Obviously we could end up establishing *only part* of "the test proposed." Thus we might establish antiquity without universality and consent. Something was believed always but not everywhere and by everyone. Or we might prove universality without antiquity and consent. Something has been believed everywhere but not always and by everyone. Or again we might demonstrate a general consent (either now or in the recent past), but have to admit that we cannot do the same for antiquity and universality. Something is now believed by everyone but this has not always and everywhere been the case.

In brief, the three elements that make up the Canon are not only distinguishable but also separable, as Vincent of Lerins himself realized. On the one hand, he knew that Arianism had spread very widely and so he could only invoke antiquity ("always") but not universality ("everywhere") against that heresy.[16] On the other hand, Donatism may have won a broad following in Christian Africa but it remained geographically confined. Hence Vincent appealed to universality ("everywhere") but not consent ("everyone") against the Donatists.[17]

(f) So far this discussion of the Vincentian Canon has had the effect of filling it out into a larger and more flexible shape: "What has been believed—at least implicitly—always, everywhere and by everyone precisely as part of Christ's saving Gospel—at least *that* is truly and properly Catholic." Yet even in this larger shape, it may not function too well as a total entity and, as we have just seen, the separable elements of "always, everywhere and by everyone" may have to set up on their own or as pairs rather than as a triad.

If then the Vincentian Canon requires so many qualifications and adjustments to avoid being patently useless and false, is it any real help? Newman did not think so. The Canon, he concluded, hardly yields "any satisfactory result. The solution it offers is as difficult as the original problem."[18] Yet I wonder whether the Canon has worn so badly that it is no longer workable.

Ultimately, it seems to me, the Vincentian Canon classically recalls that intersubjective nature of inherited Christian truth and life which must play an essential part in any discernment of traditions. Such discernment takes place in a Church community bonded together by a complex history of belief and practice. Any judgments and decisions about inherited traditions must be seriously checked against the collective experience of earlier Christians. Certain movements and trajectories can suggest ways in which the enduring presence of Christ's Spirit has shaped different Christian traditions. Even if it does not explicitly invoke the Holy Spirit, the Vincentian Canon reminds us that we must search for signs of the Spirit's enduring guidance in *past* generations of Christians. God is faithful. We can expect that we will find help by examining the ways our Christian predecessors experienced and expressed God's revelation and grace.

A few remarks about this scrutiny of the past. First, if something has been accepted, believed and practiced "never, nowhere and by no one," that should give us pause in our endorsement of some current traditions. Then too in searching for a usable past, we need to be on our guard against simply looking for what we want to find, tracking down traditions to support judgments we have already discreetly made, and hence being committed to accept lesser hints rather than follow the general weight of testimony. Newman articulates this warning, albeit with a somewhat different purpose: "And do not the same ancient Fathers bear witness to another doctrine, which you disown? Are you not as a hypocrite, listening to them when you will, and deaf when you will not?.... You accept the lesser evidence, you reject the greater."[19] Third, one would risk turning into an incautious *laudator temporis acti* who blandly idealizes the past, if one ignored the fact that every tradition is historically conditioned, even those at the very origins of Christianity. For instance, was the "loyal" attitude of the first Christians toward the Romans (reflected in Luke/Acts, 1 Peter, Romans 13 and elsewhere in the New Testament) a normative, intrinsic consequence of their experience of Jesus or simply a prudent stance dictated by the circumstances?

Granted all these cautionary remarks, the traditions of the Christian past, despite all the sinful corruptions, will, nevertheless, disclose the unfailing influence of Christ's Spirit and not just "the dust and debris of two thousand years."[20] As we seek help in discerning particular issues in our present traditions and experiences, we may find only thin trajectories, small hints and minor signs in the past. But some usable traditions will be there to challenge and illuminate us. For example, present experience of the women's movement in the Church—or would it be more accurate to say "women's movements"?—have prompted some to turn back to Julian of Norwich, St. Anselm of Canterbury, Isaiah and others for their use of feminine imagery in speaking of God and/or Jesus. Here and elsewhere, the records of past Christian experience will help us to discern and interpret the present.

To conclude this treatment of the Vincentian Canon. It could ultimately be rephrased this way: "What we can discover to have been believed and practiced *at least* sometimes, in some places and by some Christians as part of the good news and which promises once again to be *life-giving*—that can truly and properly direct our discernment of present traditions and experiences." "Life" in the mere sense of quantitative success is no necessary guide to truth, as Newman warned: "Life is no criterion of truth, for unreal, but plausible or isolated, ideas may powerfully affect multitudes."[21] However, what has once given and now promises again to give and enhance genuine life in Christ can be safely followed. Thus the Vincentian Canon, if it encourages an interest in earlier Christian experience, it does this in order to find and accept life-giving sources and not simply to augment "objective" historical knowledge.

e. *The "Sensus Fidei"*

Where the Vincentian Canon, despite the tense of "creditur (is believed)," focuses on the *past,* the *sensus fidei* looks to the *present* sensitivity found in the whole body of believers. Here and now the Holy Spirit guides their instinctive discernment in matters of faith. As constituting the body of Christ they enjoy an "intimate sense" of the "spiritual realities which they experience."[22] Thus the Holy Spirit, by shaping the corporate mind of the Church, provides a further criterion for testing and scrutinizing inherited traditions.

Inasmuch as the *sensus fidei* involves the Holy Spirit, it can seem obscurely dangerous to some people. By appealing to something invisible, does this criterion provide a warrant for intolerable excesses of all kinds? However, in the long run or even in the short run two safeguards are available. Do we see that a given discernment of inherited traditions which primarily appeals to the Holy Spirit in fact brings the visible fruits of the Spirit (Gal 5, 22f.)? By its fruits we can know the presence of a true *sensus fidei.*

Second, this criterion must ultimately look to the Spirit's impact on the *collective* mind of the *whole* Church. It does not justify the aberrations of small groups nor does it support a discernment which makes no attempt to reflect on world Christianity and takes the traditions of one continent or even one country as decisive. Of course, there are immense difficulties here. How do we establish the *sensus fidei* of Christians or even simply of Roman Catholics, who across the world exhibit many cultural diversities and divisions? Nevertheless, this third criterion rightly directs us to examine the faith and practice of the *whole* Church—"from the bishops to the last of the faithful."[23]

At times, however, we may want a unified *sensus fidei* which we cannot get. Just as in the past, so now difficulties will flare up precisely when the whole Church does not appear to judge matters of faith in the same way. In this century the discernment of small groups eventually led the majority to find richer peace, joy and life through the liturgical and ecumenical movements. We can readily agree that those groups of pioneers who brought the Church at large to a greater sensitivity in fact constituted genuine prophetic minorities. How can we discern and interpret other innovating groups who today challenge various inherited attitudes and practices? They do not represent the general consensus and yet some of them may turn out to be prophetic minorities, who are experiencing in a special way the guidance of the Holy Spirit and are called to prompt others into a more Christian discernment about the life of faith.

Once again we have no other means for assessing whether such innovating groups genuinely do express a true *sensus fidei* than by (a) checking the visible fruits of the Spirit, and (b) analyzing them in the light of the other seven criteria discussed in this chapter.

4. *Continuity*

Right from the early centuries of Christianity continuity has proved a constant concern. At times true continuity with the Apostolic Church was misunderstood as immobility by those who identified all change with heresy. They supposed that the "content" of Christian revelation had been clearly and comprehensively defined at the outset. Hence they believed it possible to maintain a complete, transhistorical continuity with what came to the apostles from Christ.

In its turn the modern magisterium has often been parodied for its constant recourse to continuity as a criterion for judgment. Wits have suggested a whole range of pronouncements which, even if they entail a change in policy, will, nevertheless, begin: "As the Church has constantly taught and practiced. . . ." However, this criterion, to which the magisterium gives an instinctive preference and which goes back in various guises to the origins of Christianity, houses no wishful assumption but a sound (formal) principle for evaluating traditions and introducing changes.

Jesus spoke of acting "like a householder who can produce from his store both the old and the new" (Mt 13, 52). Changes in contemporary experiences, questions, interests and language can demand that certain Christian traditions be revived, modified or dropped, but without losing continuity with the essential message inherited from the past. Continuity does not in fact mean immobility, "the dead hand of tradition," and a rigidity which upholds the letter at the expense of the spirit. At the same time, however, there will inevitably be some tension between the demands of continuity and those of innovation. Two questions must be responsibly answered: Faced with possible changes in these or those traditions, what do we judge will count as proper continuity? What will prove faithful innovations? There is no easy way of clearly and fully predicting in advance the precise ways in which authentic identity should be preserved and real continuity maintained in and through historical changes.

We could, for example, spot the false continuity involved in artificially retaining traditions that have become petrified and even oppressive. Or we could note how certain traditional concepts drawn from earlier experiences fail to fit present experiences. But in both cases we would need to establish what such a "fit" entails and what counts for petrification and oppression.

We might want to describe proper continuity as a homogeneous development as opposed to a heterogeneous development that introduces alien and unfaithful innovations. But this terminology simply shifts the question slightly to leave us with what is the same issue: What will count as homogeneous as opposed to heterogeneous development?

Some versions of this criterion for evaluating traditions lean more toward the preservation of what is already there—for example, the admonition of Pope Stephen the First: "Nihil innovetur nisi quod traditum est (let there be no innovations except on the basis of what has been handed down)" (Denz.-Schön . . . 110). Other versions like the analogy of organic growth used by Newman among others highlight progress and change. But in both cases the key appeal is to a continuity which—through all the changes in particular traditions—preserves the essential identity in the Church, guided yesterday, today and forever by the Holy Spirit.

5. *Creed As Criterion*

From the early centuries of Christianity the Apostles' Creed, the Nicene Creed and other brief summaries of faith have supplied a workable means for testing inherited traditions, assessing experiences and judging proposed innovations—specifically, at the level of *doctrinal* traditions. The confession of the key articles of belief helped to ensure an essential continuity in the Church's life of faith. In every age attention to the creeds will disclose the relativity and contingency of some doctrinal features of contemporary Christianity. In fact, there are few more effective ways of combating the persistent temptation to absolutize a whole range of particular doctrinal traditions that we receive from previous generations of believers than to lay them alongside some classical creed.

It was to "the essential elements and vital substance of the gospel message" communicated by the Creed that the 1977 Synod of Bishops in Rome pointed in their closing message. The synod found in the Creed "the basic nucleus" which should guide catechetics (8), and—one might add—the evaluation of inherited doctrines, formulations and attitudes in the area of traditional beliefs.

6. *Apostolicity*

Although, as such, it is not of apostolic origin, the Apostles' Creed refers us, of course, to those first Christians who experienced the life, death and resurrection of Jesus in a peculiarly direct way, witnessed to that experience and under the guidance of the Holy Spirit set the Church going. The apostolic experience, faith and proclamation remain uniquely informative, because of the special connection with Jesus Christ enjoyed by Peter, Paul and their colleagues. This norm of judgment found its classical champion of St. Irenaeus.

At one level this criterion of apostolicity relates back to the first, inasmuch as it indicates the basis for the magisterium's *authority*. The bishops enjoy a special share in apostolic authority, since they inherit—within the historical continuity of the Church's life—a particular responsibility for the apostolic mission and hence a particular responsibility to scrutinize, preserve and modify Christian traditions, be they doctrinal, liturgical or moral.

As regards the *information* it provides, the criterion of apostolicity reduces to the next criterion, the Bible. First, the Jewish scriptures provided the biblical mirror in and through which the apostolic community interpreted their experience of Jesus and confessed him as the Christ of God. Then they recorded that experience and the faith it initiated in the writings which eventually came together to form the New Testament. Thus "the faith that comes to us from the apostles" comes to us through a scriptural record. The Bible—and, in particular, the New Testament—attests and makes present for us the experience, faith and preaching of the Apostolic Church. The scriptures are the sign and guarantee of the apostolicity of the tradition and some traditions. In certain theological circles it has been conventional to refer to the Bible as "the Book of the Church." It might be more accurate to call it "the Book of the Apostolic Church." Whatever our terminology here, that permanent and inspired record of Christian origins stands out from all the norms already mentioned, inasmuch as it is formally the word of God.[24]

To sum up. Apostolicity, even more than any of the other criteria for discerning and interpreting the Church's traditions, lacks any independent force of its own. It can be either reduced to the first criterion (the magisterium) or to the seventh (the apostolic scriptures). The bishops succeed to apostolic authority, but have no extra information derived from the apostles that might go beyond the inspired record available to all believers.

7. *The Scriptures*

Both in its explicit teaching[25] and in its actual practice the Second Vatican Council appealed to the scriptures as decisively important in guiding the belief and life of the faithful. Whether in testing established traditions, interpreting experience, and judging proposed innovations or other Christian activities, the Bible is vital. It normatively records the origins of faith in the experience, testimony and preaching of the apostolic Church and in the history of Israel.

To say this is to let loose at once a swarm of questions. As the Bible does not interpret itself, how do we know that our scriptural evidence is being truly guided by the Holy Spirit and is not just another tedious example of arbitrary exegesis or of an historical approach which respects the letter but misses the spirit? More and more—not only among Roman Catholics, Anglicans and the Orthodox but also among Protestants—the conviction has developed that the lived transmission of the Church's faith provides an indispensable commentary on the scriptures. In other words, the interpretation of the Bible must take place in a traditional context. But in practice how will this help to evaluate the baptism of infants, the non-ordination of women, forms of papal government, developments in canon law and other particular traditions? However, a thousand difficulties should not make a doubt. No matter what precise approach we adopt to biblical interpretation, the scriptures must remain decisive for Christian decision-making.

8. *The Risen Lord*

Hugh of St. Victor pointed to the deepest unity of the scriptures when he wrote: "Omnis Scriptura unus liber est, et ille unus liber Christus est (the whole of scripture is one book, and that one book is Christ)."[26] Not only the Bible but also all the other criteria we have discussed should ultimately bring us to the crucified and risen Christ who remains living and present to communicate his truth and grace. Any indications to the contrary notwithstanding, the magisterium is in the business of serving and proclaiming Christ (criterion 1). The faith and life of past and present Christians have centered on Christ, whose death they proclaim until he comes (1 Cor 12, 26)). The Holy Spirit who has directed them and continues to direct them does nothing else than bring them to praise the glorified Son of God (1 Cor 12, 3) (criteria 2 and 3). Ultimately Christian continuity derives from Jesus Christ, "the same yesterday and today and forever" (Hebr 13, 8) (criterion 4). Any creed of the Church turns on the mystery of Christ, the center of salvation history (criterion 5). The unique experience and role of the apostles derived from the unique and definitive nature of God's self-communication in Christ's incarnation, life, death, resurrection and sending of the Holy Spirit (criterion 6). The scriptures find their final and proper focus in the Word made flesh (criterion 7).

In their special way St. Paul's two letters to the Corinthians encourage us to make an explicitly christological criterion *the* key to the discernment of traditions. At our peril we let Christ get shaded and even lost in our Christian decision-making, at whatever level. The apostle points toward the Eucharist where we find the *traditum* par excellence: the crucified and risen Christ handed over for us (1 Cor 11, 23). In Second Corinthians Paul reflects on his "weaknesses"—what we could call his sufferings or vulnerability (4, 8ff.; 6,4ff.; 11, 23ff.; 12, 10). In the painful weakness of his ministry the apostle sees himself conformed to Christ and recognizes the ultimate touchstone in the principle of "power made perfect in weakness" (12, 9). To put all this in the perspective of this chapter: We can devise no more Christian way of reflecting on our inherited traditions than by asking two questions. Do these traditions and/or these proposed innovations help us to celebrate better the Eucharist and thus proclaim more powerfully the death of the Lord until he comes? (1 Cor 11, 26). What judgments and decisions about our established traditions will conform us more clearly to the mystery of Christ, who "was crucified in weakness, but lives by the power of God" (2 Cor 13, 4)?

Reading over this piece, I realize two things. First, I might have added endless references to the immense theological literature that attaches to each of the criteria. But by overloading the text with detail I could have distracted the reader from the main, and, it seems, the original point of the chapter: a statement of *all* the criteria for interpreting our inherited traditions, both in themselves and in their convergence toward the ultimate criterion, Christ himself. Second, the search for *the* Tradition within the traditions, the "purity of the Gospel" or call it what you will is finally—as William Reiser pointed out to me—another version of the classic quest for the essence of Christianity.[27] Like that quest the search for *the* Tradition finds its ultimate goal in the person of Jesus Christ risen from the dead.

9. To Conclude

The future of the Church can only be guessed at, not foretold. What Christian faith holds for certain, however, is that as long as the world survives the Church will too. But if the Church is going to face satisfactorily the challenges posed by the forces that currently move and change the world, both fidelity and freedom are needed. If "the purity of the Gospel" inherited from the Apostolic Church is to be fully effective, the various traditions through which the gospel has been expressed must be interpreted, translated, modified, or renewed. Some of those traditions may prove to be mere traditions of men (Mk 7, 8) which should be dropped. For this process of discernment Christian faith suggests a number of criteria which finally converge toward one point—not toward the claims of efficiency, the voice of democracy, or any other immediately attractive principle, but toward the crucified and risen Lord. The ultimate question must be: In the face of these or those particular traditions, what does obedience to the crucified and risen Jesus demand of us? Every faithful response here carries with it an enhanced life in him who came to bring us life and bring it in abundance.[28]

Bibliography

A. Anton, "La comunidad creyente, portadora de la revelación," in L. Alonso-Schökel (ed.), *Comentarios a la constitución "Dei Verbum" sobre la divina revelación* (Biblioteca de autores cristianos 284; Madrid, 1969), pp. 331–64.

K. Baus, "Vinzens von Lerins," LTK 10:800–1.

Y. Congar, *Tradition and Traditions: An Historical and a Theological Essay,* tr. by M. Naseby and T. Rainborough (New York, 1966).

Faith and Order, Louvain 1971 (Geneva, 1971), pp. 9–34 and 212–15, on "Interpreting the Sources of Our Faith."

W. Pannenberg, "The Crisis of the Scripture Principle," in his *Basic Questions in Theology,* tr. by G. H. Kehm (2 vols.; Philadelphia, 1970–71), 1:1–15.

K. Rahner, "Magisterium," in *Sacramentum Mundi* 3:351–38.

G. Sala, "Magistero," *Dizionario Teologico Interdisciplinare* 2:423–34.

See also the bibliography for the essay of J. Alfaro.

⑲
Theology and the Magisterium

Juan Alfaro

I. The Problem: Faith, Reason, Theology

1. Catholicism acknowledges the ecclesial magisterium as the binding and even "infallible" interpreter of Christian revelation. Protestantism rejects such a magisterium as incompatible with the primacy of God's word, on the grounds that the ecclesial institution claims parity with divine revelation.[1]

Catholic theology must take seriously a problem that thus touches the very heart of Christianity: the unconditional primacy of Christ (the revealer and definitive revelation of God) over the Church, and the person's relation to Christ as the absolutely primordial element in Christian existence. It is evident that the problem raised by the mediation of the ecclesial magisterium is profoundly connected with the basic themes of theology: Christ and the Church, scripture and ecclesial tradition, God's revelation in Christ and Christian faith (christology, ecclesiology, anthropology). Any solution must leave intact the uniqueness of the Christ event and the original character of Christian existence, the ultimate meaning of which is to be found in its relation to Christ.

The mediation of the ecclesial magisterium in regard to Christian faith inevitably influences theology in the exercise of its proper function, since in his effort to understand the Christian faith the Catholic theologian is faced with magisterial interpretations that are binding on his faith and therefore on his theological reflection as well; in other words, the definitions issued by the magisterium set limits for the proper function of theology. The result is a tension between human reason as exercised in theological reflection and the magisterium's binding authority, in which the Catholic theologian believes. The problem of theology and magisterium is part of the broader and more radical problem of faith and reason. We are dealing, therefore, with a basic theological problem, namely, with the task proper to theology and, above all, with its relation to faith.

2. Almost nine centuries have passed since Anselm of Canterbury defined theology in a phrase that can without exaggeration be called lapidary: *fides quaerens intellectum* (faith seeking understanding).[2] In three words, all

of them necessary and sufficient, each of them in the order that befits it, the phrase expresses the essential task of theology. Surprising though it seems, Anselm's definition has never been bettered; it could, and would have to be, reinterpreted, but down to our time it has not been replaced, and it is hard to see how in fact it could be improved.

The first word, *fides,* indicates that theology starts with faith, presupposes it, and is required by it. If faith includes knowledge of a content and of the motive which justifies the decision to believe, then it must be possible and, in addition, humanly necessary for the believer (as believer) to reflect on what he believes and on the motives for his decision to believe: this is a demand created by the presence of reason within faith itself. Then this human reflection which is the special attribute of the believer as believer, calls for a special name: *theology.* If belief and unbelief are two distinct things and if faith itself calls for reflection on it, then it must be acknowledged that the kind of reflection we call theology has its own character, distinct from any other. The man who believes and endeavors to understand himself as a believer cannot act *as though he were not a believer;* such an attitude would be unauthentic and illusory. The fact that the theologian believes (is a Christian) cannot be merely accidental in relation to his theology;[3] rather it belongs to the very essence of this theology.

The Anselmian formula speaks of theology as *quaerens,* in the two senses of this Latin word: to *ask* and to *seek out.* Theology springs from faith insofar as faith *asks itself* about itself and *seeks* to understand itself; faith turns into theology to the extent that it asks endless questions and seeks without acknowledging limits. The *quaerere* proper to theology cannot draw back from any questions. That which is believed and the very act of believing transcend human reason; for this reason theology can never stop asking and seeking, finding itself, as it does, always confronted with the mystery of God who is both revealed and hidden in Christ.

The mental process that acknowledges no boundaries but constantly sets out from faith which seeks understanding of itself (*quaerens* INTELLECTUM) formally constitutes theology; to engage in the process is to "do theology."

Today, however, a simple repetition of the Anselmian formula is not enough. Each of its terms as well as its overall meaning must be interpreted.

The word *fides* must be understood in its totality and unity, which embrace both *fides quae and fides qua.* In other words, faith must be understood as the total response of the human person to the saving action which God has accomplished and revealed in Christ. Assent, choice, and action are the reciprocally immanent dimensions of a single undivided vital act: an assent (to the content of Christian revelation) that is formed by the decision to hope (eschatological dimension of faith) and completed by the practice of love (therefore, faith, hope, and charity as different but reciprocally implied aspects of a single existential Christian attitude). In the terminology of linguistic analysis there are cognitive-assertive, fiducial-self-implicative, and practical-operative aspects. Theology, then, is this *fides* which, in its totality and unity of knowing, hoping, and loving seeks a reflective understanding of itself.

The theological *quaerere,* which by its nature tends to its own fulfillment as a form of human reflection, will be a search that is *critical,* that is, aware of its presuppositions and of the requirements of its mental process as universally valid; *methodical,* that is, carried on in accordance with the norms set by its object, its character as reflection on faith, and its purpose; and *systematic,* that is, directed to a coherent understanding of the revealed contents in their mutual connections, their relation to the center of faith which is Christ, and their significance for man's salvation.

In its search for an understanding (*intellectum*) of faith, theology today is aware that it encounters Christian revelation in a written text (the biblical writings) which is itself the result of a process of interpretation and which has in addition been constantly reinterpreted by the faith of the Church over the centuries (tradition) and therefore been reexpressed in various historical (cultural, linguistic) contexts. Theology must take this process of interpretation into account and try to retrieve it and integrate it into a current reinterpretation that fits in with the conditions of understanding and expression proper to our age. Hermeneutics and linguistic analysis are thus indispensable for the task of theology, which is a *contemporary* understanding of faith and Christian revelation.

Faith itself, then, implies a comprehensive and radical question regarding itself and thus gives rise to theological reflection. The question takes concrete shape in several queries: *What do I believe? How do I believe? Why do I believe?* (content of belief; peculiar structure of the act of believing, and finality of faith). Because theology is rooted in faith, it enjoys the same legitimacy, freedom, and boundless right to question that faith does. The attitude of Christian faith understands itself to be authentically human, because it is a response to the basic question the human person asks regarding the meaning of life. It is a question the person cannot avoid, and no response can be given to it except in a comprehensive act that includes knowing, deciding, and acting. An attitude of purely neutral rationality in the face of the ultimate question is existentially impossible; the possibility of obtaining compelling evidence is eliminated. This human attitude to the question of the meaning of life prefigures and renders intelligible the characteristic structure of faith.[4]

Now that the specific function of theology has been indicated, it is possible to identify its tasks in relation to the ecclesial magisterium: (a) to seek an understanding of the magisterium in the context of Christian revelation; (b) and to interpret the content of the definitions issued by the magisterium.

II. Theological Understanding of an Infallible Magisterium

3. The New Testament writers, each adopting his own perspective, present the Christ-event as God's definitive act of salvation and revelation. The event is absolutely unparalleled, unique, and nonrepeatable (eschato-

logical) because in it God has spoken his final word as a word of salvation. The totality-unity of the event includes the coming of Christ into the world, his action and his message, his death and resurrection; it is therefore both immanent and transcendent in relation to history upon which it bestows an ultimate significance for salvation. Within the process of progressive understanding of the Christ-event as presented to us in the New Testament two moments (the last the first) stand out: the resurrection and the incarnation (decisive expression of the divinity of Christ).

Neither the resurrection of Christ nor the incarnation of the Son of God could be the products of historical becoming; they can only result from the absolutely free intervention of God, as God, in history. Both are self-grounding; that is, they carry with them the ground of their reality and truth. The risen Jesus manifests himself to his disciples and thus creates in them an experiential certitude regarding his resurrection; this certitude then finds expression in the Christian kerygma, which has as its focal point the confession of Christ's death and resurrection. The resurrection of Christ thus shows its character as revelation (event and word of God as God) *which grounds its own reality and truth and its expression in human propositions.*

Meditating, in the perspective of the incarnation, on the unparalleled experience which the historical Jesus has of God (the *Abba* of the Synoptics), the fourth gospel sees the Son of God made man as the revealer of God, who carries in himself (in his divine sonship) the very ground of his revelation and the reality and truth of his testimony. The incarnation is the supreme revelation of God *because by itself it grounds its own reality and truth and the human expression of this reality and truth:* Christ is not only the center but also the self-grounding ground of faith. Christian revelation and Christian faith have a christological structure, Christ being both revealer and revealed (self-revelation, foundation and content of faith).[5]

The Christ-event claims for itself an absolute primacy in revelation and faith, and this primacy is the primacy not simply of a norm but of a *foundation.* The divinity of the man Jesus is the essence of Christianity and constitutes the originality of Christian revelation and Christian faith. In the final analyses Christian faith has only one foundation: Christ himself.

Only if we take account of the Christ-event as grounding its own reality and its human expression can we speak (meaningfully) of the "authority" proper to Christian revelation. "Authority" here means to be "author," to create, to ground (in an ontological, not a juridical sense). Christian revelation is "authoritative" to the extent that it presents itself as a self-grounding event which therefore calls man to faith in an unconditional manner. Only in the context of this "authority" that attaches to God's revelation in Christ is it possible to speak of a (derived) "authority" of the Church and the magisterium.

4. The absolute uniqueness of the Christ-event gives rise to the uniqueness proper (here: relative to Christ) to the apostolic Church; the primacy of the latter in relation to the post-apostolic Church is not merely temporal but

qualitative, and this precisely because of its unique connection with Christ. The experience of the risen Lord, the gift of the Spirit, and the apostolic mission constitute the unique character of the apostolic Church as a grace received from Christ. For this reason, the apostolic Church is normative for the Christian faith of every age, not simply because it is not possible to come in touch with the Christ-event except through the testimony of the apostolic Church but also and above all because the apostolic Church came into being through a privileged grace and revelation of Christ.

From the uniqueness and resultant normative character of the apostolic Church comes the normative value of the New Testament scriptures for Christian faith. These writings transmit the Christ-event to us as attested and more fully understood by the apostolic Church, and for this reason they have been accepted by the post-apostolic Church as the norm of its faith.[6]

From Christ to the apostolic Church and from the latter to the New Testament writings there is a derivation of normativeness and "authority" in regard to Christian faith, with Christ continuing to be at every point the ultimate foundation.

Christian revelation does not reach us simply as a content transmitted in the New Testament writings. It also comes to us insofar as it is accepted and attested by the living faith of the Church. The claim of *Sola Scriptura* contradicts the historical character of Christianity and ignores New Testament ecclesiology.

In full accord with the New Testament, Vatican II sees the Church as being the primordial sacrament of Christ, "the community of faith, hope, and charity," which is sustained by the presence of Christ through his Spirit. The Council asserts that this community ("the holy people of God") "cannot err in matters of belief"; that is, it is "indefectible" in its adherence to the Christian message.[7]

"Infallibility" or "indefectibility" means that the Church, as the community of those who believe in Christ and in human words confess their faith in him, cannot perish. The Church will always perdure in the truth of Christ and in the human proclamation of this truth. Without this permanent communion in the propositionally stated confession of one and the same faith in Christ there can be no Church.

The foundation of the "infallibility" of the believing Church is in Christ as God's definitive revelation and salvation for the human race, for since the Christ-event is intrinsically a "once and for all" affair (that is, it can never lose its power), neither can the community of those who believe in him disappear from history. If this community did disappear it would mean the disappearance of Christ's presence, through his Spirit, in the midst of the human race. Evidently, then, the "infallibility" of the Church is not something the Church possesses as its own, so that it can dispose of it as it wishes or make human forecasts regarding it. It is solely a gift of Christ, a promise he made which the Church accepts and acknowledges as such through faith and hope. For this reason, the very assertion of its "infallibility" is an expression of its faith and hope in Christ.

The gift of "indefectibility" in faith is not promised to the individual Christian but the ecclesial community as such; the faith of the Church is therefore binding and normative for each member. But this *mediation* of the ecclesial community in relation to the personal faith of the individual Christian must be properly understood: it is a mediation that is continuously being created by Christ and has its foundation in him. Adherence to the Church and adherence to Christ are thus inseparable, but they are by no means identical: Christ is not the Church (but the Lord of the Church) and the Church is not Christ (but the community that receives its life from Christ). By its nature, then, the mediation of the Church points to Christ as its origin and foundation. Christ alone is the foundation of Christian faith in both its communal and individual dimensions; in the last analysis, he is the object of faith. With the same radical freedom with which the Christian believes in Christ, he believes in the normative and binding character of the Church's faith. Both in revelation and in faith absolute primacy belongs to Christ alone (as both ground and goal).

5. The connection between the faith of each Christian (and therefore of the theologian and his theologizing) and the "indefectible" faith of the Church is an indispensable datum for the possibility of a theological understanding of the magisterium. If we are to make progress toward such an understanding we must examine the relation between the Church's faith (ecclesial "tradition") and scripture, as set forth with notable exactitude by Vatican II.

Fully in keeping with its comprehensive concept of faith (knowledge, decision, action), the Council does not reduce "tradition" to the simple transmission of a doctrinal content, but rather identifies it with the very being of the Church, with the life and action of the Church as expressed in her confession of faith. Down the centuries, under the interior guidance of the Spirit, the Church has grown in understanding and formulation of Christian revelation. This interpretative activity of ecclesial faith has unfolded in a dialectic of continuity and novelty, and the impulse for it has come from the eschatological thrust of faith and hope toward the future fullness of God's salvific revelation.[8]

The Council has formulated, with proper clarity, the fundamental distinction between scripture and ecclesial "tradition": only scripture is the word of God (*locutio Dei*); "tradition" is the living transmission of this word of God. Any identification of the Church (ecclesial "tradition") with the revelation of God is excluded. But non-identification does not mean separation. There is a close and reciprocal connection between scripture and "tradition," with each of the two playing a different role. Insofar as scripture contains the Christian revelation it is the norm for the Church and its faith; on the other hand, it is as it is understood in the living faith of the Church that scripture becomes the living word of God to us here and now. Both scripture and tradition are required in order that the revelation of God in Christ may become God's word for us at our present moment of history.[9]

It must therefore be said that both the faith of the Christian and theology are inseparably bound up with scripture and ecclesial "tradition," but in different ways: they are bound up with the scriptures as with a norm that is normative even for ecclesial "tradition"; they are bound up with "tradition," on the other hand, as a norm that is itself normed by the scriptures. But it would be a mistake to think that this statement says everything. It must not be forgotten that neither the Christian generally nor the theologian can ever stand before "Scripture *Alone*." Rather, they stand before scripture within the bonds of communion with the faith of the Church, because their own personal faith implies a link with the Church and the Church's understanding of the revelation contained in scripture. It is precisely here, in the existential situation of Christian faith as indivisibly personal and communal, that the normative dyad "scripture-tradition" shows its profound unity-in-diversity.

A theological understanding of the scripture-tradition relationship must take into account the historical dimension of the entire cognitive process. All human knowledge receives something from history, develops within history, and thus contributes to the historical process; it is conditioned not only by the constitutive (transcendental) structures of the human person but also by the concrete (cultural and linguistic) historical context in which it arises. The person asks questions and achieves understanding within this prior horizon ("preunderstanding") in which he experiences himself and his relation to the world. In other words, human understanding is interpretation. Human understanding, therefore, is a process involving continuity with the past and creative openness to the future (the new forth-coming); here we see the paradox and truth of the process, since it can maintain its continuity with the past only through a constantly renewed comprehension, a permanent act of interpretation.

Because it is conditioned by the changing historical context, ecclesial tradition cannot abide in the revealed truth unless it ever anew understands and expresses the Christ-event and the word of God that is contained in the scriptures. But its permanence in the truth of Christian revelation has its own proper foundation and character. In the last analysis, this permanence is based on the absolute uniqueness of the Christ-event as definitive anticipation of the fullness that is to come. It is also based on a constant verificatory reference to its norm, which is scripture. That which ecclesial tradition transmits is not merely something now past but the reality of Christ who is ever present through his Spirit in a permanent communion of life with Christ. This communion represents the experiential aspect of ecclesial faith and keeps this faith ever in movement toward the coming fullness of God's revelation and therefore toward an ever-renewed proleptic understanding of it.

6. A theological understanding of an authoritative and infallible ecclesial magisterium is possible only within the global christological and ecclesiological context which I have been explaining. Any understanding of it must keep in mind the eschatological (self-grounding and imperishable) character of the Christ-event and of its privileged expression in scripture (which be-

longs among the foundational elements of the Church) and the indefectibility of the Church as permanently ensured by the presence of Christ through his Spirit; the Church is thus established as "universal sacrament" of God's revelation and salvation in Christ, precisely insofar as she is a "community of faith, hope, and charity" (or: insofar as she is a "communion").

Within this global context we must examine, above all, the way in which the magisterium understands itself in the exercise of its acts, that is, the way in which this self-understanding is manifested in the language the magisterium uses in its definitions. An analysis of this language in all the conciliar and pontifical definitions yields the following results: (a) the act of defining is almost always expressed by means of the verbs proper to the profession of faith (*credere, profiteri, confiteri*); in addition, the formula used not infrequently describes the confession as a definition and vice versa (*confitetur definiens; credentes asserimus*), thus uniting in one act a definition and a profession of faith on the part of the definer. (b) This indivisible act of "believing-defining" asserts that a propositional content is included in Christian revelation, for the act of defining, being itself an act of faith, supposes the revealed character of the "defined-believed" content; the act is thus not an act of revelation but of acceptance (which implies understanding-interpretation) of God's word. (c) The act of "defining-believing" is based on scripture and tradition and thus acknowledges its dependence on these. (d) The act of defining is not merely assertive but also authoritative, since it makes the acceptance of what is defined a necessary condition for belonging to the Church as a community of faith and salvation; it thus shows awareness of an "authority" which the magisterium in its exercise believes and proclaims to have been received from Christ.[10] But in its intention of asserting the defined content to be *revealed,* the magisterium acknowledges the primacy of the "authority" of God's word as well as the primacy of the content of revelation. The content is not revealed because it is defined, but vice versa. The definition is not the word of God but an authoritative interpretation of that word.

The language proper to definitions is thus self-implicative, assertive, and operative; by these three dimensions it shows its ecclesial and christological structure. It implies in itself an ecclesial faith (the act of faith made in communion with the Church); it affirms the absolute primacy and authority of God's word in Christ; it is directed to the community of those who believe in Christ and calls for a response of faith. Clearly, a definition of the magisterium has meaning only within the "vital form" of ecclesial faith and the context of communion in one and the same faith in Christ.

The very language used in definitions shows, therefore, the self-transcendence and self-relativization of the "authority" of the magisterium. The presence in these definitions of an act of faith, as well as their intention of declaring their content to be revealed by God imply an acknowledgment of the transcendence of God's word and of their own relativity in relation to this word. What is being demanded of the faithful is, in the final analysis, an assent to the word of God as such. A definition has, for its condition, communion in the faith of the Church; it participates in and is ordered to this faith. It thus presupposes a more profound reality that is transcendent over it, namely, the sacramentality of the Church as community of faith that is sustained by the permanent presence of Christ through his Spirit. Finally, a definition is binding even on its authors, thus proving its self-transcendence in relation to the highest court of appeal in the ecclesial communion and to the self-grounding "authority" of God's revelation in Christ.

In its definitory acts throughout history the ecclesial magisterium has shown itself aware that it is not to be identified with revelation and that it is subordinate to the sovereignty of God's word, just as the Church has always recognized itself to be distinct from and absolutely dependent on Christ. This consciousness has itself reached the level of doctrinal explicitation at the last two councils.

According to Vatican I the definitions of the magisterium are not divine revelations; they have a norm, which is the word of God as contained in scripture and transmitted by tradition. Their function is to protect and faithfully expound the content of revelation (the *depositum*). Consequently, definitions call for an assent of faith to the content of revelation precisely as revealed (*tamquam divinitus revelata credenda*); this is to say that they call for an assent that is based on the word of God.[11]

As was expected, Vatican II locates the function of the magisterium in a broad christological and ecclesiological framework. The Church is established and permanently sustained by Christ as universal sacrament (effective sign) of salvation; this sacramentality is identical with the very being of the Church as a "community of faith." "The people of God" receives from Christ, through his Spirit, the grace of indefectibility in its faith; this indefectibility implies the bond of communion (*consensus, conspiratio*) in the common confession (by all: faithful and bishops) of Christian revelation.[12]

The primatial-episcopal institution (with its three inseparable functions of sanctifying, governing and teaching) derives in the final analysis from Christ; its "authority" is based on the self-grounding "authority" of the total Christ-event. In relation to the universal and primordial sacramentality of the Church itself the episcopate is a particular sacrament.[13]

I have now pointed out the limiting conditions and specific function of the magisterium. In their definitions the pope and the episcopate are subject (*stare et conformari* TENENTUR) to divine revelation as contained in scripture and transmitted by tradition. The magisterium is beneath the word of God, and its attitude is one of faith (*pie audit*) and service; that is, it is unconditionally subject to the supreme authority and content of revelation, has scripture for its norm, and is linked to communion in the faith of the Church. Its function is to provide an interpretation that is faithful and "authentic" (authoritative, in virtue of authority received from Christ) of the content of revelation as such; for this reason it can demand of the faithful a response of faith that is based on the word of God. The "irreformability" of definitions and the fact that they bind all members of the Church show that the magisterium receives its authority from Christ and not from the ecclesial community; in other words, the magisterium belongs to the very being of the Church as founded on the Christ-event.[14]

Vatican II has something important to say on the question (not raised at Vatican I) of ecclesial acceptance (*receptio*) of definitions: "To the resultant definitions the assent of the Church can never be wanting, on account of the activity of the same Holy Spirit, whereby the whole flock of Christ is preserved and progresses in unity of faith."[15] The Council considers the Church's indefectible unity in faith, a unity deriving from the interior action of the Spirit (who according to the same Council is an absolute gift from Christ), to be the reason why the Church's assent to definitions "can never be wanting." The words "can never be wanting" express, therefore, neither a necessary logical connection nor mere human foresight; they express only the attitude of faith-hope in the grace of Christ, which, as such, transcends the dispositions and calculations of human beings. As acts of the magisterium, definitions include within themselves faith and hope in the gift of ecclesial indefectibility which finds concrete application in the acceptance of what is defined. Clearly, then, the infallibility of the magisterium and its definitions is intelligible only in light of the Church's indefectibility in its communion of faith or, to put it differently, in light of the Church's sacramentality. Ecclesial communion, which is brought into being by the grace of Christ, is the vital matrix which gives meaning to both the indefectibility of the Church's faith and the infallibility of the magisterium. It is not enough, then, to say with John Henry Newman that "reception" by the Church is a sign of the truth of the definitions;[16] it must rather be said that the truth of what is defined asserts itself as present and alive in its reception, just as the content of revelation remains present and alive in the faith of the Church.

The foregoing reflections show that a theological understanding of the Church's infallible magisterium is based concretely on two facts which the Catholic theologian believes to be contained in Christian revelation: the indefectibility of the Church as a community of faith, and the primatial-episcopal institution as a fundamental element in the being of the Church.[17] Both of these realities are based (though in different ways) on the self-grounding character ("authority") of the Christ-event.

The binding indefectibility of the ecclesial community enables us to understand the possibility that, if there is an institutional magisterium in the Church, then its action is binding and infallible. In addition: if the ecclesial community is both indefectible in its faith and directed by the magisterium, then it is understandable that this magisterium should have received from Christ "the sure gift of truth"[18] without which it could not carry out its mission of preserving the ecclesial community in the visible unity of a single faith. History shows clearly that the visibility of the Church insofar as it is a community united in a single faith has not infrequently been obscured or rendered ambiguous or been subjected to serious uncertainties with regard to the very foundations of Christianity. It is precisely these boundary situations that render comprehensible the role of the magisterium as a concrete, visible institution which not only brings clarification but binds in an infallible way *as authoritative guide of an indefectible ecclesial faith.* How could the magisterium provide unifying certainty if its definitions did not carry with them the assurance of truth? And how could it decide (the "operative-performative" aspect of definitions) on whether those maintaining certain views belong to the Church as visible community of salvation if its definitions could be erroneous interpretations of Christian revelation?

Theological reflection thus sees the magisterium as being similar to and closely bound up with ecclesial tradition, but not identical with this. Both of these are essentially related to (dependent on) the word of God (and therefore have scripture as their norm); both are living, actual, binding interpretations of this word. But the two interpretations are on different levels; in modern terminology we might speak of a "first order" interpretation and a "second order" interpretation. Tradition is closer to the living experience of the Church's faith, and its language reflects this vital depth; the magisterium operates at a subsequent level of reflection and expresses itself in a more developed kind of language (metalanguage). The magisterium presupposes the deeper reality of indefectible communion in the Church's faith and is at the service of this communion; correspondingly, it has a privileged visibility and concreteness within the unity of faith. Between ecclesial tradition and magisterium there is thus a close, reciprocal and varied interaction; it can be said that tradition and its binding character attain their clearest visibility in the magisterium.[19]

In summary, theology understands the magisterium as *united* to the ecclesial community by the bond of a single faith, as *presupposing* the indefectibility of the Church's faith, as *normed* by scripture, and, in the last analysis, as *founded* upon the self-grounding and imperishable Christ-event. The assent of faith to dogmatic definitions implies, therefore, the same radical choice by which Christians believe in Christ (the ultimate foundation of faith) and therefore in his visible and indefectible Church in the concrete institutional form this has received from the total Christ-event. It is in the context provided by the radical freedom of Christian faith that the Catholic theology will seek to understand and interpret the definitions issued by the magisterium.

III. Theological Interpretation of Dogmas

7. Every dogmatic definition is both a terminus and a new point of departure in the living process whereby ecclesial faith endeavors to understand its own content. The acceptance ("reception") of a dogma by ecclesial faith is always a historical event, the concrete shape of which eludes human foreknowledge. In following its inherent tendency to seek self-understanding within the cultural and linguistic context of the moment, faith must inevitably reinterpret and re-express itself. Not only the definitions of the magisterium but even the very word of God are structured as human propositions and are therefore subject to a continuous process of interpretation in faith (it

is no accident that the magisterium has reinterpreted its own dogmas and therefore the revealed content of these).

Theology therefore has as part of its proper task to undertake a *critical, methodical, systematic* (and, in this sense, scientific) understanding—misinterpretation of dogmas. The Catholic theologian, as a believer, accepts the definitions of the magisterium as being an "authentic" interpretation of revelation; he then tries to determine exactly the original sense of the text of the definition, to integrate its contents with scripture and tradition, and to understand and express this content in current concepts and language that are open to the future of the faith. In this task (which is carried out in communion with and as a service to the faith of the Church) we may distinguish three phases (which are not successive in time): *retrospective, introspective,* and *prospective.*

Dogmas always rise out of a prior theology whose concepts and language the dogmas make their own. The interpretation of dogmas therefore requires a knowledge of the theology in question, of the limitations proper to the problematic of such a theology, of the kind of thinking (*Denkform*) that its categories reveal, and of the varied and even contrary positions taken on one and the same question.

Unless this theology is known and understood, it will not be possible to take the next and decisive step in the proper manner: I am referring to the analysis of the genesis of the definition, this analysis being made with the help of the documents that show the gradual gestation of the definition. Only this kind of careful and rigorous analysis will enable us to determine several points: what the question was on which the magisterium intended to take a position; what the concrete teaching was which it meant to condemn as irreconcilable with the Christian faith, and how this teaching was understood; what the meaning was of the terms that then appeared in the definitory formula. A determination can also be made of whether some aspects of the question were overlooked or rather were simply omitted (sometimes the very terms used in formulating the question implied a limited vision of this question); what theological opinions were left open (neither rejected nor approved); what presuppositions, not recognized as being present, may have exercised a hidden (but decisive) influence in the discussions preceding the definition; and, finally, whether there may not have been at times a deeper and more fundamental perspective which was common both to dogma and to condemned doctrine but within which the parties could not reach mutual understanding because they lacked adequate concepts and an adequate vocabulary. These various questions are not arbitrarily put down here, for they express concrete aspects of the historical conditioning which no human thinking can escape, and of the insuperable limits of all human thinking, limits which make themselves known chiefly in the impossibility of eliminating all presuppositions, that is, of justifying in an explicit way all the implications of the problems and therefore of the answers as well.

While such an analysis of the genesis of a definition is indispensable and of decisive importance, we may not forget that the content of a dogma is identical with what is in fact expressed in the terms of the definitory formula. Whatever else the authors of the definition may have been thinking but did not in fact express in the dogmatic formula itself does not belong to the definition (although it may help in the understanding of the definition). This shows the exceptional importance of interpreting the text itself of the definition.

The practice of Catholic theologians has established the following interpretive norms, which take into account the basic intention of the magisterium in its definitory acts. Only that is defined which is the direct concern of the assertion (positive or negative) made in the definitory act. Subordinate propositions which are given as justifications for the definition or simply as further explanations of what is defined, do not themselves have a dogmatic character. Nor does a definition include that which is explicitly offered as a presupposition or foundation of the definition. In addition, a definitory formula may contain expressions which go beyond the question being decided and are therefore to be regarded as further explanations in terms of the theology of the time. The Code of Canon Law has anticipated the case in which, despite careful study, some doubt remains about the definitory act itself or some aspect of its content; Canon 1323 says: "Nothing is to be understood as dogmatically declared or defined, unless it is beyond a doubt so declared or defined."

The sole purpose of this "retrospective" phase in theological understanding of dogmas is to delimit exactly the defined content that calls for an assent of faith. But such a determination is already an act of interpretation, since it expresses the content of the definition in new propositions; the interpretation can be validated only a posteriori, by showing that the new propositions are in agreement with the text of the dogmatic formula.[20]

8. The content of dogmas is not revealed by God because the magisterium has defined it as revealed, but vice versa. A definition does not make its content to be revealed but rather presupposes and recognizes that it is revealed; in other words, the definition serves only as a formal (binding and infallible) criterion for determining whether a particular content belongs to revelation. The definitions themselves, therefore (both in the intention of the magisterium which does the defining, and in their contents which "are proposed as divinely revealed and to be believed"[21]), refer to the word of God as the original foundation which establishes what divine truth is and as consequently the foundation of the credibility and intelligibility of the dogmas. Far from excluding the word of God, dogma includes in its very structure an appeal to the "unnormed norm" which is scripture, and to the understanding of scripture which is given in ecclesial tradition. Theology is therefore called upon to interpret and show the truth of dogma by relating it to scripture and tradition. This task is part of the theological understanding of dogmas, since the truth of these is established by revelation; the understanding here is an introspective understanding (in-sight, *Ein-sicht*) of the truth of the defined content as revealed.

By their own finality dogmas are limited to concrete and partial aspects of revealed truth, which are therefore inevitably presented in separation from the total context of revelation and from the historical process of revelation. A theological understanding of dogmas demands, then, that they be inserted into the total process of biblical revelation and of tradition; such an insertion is by its nature an interpretation of the dogmatic content. This is the method (it might be called "genetic-progressive") which Vatican II has called to the attention of theologians as being implied by its teaching on scripture, tradition, and the magisterium (primacy of scripture, and connection of the magisterium with ecclesial tradition[22]); it is a method that is called for by the sovereignty of God's word and by the historical development that is the mark of biblical revelation and tradition. Only by respecting this entire process can theology situate dogmas within their broadest and solely valid horizons and understand-interpret their content as revealed by God and transmitted by the Church's faith. The investigation of this process is theology done in an attitude of faith and with the care shown by human thinking that honestly seeks truth in its full depth while excluding any pretense of "demonstrating" the defined content to be revealed. The process of which I am speaking is, after all, an historical process involving the Christian faith, which as such transcends human reason and therefore cannot be adequately translated into human reflective knowledge.

In this introspective-integrative phase of the theological interpretation of dogmas a great deal of helpful guidance is provided by two points made in Vatican II: (a) In the truths of the Christian faith there is a "gradation" according to the varied connection each has with the foundation of faith, namely, Christ; the importance of dogmas varies according to their connection with the history of salvation and the mystery of Christ;[23] (b) revelation is saving truth, manifested by God for the salvation of the human race.[24] By means of these two closely connected statements the Council shaped its christocentric vision of revelation and salvation, that is, of the absolute primacy of the Christ-event as God's definitive salvation and revelation. It is easy to see that in these statements Vatican II has set down an important new hermeneutical norm for the interpretation of dogmas. The magisterium's definition neither creates nor alters the connection of the defined content with the mystery of Christ, nor gives it a higher place in the "gradation" of the truths of the Christian faith. Nor does the mere fact of the definition prove that the magisterium has followed in its definitions the criterion of closer connection with the mystery of Christ. It cannot therefore be either claimed or supposed that every content of a dogma is more important for Christian faith and for salvation than what is not defined, nor that all dogmas are of the same importance in this respect. A dogmatic definition does not ground the revealed character of what is defined but rather presupposes and acknowledges it; it therefore leaves intact the "gradation" of importance which attaches to various truths in the totality of revelation, which has Christ for its center. Theologians must therefore try to understand (interpret) dogmas according to their connection with the Christ-event and their significance for the salvation of human beings.

9. Because dogmas are binding on the Church's faith present and future, they require that the understanding of their content be constantly renewed, so that they may be assimilated in a living way in Christian faith and practice. The pure and simple verbal repetition of dogmatic formulas in a changed cultural and linguistic setting would produce an illusory orthodoxy.

The task of rendering the content of dogmas accessible (believable-understandable) to the people of today and tomorrow lays upon theologians the responsibility of providing the magisterium, and thus the ecclesial community, with an indispensable service: a service of *creative fidelity* in the search for an interpretation whose concrete configuration cannot be established in advance. No dogmatic formulation can provide an exhaustive and fully adequate (and in this sense ultimate and definitive) knowledge of the defined reality, because in this reality there is always present, at least implicitly, the mystery of God in Christ, and this mystery transcends any possible human formulation.

The "charism of truth" that belongs to the magisterium does not guarantee that the formulation of a dogma was the best or the only one possible at the historical moment in which it was issued, nor that it will necessarily be understood without difficulty in the future. It may even happen that the historical context in which the dogma originated (limitations already present in the manner of asking the question; the concepts then available; the underlying vision of the world; the language; the very concept had of truth; and so on) was an obstacle to its acceptance (credibility-intelligibility) by future generations. The result would then be what we call today a "communications breakdown"[25] between the dogmatic formulation and the present situation of believers, with the resultant risk that the dogmatic content might for practical purposes be relegated to a marginal place in Christian life.

The basic demand which the interpretation of dogmas makes on today's theologian is an acute sensitivity to the concrete difficulties which not a few sincere Christians have with particular dogmatic formulas, as well as a thorough examination of the origin of these difficulties, which must be sought in the difference between contemporary culture and that of the age in which the dogmas originated.

Dogmas have exchanged the history-of-salvation and personalist mode of thought that is proper to biblical revelation for another that is "essentialist" and is reflected in such concepts as "nature," "subsistence," "substance," "form," and "disposition." Contemporary theology can and must reverse the process and reinterpret dogmas in the history-of-salvation and personalist mode of thought which is much more accessible to the contemporary mind.

In fact, dogmas are not identified with a particular "world picture." It is no less true, however, that they are conditioned by underlying cosmological representations which have been abandoned by contemporary culture, and that they have therefore lost their meaning in the language of our day. Moreover, the language of dogmas is based on the theological language of the past, which developed unilaterally within the "logical function" of language and thus ran the risk of reducing revelation to a set of truths; in the process, the language of faith suffering a weakening of its meaning; it is the theologian's task to restore their full meaning to such dogmas.

In their work of interpreting dogmas theologians must remain fully aware that the very passage to transcendence (to transcendent personal reality) has become more difficult and makes greater demands on the people of our time. Various factors have contributed to this stage of affairs.

Our age is characterized by advances in the natural sciences and therefore in human technology; the result has been a new experience of the world, of the human person, and of history ("secularization") that now forms the only possible basis for a religious attitude. The daily more predominant mentality peculiar to the natural sciences, the growing influence of "logical neopositivism," and the critical approach to subjectivity (depth psychology and structuralism) require that any question be radically justified (as a question) which moves beyond the realm of empirical verifiability (or falsifiability) and the formal nomology of the corresponding cognitive process. This predominantly scientifico-empirical culture has given rise to the rather widespread phenomenon of distrust ("suspicion") toward any question that looks beyond the boundaries of the empirical.[26] To this must be added the wide diffusion of philosophical systems which, though different and even opposed among themselves, are at one in excluding a personal God and in refusing to acknowledge any reality not immanent in the world and history (Marxism, agnostic or atheistic existentialism). We can no longer count on a Christian faith which society safeguards, and we can anticipate that in the time ahead the question of God (of the very possibility of speaking meaningfully of God) will be asked in an increasingly radical way.

In this situation there is only one road theology may follow: it must confront, in depth, the question of the human person and of the ultimate meaning of human existence. Only from this vantage point will it be possible to discover the signs of transcendence that are implicit in human existence, to justify the meaningfulness of meta-empirical language, and to justify the God-question and the special nature of religious language. At the bottom of every theological and christological question the question of man lurks; starting from the human and from the unbridgeable gap between the threatened existence of the human person (his finiteness, his inability to save himself) and the limitless hope that sustains it, it can be shown that the person is open to a possible revelation of God and to his liberating grace. The Christ-event itself is intelligible, in the final analysis, only in this anthropological perspective. Talk of God and Christ can have meaning only in the context of salvation; that is, when it is understood and lived in light of the fundamental experience of the human person as in need of salvation and as therefore open to the absolute gratuitousness of hope.

As it looks ahead to the future of faith, theology must seek an understanding of dogmas in their two inseparable dimensions: the christological and the anthropological, that is, in their connection with the total Christ-event (his historical existence and his resurrection) and with the complete salvation of man (present anticipation and future fulfillment). In the basic intention they all share the dogmas are related to the definitive revelation and grace of God in Christ as being the salvation of the human person; this is the basis of the truth of their content and indeed their very character as dogmas. Their interpretation in the direction of the future is guided by the "once and for always" aspect of the Christ-event (as revelation of God and salvation of man), which is always present in the Church and always in progress toward its future fullness.

To seek for the future of the Christian faith means to seek the unity of Christians in the faith, and this quest identifies the ecumenical task of the Catholic theologian precisely in his work of interpreting the dogmas which at present establish the boundaries dividing the Christian confessions. He must get to the roots of the division and try to find in the shared Christian essence new and more comprehensive perspectives that will open ways to mutual understanding.

Bibliography

Y. Congar, "Apostolicité du ministère et apostolicité de doctrine," in K. Bäumer (ed.), *Volk Gottes* (Freiburg, 1967), pp. 84–112; "La réception comme réalité ecclésiologique," RSPT 56 (1972), 169–203; "Pour une histoire 'sémantique' du terme 'magisterium,'" RSPT 60 (1976), 64–98; "Bref historique des formes du 'magistère' et de ses rélations avec les doctrines," RSPT 60 (1976), 98–112.

K. Rahner, "The Teaching Office of the Church in the Present-day Crisis of Authority," in his *Theological Investigations* 12, tr. by D. Bourke (New York, 1974), pp. 3–30; "Theology and the Church's Teaching Authority after the Council," *Theological Investigations* 9, tr. by G. Harrison (New York, 1972), pp. 83–100; "Magisterium" in *Sacramentum Mundi* 3:351–58.

O. Rousseau (ed.), *L'infaillibilité de l'Eglise* (Chevetogne, 1965).

M. Löhrer, "Träger der Vermittlung," in *Mysterium Salutis* 1 (Freiburg, 1965), pp. 545–87; "Überlegungen zur Interpretation lehramtlicher Aussagen als Frage des ökumenischen Gesprächs," in H. Vorgrimler (ed.), *Gott in Welt: Festgabe für Karl Rahner* (Freiburg, 1964), 2:499–523.

E. Castelli (ed.), *L'infallibilità. L'aspetto filosofico e teologico* (Padua, 1970).

E. Schillebeeckx, *The Understanding of Faith: Interpretation and Criticism,* tr. by N. D. Smith (New York, 1974).

A. Descamps, "Théologie et magistère," ETL 52 (1976), 82–133.

J. Alfaro, "Problema theologicum de munere theologiae respectu magisterii," Greg 57 (1976), 39–79.

International Theological Commission, "Theses de magisterii ecclesiastici et theologiae ad invicem relatione," Greg 57 (1976), 549–63.

Notes

Abbreviations

AAS	*Acta Apostolicae Sedis*
Abbott	*The Documents of Vatican II*, ed. by W. M. Abbott (New York, 1966)
Ang	*Angelicum*
Bib	*Biblica*
BLE	*Bulletin de littérature ecclésiastique*
CT	*Ciencia Tomista*
DS	*Enchiridion symbolorum*, ed. by H. Denzinger; 32nd ed. by A. Schönmetzer (Freiburg, 1963)
EnciCatt	*Enciclopedia Cattolica*
ETL	*Ephemerides Theologicae Lovanienses*
ETR	*Etudes théologiques et religieuses*
EvQu	*Evangelical Quarterly*
Flannery	*Vatican Council II: The Conciliar and Postconciliar Documents*, ed. by A. Flannery (Collegeville, 1975)
FZPT	*Freiburger Zeitschrift für Philosophie und Theologie*
GCS	*Die griechischen christlichen Schriftsteller der ersten drei Jahrhunderte*
Greg	*Gregorianum*
HZ	*Historische Zeitschrift*
Irén	*Irénikon*
Ist	*Istina*
ITQ	*Irish Theological Quarterly*
JRel	*Journal of Religion*
KD	*Kerygma und Dogma*
LTK	*Lexikon für Theologie und Kirche*, 2nd ed.
LTP	*Laval théologique et philosophique*

MTZ	*Münchener theologische Zeitschrift*
NCCHS	*New Catholic Commentary on Holy Scripture*
NRT	*Nouvelle revue théologique*
NTS	*New Testament Studies*
NZST	*Neue Zeitschrift für systematische Theologie*
ParVi	*Parole di Vita*
PL	*Patrologia Latina*
RassTeol	*Rassegna Teologica*
RBiblIt	*Rivista Biblica Italiana*
REG	*Revue des études grecques*
RevMétaMor	*Revue de métaphysique et de morale*
RGG	*Die Religion in Geschichte und Gegenwart,* 3rd ed.
RSPT	*Revue des sciences philosophiques et théologiques*
RSR	*Recherches de science religieuse*
RT	*Revue thomiste*
RThPh	*Revue de théologie et de philosophie*
Sal	*Salesianum*
SC	*Sources chrétiennes*
ScCatt	*Scuola Cattolica*
Schol	*Scholastik*
TLZ	*Theologische Literaturzeitung*
TPS	The Pope Speaks
TQ	Theologische Quartalschrift
TTZ	*Trierer theologische Zeitschrift*
TvF	*Tijdschrift voor Filosofie*
TZ	*Theologische Zeitschrift*
ZKG	*Zeitschrift für Kirchengeschichte*
ZNW	*Zeitschrift für die neutestamentliche Wissenschaft*
ZTK	*Zeitschrift für Theologie und Kirche*

Introduction

1. We have in mind the *Chroniques de théologie fondamentale* which Jean-Pierre Torrell has been publishing regularly in RT since 1964, and the bulletins of Henri de Lavalette in RSR since 1971.

2. Symposium held at Gazzada, Italy, September 6–11, 1964, with papers by H. Bouillard, G. Colombo, A. M. Javierre, R. Latourelle and J.-B. Metz; the papers are published under the title of *Le Deuxième Symposium international de théologie dog-matique fondamentale* in *Biblioteca del Salesianum,* vol. 71, 1965. In 1969 a confer-

ence on fundamental theology was held at the Gregorian University in Rome, with J. Alfaro, H. Bouillard, H. Carrier. G. Dejaifve, R. Latourelle and G. Martelet participating; cf. "La théologie fondamentale á la recherche de son identité," Greg 50 (1969), 757–76.

3. J. Schmitz, "La théologie fondamentale," in R. V. Gucht and H. Vorgrimler (eds.), *Bilan de la théologie au XXe siècle* (Paris—Tournai, 1970), pp. 9–51; V. Boublik, "Orientamenti attuali della teologia fondamentale," in A. Marranzini (ed.), *Correnti teologiche postconciliari* (Rome, 1974), pp. 139–47; F. Ardusso, "Teologia fondamentale," in L. Pacomio (ed.), *Dizionario teologico interdisciplinare* 1 (Rome, 1977), pp. 182–202; J.-B. Metz (ed.), *The Development of Fundamental Theology* (Concilium 46; New York, 1969).

4. A. Dulles, *A History of Apologetics* (Philadelphia, 1971); H. Stirnimann, "Erwägungen zum Fundamentaltheologie. Problematik, Grundfragen, Konzept," FZPT 24 (1977), 291–365; C. Geffré, "Recent Developments in Fundamental Theology: An Interpretation," *Concilium* 46, pp. 5–27, now in his book *A New Age in Theology,* tr. by R. Shillenn et al. (New York, 1974).

Chapter 1

1. Cf. "Chronique de théologie fondamentale," RT 64 (1964), 97–127; 66 (1966), 63–107, 239–76; 67 (1967), 439–65; 69 (1969), 61–92; 71 (1971), 61–98; 75 (1975), 599–624; 76 (1976), 97–125; 78 (1978), 430–63; 79 (1979), 273–314.

2. *Concilium,* no. 46: *The Development of Fundamental Theology.*

3. H. Fries, "Zum heutigen Stand der Fundamentaltheologie," TTZ 84 (1975), 351–63.

4. H. Stirnimann, "Erwägungen fur Fundamentaltheologie. Problematik, Grundfragen, Konzept," FZPT 24 (1977), 291–365.

5. Ibid., pp. 308–17. To these studies of Fries and Stirnimann we may add the rather hasty but relatively complete survey, in Italian, of V. Boublík, "Orientamenti attuali della teologia fondamentale," in A. Marranzini (ed.), *Correnti teologiche postconciliari* (Rome, 1974), pp. 139–47.

6. J.-B. Metz, "Editorial," *Concilium,* 6, p. 1.

7. K. Rahner, *Est-il possible aujourd'hui de croire? Dialogue avec les hommes de ce temps* (Paris, 1966); citation from p. 198. Cf. the discussion of this book in RT 67 (1967), 439–42.

8. "Editorial," *Concilium,* 46, p. 1.

9. J. Alfaro, H. Bouillard, H. Carrier, G. Dejaifve, R. Latourelle, and G. Martelet, "La théologie fondamentale á la recherche de son identité. Un carrefour," Greg 50 (1969), 757–76.

10. C. Geffré, "Recent Developments in Fundamental Theology: An Interpretation," *Concilium,* 46, pp. 5–27; now in his book *A New Age in Theology,* tr. by R. Shillenn et al. (New York, 1974), pp. 11–30.

11. H. Bouillard, "De l'apologétique á la théologie fondamentale," in his *Les quatre fleuves* 1. *Dieu connu en Jésus-Christ* (Paris, 1973), pp. 57–70. For a complementary survey of J. Schmitz, "La théologie fondamentale," in H. Vorgrimler and R. van der Gucht (eds.), *Bilan de la théologie au XXe siècle* 2 (Tournai—Paris, 1970), pp. 9–51.

12. Cf. my "Chronique," RT 64 (1964), 97–103.

13. H. Bouillard, "La tâche actuelle la théologie fondamentale," in *Recherches Actuelles II* (Le point théologique 2; Paris, 1972), pp. 7–49. My citations in this and

the preceding two paragraphs are from pp. 7–9 of the essay; I have inverted the order of the first two trends as given by Fr. Bouillard.

14. Cf. above, n. 4. In an article, "Teologia fondamentale," in G. Barbaglio and S. Dianich (eds.), *Nuovo Dizionario di Teologia* (Alba, 1977), pp. 1754–67, G. Ruggieri likewise sees a threefold division within fundamental theology, but he distinguishes the branches as "models": the neoscholastic model, the immanence model, the political model (cf. pp. 1756ff.).

15. Cf. *Concilium,* 6, pp. 1–2.

16. In the editorial for *Concilium,* 6, Metz remains vague about the definition of fundamental theology. He is clearer on the need of renewal in this discipline (cf. n. 6, above), but we may legitimately doubt that its specific mission is "a more effective proclamation of our faith in its confrontation with contemporary philosophical and theological problems" (p. 1).

17. Cf. A. Gardeil, *La crédibilité et l'apologétique* (2nd ed.; Paris, 1912), p. 205.

18. Cf. H. Bouillard, "La tâche actuelle . . .," pp. 25–26.

19. This is not the place for explaining my own position; I refer the reader to the pages referred to in n. 12, above.

20. J.-B. Metz, *Faith in History and Society: Toward a Practical Fundamental Theology,* tr. by. D. Smith (New York, 1980); the German original was published at Mainz in 1977. There is a detailed review of the book in RT 79 (1979), 286–94.

21. Despite his effort to separate himself from the political theology of J. B. Metz, Antonio Osuna adopts almost the same position in his article, "La función crítica de la teología. Reflexiones para una teología fundamental," CT 103 (1976), 577–622. The reservations expressed by G. Ruggieri seem to me much more pertinent (n. 14, above, pp. 1758–60).

22. Cf. n. 4, above.

23. The reader will see how sound the methodology of this position is by contrasting it with that of David Tracy, according to whom the practioner of fundamental theology need not be a believing member of the Christian community: "The Task of Fundamental Theology," JRel 54 (1974), 13–34, at p. 14, n. 2. Tracy repeats this statement in his book *Blessed Rage for Order: The New Pluralism in Theology* (New York, 1975); cf. p. 36, n. 16; p. 57 n. 3. There is a good critique of this position in G. O'Collins' review in Greg 57 (1976), 779. We used to think that the unbelieving theologian of decadent Scholasticism was a figment of the imagination, but here he is *redivivus!*

24. There is a lengthy presentation of Stirnimann's views, followed by some critical queries, in RT 79 (1979), 273–86.

25. A Protestant author, Karl Nitzschke, wrote in 1956: "Fundamental theology, also known as apologetics, is a basic discipline of Roman Catholic theology" (cited in Stirnimann, art. cit., p. 291, n. 1; I owe to Stirnimann many of my references in this section of my essay). An analogous judgment appeared in 1970 from the pen of Josef Schmitz: "In German-speaking countries . . . apologetics or fundamental theology is almost universally rejected as a strictly theological discipline" (cf. art. cit. in n. 11, above, p. 38).

26. G. Ebeling, "Erwägungen zu einer evangelischen Fundamentaltheologie," ZTK 67 (1970), 479–524.

27. *Wort und Glaube* 3 (Tübingen, 1975). Although this collection bears the subtitle: "Contributions to Fundamental Theology, Soteriology and Ecclesiology," it does not contain the article cited just now in n. 26. In his Preface (p. III) Ebeling explains that he intends to expand that article as part of a larger work.

28. W. Joest, *Fundamentaltheologie. Theologische Grundlagen- und Methoden-problemenlehre* (Stuttgart, 1974), p. 9. On the work of Ebeling and Joest cf. Stirnimann's review: "Evangelische Fundamentaltheologie," FZPT 22 (1975), 378–83, which fills out the briefer comments in the study I am citing here.

29. M. Seckler, "Evangelische Fundamentaltheologie. Erwägungen zu einem Novum aus katholischer Sicht," TQ 155 (1975), 281–99. H. Fries, "Zum heutigen Stand . . .," p. 363, also stresses the importance of this Protestant interest in fundamental theology.

30. Cf. Ebeling, "Erwägungen . . .," p. 505.

31. Cf. Stirnimann, "Erwägungen . . .," p. 300 and n. 42; cf. pp. 293–301.

32. F. Hahn, "Exegese und Fundamentaltheologie. Die Rückfrage nach Jesus in ihrem Verhältnis zu Kerygma und Heiliger Schrift. Ein Beitrag zu Grandfragen der Theologie aus evangelischer Sicht," TZ 155 (1975), 262–80.

33. J. Flury, "Was ist Fundamentaltheologie?" TZ 31 (1975), 351–67.

34. H. Beintker, "Verstehen und Glauben. Grundlinien einer evangelischen Fundamentaltheologie," KD 26 (1976), 22–40.

35. B. Reymond, B. Morel, P.-A. Stucki, A. Gonnelle, U. Neuenschwander and L. Gagnebin, "L'apologétique aujourd'hui," ETR 47 (1972), 161–208. In his book on A. Sabatier, B. Reymond calls attention to the apologetic dimension of Sabatier's work; cf. RT 78 (1978), 440.

36. This bond has long been acknowledged by Catholic theologians; R. Latourelle gives a fine exemplification of it in his book, *Finding Jesus through the Gospels: History and Hermeneutics,* tr. by A. Owen (Staten Island, N.Y., 1979); cf. RT 78 (1978), 657–60.

37. For this summary cf. Stirnimann, "Erwägungen . . .," pp. 318–19.

38. See, e.g., the article of Bouillard cited above in n. 13. G. Ruggieri seems to be thinking along the same lines when he includes "the other" in the horizon of his definition of fundamental theology; but we may note that this "other" is "inside" as well as "outside" (cf. art. cit. in n. 14, above, pp. 1754–55 and 1764–65).

39. Sometimes it even shows a polemical tone that is in the direct line of classical apologetics, as in John King-Farlow and William D. Christensen, *Faith and the Life of Reason* (Dordrecht, 1972).

40. Schubert M. Ogden, *The Reality of God* (London, 1967).

41. Gustaf Aulén, *The Drama and the Symbols* (Philadelphia, 1970).

42. John Macquarrie, *God-Talk. An Examination of the Language and Logic of Theology* (London, 1967).

43. H. Bouillard, "La tâche actuelle . . .," p. 34, and H. Fries, "Zum heutigen Stand . . .," p. 355, have called attention to the relevance of this method.

44. There is an interesting survey of Protestant apologetics, chiefly in the English-speaking countries, in Langdon Gilkey, "Trends in Protestant Apologetics," *Concilium,* 46, pp. 127–57.

45. I might also mention Maurice Blondel, to whom H. Bouillard owes so much (cf. "La tâche actuelle . . .," pp. 36–37). With regard to Pascal the reader should consult the important book of Pierre Magnard, *Nature et histoire dans l'apologétique de Pascal* (Paris, 1975).

46. Cf. Stirnimann, "Erwägungen . . .," pp. 319–21.

47. J.-B. Metz, *Faith in History and Society,* p. 14. And cf. earlier, on p. 3: "Any Christian theology . . . can be defined, at least in its task and intention, as the defense of hope."

48. Ibid., pp. 8–10; Metz refers here to Ebeling.

49. Cf. A. Patfoort, "Nouvel âge de la théologie ou . . . de l'apologétique?" *Ang* 50 (1973), 243–48. Speaking of Geffré's book, *A New Age in Theology* (the French original appeared in 1972), Patfoort observes that a number of traits presented as specific to a renewed theology are in fact typically apologetic attitudes (cf. pp. 244–45).

50. Cf. 1 Corinthians 15. As early as the end of the apostolic age, and even before the time of the Fathers known as the Apologists, Christians had to defend their faith by means of writings; cf. H. Paulsen's recent essay on one such undertaking: "Das Kerygma Petri und die urchristliche Apologetik," ZKG 88 (1977), 1–37.

51. Cf. J. de Ghellinck, *Le mouvement théologique du XIIe siècle* (1st ed.; Paris, 1948), pp. 279–84.

52. Peter the Venerable, for example, one of the most important apologetes of the twelfth century, often cites this verse; cf. J. P. Torrell, "La notion de prophétie et la méthode apologétique dans le *Contra Saracenos* de Pierre le Vénérable," *Studia Monastica* 18 (1975), 257–82, at p. 274.

53. A. Gardeil, *La structure de l'âme et l'expérience mystique* (Paris, 1927). I mention the title here simply as representative of a theological preoccupation that was very strong at that time and that could be the subject of a very full bibliography.

54. Jean Mouroux, *The Christian Experience. Introduction to a Theology,* tr. by G. Lamb (New York, 1954).

55. H. Bouillard, "Human Experience as the Starting Point of Fundamental Theology," *Concilium,* 46, pp. 79–91. Bouillard had developed this theme at greater length in his *The Logic of Faith* (New York, 1967); he has touched on it once again in his essay, "La tâche actuelle. . . ."

56. A few titles: Gregory Baum, "Religious Experience and Religious Statement," and Seely Beggiani, "Revelation and Religious Experience," in G. Devine (ed.), *New Dimensions in Religious Experience* (New York, 1970), pp. 3–11 and 31–51. Although the word "experience" does not appear in the title of Gabriel Moran's *The Present Revelation: The Search for Religious Foundations* (New York, 1972), the book is concerned throughout with the subject of "revelation and experience." On Moran's book cf. A. Dulles, "The Problem of Revelation," *Proceedings of the Twenty-ninth Annual Convention of the Catholic Theological Society of America (Chicago, 1974),* pp. 77–106, at pp. 92–97, as well as my own review in RT 78 (1978), 440–49. More recently, there is Gerald O'Collins' article, "Theology and Experience," ITQ 44 (1977), 279–90.

57. P. Schoonenberg, "Revelation and Experience," *Lumen vitae* 25 (1970), 551–60.

58. G. Ebeling, "Die Klage über das Erfahrungsdefizit in der Theologie als Frage nach ihrer Sache," in his *Wort und Glaube* 3 (Tübingen, 1975), pp. 3–28. On experience in Ebeling cf. a few remarks in RT 76 (1976), 120–21. Ebeling has recently returned to this subject in order to show that the scriptural principle, which is traditional in Protestant theology, does not exclude an appeal to experience, as the example of Luther himself shows: "Schrift und Erfahrung als Quellen theologischer Aussage," ZTK 75 (1978), 99–106.

59. P. Jacquemont, J.-P. Jossua and B. Quelquejeu, *Une foi exposée* (Paris, 1972).

60. J.-P. Jossua, "Théologie et expérience chrétienne," in *Le service théologique dans l'Eglise: Mélanges offerts au Père Yves Congar* (Cogitatio fidei 76; Paris, 1974), pp. 113–29. Jossua has written several other articles on the same subject; cf. ibid., p. 113, n. 1.

61. J. B. Metz, "Excursus: Theology as Biography," in his *Faith in History and Society,* pp. 219–28.

62. Stirnimann, "Erwägungen . . .," pp. 343–47.

63. J.-P. Torrell, "Chronique," RT 76 (1976), 118–20; 78 (1978), 446–49.

64. Cf. Ebeling, "Die Klage . . .," pp. 6ff.

65. Cf. ibid., pp. 8–9, n. 11.

66. In the margin of his Commentary on Romans 5:4 (in which he translates the Greek *dokimē* by the German *Erfahrung*), Luther wrote: "Experience is when a person has been well tested and can speak about a subject as one who has been there" (cited by Ebeling, "Die Klage . . .," p. 6, n. 3). Thomas Aquinas, for his part, speaks of things that intensify faith because they resist it or put it to the test: "For this reason the martyrs gain greater merit in their faith . . . as do the learned [that is, the theologians], who do not abandon the faith in the face of arguments offered by the philosophers . . ." (*Summa theologiae,* 2-2, q. 2, a. 10, ad 3).

67. Cf. the texts cited by Stirnimann, "Erwägungen . . .," p. 345, n. 220.

68. "A theologian reaches maturity only through doubt and temptation: that is an ancient and splendid saying" (cited by Ebeling, "Die Klage . . .," p. 11).

69. E. Hocedez, *Histoire de la théologie au XIX ͤ siècle* 1 (Paris, 1948), pp. 179–80, tells us that Hermes' "method was inspired chiefly by his religious experience."

70. The literature is far too extensive for me to give even an idea of it here. As but one example, cf. J.-P. Torrell, "Le projet de Dieu: Former un Peuple; comment la J. O. C. la réalise dans la jeunesse ouvrière," *Masses ouvrières,* no. 239 (April, 1967), pp. 28–45.

71. The term is Ebeling's, in "Die Klage . . .," p. 5; he also cites H.-G. Gadamer, who regards the concept of experience as one of the most obscure we have (ibid., n. 2).

72. Cf. Ebeling, ibid., p. 25 and, at greater length, pp. 16–24.

73. Cf. ibid., p. 25.

74. Cf. Stirnimann, "Erwägungen . . .," pp. 345–47. Stirnimann returns to the theme of experience in "Language, Experience and Revelation," *Concilium,* no. 133, pp. 117–30.

75. Cf. J.-P. Torrell, "Chronique," RT 76 (1976), 119–20.

76. On this distinction cf. the explanations given by G. Geffré in the collective volume *Le déplacement de la théologie* (Le Point Théologique 21; Paris, 1977), pp. 6 and 175–77.

Chapter 2

1. The term "disclosure" refers to the *cognitive* side of religious truth; the term "transformation" to the ethical (both personal and social) side of that truth.

2. The term "discipline" allows for a wider range in the English-speaking world than the more familiar term "science." The latter term, which retains its expansive meaning in the Scholastic notion of *scientia* and the German notion of *Wissenschaft,* has become largely identified with the methods of natural science (and their analogues in social science) in the English-language discussion. On the notion of "discipline," see Stephen Toulmin, *Human Understanding* 1: *The Collective Use and Evolution of Concepts* (Princeton, 1972), espec. pp. 145–200 and 364–412.

3. The assumption here is that any theology is related in some manner to all three publics (church, academy, society) from the viewpoint of sociology of knowl-

edge. Theologically formulated, every theology is related to both "church" and "world."

4. This notion of "church" is a social scientific one; for its use in theology proper, see James Gustafson, *Treasure in Earthen Vessels* (New York, 1967). A properly theological notion of church includes the former, yet insists that the church is also a strictly theological reality, i.e., the church participates in the ultimate mystery of God's self-revelation in Jesus Christ.

5. The notion of "public argument" need not take either a conceptualist or a rationalist cast. For a classical study of the full range of truly critical reason, see Bernard Lonergan, *Insight* (London, 1957); on the nature of argument, see Stephen Toulmin, *The Uses of Argument* (New York, 1958).

6. For a contemporary treatment of the issue, see Paul Ricoeur, *Interpretation Theory: Discourse and the Surplus of Meaning* (Fort Worth, 1976).

7. Contrast, for example, Dorothee Soelle's critical fairness to Bultmann in *Political Theology*, tr. by J. Shelley (Philadelphia, 1971), pp. 19–31, with José Miranda's critical unfairness to Rahner in *Marx and the Bible: A Critique of the Philosophy of Oppression*, tr. by J. Eagelson (Maryknoll, 1974), pp. 247, 249.

8. For the concept "situation" in its theological meaning, see Paul Tillich, *Systematic Theology* 1 (Chicago, 1951), pp. 3–66. One need not accept Tillich's own program to agree with his important analysis of the theological relevance of the central category "situation."

9. The dominant characteristic of *Gaudium et Spes* heads in this direction, as indeed does the mainline Catholic theological tradition and its formulation of the relationships of "faith" and "reason" and its distrust (in principle, if not always in fact) of any strictly sectarian notion of "church."

10. The relationships of "religious studies" and "theology" is one of the most pressing intellectual concerns in the English-speaking theological world. The same kind of concern is often articulated in European contexts under the rubrics of "theology" and the "scientific study of religion." For one example, see Wolfhart Pannenbert, *Theology and the Philosophy of Science*, tr. by F. McDonagh (Philadelphia, 1976).

11. For a longer defense of this position, see my *Blessed Rage for Order: The New Pluralism in Theology* (New York, 1975); the companion volume on systematic theology, *The Analogical Imagination* (New York, 1980), provides the needed longer defense of the model of systematics outlined here. The present article intends only a summary of the main notions of fundamental and systematic theology and their dual necessity. The more extensive warrants for each position may be found in the works cited above.

12. Alternative expressions include "doctrinal theology," "dogmatics," "Christian theology," "Catholic theology," etc.

13. The first two characteristics are more familiar in many Reformed theologies; the third in most Catholic theologies.

14. See H. Richard Niebuhr, *The Meaning of Revelation* (New York, 1946).

15. My own position on the role of metaphysics in a historically-conscious theology (a position contrary to Niebuhr's) may be found in *Blessed Rage for Order*, pp. 146–87.

16. See Hans-Georg Gadamer, *Truth and Method*, tr. by G. Barden and J. Cumming (New York, 1975), espec. pp. 235–74 and 325–45, for this and the following discussion of the *truth*-character of hermeneutics.

17. The theory of the "classic" backing of this definition may be found in *The Analogical Imagination* (n. 11, above), chapters 3 and 4.

18. Here, of course, the concept "church" would need to possess a properly theological and not only sociological character; cf. n. 4, above.

19. For a sustained analysis of the role of *praxis* for fundamental theology itself, see Johann Baptist Metz, *Faith in History and Society: Toward a Practical Fundamental Theology,* tr. by D. Smith (New York, 1979). Present limitations of space foreclose an extensive development of the notion of practical theology implied in the present article. For the moment, it may suffice to state that both fundamental and systematics call for practical theology related to *praxis* for their own sufficiency. When that fuller picture is completed, one can also speak, with Metz, of a "practical fundamental theology," as long as, again with Metz, Rahner, and Küng—despite their other differences—one may also recognize the *necessity* from the viewpoint of both systematic and practical theologies for fundamental theology: for responses to the questions inevitably posed in our situation to both systematic and practical theologies. In sum, insofar as all theologies need to take seriously the evangelical call "Always be prepared to make a defense to anyone who calls you to account for the hope that is in you" (1 Pet 3:15), they *need* to engage in fundamental theology.

Chapter 3

1. R. Latourelle, "Apologétique et fondamentale," Sal 27 (1965), 256; C. Geffré, "Recent Developments in Fundamental Theology," *Concilium,* 46, pp. 13–14 (= A New Age in Theology, pp. 11–30); H. Bouillard, "La tâche actuelle de la théologie fondamentale," in *Recherches Actuelles II* (Le point théologique 2; Paris, 1972), pp. 11–14; idem, "De l'apologétique à la théologie fondamentale," in his *Les Quatre Fleuves* 1. *Dieu connu en Jésus-Christ* (Paris, 1974), pp. 57–70.

2. A . Gardeil, *La crédibilité et l'apologétique* (Paris, 1908); R. Garrigou-Lagrange, *De revelatione per Ecclesiam catholicam proposita* (Rome, 1950⁵).

3. N. Dunas, "Le probléme et le statut de l'apologétique," RSPT 43 (1959), 658.

4. A. de Bovis, "Bulletin d'apologétique," RSR 43 (1955), 624.

5. R. Latourelle, art. cit., pp. 257–60.

6. Ibid. pp. 260–61.

7. Dunas, art. cit., p. 680.

8. Y. Congar, *La foi et la théologie* (Bruges—Paris, 1962), p. 183.

9. Ibid.

10. Ibid., pp. 184, 198.

11. J.-P. Torrell, "Chronique de théologie fondamentale," RT 64 (1964), 100.

12. Ibid.

13. Ibid.

14. Ibid., p. 102.

15. Latourelle, art. cit., pp. 267–68.

16. Ibid., p. 268. Same idea in idem, "Dismemberment or Renewal of Fundamental Theology?" *Concilium,* 46, pp. 29–30. In 1930 H. de Lubac was already saying that "the compenetration of apologetics and theology [= dogmatic theology in this context], which often seems necessary in practice, is also fully justified in theory. Only barren prejudice and a false conception of their nature causes the two to be set in opposition to one another. In fact, they complement one another, they vitalize one

another. The place where they meet and enter into the most fruitful collaboration is fundamental theology": "Apologétique et théologie," NRT 57 (1930), 378. H. Urs von Balthasar remarks: "I will have to speak of many subjects that are usually treated in what is called 'Fundamental Theology.' But this should not lead the reader to believe that I am here undertaking to elaborate a fundamental theology that would be distinct from and opposed to dogmatic theology; in my study I will rather be trying to convince the reader that these two aspects of theology are inseparable": *La gloire et la croix* 1 (Paris, 1965), pp. 11–12.

17. V. Boublik, *Incontro con Cristo* (Rome, 1968); idem, "Orientamenti attuali della teologia fondamentale," in A. Marranzini (ed.), *Correnti teologiche postconciliari* (Rome, 1974), p. 145.

18. H. Bouillard, *The Logic of Faith* (New York, 1967), pp. 34–35.

19. H. Bouillard, "Human Experience as the Starting Point of Fundamental Theology," *Concilium*, 6 (1965), 83–92.

20. J. Alfaro, H. Bouillard, H. Carrier, G. Dejaifve, R. Latourelle, and G. Martelet, "La théologie fondamentale à la recherche de son identité," Greg 50 (1969), 765.

21. H. Bouillard, "La tâche actuelle . . .," p. 24.

22. Ibid., pp. 42 and 25.

23. Ibid., p. 26.

24. Ibid., p. 42.

25. Ibid., p. 26.

26. K. Rahner has explained what he intends in his *Foundations of Christian Faith: An Introduction to the Idea of Christianity*, tr. by W. V. Dych (New York, 1978). This "foundational course" includes fundamental theology and dogmatic theology in close unity; it includes both the *motivation* for faith and the *content* of faith. "The point of our foundational course in theology is precisely this, to give people confidence from the very *content* of Christian dogma itself that they can believe with intellectual honesty" (p. 12). This basic course rightly does not bear the title "Fundamental Theology," since it contains both more and less than classical fundamental theology. It contains *more* because it studies not only the fact but the content of revelation. It contains *less* because it chooses among the problems of classical fundamental theology. Its norm for selection is this: It studies those mysteries and motives of credibility that have an *existential* resonance in the life of people today.

27. H. Fries, "Fundamental Theology," in *Sacramentum Mundi* 2 (New York, 1968), pp. 368–72.

28. H. Fries, "From Apologetics to Fundamental Theology," *Concilium*, pp. 57–67.

29. Ibid., p. 67.

30. C. Geffré, "Recent Developments . . .," p. 20.

31. P. Ricoeur, C. Geffré, E. Levinas, E. Haulotte, and E. Cornélis, *La révélation* (Brussels, 1977), p. 171.

32. G. Söhngen, "Fundamentaltheologie," LTK 4:452–59.

33. H. Stirnimann, "Erwägungen zur Fundamentaltheologie: Problematik, Grundfragen, Konzept," FZPT 24 (1977), 291–317. A detailed study of this article is provided by J.-P. Torrell, "Questions de théologie fondamentale," RT 79 (1979), 273–86.

34. Stirnimann, ibid., pp. 322–23.

35. Ibid., pp. 334–50.

36. Ibid., pp. 351–57.

37. J.-B. Metz, Editorial in *Concilium,* 6 (1965), p. 7 (French edition).

38. Ibid., p. 8.

39. R. Latourelle, *Théologie de la Révélation* (Bruges—Paris—Montreal, 1969³), pp. 231–62. [This is a later, revised edition of the work cited below, n. 57, in an English translation.]

40. Ibid., pp. 369–73.

41. There is a bibliography on the subject in R. Latourelle, *Finding Jesus through the Gospels: History and Hermeneutics,* tr. by A. Owen (Staten Island, N.Y., 1979), pp. 273–84.

42. R. Latourelle, "Dismemberment or Renewal . . .," pp. 38–40; idem, *Christ and the Church: Signs of Salvation,* tr. by E. D. Parker (Staten Island, N.Y., 1972), pp. 9–73.

43. This broad spectrum of partners and addressees of fundamental theology has been emphasized especially by H. Bouillard, "La tâche actuelle . . .," p. 23; H. Stirnimann, "Erwägungen . . .," p. 360; H. Fries, "Zum heutigen Stand der Fundamentaltheologie," TTZ 84 (1975), 357.

44. H. Bouillard, "La tâche actuelle . . .," p. 24.

45. For example, there are two full pages on the nature, object and method of fundamental theology in *The Theological Formation of Future Priests* (February 22, 1976), tr. in *The Pope Speaks* 21 (1976), 373–74. The term "fundamental theology" is officially recognized in the *Ordinationes* (April 29, 1979), Part II, art. 51, that accompanied the recent Apostolic Constitution *Sapientia Christiana* (April 15, 1979), in *Osservatore Romano,* May 25–26, 1979, p. 4.

46. R. Latourelle, "Dismemberment or Renewal . . .," pp. 29–30; idem, "La théologie fondamentale à la recherche de son identité," Greg 50 (1969), 757–58; H. Bouillard, "La tâche actuelle . . .," pp. 20–21.

47. R. Latourelle, "Apologétique et Fondamentale," pp. 259–60; A. Manaranche, *Les raisons de l'espérance: Theologie fondamentale* (Paris, 1979), p. 8.

48. For example, H. Bouillard, "Esquisse d'un traité de la révélation," *Bulletin du Comité des études,* no. 61 (July–October, 1970), 249; H. Stirnimann, "Erwägungen . . .," pp. 363–65.

49. "Die Fundamentaltheologie ist der heute gefragteste theologische Disziplin," in "Zum heutigen Stand . . .," p. 351. More recently, in 1979, A. Manaranche has observed: "I and many others think that fundamental theology is *a discipline in its own right,* even if it must be concerned with all the other treatises as well. Its aim is to be an apologia or defense dealing with the foundations of faith and especially with the act of revelation. If Christians, who constantly include themselves in the discourse, neglect it, they will find obscurity descending on a certainty that will then prove to have an imposing body but feet of clay. The dialogical dimension of dogmatic theology cannot do without this kind of reflection" (op. cit., pp. 76–77).

50. Schubert M. Ogden, *The Reality of God* (London, 1967), p. 120.

51. G. Ebeling, "Erwägungen zu einer evangelischen Fundamentaltheologie," ZTK 67 (1970), 479–524.

52. Concerning this renewal of interest in apologetics and fundamental theology among both Protestants and Catholics cf. the second and third parts of Jean-Pierre Torrell's essay in this volume.

53. This is something which Karl Rahner, for example, does in a first-rate manner.

54. H. Fries, "Zum heutigen Stand . . .," p. 352, is in agreement here.

55. G. de Fois, "Révélation et société: La Constitution *Dei Verbum* et les fonctions sociales de l'Ecriture," RSR 63 (1975), 457–503.

56. On this theme cf. *Revelation and Experience,* Concilium, 133 (1978), and J.-P. Torrell, "Révélation et expérience. Chronique de théologie fondamentale," RT 78 (1978), 430–63. This aspect is particularly emphasized in such writers as H. Bouillard, G. Baum, G. Moran, A. Dulles, J.-P. Jossua, G. O'Collins, J.-B. Metz, and H. Stirnimann.

57. In the introduction to my *Theology of Revelation* (Staten Island, N.Y., 1966), I wrote: "Side by side with the apologetic study of revelation, there is thus room for a dogmatic study of revelation. . . . This dogmatic treatise on revelation will appear as a *complement* to the treatise on apologetics and also as a preparation to the treatise on faith" (p. 15; italics added). That book was thus intended as a contribution to such a dogmatic theology of revelation; it seeks to meet a need and does not claim to replace an apologetics of revelation.

58. In section III, above, I indicated the content of these three approaches.

59. In his review of (the French original of) C. Geffré's *A New Age in Theology* A. Patfoort legitimately asks whether a number of traits regarded today as characteristic of a renewed theology are not in fact signs of a new age of *apologetics,* since in the last analysis the point being made is that the people of *our day* must be shown the credibility of the Christian faith, that is, the *meaning* which the Christian faith has for each of us. Cf. A. Patfoort, "Nouvel âge de la théologie ou . . . de l'apologétique," Ang 50 (1973), 243–48.

Chapter 5

1. Cf. Henri de Lubac, *The Sources of Tradition,* tr. by L. O'Neill (New York, 1968); idem, *Exégèse médiévale: Les quatre sens de l'Ecriture* (4 vols.; Paris, 1959–64).

2. Cf. R. Marlé, *Au coeur de la crise moderniste. Le dossier inédit d'une controverse.* Lettres de M. Blondel, H. Bremond, et al., présentés par René Marlé, S.J. (Paris, 1960).

3. M. Blondel, *History and Dogma,* in *The Letter on Apologetics and History and Dogma,* tr. by A. Dru and I. Trethowan (New York, 1964).

4. M. Kähler, *The So-called Historical Jesus and the Historic, Biblical Christ,* tr. by C. E. Braaten (Philadelphia, 1964).

5. I am evidently referring here to the famous *Römerbrief,* especially the second edition of 1921, the Preface of which is a full-fledged hermeneutical manifesto on a small scale. English translation: K. Barth, *The Epistle to the Romans,* tr. from the 6th ed. by E. C. Hoskyns (London, 1933).

6. This thesis of Bultmann on demythologization and existential interpretation is the subject of my book *Bultmann et l'interprétation du Nouveau Testament* (Paris, 1956; 2nd ed.: 1966).

7. In *Kerygma und Mythos* III, ed. by H. W. Bartsch (Hamburg, 1952), p. 51.

8. G. Ebeling, *The Word of God and Tradition: Historical Studies Interpreting the Divisions of Christianity,* tr. by S. H. Hooke (Philadelphia, 1968), p. 116.

9. Ibid., p. 119.

10. Ibid., p. 133.

11. Ibid., p. 136.

11a. Ibid., pp. 133–34.

12. E. Käsemann, in E. Käsemann (ed.), *Das Neue Testament als Kanon* (Göttingen, 1970), p. 407.

13. E. Käsemann, *Perspectives on Paul*, tr. by M. Kohl (Philadelphia, 1971), pp. 164, 165.

14. The document, "L'autorité de la Bible," was published in a special number of *Istina* 16 (1971), 312–25.

15. Vatican II, *Dogmatic Constitution on the Sacred Liturgy*, in W. M. Abbott (ed.), *The Documents of Vatican II* (New York, 1966), p. 120.

16. W. Kasper, *Dogme et Evangile* (Paris—Tournai, 1967), pp. 109–112. [Translation by F. van Groenendahl of *Dogma under dem Wort Gottes* (Mainz, 1965).]

17. M. de Certeau, "Autorités chrétiennes," *Etudes* 332 (1970), 269.

18. Ibid., p. 271.

19. Ibid., p. 275.

20. Ibid.

21. Paris, 1950.

22. Paul Beauchamp, *L'un et l'autre Testament. Essai de lecture* (Paris, 1976), p. 296.

23. Ibid., p. 298.

24. Ibid., p. 294.

25. D. Bonhoeffer, *Letters and Papers from Prison*, tr. by R. H. Fuller (rev. and enlarged ed.; New York, 1967), pp. 103 and 155.

26. This is the view of, for example, Hans Albert in his *Traktat über Kritische Vernunft* (Tübingen, 1968).

27. Cf. R. Bultmann, "The Significance of the Historical Jesus for the Theology of Paul," in his *Faith and Understanding*, tr. by L. Pettibone Smith (New York, 1969), p. 237.

28. In *Faith and Understanding*, pp. 53–65.

29. In Roland Barthes, Paul Beauchamp, et al., *Exégèse et Herméneutique* (Paris, 1971), pp. 291–95.

Chapter 6

1. Cf. Paul Ricoeur, *History and Truth*, tr. by C. A. Kelbley (Evanston, 1965); H. Kuhn, "Wahrheit und geschichtliches Verstehen," HZ 193 (1961), 376–89; K. Oedingen, "Das Problem der Wahrheit in der Erforschung der Geschichte," TvF 32 (1970), 494–520.

2. P. Gisel, "Ernst Käsemann ou la solidarité conflictuelle de l' histoire et de la vérité," ETR 51 (1976), 21–37; cf. p. 31: "The coming of modernity . . . could not but call attention once again to the question of the relation between history and truth. And if people commonly speak today of a crisis in metaphysics, the roots of it are certainly in this question of history and truth. What relations exist between the two? This question has been asked for two or three centuries now. Under the surface it obsesses our culture and politics. . . . It even crops up today in the debates (whose premises are poorly thought out) that sometimes preoccupy our synods or control the positions we take in politics or theology." Cf. the same author's *Vérité et histoire. La théologie dans la modernité: Ernst Käsemann* (Paris, 1977), ch. 1 (pp. 39–132).

3. Cf. M. Blondel, *History and Dogma*, in *The Letter on Apologetics and History and Dogma*, tr. by A. Dru and I. Trethowan (New York, 1964); Chr. Théobald, "L'entrée de l'histoire dans l'univers religieux et théologique au moment de la 'crise

moderniste,' " in J. Greisch et al., *La crise contemporaine: Du modernisme à la crise des herméneutiques* (Théologie historique 24; Paris, 193-73), pp. 7–85; J. Hulshof, *Wahrheit und Geschichte. Alfred Loisy zwischen Tradition und Kritik* (Essen, 1973).

4. Cf. Cl. Geffré, "Esquisse d'une théologie de la révélation," in the collection of essays entitled *La révélation* (Brussels, 1977), pp. 171–205 at p. 174.

5. Art. cit. (n. 2, above), p. 32. For a short critical discussion of Gisel's position see my *La vérité dans Saint Jean* 2 (Analecta Biblica 74; Rome, 1977), pp. 784–85, n. 418.

6. C.-J. Pinto de Oliveria, "Bilan et perspectives," which provides the conclusion for the collection of essays entitled *Hegel et la théologie contemporaine* (Bibliothèque théologique; Neuchâtel—Paris, 1977), pp. 229–54 at p. 247 (italics added). There is already an excellent statement of the problem in M. Blondel, *History and Dogma* (n. 3, above), p. 223: "Historical facts are the foundations of the Catholic faith."

7. On the one hand, cf. J. B. Lotz, "Von der Geschichtlichkeit der Wahrheit," Schol 27 (1952), 481–503; J. Möller, "Die Geschichtlichkeit und Einheit der Wahrheit," in *Die Wissenschaften und die Wahrheit* (Stuttgart, 1966), pp. 185–200; W. Hirsch, "La tesi di Heidegger sulla storicità della verità," Rass Teol 19 (1978), 258–62. On the other hand, cf. B. Garceau, "Historicité et transcendance de la vérité," in *Actes du VIIe Congrès interaméricain de philosophie* (Quebec, 1967); R. Lauth, *Die absolute Ungeschichtlichkeit der Wahrheit* (Stuttgart, 1966). The two theses are well presented in V. Subilia, *I tempi di Dio* (Turin, 1970), pp. 179–93; "La verità è nella storia," and pp. 194–95: "La verità non è nella storia." Cf. also J. Möller, "Geschichtlichkeit und Ungeschichtlichkeit der Wahrheit," in *Theologie im Wandel. Festschrift zum 150-jahrigen Bestehen der Kath.-theol. Fakultät der Universität Tübingen* (Freiburg i. B., 1967), pp. 15–40.

8. E. des Places, "La langue philosophique de Platon. Le vocabulaire de l'accès au savior et la science," *Siculorum Gymnasium* 16 (1961), 71–83: "The truth of things is the truth of the Ideas" (p. 80).

9. Cf. M. Detienne, "La notion mythique d'Alétheia," REG 73 (1960, 27–35: "*Aiōn* [eternity] measures the plain of *Alétheia,* from which the river of *Chronos* runs out. *Alétheia* therefore has no temporal dimension; it transcends human time, since it contains both past and future" (p. 32).—N.B. In the course of this article I shall be repeating points already made in connection with another problem and in another perspective; cf. "La notion biblique de vérité et sa rencontre avec la notion héllénistique dans l'Englise ancienne" (to appear in a volume of essays produced by the Pontifical Biblical Commission on the problem of inculturation).

10. *Extraits de Stobée* II, B, 5 (ed. by A. Festugière in the Budé collection, III, 14). The theme of Plato's *Phaedrus* is also found there: the soul, once initiated, "travels across the Plain of Truth" (XXV, 4; Budé, IV, 69). It is not surprising that this Platonic theme should have been enthusiastically received by the gnostics, since in gnosticism dualism was pushed to extremes: the world below is "the totality of evil" (*Corpus Hermeticum* 6, 4; Budé, I, 74); the Pleroma is "the place of the Truth" (*Pistis Sophia* 5 and 143).

11. Plato, *Phaedrus,* 246d and 247c, tr. by R. Hackforth, *Plato's Phaedrus* (Cambridge, 1952), reprinted in E. Hamilton and H. Cairns (eds.) *Plato: The Collected Dialogues* (Bollingen Series 71; New York, 1961), pp. 493–94.

12. Gregory of Nyssa, *Vita Moysis,* 2, 19 (PG 44:332C; SC lbis:37); Maximus the Confessor, *Mystagogia* 5 (PG 91:677A).

13. Cf. *La vérité dans Saint Jean* 1:243, n. 374.

14. *In Joannem* VI, 6, 38, (GCS Orig. IV, 114, 22–23).

15. Ibid. (GCS Orig. IV, 114, 19–25).

16. J. D. Zizioulas, "Vérité et Communion dans la perspective de la pensée patristique grecque," Irén 50 (1977), 451–510 at p. 462.

17. J. Goimard, review of T. Todorov, *Symbolisme et interprétation* (Paris, 1978), in *Le Monde*, April 27, 1979, p. 25 (italics added).

18. M. F. Sciacca, "Razionalismo," EnciCatt 10:580.

19. *Oeuvres et lettres* (éd. de la Pléiade; Paris, 1949), p. 18, cited in J.-L. Allard, *Le Mathématisme de Descartes* (Ottawa, 1963), p. 129.

20. Leibniz, *Theodicy*, tr. by E. M. Huggard (New Haven, 1952), p. 73. Cf. also *Monadology*, no. 29, in *Leibniz: Philosophical Writings* (London, 1934): "It is the knowledge of necessary and eternal truths which distinguishes us from mere animals, and gives us *reason* and the sciences, raising us to knowledge of ourselves and God. It is this in us which we call the rational soul or *mind*" (p. 8).

21. "Accidental truths of history can never become the proof of the necessary truths of reason," in *On the Proof of the Spirit and of Power*, translated in H. Chadwick (ed.), *Lessing's Theological Writings* (London, 1956), p. 53. On this subject cf. G. W. Bromiley, "History and Truth: A Study of the Axiom of Lessing," *EvQ* 18 (1946), 191–98.

22. P. Gisel, *Vérité et histoire*, p. 57.

23. For more details cf. *La vérité dans Saint Jean* 2:1048–52. There I cite many texts of the post-tridentine period. It should be noted that the habit of speaking of *veritates* (plural) is very like the way in which Leibniz and Lessing expressed themselves in the texts cited a little earlier.

24. Cf. the sometimes very incisive thoughts of J. Doyon, "Théologie catholique et discours idéologique," LTP 36 (1978), 179–95, especially p. 192.

25. Pius IX, Letter *Tuas libenter* to the Archbishop of Munich-Freising (December 21, 1863): "ineffabiles veritates ab ipsa divina revelatione propositas" (DS, no. 2878).

26. Pius XII, Encyclical Letter *Humani generis* (August 12, 1950): "veritas divinitus revelata" (DS, no. 2887).

27. M. Blondel, *History and Dogma*, pp. 226–31: "Extrinsicism." But Blondel dwells at much greater length on another deviation that became a real threat in Loisy's day: "Historicism" (pp. 231–64). I shall speak of this in a moment.

28. Ibid., p. 230.

29. Ibid., p. 229.

30. Cf. the very enlightening study by K. Löwith, "Vicos Grundsatz: Verum et factum convertuntur. Seine theologische Prämisse und seine säkulare Konsequenzen," *Sitzungsberichte der Heidelbergschen Akademie der Wissenschaften* (Heidelberg, 1968), Heft 1, pp. 5–36.

31. In *De Antiquissimorum Italorum Sapientia* (ed. 1914), pp. 131–32, he wrote: "The criterion of truth is to have brought it into being (*Veri criterium est id ipsum fecisse*)" (cited in Löwith, art. cit., p. 9); or again: "To establish the truth and to make it are one and the same thing (*Etenim habes verare et facere idem esse*)," ibid., p. 191 (Löwith, p. 9).

32. For Blondel, cf. n. 27, above. Among later works cf. especially E. Troeltsch, *Der Historismus und seine Probleme* (Tübingen, 1922); idem, *Der Historismus und seine Überwindung* (Berlin, 1924); F. Meinecke, *Historicism: The Rise of a New His-*

torical Outlook (1936), tr. by J. E. Anderson (New York, 1972).

33. B. Croce, "La naissance de l'historisme," RevMetaMor 44 (1937), 603–21 at p. 603 (italics added).

34. Gisel, *Vérité et histoire,* pp. 62–74, especially pp. 72–74. See the more precise definition given by J. H. Walgrave, *Newman the Theologian,* tr. by A. V. Littledale (New York, 1960), p. 82: "Historicism is the claim to deal exhaustively with all intellectual problems by the study of their history."

35. *De la connaissance historique* (Paris, 1954), pp. 222–23. [I have translated directly from Marrou's French text instead of using the English version, *The Meaning of History,* tr. by R. J. Olsen (Baltimore, 1966), p. 231.—Tr.]

36. I am alluding here to the fruitful distinction introduced by Blondel between history as reality and history as science; the main point of this distinction has been taken over by H. Marrou.

37. Quite recently, B. Welte has proposed to revitalize christology by highlighting the "events" or "facts" related in the gospels; cf. *Jesus Christus und die Theologie* (Freiburg, 1977), pp. 151–54. But once again we must ask: What is meant by "facts"? And is it possible simply to *replace* metaphysical categories with categories referring to events? If we think a little more deeply about events and their *meaning,* we will necessarily raise the further question of the ultimate identity of the persons involved.

38. Gisel, *Vérité et histoire,* p. 62.

39. Chr. Théobald, art. cit. (n. 3, above), p. 41.

40. On this subject of the criticisms offered by Blondel (n. 27, above) and many recent students in regard to the limitations of the critical historical method. I shall cite only one of the most recent: E. Biser, "Postkarte genügt nicht! Auf der Suche nach Alternativen zur historisch-kritischen Methode," in J. Sauer (ed.), *Mehrdimensionale Schriftauslegung?* (Karlsruhe, 1977), pp. 9–34. Cf. also this statement of Ch. Pietri, "Henri-Irénée Marrou. In Memoriam," *Communio* 2/4 (1977), 90–96 at p. 93: "The epistemological difficulties in which 'critical historical exegesis' often finds itself floundering are due in part to the positivist type of history whose epitaph was written by H. Marrou." For the philosophical presuppositions of this approach cf. X. Tilliette's lecture at Rome, May 8, 1979: "The Jesus of History and the Christ of Faith in the Light of Philosophical Christology."

41. Cf. J.-M. Beaude, *Jésus oublié. Les évangiles et nous* (Paris, 1977).

42. Cited by G. Morel, *Problèmes actuels de la théologie* (Paris, 1968), pp. 149–50. The text is from Hegel's *Philosophy of Religion.*

43. Hegel, *The Phenomenology of Mind,* tr. by J. Baillie (2nd ed.; New York, 1949), p. 81. Here is the German text (extended a bit further than the passage quoted in English): "Das Wahre ist das Ganze. Das Ganze aber ist nur das durch seine Entwicklung sich vollendende Wesen. Es ist von dem Absoluten zu sagen, dass es wesentlich *Resultat,* dass es erst am *Ende* das ist, was es in Wahrheit ist; und hierin eben besteht seine Natur, Wirkliches, Subjekt oder Sichselbstwerden zu sein ist": *Die Phänomenologie des Geistes,* Vorrede, ed. by J. Hoffmeister (Hamburg, 1952), p. 21.

44. Tr. by J. Baillie, p. 81. German test: "(Das Wahre) ist das Werden seiner selbst, der Kreis, der sine Ende als seinen Zweck voraussetzt und zum Anfange hat und nur die Ausführung und seine Ende wirklich ist" (ed. Hoffmeister, p. 20) Cf. A. Gilliéron, review of F. Guibal, *Dieu selon Hegel* (Paris, 1975), in RThPh 27 (1977), 169: "There is no . . . truth that is not in movement, that has not undergone a process of becoming, and that is not accompanied by a consciousness of this truth."

45. Cf. Hegel, *Leçons sur Platon,* an unpublished text of 1825–26, edited, trans-

lated and annotated by J. L. Vieillard-Baron (Paris, 1976), and R. Scherer's review in RThPh 27 (1977), 260.

46. E. Brito, "Le Modèle hégélien des christologies contemporaines," *Communio* 2/2 (1977), 84–92, at p. 87.

47. Gisel, *Vérité et histoire,* p. 645; but he too expresses some reservations.

48. Cf. also P. Chapelle, "Hegel et la théologie catholique," in *Hegel et la théologie contemporaine* (n. 6, above), pp. 205–18, and C.-J. Pinto de Oliveria, ibid., pp. 229–54.

49. J. Lacroix, *The Meaning of Modern Atheism,* tr. by G. Barden (New York, 1965), p. 39.

50. In *Karl Marx: Selected Writings,* ed. by D. McLellan (New York, 1977), p. 156. German text in *Die Frühschriften,* ed. by S. Landshut (Stuttgart, 1953), p. 339: "In der Praxis muss der Mensch die Wahrheit, i.e. die Wirklichkeit und Macht, Diesseitigkeit seines Denkens beweisen."

51. Lacroix, op. cit., p. 39.

52. As W. Pannenberg has correctly observed, the contemporary mind is shaped by the "subjectivization of truth"; cf. *Basic Questions in Theology,* tr. by G. H. Kehm, 2 (Philadelphia, 1971), pp. 1–27 at p. 13.

53. M. F. Sciacca, *L'interiorità oggettiva,* in *Opere* 1 (Milan, 1965⁵), p. 20: "Pensiero e verità s'identificano nell'immanenza assoluta della verità nel pensiero e del pensiero nella verità." One of Sciacca's most important ideas was that we are faced today with two radically opposed conceptions of interiority: that of modern subjectivism ("subjective interiority"), for which truth is created by the subject's activity, and that of Christian spiritualism ("objective interiority"), for which interiority is an experience of truth, an interior presence of objective truth in the human mind. According to Sciacca, one of the most important tasks of Christian thinkers today is to recover the authentic notion of interiority; cf. *Dalla spiritualismo critico allo spiritualismo cristiano,* II (*Opere* 24;Milan, 1965), p. 307. I shall return to the idea of objective interiority in the fourth part of this essay.

54. Cf. his only book, *Der Einzige und sein Eigenthum* (Leipzig, 1845). [The book was translated into English in 1907 by S. T. Byington as *The Ego and His Own,* but the translation was not available to me.—Tr.]

55. Cf. H. Arvon, *Aux sources de l'existentialisme: Max Stirner* (Paris, 1954); G. Penzo, *Max Stirner: La rivolta esistenziale* (Turin, 1971). I draw my information directly from Penzo's book.

56. Cf. A. Plebe, "Max Stirner e le origini dell'anarchismo," in *Anarchismo vecchio e nuovo* (Florence, 1971), pp. 11–25.

57. Cf. Penzo, op. cit., pp. 169–75: "Egoismo e verità.

58. *Der Einzige . . . ,* p. 415; cf. Penzo, op. cit., p. 171, n. 17.

59. "Wahr ist, was mein ist, unwahr das, dem Ich eigen bin," ibid., p. 416; Penzo, op. cit., p. 173, n. 21.

60. Ibid.: "Ich bin das Kriterium der Wahrheit"; Penzo, op. cit., p. 173, n. 24. At this point we are not far from Nietzsche who identifies truth with the will to power; cf. *The Will to Power,* tr. by W. Kaufmann and R. J. Hollingdale (New York, 1967), p. 290, no. 534: "The criterion of truth resides in the enhancement of the feeling of power." And cf. the commentary of J. Granier, *Le problème de la vérité dans la philosophie de Nietzsche* (Paris, 1966), pp. 494ff.

61. Penzo, op. cit., pp. 336–55: "Critica interna alla filosofia stirneriana."

62. W. Barrett says: "One great achievement of existential philosophy has been a new interpretation of the idea of truth in order to point out that there are different

kinds of truth, where a rigid scientific rationalism has postulated but one kind of objective scientific truth." Cited in P. Edwards, "Kierkegaard and the 'Truth' of Christianity," *Philosophy* 46 (April, 1971), 89–108 at p. 89.

63. Penzo, op. cit., pp. 344–47.

64. Penzo, ibid., p. 348: "This is the basis for concluding that Stirnerian self-centeredness is a new form of idealism; that is the conclusion reached by Engels and Marx, although by way of quite different reflections."

65. Cf. N. Viallaneix, *Kierkegaard. L'Unique devant Dieu* (Horizon philosophique; Paris, 1974). Note that "the individual" or "the unique one" also occurs as part of the German title of Stirner's book, n. 54, above.

66. S. Kierkegaard, *Training in Christianity*, tr. by W. Lowrie (London, 1941), p. 201.

67. Cf. L. Malevez, "Subjectivisme et vérité dans Kierkegaard et dans la théologie chrétienne," in *Mélanges Joseph Maréchal* 2 (Brussels—Paris, 1950), 408–23. Cf. also H. Bouillard, "La foi d'après Kierkegaard," BLE (48 (1947), 18–30, and J. Collins, *The Mind of Kierkegaard* (Chicago, 1953), pp. 137–45: "Truth and Existence."

68. *Concluding Philosophical Postscript*, tr. by D. F. Swenson and W. Lowrie (Princeton, 1941), p. 181.

69. Ibid., pp. 179–80.

70. Cf. Malevez, art. cit., pp. 409–11, who cites as representatives of this interpretation: J. Wahl (1938), W. Perpeet (1939), M. De Waelhens (1940), and A.-D. Sertillanges (1941).

71. Cf. Collins, op. cit., p. 142.

72. Cf. the authors named in n. 67, and Viallaneix, op. cit.

73. Bouillard, art. cit., p. 21.

74. Malevez, art. cit., p. 416.

75. Bouillard, art. cit., p. 23; cf. Collins, op. cit., p. 141.

76. Cf. the general conclusion of my book *La vérité dans Saint Jean* (n. 5, above, 2:1023–57).

77. The linking of "mystery" and "truth" is especially characteristic of the apocalyptic tradition; cf. e.g., Tb 12:11 (S); Wis 6:22; the *Hymns* from Qumran, 1QH XI, 7–10: "Thou hast made known to them Thy secret of truth and given them understanding of all Thy marvelous mysteries" (in A. Dupont-Sommer, *The Essene Writings from Qumran*, tr. by G. Vermès [London, 1961]), p. 237.

78. Cf. above, p. 87.

78a. Abbott, p. 112 (italics added).

79. This formula ("the truth of the facts") comes to us from the historiography and juridicial language of the Greeks; cf., e.g., Thucydides, *De Bello Pelop.* II, 41, 2. 4: *(tōn) ergōn (hē) alētheia;* Demosthenes, *Contra Aphobos* III, 5: *tēn alētheian tōn pragmatōn;* Josephus, *Contra Apionem* I, 217: *tēn men alētheian tōn pragmatōn.*

80. J. Lacroix, *Histoire et vérité* (Tournai, 1962), p. 7: "Mystery is what opens up the temporal realm and gives it depth; it introduces a vertical dimension into the temporal order and makes the latter a time of revelation and manifestation."

81. For a detailed exegesis of this verse I refer the reader to my *La vérité dans Saint Jean* 1:158–69.

8la. *Decree on the Missionary Activity of the Church*, no. 8 (Abbott, pp. 594–95).

82. There are several instances of this traditional use of the word "truth" in liturgical and conciliar texts; cf. *La vérité dans Saint Jean* 2:1041–45 and 1055.

83. Cf. above, n. 77.

84. Cf. Dan 10:21: "But I will tell you what is inscribed in *the book of truth.*" The mystery is to be revealed to human beings; this book of God's truth is the book of predestination.

85. The expression already occurs in Ps 30[31]:6 of the LXX: "Lord God of truth, you set me free (*elutrōsō me, Kurie ho Theos tēs alētheias*)," and then frequently in early Christian texts: *Ascension of Isaiah* 6, 8; *Acts of Thomas* 25; *Apostolic Constitutions* V, 3; XIII, 13. 15; XIV, 1; etc. Cf. *La vérité dans Saint Jean* 1:32–34.

86. The expression "the Father of truth" quickly became a favorite of the gnostics; this probably explains why it was avoided in Christian circles. Cf. *La vérité dans Saint Jean* 1:35 and n. 30.

87. Cf. in the Neo-vulgate: Ps 24:5; 25:3; 29:10; 35:6; 39:11–12; 42:3; 53:7; etc.

88. Cf. J. Deshusses, *Le Sacramentaire Grégorien: Ses formes principales d'après les plus anciens manscrits* (Spicilegium Friburgense 16; Fribourg, 1971), p. 481: "Orationes matutinales," no. 1498 (this prayer is from the early Gelasian Sacramentary).

89. Cf. in the Book of Wisdom the contrast between the eschatological situation of the just (they *"will understand truth,"* 3:9) and that of the wicked ("they will see the end of the wise man, and *will not understand what the Lord purposed for him,"* 4:17).

90. Cf. above, p. 88.

91. Cf. G. Chantraine, *Vraie et fausse liberté du théologien* (Paris, 1969), p. 98: "Insofar as it is completely original and utterly unique, the historicity of Jesus eludes simple historical testimony. It is the provinces of witnesses who know it in what is special to it . . .; it is mediated only through the testimony of the apostles."

92. Vatican Council II, *Constitution on Divine Revelation,* no. 4 (Abbott, p. 113).

93. Cf. above, n. 89.

94. This is a better translation than the one in the Vulgate, which has: "He will teach you all truth (*docebit vos omnen veritatem*)"; the Neo-Vulgate is more accurate: "He will guide you into all the truth (*deducet vos in omnem veritatem*)."

95. *Adversus Praxean* 2, 1; 30, 5 (CCL 2:1160 and 1204).

95a. No. 8 (Abbot, p. 116).

96. On this subject cf E. Brito, art. cit. (n. 46, above), especially pp. 91–92: "The limits of the Hegelian model." Cf. the same author's *Hegel et la Tâche actuelle de la christologie* (Paris—Namur, 1979), and the article of C. J. Pinto de Oliveria cited earlier (n. 7).

97. Clement of Alexandria, *Paedadogus* I, 5, 20 (SC 70:147).

98. St. Augustine, *De vera religione* 39, 72 (PL 34:154): "Noli foras ire, in teipsum redi: in interiore homine habitat veritas; et si tuam naturam mutabilem inveneris, transcende et teipsum."

99. St. Gregory the Great. *Moralia in Job* 26, 32 (PL 76:368A).

100. Ibid., 19, 17 (PL 76:106D).

101. The formula is from Nicole's *Traité de l'oraison;* cf. A. Forest, *Pascal ou l'intériorité révélante* (Paris, 1971), p. 71.

102. *Concluding Philosophical Postscript* (n. 68, above), p. 71.

103. On the "passion of the infinite" cf. above, p. 153 and n. 69. For the identification of truth and "life" cf. *Training for Christianity* (n. 66, above), p. 199: "Christ's life was the truth. . . . Christ's life upon earth, every instant of this life, was the truth"; p. 201: "Truth . . . is a *life,* as the truth was in Christ, for he was the truth." But in John 14:6 "truth" and "life" are not synonyms: "truth" is the self-

manifestation of Jesus; "life" is his own life as Son, which he desires to share with us by revealing it to us in himself (=the truth).

104. Cf. n. 53, above on M. F. Sciacca and "objective interiority."

105. Cf. N. H. Giao. *Le Verbe dans l'histoire. La philosophie de l'Historicité du P. Gaston Fessard,* with a preface by J. Ladrière (Paris, 1974). Cf. the review by M. Corvez, RT 77 (1977), 677–78, which gives an accurate summation of Fessard's aim: "The movement of the Concept according to Hegel, the movement of Faith according to Kierkegaard, and the movement of History according to Marx must combine to effect a symbolic understanding of the human condition."

For my part, I would add two further dimensions as being equally necessary for a Christian vision of truth: the movement toward the originating reality, toward Christ "who was in the beginning," and the movement toward the Transcendant, toward God, to whom we are led by him who is "the way."

106. Preface to the book by N. H. Giao cited in n. 105.

Chapter 7

1. A. Schweitzer, *Von Reimarus zu Wrede* (Tübingen, 1906); English tr. by W. Montgomery, *The Quest of the Historical Jesus* (London, 1910).

2. M. Dibelius, *Die Formgeschichte des Evangeliums* (Tübingen 1919; 1933²); English tr. by B. L. Woolf, *From Tradition to Gospel* (London, 1934). K.-L. Schmidt, *Die Rahmen der Geschichte Jesu* (Berlin, 1919). R. Bultmann, *Die Geschichte der synoptischen Tradition* (Göttingen, 1921; 1931²); English tr. by J. Marsh, *The History of the Synoptic Tradition* (Oxford, 1963).

3. Schweitzer, op. cit.

4. E. Renan, *La vie de Jésus* (Paris, 1863); English tr. by C. E. Wilbour, *The Life of Jesus* (London, 1864).

5. *Die Predigt vom Reiche Gottes* (Göttingen, 1892); English tr. by R. H. Hiers and D. L. Holland, *Jesus' Proclamation of the Kingdom of God* (Philadelphia, 1971).

6. *Leben Jesu* (Tübingen, 1835–36); English tr. by G. Eliot, *The Life of Jesus Critically Examined* (London, 1846); reissued: Philadelphia, 1972.

7. *Der sogennante historische Jesus und der geschichtliche, biblische Christus* (Leipzig, 1892); English tr. by C. E. Braaten, *The So-called Historical Jesus and the Historic, Biblical Christ* (Philadelphia, 1964).

8. This school is connected with the names of R. Reitzenstein and W. Bousset. The results of their researches are given in C. Clemen, *Religionsgeschichtliche Erklärung des Neuen Testaments* (Berlin, 1924).

9. In addition to this classical book named above in n. 2, Bultmann has given a synthesis of his method in his *Die Erforschung der Synoptischen Evangelien* (Berlin, 1925). There is an Italian translation of this book, *Storia dei Vangeli Sinottici* (Bologna, 1969) to which reference will be made in subsequent notes.

10. One of the first was V. Taylor, who in 1933 launched a more moderate type of form criticism in his *The Formation of the Gospel Tradition*

10a. No. 19 (Abbott, p. 124).

11. Perrin did not invent these criteria; some of them are already to be found in Bultmann and Dibelius, but Perrin was the first to codify them with greater precision in his *Rediscovering the Teaching of Jesus* (London, 1967), pp. 39–49.

12. Cf. R. Bultmann, *Jesus and the Word,* tr by T. P. Smith and C. H. Lantero

(New York, 1934), p. 173: "But there can be no doubt that Jesus did the kind of deeds which were miracles to his mind and to the minds of his contemporaries, that is, deeds which were attributed to the supernatural, divine cause; undoubtedly he healed the sick and cast out demons." L. Goppelt, *Theologie des Neuen Testaments* 1 (Göttingen, 1975), pp. 194–95, is much closer to the Catholic position.

13. *Storia dei Vangeli Sinottici,* p. 89.

14. Cf. R. H. Fuller, *The Foundations of New Testament Christology* (New York, 1965), p. 109.

15. Ibid., pp. 114–15.

16. Cf. E. Lohse, *Grundriss der neutestamentlichen Theologie* (Stuttgart, 1964), p. 49.

17. Cf. R. Bultmann, *Theology of the New Testament,* tr. by K. Grobel, 1 (New York, 1951), pp. 26–32.

18. "The Problem of the Historical Jesus," in his *Essays on New Testament Themes,* tr. by W. J. Montague (London, 1964), pp. 15–47.

19. Bultman deals with the problem at length in his *Das Verhältnis der urchristlichen Botschaft zum historischen Jesus* (Heidelberg, 1960).

20. *Jesus Christ and Mythology* (New York, 1958), pp. 35–36.

21. *The Communion of the Christian with God,* tr. by J. S. Stanyon and R. W. Stewart (Philadelphia, 1971), pp. 224–26.

22. Op. cit., p. 60.

23. For the explanations offered by the rationalists cf. Schweitzer, *The Quest . . .,* pp. 48–67.

24. Cf. Strauss, *The Life of Jesus Critically Examined,* pp. 86–87.

25. *Jesus,* tr. by C. B. Hedrick and F. C. Grant (Philadelphia, 1949), pp. 79 and 82.

26. Bultmann, *Storia dei Vangeli Sinottici,* pp. 54–56.

27. "Bultmann Replies to His Critics," in H. W. Bartsch (ed.), *Kerygma and Myth: A Theological Debate,* tr. by R. H. Fuller (rev. ed.; New York, 1961), p. 199.

28. Ibid., p. 211.

29. Willi Marxsen, "The Resurrection of Jesus as a Historical and Theological Problem" (tr. by D. M. Barton), in C. F. D. Moule (ed.), *The Significance of the Message of the Resurrection for Faith in Jesus Christ* (Studies in Biblical Theology, Second Series, 8; Naperville, Ill., 1969), pp. 37–38.

30. Bultmann, *Theology of the New Testament,* 1:130. On this problem cf. P. Grech, "L'inno Christologico di Col 1 e la gnosi," in *La Cristologia di S. Paolo* (Atti XXIII Settimana A.B.I.; Brescia, 1976), pp. 81–96.

31. Bultmann, *Jesus Christ and Mythology,* pp. 16–17.

32. Weimar edition, 16:217, lines 33–34.

33. "New Testament and Mythology," in *Kerygma and Myth,* p. 41.

34. Ibid., p. 44.

35. G. Ebeling, *Theology and Proclamation: Dialogue with Bultmann,* tr. by J. Riches (Philadelphia, 1966), pp. 82ff.

36. P. van Buren, *The Secular Meaning of the Gospel* (New York, 1963).

37. F. Belo, *Lecture matérialiste de l'évangile de Marc* (Paris, 1975); English tr. by M. J. O'Connell, *A Materialist Reading of the Gospel of Mark* (Maryknoll, N.Y., 1981).

38. W. Pannenberg, *Jesus—God and Man,* tr. by L. L. Wilkens and D. A. Priebe (Philadelphia, 1968); J. Moltmann, *The Theology of Hope,* tr. by J. Leitch (New York, 1967).

39. Cf. E. H. Cousins (ed.), *Process Rheology: Basic Writings* (New York, 1971).

40. 6 (1966).

41. AAS 65 (1973), 396–408; tr. in TPS 18 (1973–74), 145–57.

42. *Die Gleichnisse Jesu* (Göttingen, 1964); English tr. by S. H. Hooke, *The Parables of Jesus* (rev. ed.; New York, 1963).

43. "Die vorösterlichen Angänge der Logientradition," in H. Ristow and K. Matthiae (eds.), *Der historische Jesu und der kergymatische Christus* (Berlin, 1961²).

44. *Exegese des Neuen Testaments* (Heidelberg, 1977), pp. 33–85.

45. Cf. also B. Gerhardsson, *The Origin of the Gospel Tradition* (Philadelphia, 1978), in which the author answers criticisms of his earlier book.

46. Society for New Testament Studies Monograph Series; Cambridge, 1974.

47. For a complete bibliography cf. L. Sabourin, *The Divine Miracles Discussed and Defended* (Rome, 1977), pp. 237–71.

48. Cf. above, nn. 12 and 25.

49. Cf. above, n. 18.

50. "Blind Alleys in the 'Jesus of History' Controversy," in his *New Testament Questions of Today,* tr. by W. J. Montague (London, 1967), pp. 23–65.

51. *The Problem of the Historical Jesus,* tr. by N. Perrin (Philadelphia, 1964).

52. *A New Quest of the Historical Jesus* (London, 1969), p. 94.

52a. Op. cit. [but this citation seems to be from the updated German edition of 1967].

53. Cf. above, n. 35. On the subject cf. also P. Grech, "La Nuova Hermeneutica: Fuchs e Ebeling," in *Esegesi ed Ermeneutica* (Atti XXI Settimana A.B.I.; Brescia, 1972), pp. 41–70.

54. For my own views on these titles cf. P. Grech "Sviluppo della Cristologia nel Nuovo Testamento," in *Problemi Attuali di Cristologia* (Rome, 1975), pp. 59–74.

55. Cf., e.g., J. A. Fitzmyer, "The Contribution of Qumran Aramaic to the Study of the New Testament," NTS 20 (1974), 382–407, against certain positions of G. Vermès.

56. Cf. above, n. 17, and the studies in *Jesus und der Menschensohn* (Freiburg, 1975).

57. *New Testament Theology* 1. *The Proclamation of Jesus,* tr. by J. Bowden (New York, 1971), pp. 272–76.

58. *Das Messiasgeheimnis in den Evangelien: Zugleich ein Beitrag zum Verständnis des Markusevangeliums* (Göttingen, 1901); English tr. by J. C. G. Greig, *The Messianic Secret* (Cambridge and London, 1971).

59. Cf., e.g., J. Jeremias, "Zur Geschichtlichkeit des Verhörs Jesu vor dem Hohen Rat," ZNW 43 (1950–51), 145–50; P. Lamarche, "Le 'blasphème' de Jésus devant le Sanhédrin," RSR 50 (1952), 74–85; D. E. Nineham, *Saint Mark* (London, 1963), on this passage.

60. C. F. D. Moule's recent *The Origin of Christology* (Cambridge, 1977), p. 35, returns to this explanation.

61. Cf. B. van Iersel, *"Der Sohn" in den synoptischen Jesusworten* (Leiden, 1961); Th. de Kruijff, *"Der Sohn des lebendigen Gottes": Ein Beitrag zur Christologie des Matthäusevangeliums* (Rome, 1962); J. Jeremias, *New Testament Theology* 1: 56–59.

62. G. Bornkamm, *Jesus of Nazareth,* tr. by I. and F. McLuskey with J. M. Robinson (New York, 1960), p. 178.

63. The first publications to make available the initial debates on the program

of demythologization are the four volumes entitled *Kerygma und Mythos*, ed. by H. W. Bartsch (Hamburg, 1948–55); other volumes followed. Bultmann gives a simple yet profound explanation of his thought in *Jesus Christ and Mythology* (New York, 1958; tr. into German in 1964). But his deepest theological thinking is to be found in the four volumes of *Glauben und Verstehen* (Tübingen, 1933–65).

64. For a bibliography cf. N. Heinrichs, *Bibliographie der Hermeneutik* (Düsseldorf, 1972).

65. This is the most fundamental of the criticisms made by P. Henning Jørgensen, *Die Bedeutung des Subjekt-Objektverhältnisses für die Theologie* (Hamburg, 1967), pp. 442–47.

66. This is the criticism made by Käsemann and Jeremias and, in general, by the other contributors to the Ristow-Matthiae volume cited in n. 43.

67. Cf. J. Macquarrie, *The Scope of Demythologizing* (New York, 1960), pp. 230–39.

68. "The Language of Scripture and Its Interpretation," *Biblical Theology Bulletin* 6 (1976), 161–76.

69. Structuralist hermeneutics lays great stress on this aspect; it is also the central thesis of Paul Ricoeur in *Ermeneutica filosofica ed ermeneutica biblica* (Brescia, 1977).

Chapter 8

1. This advent is solemnly proclaimed in, for example, the Erlangen lectures of 1821 (first text in volume 5 of the Jubilee Edition).

2. Letter to Madame Ven-Wisine of Omsk, end of February, 1854, in A. S. Dolinine, *Lettres de F. M. Dostoïevski* I, no. 61.

3. *Il Cristo dei filosofi. Atti del XXX Convegno di Gallarate* (Brescia, 1976). My contribution is on pp. 39–50 and 333–34.

4. Cf. the fine book of Father Georges Chantraine, *"Mystère" et "Philosophie du Christ" selon Erasme* (Namur—Gembloux, 1971).

5. Cf. Rudolf Haubst, *Die Christologie des Nikolaus von Kues* (Freiburg i. B., 1956).

6. The distinction was thematized by D. F. Strauss and forcefully repeated by Martin Kähler at the end of the nineteenth century.

7. For example, in *Von der Wahrheit* (Munich, 1947), p. 1052. But the formula is repeated in *Philosophical Faith and Revelation,* tr. by E. B. Ashton (New York, 1967).

8. *The Great Philosophers,* tr. by R. Manheim, 1 (New York, 1962), pp. 74–96.

9. In *The Two Sources of Religion and Morality.* See the very valuable book of Henri Gouhier, *Bergson et le Christ des Evangiles* (Paris, 1961).

10. Cf. especially the *Traité de la Nature et de la Grâce.* I call the reader's attention to the divergent interpretations given by M. Gueroult and H. Gouhier of the Oratorian's philosophical christology.

11. Cf. the final section (XXXVII) of the *Discours de métphysique.*

12. *Une énigme historique: le Vinculum substantiale d'après Leibniz et l'ébauche d'un réalisme supérieur* (Paris, 1930). Cf. pp. 73, 96, 127–30.

13. In his *Bergson et le Christ des Evangiles.*

14. Letter to Henri Oldenbourg (LXXIII).

15. *Traité Théologique-Politique* (Oeuvres Complètes de Spinoza, édition de la Pléide; Paris, 1954), p. 730.

16. In the notes of a conversation of the young Leibniz with Tschirnhaus, in Eduard Bodemann (ed.) *Die Leibniz-Handschriften zu Hannover* (Hannover, 1889), re-edited by G. Olms (Hildensheim, 1966), p. 103.

17. In a lecture at the Institut Catholique de Paris, January 19, 1977, published as "Spinoza devant le Christ," Greg 58 (1977), 221–37.

18. Letter LXXIII.

19. *Die Religion innerhalb der Grenzen der blossen Vernuft* (Königsberg, 1793); English tr., *Religion Within the Limits of Reason Alone*, by T. M. Greene and H. H. Hudson (Chicago, 1934). Kant's work appeared shortly after Fichte's *Critique of All Revelation* (*Versuch einer Kritik aller Offenbarung*).

20. *Religion*, Book II, Section One, A and B.

21. Ibid., Book II, Section One, C. Solution of difficulties.

22. That is, by leaving statutory faith to its own devices. Cf. ibid., Book III, Division One, VI ("Human skill and wisom cannot ascend so far as heaven in order itself to inspect the credentials validating the mission of the first Teacher," in Greene and Hudson, op. cit., p. 103).

23. In the sixth lecture of the *Answeisung zum seligen Lebel* (Initiation to the Blessed Life) (1806), and especially in the appendix added to these lectures (Medicus edition, V: 187–203, 279–86; I. H. Fichte edition, V: 475–91, 567–74).

24. In the edition of Fritz Medicus, V:103–308; also in the edition of I. H. Fichte, V:397–574, where the second appendix does not have numbered sections.

25. Published posthumously (1820). The title given them by I. H. Fichte is: *The Doctrine of the State* or *On the Relation of the Original State to the Kingdom of Reason* (V:369–600). Medicus uses Fichte's own formulation in the prospectus for the course: *Lectures on Various Subjects Taken from Applied Philosophy* (VI:417–625).

26. Medicus edition, VI 586 (IV:550).

27. Ibid., 565 (IV:521).

28. Ibid., 585 (IV:549).

29. Ibid., 599 (IV:569).

30. Ibid., 576 (IV:537).

31. Ibid., 581 (IV:544).

32. In the dialogue *Bruno*, Schröter ed., III:148; Cotta ed., IV:252; cf. 316 (294).

33. Ibid., 320 (V:298).

34. David Friedrich Strauss, "Hegel über die evangelische Geschichte," in his *Streitschriften zur Vertheidigung meiner Schrift über das Leben und zur Charakteristik der gegenwärtigen Theologie*, Bd. I, Heft 3 (Tübingen: C. F. Osiander, 1838), especially pp. 88–94.

35. Ibid., pp. 80–81, 93–94.

36. Jules Lequier, *Oeuvres Complètes*, ed. by J. Grenier (Neuchâtel, 1952), p. 304 n.

37. *La Philosophie et l'Esprit chrétien* I. *Autonomie essentielle et connexion indéclinable* (Paris, 1944); II. *Conditions de la symbiose seule normale et salutaire* (1946); *Exigences philosophiques du christianisme* (Paris, 1950).

38. Cf. "Le dernier chapitre de *L'Action*. Manuscrit Boutroux," edited by Henri Bouillard in *Archives de Philosophie*, January–March, 1961.

39. "Le lieu de la connaissance et de l'action dans l'être," in *L'Action* (1893, 1950), pp. 424–65.

40. In *The Idiot*, Part III, chapter 6: contemplation of the dead Christ as paint-

ed by Holbein; pp. 446–47 in the translation by David Magarshack (Baltimore: Penguin, 1955).

Chapter 9

1. "Current Problems in Christology," in his *Theological Investigations* 1, tr. by C. Ernst (Baltimore, 1961), pp. 149–200.

2. Cf. Henri Gouhier, *La philosophie de Malebranche et son expérience religieuse* (Paris, 1926).

3. Cf. Xavier Tilliette, *Le Christ des philosophes* (course at the Institut Catholique de Paris, 1974 and 1976).

4. Cf. Paul Evdokimov, *Le Christ dans le pensée russe* (Paris, 1970).

5. Cf. Paul Hazard, *The European Mind, 1680–1715,* tr. by J. L. May (London, 1953). Idem, *European Thought in the Eighteenth Century from Montesquieu to Lessing,* tr. by J. L. May (New Haven, 1954). Ernst Cassirer, *The Philosophy of the Enlightenment,* tr. by F. C. A. Koelin and J. P. Pettegrove (Princeton, 1951). Georges Gusdorf, *Les principes de la pensée au siècle des lumières* (Paris, 1971).

6. "Sur de motif de l'Incarnation," in H. Bouëssé and J. J. Latour (eds.), *Problèmes actuels de christologie. Trauvaux du symposium de l'Arbresle 1961* (Paris, 1965), pp. 35–80; *L'au-delà retrouvé. Christologie des fins dernières* (Paris, 1965), pp. 33–62; "Le Premier-né de toute créature. Esquisse d'une vision christologique de la création," *Communio* 3 (1976), 30–48, *Vivre aujourd'hui la foi de toujours. Relecture du Credo* (Paris, 1978), pp. 13–43.

7. Cf. Emile Benveniste, *Problèmes de linguistique générale* 1 (Paris, 1966).

8. Cf. André Leroi-Gourhan, *Le geste et la parole* (Paris, 1964), pp. 261–300.

9. The word "sphere" is meant here to assert that human development does not take place in a Euclidean two-dimensional world but has "volume," as it were, and involves a real expansion.

10. This deficiency is clearly identified but not completely overcome by Gaston Fessard in his "Le mystère de la société," RSR 35 (1948), 161–226, which appears in a revised form in Fessard's *De l'actualité historique* (Paris, 1951), p. 159–75. The article in RSR contains considerations on *generic life* and *generic being* in the light of the young Marx's thinking; I do not discuss these here, but they were in fact the remote source of what I am here calling "the generic."

11. Cf. B. Malinowski, *Sex and Repression in Savage Society* (New York, 1927), pp. 135–78.

12. Cf. Claude Lévi-Strauss, *The Elementary Structures of Kinship,* tr. by J. H. Bell, J. R. von Sturmer, and R. Needham (rev. ed.; Boston, 1969), pp. 478–98.

13. Cf. Emmanuel Levinas, *Totality and Infinity: An Essay on Exteriority,* tr. by A. Lingis (Pittsburgh, 1969); Eliane Amada Lévi-Valensi, *Les voies et les pièges de la psychanalyse* (Paris, 1970).

14. Cf. André Leroi-Gourhan, *Evolution et technique* 1. *L'homme et la matière;* 2. *Milieu et techniques* (Paris, 1971–73). For a more informal review, cf. Arnold Toynbee, *La grande aventure de l'histoire* (Paris—Brussels, 1977) pp. 46–76.

15. Cf. Claude Bruaire, *La raison politique* (Paris, 1974).

16. Cf. J. L. Talmon, *The Origins of Totalitarian Democracy* (New York, 1960).

17. Cf. Mircea Eliade, *Histoire des croyances et des idées religieuses* (Paris, 1978ff.). Two volumes have thus far appeared.

18. Cf. Paul Vernière, *Spinoza et la pensée française avant la révolution* (Paris, 1954).

19. Cf. Claude Bruaire, *Le droit de Dieu* (Paris, 1974), and the last chapter of *La raison politique* (n. 15, above).

Chapter 10

1. A. Grillmeier, "The Figure of Christ in Catholic Theology Today," in *Theology Today* 1: *Renewal in Dogma,* tr. by P. White and R. H. Kelly (Milwaukee, 1965).

2. On the other hand, the principles governing a possible christocentrism in theology generally and those governing it in fundamental theology in particular will not be heterogeneous in the final analysis. In fact, in regard to theology and to any and every theologoumenon, the person of Christ lays claim to an absoluteness which extends to both content and form.

3. I am referring to *structuration* and therefore to the effective ability of the christocentric principle to give explicit form to the discourse of fundamental theology. The correctness of our appreciation of the person of Christ and of the relations to it of the various mysteries of faith is not formally tackled here, since if it were I might find myself forced to pass judgment on the general value of any theology actually proposed.

4. Some suggestions are made in passing in H. Küng, "Christozentrik," LTK 2:1172, and in Grillmeier, art. cit., pp. 267ff.

5. Splendidly symptomatic in this area is the Dogmatic Constitution *Dei Filius* of Vatican I, which became a classical locus for fundamental theology.

6. It is as viewed from this angle that I speak of it in a context in which I am dealing strictly with fundamental theology. Any consideration that helps faith in its self-presentation is clearly relevant to the problem of credibility.

7. The criticism should not have struck people as a novelty. Rousselot's *analysis fidei,* for example, had appeared a quarter century earlier.

8. It was also, of course, a homage to the original form which revelation had taken. But there was a failure to draw the very logical conclusion that the exigencies which had emerged could be proposed as meaningful (if not strictly normative) for theology *as such* and therefore for *every* theology.

9. It is not easy to determine whether the "difficulty" was regarded as resident in the Christ-sign itself or in the arduousness of the *demonstratio catholica*. The anti-hermesian context suggests a more general perspective, but one thing is sure: that for a long time after Vatican I there would be a tendency to brand as "Protestant" any objection leveled at Catholic theology by Enlightenment thinking. The specific emphases on the "Catholic" (in the confessional sense) character of the discourse that unfolds in the last part of Chapter III of *Dei Filius* (DS, nos. 3012–14) are relevant here.

10. Cf. H. de Lubac, *Histoire et esprit. L'intelligence de l'Ecriture d'après Origène* (Paris, 1971). Idem., *Exégèse médiévale, Les quatre sens de l'Ecriture* (4 vols.; Paris, 1959–64).

11. Cf. H. Strathmann, "Die Krisis des Kanons der Kirche. Joh. Gerhards und Joh. Sal. Semlers Erbe," in E. Käsemann, ed., *Das Neue Testament als Kanon* (Göttingen, 1970), pp. 41–61. Strathmann's essay dates from 1941.

12. *Dei Verbum,* no. 18: "The Gospels have special preeminence, and rightly so" (Abbott, p. 122). Latin text: "Evangelia merito excellere."

13. Cf. the teaching on the *gratia capitis* ("the grace of [Christ] the Head"). It is difficult to imagine a theological thesis being developed with a greater disregard of the historical character of salvation. It should be noted, however, that this a-historicalness has nothing to do with the transcendence of the risen Lord ("head" of the body which is the Church) in relation to history.

14. This passage is cited in *Dei Verbum,* no. 6.

15. DS, nos. 3005, 3008, 3015.

16. See, at an earlier time, Blondel's lecture on the necessity of what is inaccessible.

17. K. Rahner, "Anthropologie," LTK 1:626. German: "Das mögliche Anderssein der Selbstentäusserung Gottes und der mögliche Bruder Christi."

18. G. Moioli, "Christocentrismo," in *Nuovo Dizionario di Teologia* (Alba, 1979), p. 218.

19. K. Rahner, "Dogmatic Reflections on the Knowledge and Self-consciousness of Christ," in his *Theological Investigations* 5, tr. by Karl-H. Kruger (Baltimore, 1966), pp. 193–215.

20. Without however believing, with incredible ignorance of history, that the conciliar text in questions represents the first opening in this direction. —The quotation is from *Dei Verbum,* no. 2 (Abbott, p. 112).

21. In using the word "analytic" (which, to tell the truth, is a bit pretentious in view of its historical connotations), I am pointing to the area of fundamental theology in which reflection on faith and revelation (and perhaps on the dynamics of tradition and scripture as mediations of revelation) is developed in the form of an analysis of the believer's act of faith. This area has often been described by the adjective "theological" (reflection, part, etc.) as distinguished from "apologetic" (where "apologetic" = rational in method and therefore pretheological). The genuinely (even if *sui generis*) theological character of apologetics itself is now taken for granted, so that the adjective "theological" is ill-adapted to indicate the specific difference marking a non-apologetic area within fundamental theology. Similarly, the adjective "dogmatic" is not very appropriate. Apart from the debatable (but now almost exclusively etymological) reference to "dogma," this adjective already distinguishes fundamental theology in its entirety from other "fundamental" areas of theology (fundamental moral theology, etc.); nor do we avoid a certain degree of kitsch when we distinguish a dogmatic fundamental theology within a fundamental dogmatic theology. As is clear from the scheme of the present article, Analysis, Apologetics, and Hermeneutics (with, perhaps, some further headings) could in my view supply the chapter headings for an effective fundamental theology.

22. It is still necessary to resist the temptation to a neutral objectivism that can become automatic for a theology "of the schools." The need is, on the one hand, not to absolutize the historical uniqueness of the individual believer, and, on the other, not to make this singularity meaningless by cultivating an abstractness that is anything but the domain of the clear and unequivocal. Cf. J. B. Metz, *Faith in History and Society: Toward a Practical Fundamental Theology,* tr. by D. Smith (New York, 1980).

23. Cf. *Mysterium Salutis. Grundriss heilsgeschichtlicher Dogmatik* 1 (Einsiedeln, 1965), pp. 919–21.

24. This is certainly *not* what Söhngen intended. But it is not a merely abstract temptation, if at least the history of the treatise *De Deo Uno* has anything to teach us. Barth's reproof cannot be idly rejected.

25. Cf. K. Rahner, "The Theology of the Symbol," in his *Theological Investiga-*

tions 4, tr. by K. Smyth (Baltimore, 1966), pp. 221–52; idem, "On the Theology of the Incarnation," ibid., pp. 105–20.

26. Cf. St. Thomas, *Summa theologiae* II–II 1. 4, a. 1.

27. The problem of tradition is only the diachronic form of the consensus as authoritatively oriented in the unidirectionality of history; in the form of this consensus revelation is transmitted to us, and, conversely, the "we" of faith reaches back to Christ. (I am obviously leaving aside here the phenomenon of Old Testament tradition, which is given to us only as something complete and historically finished.)

28. Cf. T. Citrini, "Tradizione," in *Dizionario teologico interdisciplinare* 3 (Turin, 1977), pp. 448–63.

29. I refer the reader here especially to G. Ebeling.

30. According to Luther the christological criterion is applied in a dynamic process of *urgere* (*treiben,* urge, press, compel). The scriptures "urge" Christ, but in a more radical way Christ "urges" the scriptures; adversaries "urge" the scriptures against Luther, who replies by "urging" Christ against even the scriptures. Cf. G. Gloege, "Zur Geschichte des Schriftverständnisses," in *Das Neue Testament als Kanon* (n. 11, above), pp. 13–40 (at 28–29); N. Appel, *Kanon und Kirche. Die Kanonkrise im heutigen Protestantismus als kontroverstheologisches Problem* (Paderborn, 1964), pp. 240–46.

31. Cf. K. H. Ohlig, *Woher nimmt die Bibel ihre Autorität? Zum Verhältnis von Schriftkanon, Kirche und Jesus* (Düsseldorf, 1970).

32. The point at issue in the discussion of a possible *fides ecclesiastica* should not be primarily the attitude to be taken toward the Church when it proposes themes connected with revelation, but rather the general attitude to be taken toward the ecclesial mediation of revelation itself.

33. R. Latourelle, *Christ and the Church: Signs of Salvation* (Staten Island, N.Y., 1972).

34. On this whole subject cf. T. Citrini, "La singolaritá di Cristo come chiave di volta della teologia fondamentale," ScCatt 103 (1975), 699–724.

35. Does the Old Testament pre-reveal the divine subject who then makes himself definitively known in Christ? Or does the Old Testament rather prepare the way for a revelation which, "although the law and the prophets bear witness to it," has been given "apart from the law" (cf. Rom 3:21, since, by any accounting, revelation and salvation may not be excessively compartmentalized)? And what relation does this "apartness" create between the form taken by the kerygma to the Jews and the form taken by the kerygma to the Greeks?

Chapter 11

1. On this point cf. G. Quell and J. Behm, "diathēkē," TDNT 2:106–34; C. Spicq, *L'épître aux Hébreux* 2 (Paris, 1953), pp. 262–63 (where two terms are successively used to translate *diathēkē:* "testamentary disposition" and "covenant"); *Translation Oecuménique de la Bible: Nouveau Testament,* p. 686 (where two translations are given in v. 15, with justification for the procedure in note *r:* "This is why he is mediator of a new covenant, a new testament"). The word "testament" is used again in Galatians 3:15–17, but it is clear that we cannot think that the principle of the death of a testator is being again invoked here, since the reference is to God's "disposition" in Genesis 15 and 17. In connection with all the texts cited in this essay the reader may consult the critical commentaries, which are too numerous to list here.

2. The word "economy," so often used by the Father, corresponds to the Greek *oikonomia* as used in Ephesians 3:9.

3. St. Irenaeus, *Demonstratio apostolica* 3. Irenaeus speaks elsewhere of "the rule (*kanōn*) of truth" (*Adversus haereses* I, 1, 20; II, 4, 1; III, 2, 2; III, 11, 1; etc.) Against the gnostics Irenaeus appeals above all to the "true tradition that comes from the apostles and, thanks to the presbyters, is preserved in the Church" (ibid. III, 3, 1). The New Testament books are the competent and (in the juridical sense) authentic witnesses to this foundational tradition of the faith.

4. For a summary presentation of this preaching on scripture as used in proclaiming the gospel cf. P. Grelot, *L'achèvement des Ecritures* (Introduction critique au Noveau Testament 5; Tournai—Paris, 1977), pp. 60–68, 96–100.

5. This point is developed in my "La deuxième épître de Pierre et la tradition apostolique," *L'année canonique* 23 (1979).

6. For a study of the theological terms cited here I refer the reader once and for all to the relevant articles in the TDNT.

7. I use here the major divisions adopted in my *Sens chrétien de l'Ancien Testament*, chapters 4–6. However, the material is classified somewhat differently here and is analyzed at the New Testament level rather than being organized in a systematic fashion.

8. This expression, dear to the Greek Fathers, is to be preferred to "history of salvation," which is a translation of the German *Heilsgeschichte*. Oscar Cullmann accepts the criticism of the German term in his *Salvation in History,* tr. by S. C. Sowers and the SCM staff (New York, 1967), pp. 74–78.

9. G. von Rad brings this point out very well in the conclusion of his *Old Testament Theology,* tr. by D. M. G. Stalker, 2 (New York, 1965), pp. 319–35; the body of volume 2 is devoted to "The Theology of Israel's Prophetic Traditions."

10. St. Thomas' interpretation of "the old law" in the *Summa theologiae* I–II, 98–100, is based on this distinction. On this point the reader may consult the explanatory notes and technical essays of J. Tonneau in his edition of *Saint Thomas: Somme théologique—La loi ancienne* (2 vols.; Tournai—Paris, 1971).

11. This "law of Christ" has, of course, practical consequences which St. Paul presents under the rubric of "the law of the Spirit of life" (Rom 8:2). On this point see the convergent studies of S. Lyonnet, "Liberté chrétienne et Loi de l'Esprit selon saint Paul," in *La vie de Esprit, condition du chrétien* (Unam sanctam 55: Paris, 1965), pp. 169–95, and C. H. Dodd, "Ennomos Christou" (1953), in his *More New Testament Studies* (Manchester, 1968), pp. 134–48.

12. Cf. especially Spicq, op. cit., 2:214–25, Excursus VI (with references to the commentaries on the passages); cf. 1:64–65, 282–83, 310. We should add his study of the passages that use the vocabulary of "stability" (*bebaio-ō, bebaiōsis*), which calls attention to the continuity of God's plan from the time of the promises made on oath down to their fulfillment by Christ (ibid., 1:64–66).

13. The idea of "proof," which is based on a rational understanding of the texts and an examination of them in the light of a critical study of history invaded the field of apologetics. Having acquired a presence in theology from the time when the preaching of the gospel came into contact with Greek culture, this concept has become rigid and inflexible in modern times (from the eighteenth century on). On the contrary, the "fulfillment of the scriptures" approach presupposed a prior understanding of scripture as the word of God and a reading of in the context of Jewish culture. It is to this perspective that we must return if we are to understand what is meant by the fulfillment of the scriptures, not only in the New Testament but in the

early patristic period as well, for example, in St. Justin (especially his *Dialogue with Trypho*).

14. Cf. P. Grelot, *La Bible, Parole de Dieu* (Tournai—Paris, 1965), pp. 238–44.

15. R. Bultmann, *Theology of the New Testament,* tr. by K. Grobel, 1 (New York, 1951), pp. 3–32.

16. Cf. R. Bultmann, *Foi et compréhension* (French tr. of essays from *Glauben und Verstehen*) 1:570–73: "In what sense is Old Testamental and Jewish history a prophecy that is fulfilled in the history of the New Testament community? It is such a prophecy by reason of its internal contradiction and failure" (p. 570).

17. R. Bultmann, "The Significance of the Old Testament for the Christian Faith," in B. W. Anderson (ed., *The Old Testament and Christian Faith: A Theological Discussion* (New York, 1963), p. 22.

18. Ibid., p. 23.

19. Cf. *Sens chrétien de l'Ancien Testament,* pp. 125–65.

20. Leo the Great, *Sermo 50, 2 = Sermons 3. Sermons sur la Passion,* text and tr. by R. Dolle (SC 74bis; Paris, 1976), pp. 152–53.

21. *Stromata* VI, xiii, 106, 3; cf. C. Mondésert, *Clément d'Alexandrie: Introduction à l'étude de sa pensée religieux à partir de l'Ecriture* (Théologie 4: Paris, 1944), p. 104.

22. Cf. Spicq, op. cit., 1:345–50.

23. Cf. *Sens chrétien de l'Ancien Testament,* pp. 209–47 (institutions), 286–326 (history), 363–403 (promises). In these various sections an attempt is made to formulate a theory of biblical "figures" along the lines of some suggestions in St. Thomas. The theory is summarized in *La Bible, Parole de Dieu,* pp. 265–87.

24. The basic presentations are still those of H. de Lubac, *Histoire et Esprit, L'intelligence de l'Ecriture d'après Origène* (Paris, 1950), and *Exégèse médiévale. Les quatre sens de l'Ecriture* (4 vols.; Paris, 1959–64).

25. *Enchiridion biblicum* (3rd ed.; Naples—Rome, 1956), nos. 555–59.

26. Cf. *La Bible, Parole de Dieu,* pp. 46–47, 62–71.

27. Cf. *Divino afflante Spiritu,* in *Enchiridion biblicum,* no. 567.

28. Cf. *La Bible, Parole de Dieu,* pp. 312–27 (concept of the *sensus plenior* or "fuller sense") and 367–84 (outline of a methodology).

29. We must distinguish this "theological demonstration" from the expression of faith that is based on scripture and has recourse to the "symbolic systems" which are established and used by scripture. The employment of this type of expression was traditional in the patristic period and in medieval theology. The latter connected it with what it called "the analogy of faith." There is in fact a close connection between the structure of faith in the two Testaments and the various symbolic systems which provide them with their religious language. But it is one thing to discover this universal presence of Christ under the veil of symbols in all the texts of both Testaments; it is another to show the reality of this presence as an object of revelation. The first of these two operations is a "rereading" which supposes the second.

30. Cf. P. Grelot, "L'exégèse biblique au carrefour," NRT 108 (1976), 416–34 and 481–511. The first part of this study examines three examples from the past; the second looks at the problems of the present time, without making any claim to solve them.

Chapter 12

1. T. Pröpper, *Jésus: Raison et foi. Théologiens et philosophes dans le débat christologique contemporain* (tr. from the German; Collection Jésus et Jésus-Christ; Paris, 1978) presents seven contemporary readings of the person of Jesus from non-Christian points of view: the existential philosophy of K. Jaspers; E. Bloch's philosophy of hope; the Marxist critique of ideologies as given by L. Kolakowski, V. Gardavski, and M. Machovec; E. Fromm's application of Freudian psychoanalytic theory; rabbinic Judaism as represented by S. Ben-Chorin. Cf. also M. Machovec, *A Marxist Looks at Jesus* (Philadelphia, 1976).

2. R. Bultmann, *Das Verhältnis der urchristlichen Botschaft zum historischen Jesus* (Abhandlungen der Heidelberger Akademie der Wissenschaften, Phil-Hist. Klasse, H. 3; Heidelberg, 1960), p. 11: "The chief hindrance felt by anyone attempting to reconstruct the moral portrait of Jesus is the fact that we have no way of knowing how Jesus understood his end, his death. . . . Did he find a meaning in it? If so, what was this meaning? We have no way of knowing."

3. R. Bultmann, *The History of the Synoptic Tradition,* tr. by J. Marsh (Oxford, 1963), p. 247.

4. R. Bultmann, *The Theology of the New Testament,* tr. by K. Grobel, 1 (New York, 1951), p. 43.

5. H. Conzelmann, *An Outline of the Theology of the New Testament,* tr. by J. Bowden (New York, 1969), p. 127: "All parts of Jesus' teaching are stamped with an indirect christology. Jesus does not teach expressly who he is, but he acts in his proclamation as one who opens up immediacy to God in every relationship. After his death, this indirect christology is transposed into the direct christology of the community's faith."

6. R. Bultmann, *Jesus Christ and Mythology* (New York, 1958), p. 84: "De-mythologizing is the radical application of the doctrine of justification by faith to the sphere of knowledge and thought. . . . There is no difference between security based on good works and security based on objectifying knowledge."

7. H. Schürmann, *Comment Jésus a-t-il véca sa mort* (Lectio divina 93; Paris 1977), p. 64. This book is a translation of *Jesu ureigener Tod* (Leipzig, 1975).

8. Ibid., p. 32, n. 39a.

9. Ibid., pp. 29–30.

10. H. Schürmann, "L'herméneutique de la prédication de Jésus," in R. Schnackenburg et al., *Le message de Jésus et l'interprétation moderne* (Cogitatio fidei 37; Paris, 1969), pp. 140–43. This book is a translation of *Gott in Welt. Festgabe für Karl Rahner* (Freiburg, 1964), where Schürmann's essay appears in 1:579–607.

11. H. Schürmann, *Traditionsgeschichtliche Untersuchungen zu den synoptischen Evangelien: Beiträge* (Düsseldorf, 1969), pp. 137–49.

12. H. Schürmann, *Le récit de la derniére Céne* (Lyons—Le Puy, 1966). This is a translation of *Der Abendmahlsbericht Lucas 22, 7–38* (Leipzig, 1955, 1967⁴).

13. H. Schürmann, *Comment Jésus a-t-il vécu sa mort?,* pp. 63, 78.

14. J. Dupont, "Les pèlerins d'Emmaüs," in *Miscellanea Biblica B. Ubach* (Monserrat, 1953), pp. 349–74.

15. Schürmann, *Comment Jésus a-t-il vécu sa mort?,* pp. 59–63.

16. X. Léon-Dufour, "Jésus devant sa mort à la lumière des textes de l'Institution eucharistique et des discours d'adieu," in J. Dupont (ed.), *Jésus aux origines de la christologie* (Journées bibliques de Louvain, 1974; Gembloux, 1975), pp. 141–68.

17. O. de Dinechin, "La similitude dans l'évangile selon saint Jean," RSR 58 (1970), 195–236.

Chapter 13

1. A very good summary of these conclusions is available in the recent collective volume edited by E. Dhanis, *"Resurrexit"*: *Actes du symposium international sur la Résurrection de Jésus (Rome 1970)* (Vatican City, 1974). I shall refer to this book simply as *Resurrexit.* In attempting my own synthesis I have kept constantly in mind the contributions and proposals made in *Resurrexit;* my work is also inspired by the grateful remembrances of the very kindly organizer of the symposium, Father E. Dhanis, and of other participants in it who have since departed from our midst, especially Josef Blinzler, Donatien Mollat, and Joachim Jeremias.

2. It will not be possible to supply an extensive bibliography. I refer the reader to my "Bibliografia sulla risurrezione di Gesù (1920–1973)," in *Resurrexit,* pp. 645–764, and its continuation, "Aggiornamento della bibliografia," in RBibIt 23 (1975), 424–40. I refer the reader also to two surveys of mine: RBibIt 17 (1969), 393–419 (discussion of the empty tomb); 23 (1975), and 24 (1976), 57–93 (the Acts of the symposium and the subsequent discussion). Finally, there is my "Testimonianze sulla risurrezione di Gesù," in the collective volume, *Il Messagio della Salvezza,* VI (Turin—Leumann, 1979), pp. 382–424.

3. Soon to be published in the *Scienze bibliche* series of the Editrice Queriniana.

4. Cf. G. Segalla, "Cristologia del Nuovo Testamento," in G. Segalla, R. Cantalamessa and G. Moioi, *Il problema cristologico oggi* (Assisi, 1973), pp. 13–142.

5. Cf. K. Rahner and W. Thüsing, *Cristologia. Prospettiva sistematica ed esegetica* (Brescia, 1974); W. Thüsing, *Erhöhung-Vorstellung und Parusie-Erwartung in der ältesten nachösterlichen Christologie* (Stuttgart, 1969).

6. I shall mention only R. Güttegemanns, " 'Text' und 'Geschichte' als Grundkategorien der generativen Poetik. Thesen zur aktuellen Diskussion um die 'Wirklichkeit' der Auferstehung," *Linguistica Biblica* 2 (1972), nos. 11–12, pp. 2–12; J. van der Veken, "Theologische Sprachlogik der Auferstehungsverkündigung," *Forum Theol. Linguisticae* 3 (1972), 176–96; D. Minguez, *Pentecostés. Ensayo de Semiótica narrativa en E(e)ch(os) 2* (Rome, 1975).

7. Y. M. -J. Congar, *Situation et tâches présentes de la théologie* (Paris, 1967), p. 71.

8. In addition to the scholars who have dealt with the general problem (M. Dibelius, P. Vielhauer, U. Wilckens, J. Dupont, and others) I may mention the following on the problem of the resurrection: H. Braun, "Zur Terminologie der Acta von der Auferstehung Jesu," TLZ 77 (1952), 533–36; I. H. Marshall, "The Resurrection in the Acts of the Apostles," in W. Gasque (ed.), *Apostolic History and the Gospels* (Exeter, 1970), pp. 91–107.

9. We need only compare the use made of it in Romans 1:4; 4:24–25; 6:4, 9; 7:4; 8:11, 34; 10:9.

10. Cf. G. Ghiberti, *I racconti pasquali del cap. 20 di Giovanni confrontati con le altre tradizioni neotestamentarie* (Brescia, 1972), pp. 79–99.

11. Cf. E. Lohmeyer, "Mir ist gegeben alle Gewalt. Eine Exegese von Mt. 28, 16–20," in *In Memoriam Ernst Lohmeyer* (Stuttgart, 1951), pp. 22–49.

12. Cf. M. Albertz, "Zur Formgeschichte der Auferstehungsberichte," ZNT 21 (1922), 259–69; C. H. Dodd, "the Appearances of the Risen Christ," in his *Studies in the Gospels* (Oxford, 1955), pp. 9–35.

13. The question of methodology is treated in A. Vögtle, "Ekklesiologische Auftragsworte des Auferstandenen," in J. Coppens et al. (eds.), *Sacra Pagina: Mis-*

cellanea Biblica Congressus Internationalis Catholici de Re Biblica (2 vols.; Gembloux, 1959), 2:280–94.

14. Cf. J. Jeremias, *New Testament Theology* 1. *The Proclamation of Jesus,* tr. by J. Bowden (New York, 1971), pp. 276–99; J. Guillet, *The Consciousness of Jesus,* tr. by E. Bonin (New York, 1972), pp. 140–60. Within the general discussion special interest attaches to the meaning of the Last Supper: cf. E. Dhanis, "La résurrection de Jésus et l'histoire. Un mystère éclairant," in *Resurrexit,* pp. 555–641 (especially 586–97); R. Pesch, "Das Abendmahl und Jesu Todesverständnis," in K. Kertelge (ed.), *Der Tod Jesu. Deutungen im Neuen Testament* (Freiburg, 1976), pp. 137–87.

15. J. Comblin, *Le Christ dans l'Apocalypse* (Tournai, 1965), p. 73.

16. Cf. J. Dupont, " 'Assis à droite de Dieu.' L'interprétation du ps. 110, 1 dans le Nouveau Testament," in *Resurrexit,* pp. 340–422.

17. Cf. G. Lohfink, *Die Himmelfahrt Jesu. Untersuchungen zu Himmelsfahrtsund Erhöhungstexten bei Lukas* (Munich, 1971).

18. In addition to the accounts of the institution of the Eucharist at the Last Supper cf. John 20:22; Romans 8:19–25.

19. S. Tromp, *De revelatione christiana* (Rome, 1950[6]), p. 273, provides a substantial list of patristic apologetic (and polemical) treatises on the resurrection. In his own treatment of the objections (including modern ones) raised against the resurrection he notes how often they are theories already present in the discussion which Origen (*Contra Celsum*), Justin (*Dialogus cum Tryphone*) and even the gospels reflect.

20. Cf. the reproach in Mark 16:14 (a tradition which does not seem to derive from the other gospels).

21. This is somewhat true of the entire gospel presentation, but evidently it is especially true of John. I have tried to show this in my article "Giovanni" in *Dizionario teologico interdisciplinare* 2 (Turin, 1979), pp. 218–35.

21a. Cf. G. Ghiberti, "Il dono dello Spirito e i poteri di Giov. 20, 21–23," in the collective volume *Segni e Sacramenti nel Vangelo di Giovanni* (Rome, 1977), pp. 183–220.

22. A valuable demonstration of this on the basis of the general state of Judaism is given by K. Schubert, " 'Auferstehung Jesu' im Lichte der Religionsgeschichte des Judentums," in *Resurrexit,* pp. 209–29.

23. Meanwhile it will be necessary, as a rule, to give up any claim of identifying particular passages for the New Testament argument from the scriptures. It seems that in the beginning there was a global persuasion that the experience of Jesus corresponded to the Father's plan and therefore in a general way to the scriptures; only gradually was attention focused on particular passages.

24. For a quick survey of the discussion of the "historical Jesus" cf. G. Ghiberti, "Gesù della storia, Cristo della fede," *Par* VI 20 (1975), 45–72.

25. Cf. the works of W. Marxsen, K. Berger, U. Wilckens, R. Pesch, and X. Léon-Dufour (cf. nn. 28, 37, 39, and 43, below).

26. I refer the reader to my 1969 survey (n. 2, above), especially in connection with the works of L. Schenke, P. Seidensticker, and others. Some more recent publications: E. Bode, *The First Easter Morning: The Gospel Accounts of the Women's Visit to the Tomb of Jesus* (Rome, 1970); J. Broer, *Die Urgemeinde und das Grab Jesu. Eine Analyse der Grablegungsgeschichte im Neuen Testament* (Munich, 1972).

An up-to-date and balanced discussion is provided in J. Kremer, "Zur Diskussion über 'das leere Grab,' " in *Resurrexit,* pp. 137–59.

27. The interpretation of Mark 16:1–8 as being the fruit of a cultic *Sitz im Leben* was proposed by G. Schille, "Das Leiden des Herrn," ZTK 52 (1953), 161–205, and developed further by L. Schenke, *Auferstehungtsverkündigung und leeres Grab. Eine traditionsgeschichtliche Untersuchung von Mk 16, 1–8* (Stuttgart, 1968). It was as a result of Schenke's study that the theory became widely known.

28. Some well-known supporters of the theory that the appearances are *Legitimationsformeln* are: W. Marxsen, *The Resurrection of Jesus of Nazareth,* tr. by M. Kohl (Philadelphia, 1970), cf. chapter 4; U. Wilckens, *Resurrection. Biblical Testimony to the Resurrection: An Historical Examination and Explanation,* tr. by A. M. Steward (Atlanta, 1978), cf. p. 13; R. Pesch (cf. n. 37, below).

29. E. Hirsch, *Die Auferstehungsgeschichten und der christliche Glaube* (Tübingen, 1940), pp. 8, 15, 33.

30. W. Michaelis, *Die Erscheinungen des Auferstandenen* (Basel, 1944); cf. idem, "horaō," TDNT 5:355–61.

31. K. Barth, *Rudolf Bultmann, ein Versuch, ihn zu verstehen* (Zürich, 1952), p. 33.

32. Marxsen, op. cit., pp. 109–11; the quotation is from p. 111.

33. Cf. B. Spörlein, *Die Leugnung der Auferstehung. Eine historisch-kritische Untersuchung zu 1 Kor 15* (Regensburg, 1971), pp. 51–63.

34. A. Pelletier, "Les apparitions du Ressuscité en terms de la Septante," Bib 51 (1970), 76–79.

35. K. H. Rengstorf, *Die Auferstehung Jesu. Form, Art und Sinn der urchristlichen Osterbotschaft* (Witten/Rhur, 1967), pp. 24–25.

36. H. Schlier, "Die Anfänge des christologischen Credo," in the collective volume, *Zur Frühgeschichte der Christologie* (Freiburg, 1970), pp. 37–38.

37. R. Pesch, "Zur Entstehung des Glaubens an die Auferstehung Jesu. Ein Vorschlag zur Diskussion," TQ 153 (1973), 201–28.

38. He cites especially his own teacher, A. Kolping. In a later comment however, Kolping does not accept this interpretation of himself, though he does favor Pesch's views; cf. A. Kolping, "Zur Entstehung des Glaubens an die Auferstehung Jesu," MTZ 26 (1975), 56–69.

39. K. Berger, *Die Auferstehung des Propheten und die Erhöhung des Menschensohnes. Traditionsgeschichtliche Untersuchung zur Deutung des Geschickes Jesu in frühchristlichen Texten* (Göttingen, 1976). This study had already been completed in 1968, and Wilckens and Pesch were inspired by it, as they themselves acknolwedge.

40. On this point Pesch refers the reader to his book (written in collaboration with H. A. Zwergel), *Kontinuität in Jesus. Zugänge zu Leben, Tod und Auferstehung* (Freiburg, 1974).

41. The issue of TQ in which Pesch's interpretation appeared contains the comments of K. H. Schelkle, P. Stuhlmacher, ana M. Hengel (exegetes), and of W. Kaiser and H. Küng (systematic theology). Some other comments are reported in the survey (n. 2, above) in RBiblIt 24 (1976), 87–88.

42. J. Guitton, "Epistémologie de la résurrection, Conecpts préalables et programmes de recherches," in *Resurrexit,* pp. 108–31.

43. X. Léon-Dufour, *Resurrection and the Message of Easter,* tr. by R. N. Wilson (New York, 1974); the quotations are from pp. 239–40. The discussion is documented in RBiblIt 24 (1976), 59–61.

44. This statement is made in a sense contrary to the thesis of R. Pesch, dis-

cussed above; its meaning is rather the one given by H. Schürmann, in his *La tradizione dei detti di Gesù* (Brescia, 1966).

45. John explicitly calls for an acceptance that is mediated by a qualified witness (20:24–29). Luke speaks of witnessing as a commission given by Jesus to the apostles with regard to "these things" (Lk 24:48) that are contained in the message of the kerygma and derive their meaning from the resurrection. The other evangelists have no explicit passages on this theme, but the connection between the resurrection, the confirmation of the mission received from the Father, and the consequent obligation to communicate the message suggests that this obligation is basic and required so that all peoples may know the messenger of salvation who has been raised up by God.

Chapter 14

1. Vatican I, Dogmatic Constitution *Dei Filius,* chapter 3 (DS, no. 3009).

2. Ibid. (DS, no. 3013).

3. J. H. Newman, *Essay in Aid of a Grammar of Assent* (Doubleday Image ed.; Garden City, N. Y., 1955), p. 229

4. Ibid., p. 330.

5. Ibid., p. 90.

6. D. Hume, Essay on Miracles," quoted by Newman, *Grammar,* p. 243.

7. Barth's opposition to apologetics, very sharp in his "dialectical" period, was moderated in his later study of Anselm and in his *Church Dogmatics* 2/1. See A. Dulles, *A History of Apologetics* (London and Philadelphia, 1971), p. 232.

8. K. Barth, *Protestant Theology in the Nineteenth Century,* tr. (Valley Forge, 1973), pp. 442–43.

9. M. Blondel, *The Letter on Apologetics,* in *The Letter on Apologetics & History and Dogma,* tr. by A. Dru and I. Trethowan (New York, 1964), p. 226. This is a theme to which Blondel frequently returns.

10. See, for instance, H. Bouillard, "De l'apologétique à la théologie fondamentale," in his *Les Quatre Fleuves* 1 (Paris, 1973), pp. 57–70. This movement is well documented by earlier chapters in the present volume.

11. Newman in his *Grammar,* pp. 136–39, quotes extensively from Locke's denunciation of the entertaining of any proposition "with greater assurance than the proofs it is built on will permit." A major concern of the *Grammar* was to reply to that objection.

12. M. Polanyi, *Personal Knowledge* (Harper Torchbooks ed.; New York, 1964), pp. 126–27.

13. M. Polanyi, "The Creative Imagination," *Chemical and Engineering News* 44 (April 25, 1966), pp. 85–92 (at p. 88).

14. Polanyi, *Personal Knowledge,* p. 130.

15. See, for example, Arthur Koestler, *The Act of Creation* (New York, 1967); also N. R. Hanson, *Patterns of Discovery* (Cambridge, Eng., 1958); W. I. B. Beveridge, *The Art of Scientific Investigation* (New York, 1961); T. S. Kuhn, *The Structure of Scientific Revolutions* (2nd ed.; Chicago, 1970).

16. St. Augustine, *Confessions,* Bk. I, chap. 1.

17. *Ibid.*

18. On the inseparability of the Bible from the Church see K. Rahner, *Inspiration in the Bible,* 2nd ed. with revised translation (New York, 1964).

19. Vatican II, *Gaudim et Spes,* no. 22 (Abbott, p. 222).

20. Vatican II, *Dei Verbum,* no. 2 (Flannery, p. 751).

21. The central importance of this theme for Vatican II's ecclesiology is indicated by *Lumen gentium,* no. 1. For a thorough study of this theme see L. Boff, *Die Kirche als Sakrament* (Paderborn, 1972).

22. An apologetical reflection may be found in R. Latourelle, *Christ and the Church: Signs of Salvation* (Staten Island, N.Y., 1972).

23. Paul VI, Opening Address at the Second Session, in H. Küng and others (eds.), *Council Speeches of Vatican II* (Glen Rock, N.J., 1964), p. 26.

24. P. Ricoeur, *The Symbolism of Evil,* tr. by E. Buchanan (Boston, 1967), pp. 347–57.

25. Rosemary Haughton, *The Transformation of Man: A Study of Conversion and Community* (Paramus, N.J., 1967), p. 269.

26. Polanyi, *Personal Knowledge,* pp. 198–99.

27. Vatican II, *Lumen gentium,* no. 8.

28. Ibid.

29. Vatican II, *Unitatis redintegratio,* no. 4; cf. no. 6.

30. Vatican II, *Lumen gentium,* nos. 14–16; *Unitatis redintegratio,* no. 22. On the various dimensions of incorporation see A. Dulles, *Church Membership as a Catholic and Ecumenical Problem* (Milwaukee, 1974).

Chapter 15

1. J. Beumer, "Glaubensgewissheit," LTK 4:942.

Chapter 16

1. For this history cf. C. G. Hallencreuz, *New Approaches to Men of Other Faiths* (Geneva, 1970); A. Richardson, *Religion in Contemporary Debate* (London, 1956); P. Knitter, "What Is German Protestant Theology Saying about Non-Christian Religions?" NZST 15 (1973), 38–64.

2. It will be enough to mention: O. Karrer, *Religions of Mankind,* tr. by E. I. Watkin (New York, 1943); M. Seckler, *Instinkt und Glaubens-Wille nach Thomas von Aquin* (Mainz, 1961); L. Capéran, *Le problème du salut des infidèles* (2 vols.; Tournai, 1934); J. Maritain, "The Immanent Dialectic of the First Act of Reason," in his *The Range of Reason* (New York, 1952), pp. 66–85; R. Lombardi, *The Salvation of the Unbeliever,* tr. by D. M. White (Westminster, Md., 1956); C. Colombo, "Reflessioni sul problema dei bambini che muoiono senza battesimo," in *Miscellanea Carlo Figini* (Venegono Inferiore, 1964), pp. 573–604.

3. H. Bürkle, *Einführung in die Theologie der Religionen* (Darmstadt, 1977); p. 25; C. F. Hallencreuz, *Dialogue and Community* (Uppsala—Geneva, 1977), p. 35.

4. There is still no history of the Church's relations with the religions, but only limited essays on one or other historical period. Who will be courageous enough to take on this task?

5. On *homo religiosus* I will mention here only: G. Zunini, *Homo religiosus* (Milan, 1966); idem, "L'esperienza religiosa dal punto di vista psicologico," in *Miscellanea Carlo Figini* (n. 2, above), pp. 759–81; P. Rossano, *L'uomo e la religione* (Fossano, 1968); G. Milanesi and M. Alletti, *Psicologia della religione* (Rome, 1973), with extensive bibliography.

6. It will be enough to mention: V. Boublik, *Teologia delle religioni* (Rome,

1973); M. Flick and Z. Alszeghy, *Fondamenti di una antropologia teologica* (Florence, 1970); idem, *L'uomo nella teologia* (Rome, 1971); H. de Lubac, *Athéisme et sens de l'homme* (Paris, 1968).

7. De Lubac, ibid., p. 98.

8. Cf. Boublik, op cit., pp. 48–49.

9. Cf. K. Rahner, *Hearers of the Word,* tr. by M. Richards (New York, 1969); for the Ebnerian inspiration cf. e.g., Ebner's notes in his *Schriften* 2 (Munich, 1963), pp. 195 (April, 1920); 267 (February, 1921); 284 (September, 1921);303 (November, 1922).

10. Among many passages of Ebner on this subject cf. ibid. 2:194, 266, 268, 275.

11. The distinction between "personal faith" and "cumulative traditions" is from W. Cantwell Smith; it is the foundation of his work *The Meaning and End of Religion: A New Approach to the Religious Traditions of Mankind* (New York, 1964).

12. Cf. e.g., P. Berger, *The Sacred Canopy: Elements of a Sociological Theory of Religion* (Garden City, N.Y., 1967); R. J. Zwi Werblowsky, *Beyond Tradition and Modernity: Changing Religions in a Changing World* (London, 1976); R. N. Bellah, *Beyond Belief: Essays on Religion in a Post-traditional World* (New York, 1970).

13. Werblowsky, op. cit., pp. 109–10.

14. H. Fries, "Das Christentum und die Religionen der Welt," in *Das Christentum und die Weltreligionen* (Würzburg, 1965), pp. 15–37 at p. 25. On the same theme cf. J. Heilsbetz, *Theologische Gründe der nichtchristlichen Religionen* (Frieburg, 1967), pp. 144–75; Boublik, op. cit., pp. 143–94.

15. Fries, art. cit., p. 24.

16. The problem has been carefully set forth by J. Jomier, O.P., with reference to Muhammad, in his article "Le dialogue et les religions," *Sources,* January–February, 1979, pp. 10–13.

17. Revelations 6:9–11 may be referring to non-Christian witnesses and spiritual leaders according to A. Feuillet, "Les martyrs de l'humanité et de Agneau égorgé. Une interprétation nouvelle de la prières de égorgés," NRT 99 (1977), 189–207.

18. The bibliography on the relation of the Church to Israel is very extensive. The reader may consult the following on the theological themes mentioned in the text: J. T. Pawlikowski, *Sinai and Calvary: A Meeting of Two Peoples* (Beverly Hills, 1976); D. Flusser, *Jesus,* tr. by R. Walls (New York, 1969); J. Isaac, *Jesus and Israel,* tr. by S. Gran (New York, 1971); J. Munck, *Christ and Israel. An Interpretation of Romans 9–11,* tr. by I. Nixon (Philadelphia, 1967); D. Judant, *Jalons pour une théologie chrétienne d'Israël* (Paris, 1975); P. E. Lapide, *Three Popes and the Jews* (New York, 1967). For identification of the major problems cf. the working document of the Committee on Jews and Christians of the Central Commission of German Catholics, published at Bonn—Bad Godesberg on May 8, 1978 under the title *Theologische Schwerpunkte der Jüdisch-Christlichen Gesprächs.*

19. For a survey of theological and practical problems cf. *Concilium,* 6 for 1976 (Italian ed.), entitled *Cristiani e musulmani;* also the document entitled *Guidelines for the Dialogue between Muslims and Christians,* issued by the Secretariat for non-Christians (Vatican City, 1969), and the annual journal *Islamochristiana,* published since 1975 by the Pontifical Institute for Arabic Studies (Rome).

20. J. N. Farquhar, *The Crown of Hinduism* (Oxford, 1913); H. Le Saux, *Sagesse hindoue, mystique chrétienne: Du Vedanta à la Trinité* (Paris, 1965); B. Griffiths, *Christian Ashram: Essays towards a Hindu-Christian Dialogue* (London, 1966);

R. Panikkar, *The Unknown Christ of Hinduism* (London, 1964); idem, *Kultmysterium in Hinduismus und Chrisentum* (Freiburg—Munich, 1964); S. J. Samartha, *Hindus vor dem universalem Christus* (Stuttgart, 1970).

21. R. de Smedt, S.J., "Ein Weg zu Christus durch Indiens Religionsgeschichte," *Orientierung* 39 (1975), 105–8.

22. R. Guardini, *The Lord,* tr. by E. C. Briefs (Chicago, 1954), p. 305. For a general introduction to Buddhist-Christian relations cf. no. 67 (July–August, 1967) of the *Pro Mundi Vita Bulletin. Concilium,* 116, is entitled *Buddhism and Christianity.* Cf. also V. Raguin, *Buddhisme, Christianisme* (Paris, 1973); H. Dumoulin, *Östliche Meditation und christliche Mystik* (Munich, 1966); Secretariat for non-Christians, *A la rencontre du Bouddhisme* (2 vols.; Rome, 1970).

23. There is a vast bibliography on the African religions and Christianity. I shall mention only: A. Shorter, *African Culture and the Christian* Church (London, 1973); C. M. Mulogo, *La religion traditionnelle des Bantu et leur vision du monde* (Kinshasa, 1973); the Abijdan Colloquium of 1977, *Black Civilization and the Catholic Church* (Paris, 1978); H. Bürkle, *Theologie und Kirche in Afrika* (Stuttgart, 1968). The *Bulletin of African Theology* has been published at Kinshasa since 1979.

24. R. Penna, *Il "mysterion" paolino* (Brescia, 1978).

25. Cf. A. Maddalena, *Il prologo e la testimonianza del Battista nel IV Vangelo* (Turin, 1976), p. 34.

26. Cf. G. Fohrer, "sophia," TDNT 7:465–96.

27. Cf. P. Rossano, "God, Israel and the Peoples: Theological Meditation on J E P D," *Bulletin Secretariatus pro non christianis,* no. 14 (1970), 93–101.

28. Cf. A. Feuillet, *Le Christ Sagesse de Dieu d'après le épîtres pauliniennes* (Paris, 1966).

29. Cf. Heinz-Horst Schrey, *Dialogische Denken* (Darmstadt, 1970).

30. Cf. H. Bürkle, op. cit., pp. 27–28.

31. According to St. John the Word "enlightens every man" (Jn 1:9). It is significant that in his Letter to the Romans St. Paul uses the same Greek word, *phaneroō,* for the self-manifestation of God in the cosmos (Rom 1:19) and in the sacred scriptures (Rom 16:26); this suggests that the two manifestations are connected.

32. An important theological seminar on the problem of revelation and inspiration in the sacred books of the various religions was held at Bangalore in 1973; the papers were published in the following year as *Research Seminar on Non-biblical Scriptures* (Bangalore, 1974).

33. Cf. U. Mann, "Religion als theologisches Problem unserer Zeit," in *Christentum und Religion* (Regensburg, 1966), pp. 53–89. On the relation of the Bible to the religions cf. P. Stockmeier, *Glaube und Religion in der frühen Kirche* (Freiburg, 1973); P. Rossano, "La Bibbia e le religioni," *Seminarium* 24 (1972), 244–55. But it must be admitted that we still have no thorough and comprehensive study of the relation of the Bible to the religions.

34. This is the thesis of J. Hick, *God and the Universe of Faith* (New York, 1973).

35. Cf. AAS 66 (1974), 561–62, tr. in TPS 19 (1975), 188.

36. H. Bouillard, "Croire et comprendre," in E. Castelli (ed.), *Mythe et foi* (Paris, 1966), pp. 294ff, cited by H. de Lubac, op. cit. (n. 6, above), p. 107.

Chapter 17

1. M. Seckler, "Katholisch als Konfessionsbezeichnung," TQ 115 (1903), 404. For a general discussion of our problem cf. O. Thils, *Les notes de l'Eglise dans l'apo-*

logétique catholique depuis le réforme (Gembloux, 1937); A. Kolping, "Notae Ecclesiae," LTK 7:1044–48.

2. J. Brunsmann in his *Lehrbuch der Apologetik* 2 (Vienna, 1930) sums up as follows the results of study of the *Notae:* "Only the Roman Catholic Church possesses all the characteristics that Christ bestowed on the Church which he instituted. For this reason it alone is the true Church" (p. 265). J. Brinktrine speaks in similar terms in his *Offenbarung und Kirche* 2 (Paderborn, 1949), pp. 232–84. See also the *Katholischer Katechismus,* p. 105.

3. A. Lang, *Die Kirche Jesu Christi* 2 (Munich, 1963), p. 176.

4. H. de Lubac, *Catholicism. A Study of Dogma in Relation to the Corporate Destiny of Mankind,* tr. by L. C. Sheppard (London, 1949), p. 118.

5. M. Schmaus, *Katholische Dogmatik* III/1 (Munich, 1958), p. 830.

6. A. Grillmeier on Chapter 1 of *Lumen gentium* in H. Vorgrimler (ed.), *Commentary on the Documents of Vatican II,* tr. by L. Adolphus, K. Smyth, and R. Strachan, 1 (New York, 1967), pp. 149–50.

7. On the entire questions cf K. Mörsdorf, *Lehrbuch des Kirchenrechts* 1 (11th ed.; 1964), pp. 175–84.

8. *Das neue Volk Gottes* (Düsseldorf, 1969), pp. 101–2.

9. J. Ratzinger, "Die Kirche und die Kirchen," *Reformatio* 2 (1964), 104.

10. Ibid., p. 105.

11. J. Ratzinger, "Prognosen für die Zukunft des Ökumenismus," in *Ökumenisches Forum* Grazer Hefte für konkrete Ökumene (Graz, 1977), p. 36.

12. E. Käsemann, "The Canon of the New Testament and the Unity of the Church," in E. Käsemann, *New Testament Essays,* tr. by W. J. Montague (Naperville, Ill., 1964), pp. 95–107.

13. H. Fries, *Ökumene statt Konfessionen?* (Frankfurt, 1977).

14. *Gemeinsame Synode der Bistümer in der Bundesrepublik Deutschlands* (Gesamtausgabe 1; Freiburg—Basel—Vienna, 1976), p. 785.

Chapter 18

1. Penguin edition (Harmondsworth, 1974), p. 100; hereafter: *Development.*

2. Dogmatic Constitution on Divine Revelation (*Dei Verbum*), no. 8 (Abbott, p. 116).

3. Vatican II, Decree on Ecumenism (*Unitatis redintegratio*), no. 6.

4. DS, no. 1501.

5. P. C. Rodger and L. Vischer (eds.) *The Fourth World Conference on Faith and Order,* Montreal, 1963 (London, 1964), pp. 50, 52; hereafter: *Montreal.*

6. *Acta Synodalia Concilii Vaticani II,* vol. III, pars III, pp. 150–51.

7. *Montreal,* p. 52.

8. Dogmatic Constitution on the Church (*Lumen gentium*), no. 25.

9. *Dei Verbum,* no. 10 (Flannery, p. 755).

10. PL 50:639.

11. *Contra Epistulam Parmeniani* III, 3.

12. "Omnium consensus vox naturae est" (*Tuscul. Disput.* I, 26, 35). "Vetus opinio est iam usque ab heroicis ducta temporibus eaque et populi Romani et omnium gentium firmata consensu versari quandam inter homines divinationem . . . id est praesensionem et scientiam rerum futurarum" (*De divin.,* I, 1).

13. H. Fries, *Ökumene statt Konfessionen?* (Frankfurt, 1977).

14. *Gemeinsame Synode der Bistümer in der Bundesrepublik Deutschlands*

15. *Development,* p. 76.
16. *Commonitorium* IV, 6.
17. Ibid., IV, 2.
18. *Development,* p. 88.
19. Ibid., p. 84.
20. Hans Küng, *On Being a Christian,* tr. by E. Quinn (Garden City, N.Y., 1976), p. 20.
21. *Development,* p. 104.
22. *Dei Verbum,* no. 8 (Flannery, p. 754).
23. *Lumen gentium,* no. 12 (Flannery, p. 363); the constitution here cites Augustine.
24. *Dei Verbum,* no. 9.
25. Ibid., nos. 9 and 24.
26. Cited by J. Scullion, *The Theology of Inspiration* (Cork, 1970), p. 90.
27. See H. Wagenhammer, *Das Wesen des Christentums* (Mainz, 1973).
28. An earlier form of this piece appeared as "Criteria for Discerning Christian Traditions" in *Science et Esprit* 30 (1978), 295–302.

Chapter 19

1. Cf. K. Barth, *Kirchliche Dogmatik* I/2, pp. 509, 634–36; G. Ebeling, *The Problem of the Historicity of the Church and Its Proclamation,* tr. by G. Foley (Philadelphia, 1967), p. 56; K. G. Steck, *Das römische Lehramt und die Heilige Schrift* (Munich, 1963); idem, *Kirche des Wortes oder Kirche des Lehramts?* (Zürich, 1962).
2. Cf. G. Söhngen, "Fides quaerens intellectum," LTK 4:120.
3. I am alluding here to the view of theology that is presented by W. Pannenberg and discussed in my article "Problema theologicum de munere theologiae respectu magisterii," Greg 57 (1976), 40–47.
4. Cf. G. Ebeling, "Theologie und Philosophie," RGG 7 (1962), 819–29.
5. Cf. J. Alfaro, "Encarnación y revelación," Greg 49 (1968), 435–40.
6. Cf. K. Rahner, *Inspiration in the Bible,* tr. by C. H. Henkey (Quaestiones Disputatae 1; New York, 1961; rev. tr., 1964).
7. Vatican II, Constitution *Lumen gentium,* nos. 8 and 12 (Abbott, pp. 22 and 29). The term "indefectibility" applies better to the total reality of the Church, while the term "infallibility" is better reserved for a partial aspect of the total reality, namely, the abiding fidelity of the Church to the confession of Christian truth. But if the two terms are understood in the light of the comprehensive concept of faith and ecclesial tradition found in Vatican II (*Dei Verbum,* nos. 5 and 8), they can be regarded as equivalents.
8. *Dei Verbum,* nos. 5 and 8.
9. Ibid., nos. 9–10.
10. Cf. DS, nos. 125–26, 150, 300–2, 437–38, 544–57, 600, 800, 850–54, 900, 902, 1300, 1307, 1330–38, 1347–51, 1510, 1520, 1600, 1803, 2803, 2903, 3000, 3007, 3011. Cf. also Vatican II, *Lumen gentium,* no. 25; *Dei Verbum,* no. 10.
11. DS, nos. 3070, 3011. In his final reply to the objections of the "minority," which insisted on the connection between the pontifical magisterium and the living faith of the Church, the official expositor, V. Gasser, made an express acknowledgment: "Everything which the universal Church assents to and receives and venerates as revealed when preached, is true and catholic" and "is the rule of faith even for pontifical definitions" (Mansi 52:1217). Gasser repeatedly emphasizes the fact that

the pope "in accordance with his office and the gravity of the subject is obliged to investigate the [revealed] truth in a proper manner," but he adds that this step is a matter solely of the pope's conscience and belongs therefore "to the moral order rather than to the dogmatic" (Mansi 51:1213–14). Y. Congar has justifiably commented: "These ethical elements must be integrated into the very ontology of the mission received" ("Apostolicité du ministère et apostolicité de doctrine," in R. Bäumer [ed.], *Volk Gottes* [Freiburg, 1967], p. 110).

12. Vatican II, *Lumen gentium,* nos. 1, 8, 12; *Dei Verbum,* no. 10.

13. *Lumen gentium,* nos. 19–24.

14. Ibid., no. 25; *Dei Verbum,* no. 10.

15. *Lumen gentium,* no. 25 (Abbott, p. 49). Latin text: "Iis autem definitionibus assensus Ecclesiae deesse non potest propter actionem Spiritus Sancti, qua universus Christi grex in unitate fidei servatur et proficit."

16. Y. Congar, "La réception comme réalité ecclésiologique," RSPT 56 (1972), 375.

17. These are the two basic points for dialogue on the infallibility of the Church's magisterium. The infallibility of the Church as a community of faith is acknowledged by a number of non-Catholic theologians. Cf. H. Ott, *Die Lehre des I. Vatikanischen Konzils* (Basel, 1963), pp. 162–63.

18. Vatican II, *Dei Verbum,* no. 8 (Abbott, p. 116)

19. The magisterium is therefore a vital organ that is endowed with a special function *within the total organism which is the Church;* this means that it shares in the indefectible faith of the Church and, by reason of its privileged visibility, "symbolizes" (in the full sense of the word: expresses and makes real) the unity of the Church's faith.

20. Theologians have not as yet applied linguistic (semantic and syntactic) analysis to the interpretation of dogmatic formulas. Such an application might well have fruitful results. Cf. A. Grabner-Haider, *Semiotik und Theologie* (Munich, 1973), pp. 145–211.

21. Vatican I, Constitution *Dei Filius,* ch. 3 (DS, no. 3011).

22. Vatican II, *Dei Verbum,* nos. 9, 21, 24; Decree *Optatam totius,* no. 16.

23. Decree *Unitatis redintegratio,* no. 11. Cf. U. Valeske, *Hierarchia Veritatum* (Munich, 1968), pp. 28–29.

24. *Dei Verbum,* nos. 2, 4, 7, 11. Cf. I de la Potterie, "La vérité de la sainte écriture," NRT 88 (1966), 149–69.

25. Cf. Grabner-Haider, op. cit., pp. 106–7.

26. Cf. J. Alfaro, "Teología, filosofía y ciencias humanas," Greg 55 (1974), 224–36.

Contributors

JUAN ALFARO:Born in 1914 at Carcastillo-Navarra, Spain. Licentiates in philosophy and theology at the respective Faculties of the Spanish Jesuits (1935–44). Doctorate in theology at the Gregorian University; two years of courses at the Pontifical Biblical Institute (Rome). Since 1952 professor of systematic theology at the Gregorian University, a co-director of *Sacramentum Mundi* and *Concilium*. Since 1974 a member of the International Theological Commission.

Numerous articles in journals and international dictionaries. Principal published works: *Lo natural y lo sobrenatural* (Madrid, 1952); *Fides, spes, caritas* (Rome, 1964); *Hacia una teología del progreso humano* (Barcelona, 1969); *Esperanza cristiana y liberación del hombre* (Barcelona, 1972); *Cristianisma y justicia* (Madrid, 1972), *Cristología y anthropología* (Madrid, 1973); *Renovación de la vida religiosa* (Bilbao, 1975).

TULLIO CITRINI: Born at Milan in 1942. Licentiate in theology at the Theological Faculty of Milan; doctorate in theology in 1968 at the Gregorian University with a thesis directed by R. Latourelle and published as *Gesù Cristo revelazione di Dio. Il tema negli ultimi decenni della teologia cattolica* (Venegono Inferiore, 1969). Teaches fundamental theology and ecclesiology at the Seminario Arcivescovile of Milan. Has published *Discorso sul sacramento dell'ordine* and articles in theological journals, especially *La Scuola Cattolica* and *Rivista del Clero Italiano*. Has contributed the articles on "Apostolo/Apostolicità della Chiesa" and "Tradizione" to the *Dizionario Teologico Interdisciplinare* (published by Marietti).

AVERY DULLES: Born in 1918. After university studies and service as naval officer in World War II, he entered the Society of Jesus in 1946. Ordained to the priesthood in 1956, he worked for a year in Münster, Germany (1957–58) and then pursued his doctoral studies at the Gregorian University, Rome (S.T.D., 1960). He taught systematic theology at Woodstock College, a Jesuit house of studies, first in Maryland (1960–69), then in New York City (1969–74). Since 1974 he has been a professor of theology at The Catholic University of America, Washington, D.C.

He is the author of many articles and of eleven books, including: *The Survival of Dogma* (Garden City, N.Y., 1971); *A History of Apologetics* (London and Philadelphia, 1971); *Models of the Church* (Garden City, N.Y., 1974; Dublin, 1976; London, 1978); *The Resilient Church* (Garden City, N.Y., 1977; Dublin, 1978). Several of these have been translated into other languages

HEINRICH FRIES: Born on December 31, 1911 in Mannheim, he pursued his theological studies at the University of Tübingen, 1931–35 and was ordained a priest in 1936. He received his doctorate in theology in 1942 and qualified as a university lecturer in 1945. Appointed Dozent at the University of Tübingen in 1946, and Ordinary Professor of the Philosophy of Religion and Fundamental Theology at Tübingen in 1950. Since 1958 he has been Ordinary Professor of Fundamental Theology at the University of Munich; since 1964 he has also been President of the Institut für Ökumenische Theologie at the University of Munich.

Among his publications: *Die Religionsphilosophie Newmans* (Stuttgart, 1948); *Die katholische Religionsphilosophie der Gegenwart: Der Einfluss Max Schelers auf ihre Formen und Gestalten. Eine problemgeschichtliche Studie* (Heidelberg, 1949); *Bultmann—Barth und die katholische Theologie* (Stuttgart, 1955. Tr. into Spanish and English: *Bultmann—Barth and Catholic Theology*, tr. by L. Swidler [Pittsburgh, 1967]); *Glauben—Wissen. Wege zu einer Lösung des Problems* (Berlin, 1960. Tr. into Dutch and Spanish); *Aspekte der Kirche* (Stuttgart, 1963. Tr. into Dutch, French, Spanish, Italian, and English: *Aspects of the Church*, tr. by T. O'Meara [Westminster, Md., 1966]); *Ärgernis und Widerspruch: Christentum und Kirche im Spiegel gegenwärtiger Kritik* (Würzburg, 1965, 1968.[2] Tr. into Italian); *Wir und die andern. Beiträge zu dem Thema: Die Kirche in Gespräch und Begegnung* (Stuttgart, 1966. Tr. into Spanish and Italian); *Herausgeforderter Glaube* (Munich, 1968; Tr. into French, Spanish, Italian, Polish, and English: *Faith under Challenge*, tr. by W. D. Seidensticker [New York, 1969]); *Glaube und Kirche auf dem Prüfstand. Versuche einer Orientierung* (Munich, 1970. Tr. into Spanish); *Ein Glaube—Eine Taufe—Getrennt beim Abendmahl?* (Graz, 1971); *Abschied von Gott? Eine Herausforderung—Versuch einer Antwort* (Freiburg, 1971, 1977[5]); *Von der Partnerschaft Gottes. Wir sind nicht allein* (Freiburg, 1975); *Glaube und Kirche als Angebot* (Graz, 1976); *Ökumene statt Konfessionen? Das Ringer der Kirche um Einheit* (Frankfurt, 1977).

Editor of: *Newman-Studien*, vols. 1–10 (Nürnberg, 1948–78); *Handbuch theologischer Grundbegriffe* (2 vols.; Munich, 1962–63. Tr. into French, Spanish, Italian); *Beiträge zur ökumenischen Theologie*, vols. 1–18 (Munich, 1967–78); with Johann Finsterhölzl, *Wegbereiter heutiger Theologie*, vols. 1–9 (Graz, 1969–76); with Georg Schwaiger, *Katholische Theologen Deutschlands* (3 vols.; Munich, 1975).

GIUSEPPE GHIBERTI: Born at Murello (Cuneo) on September 15, 1934. Licentiate in biblical studies at the Pontifical Biblical Institute, Rome (1960); doctorate in theology with emphasis on the Bible at the Gregorian University (1966). Since 1963 has taught New Testament exegesis in the Turin section of the Theological Faculty of Northern Italy (president of the same, 1977–79); since 1974, professor of New Testament philology in the Faculty of Letters of the Catholic University of Milan, appointment made permanent in 1979. Since 1971, a member of the *Studiorum Novi Testamenti Societas* at Cambridge, Eng.; editor of *Parole di Vita* (1972–76) and, since

1973, of *Rivista biblica,* the scientific journal of the Italian Biblical Association; substitute professor of the History of Christianity at the Faculty of Letters of the University of Turin (1978–79).

Publications: Articles in *Parole di Vita, Rivista biblica, Assemblées du Seigneur, Scuola Cattolica, Rivista diocesana torinese;* in *Atti della Settimana Biblica Italiana, Studi Biblici,* and *Studia Pataviana.* Editor of collaborative works (*Miscellanea Card. Pellegrino;* scripture section of the *Dizionario Teologico Interdisciplinare*). Author of biblical studies ("Bibliografia sulla risurrezione di Gesù," in *Resurrexit* [Rome, 1964]; "Bibliografia sull'esegesi dei racconti pasquali e sul problema della risurrezione di Gesù," in *Scuola Cattolica,* 1969). Contributor to various volumes, such as *Segni e Sacramenti nel Vangelo di Giovanni* (Rome, 1977); *Chiesa per il mondo,* vol. 1 (Bologna, 1974); *Laicità nella Chiesa* (Milan, 1977); *Nuovo Dizionario di Teologia* (Rome, 1976); *Il messagio della salvezza,* vol. 8 (Turin. 1978) and 6 (Turin, 1979).

PROSPER GRECH: Was born in Malta (1925) and is a member of the Order of St. Augustine. Studied at the University of Malta, the Collegio Internazionale S. Monica, the Gregorian, the Biblical Institute, and at Fribourg, Oxford, and Cambridge. Since 1965, has been professor of New Testament studies at the Augustinianum. Presently head of the Institute Patristico Augustinianum. Guest professor at the Pontifical Biblical Institute, Rome (hermeneutics) and at the Pontifical Lateran University (biblical theology).

Publications: *Le idee fondamentali del Nuovo Testamento* (Modena, 1970²); with G. Segalla, *Methodologia per lo studio della teologia neotestamentaria* (Turin, 1978); *Acts of the Apostles: A Doctrinal Commentary* (Staten Island, N.Y., 1966). Articles in: *Catholic Biblical Quarterly, New Testament Studies, Biblical Theology Bulletin.* Contributor to: *New Catholic Commentary on Holy Scripture; Atti della Settimana Biblica Italiana,* 1970, 1972, 1976; *Problemi attuali di cristologia* (Rome, 1976); *Incontro con la Bibbia* (Rome, 1948).

PIERRE GRELOT: Born 1917, is a priest of the Orléans diocese (1941). Studied at the Institut Catholique de Paris (licentiate in theology, 1942; doctorate in theology, 1949; diplomas in the ancient Eastern languages). Engaged in various catechetical ministries until 1955. Has taught sacred scripture: at the major seminary of the Orléans diocese (1943–45); courses for the formation of catechists and religious women at the Institut Catholique de Paris (since 1950), at the Seminaire de Saint-Sulpice in Paris (1955–61), in the Faculty of Theology and then in the U. E. R. of theology and religious sciences at the Institut Catholique de Paris (since 1962). Teaches Aramaic (in the Ecole des langues orientales anciennes at the Institut Catholique de Paris (since 1952). Member of the Pontifical Biblical Commission (since 1972).

Publications: *Introduction aux livres saints* (Paris, 1963; Eng. tr.: *Intro-*

duction to the Bible, tr. by G. F. Campbell [New York, 1967]); *Le couple humain dans l'Ecriture* (Paris, 1964;[2] Eng. tr.: *Man and Wife in Scripture,* tr. by R. Brennan [New York, 1964]); *Sens chrétien de l'Ancien Testament* (Tournai, 1962); *La Bible. Parole de Dieu* (Paris, 1965); *Bible et théologie* (Paris, 1965); *Réflexions sur le problème du peché originel* (Tournai, 1967); *Péché originel et rédemption examinés à partir de l'épître aux Romains* (Paris, 1973); *Documents araméens d'Egypte* (Paris, 1972); *De la mort à la vie éternelle* (Paris, 1971); *Le ministère de la nouvelle alliance* (Paris, 1967); *Ecouter l'Evangile* (Paris 1974); *Le monde à venir* (Paris, 1974). To be published: *L'espérance juive à l'heure de Jésus.*

Co-editor with A. George of the *Introduction critique au Nouveau Testament,* with contributions in vols. 1 and 2.

Contributor to the collaborative volume *La "verità" della Bibbia nel dibattito attuale* (Brescia, 1968), and to various journals.

JACQUES GUILLET: Born at Lyons in 1910; ordained a priest of the Society of Jesus in 1945. Biblical studies at Jerusalem and Rome. Professor of exegesis and fundamental theology in the Faculty of Theology at Lyon-Fourvière from 1951 to 1972, then at the Centre-Sèvres in Paris since 1972.

Principal works: *Thèmes bibliques* (Paris, 1951; Eng. tr by A. J. La-Mothe *Themes of the Bible* [Notre Dame, Ind., 1961]); *Jésus devant sa vie et sa mort* (Paris, 1971; Eng. tr.: *The Consciousness of Jesus,* tr. by E. Bonin [New York, 1972]); *Jésus-Christ hier et aujourd'hui* (Paris, 1974;[4] Eng. tr.: *Jesus Christ Yesterday and Today: Introduction to Biblical Spirituality,* tr. by J. Duggan [Chicago, 1965]); *Jésus-Christ dans notre monde* (Paris, 1974; Eng. tr.: *Jesus Christ in Our World,* tr. by M. J. O'Connell [St. Meinrad, 1977]); *Les premiers mots de la foi* (Paris, 1977).

IGNACE DE LA POTTERIE: Born at Waregem, Belgium on June 24, 1914; entered the Society of Jesus in 1932. Studied philosophy and theology at Louvain and scripture at the Pontifical Biblical Institute in Rome. Professor of New Testament exegesis at Louvain (1950–60), then at the Biblical Institute (since 1960). Member of the *Studiorum Novi Testamenti Societas* and of the Pontifical Biblical Commission.

Publications: *Getuige van het Woord. Inleiding op de geschriften van Johannes* (Antwerp, 1961); with S. Lyonnet, *La vie selon l'Esprit, condition du chrétien* (Unam sanctam 55; Paris, 1965; Tr. into Spanish, Italian and English: *The Christian Lives by the Spirit,* tr. by J. Morriss [Staten Island, N.Y., 1971]); *Gesù Verità. Studi di cristologia giovannea* (Turin, 1973), with expanded Spanish edition: *La verdad de Jesús. Estudio de cristología joanea* (Biblioteca de autores cristianos; Madrid, 1979); *La vérité dans saint Jean* (2 vols., Analecta biblica 73–74; Rome, 1977); *¡ Maria-Virgen ! en el IV Evangelio. La Madre de Jesús y la Concepción virginal del Hijo de Dios. Estudio de teología joanea* (Madrid, 1979). Editor of *La "verità" della Bibbia nel dibattito attuale* (Brescia, 1968, 1979[2]).

Articles on exegesis and biblical theology, especially in: *Civiltà Cattolica, Biblica, Gregorianum, Nouvelle revue théologique,* and *Vocabulaire de theologie biblique* (ed. by X. Léon-Dufour).

RENE LATOURELLE: Born at Montreal in 1918; entered the Society of Jesus in 1938. After obtaining a doctorate in history (University of Montreal, 1950) and in theology (Gregorian University, 1957), he taught fundamental theology in the Facultés S.J. at Montreal (1956–59). Since 1959 he has taught fundamental theology at the Gregorian University, where he has also been Dean of the faculty of theology for nine years.

Publications: In addition to two works of a more directly historical character (*Etudes sur les écrits de S. Jean de Brébeuf* [2 vols.; Montreal, 1952–53] and *Brébeuf* [Montreal and Paris, 1958]), he has published a number of books on theology: *Théologie de la Révélation* (Bruges-Brussels-Paris-Montreal, 1969.[3] Eng. tr.: *Theology of Revelation* [Staten Island, N.Y., 1966]) *Theologie, science de salut* (Bruges-Brussels-Paris-Montreal, 1968. Eng. tr.: *Theology: Science of Salvation* [Staten Island, N.Y., 1970]); *Le Christ et l'Eglise: Signes de salut* (Tournai-Paris-Montreal, 1971. Eng. tr.: *Christ and the Church: Signs of Salvation* [Staten Island, N.Y., 1972]); *Le témoignage chrétien* (Tournai-Paris-Montreal, 1971); *Nuova immagine della Facoltà di teologia* (Rome, 1974); *L'accès à Jésus par les Evangiles. Histoire et herméneutique* (Tournai-Paris-Montreal, 1978. Eng. tr.: *Finding Jesus through the Gospels: History and Hermeneutics,* tr. by A. Owen [Staten Island, N.Y., 1979]). Most of these books have been translated into several languages.

The author has contributed to the various European and American journals, to dictionaries of theology and spirituality, and to collaborative volumes.

RENE MARLE: Born in Normandy (France) in 1919; entered the Society of Jesus in 1937. Theological studies at Lyon-Fourvières; ordained in 1950. Doctorate in theology at the Institut Catholique de Paris in 1950 with a thesis on *Bultmann et l'interprétation du Nouveau Testament* (Paris, 1956; 1966[2]). Professor in the Facultés Catholiques de l'Ouest, then at the Catholic Institute of Paris, where he directs the Institut Supérieur de Pastorale Catéchétique. Regular contributor to *Etudes* and *Recherches de science religieuse.*

In addition to his dissertation on Bultmaan, he has published the following books: *Le problème théologique de l'herméneutique* (Paris, 1963, 1968.[2] Eng. tr.: *Introduction to Hermeneutics,* tr. by E. Froment and R. Albrecht [New York, 1967]); *Bultmann et la foi chrétienne* (Paris, 1967. Eng. tr.: *Bultmann and Christian Faith,* tr. by T. DuBois [Westminster, Md., 1968]); *Dietrich Bonhoeffer, témoin de Jésus Christ parmi ses frères* (Paris, 1967, 1968.[2] Eng. tr.: *Bonhoeffer: The Man and His Work,* tr by R. Sheed [New York, 1968]): *Herméneutique et catéchèse* (Paris, 1970); *La singularité chrétienne* (Paris, 1970. Eng. tr. *Identifying Christianity,* tr. by Sr. J.

M. Lyons [St. Meinrad, 1975]); *Parler de Dieu aujourd'hui. La théologie herméneutique de Gerhard Ebeling* (Paris, 1975). Most of these books have been translated into several languages.

GUSTAVE MARTELET: Born in 1916; entered the Society of Jesus in 1935. After a lengthy formation in the literary, philosophical, and scientific disciplines, he concentrated on theology which, from 1952 on, he taught first at Lyon-Fourvière, then at the Centre-Sèvres in Paris. Focusing by profession and personal interest on the problems of fundamental and dogmatic theology, he has endeavored never to separate the realities of faith from those of human life. Having been present throughout Vatican II as a theologian of the French-speaking bishops of Equatorial Africa, he insists that not everything in the doctrinal work of the Council has as yet received the treatment it calls for.

Among his writings: *Victoire sur la mort. Essai d'anthropologie chrétienne* (Lyons, 1962); *Sainteté d l'Eglise et vie religieuse* (Toulouse, 1964. Eng. tr.: *The Church's Holiness and Religious Life,* tr. by R. L. Sullivan [St. Mary's, Kansas, 1966]); *Les idées maîtresses de Vatican II: Introduction à l'esprit du Concile* (Paris, 1967); *L'existence et l'amour: Pour mieux comprendre l'encyclique Humanae Vitae* (Paris, 1969); *Eucharistie, Résurrection et Genèse de l'homme* (Paris, 1972. Eng. tr.: *The Risen Christ and the Eucharistic World,* tr. by R. Hague [New York, 1976]); *2000 ans d'accueil à la vie* (Paris, 1973); *L'au-delà retrouvé: Christologie des fins dernières* (Paris, 1975); *Vivre aujourd'hui la foi de toujours: Relecture du Credo* (Paris, 1977); *Oser croire en l'Eglise* (Paris, 1979). Has published, and continues to publish, articles in *Nouvelle revue théologique and Communio.* Is a member of the International Theological Commission.

CARLO M. MARTINI: Born in Turin on February 13, 1927; entered the Society of Jesus in 1944. Specialized in fundamental theology at the Gregorian University, 1956–59, obtaining a doctorate in theology there; specialized also in the biblical sciences at the Pontifical Biblical Institute in Rome and at the University of Münster, 1954–56 and 1962–65, obtaining a doctorate in sacred scripture. Taught fundamental theology in the theological faculty at Chieri, 1959–62, and general introduction to scripture at the Biblical Institute from 1962 on. Was Rector of the Biblical Institute from 1969 to 1978. Member of the Pontifical Biblical Commission, the Vatican Commission for Catholic-Jewish Relations, and the Pontifical Commission for the Neo-Vulgate; as a member of an interconfessional committee, helped edit the critical *Greek New Testament* published by the various Bible Societies. Rector of the Gregorian University from September 8, 1978. Appointed Archbishop of Milan on December 28, 1979.

Some publications: *Il problema storico della risurrezione negli studi recenti* (Rome, 1959); *Il problema della recensionalità del codice B alla luce del papiro Bodmer XIV* (Rome, 1966); with K. Aland and M. Black, *The Greek New Testament* (Stuttgart, 1969); *Atti degli Apostoli* (Rome, 1970).

GERALD GLYNN O'COLLINS: Born in 1931 in Melbourne, Australia. Studied in Australia, Germany, and England; Ph.D. (Cantab., 1968). 1968–73 taught at the Weston School of Theology (Boston Theological Institute) and the United Faculty of Theology (Melbourne). Since 1974 professor of fundamental theology at the Gregorian University. Numerous articles in *Gregorianum, Heythrop Journal, Interpretation, Irish Theological Quarterly, Rassegna di Teologia, Science et Esprit, Theological Studies, The Way*, and others.

Published works include: *Theology and Revelation* (Cork and South Bend, 1968); *Man and His New Hopes* (New York, 1969); *Foundations of Theology* (Chicago, 1971); *The Easter Jesus* (London, 1973; published in the United States as *The Resurrection of Jesus Christ*); *Theology of Secularity* (Cork and South Bend, 1974); *Has Dogma a Future?* (London, 1975; published in the United States as *The Case against Dogma*); *What Are They Saying about Jesus?* (New York, 1977); *The Calvary Christ* (London and Philadelphia, 1977); *What Are They Saying about the Resurrection?* (New York, 1978); *The Second Journey* (New York, 1978; Dublin, 1979).

KARL RAHNER: Born in 1904 at Freiburg in Breisgau (Germany); entered the Society of Jesus in 1922. Philosophical studies at Pullach (Munich) and theological studies at Valkenburg (Holland). After studies under Martin Heidegger, qualified in theology (1937) at Innsbruck, where he taught until 1939, when the Nazis suppressed the Faculty and expelled Rahner from the Tyrol. He taught again at Innsbruck 1948–64 (appointed Ordinary Professor in 1949); in 1964 he succeeded Guardini at Munich; Münster, 1967–70; from 1971 at Munich (as emeritus). He was a theological peritus at the Second Vatican Council, a member of the International Theological Commission, and a guest professor at the Gregorian and other universities.

2857 titles are listed in R. Bleistein and E. Klinger, *Bibliographie K. Rahners* (2 vols.; Freiburg, 1969 and 1974).

Some major works: *Schriften zur Theologie* (14 vols; 1954—; in English as *Theological Investigations*); *Hearers of the Word*, tr. by M. Richards (New York, 1969); *Foundations of Christian Faith: An Introduction to the Idea of Christianity*, tr. by W. V. Dych (New York, 1978); important chapters in *Mysterium Salutis* I/2, II/1, and II/2 (1968–70).

With others he has edited, and contributed articles and essays on many subjects and important questions in, the second edition of the *Lexikon für Theologie und Kirche, Sacramentum Mundi*, the *Quaestiones Disputatae* series, and others. In 1963 he and E. Schillebeeckx founded *Concilium*.

PIETRO ROSSANO: Born in 1923. Secretary of the Secretariat for Non-Christians. Professor of the theology of religions at the Gregorian University and the Urbanianum.

Publications in the biblical field: a translation-commentary, *Nuovo Testamento* (Turin, 1963; 1979³); commentaries on the *Lettere ai Tessalonicesi* (Turin, 1964) and the *Lettere ai Corinti* (Rome, 1973). Contributor to the

Introduzioni al Nuovo Testamento published by Marietti and Morcelliana. Publications in the field of the science and theology of religions: *L'uomo e la religione* (Fossano, 1968); "Theologie der Mission," in *Mysterium Salutis* IV/1 (Einsiedeln, 1972); *Il problema teologico delle religioni* (Rome, 1975); many articles of the dialogue with and the theology of the religions in the *Bulletin Secretariatus pro non christianis*.

Contributor to: *Biblica, Verbum Domini, Rivista Biblica, Bibbia e Oriente, Scuola Cattolica, Studium, Vita e pensiero, Orientamenti pedagogici, Seminarium,* and to the *Dizionario dei temi conciliari* (Vatican City, 1969), the *Nuovo Dizionario di Teologia* (Rome, 1977), and the *Enciclopedia Europea* (Milan, 1979).

XAVIER TILLIETTE: Born at Gorbie, France, in 1921; entered the Society of Jesus in 1938, was ordained priest in 1951, obtained his doctorat-ès-lettres (in philosophy) in 1970. Professor of philosophy at the Collège Saint-Louis-de-Gonzague in Paris, 1947–49 and 1954–57. Theological studies at Lyon-Fourvière, 1949–53. Became editor of *Etudes* (1957–61), professor of philosophy at the scholasticate in Chantilly (1964–70), while being at the same time (1964–70) editor of *Etudes* and secretary of the *Archives de philosophie*. Has taught at the Institut Catholique de Paris since 1969 and at the Gregorian University since 1972.

Some publications: *Karl Jaspers* (1960); *Jules Lequier ou le tourment de la liberté* (1964); *Maurice Merleau-Ponty* (1970); *Schelling. Une philosophie en devenir* (2 vols. 1970); *Attualità di Schelling* (1972); *Schelling im Spiegel seiner Zeitgenossen* (vol. 1, 1974). Regular collaborator in the *Archives de philosophie*. Many articles in *Etudes, Archives de philosophie, Recherches de science religieuse, Archivio di filosofia, Gregorianum, Actes des colloques* of the Instituto Romano di studi umanistici, *Hegel-Studien, Revue de métaphysique et de morale, Studia philosophica, Rivista di estetica,* and other periodicals. Has written an introduction and commentary on the *Textes esthétiques* of Schelling (1978). In preparation: *Le Christ des philosophes: L'intuition intellectuelle.*

JEAN-PIERRE TORRELL: Born in 1927; a Dominican since 1952. Since 1961, teacher of philosophy at the Dominican Studium of the Toulouse Province and at the Ecole Théologique of the Little Brothers of Jesus (Charles de Foucauld). Since 1975, guest professor at the Gregorian University; in 1977, visiting professor at St. Michael's College, Toronto.

In addition to his scientific books—*La théologie de l'épiscopat au premier concile du Vatican* (Unam sanctam 37; Paris, 1961); *Théorie de la prophétie et philosophie de la connaissance aux environs de 1230* (Spicilegium Sacrum Lovaniense 40; Louvain, 1977)—he has published two essays: *Inutile sainteté? L'homme dans le miroir de Dieu* (Paris, 1971); *Dieu qui es tu? Un homme et son Dieu* (Paris, 1974).

Since 1964 has written the *Chronique de théologie fondamentale* in the *Revue thomiste*. Numerous articles in the *Revue thomiste* and other journals.

DAVID TRACY: Born 1939; ordained in 1963; S.T.D. at the Gregorian University, Rome. Now professor of philosophical theology at the University of Chicago Divinity School.

Co-editor of the *Journal of Religion* and a member of the editorial boards of the *Journal of the American Academy of Religion* and *Concilium*. Author of many articles and the following books: *The Achievement of Bernard Lonergan* (1970), *Blessed Rage for Order* (1975), and *The Analogical Imagination* (1981). Co-editor of *Toward Vatican III* (1977).

Index of Authors